Frommer's

Portugal

18th Edition

by Darwin Porter &
Danforth Prince

Here's what the critics say about Frommer's:

"Amazingly easy to use. Very portable, very complete."

—*Booklist*

"Detailed, accurate, and easy-to-read information for all price ranges."

—*Glamour Magazine*

"Hotel information is close to encyclopedic."

—*Des Moines Sunday Register*

"Frommer's Guides have a way of giving you a real feel for a place."

—*Knight Ridder Newspapers*

Wiley Publishing, Inc.

About the Authors

Veteran travel writers **Darwin Porter** and **Danforth Prince** have written numerous bestselling Frommer's guides, notable to Germany, France, Italy, England, and Spain. Porter, who was bureau chief for the *Miami Herald* when he was 21, wrote the first Frommer's guide to Germany; Prince, who began writing with Porter in 1982, worked for the Paris bureau of the *New York Times.*

Published by:

Wiley Publishing, Inc.

111 River St.
Hoboken, NJ 07030-5774

ISBN 0-7645-4282-6

Editor: Billy Fox
Production Editor: M. Faunette Johnston
Cartographer: John Decamillis
Photo Editor: Richard Fox
Production by Wiley Indianapolis Composition Services

For information on our other products and services or to obtain technical support, please contact our Customer Care Department within the U.S. at 800/762-2974, outside the U.S. at 317/572-3993 or fax 317/572-4002.

Wiley also publishes its books in a variety of electronic formats. Some content that appears in print may not be available in electronic formats.

Manufactured in the United States of America

5 4 3 2 1

Contents

4 Exploring Lisbon 106

5 Estoril, Cascais & Sintra 144

6 South of the Tagus 177

7 Estremadura 190

8 The Algarve 208

9 Alentejo & Ribatejo 255

10 Coimbra & the Beiras 277

11 Porto & Environs 307

12 The Minho Region & Trás-os-Montes 342

13 Madeira & Porto Santo 370

Appendix: Portugal in Depth 405

Index 416

List of Maps

An Invitation to the Reader

In researching this book, we discovered many wonderful places—hotels, restaurants, shops, and more. We're sure you'll find others. Please tell us about them, so we can share the information with your fellow travelers in upcoming editions. If you were disappointed with a recommendation, we'd love to know that, too. Please write to:

Frommer's Portugal, 18th Edition
Wiley Publishing, Inc. • 111 River St. • Hoboken, NJ 07030-5774

An Additional Note

Please be advised that travel information is subject to change at any time—and this is especially true of prices. We therefore suggest that you write or call ahead for confirmation when making your travel plans. The authors, editors, and publisher cannot be held responsible for the experiences of readers while traveling. Your safety is important to us, however, so we encourage you to stay alert and be aware of your surroundings. Keep a close eye on cameras, purses, and wallets, all favorite targets of thieves and pickpockets.

Frommer's Star Ratings, Icons & Abbreviations

Every hotel, restaurant, and attraction listing in this guide has been ranked for quality, value, service, amenities, and special features using a **star-rating system.** In country, state, and regional guides, we also rate towns and regions to help you narrow down your choices and budget your time accordingly. Hotels and restaurants are rated on a scale of zero (recommended) to three stars (exceptional). Attractions, shopping, nightlife, towns, and regions are rated according to the following scale: zero stars (recommended), one star (highly recommended), two stars (very highly recommended), and three stars (must-see).

In addition to the star-rating system, we also use **seven feature icons** that point you to the great deals, in-the-know advice, and unique experiences that separate travelers from tourists. Throughout the book, look for:

Finds	Special finds—those places only insiders know about
Fun Fact	Fun facts—details that make travelers more informed and their trips more fun
Kids	Best bets for kids and advice for the whole family
Moments	Special moments—those experiences that memories are made of
Overrated	Places or experiences not worth your time or money
Tips	Insider tips—great ways to save time and money
Value	Great values—where to get the best deals

The following **abbreviations** are used for credit cards:

AE American Express
DC Diners Club
DISC Discover
MC MasterCard
V Visa

Frommers.com

Now that you have the guidebook to a great trip, visit our website at **www.frommers.com** for travel information on more than 3,000 destinations. With features updated regularly, we give you instant access to the most current trip-planning information available. At Frommers.com, you'll also find the best prices on airfares, accommodations, and car rentals—and you can even book travel online through our travel booking partners. At Frommers.com, you'll also find the following:

- Online updates to our most popular guidebooks
- Vacation sweepstakes and contest giveaways
- Newsletter highlighting the hottest travel trends
- Online travel message boards with featured travel discussions

What's New in Portugal

As Portugal moves deeper into a new century with a new currency, the landscape is forever changing, although the old-fashioned traditions such as handcrafts and architecture remain to delight new visitors every year. Experiencing the greatest changes are Lisbon, the Costa do Sol (Estoril and Cascais), the emerging city of Porto, and the forever volatile Algarve, the beachfront strip along the southern coast. Here are some major developments that could have an impact on your trip.

LISBON ACCOMMODATIONS In the heart of Lisbon, **VIP Eden** (Lisbon; ✆ **21/321-66-00**) has opened and has won architectural awards for its recycling of an Art Deco landmark, the Eden Theatre. Now converted to a sleek new 134-room apartment house, it offers suitelike living arrangements complete with fully equipped kitchenettes ideal for families. Even bigger excitement is being generated by the opening of the 14-room **Solar do Castelo** (Lisbon; ✆ **21/887-09-09**) within the walls of St. George's Castle, crowning the Alfama hilltop overlooking the city. This atmospheric and first-rate hotel was constructed on the site of the former kitchens of Lisbon's first Royal Palace, offering beautifully furnished bedrooms. At Parque das Nações, Lisbon has its third Tivoli Hotel, this one called **Tivoli Tejo,** Avenida D. João II (✆ **21/891-51-00**), a glistening 279-room hotel just a 2-minute walk from the splendid new transportation hub, Estação do Oriente. Offering rooms in a wide range of sizes and configurations, this is one of the best equipped hotels in Lisbon, complete with a 16th-floor gourmet restaurant and a dramatic indoor pool. See chapter 3.

LISBON DINING Standing virtually under the Ponte do 25 de Abril (25th of April Bridge), **Doca Peixe** (Lisbon; ✆ **21/397-35-65**) means "Fish Dock" in Portuguese, and that aptly describes the first-rate offerings served here nightly in an evocative nautical ambience. Check out the wide range and variety of offerings in the aquarium at the entrance. In the increasingly fashionable Parque das Nações district, **Restaurante Panoramico Torre Vasco da Gama** (Lisbon; ✆ **21/893-95-50**) has become the restaurant of choice, not only for its exciting international menu, but also for its panoramic seascape views that include the vast span of the Vasca da Gama Bridge stretching over the Tagus river. The restaurant is installed atop a new landmark built for the World Expo show. See chapter 3 for more details.

ESTORIL DINING In what used to be the playground of kings (most often exiled royalty), the beach resort of Estoril outside Lisbon has had its dining scene vastly improved with the opening of **La Villa** (Estoril; ✆ **21/468-00-33**), fronting Praia do Tamariz. The chefs concoct a Mediterranean menu that includes some savory Moroccan specialties as well, with everything served in a restored 18th-century palace. See chapter 5 for more details.

CASCAIS ACCOMMODATIONS The big news along the Costa do Sol

(Lisbon's beach strip) is the opening of a government-rated, 5-star hotel, **Farol Design Hotel** (Cascais; ✆ **21/482-34-90**), in a restored 19th-century mansion along the waterfront. This stylish boutique hotel has been an instant hit since its opening to a beach- and fun-loving crowd attracted to this resort, which is far livelier than in Estoril. More hotel news is generated by the opening of **Village Cascais** (Cascais; ✆ **21/482-60-60**), a stunningly modern first-class hotel in the historic district of this old fishing port. The hotel offers beautifully furnished bedrooms and is one of the best equipped in the area, with such luxuries as two pools. See chapter 5 for more data.

SESIMBRA ACCOMMODATIONS The opening of the completely modern 100-room **Sana Park Sesimbra Hotel** (Sesimbra; ✆ **21/228-90-00**) is luring more beach devotees to this little fishing port south of Lisbon. The government-rated four-star hotel serves as a beach escape from Lisbon for those not wanting to patronize the more overcrowded Estoril and Cascais on the immediate doorstep of Lisbon. The fresh seafood served in its topnotch restaurant is another reason to stay here. See chapter 6 for more details.

SETÚBAL ACCOMMODATIONS In this ancient city south of the Tagus, a government-rated four-star hotel, **Estalagem Do Sado** (Setúbal; ✆ **26/554-28-00**), has opened with 66 handsomely furnished and impressive bedrooms. Bedrooms are divided between an older restored building and a more modern wing, and there's an on-site restaurant with a panoramic view over the cityscape. See chapter 6 for more details.

ALGARVE DINING Outside the Algarvian town of Almancil, in the scenic Vale do Lobo to its southeast, a series of restaurants has opened to earn Michelin stars, unique outside of Lisbon. Today this Valley of the Wolf offers the best dining in the south of Portugal in a rather amazing concentration of top restaurants. **Casa Velha** (Quinta do Lago; ✆ **28/939-49-83**) lures with some of the most refined and finely tuned French cuisine along the coast. It enjoys a lakeside setting in a restored century-old farmhouse. In Vale Formoso, 3.2km (2 miles) from Almancil, **Henrique Leis** (Vale Formosa; ✆ **28/939-34-38**) is one of the region's most outstanding restaurants, attracting serious foodies to its world-class French and international cuisine. Chef Henrique Leis is a master of the kitchen, insisting on market-fresh ingredients that he concocts into sublime offerings. Finally, there is **São Gabriel** (Quinto do Lago; ✆ **28/939-45-21**), an elegant citadel of fine Swiss and Continental cuisine in a setting southeast of the center of Almancil. The cuisine here is so well crafted and daringly original that it attracts discerning palates up and down the coast. See chapter 8 for more details.

ESTREMOZ ACCOMMODATIONS In the Alentejo city of Estremoz, long known for its deluxe pousada, a challenger has risen. Although it has been open for some time, **Estalgem Páteo dos Solares** (Estremoz; ✆ **26/833-84-00**) is just now becoming known among savvy travelers to this region. Evoking old Portugal, it is a restored 41-room manor house that has been completely brought up-to-date with such added luxuries as hydromassages. See chapter 9 for more details.

VISEU DINING The provincial city of Viseu, capital of the region of Portugal known as Beira Alta, has gained a new leading restaurant, **Muralha da Sé** (Viseu; ✆ **23/243-77-77**), serving a most rewarding and authentic Portuguese cuisine in the heart of the historic district. Its grilled lamb dishes and grilled baby beef are the finest meat platters served in the region, and the menu is backed up by a reasonably priced wine list. See chapter 10 for more details.

PORTO DINING A refined Japanese cuisine has finally invaded this northern city famous for its production of port wine. Amid a minimalist décor, **Itmae** (Porto; ✆ **22/205-12-40**) offers superb Japanese dishes, attracting all sushi lovers and devotees of the freshest of fish. Highly trained chefs are acquainting local palates with some real Asian treats such as ruby-red raw tuna. See chapter 11 for more details.

BRAGA ACCOMMODATIONS More travelers to the far northern city of Braga are learning about the opening of a good and most affordable budget hotel, **Albergaria Senhora a Branca** (Braga; ✆ **25/326-99-38**). Modern comforts have been installed in this restored hotel, along with a bounty of antiques—the owner was a former dealer. See chapter 12.

MADEIRA ACCOMMODATIONS **Choupana Hills Resort & Spa** (Funchal; ✆ **29/120-60-20**) is an elegant new hotel with a first-rate spa that has opened in the mountains overlooking the city of Funchal and the bay. The resort offers understated luxury, a fusion cuisine, and a romantic hideaway. There's nothing quite like it on the island of Madeira. See chapter 13.

1

The Best of Portugal

Centuries ago, Portugal was a pioneer of worldwide exploration. Until recently, however, it was never as successful in attracting visitors to its own shores. Outside of greater Lisbon, the Algarve, and the island of Madeira, Portugal remained unknown and undiscovered by the mainstream visitor for many decades.

Today's travelers are beginning to realize that Portugal was unjustly overlooked. It offers sandy beaches, art treasures, flavorful cuisine, a unique form of architecture (Manueline), charming handcrafts, a mild climate, relatively moderate hotel rates, and polite and friendly people. Only 2 million annual visitors came to Portugal in the late 1970s. The number swelled to 20 million in the mid-1990s, and an explosion of hotel and resort building has kept pace.

Despite its small size—225km (140 miles) wide and 612km (380 miles) long—Portugal is one of the most rewarding travel destinations in Europe. Exploring its towns, cities, villages, and countryside will likely take longer than expected because there is so much richness and variety along the way.

The people, whose warmth is legendary, inhabit a majestic land of extraordinary variety. You'll see almond trees in the African-looking Algarve; cork forests and fields of golden wheat in Alentejo; ranches in Ribatejo; narrow, winding streets in the Alfama in Lisbon; ox-drawn carts crossing the plains of Minho; and vineyards in the Douro. Azaleas, rhododendrons, and canna grow for miles on end; the sound of fado music drifts out of small cafes; windmills clack in the Atlantic breezes; sardine boats bob in the bays; and gleaming whitewashed houses glisten in the sun. The sea is never far away.

This list is an embarkation point for the discoveries, like those by the mariners of old, that you'll eventually make on your own.

1 The Best Travel Experiences

- **Hiking in the Algarve:** Portugal's incredible physical beauty makes it a spectacular place for outdoor activities. In the southern Algarve region's low-lying lagoons and rocky highlands, the panoramas extend for miles over the nearby ocean. Especially rewarding is trekking through the territory near Sagres, which has retained its mystical hold on journeyers since it was known as the end of the world. Other worthwhile hikes include the footpaths around the villages of Silves and Monchique, where eroded river valleys have changed little since the Moorish occupation. See chapter 8.
- **Pousada-Hopping:** After World War II, the Portuguese government recognized that the patrimony of its great past was desperately in need of renovation. It transformed dozens of monasteries, palaces, and convents into hotels, honoring the historical authenticity of their architectural cores. Today's travelers can intimately experience some of Portugal's greatest architecture by staying in a *pousada,* part of a

Portugal

0
30 mi
0
50 km
N
N101
Viana do Castelo
Bragança
Braga
N103
Porto
Vila Real
Rio Douro
Rio Duero
Espinho
N2
N102
E802
ATLANTIC
OCEAN
Aveiro
Viseu
Guarda
Coimbra
Figueira da Foz
E80
E1
SPAIN
Leiria
Batalha
Fátima
Castelo
Branco
Nazaré
Tomar
N109
Rio Tejo (River Tagus)
Peniche
N118
Cáceres
Santarém
Portalegre
Estoril
Sintra
LISBON
Cascais
E90
Badajoz
N4
N18
Elvas
Mérida
Setúbal
Cabo
Espichel
Évora
E1
N120
N18
E802
Cabo de Sines
Sines
Beja
Rio Guadiana
FRANCE
N259
PORTUGAL
SPAIN
N120
E1
N264
Cabo de
S. Vicente
Portimão
Vila Real de
S. António
E1
Sagres
Lagos
N125
Huelva
Seville
Faro
Olhão

chain of state-owned and operated hotels. The rooms might not be as opulent as you'd hoped, and the government-appointed staffs will probably be more bureaucratic than you'd care to encounter. Nonetheless, pousada-hopping rewards the visitor with insights into the Portugal of long ago.

- **Playing Golf by the Sea:** British merchants trading in Portugal's excellent wines imported the sport of golf around 1890. Until the 1960s, it remained a diversion only for the very wealthy. Then an explosion of interest from abroad led to the creation of at least 30 major courses. Many courses lie near Estoril and in the southern Algarve. The combination of great weather, verdant fairways, and azure seas and skies is almost addictive (as if golf fanatics needed additional motivation).
- **Swooning to Fado:** After soccer, *fado* (which translates as "fate") music is the national obsession. A lyrical homage to the bruised or broken heart, fado assumes forms that are as old as the troubadours. Its four-line stanzas of unrhymed verse, performed by such legendary stars as Amália Rodrigues, capture the nation's collective unconscious. Hearing the lament of the *fadistas* (fado singers) in clubs is the best way to appreciate the melancholy dignity of Iberia's western edge.
- **Finding a Solitary Beach:** Portugal has long been famous for the glamour and style of the beaches near Estoril, Cascais, Setúbal, and Sesimbra. More recently, the Algarve, with its 200km (124 miles) of tawny sands, gorgeous blue-green waters, and rocky coves, has captivated the imagination of northern Europeans. While the most famous beaches are likely to be very crowded, you can find solitude on the sands if you stop beside lonely expanses of any coastal road in northern Portugal.
- **Fishing in Rich Coastal Waters:** Portugal's position on the Atlantic, its (largely) unpolluted waters, and its flowing rivers encourage concentrations of fish. You won't be the first to plumb these waters—Portugal fed itself for hundreds of generations using nets and lines, and its maritime and fishing traditions are among the most entrenched in Europe. The mild weather allows fishing year-round for more than 200 species, including varieties not seen anywhere else (such as the 2m/6-ft.-long). The country's rivers and lakes produce three species of trout, black bass, and salmon; the cold Atlantic abounds in sea bass, shark, tope, grouper, skate, and swordfish.
- **Trekking to the End of the World:** For medieval Europeans, the southwestern tip of Portugal represented the final frontier of human security and power. Beyond that point, the oceans were dark and fearful, filled with demons waiting to devour the bodies and souls of mariners foolhardy enough to sail upon them. Adding Sagres and its peninsula to the Portuguese nation cost thousands of lives in battle against the Moors, and getting there required weeks of travel over rocky deserts. Making a pilgrimage to this outpost is one of the loneliest and most majestic experiences in Portugal. Come here to pay your respects to the navigators who embarked from Sagres on journeys to death or glory. Half a millennium later, the excitement of those long-ago voyages still permeates this lonely corner. See chapter 8.
- **Losing It at a Spa:** Compared to the sybaritic luxury of spas in Germany and France, Portuguese spas are underaccessorized, and by

California's frenetic standards, they're positively sleepy. Still, central and northern Portugal share about half a dozen spas whose sulfur-rich waters have been considered therapeutic since the days of the ancient Romans. Luso, Monte Real, and Curia are the country's most famous spas, followed closely by Caldas do Gerês, Vimeiro, and São Pedro do Sul. Don't expect the latest in choreographed aerobics and spinning classes; instead, sink into communion with nature, rid your body of the toxins of urban life, and retire early every night for recuperative sleep.

- **Tasting & Touring in Port Wine Country:** Across the Rio Douro from the heart of the northern city of Porto lies Vila Nova de Gaia, the headquarters of the port-wine trade since the 1600s. From vineyards along the Douro, wine is transported to "lodges" (warehouses), where it is matured, bottled, and eventually shipped around the world. More than 25 companies, including such well-known names as Sandeman, maintain port-wine lodges here. Each offers free guided tours, always ending with a tasting of one or two of the house wines. The tourist office in Porto will provide you with a map if you'd like to drive along the Douro to see the vineyards. See chapter 11.

2 The Best Towns to Visit

- **Sintra:** Since the Moorish occupation, Portuguese kings and nobles have recognized this town's irresistible charm. You'll find a denser concentration of beautiful villas and gardens here than you'll find anywhere else in Portugal. At least five major palaces and convents are tucked amid the lush vegetation. See section 5 in chapter 5.
- **Óbidos:** This town is the most perfectly preserved 13th-century village in central Portugal. Its historic authenticity is the primary concern of the population of less than 5,000. For 600 years, Óbidos was the personal property of Portuguese queens, a symbolic love offering from their adoring husbands. Óbidos has always breathed romance. See section 1 in chapter 7.
- **Nazaré:** This folkloric fishing village in central Portugal produces wonderful handcrafts. The town has a strong sense of traditional culture that's distinctly different from that of nearby communities. See section 3 in chapter 7.
- **Fátima:** In 1913, an apparition of the Virgin Mary appeared to three shepherd children from Fátima, who were called upon to spread a message of peace. Their story was at first discounted and then embraced by a church hierarchy under assault by the ravages of World War I. Later, 70,000 people who were assembled on the site claimed to witness miracles. Today Fátima is the most-visited pilgrimage site in Iberia, home to dozens of imposing churches and monuments. See section 5 in chapter 7.
- **Évora:** A well-preserved ancient Roman temple rises across the street from convents and monasteries that flourished when the kings of Portugal used this town as their capital in the 12th century. These buildings combine with remnants of the Moorish occupation to form one of the most alluring architectural medleys in Europe. Although not large, Évora is one of the country's most perfectly preserved architectural gems. See section 4 in chapter 9.

- **Tomar:** Beginning in the 12th century, the Knights Templar and later the Knights of Christ (two warlike and semimonastic sects) designated Tomar as their Portuguese headquarters. They lavished the town with adornments over the centuries until it looked, as it does today, like a living monument to the architecture of medieval Portugal. See section 1 in chapter 9.
- **Coimbra:** The country's academic center, this town boasts a university with roots in the Middle Ages, a rich historic core, and a tradition of troubadour-style singing that's one of the most vital in Iberia. See section 3 in chapter 10.
- **Porto:** The second city of Portugal, Porto has rich associations with the port-wine trade. Entrepreneurs who returned home after making their fortunes in Brazil built some of the town's most imposing villas in the late 19th century. See section 1 in chapter 11.
- **Guimarães:** The birthplace of the country's first king, Afonso Henríques, and the core from which the country expanded, Guimarães is the cradle of Portugal. Its medieval core is one of the most authentic anywhere. The town was also the birthplace of Gil Vicente (1470?–1536?), a playwright referred to as the Shakespeare of Portugal. See section 1 in chapter 12.
- **Viana do Castelo:** This northern town with strong folkloric traditions is noted for pottery, women's regional dresses, abundant rainfall, and a collection of distinctive and dignified public buildings. Its heyday was in the 1500s, when fleets departed from here to fish for cod as far away as Newfoundland. Profits from their activities helped pay for the town's handsome collection of Manueline buildings. See section 5 in chapter 12.

3 The Best Beaches

- **Costa do Sol:** Sometimes called the Estoril Coast, this stretch of seafront extends 32km (20 miles) west of Lisbon. Its two major resorts are Estoril and Cascais. Once the playground of the wintering wealthy, the area now attracts throngs of tourists, mainly from northern Europe. See sections 1 and 2 in chapter 5.
- **The Algarve:** This region at the southern tip of Portugal gained its place on world tourist maps because of its string of beautiful, clean, sandy beaches. Lovely coves, caves, and grottos—some accessible only by boat—add to the region's allure. There are hundreds of beaches to choose from. Albufeira and Praia da Rocha are set against a backdrop of towering rock formations; the best cove beach is at Lagos, a former Moorish town with a deep-water harbor and wide bay. See chapter 8.
- **The Beiras:** In central Portugal, north of Lisbon, some of the finest beaches in Europe open onto the Atlantic. Like gems in a necklace, good, sandy beaches stretch from Praia de Leirosa north to Praia de Espinho. The surf can be heavy and the undertow strong. Major resorts include Figueira da Foz and nearby Buarcos. The beaches between Praia de Mira and Costa Nova are more secluded. See section 2 in chapter 10.
- **Costa Verde:** As the northern coastline approaches Galicia in Spain, the Atlantic waters grow colder, and even in summer, they're likely to be windswept. But on certain days they're among the most

dramatic in Europe. We like the wide, sandy beach at Ponte de Lima, but there are many others. Notable destinations are the resort of Espinho, south of Porto, and other beach meccas, including Póvoa do Varzim and Ofir, which have some of the best hotels, restaurants, and watersports equipment in the country. See sections 2 and 4 in chapter 11.

4 The Best Hotels

- **Pestana Carlton Palace (Lisbon; ✆ 21/361-56-00):** One of the grandest hotels to open in Portugal in years, this hotel lies in an upscale residential section 5km (3 miles) from the historic center. It was carved out of a former villa built in 1907. It's a stunning example of the romantic revival architectural style. See p. 88.
- **Four Seasons Hotel The Ritz Lisbon (Lisbon; ✆ 800/332-3442 in the U.S., or 21/383-20-20):** Built in the 1950s and host to a roster that reads like a who's who of international glamour, the Ritz is one of Portugal's legendary hotels. Everywhere in the hotel, you'll get the impression that a swanky reception is about to begin. See p. 78.
- **York House (Lisbon; ✆ 21/396-24-35):** A former 17th-century convent and private home, York House is the place to stay in Lisbon. It abounds with climbing vines, antiques, four-poster beds, and oriental carpeting—fittings and furnishings that maintain the building's historic character without flattening your wallet. See p. 84.
- **Albatroz (Cascais; ✆ 21/484-73-80):** In a garden overlooking the Atlantic, this inn was originally built as the summer residence of the dukes of Loulé. Since its transformation into a stylish hotel, its aristocratic elegance has drawn guests from throughout Europe. Service is impeccable. See p. 154.
- **Palácio Hotel (Estoril; ✆ 21/464-80-00):** The Palácio enjoyed its heyday during the 1950s and 1960s, when every deposed monarch of Europe seemed to disappear into the Art Deco hotel's sumptuous suites. The result: the curious survival in Estoril of the royal ambience of a Europe gone by. Today "the Palace" maintains a staff whose old-timers are among the best in Europe at offering royal treatment to guests. See p. 147.
- **Tivoli Palácio de Seteais (Sintra; ✆ 21/923-32-00):** One of the most elegant hotels in Portugal bears one of the country's most ironic names. In 1807, a treaty ending the Napoleonic campaign in Portugal was signed here, with terms so humiliating to the Portuguese that they labeled the building the Palace of the Seven Sighs. Any sighing you're likely to do today will be from pleasure—at the setting, the lavish gardens, and the reminders of an old-world way of life. See p. 169.
- **Le Méridien Dona Filipa (Almancil; ✆ 28/935-72-00):** Rising above the sea, this hotel is comfortable, modern, well designed, and sophisticated, but the most stunning feature is the 180 hectares (445 acres) surrounding it. Part of the land is devoted to a superb golf course. Don't let the severe exterior fool you—the inside is richly appointed with Chinese and Portuguese accessories, many of them antique. See p. 242.

- **Monte do Casal (Estói; ✆ 28/999-15-03):** An 18th-century country house on the Algarve has been converted into one of the most charming and tranquil places along the coast. Set on 3 hectares (7.4 acres) of flowering trees, it offers a chance to escape from the curse of the high-rise sea resort hotels and into an inn of style that captures some of the spirit of the region itself. See p. 251.
- **Palace Hotel do Buçaco (Buçaco; ✆ 23/193-79-70):** This palace, built between 1888 and 1907 as a sylvan refuge for the royal family, saw tragedy early. A year after its completion, the king and his oldest son were assassinated, leaving Queen Amélia to grieve within its *azulejo*-sheathed walls. In 1910, the palace's enterprising Swiss chef persuaded the government to allow him to transform the place into an upscale hotel. Bittersweet memories of its royal past still seem to linger within the thick walls. See p. 295.
- **Ipanema Park Hotel (Porto; ✆ 22/532-21-00):** One of the leading government-rated five-star hotels in the north of Portugal offers 15 floors of grand comfort with the largest roster of facilities in the city, including an outdoor pool with a panoramic view on the 15th floor. This bastion of good taste and luxury is as popular with tourists as it is with its business clients. See p. 321.
- **Infante de Sagres (Porto; ✆ 22/339-85-00):** A textile magnate built this hotel in 1951 in the style of a Portuguese manor house. Its elegant detailing makes it appear much older than it is. It's the most nostalgic, elegant, and ornate hotel in Porto. The managers began their careers here as teenage bellboys, and the staff members have obvious pride in their hotel. See p. 320.
- **Reid's Palace (Funchal; ✆ 800/223-6800 in the U.S., or 29/171-71-71):** For more than a century, Reid's has fulfilled the colonial fantasies of every British imperialist abroad. Set on a rocky promontory, it serves tea promptly at 4pm, contains English antiques that the Portuguese staff waxes once a week, and plays chimes to announce the beginning of the dinner service. Founded in 1891 and enlarged in 1968, it features terraced gardens spilling down to the sea and a very correct clientele that once included Winston Churchill. See p. 380.

5 The Best Pousadas

- **Pousada de São Filipe (Setúbal; ✆ 26/552-38-44):** During the 1500s, this structure served as a defensive link in a chain of fortresses surrounding Lisbon. Today it boasts antique *azulejos* (glazed earthenware tiles), panoramic views of the town, and a keen sense of Portuguese history. The rooms are simple (some might say monastic) but comfortable and tidy. See p. 187.
- **Pousada do Castelo (Óbidos; ✆ 26/295-50-80):** This pousada lies in a wing of the castle that protects one of the most perfectly preserved medieval towns in Portugal. In 1285, King Dinis offered the castle—along with the entire village—to his beloved Queen Isabel. Inside, the medieval aesthetic coexists with improved plumbing, electricity, and unobtrusive contemporary comforts. See p. 193.
- **Pousada de Santa Luzia (Elvas; ✆ 26/863-74-70):** This pousada opened in 1942 during the most

horrible days of World War II, near the strategic border crossing between neutral Portugal and Fascist Spain. Vaguely Moorish in design, with two low-slung stories, it was most recently renovated in 1992. It offers comfortable, colorful lodgings. See p. 266.

- **Pousada da Rainha Santa Isabel (Estremoz; ✆ 26/833-20-75):** Housed in a structure originally built during the Middle Ages, the Santa Isabel is the most lavish pousada in Portugal. Reproductions of 17th-century antiques, about .5 hectares (1.2 acres) of gleaming marble, and elaborately detailed tapestries create one of the most authentic old-fashioned decors in the region. Guests have included Vasco da Gama, who was received here by Dom Manuel before the explorer's departure for India. See p. 263.
- **Pousada dos Lóios (Evora; ✆ 26/673-00-70):** This pousada was conceived as a monastery and rebuilt in 1485 adjacent to the town's ancient Roman temple. The purity of its design and the absence of encroachments from the modern world contribute to one of the most aesthetically thrilling experiences in Portugal. Inside there are no traces left of its original austerity—everything is luxurious and comfortable. See p. 269.

6 The Best Restaurants

- **Clara (Lisbon; ✆ 21/885-30-53):** This elegant citadel with its soft piano music is a refined dining room serving a remarkable Portuguese and international cuisine that has made it a favorite among serious palates. The chefs take special care with all their ingredients, and we sing their praise year after year for their impeccable offerings. See p. 92.
- **Gambrinus (Lisbon; ✆ 21/342-14-66):** It isn't as upscale as some of its competitors or the preferred rendezvous of the country's most distinguished aristocrats. Nonetheless, this is one of the hippest, best-managed seafood restaurants in Lisbon; the stand-up bar proffers an astonishing array of shellfish. Enjoy a glass of dry white port accompanied by some of the most exotic seafood in the Atlantic. See p. 90.
- **Casa da Comida (Lisbon; ✆ 21/388-53-76):** This restaurant is probably at its best on foggy evenings, when roaring fireplaces remove the damp chill from the air. Don't let the prosaic name fool you—some visitors prefer its Portuguese-French cuisine over the food at any other restaurant in Lisbon. Portions are ample, and the ambience is bracing and healthful. See p. 92.
- **Conventual (Lisbon; ✆ 21/390-91-96):** The facade that shields this restaurant from the medieval square is as severe as that of a convent—which, in fact, it used to be. Inside you're likely to find the prime minister of Portugal dining with assorted ministers. You'll always find a collection of panels from antique churches, and rich but refined cuisine based on the bourgeois traditions of Old Portugal. See p. 94.
- **Cozinha Velha (Queluz; ✆ 21/435-02-32):** During the 1700s, food for the monarchy's most lavish banquets was prepared here (the name means "old kitchen"). Today the high-ceilinged kitchens serve an unusual restaurant whose cuisine reflects the old days of Portuguese royalty. Dishes include

cataplana, a savory fish stew with clams, shrimp, and monkfish. Equally outstanding is soufflélike *bacalhau espiritual* (codfish), which takes 45 minutes to prepare and should be ordered when you make your reservation. The restaurant is celebrated for its desserts, many of which are based on ancient convent recipes. See p. 164.

- **Restaurante Porto de Santa Maria (Guincho; ✆ 21/487-10-36 or 21/487-02-40):** The understated beige-and-white decor highlights the restaurant's bubbling aquarium and sea view. The menu lists nearly every conceivable kind of shellfish, served in the freshest possible combinations in a justifiably popular dining room. See p. 162.
- **Four Seasons (in the Palácio Hotel, Estoril; ✆ 21/464-80-00):** This tranquil restaurant, with its rich colors and artful accents, has been a fixture in Estoril since the days when deposed European monarchs assembled here with their entourages. High glamour, old-world service, and impeccably prepared international cuisine are this place's hallmarks. See p. 149.
- **Casa Velha (Quinta do Lago, near Almancil; ✆ 28/939-49-83):** On a rocky hilltop above the modern resort of Quinta do Lago (with which it is not associated), this restaurant occupies a century-old farmhouse, with kitchens modernized for the preparation of gourmet food. The sophisticated cuisine includes preparations of upscale French and Portuguese recipes. See p. 243.
- **Churrascão do Mar (Porto; ✆ 22/609-63-82):** Porto's most elegant restaurant, serving a Brazilian cuisine, is housed in a 19th-century antique manor restored to its Belle Epoque glory. The town's finest chefs turn out a savory cuisine specializing in grilled seafood. See p. 325.

7 The Best Romantic Getaways

- **Guincho:** On the Estoril Coast, 9km (5½ miles) northwest of Cascais, this is the westernmost point in continental Europe. It's a dramatic, spectacular site where waves crash against three sides of a restored 17th-century fortress (now the Hotel do Guincho, one of the most unusual, luxurious hotels in Europe). Balconies—best shared with a loved one—overlook the panoramic scene, with beaches on both sides. The crashing surf makes good background music for a torrid affair straight out of a romance novel. See section 3 in chapter 5.
- **Sintra:** Since the time of the Moorish occupation, Sintra has been considered one of the most beautiful and desirable sites in Portugal. Sintra has been favored by Catholic monarchs, industry moguls, and members of the Portuguese gentry. See section 5 in chapter 5.
- **Serra de Arrábida:** This whale-shape ridge never exceeds 1,525m (5,000 ft.) in height. The masses of wildflowers that flank its sides are among the most colorful and varied in Iberia. The Serra lies between Sesimbra and Setúbal, across the estuary of the Tagus from Lisbon. En route from Lisbon, you'll find crowded and secluded beaches, a medieval Capuchin monastery (the Convento Novo), and a smattering of good restaurants. The town of Sesimbra, with its historic, sleepy main square and ruined fortresses,

offers bars, restaurants, and insight into the Iberia of a bygone era. See sections 2 through 4 in chapter 6.

- **Óbidos:** After Dom Afonso Henríques wrenched the village from the Moors, he offered Óbidos as a wedding gift to his betrothed, his beloved Isabel. The village remained the personal property of the queens of Portugal until 1834. Today the town's ramparts, cobblestone streets, and 14th-century facades make Óbidos the most romantic spot in Portugal. See section 1 in chapter 7.
- **Buçaco:** This forest figures more prominently in the national psyche than any other in Portugal, partly because of its association with the doomed royal family. In the 7th century, Benedictine and Capuchin monks labored to diversify the number of exotic trees that flourish in the forest. Around 1900, the Portuguese royal family built a palace here—but spent only a few summers before assassinations and revolutions changed the role of the monarchy forever. Today the palace functions as a supremely romantic hotel. See section 4 in chapter 10.

8 The Best Palaces & Castles

- **Castelo de São Jorge (the Alfama, Lisbon; ✆ 21/887-72-44):** This hilltop has long been valued as a fortification to protect settlements along the Tagus. Today the bulky castle crowns one of the most densely populated medieval neighborhoods of Lisbon, the Alfama. It encompasses a nostalgic collection of thick stone walls, medieval battlements, Catholic and feudal iconography, verdant landscaping, and sweeping views of one of Europe's greatest harbors. See p. 108.
- **Palácio Nacional de Queluz (near Lisbon; ✆ 21/434-38-60):** Designed for the presentation of music and royal receptions in the 1700s, this castle was modeled as a more intimate version of Versailles. It's a symmetrical building ringed with gardens, fountains, and sculptures of mythical heroes and maidens. Although gilt, crystal, and frescoes fill its interior, most Portuguese are proudest of the *azulejos* room, where hand-painted blue-and-white tiles depict day-to-day life in the Portuguese colonies of Macao and Brazil. See p. 163.
- **Palácio Nacional de Pena (Sintra; ✆ 21/923-73-00):** Only a cosmopolitan 19th-century courtier could have produced this eclectic, expensive melange of architectural styles. Set in a 200-hectare (495-acre) walled park, it was commissioned by the German-born consort of the Portuguese queen; it reminds some visitors of the Bavarian castles of Mad King Ludwig. Appointed with heavy furnishings and rich ornamentation, it's a symbol of the Portuguese monarchs in their most aesthetically decadent stages. See p. 167.
- **Castelo dos Mouros (Sintra; ✆ 21/923-73-00):** In the 19th century, the monarchs ordered that this castle, evocative of the Moorish occupation of Portugal, remain as a ruined ornament to embellish their sprawling parks and gardens. Set near the much larger, much more ornate Pena palace (see above), the squat, thick-walled fortress was begun around A.D. 750 by the Moors and captured with the help of Scandinavian Crusaders in 1147. It retains its jagged battlements, a quartet of eroded towers, and a ruined Romanesque chapel

erected by the Portuguese as a symbol of their domination of former Moorish territories. See p. 168.

- **Palace Hotel do Buçaco (Buçaco; ✆ 23/193-79-70):** Of all the buildings in this list, the Palace of Buçaco is the most important national icon. Completed in 1907, it's also the only one that operates as a hotel, allowing visitors to sleep within the walls of a former royal palace. Constructed from marble, bronze, stained glass, and exotic hardwoods, and inspired by the greatest buildings in the empire, it represents more poignantly than any other Portuguese palace the final days of the doomed aristocracy. See p. 295.

9 The Best Museums

- **Museu da Fundação Calouste Gulbenkian (Lisbon; ✆ 21/782-30-00):** Its namesake was an Armenian oil czar, Calouste Gulbenkian (1869–1955), whose fortune derived from a 5% royalty on most of the oil pumped out of Iraq. His eclectic collections of Asian and European sculpture, paintings, antique coins, carpets, and furniture are on display in a modern compound in a lush garden. See p. 114.
- **Museu Nacional dos Coches (Lisbon; ✆ 21/361-08-50):** Founded by Queen Amélia in 1904, when the horse-drawn buggy was becoming obsolete, this museum is on the premises of the riding school of the Palácio do Belém (the official home of the Portuguese president). It contains dozens of magnificent state carriages, some decorated with depictions of Portugal's maritime discoveries. See p. 112.
- **Museu Nacional de Arte Antiga (Lisbon; ✆ 21/391-28-00):** In the 1830s, the power of many of Portugal's fabulously wealthy monasteries was violently curbed. Many of the monasteries' art treasures, including the country's best collection of Portuguese primitives, as well as gold and silver plate crafted from raw materials mined in India, are displayed at the 17th-century palace of the counts of Alvor. See p. 113.
- **Museu de Marinha (Lisbon; ✆ 21/362-00-19):** The most important maritime museum in the world—a rich tribute to Portugal's Age of Exploration—is in the west wing of the Jerónimos Monastery. The thousands of displays include royal galleons dripping with gilt and ringed with depictions of saltwater dragons and sea serpents. See p. 112.

10 The Best Churches & Abbeys

- **Mosteiro dos Jerónimos (Belém; ✆ 21/362-00-34):** More than any other ecclesiastical building in Portugal, this complex represents the wealth that poured into Lisbon from the colonies during the Age of Discovery. Begun in 1502 in Belém, the seaport near the gates of Lisbon, it's the world's most distinctive Manueline church. Richly ornate and unlike any other building in Europe, it has, among other features, columns carved in patterns inspired by the rigging of Portuguese caravels laden with riches from Brazil and India. See p. 110.
- **Palácio Nacional de Mafra (Mafra; ✆ 26/181-75-50):** The convent was originally intended to house only about a dozen monks, but after the king of Portugal was

blessed with an heir, he became obsessed with its architecture and vastly augmented its scale. Construction began in 1717, and funding came from gold imported from Portuguese settlements in Brazil. Some 50,000 laborers toiled more than 13 years to complete the convent. Today the buildings alone cover 4 hectares (9.9 acres) and include a royal palace as well as accommodations for 300 monks. A park whose outer wall measures 19km (12 miles) surrounds the complex. See p. 174.

- **Mosteiro de Santa Maria (Alcobaça; ✆ 26/250-51-20):** More closely associated with the Portuguese wars against the Moors than almost any other site in Iberia, this monastery was a gift from the first Portuguese king (Afonso Henríques) to the Cistercians in 1153. As part of one of the most dramatic land-improvement projects in Portuguese history, a community of ascetic monks cleared the surrounding forests, planted crops, dug irrigation ditches, and built a soaring church (completed in 1253) that critics cite as one of the purest and most artfully simple in Europe. See p. 197.
- **Mosteiro de Santa Maria da Vitória (Batalha; ✆ 24/476-54-97):** In 1385, the Castilian Spaniards and the Portuguese, led by a youth who had been crowned king only a week before, fought one of the most crucial battles in Iberian history. The outcome ensured Portugal's independence for another 200 years. It was celebrated with the construction of the monastery at Batalha, whose style is a triumph of the Manueline and Flamboyant Gothic styles. See p. 203.
- **Convento da Ordem de Cristo (Tomar; ✆ 24/931-34-81):** Built in 1160 along the most hotly contested Muslim-Christian border in Iberia, this convent was originally intended as a monastic fortress. Successive building programs lasted half a millennium, ultimately creating a museum of diverse architectural styles. Some of the interior windows, adorned with stone carvings of ropes, coral, frigate masts, seaweed, cables, and cork trees, are the most splendid examples of Manueline decoration in the world. See p. 256.

11 The Best Wines

For generations, much of what the English-speaking world knew about Portugal came from the reports that wine merchants brought back to Britain from the wineries of the Douro Valley. Today Portugal is famous throughout the world for its port wines, and many parts of central and northern Portugal are covered with well-tended vines sprouting from intricately laid-out terraces that descend verdant hillsides.

- **Port:** Known for decades as the Englishman's wine, port was once the drink uncorked for toasting in England. In gentlemen's clubs, vintage port (only 1% of all port made) was dispensed from a crystal decanter. Later, when the English working classes started drinking less superior port in Midland mill towns, they often spiked it with lemon. Today the French consume almost three times the amount of port that the British do.

  Some 40 varieties of grape go into making port. Made from grapes grown in rich lava soil, port today is either vintage or blended, and ranges from whites to full-bodied tawnies and reds. The latter is often consumed at the end of a meal with cheese, fruit, or nuts. You can visit a port-wine lodge to learn more about port—and, more important, to taste it. The best lodges to visit are concentrated in Vila Nova de Gaia, a suburb of Porto across the Douro from Porto's commercial center.

- **Vinhos Verdes (pronounced "veen-yosh vair-desh"):** These "green wines" are more lemony in color. Many come from the Minho district in northwest Portugal, which, like Galicia in the north of Spain, gets an abundance of rain. Cultivated in a humid atmosphere, the grapes are picked while young. Some wine aficionados don't consider this wine serious, finding it too light. With its fruity flavor, it's said to suggest the cool breezes of summer. It's often served with fish, and many Portuguese use it as a thirst quencher in the way an American might consume a soft drink. The finest vinhos verdes are from Monção, just south of the river Minho. Those from Amarante are also praised.
- **Dão:** Dão is produced from grapes grown just south of the Douro in the north's mountainous heartland. "Our vines have tender grapes" goes the saying throughout the valleys of Mondego and Dão, each split by a river. Summers are fiery hot and winters wet, cold, and often bitter. A lot of Dão wine is red, notably the vinhos maduros, matured in oak casks for nearly 2 years before being bottled. The wine is velvety in texture and often accompanies roasts. At almost every restaurant in Portugal, you'll encounter either branco (white) or Dão tinto (red). The best bottles of red Dão wine are the reserve ("reserva" is printed on the label). Other names to look for include Porta dos Cavaleiros and Terras Altas. (No one seems to agree on how to pronounce the name—*daw-ng, da-ow,* or, least flattering, *dung.*)
- **Madeira:** Grown from grapes rooted in the island's volcanic soil, this wine traces its origins to 1419. Its history is similar to that of port, in that it was highly prized by aristocratic British families. George Washington was among the wine's early admirers, although the Madeira he consumed little resembled the product bottled today. Modern Madeira wines are lighter and drier than the thick, sweet kinds favored by generations past.

  The wine, which is fortified and blended, includes such varieties as Malmsey, Malvasia, and Boal—sweet, heavy wines usually served with dessert or at the end of a meal. The less sweet Verdelho is often consumed as a light drink between meals, in much the same way that a Spaniard downs a glass of sherry. Dry and light, Sercial is best as an aperitif and is often served in Portugal with toasted and salted almonds. None of these wines is likely to be consumed with the main dish at dinner.

12 The Best Offbeat Trips

- **Horseback Riding Along the Coast:** The Atlantic Ocean is the livelihood of many Portuguese and the inspiration for a number of rides along its beaches. An American company, Equitour, offers these treks. (For more details, refer to section 14 in chapter 2). In addition to beach riding, there is trekking through olive groves, vineyards, pine forests, and lagoons. Seeing this beautiful country from the back of a well-trained, even-tempered Lusitano is a rewarding experience.

- **Appreciating Manueline Architecture:** Manuelino—as it's known in Portuguese—marked a dramatic artistic shift from the late Gothic style prevalent during the reign of King Dom Manuel. It mixes Christian motifs with shells, ropes, and strange aquatic shapes and is usually crowned with heraldic or religious symbols. The best example is the grand Monastery of Jerónimos in Belém, outside Lisbon, dating from the 16th century. Another towering example is the mysterious and astrologic visions of the famous window of the Convent of Christ in Tomar, the bastion of the Knights Templar in days gone by.
- **Visiting the Lost Continent of Atlantis:** One of the most offbeat travel experiences in Europe is a trip to the Azores. Mythologists believe the remote Portuguese islands in the mid-Atlantic are the only remnants of the lost continent of Atlantis. For hundreds of years they were considered the end of the Earth, the outer limits of the European sphere of influence, beyond which ships could not go. Even today they're a verdant but lonely archipelago where the winds of the ocean meet, cyclones call on each other, and urbanites can lose themselves in fog-bound contact with the sea. Although space limitations do not allow us to document these fascinating islands in this guide, any branch of a Portuguese national tourist office can provide you with information.
- **Paying a Call on Berlenga Island:** Berlenga is a granite island 11km (7 miles) west of the Portuguese coastline. The island has always been the first line of defense against invaders from the sea. In 1666, 28 Portuguese tried to withstand 1,500 Spaniards who bombarded the site from 15 ships. A medieval fortress demolished in the battle was rebuilt several decades later and today houses a no-frills hostel. The entire island and the rocky, uninhabited archipelago that surrounds it are a designated nature reserve whose flora and fauna—both above and below the surface of the sea—are protected from development and destruction. Boat transport departs from the Peniche Peninsula, about 92km (57 miles) north of Lisbon. See chapter 7.
- **Heading "Beyond the Mountains":** The northernmost district of Trás-os-Montes is a wild, rugged land whose name means "beyond the mountains." Exploring this region provides a glimpse into a Portugal infrequently seen by outsiders. Most of the population lives in deep valleys, often in traditional houses built of shale or granite, and speaks a dialect of Galician similar to that spoken just across the border in northwestern Spain. Much of the plateau is arid and rocky, but swift rivers and streams provide water for irrigation, and thermal springs have bubbled out of the earth since at least Roman times. You can drive through these savage landscapes, but don't expect superhighways. What you'll find are ruins of pre-Roman fortresses, dolmens, and cromlechs erected by prehistoric Celts, and decaying old churches. See chapter 12.

13 The Best Shopping

Here's a list of some of the more enchanting artifacts and handcrafts produced in Portugal:

- **Arraiolos Carpets:** The Moorish traditions that once prevailed in the town of Arraiolos, where the carpets are still manufactured, inspired their intricate stitching. Teams of embroiderers and weavers work for many days, using pure wool in combinations of petit point with more widely spaced ponto largo cross-stitches. The resulting depictions of garlands of fruit and flowers (a loose interpretation of French Aubusson carpets) and animals scampering around idealized gardens (a theme vaguely inspired by carpets from Persia and Turkey) are some of the most charming items for sale in Portugal. The size of the piece and the intricacy of the design determine the price, which is often less than half what you'd pay in North America. If you can't make it to Arraiolos, you'll find the carpets for sale at outlets in Lisbon.

- **Ceramics & Tiles:** Early in Portugal's history, builders learned to compensate for the lack of lumber by perfecting the arts of masonry, stuccoing, and ceramics. All were used to construct the country's sturdy, termite-proof buildings. After the ouster of the Moors, their aesthetic endured in the designs painted on tiles and ceramic plates, vessels, and jugs. Later, styles from Holland, England, and China combined to influence a rich tradition of pottery-making. The most prevalent of these appear as the blue-and-white *azulejos* (tiles), each with an individual design, which adorn thousands of indoor and outdoor walls throughout the country. Equally charming are the thousands of plates, wine and water jugs, and vases adorned with sylvan landscapes populated with mythical creatures. New and (to a lesser extent) antique samples of any of these items can be acquired at outlets throughout Portugal.
- **Jewelry:** In Portugal, any piece of jewelry advertised as "gold" must contain at least 19.2 karats. This purity allows thousands of jewelers to spin the shining stuff into delicate filigree work with astounding detail. Whether you opt for a simple brooch or for a depiction in gold or filigreed silver of an 18th-century caravel in full four-masted sail, Portugal produces jewelry worthy of an infanta's dowry at prices more reasonable than you might expect. The country abounds in jewelry stores.
- **Handcrafts:** For centuries, the design and fabrication of lace, rugs, hand-knit clothing, wood carvings, and embroidered linens have evolved in homes and workshops throughout Portugal. Although some of the cruder objects available for sale are a bit clunky, the best can be called art. From the north to the south, store after store offers regional handcrafts.
- **Leather Goods:** Iberia has always been a land of animal husbandry, bullfighting, and cattle breeding, and the Portuguese leather-making industry is known throughout the world. Its products include jackets, shoes, pocketbooks, and wallets, all of which sell for prices much more reasonable than those outside Portugal. The best stores are concentrated in Lisbon.

2

Planning Your Trip to Portugal

Just getting started is the difficult part for many travelers. This chapter addresses the where, when, and how of visiting Portugal—all the logistics of putting your trip together and taking it on the road.

1 Regions in Brief

Portugal's coastline stretches some 800km (496 miles). The country is bounded on the south and west by the Atlantic Ocean and on the north and east by Spain. Continental Portugal totals some 55,000 sq. km (21,450 sq. miles); its Atlantic islands, including Madeira and the Azores, add 1,935 sq. km (755 sq. miles). The Azores lie some 1,130km (701 miles) west of Lisbon (Lisboa), the capital of the country. Portugal's population is about 10.3 million.

Portugal has four major rivers—the Minho in the north, which separates the country from Spain; the Douro, also in the north, known for vineyards that produce port wine; the Tagus, which flows into the Atlantic at Lisbon; and the Guadiana, in the southeast. Part of the Guadiana forms an eastern frontier with Spain.

LISBON & THE COSTA DO SOL Portugal's capital is on hilly terrain beside one of the finest harbors in Europe—the estuary of the Tagus (Tejo) River. Within a few miles of the city limits, the beaches of the Costa do Sol cater to residents of the capital, who easily reach them by bus and train. Until the development of beaches in the Algarve, those on the Costa do Sol were among the most crowded and glamorous in the country. The best-known resorts include Estoril and Cascais, long playgrounds of the wintering wealthy.

ESTREMADURA The name translates as "the extremity," but it has radically different connotations from those associated with the harsh landscapes of Estremadura in neighboring Spain. Early in the development of the Portuguese nation, rulers based in the country's north-central region coined the term to refer to the Moorish territories to the south that the Portuguese eyed enviously. Technically, those territories included Nazaré, Obidos, and Fátima; in many cases, the word is now used to include the territory around Lisbon as well. Estremadura's coastline is flanked by some of the country's richest fishing banks.

THE ALGARVE Encompassing the extreme southwestern tip of Europe, the Algarve boasts a 161km (100-mile) coastline with some of the best beaches in Europe. It's permeated with memories of the long-ago Moorish occupation, when the region was called Al-Gharb. The garden of Portugal, this naturally arid district is laced with large-scale irrigation projects. Except for the massive development of beach resorts since the late 1960s, the landscape in many ways resembles the coast of nearby Morocco, with which it has much in common.

ALENTEJO & RIBATEJO East and southeast of Lisbon, these regions form the agrarian heartland of Portugal. Underpopulated but fertile, and marked mostly by fields and grasslands, these are horse- and bull-breeding territories, with some of the most idyllic landscapes in Iberia. Their medieval cities, including Evora, Tomar, Beja, Elvas, and Estremoz, contain famous examples of Roman and Manueline architecture.

COIMBRA & THE BEIRAS Between two of the country's most vital rivers, the Beiras were incorporated into the medieval kingdom of Portugal earlier than the territories farther south, including Lisbon. Given their history, they're among the most traditional Portuguese areas in the country. The medieval university town of Coimbra is the highlight of the region; a cluster of spas and the legendary forest of Buçaco also draw visitors. The region technically consists of three districts: Coastal Beira (Beira Litoral), Low Beira (Beira Baixa), and High Beira (Beira Alta). The Beiras contain the country's highest peaks—the Serra de Estrêla—and the Mondela River.

PORTO & THE DOURO Porto, Portugal's second-largest city, has thrived as a mercantile center since English traders used it as a base for the export of port, London's favorite drink during the Regency. The river that feeds it, the Douro, flows through some of the world's richest vineyards before emptying into the Atlantic in Porto's harbor. Porto abounds with the 19th-century mansions of merchants who grew wealthy from growing wine grapes or through investments in such colonies as Brazil. The most popular resort in the region is the once-sleepy former fishing village of Póvoa de Varzim.

THE MINHO This is the northernmost region of Portugal, an isolated, idiosyncratic area with a population descended more or less directly from Celtic ancestors. The local tongue is a tricky dialect that more closely resembles that of Galicia (in northwestern Spain) than it does Portuguese. The Minho is almost a land unto itself; with most of the population centered in Viana do Castelo, Guimarães, and Braga. Ardently provincial and suspicious of outsiders, the district figured prominently in the development of medieval Portugal as a kingdom separate from Spain, producing early kings who moved south in their conquest of territories held until then by the Moors.

TRAS-OS-MONTES This far northeastern and least visited corner of Portugal is a wild, rugged land whose name translates literally as "beyond the mountains." Aggressively provincial, the region nevertheless has strong ties to its neighbor, the Minho. Local granite dominates the architecture. The district stretches from Lamego and the Upper Douro to the Spanish border. Vila Real is the largest town.

MADEIRA Near the coast of Africa, 855km (530 miles) southwest of Portugal, Madeira is the much-eroded peak of a volcanic mass. Wintering English gentry first discovered the island's recreational charms; today it's one of the world's most famous islands, known for the abundant beauty of its gardens. Only 57km (35 miles) long and about 21km (13 miles) across at its widest point, the island is an autonomous region of Portugal and has a year-round population of 255,000.

THE AZORES This island chain is one of the most isolated in the Atlantic Ocean. It constitutes an autonomous region and has some 240,000 year-round occupants who live amid rocky, moss-covered landscapes closely tied to the sea. The archipelago spans more than 800km (496 miles) that stretch from the southeastern tip of Santa Maria to the northwestern extremity of

Regions of Portugal

Destination Portugal: Red Alert Checklist

- If you purchased traveler's checks, have you recorded the check numbers and stored the documentation separately from the checks?
- Did you stop the newspaper and mail delivery, and leave a set of keys with someone reliable?
- Did you pack your camera and an extra set of camera batteries and purchase enough film? If you packed film in your checked baggage, did you invest in protective pouches to shield film from airport x-rays?
- Do you have a safe, accessible place to store money?
- Did you bring your ID cards, such as AAA and AARP cards and student IDs, that could entitle you to discounts ?
- Did you bring emergency drug prescriptions and extra glasses and/or contact lenses?
- Did you find out your daily ATM withdrawal limit?
- Do you have your credit card PINs? Is there a daily withdrawal limit on credit card cash advances?
- If you have an E-ticket, do you have documentation?
- Did you leave a copy of your itinerary with someone at home?
- Do you have the measurements for those people you plan to buy clothes for on your trip?
- Do you have the address and phone number of your country's embassy with you?

the island of Corvo. The chain's largest island is São Miguel, which lies a third of the way across the Atlantic, about 1,200km (744 miles) west of Portugal and 3,400km (2,108 miles) east of New York. Today the Azores are widely known within yachting circles as the final destination for annual sailboat races from Newport and Bermuda.

2 Visitor Information

SOURCES OF INFORMATION

Before you go, contact one of the overseas branches of the **Portuguese National Tourist Office.** The main office in the **United States** is at 590 Fifth Ave., 4th Floor, New York, NY 10036-4704 (✆ **212/354-4403**). In **Canada,** the office is at 600 Bloor St. W., Suite 1005, Toronto, ON M4W 3B8 (✆ **416/921-7376**). In the **United Kingdom,** contact the Portuguese Tourist Office, 22-25A Sackville St., 2nd Floor, London W1X 1DE (✆ **020/7494-1441**). In **Australia,** information is available at the Embassy of Portugal, 6 Campion St., Deakin (Canberra) (✆ **02/6290 1733**).

HELPFUL WEBSITES

- **www.portugal.org:** Investments, Trade, and Tourism of Portugal, a government agency, maintains this site. It is a general information resource, providing data about tourism and attractions, among other information.
- **www.portugal-info.net:** This site provides an encyclopedic range of information about accommodations, restaurants and cuisine, events, entertainment, and sports. Its focus is on Lisbon and the Algarve, and it's of special use to the visitor from the United Kingdom.

- **www.pousadas.pt/:** This site provides the best details on *pousadas* (government-sponsored inns scattered throughout the country). It offers geographic details, current rates, information on online bookings, and even photographs.
- **www.tap-airportugal.us:** This site provides data about TAP's (Portuguese Air Transportation) flights in Portugal and online reservations. New features include all published fares and data about how to change reservations.

3 Entry Requirements & Customs

ENTRY REQUIREMENTS

Visas are not needed by U.S., Canadian, Irish, Australian, New Zealand, or British citizens for visits of less than 3 months. You do need a valid passport unless you're a citizen of another EU country (in which case, you need only an identity card, although we always recommend that you carry a passport anyway).

Safeguard your passport in an inconspicuous, inaccessible place like a money belt. If you lose it, visit the nearest consulate of your native country as soon as possible for a replacement.

For information on how to get a passport, go to the "Fast Facts" section of this chapter—the websites listed provide downloadable passport applications as well as the current fees for processing passport applications. For an up-to-date country-by-country listing of passport requirements around the world, go the "Foreign Entry Requirement" Web page of the U.S. State Department at **http://travel.state.gov/foreignentryreqs.html**.

CUSTOMS

WHAT YOU CAN BRING INTO PORTUGAL

You can take into Portugal most personal effects and the following items duty-free: a portable typewriter and 1 video camera or 2 still cameras with 10 rolls of film each; a portable radio, a tape recorder, and a laptop PC per person, provided that they show signs of use; 200 cigarettes, or 50 cigars, or 250 grams of tobacco; 2 liters of wine or 1 liter of liquor per person over 17 years old; and sports equipment, including fishing gear, 1 bicycle, skis, tennis or squash racquets, and golf clubs.

WHAT YOU CAN TAKE HOME FROM PORTUGAL

Returning **U.S. citizens** who have been away for at least 48 hours are allowed to bring back, once every 30 days, $800 worth of merchandise duty-free. You'll be charged a flat rate of 4% duty on the next $1,000 worth of purchases. Be sure to have your receipts handy. On mailed gifts, the duty-free limit is $100. With some exceptions, you cannot bring fresh

Tips Passport Savvy

Allow plenty of time before your trip to apply for a passport; processing normally takes 3 weeks but can take longer during busy periods (especially spring). And keep in mind that if you need a passport in a hurry, you'll pay a higher processing fee. When traveling, safeguard your passport in an inconspicuous, inaccessible place like a money belt, and keep a copy of the critical pages with your passport number in a separate place. If you lose your passport, visit the nearest consulate of your native country as soon as possible for a replacement.

fruits and vegetables into the United States. For specifics on what you can bring back, download the invaluable free pamphlet *Know Before You Go* online at **www.customs.gov**. (Click on "Traveler Information" and then "Know Before You Go.") Or, contact the **U.S. Customs Service,** 1300 Pennsylvania Ave., NW, Washington, DC 20229 (© **877/287-8667**), and request the pamphlet.

For a clear summary of **Canadian** rules, write for the booklet *I Declare,* issued by the **Canada Customs and Revenue Agency** (© **800/461-9999** in Canada, or 204/983-3500; www.ccra-adrc.gc.ca). Canada allows its citizens a C$750 exemption, and you're allowed to bring back duty-free 1 carton of cigarettes, 1 can of tobacco, 40 imperial ounces of liquor, and 50 cigars. In addition, you're allowed to mail gifts to Canada valued at less than C$60 a day, provided that they're unsolicited and don't contain alcohol or tobacco (write on the package "Unsolicited gift, under $60 value"). All valuables should be declared on the Y-38 form before departure from Canada, including serial numbers of valuables you already own, such as expensive foreign cameras. ***Note:*** The $750 exemption can be used only once a year and only after an absence of 7 days.

Citizens of the U.K. who are **returning from a European Union (EU) country** will go through a separate Customs exit (called the Blue Exit) especially for EU travelers. In essence, there is no limit on what you can bring back from an EU country, as long as the items are for personal use (this includes gifts) and you have already paid the necessary duty and tax. However, Customs law sets out guidance levels. If you bring in more than these levels, you might be asked to prove that the goods are for your own use. Guidance levels on goods bought in the EU for your own use are 3,200 cigarettes, 200 cigars, 400 cigarillos, 3kg of smoking tobacco, 10 liters of spirits, 90 liters of wine, 20 liters of fortified wine (such as port or sherry), and 110 liters of beer.

The duty-free allowance in **Australia** is A$400 or, for those under 18, A$200. Citizens can bring in 250 cigarettes or 250 grams of loose tobacco, and 1,125 milliliters of alcohol. If you're returning with valuables you already own, such as foreign-made cameras, you should file form B263. A helpful brochure available from Australian consulates or Customs offices is *Know Before You Go.* For more information, call the **Australian Customs Service** at © **1300/363 263,** or log on to www.customs.gov.au.

The duty-free allowance for **New Zealand** is NZ$700. Citizens over 17 can bring in 200 cigarettes, 50 cigars, or 250 grams of tobacco (or a mixture of all 3 if their combined weight doesn't exceed 250g), plus 4.5 liters of wine and beer, or 1.125 mililiters of liquor. New Zealand currency does not carry import or export restrictions. Fill out a certificate of export listing the valuables you are taking out of the country; that way, you can bring them back without paying duty. Most questions are answered in a free pamphlet available at New Zealand consulates and Customs offices: *New Zealand Customs Guide for Travelers, Notice no. 4.* For more information, contact **New Zealand Customs,** The Customhouse, 17–21 Whitmore St., Box 2218, Wellington (© **04/473-6099** or 0800/428-786 in New Zealand; www.customs.govt.nz).

4 Money

There are no limits on foreign currency brought into Portugal, but visitors are advised to declare the amount carried. That proves to the Portuguese Customs Office that the currency came from outside the country, and it

The U.S. Dollar, the British Pound, the Canadian Dollar & the Euro

The U.S. Dollar and the Euro. One U.S. dollar was worth approximately 1.15€ at the time of this writing. (Inversely stated, that means that 1€ was worth approximately US87¢.)

The British Pound, the U.S. Dollar, the Euro. At press time, £1 equaled approximately US$1.61 or approximately 1.40€.

The Canadian Dollar, the U.S. Dollar, and the Euro. At press time, C$1 equaled approximately US72¢ and approximately .63€.

US$	£	C$	Euro	US$	£	C$	Euro
1	.60	1.40	1.15	75	47	105	86
2	1.25	2.80	2.30	100	62	140	115
3	1.90	4.20	3.45	125	78	175	144
4	2.50	5.60	4.60	150	93	210	173
5	3.10	7.00	5.75	175	109	245	201
6	3.70	8.40	6.90	200	124	280	230
7	4.35	09.80	8.05	225	140	315	259
8	4.95	11	09.20	250	155	350	287
9	5.60	13	10	275	171	385	316
10	6.20	14	12	300	186	420	345
15	09.30	21	17	350	217	490	403
20	13	28	23	400	248	560	460
25	16	35	29	500	310	700	575
50	31	70	58	1000	620	1400	1150

allows you to take out the same amount or less.

EURO CURRENCY

The euro, the new single European currency, became the official currency of Portugal and 11 other countries on January 1, 1999, but not in the form of cash. On January 1, 2002, euro bank notes and coins were introduced. During a 2-month transition period, escudo notes, the old currency of Portugal, were withdrawn from circulation. The symbol of the euro is €; its official abbreviation is EUR.

FOREIGN CURRENCIES VS. THE US DOLLAR

Conversion ratios between the U.S. dollar and other currencies fluctuate, and their differences could affect the relative costs of your holiday. The figures reflected in the currency chart below were valid at the time of this writing, but they might not be valid by the time of your departure. This chart is useful for conversions of small amounts of money, but if you're planning on any major transactions, check for more updated rates before making any serious commitments.

It's a good idea to exchange at least some money—just enough to cover airport incidentals and transportation to your hotel—before you leave home so you can avoid lines at airport ATMs. You can exchange money at your local American Express or Thomas Cook office or your bank. If you're far from a bank with currency-exchange services, American Express offers traveler's checks and foreign currency, though with a $15 order fee and additional shipping costs, at www.americanexpress.com or **800/807-6233.**

ATMS

The easiest and best way to get cash away from home is from an ATM. The **Cirrus** (✆ **800/424-7787** in the U.S.; www.mastercard.com) and **PLUS** (✆ **800/843-7587** in the U.S.; www.visa.com) networks span the globe; look at the back of your bank card to see which network you're on, and then call or check online for ATM locations at your destination. Be sure you know your personal identification number (PIN) before you leave home, and be sure to find out your daily withdrawal limit before you depart. Also keep in mind that many banks impose a fee every time a card is used at a different bank's ATM, and that fee can be higher for international transactions (up to $5 or more) than for domestic ones (where they're rarely more than $1.50). On top of this, the bank from which you withdraw cash might charge its own fee. To compare banks' ATM fees within the U.S., use www.bankrate.com. For international withdrawal fees, ask your bank.

You can also get cash advances on your credit card at an ATM. Keep in mind that credit card companies try to protect themselves from theft by limiting the funds cardholders can withdraw outside their home country, so call your credit card company before you leave home.

If you have a PIN and a Visa, MasterCard, or EuroCard, you can head for the main office of **Unicre-Unibanco,** Avenida Antonio Augusto de Aguiar 122, 1050-019 Lisbon (✆ **21/350-9500**). ATMs are in a generally secure area that's accessible 24 hours a day from the sidewalk. Some branches also have ATMs.

If you have an American Express card and a PIN, you can use almost any ATM in Portugal, including the Unicre-Unibanco location listed above. Machines are usually reliable, but it's best to have a backup system for getting cash in case the ATMs in Portugal can't decipher the numbers on your card.

If you want to get cash as a debit against your American Express account, consult Amex's Portuguese representative, **Top Tours** (see "American Express" in "Fast Facts: Portugal," later in this chapter). Bring your Amex card, a photo ID or passport, and one of your personal checks drawn on virtually any bank in the world.

TRAVELER'S CHECKS

Traveler's checks are something of an anachronism from the days before the ATM made cash accessible at any time. Traveler's checks used to be the only sound alternative to traveling with dangerously large amounts of cash. They were as reliable as currency but, unlike cash, could be replaced if lost or stolen.

These days, traveler's checks are less necessary because most cities have 24-hour ATMs that allow you to withdraw small amounts of cash as needed. However, keep in mind that you will likely be charged an ATM withdrawal fee if the bank is not your own, so if you're withdrawing money every day, you might be better off with traveler's checks—provided that you don't mind showing identification every time you want to cash one.

Tips **Small Change**

When you change money, ask for some small bills or loose change. Petty cash will come in handy for tipping and public transportation. Consider keeping the change separate from your larger bills so that it's readily accessible and you'll be less of a target for theft.

Tips Dear Visa: I'm Off to Madeira!

Some credit card companies recommend that you notify them of any impending trip abroad so that they don't become suspicious and block charges when the card is used numerous times in a foreign destination. Even if you don't call your credit card company in advance, you can always call the card's toll-free emergency number (see "Fast Facts," later in this chapter) if a charge is refused—a good reason to carry the phone number with you. But perhaps the most important lesson here is to carry more than one card with you on your trip; a card might not work for any number of reasons, so having a backup is the smart way to go.

You can get traveler's checks at almost any bank. **American Express** offers denominations of $20, $50, $100, $500, and (for cardholders only) $1,000. You'll pay a service charge ranging from 1% to 4%. You can also get American Express traveler's checks over the phone by calling ✆ **800/221-7282** in the U.S.; Amex gold and platinum cardholders who use this number are exempt from the 1% fee. AAA members can obtain checks without a fee at most AAA offices.

Visa offers traveler's checks at Citibank locations nationwide, as well as at several other banks. The service charge ranges between 1.5% and 2%; checks come in denominations of $20, $50, $100, $500, and $1,000. Call ✆ **800/732-1322** in the U.S. for information. **MasterCard** also offers traveler's checks. Call ✆ **800/223-9920** in the U.S. for a location near you.

Foreign currency traveler's checks are useful if you're traveling to one country or to the Euro zone; they're accepted at locations such as B&Bs where dollar checks might not be, and they minimize the amount of math you have to do at your destination. **American Express** offers checks in Australian dollars, Canadian dollars, British pounds, euros, and Japanese yen. **Visa** checks come in Australian, Canadian, British, and euro versions; **MasterCard** offers those four plus yen and South African rands.

If you choose to carry traveler's checks, be sure to keep a record of their serial numbers separate from your checks, in case they are stolen or lost. You'll get a refund faster if you know the numbers.

CREDIT CARDS

Credit cards are a safe way to carry money, they provide a convenient record of all your expenses, and they generally offer good exchange rates. You can also withdraw cash advances from your credit cards at banks or ATMs, provided you know your PIN. If you've forgotten yours or didn't even know you had one, call the number on the back of your credit card and ask the bank to send it to you. It usually takes 5 to 7 business days, though some banks will provide the number over the phone if you tell them your mother's maiden name or some other personal information. Your credit card company will likely charge a commission (1 or 2%) on every foreign purchase you make, but don't sweat this small stuff; for most purchases, you'll still get the best deal with credit cards when you factor in things like ATM fees and higher traveler's check exchange rates.
In Portugal, American Express, Diners Club, MasterCard, and Visa are commonly accepted, with the latter two cards predominating.

What Things Cost in Lisbon	Euro €	US $	U.K. £
Taxi from the airport to the city center	7.50€	8.60	7.10
Average Metro ride	.50€	.55	.50
Double room at Four Seasons Hotel The Ritz Lisbon (very expensive)	284€	327	270
Double room at the Janelas Verdes Inn (moderate)	90€	103	85
Double room at the Residência Nazareth (inexpensive)	36€	41	34
Lunch for one, without wine, El Bodegón (moderate)	18€	21	17
Lunch for one, without wine, at António (moderate)	7.50€	8.60	7.10
Dinner for one, without wine, at António Clara (expensive)	30€	34	28
Dinner for one, without wine, at Conventual (moderate)	23€	26	21
Dinner for one, without wine, at Bonjardim (inexpensive)	14€	16	13
Glass of beer	1.90€	2.15	1.80
Coca-Cola in a restaurant	1.50€	1.75	1.45
Cup of coffee in a cafe	.40€	.45	.35
Roll of ASA 100 color film, 24 exposures	6€	6.90	5.70
Admission to the Museu Nacional dos Coches	2.25€	2.60	2.15
Movie ticket	3.70€	4.30	3.50
Theater ticket	7.50€	8.60	7.10

5 When to Go

CLIMATE

"We didn't know we had an April," one Lisbon resident said, "until that song came out." As a song and a season, "April in Portugal" is famous. Summer might be the most popular time to visit, but for the traveler who can chart his or her own course, spring and autumn are the most delectable seasons.

To use a North American analogy, the climate of Portugal most closely parallels that of California. There are only slight fluctuations in temperature between summer and winter; the overall mean ranges from 77°F (25°C) in summer to about 58°F (14°C) in winter. The rainy season begins in November and usually lasts through January. Because of the Gulf Stream, Portugal's northernmost area, Minho, enjoys mild (albeit very rainy) winters, even though it's at approximately the same latitude as New York City.

Snow brings many skiing enthusiasts to the Serra de Estrêla in north central Portugal. For the most part, however, winter means only some rain and lower temperatures in other regions. The Algarve and especially Madeira enjoy temperate winters. Madeira, in fact, basks in its high season in winter. The

Algarve, too, is somewhat of a winter Riviera that attracts sun worshipers from North America and Europe. Summers in both tend to be long, hot, clear, and dry.

Lisbon and Estoril enjoy 46°F (8°C) to 65°F (18°C) temperatures in winter and temperatures between 60°F (16°C) and 82°F (28°C) in summer.

Average Daytime Temperature (°F & °C) & Monthly Rainfall (Inches) in Lisbon

	Jan	Feb	Mar	Apr	May	June	July	Aug	Sept	Oct	Nov	Dec
Temp.(°F)	57	59	63	67	71	77	81	82	79	72	63	58
Temp.(°C)	13.8	15	17.2	19.4	21.6	25	27.2	27.7	26.1	22.2	17.2	14.4
Rainfall	4.3	3.0	4.2	2.1	1.7	.6	.1	.2	1.3	2.4	3.7	4.1

HOLIDAYS

Watch for these public holidays, and adjust your banking needs accordingly: New Year's Day and Universal Brotherhood Day (January 1); Carnaval (early March—dates vary); Good Friday (March or April—dates vary); Liberty Day, anniversary of the revolution (April 25); Labor Day (May 1); Corpus Christi (June—dates vary); Portugal Day (June 10); Feast of the Assumption (August 15); Proclamation of the Republic (October 5); All Saints' Day (November 1); Restoration of Independence (December 1); Feast of the Immaculate Conception (December 8); and Christmas Day (December 25). The Feast Day of St. Anthony (June 13) is a public holiday in Lisbon, and the Feast Day of St. John the Baptist (June 24) is a public holiday in Porto.

PORTUGAL CALENDAR OF EVENTS

We suggest that you verify dates with a tourist office because festival dates can vary greatly from year to year. Sometimes last-minute adjustments are made because of scheduling problems.

January

Festa de São Gonçalo e São Cristovão, Vila Nova de Gaia, across the river from Porto. These resemble fertility rites and are two of the most attended religious festivals in Portugal. An image of São Gonçalo is paraded through the narrow streets as merrymakers beat drums. Boatmen along the Douro ferry a figure of São Cristovão with a huge head down the river. Much port wine is drunk, and cakes baked into phallic shapes are consumed by all. Early January. Call ✆ **22/375-19-02** for more information.

February/March

Carnaval (Mardi Gras), throughout the country, notably in Nazaré, Ovar, Loulé, and Funchal (Madeira). Each town has its unique way of celebrating. Masked marchers, flower-bedecked floats, and satirically decorated vehicles mark the occasion. Food and wine are consumed in abundance. This is the final festival before Lent. For more details, check with the Portuguese National Tourist Office (see "Visitor Information," earlier). February or March.

Easter, all over Portugal. Some of the most noteworthy festivities take place at Póvoa de Varzim, Ovar, and especially the town of Braga, where Holy Week processions feature masked marchers and bejeweled floats along with fireworks, folk dancing, and torch parades. For more details, check with a Portuguese national tourist office (see "Visitor Information," earlier).

May

Festas das Cruzes, Barcelos on the river Cávado, near Braga. Since 1504, this festival has been celebrated with a Miracle of the Cross procession centered on a carpet made of millions of flower petals. Women in colorful regional dress adorn themselves with large gold chains. A giant fireworks display on the river signals the festival's end. Call ✆ **25/381-18-82** for more information. Early May.

First pilgrimage of the year to Fátima. In 1930, the bishop of Leiria authorized pilgrimages to this site. Today people from all over the world flock here to commemorate the first apparition of the Virgin to the little shepherd children in 1917. The year's last pilgrimage is in October (see below). Make hotel reservations months in advance, or plan to stay in a neighboring town. For more information, call the Fátima tourist office (✆ **24/953-11-39**). Mid-May.

June

Feira Nacional da Agricultura (also known as the Feira do Ribatejo), Santarém, north of Lisbon on the river Tagus. This is the most important agricultural fair in Portugal. The best horses and cattle from all provinces are on display, and horse shows and bullfights enliven the festival. Food pavilions feature various regional cuisines. For more information, call ✆ **24/330-03-00.** June 7 to 15.

Feast of St. John, Porto, home of the famous port wine. Honoring São João (St. John), this colorful festival features bonfires, all-night singing and dancing, and processions of locals in colorful costumes. Call ✆ **22/205-27-40;** www.portoturismo.pt, for more information. June 23 and 24.

Festas dos Santos Populares, throughout Lisbon. Celebrations begin on June 13 and 14 in the Alfama, with feasts honoring Saint Anthony. Parades commemorating the city's patron saint feature *marchas* (parading groups of singers and musicians) along Avenida da Liberdade, and there is plenty of singing, dancing, drinking wine, and eating grilled sardines. On June 23 and 24, for the Feast of St. John the Baptist, bonfires brighten the night and participants jump over them. The night of the final celebration is the Feast of St. Peter on June 29. The Lisbon tourist office (✆ **21/346-63-07;** www.egeac.pt) supplies details about where some of the events are staged, although much of the action is spontaneous. Mid-June to June 30.

Festas do São Pedro, Mintijo, near Lisbon. This festival honoring St. Peter has been held since medieval times. On the final day there's a blessing of the boats and a colorful procession. Grilled sardines are the main item on the menu. Bull breeders bring their beasts into town and release them through the streets to chase foolish young men, who are often permanently injured or killed. There are also bullfights. On the final night, participants observe the pagan rite of setting a skiff afire and offering it as a sacrifice to the river Tagus. Call ✆ **21/346-63-07** for more information. June 28 and 29.

July

Colete Encarnado (Red Waistcoat), Vila Franca de Xira, north of Lisbon on the river Tagus. Like the more famous *feria* in Pamplona, Spain, this festival involves bulls running through narrow streets, followed by sensational bullfights in what aficionados consider the best bullring in Portugal. Fandango dancing and rodeo-style competition among the *Ribatejo campinos* (cowboys) mark the event. For more information, call ✆ **26/327-76-53.** First or second Sunday in July.

Estoril Festival. Outside Lisbon at the seaside resort of Estoril, this festival of classical music occupies two concert halls that were built for the

500th anniversary of Columbus's first voyage to the New World. For information, write **Associação Internacional de Música da Costa do Estoril,** Casa Museu Verdades de Faria, Av. de Saboia, 2765–277 Monte Estoril (✆ **21/468-51-99;** fax 21/468-56-07; www.estorilfestival.net). Mid-July to first week in August (dates vary).

August

Feast of Our Lady of Monte, Madeira. On Assumption Eve and Day (Aug 14–15), the island's most important religious festival begins with devout worship and climaxes in an outburst of fun. There's music, dancing, eating, and general drinking and carousing until dawn. For more information, call ✆ **21/346-91-13.**

Festas da Senhora da Agonia, Viana do Castelo, at the mouth of the river Lima, north of Porto. The most spectacular festival in the north honors Our Lady of Suffering. A replica of the Virgin is carried through the streets over carpets of flowers. The bishop directs a procession of fishers to the sea to bless the boats. Float-filled parades mark the 5-day-and-night event as a time of revelry and celebration. A blaze of fireworks ends the festival. Call the tourist office (✆ **25/882-26-20**) for exact dates, which vary from year to year. Reserve hotel rooms well in advance or be prepared to stay in a neighboring town. Mid-August.

September

Romaria da Nossa Senhora de Nazaré, Nazaré, Portugal's most famed fishing village. The event (Our Lady of Nazaré Festival) includes folk dancing, singing, and bullfights. The big attraction is the procession carrying the image of Nossa Senhora de Nazaré down to the sea. For more information, call ✆ **262/56-11-94.** Early to mid-September.

October

Last Pilgrimage of the Year to Fátima. Thousands of pilgrims from all over the world descend on Fátima to mark the occasion of the last apparition of the Virgin, which is said to have occurred on October 12, 1917. Call ✆ **24/953-11-39** for more information. October 12.

6 Travel Insurance

Since Portugal for most of us is far from home, and a number of things could go wrong—lost luggage, trip cancellation, a medical emergency—consider the following types of insurance.

Check your existing insurance policies and credit-card coverage before you buy travel insurance. You might already be covered for lost luggage, cancelled tickets, or medical expenses. The cost of travel insurance varies widely, depending on the cost and length of your trip, your age, your health, and the type of trip you're taking.

TRIP-CANCELLATION INSURANCE Trip-cancellation insurance helps you get your money back if you have to back out of a trip, if you have to go home early, or if your travel supplier goes bankrupt. Allowed reasons for cancellation can range from sickness to natural disasters to the State Department declaring your destination unsafe for travel. (Insurers usually won't cover vague fears, though, as many travelers discovered who tried to cancel their trips in October 2001 because they were wary of flying.) In this unstable world, trip-cancellation insurance is a good buy if you're getting tickets well in advance—who knows what the state of the world, or of your airline, will be in 9 months? Insurance policy details vary, so read the fine print—and especially make sure that your airline or cruise line is on the list of carriers covered in case of bankruptcy. For information, contact one of the following insurers: **Access America** (✆ 800/284-8300 in the U.S.; www.accessamerica.com), **Travel Guard International** (✆ 800/826-1300 in the U.S.; www.travelguard.com), **Travel Insured International** (✆ 800/243-3174 in the U.S.; www.travelinsured.com), **or Travelex Insurance Services** (✆ 800/228-9792 in the U.S.; www.travelex-insurance.com).

MEDICAL INSURANCE Most health insurance policies cover you if you get sick away from home—but check, particularly if you're insured by an HMO. With the exception of certain HMOs and Medicare/Medicaid, your medical insurance should cover medical treatment—even hospital care—overseas. However, most out-of-country hospitals make you pay your bills up front and send you a refund after you've returned home and filed the necessary paperwork. And in a worst-case scenario, there's the high cost of emergency evacuation. If you require additional medical insurance, try **MEDEX International** (✆ **888/MEDEX-00** in the U.S., or 410/453-6300; www.medexassist.com) or **Travel Assistance International** (✆ **800/821-2828** in the U.S.; www.travelassistance.com); for general information on services, call the company's **Worldwide Assistance Services, Inc.,** at ✆ **800/777-8710** in the U.S.

LOST-LUGGAGE INSURANCE On international flights (including U.S. portions of international trips), baggage is limited to approximately $9.05 per pound, up to approximately $635 per checked bag. If you plan to check items more valuable than the standard liability, see if your valuables are covered by your homeowner's policy, get baggage insurance as part of your comprehensive travel-insurance package, or buy Travel Guard's (see above) BagTrak product. Don't buy insurance at the airport because it's usually overpriced. Be sure to take any valuables or irreplaceable items with you in your carry-on luggage because many valuables (including books, money, and electronics) aren't covered by airline policies.

If your luggage is lost, immediately file a lost-luggage claim at the airport, detailing the luggage contents. For most airlines, you must report delayed, damaged, or lost baggage within 4 hours of arrival. The airlines are required to deliver luggage, once found, directly to your house or destination free of charge.

7 Health & Safety

STAYING HEALTHY

Portugal does not offer free medical treatment to visitors, except for citizens of certain countries, such as Great Britain, which have reciprocal health agreements. Nationals from such countries as Canada and the United States have to pay for medical services rendered.

You should encounter few health problems traveling in Portugal. The tap water is generally safe to drink, the milk is pasteurized, and health services are good. Occasionally, the change in diet can cause some minor diarrhea, so you might want to take along some antidiarrhea medicine.

Limit your exposure to the sun, especially during the first few days of your trip and thereafter from 11am to 2pm. Use a sunscreen with a high protection factor and apply it liberally. Remember that children need more protection than adults do.

WHAT TO DO IF YOU GET SICK AWAY FROM HOME

Medical facilities are generally available in Portugal but, in many cases, might not meet U.S. standards. If a medical emergency arises, your hotel staff can usually put you in touch with a reliable doctor. If not, contact the American embassy or a consulate; each one maintains a list of English-speaking doctors. Medical and hospital services aren't free, so be sure that you have appropriate insurance coverage before you travel.

In most cases, your existing health plan will provide the coverage you need. But double-check; you might want to buy **travel medical insurance** instead. (See the section on insurance, above.) Bring your insurance ID card with you when you travel.

If you suffer from a chronic illness, consult your doctor before your departure. For conditions like epilepsy, diabetes, or heart problems, wear a **Medic Alert Identification Tag** (© **800/825-3785** in the U.S.; www.medicalert.org), which will immediately alert doctors to your condition and give them access to your records through Medic Alert's 24-hour hot line.

Pack **prescription medications** in your carry-on luggage, and carry prescription medications in their original containers, with pharmacy labels—otherwise, they won't make it through airport security. Also bring along copies of your prescriptions in case you lose your pills or run out. Don't forget an extra pair of contact lenses or prescription glasses. Carry the generic name of prescription medicines, in case a local pharmacist is unfamiliar with the brand name.

Contact the **International Association for Medical Assistance to Travelers (IAMAT)** (© **716/754-4883** in the U.S. or 416/652-0137; www.iamat.org) for tips on travel and health concerns in the countries you're visiting and for lists of local, English-speaking doctors. The **Centers for Disease Control and Prevention** (© **800/311-3435** in the U.S.; www.cdc.gov) provide up-to-date information on necessary vaccines and health hazards by region or country. Any foreign consulate can provide a list of area doctors who speak English. If you get sick, consider asking your hotel concierge to recommend a local doctor—even his or her own. You can also try the emergency room at a local hospital; many have walk-in clinics for emergency cases that are not life-threatening. You might not get immediate attention, but you won't pay the high price of an emergency room visit.

STAYING SAFE

Though Portugal has a relatively low rate of violent crime, petty crime against tourists is on the rise in continental Portugal. Travelers can become targets of pickpockets and purse-snatchers, particularly at popular sites, in restaurants, and on public transportation. Rental cars and vehicles with nonlocal license plates are targets for break-ins, and travelers should remove all luggage from vehicles upon parking. Travelers should also avoid using ATMs in isolated or poorly lit areas. Drivers in continental Portugal should keep car doors locked when stopped at intersections. In general, visitors to Portugal should carry limited cash and credit cards and should leave extra cash, credit cards, and personal documents at home or in a hotel safe. While thieves can operate anywhere, the U.S. Embassy receives frequent reports of theft from the following areas:

Lisbon Area: Pick-pocketing and purse-snatching in the Lisbon area occur in buses, restaurants, the airport, trains, train stations, and trams, especially tram no. 28 to the Castle of São Jorge. Gangs of youths have robbed passengers on the Lisbon–Cascais train. At restaurants, thieves snatch items hung over the backs of chairs or placed on the floor. There have been reports of theft of unattended luggage from the Lisbon Airport. Special care should be taken at the Santa Apolonia and Rosso train stations, the Alfama and Bairro Alto districts, the Castle of São Jorge, and Belem.

Other Areas: Thefts have been reported in Sintra, Cascais, Mafra, and Fátima. Automobile break-ins occur in parking areas at attractions and near restaurants. Special care should be taken in parking at the Moorish Castle and Pena Palace in Sintra, and at the beachfront areas of Quincho, Cabo da Roca, and Boca do Inferno.

8 Specialized Travel

TRAVELERS WITH DISABILITIES

Most disabilities shouldn't stop anyone from traveling. There are more options and resources out there than ever.

Because of Portugal's many hills and endless flights of stairs, visitors with disabilities might have difficulty getting around the country, but conditions are slowly improving. Newer hotels are more sensitive to the needs of those with disabilities, and the more expensive restaurants, in general, are wheelchair-accessible. However, since most places have limited, if any, facilities for people with disabilities, you might consider taking an organized tour specifically designed to accommodate travelers with disabilities.

Organizations that offer assistance to travelers with disabilities include the **MossRehab Hospital** (✆ **215/456-9900;** www.mossresourcenet.org), which provides a library of accessible-travel resources online; the **Society for Accessible Travel and Hospitality** (✆ **212/447-7284;** www.sath.org; annual membership fees $45 for adults, $30 for seniors and students), which offers a wealth of travel resources for all types of disabilities and informed recommendations on destinations, access guides, travel agents, tour operators, vehicle rentals, and companion services; and the **American Foundation for the Blind** (✆ **800/232-5463** in the U.S.; www.afb.org), which provides information on traveling with Seeing Eye dogs.

For more information specifically targeted to travelers with disabilities, the community website **iCan** (www.icanonline.net/channels/travel/index.cfm) has destination guides and several regular columns on accessible travel. Also check out the quarterly magazine ***Emerging Horizons*** ($15 per year, $20 outside the U.S.; www.emerginghorizons.com); **Twin Peaks Press** (✆ **360/694-2462;** http://disabilitybookshop.virtualave.net/blist84.htm), offering travel-related books for travelers with special needs; and ***Open World Magazine,*** published by the Society for Accessible Travel and Hospitality (see above; subscription $18/yr., $35 outside the U.S.).

GAY & LESBIAN TRAVELERS

Attitudes toward homosexuality vary by region, with Lisbon, naturally, being the center of gay male life (less so for lesbians). The country has a strong Catholic heritage, and public displays of same-sex affection, especially in rural areas, might bring disapproval. Even so, overt homophobia is rare in Portugal. Nearly all hotels are savvy about checking in same-sex couples, even if a double bed is requested.

The International Gay & Lesbian Travel Association (IGLTA) (✆ **800/448-8550** in the U.S. or 954/776-2626; www.iglta.org) is the trade association for the gay and lesbian travel industry, and offers an online directory of gay and lesbian-friendly travel businesses; go to the website and click on "Members."

Many agencies offer tours and travel itineraries specifically for gay and lesbian travelers. **Above and Beyond Tours** (✆ **800/397-2681** in the U.S.;

www.abovebeyondtours.com) is the exclusive gay and lesbian tour operator for United Airlines. **Now, Voyager** (✆ **800/255-6951** in the U.S.; www.nowvoyager.com) is a well-known San Francisco–based gay-owned and -operated travel service. **Olivia Cruises & Resorts** (✆ **800-631-6277** in the U.S., or 510/655-0364; www.olivia.com) charters entire resorts and ships for exclusive lesbian vacations and offers smaller group experiences for both gay and lesbian travelers.

The following travel guides are available at most travel bookstores and gay and lesbian bookstores, or you can order them from **Giovanni's Room** bookstore, 1145 Pine St., Philadelphia, PA 19107 (✆ **215/923-2960;** www.giovannisroom.com): ***Frommer's Gay & Lesbian Europe,*** an excellent travel resource; ***Out and About*** (✆ **800/929-2268** in the U.S., or 415-644-8044; www.outandabout.com), which offers guidebooks and a newsletter 10 times a year packed with solid information on the global gay and lesbian scene; ***Spartacus International Gay Guide*** and ***Odysseus,*** both good annual English-language guidebooks focused on gay men; the ***Damron*** guides, with separate annual books for gay men and lesbians; and ***Gay Travel A to Z: The World of Gay & Lesbian Travel Options at Your Fingertips,*** by Marianne Ferrari (Ferrari Publications; Box 35575, Phoenix, AZ 85069), a very good gay and lesbian guidebook series.

SENIOR TRAVEL

Mention the fact that you're a senior citizen when you make your travel reservations. Although all of the major U.S. airlines except America West have cancelled their senior discount and coupon book programs, many hotels still offer discounts for seniors. In most cities, people over the age of 60 qualify for reduced admission to theaters, museums, and other attractions, as well as discounted fares on public transportation.

Members of **AARP** (formerly known as the American Association of Retired Persons), 601 E St. NW, Washington, DC 20049 (✆ **800/424-3410** in the U.S., or 202/434-2277; www.aarp.org), get discounts on hotels, airfares, and car rentals. AARP offers members a wide range of benefits, including *AARP The Magazine* and a monthly newsletter. Anyone over 50 can join.

Many reliable agencies and organizations target the 50-plus market. **Elderhostel** (✆ **877/426-8056** in the U.S.; www.elderhostel.org) arranges study programs for those aged 55 and over (and a spouse or companion of any age) in the U.S. and in more than 80 countries around the world. Most courses last 5 to 7 days in the U.S. (2–4 weeks abroad), and many include airfare, accommodations in university dormitories or modest inns, meals, and tuition. **ElderTreks** (✆ **800/741-7956** in the U.S.; www.eldertreks.com) offers small-group tours to off-the-beaten-path or adventure-travel locations, restricted to travelers 50 and older.

Recommended publications offering travel resources and discounts for seniors include: the quarterly magazine ***Travel 50 & Beyond*** (www.travel50andbeyond.com); ***Travel Unlimited: Uncommon Adventures for the Mature Traveler*** (Avalon); ***101 Tips for Mature Travelers,*** available from Grand Circle Travel (✆ **800/221-2610** in the U.S., or 617/350-7500; www.gct.com); ***The 50+ Traveler's Guidebook*** (St. Martin's Press); and ***Unbelievably Good Deals and Great Adventures That You Absolutely Can't Get Unless You're Over 50*** (McGraw Hill).

FOR BLACK TRAVELERS

Agencies and organizations that provide resources for black travelers include **Rodgers Travel** (✆ **215/473-1775;** www.rodgerstravel.com), a Philadelphia-based travel agency with an extensive menu of tours in destinations worldwide, including heritage and private group tours.

The Internet offers a number of helpful travel sites for the black traveler. **Black Travel Online** (www.blacktravelonline.com) posts news on upcoming events and includes links to articles and travel-booking sites. **Soul of America** (www.soulofamerica.com) is a more comprehensive website, with travel tips, event and family reunion postings, and sections on historically black beach resorts and active vacations.

For more information, check out the following collections and guides: ***Go Girl: The Black Woman's Guide to Travel & Adventure*** (Eighth Mountain Press), a compilation of travel essays by writers including Jill Nelson and Audre Lorde, with some practical information and trip-planning advice; ***The African American Travel Guide,*** by Wayne Robinson (Hunter Publishing; must be bought direct at www.hunterpublishing.com), with details on 19 North American cities; ***Steppin' Out,*** by Carla Labat (Avalon), with details on 20 cities; ***Travel and Enjoy Magazine*** (✆ **866/266-6211;** www.travelandenjoy.com; subscription $24/yr), which focuses on discounts and destination reviews; and the more narrative ***Pathfinders Magazine*** (✆ **877/977-PATH;** www.pathfinderstravel.com; subscription $15/yr.), which includes articles on everything from Rio de Janeiro to Ghana.

FAMILY TRAVEL

If you have enough trouble getting your kids out of the house in the morning, dragging them thousands of miles away might seem like an insurmountable challenge. But family travel can be immensely rewarding, giving you new ways of seeing the world through smaller pairs of eyes.

On airlines, you must request a special menu for children at least 24 hours in advance. If baby food is required, however, bring your own and ask a flight attendant to warm it to the right temperature.

Arrange ahead of time for such necessities as a crib, a bottle warmer, and a car seat.

The University of New Hampshire runs **Familyhostel** (✆ **800/733-9753** in the U.S., or 603/862-1147; fax 603/862-1113; www.learn.unh.edu), an intergenerational alternative to standard guided tours. You live on a European college campus for the 2- or 3-week program, attend lectures and seminars, go on lots of field trips, and do all the sightseeing—all of it guided by a team of experts and academics. It's designed for children (ages 8–15), parents, and grandparents.

You can find good family-oriented vacation advice on the Internet from sites like the **Family Travel Network** (www.familytravelnetwork.com); **Traveling Internationally with Your Kids** (www.travelwithyourkids.com), a comprehensive site offering sound advice for long-distance and international travel with children; and **Family Travel Files** (www.thefamilytravelfiles.com), which offers an online magazine and a directory of off-the-beaten-path tours and tour operators for families.

Look also for our "Kids" icon, indicating attractions, restaurants, or hotels and resorts that are especially family-friendly.

Remember that for people 15 and under, a passport is valid for only 5 years and costs $40, whereas for those 16 and up, a passport is valid for 10 years and costs $60.

STUDENT TRAVEL

The best resource for students is the **Council on International Educational Exchange,** or CIEE (✆ **800/407-8839** in the U.S., or 207/553-7600; www.ciee.org). **STA Travel**

(✆ **800/781-4040** in the U.S.; www.statravel.com) is the biggest student travel agency in the world. It can get you discounts on plane tickets, rail passes, and the like. Ask for a list of their offices in major cities so that you can keep the discounts flowing (and aid lines open) as you travel.

From STA Travel you can get the student traveler's best friend, the **International Student Identity Card (ISIC).** It's the only officially accepted form of student identification, good for cut rates on rail passes, plane tickets, and other discounts. It also offers basic health and life insurance and a 24-hour help line. If you're no longer a student but are still under 26, you can get an **International Youth Travel Card (IYTC)** from the same people, which gets you the insurance and some of the discounts (but not student admission prices in museums).

In Canada, **Travel CUTS,** 200 Ronson Dr., Suite 320, Toronto, ON M9W 5Z9 (✆ **800/667-2887** or 416/614-2887; fax 416/614-9670; www.travelcuts.com), provides International Travel Identity cards for students and teachers ages 12 to 25.

FOR SINGLE TRAVELERS

Many people prefer traveling alone—except for the relatively steep cost of booking a single room, which is usually well over half the price of a double.

Unfortunately for the 85 million or so single Americans, the travel industry is far more geared toward couples, so singles often wind up paying the penalty. One company that resolves this problem is **Travel Companion Exchange** (TCE), which matches single travelers with like-minded companions. Jens Jurgen, who charges $159 for an annual listing in his well-publicized records, heads the Exchange. People seeking travel companions fill out forms stating their preferences and needs, and receive a listing of potential travel partners. Companions of the same or opposite sex can be requested. For $48 you can get a bimonthly newsletter averaging 70 large pages that also provides numerous money-saving travel tips of special interest to solo travelers. A sample copy is available for $6. For an application and more information, contact Jens Jurgen at Travel Companion Exchange, P.O. Box 833, Amityville, NY 11701 (✆ **631/454-0880;** fax 631/454-0170; www.travelcompanions.com).

Travel Buddies Singles Travel Club (✆ **800/998-9099** in the U.S., or 604/533-2483; www.travelbuddiesworldwide.com) runs single-friendly tours. **The Single Gourmet Club,** 510 Madison Ave., New York, NY 10022 (✆ **212/980-8788;** fax 212/980-3138; www.singlegourmetny.com), is an international social, dining, and travel club for singles. It has offices in 21 American and Canadian cities and in London.

Many British agents are keenly aware of the needs of the single traveler. One tour operator whose groups are usually at least half singles is **Explore Worldwide Ltd.,** 1 Frederick St., Aldershot, Hampshire, England GU11 1LQ (✆ **01252/760000;** www.exploreworldwide.com). It has a well-justified reputation for offering offbeat tours, including 14-day expeditions to five islands of the Azores, and motor coach tours through the highlights of "Unknown Spain and Portugal." Groups rarely include more than 16 participants; children under 14 are not allowed.

TravelChums (✆ **212/787-2621;** www.travelchums.com) is an Internet-only travel-companion matching service with elements of an online personals-type site, hosted by the respected New York–based Shaw Guides travel service.

For more information, check out Eleanor Berman's ***Traveling Solo: Advice and Ideas for More Than 250 Great Vacations*** (Globe Pequot), a guide with advice on traveling alone, whether on your own or on a group tour. (It's been updated for 2003.) Or turn to the **Travel Alone and Love It** website (www.travelaloneandloveit.com), designed by former flight attendant Sharon Wingler, the author of the book of the same name. Her site is full of tips for single travelers.

9 Planning Your Trip Online

SURFING FOR AIRFARES

The "big three" online travel agencies, **Expedia.com, Travelocity.com,** and **Orbitz.com,** sell most of the air tickets bought on the Internet. (Canadian travelers should try expedia.ca and Travelocity.ca; U.K. residents can go to expedia.co.uk and opodo.co.uk.) Each has different business deals with the airlines and might offer different fares on the same flights, so it's wise to shop around. Expedia and Travelocity will also send you **e-mail notification** when a cheap fare becomes available to your favorite destination. Of the smaller travel agency websites, **SideStep** (www.sidestep.com) has gotten the best reviews from Frommer's authors. It's a browser add-on that purports to "search 140 sites at once," but in reality it beats competitors' fares only as often as other sites do.

Also remember to check **airline websites,** especially those for low-fare carriers whose fares are often misreported or simply missing from travel agency websites. Even with major airlines, you can often shave a few bucks from a fare by booking directly through the airline and avoiding a travel agency's transaction fee. But you'll get these discounts only by **booking online:** Most airlines now offer online-only fares that even their phone agents know nothing about. For the websites of airlines that fly to and from your destination, go to "Getting There," below.

Great **last-minute deals** are available through free weekly e-mail services provided directly by the airlines. Most of these are announced on Tuesday or Wednesday and must be purchased online. Most are valid only for travel that weekend, but some can be booked weeks or months in advance. Sign up for weekly e-mail alerts at airline websites, or check megasites such as **Smarter Living** (smarterliving.com) that compile comprehensive lists of last-minute specials. For last-minute trips, **site59.com** in the U.S. and **lastminute.com** in Europe often have better deals than the major-label sites.

If you're willing to give up some control over your flight details, use an **opaque fare service** like **Priceline** (www.priceline.com; www.priceline.co.uk for Europeans) or **Hotwire** (www.hotwire.com). Both offer rock-bottom prices in exchange for travel on a "mystery airline" at a mysterious time of day, often with a mysterious change of planes en route. The mystery airlines are all major, well-known carriers. Priceline usually has better deals than Hotwire, but you have to play their "name our price" game. If you're new at this, the helpful folks at **BiddingForTravel** (www.biddingfortravel.com) do a good job of demystifying Priceline's prices. Priceline and Hotwire are great for flights within North America and between the U.S. and Europe.

For much more about airfares and savvy air-travel tips and advice, pick up a copy of *Frommer's Fly Safe, Fly Smart* (Wiley Publishing, Inc.).

SURFING FOR HOTELS

Shopping online for hotels is much easier in the U.S., Canada, and certain parts of Europe, including Spain, than it is in the rest of the world. Of the "big three" sites, **Expedia** might be the best choice, thanks to its long list of special deals. **Travelocity** runs a close second. Hotel specialist sites

Frommers.com: The Complete Travel Resource

For an excellent travel-planning resource, we highly recommend Frommers.com (www.frommers.com). We're a little biased, of course, but we guarantee that you'll find the travel tips, reviews, monthly vacation giveaways, and online-booking capabilities thoroughly indispensable. Among the special features are our popular **Message Boards,** where Frommer's readers post queries and share advice (sometimes even our authors show up to answer questions); **Frommers.com Newsletter,** for the latest travel bargains and insider travel secrets; and **Frommer's Destinations Section,** where you'll get expert travel tips, hotel and dining recommendations, and advice on the sights to see for more than 3,000 destinations around the globe. When your research is done, the **Online Reservations System** (www.frommers.com/book_a_trip/) takes you to Frommer's preferred online partners for booking your vacation at affordable prices.

hotels.com and **hoteldiscounts.com** are also reliable. An excellent free program, **TravelAxe** (www.travelaxe.net), can help you search multiple hotel sites at once, even ones you might never have heard of.

Priceline and Hotwire are even better for hotels than for airfares; with both, you're allowed to pick the neighborhood and quality level of your hotel before offering up your money. Priceline's hotel product even covers Europe and Asia, though it's much better at getting five-star lodging for three-star prices than at finding anything at the bottom of the scale. ***Note:*** Hotwire overrates its hotels by one star—what Hotwire calls a four-star is a three-star anywhere else.

SURFING FOR RENTAL CARS

For booking rental cars online, the best deals are usually found at rental-car company websites, although all the major online travel agencies also offer rental-car reservations services. Priceline and Hotwire work well for rental cars, too; the only "mystery" is which major rental company you get, and for most travelers, the difference among Hertz, Avis, and Budget is negligible.

10 The 21st-Century Traveler

INTERNET ACCESS AWAY FROM HOME

Travelers have any number of ways to check their e-mail and access the Internet on the road. Of course, using your own laptop—or even a PDA (personal desk assistant) or electronic organizer with a modem—gives you the most flexibility. But even if you don't have a computer, you can access your e-mail and even your office computer from cybercafes.

WITHOUT YOUR OWN COMPUTER

It's hard nowadays to find a city that *doesn't* have a few cybercafes. Although there's no definitive directory for cybercafes—these are independent businesses, after all—three places to start looking are at **www.cybercaptive.com**, **www.netcafeguide.com**, and **www.cybercafe.com**.

Most major airports now have **Internet kiosks** scattered throughout their gates. These kiosks, which you'll also see in shopping malls, hotel lobbies, and tourist information offices around the world, give you basic Web access for a per-minute fee that's usually higher than cybercafe prices. The kiosks' clunkiness and high price means they should be avoided whenever possible.

To retrieve your e-mail, ask your **Internet Service Provider (ISP)** if it has a Web-based interface tied to your existing e-mail account. If your ISP doesn't have such an interface, you can use the free **mail2web** service (www.mail2web.com) to view (but not reply to) your home e-mail. For more flexibility, you might want to open a free, Web-based e-mail account with **Yahoo! Mail** (mail.yahoo.com). (Microsoft's Hotmail is another popular option, but Hotmail has severe spam problems.) Your home ISP might be able to forward your e-mail to the Web-based account automatically.

If you need to access files on your office computer, look into a service called **GoToMyPC** (www.gotomypc.com). The service provides a Web-based interface for you to access and manipulate a distant PC from anywhere—even a cybercafe—provided that your "target" PC is on and has an always-on connection to the Internet (such as with Road Runner cable). The service offers top-quality security, but if you're worried about hackers, use your own laptop rather than a cybercafe to access the GoToMyPC system.

WITH YOUR OWN COMPUTER

Major Internet Service Providers (ISP) have **local access numbers** around the world, allowing you to go online by simply placing a local call. Check your ISP's website or call its toll-free number, and ask how you can use your current account away from home and how much it will cost.

If you're traveling outside the reach of your ISP, the **iPass** network has dial-up numbers in most of the world's countries. You'll have to sign up with an iPass provider, who will then tell you how to set up your computer for your destination(s). For a list of iPass providers, go to www.ipass.com and click on "Individuals." One solid provider is **i2roam** (www.i2roam.com; ✆ **866/811-6209** in the U.S. or Canada, or 920/235-0475).

Wherever you go, bring a **connection kit** of the right power and phone adapters, a spare phone cord, and a spare Ethernet network cable.

Most business-class hotels throughout the world offer dataports for laptop modems, and a few hundred hotels in Portugal now offer high-speed Internet access using an Ethernet network cable. You'll have to bring your own cables either way, so **call your hotel in advance** to find out what the options are.

CELLPHONES OUTSIDE THE U.S.

The three letters that define much of the world's **wireless capabilities** are GSM (Global System for Mobiles), a big seamless network that makes for easy cross-border cellphone use throughout Europe and in dozens of other countries worldwide. In the U.S., T-Mobile, AT&T Wireless, and Cingular use this quasi-universal system; in Canada, Microcell and some Rogers customers are GSM, and all Europeans and most Australians use GSM.

If your cellphone is on a GSM system and you have a world-capable phone such as many (but not all) Sony Ericsson, Motorola, or Samsung models, you can make and receive calls across civilized areas on much of the globe, from Andorra to Uganda. Just call your wireless operator and ask for "international roaming" to be activated on your account. Unfortunately, per-minute charges can be high—usually $1.50 to $2.50 in Portugal.

Cellphone Rental

Two good wireless rental companies are **InTouch USA** (✆ **800/872-7626** in the U.S.; www.intouchglobal.com) and **RoadPost** (www.roadpost.com; ✆ **888-290-1606** in the U.S., or 905/272-5665). Give them your itinerary, and they'll tell you what wireless products you need. InTouch will also advise you for free on whether your existing phone will work overseas; simply call ✆ **703/222-7161** between 9am and 4pm EST, or go to http://intouchglobal.com/travel.htm.

World-phone owners can bring down their per-minute charges with a bit of trickery. Call your cellular operator and say you'll be going abroad for several months and want to "unlock" your phone to use it with a local provider. Usually, they'll oblige. Then, in your destination country, pick up a cheap, prepaid phone chip at a mobile phone store and slip it into your phone. (Show your phone to the salesperson because not all phones work on all networks.) You'll get a local phone number in your destination country—and much, much lower calling rates.

Otherwise, **renting** a phone is a good idea. While you can rent a phone from any number of overseas sites, including kiosks at airports and at car-rental agencies, we suggest renting the phone before you leave home. That way you can give loved ones your new number, make sure the phone works, and take the phone wherever you go—especially helpful when you rent overseas, where phone-rental agencies bill in local currency and might not let you take the phone to another country.

Phone rental isn't cheap. You'll usually pay $40 to $50 per week, plus airtime fees of at least a dollar a minute. If you're traveling to Europe, though, local rental companies often offer free incoming calls within their home country, which can save you big bucks. The bottom line: Shop around.

11 Getting There

BY PLANE

Flying from New York to Lisbon typically costs less than from New York to Paris, Amsterdam, or Frankfurt.

In today's marketplace, one airline proposes a fare structure, and another airline follows with a competing and perhaps different fare structure. The competition might or might not result in uniform prices for all airlines flying to that particular country. It all adds up to chaos—but often beneficial chaos for the alert traveler willing to study and consider all the fares available. The key to bargain airfares is to shop around.

Flying time from New York to Lisbon is about 6½ hours; from Atlanta to Lisbon (with a stopover), it's 12 hours; from Los Angeles to Lisbon (with a stopover), it's 15 hours; and from Montreal or Toronto, it's 8 hours.

MAJOR AIRLINES When it was established in 1946, **TAP** (✆ **800/221-7370;** www.tap-airportugal.pt), the national airline of Portugal, flew only between Lisbon and Angola and Mozambique (then Portuguese colonies). Today TAP flies to four continents and has one of the youngest fleets in the airline industry—its aircraft have an average age of only 4 years. Its U.S. gateway is Newark, New Jersey. In Portugal, it flies to three destinations, the most popular of which are Lisbon, Porto and Faro.

Continental Airlines (© **800/525-0280** in the U.S.; www.continental.com) began flying to Lisbon from Newark International Airport in 1997. The increased capacity comes as a welcome addition to existing air service, particularly during heavy travel periods in summer.

Air Canada (© **800/247-2262** in the U.S. or Canada; www.aircanada.ca) no longer offers direct flights to Lisbon, but it does offer daily flights from Toronto and Montreal to Paris, where you can transfer to another carrier to reach Lisbon.

For flights from the U.K., contact **British Airways** (© **0845/773-3377**, or 0345/222-111 outside London www.british-airways.com) or **TAP**, Gillingham House, 3844 Gillingham St., London SW1V 1JW (© **0845/601-0932**).

TAP also has frequent flights on popular routes from major cities in western Europe. Its flights to Lisbon from London are an especially good deal; sometimes they're priced so attractively that one might combine a sojourn in England with an inexpensive side excursion to Portugal. TAP gives passengers the option of stopping midway across the Atlantic in the Azores, and it makes baggage transfers and seat reservations on connecting flights within Portugal much easier.

REGULAR FARES All airlines divide their calendar year into three seasons—basic, shoulder, and peak—whose dates might vary slightly from airline to airline. TAP's basic season is November 1 to December 14 and December 25 to March 31. The most expensive season is its peak season from June 1 to September 15, when passengers tend to solidly book most transatlantic flights. Other dates are shoulder season.

DISCOUNTED FARES All the major carriers offer an APEX ticket, generally the cheapest transatlantic option. Usually such a ticket must be purchased 14 to 21 days in advance, and a stay in Europe must last at least 7 days but not more than 30. Changing the date of departure from North America within 21 days of departure sometimes entails a penalty of around $150; with some tickets, no changes of any kind are permitted.

A more flexible (but more expensive) option is the regular economy fare. This ticket offers the same seating and services as the APEX ticket for a shorter stay than the 7-day APEX minimum requirement. One of the most attractive side benefits of an economy-class ticket is the absolute freedom to make last-minute changes in flight dates and unrestricted stopovers.

For families, one strong attraction of TAP is that infants under 2 years pay 10% of the adult fare. (About a half dozen bassinets are available on transatlantic flights, allowing parents to lift infants off their laps onto specially designed brackets during certain segments of the flight.) Children under 12 pay 75% of the adult price for most categories of tickets.

TAP offers a winter senior citizen fare from its three U.S. gateways to anywhere in Portugal. The discount is 10% off published fares. The discount applies for seniors (travelers 62 years of age or older) plus a companion of any age (spouse, grandchild, or friend). The maximum stay abroad with this type of ticket is 2 months. Tickets must be purchased at least 14 days before departure.

Subject to change, TAP offers a one-way youth fare. It's 50% off the regular fare, depending on the season, between New York or Boston and Lisbon. Tickets of this type can be purchased only at the last minute because they can be booked only within 72 hours of departure. Youth fares are offered only to travelers aged 12 to 24 and only if space is available. They cannot be mailed and must be purchased in person at a travel agent or any TAP counter.

None of the above options takes into account promotional fares airlines might initiate while you're planning your trip. These are usually particularly attractive during the basic season.

Clients who prefer not to specify when they'll return home, or who can't purchase their tickets within 21 days before takeoff, usually opt for TAP's excursion fare. It costs more than either APEX option but has no restrictions on advance purchases or time of travel.

The airline's most exclusive and most expensive class of service is named after the seafaring pioneers who spread Portugal's empire throughout the world. Navigator Class passengers benefit from better service and upgraded food and drink. This is TAP's version of business class, comparable to first class on other major carriers.

GETTING THROUGH THE AIRPORT

With the federalization of airport security, security procedures at U.S. airports are more stable and consistent than ever. Generally, you'll be fine if you arrive at the airport **1 hour** before a domestic flight and **2 hours** before an international flight; if you show up late, tell an airline employee and he or she will probably whisk you to the front of the line.

Bring a **current, government-issued photo ID** such as a driver's license or passport, and if you've got an E-ticket, print the **official confirmation page;** you'll need to show your confirmation at the security checkpoint and show your ID at the ticket counter or the gate. (Children under 18 do not need photo IDs for domestic flights, but the adults checking in with them do.)

Security lines are getting shorter than they were during 2001 and 2002, but some doozies remain. If you have trouble standing for long periods of time, tell an airline employee; the airline will provide a wheelchair. Speed up security by **not wearing metal objects** such as big belt buckles or clanky earrings. If you've got metallic body parts, a note from your doctor can prevent a long chat with the security screeners. Keep in mind that only **ticketed passengers** are allowed past security, except for folks escorting passengers with disabilities or children.

Federalization has stabilized **what you can carry on** and **what you can't.** The general rule is that sharp things are out, nail clippers are okay, and food and beverages must be passed through the X-ray machine—but security screeners can't make you drink from your coffee cup. Bring food in your carry-on rather than checking it because explosive-detection machines used on checked luggage have been known to mistake food (especially chocolate, for some reason) for bombs. Travelers in the U.S. are allowed one carry-on bag, plus a "personal item" such as a purse, briefcase, or laptop bag. Carry-on hoarders can stuff all sorts of things into a laptop bag; as long as it has a laptop in it, it's still considered a personal item. The Transportation Security Administration (TSA) has issued a list of restricted items; check its website (www.tsa.gov/public/index.jsp) for details.

In 2003, the TSA will be phasing out **gate check-in** at all U.S. airports. Passengers with E-tickets and without checked bags can still beat the ticket-counter lines by using **electronic kiosks** or even **online check-in.** Ask your airline which alternatives are available; if you're using a kiosk, bring the credit card you used to book the ticket. If you're checking bags, you will still be able to use most airlines' kiosks; again, call your airline for up-to-date information. **Curbside check-in** is also a good way to avoid lines, although a few airlines still ban curbside check-in entirely; call before you go.

At press time, the TSA is also recommending that you **not lock your**

Tips Don't Stow It—Ship It

If ease of travel is your main concern and money is no object, you can ship your luggage with one of the growing number of luggage-service companies that pick up, track, and deliver your luggage (often through couriers such as Federal Express) with minimum hassle for you. Traveling luggage-free might be ultraconvenient, but it's not cheap: One-way overnight shipping can cost from $100 to $200, depending on what you're sending. Still, for some people, especially the elderly or the infirm, it's a sensible solution to lugging heavy baggage. Specialists in door-to-door luggage delivery are **Virtual Bellhop** (www.virtualbellhop.com), **SkyCap International** (www.skycapinternational.com), and **Luggage Express** (www.usxpluggageexpress.com).

checked luggage so screeners can search it by hand, if necessary. The agency says to use plastic "zip ties" instead, which can be bought at hardware stores and can be easily cut off.

FLYING FOR LESS: TIPS FOR GETTING THE BEST AIRFARE

Passengers sharing the same airplane cabin rarely pay the same fare. Travelers who need to purchase tickets at the last minute, change their itinerary at a moment's notice, or fly one-way often get stuck paying the premium rate. Here are some ways to keep your airfare costs down.

- Passengers who can book their ticket **long in advance,** who can **stay over Saturday night,** or who **fly midweek** or **at less-trafficked hours** will pay a fraction of the full fare. If your schedule is flexible, say so, and ask if you can secure a cheaper fare by changing your flight plans.
- You can also save on airfares by keeping an eye out in local newspapers for **promotional specials** or **fare wars,** when airlines lower prices on their most popular routes. You rarely see fare wars offered for peak travel times, but if you can travel in the off-months, you might snag a bargain.
- Search **the Internet** for cheap fares (see "Planning Your Trip Online," earlier in this chapter).
- **Consolidators,** also known as bucket shops, are great sources for international tickets, although they usually can't beat the Internet on fares within North America. Start by looking in Sunday newspaper travel sections; U.S. travelers should focus on the *New York Times, Los Angeles Times,* and *Miami Herald.* For less-developed destinations, small travel agents who cater to immigrant communities in large cities often have the best deals. ***Beware:*** Bucket shop tickets are usually nonrefundable or rigged with stiff cancellation penalties, often as high as 50% to 75% of the ticket price, and some put you on charter airlines with questionable safety records. Several reliable consolidators are worldwide and available on the Net. **STA Travel** is now the world's leader in student travel, thanks to its purchase of Council Travel. It also offers good fares for travelers of all ages. **Flights.com** (© **800/TRAV-800** in the U.S.; www.flights.com) started in Europe and has excellent fares worldwide, but particularly to that continent. It also has "local" websites in 12 countries. **FlyCheap**

(✆ **800/FLY-CHEAP** in the U.S.; www.1800flycheap.com) is owned by package-holiday megalith MyTravel and so has especially good access to fares for sunny destinations. **Air Tickets Direct** (✆ **800/778-3447** in the U.S. or Canada; www.airticketsdirect.com) is based in Montreal and leverages the currently weak Canadian dollar for low fares; it'll also book trips to places that U.S. travel agents won't touch, such as Cuba.

- Join **frequent-flier clubs.** Accrue enough miles, and you'll be rewarded with free flights and elite status. It's free, and you'll get the best choice of seats, faster response to phone inquiries, and prompter service if your luggage is stolen, your flight is canceled or delayed, or you want to change your seat. You don't need to fly to build frequent-flier miles—**frequent-flier credit cards** can provide thousands of miles for doing your everyday shopping.

BY TRAIN

Thousands of traveling Brits (and foreigners visiting the U.K.) cross France and Spain by rail to begin their Portuguese holiday. If you opt for this, expect lots of worthwhile scenery, and be aware that you'll have to change trains in Paris.

Trains from London originate in Waterloo Station, pass through the Channel Tunnel, and arrive in Paris at Gare du Nord. Don't expect to merely cross over a railway platform to change trains: You'll have to traverse urban Paris, moving from Gare du Nord to Gare Montparnasse. You can do this for the cost of a Métro ticket, but if you have luggage, hiring a taxi makes the transit a lot easier. (Taxis line up near your point of arrival.) From Gare Montparnasse, the train continues through France but requires a change of equipment in Hendaye, on the Spanish-French border. It continues to Lisbon's St. Apolonia station. Total travel time for this itinerary is 22 hours, so we strongly recommend reserving a couchette (sleeping car). Budgeteers can save about 10% off fares by taking a slower, less convenient ferry across the English Channel. However, this option adds at least 5 hours, additional transfers, and many hassles at the docks on either side of the water, and will involve you in imbroglios that probably aren't worth the savings.

From Paris, the most luxurious way to reach Portugal is by the overnight Paris–Madrid TALGO express train. It leaves from Gare d'Austerlitz and arrives in Madrid's Chamartín Station, where you transfer to the Lisboa Express.

In Madrid, the Lusitania Express leaves the Atocha Station at 10:45pm and arrives in Lisbon at 8:15am; the 11pm train arrives in Lisbon at 8:40am. For more complete information about rail connections, contact **Caminhos de Ferro Portuguêses,** Calçada do Duque 20, 1200 Lisboa (✆ **21/321-57-00;** www.cp.pt in Lisbon).

If you plan to travel a lot on European railroads, secure the latest copy of the *Thomas Cook European Timetable of Railroads.* This comprehensive 500-plus-page timetable documents all of Europe's main-line passenger rail services with detail and accuracy. It's available exclusively in North America from the **Forsyth Travel Library,** 44 S. Broadway, White Plains, NY 10601 (✆ **800/367-7984** in the U.S.). It costs $28, plus $4.95 postage for priority airmail to the United States and $6.95 for shipments to Canada. You can buy rail passes (see below) from Forsyth.

EURAILPASSES The Eurailpass is one of Europe's greatest bargains, permitting unlimited first-class rail travel through 17 countries in Europe, including Portugal. Passes are for periods as short as 15 days or as long as 3 months and are strictly nontransferable.

Your best bet is to buy a **Eurailpass** outside Europe (it's available in Europe but costs more). It costs $588 for 15 days, $762 for 21 days, $946 for 1 month, $1,338 for 2 months, and $1,654 for 3 months. Children 3 and under travel free provided that they don't occupy a seat (otherwise, they're charged half fare); children 4 to 11 are charged half fare. If you're under 26, you can purchase a **Eurail Youthpass,** entitling you to unlimited second-class travel for $414 for 15 days, $534 for 21 days, $664 for 1 month, $938 for 2 months, and $1,160 for 3 months.

Seat reservations are required on some trains. Many of the trains have *couchettes* (sleeping cars), which cost extra. Obviously, the 2- or 3-month traveler gets the greatest economic advantages; the Eurailpass is ideal for such extensive trips. With the pass you can visit all of Portugal's major sights, from Lisbon to Porto. Eurailpass holders are entitled to considerable reductions on certain buses and ferries as well.

If you'll be traveling for 2 weeks or a month, think carefully before you buy a pass. To get full advantage of a pass for 15 days or a month, you'll have to spend a great deal of time on the train.

The **Eurail Flexipass** allows you to travel through Europe with more flexibility. It's valid in first class and offers the same privileges as the Eurailpass. However, it provides a number of individual travel days that you can use over a much longer period of consecutive days. That makes it possible to stay in one city and yet not lose a single day of travel. There are two passes: 10 days of travel in 2 months for $694, and 15 days of travel in 2 months for $914. The **Eurail Youth Flexipass** is identical except that it's sold only to travelers under 26 and costs less: $592 for 10 days of travel within 2 months, and $778 for 15 days of travel within 2 months.

A **Eurail Selectpass** allows travelers to select 3 countries linked by rail or ferry out of the 17 countries covered by Eurailpass. This is a flexipass, meaning that travel days need not be consecutive; passes are offered for 5, 6, 8, or 10 days within a 2-month period. Prices for a Eurail Selectpass begin at $356 per person for 5 days.

Portuguese Railpass offers any 4 days unlimited first-class train travel in a 15-day period for $105. Children 4 to 11 travel at half fare, and children under 4 travel for free.

The **Iberic Railpass,** good for both Portugal and Spain, offers any 3 days of unlimited first-class train travel in a 2-month period for $205 (children 4–11 pay half fare on any of these discount passes). An **Iberic Saverpass,** again including both Spain and Portugal, offers any 3 days unlimited, first-class train travel in a 2-month period for $200, or any 4 days in 2 months for $240.

WHERE TO BUY RAIL PASSES

Travel agents in all towns and railway agents in major North American cities sell all these tickets, but the biggest supplier is **Rail Europe** (**©** **800/848-7245** in the U.S.; www.raileurope.com), which can also give you informational brochures.

Many different rail passes are available in the United Kingdom for travel in Britain and continental Europe. Stop in at the **International Rail Centre,** Victoria Station, London SWIV 1JY (**©** **0870/584-8848** in the U.K.). Some of the most popular passes, including Inter-Rail and Euro Youth, are offered only to travelers under 26 years of age; these allow unlimited second-class travel through most European countries.

VIA THE CHANNEL TUNNEL

The Eurostar Express began twice-daily passenger service between London and both Paris and Brussels in 1994. The 50km (31-mile) journey

Portuguese Rail System

between France and Great Britain takes 35 minutes, although actual "Chunnel" time is only 19 minutes.

Rail Europe (✆ **800/438-7245** in the U.S. for information; ✆ **0870/530-0003** for reservations from the U.K., ✆ **800/387-6782** in the U.S.; www.raileurope.com) sells tickets on the Eurostar with direct service between Paris or Brussels and London. Your best deal is to book with the 0870 number in England. If you reserve at least 7 days in advance, you get various reductions.

BY BUS

There is no convenient bus service from other parts of Europe to Portugal. Flying, driving, and traveling by rail are the preferred methods. However, the buses that do make the trip—say, from London or France—offer somewhat lower prices (and less comfort) than equivalent journeys by rail.

The largest bus line in Europe, **Eurolines Ltd.,** 52 Grosvenor Gardens, London SW1W 0UA (✆ **01582/404511;** www.gobycoach.com), operates bus routes to Portugal that stop at several places in France (including Paris) and Spain along the way. Buses leave from London's Victoria Coach Station daily, travel by ferry across the English Channel, and arrive in Lisbon 39 hours later. Tickets from London to Lisbon cost £94 ($150) one-way and £148 ($237) round-trip.

The same company offers service from London's Victoria Coach Station to Faro, in southern Portugal, every Monday, Wednesday, and Friday at 10pm. Arrival is 2 days later, after multiple stops and delays. The cost is £102 ($163) one-way and £166 ($266) round-trip. For more detailed information, call **Eurolines** (✆ **01582/404511**) in Birmingham, England.

BY BOAT

BY FERRY **Brittany Ferries** operates from Plymouth, England, to Santander, Spain. From March through November, crossing time is 23 to 24 hours. Between October and April, the trip takes 30 to 33 hours. Contact Brittany Ferries, Millbay Docks, Plymouth, England PL1 3EW (✆ **08703/665333;** www.brittany-ferries.co.uk), for exact schedules and more information. From Santander, you can drive west to Galicia, in Spain, and then head south toward Portugal, entering through the Minho district.

BY SEACAT Traveling by SeaCat (a form of high-speed catamaran) cuts your journey time from the United Kingdom to the Continent. A SeaCat trip can be a fun adventure, especially for first-timers or children, because the vessel is technically "flying" above the surface of the water. A SeaCat crossing from Folkestone to Boulogne is longer in miles but takes less time than the Dover–Calais route used by conventional ferries. For reservations and information, call **HoverSpeed** (✆ **800/677-8585** North America or 0870/524-0241 in England).

12 Packages for the Independent Traveler

Before you start your search for the lowest airfare, you might want to consider booking your flight as part of a travel package. Package tours are not the same thing as escorted tours. Package tours are simply a way to buy the airfare, accommodations, and other elements of your trip (such as car rentals, airport transfers, and sometimes even activities) at the same time and often at discounted prices—kind of like one-stop shopping. Packages are sold in bulk to tour operators—who resell them to the public at a cost that usually undercuts standard rates.

One good source of package deals is the airlines themselves. Air/land packages are offered by most major airlines, including **Continental Airlines Vacations** (✆ **800/301-3800** in the U.S.; www.coolvacations.com) and **TAP** (✆ **800/221-7370** in the U.S.; www.tap-airportugal.us).

Miami is an increasingly popular launching pad for Iberia. The best traditional and customized tours in Florida are offered by **Latin Tour Dimensions,** 5900 Collins Ave., Suite 1502, Miami Beach, FL 33140 (✆ **800/644-0438** in the U.S., or 305/861-3069; fax 305/861-5043; www.latintourdimensions.com).

In the United Kingdom, organized tour operators include **Magic Travel Group,** Kings Place, 12–42 Wood St., Surrey KT1 1JF (✆ **020/8939-5452;** www.magictravelgroup.co.uk), and **Mundi Color Holidays,** 276 Vauxhall Bridge Rd., London SW1V 1BE (✆ **020/7828-6021;** www.mundicolor.co.uk).

Escorted tours are structured group tours with a group leader. The price usually includes everything from airfare to hotels, meals, tours, admission costs, and local transportation.

There are many escorted tour companies to choose from, each offering transportation to and within Portugal, prearranged hotel space, and such extras as bilingual tour guides and lectures. Many of these tours to Portugal include excursions to Spain.

Some of the best escorted tours are offered by **Blue Danube Holidays** (✆ **800/268-4155** in the U.S.), a long-established company since 1983. It offers a Grand Tour of Portugal along with any number of beach holidays (from Madeira to the Algarve), and even city tours of Lisbon.

Some of the most expensive and luxurious tours are run by **Abercrombie & Kent International** (✆ **800/323-7308** in the U.S., or 630/954-2944; www.abercrombiekent.com), including deluxe 13- or 19-day tours of the Iberian Peninsula by train. Guests stay in fine hotels.

Alternative Travel Group Ltd. (✆ **01865/310399;** www.atg-oxford.co.uk) is a British firm that organizes walking and cycling vacations in Portugal and Spain. Tours explore the scenic countryside and medieval towns of each country. If you'd like a brochure outlining the tours, call ✆ **01865/315663.**

Petrabax Tours (✆ **800/634-1188** in the U.S.; www.petrabax.com) attracts those who prefer to see Portugal by bus, although fly/drive packages are also offered. A number of city packages are also available, plus a 9-day trip that tries to capture the essence of Portugal and Spain.

Many people derive a certain ease and security from escorted trips. Escorted tours—whether by bus, motor coach, train, or boat—let travelers sit back and enjoy their trip without having to spend lots of time behind the wheel. All the little details are taken care of, you know your costs up front, and there are few surprises. Escorted tours can take you to the maximum number of sights in the minimum amount of time with the least amount of hassle—you don't have to sweat over the plotting and planning of a vacation schedule. Escorted tours are particularly convenient for people with limited mobility.

On the downside, an escorted tour often requires a big deposit up front, and lodging and dining choices are predetermined. As part of a cloud of tourists, you'll get little opportunity for serendipitous interactions with locals. The tours can be jam-packed with activities, leaving little room for individual sightseeing, whim, or adventure—plus they also often focus only on the heavily touristed sites, so you miss out on the lesser-known gems.

Before you invest in an escorted tour, ask about the **cancellation policy:** Is a deposit required? Can they cancel the trip if they don't get enough people? Do you get a refund if they cancel? If *you* cancel? How late can you cancel if you are unable to go? When do you pay in full? ***Note:*** If you choose an escorted tour, think strongly about purchasing trip-cancellation insurance, especially if the tour operator asks you to pay up front. See the section on "Travel Insurance," earlier in this chapter.

You'll also want to get a complete **schedule** of the trip to find out how much sightseeing is planned each day and whether enough time has been allotted for relaxing or wandering solo.

The **size** of the group is also important to know up front. Generally, the smaller the group is, the more flexible the itinerary is and the less time you'll spend waiting for people to get on and off the bus. Find out the **demographics** of the group as well. What is the age range? What is the gender breakdown? Is this mostly a trip for couples or singles?

Discuss what is included in the **price.** You might have to pay for transportation to and from the airport. A box lunch might be included in an excursion, but drinks might cost extra. Tips might not be included. Find out whether you will be charged if you decide to opt out of certain activities or meals.

Before you invest in a package tour, get some answers. Ask about the **accommodation choices** and prices for each. Then look up the hotels' reviews in a Frommer's guide and check their rates for your specific dates of travel online. You'll also want to find out what **type of room** you get. If you need a certain type of room, ask for it; don't take whatever is thrown your way. Request a nonsmoking room, a quiet room, a room with a view, or whatever you fancy.

Finally, if you plan to travel alone, you'll need to know whether a **single supplement** will be charged and whether the company can match you up with a roommate.

13 Special-Interest Trips

CULTURAL EXCHANGES

Servas ("to serve" in Esperanto), 11 John St., Room 407, New York, NY 10038 (© **212/267-0252;** fax 212/267-0292; www.usservas.org) is a nonprofit, nongovernmental, international, interfaith network of travelers and hosts. Its goal is to help build world peace, goodwill, and understanding by providing opportunities for deeper, more personal contacts among people of diverse cultural and political backgrounds. Servas travelers share living space, without charge, with members of communities worldwide. Visits last a maximum of 2 nights. Visitors pay a $75 annual fee, plus a $25 deposit for access to lists of international hosts. Visitors fill out an application and are interviewed for suitability by 1 of more than 200 Servas interviewers throughout the country. They then receive a directory listing the names and addresses of prospective hosts.

Friendship Force, 34 Peachtree St., Suite 900, Atlanta, GA 30303 (© **404/522-9490;** www.friendshipforce.org/), is a nonprofit organization intended to foster friendships among disparate peoples around the world. Dozens of branch offices throughout North America arrange en masse visits usually once a year. Because of these group bookings, the price of air transportation is usually less than what volunteers would pay if they bought advance-purchase tickets individually. Each participant is required to spend 2 weeks in the host country (in Europe and throughout the world). One stringent requirement is that a participant must spend 1 full week in the home of a family as a guest. Most volunteers spend the second week traveling.

LEARNING THE LANGUAGE

The National Registration Center for Study Abroad (NRCSA), P.O. Box 1393, Milwaukee, WI 53201 (✆ **414/278-0631;** www.nrcsa.com), allows you to experience Portugal by living and learning the language. The NRCSA has helped people of all ages and backgrounds participate in foreign travel and cultural programs since 1968. Contact the NRCSA for details about the courses and their costs.

THEME TOURS

Cycling tours are a good way to see the back roads of a country and stretch your limbs. Although dozens of companies in Britain offer guided cycling tours on foreign turf, only a handful offer itineraries through Portugal. One is the **Cyclists' Tourist Club,** 69 Meadrow, Godalming, Surrey GU7 3HS (✆ **0870/873-0060;** www.ctc.org.uk). It charges £28.50 ($46) a year for membership, which includes information and suggested cycling routes through Portugal and dozens of other countries.

In the United States, bicyclists can contact **Backroads,** 801 Cedar St., Berkeley, CA 94710 (✆ **800/GO-ACTIVE** in the U.S., or 510/527-1555; www.backroads.com). Another outfitter arranging bike tours is **Uniquely Europe,** a division of Europe Express, 19021 120 Ave. NE, Suite 102, Bothell, WA 98011 (✆ **800/426-3615** in the U.S., or 425/487-6711; www.europeexpress.com).

The best golf tours (usually in the Algarve) are arranged by **Golf International,** 14 East 38th St., New York, NY 10016 (✆ **800/833-1389** in the U.S., or 212/986-9176; www.golfinternational.com). West Coast residents can contact **ITC Golf Tours,** 4134 Atlantic Ave., Suite 205, Long Beach, CA 90807 (✆ **800/257-4981** in the U.S., or 562/595-6905; www.itcgolf-africatours.com).

Tours on the best hiking and walking trails are available through **Adventure Center,** 1311 63rd St., Suite 200 Emeryville, CA 94608 (✆ **800/227-8747** in the U.S., or 510/654-1879; www.adventurecenter.com).

With its historic sights and beautiful countryside, Portugal is an appealing place for hill climbing and hiking. In the United Kingdom, **Waymark Holidays,** 44 Windsor Rd., Slough, Berkshire SL1 2EJ (✆ **01753/516477;** www.waymarkholidays.co.uk/), offers 7-day walking tours through the verdant hills of Main Lands about four times a year. **Sherpa Expeditions,** 131a Heston Rd., Hounslow, Middlesex TW5 0RF (✆ **020/8577-2717;** www.sherpaexpeditions.com), offers trips through off-the-beaten-track regions of the world, which include the Portuguese island of Madeira.

You might have read about archaeology tours, but most permit you only to look at the sites, not actually dig. A notable and much-respected exception is **Earthwatch,** 57 Woodstock Rd., Oxford, England OX2 6HU (✆ **01865/318838;** www.earthwatch.org). It offers more than 150 programs designed and supervised by well-qualified academic and ecological authorities. At any time, at least 50 programs welcome participants for hands-on experience in preserving or documenting historical, archaeological, or ecological phenomena of interest to the global community. Projects in Portugal have included digs that uncovered a string of ancient and medieval hill forts across the country.

In the United Kingdom, for the best sampling of possibilities, contact the **Association of Independent Tour Operators,** or AITO (✆ **020/8744-9280;** www.aito.co.uk). The staff can provide names and addresses of tour operators that specialize in travel relating to your particular interest.

14 The Active Vacation Planner

BULLFIGHTS No discussion of Portuguese recreation would be complete without a reference to *la tourada* (bullfighting). Unlike the rituals in Spain and parts of South America, in Portuguese bullfighting, the bull is not killed at the end of the event, but is released to a life of grazing and stud duties. The *cavaleiros* (horsemen) dress in 18th-century costumes, which include silk jackets, tricornered hats, and tan riding breeches. Bullfights are held regularly in Lisbon's Campo Pequeno area, across the Tagus in the working-class city of Santarém, throughout the south-central plains, and in the Azores.

FISHING The northern section of Portugal receives abundant rainfall and contains rugged hills and some of the best-stocked streams in Iberia. Most noteworthy are the Rio Minho, the Ria Vouga, the Ria Lima, and the creeks and lakes of the Serra de Estrêla. For fishing in the area in and around Lisbon, contact the **Clube dos Amadores de Pesca de Lisboa,** Travessa do Adro 12, 1100 Lisbon (✆ **21/885-33-85**), or the **Clube dos Amadores de Pesca da Costa do Sol,** Rua dos Fontainhas 8, 2750 Cascais (✆ **21/484-16-91**). For information about fishing elsewhere in the country, contact regional tourist offices.

Fishing in inland waters is limited compared to fishing along the 800km (496 miles) of coastline. Deep-sea fishing, in waters richly stocked with fish swept toward Europe on northeast-flowing ocean currents, yields abundant catches. Fishing boats can be rented, with and sometimes without a crew, all along the Algarve as well.

FOOTBALL Football—called soccer in the United States—is the most popular sport in Portugal. It's taken so seriously that on Sunday afternoons during important matches (with Spain or Brazil, for example), the country seems to come almost to a standstill. Notices about the venues of upcoming matches are prominently posted with hotel concierges, in newspapers, and on bulletin boards throughout various cities. One of the most-watched teams is that of Porto, which won the European Cup in 1987. The loyalty of Lisbon fans seems equally divided between the two hometown teams, Benfica and Sporting Club.

GOLF With its sun-flooded expanses of underused land and its cultural links to Britain, Portugal has developed a passion for golf. Most of the nation's finest courses date from the late 1970s. The most important ones are in the Algarve; many are world-class. Others have been developed near Lisbon and Estoril, near Porto, and even on Madeira and the Azores. Usually within sight of the sea, most courses incorporate dramatic topography, and such famed golf-course designers as Robert Trent Jones, Henry Cotton, and Frank Pennink conceived most. For more information and an overview, contact the **Federação Portuguesa de Golf** (Portuguese Golf Federation), Avenida Lastulipas 6, Edificio 1495-161 Miraflores (✆ **21/412-37-80;** www.fpt.pt).

HORSEBACK RIDING The Portuguese have prided themselves on their equestrian skills since their earliest battles against Roman invaders. Most of the resorts along the Algarve, plus a few in Cascais, maintain stables stocked with horses for long trail rides over hills, along beaches, and through ancient sun-baked villages. For more information, contact the **Federação Equestre Portuguesa** (Portuguese Equestrian Federation), Avenida Manuel Maia 26, 1000-201 Lisboa (✆ **21/847-87-74;** www.fep.pt).

The best offering available from **Equitour,** P.O. Box 807, Dubois, WY 82513 (✆ **800/545-00-19** or 307/455-33-63; www.ridingtours.com), is a program of 8 days and 7 nights with Lisbon as a meeting point. The price is 1,150€ to 1,350€ ($1,323–$1,553) per person, and the weight limit is 170 pounds. Accommodations and special transfers are included in this tour, "The Blue Coast Ride." The rides go across some of the most scenic parts of Portugal, through valleys, along passes, and past waterfalls.

NATURE WATCHING Hiking in Portugal is great for bird-watchers. The westernmost tip of continental Europe lies along the main migration routes between the warm wetlands of Africa and the cooler breeding grounds of northern Europe. The moist, rugged terrain of northern Portugal is especially suited for nature watching, particularly around Peneda-Gerês, where wild boar, wild horses, and wolves still roam through hills and forests.

WATERSPORTS With much of its national identity connected to the sea, Portugal offers a variety of watersports. Outside the Algarve, few activities are highly organized, although the country's 800km (496 miles) of Atlantic coastline are richly peppered with secluded beaches and fishing hamlets. A recent development, especially in the Algarve, is the construction of a series of waterparks, with large swimming pools, wave-making machines, waterslides, and fun fountains.

Sailing on well-designed oceangoing craft can be arranged at the Cascais Yacht Club, at any of the marinas in the Tagus, near Lisbon, or along the Algarve—particularly near the marina at Vilamoura. The surfing along the sun-blasted, windswept coast at Guincho has attracted fans from throughout Europe. For information about sailing and water events, contact the **Associação Naval de Lisboa** (Naval Association of Lisbon), Doca de Belém, 1400-038 Lisboa (© **21/363-72-38**); the **Federação Portuguesa de Vela** (Portuguese Sailing Federation), Doca de Belém, 1300-038 Lisboa (© **21/365-85-00**); or the **Federação Portuguesa de Actividades Subaquáticas** (Portuguese Underwatersports Federation), Rua Manuel Cordozo 39, 1700-206 Lisboa (© **21/846-01-74**).

15 Getting Around Portugal

BY CAR

Many scenic parts of Portugal are isolated from train or bus stations, so it's necessary to have a private car to do serious touring. That way, you're on your own, unhindered by the somewhat fickle train and bus timetables, which often limit your excursions to places close to the beaten track.

There are few superhighways in Portugal, and they're often interrupted by lengthy stretches of traffic-clogged single-lane thoroughfares. The roads, however, provide access to hard-to-reach gems and undiscovered villages.

RENTALS Three of North America's major car-rental companies maintain dozens of branches at each of Portugal's most popular commercial and tourist centers, at rates that are usually competitive.

Budget Rent-a-Car (© **800/472-3325** in the U.S.; www.budget.com) has offices in more than a dozen locations in Portugal. The most central and most used are in Lisbon, Faro (the heart of the Algarve), Porto, Praia da Rocha (also a popular Algarve destination), and Madeira. Because Portugal has one of the highest accident rates in Europe, it's an excellent idea to buy the optional CDW (collision-damage waiver) insurance.

Note that some North American credit and charge card issuers, especially American Express, sometimes agree to pay any financial obligations incurred after an accident involving a client's rented car, but only if the imprint of the card is on the original rental contract. Because of this agreement, some clients opt to decline the extra insurance coverage offered by the car-rental company. To be sure that you qualify for this free insurance, check in advance with your card issuer. Know that even though the card's issuer might eventually reimburse you, you'll still have to fill out some complicated paperwork and usually advance either cash or a credit or charge card deposit to cover the repair cost.

Avis (✆ **800/331-1084** in the U.S.; www.avis.com) maintains offices in downtown Lisbon and at the airport, and at 17 other locations throughout Portugal. The main office is at Campo Grande 38–90, Lisbon (✆ **21/754-78-39**).

Hertz (✆ **800/654-3001** in the U.S.; www.hertz.com) has about two dozen locations in Portugal and requires a 3-day advance booking for its lowest rates. Hertz's main office is at Avenida Rua Castillo 72, Lisbon (✆ **21/381-24-30**).

Kemwel Holiday Autos (✆ **800/678-0678;** www.kemwel.com), sometimes offers a viable alternative to more traditional car rental companies. Kemwel leases entire blocks of cars a year in advance at locations throughout Portugal and then rents them back out to qualified customers who pay the entire price in advance. In Portugal, cars can be retrieved in Lisbon. Kemwel, along with its competitor, Auto Europe (see below), issues vouchers in advance of your departure. The price includes taxes, airport surcharges, unlimited mileage and, on request, insurance premiums. The result is a cost-effective car rental with few, if any, bill-related surprises when you return the car.

Auto Europe (✆ **800/223-5555;** www.autoeurope.com) leases cars on an as-needed basis from larger car rental companies throughout Europe. Its rates sometimes are less than those at Hertz and Avis. In a system that's equivalent to the one used by Kemwel (see above), vouchers are issued in advance for car rentals, with most or all incidentals included. Prepayment of 20% to 60%, depending on the value of the car, is required.

GASOLINE Unlike the situation only a few years ago, gasoline (petrol, to the British) stations are now plentiful throughout Portugal. However, if you wander far off the beaten track, it's always wise to have a full tank and to get a refill whenever it's available, even if your tank is still more than half full. The government clamps price controls on gas, and it should cost the same everywhere. Credit and charge cards are frequently accepted at gas stations, at least along the principal express routes. You should note that ever-changing gas prices are much higher than you're probably used to paying, and gas is measured in liters.

DRIVER'S LICENSES U.S. and Canadian driver's licenses are valid in Portugal. But if you're at least 18 and touring other destinations in Europe by car, you should probably invest in an international driver's permit. In the United States, apply through any local branch of the **American Automobile Association** (AAA); for a list of local branches, contact the national headquarters, 1000 AAA Dr., Heathrow, FL 32746-5063 (✆ **800/222-4357;** www.aaa.com). Include two 2-by-2-inch photographs, a $10 fee, and a photocopy of your state driver's license. In Canada, you pay C$10 and apply to the **Canadian Automobile Association** (CAA), 2 Carlton St., Toronto, ON M5B 153 (✆ **613/247-0117;** www.caa.ca).

Note that your international driver's license is valid only if it's accompanied by an authorized license from your home state or province.

In Portugal, as elsewhere in Europe, to drive a car legally you must have in your possession an international insurance certificate, known as a **Green Card** (Carte Verte or Carte Verde). The car-rental agency will provide you with one as part of your rental contract.

DRIVING RULES Continental driving rules apply in Portugal, and international road symbols and signs are used. Wearing safety belts is compulsory. Speed limits are 90 kmph (56 mph) on main roads, and 60 kmph (37 mph) in heavily populated or built-up sections. On the limited number of express highways, the speed limit is 120 kmph (74 mph).

ROAD MAPS Michelin publishes the best road maps, available at many stores and map shops throughout Europe and in the United States and Canada. If you can't find them, you can order them from Michelin, P.O. Box 19008, Greenville, SC 29602-9008 (✆ **800/423-0485** in the U.S., or 864/458-5619 in South Carolina; www.michelin.com). The maps are updated every year; always try to obtain the latest copy because Portugal's roads are undergoing tremendous change. One of the best Michelin maps to Portugal is no. 440 (on a scale of 1:400,000, or 1 inch = 9.8km/6 miles). Scenic routes are outlined in green, and major sights and national parks along the way are indicated.

BREAKDOWNS If you rent your car from one of the large companies, such as Avis or Hertz, 24-hour breakdown service is available in Portugal. If you're a member of a major automobile club, such as AA, CAA, or AAA, you can get aid from the **Automovel Clube de Portugal (ACP),** Amoreiva Shopping Center, 1270 Lisboa (✆ **21/318-02-02;** www.acp.pt). In the north, the branch office of the club is at Rua Gonçalo Cristovão 26, 4000 Porto (✆ **22/205-67-32**).

PACKAGE DEALS Many packages are available that include airfare, accommodations, and a rental car with unlimited mileage. Compare these prices with the cost of booking airline tickets and renting a car separately to see if these offers are good deals.

WEB RENTALS Internet resources can make comparison shopping easier. Microsoft Expedia (www.expedia.com) and Travelocity (www.travelocity.com) help you compare prices and locate car-rental bargains from various companies nationwide. They will even make your reservation for you once you've found the best deal.

HITCHHIKING There's no law against hitchhiking, but it isn't commonly practiced. If you decide to hitchhike, do so with discretion. Usually Portuguese auto insurance doesn't cover hitchhikers. Considering the potential danger to both the passenger and the driver, hitchhiking is not recommended by *Frommer's Portugal.*

BY PLANE

Portugal is a small country, and flying from one place to another is relatively easy. Train is the usual method of public transportation (see below). Nevertheless, **TAP Air Portugal** flies four times a day to Faro, in the Algarve, and Porto, the main city of the north. Service to Faro is likely to be more frequent in July and August. There are also four flights a day to Funchal, capital of Madeira, plus limited service to the Azores.

For more information, contact TAP Air Portugal, Gare Do Orerients, 1200 Lisboa (✆ **21/841-50-00;** www.tap-airportugal.pt).

BY TRAIN

The Portuguese railway system is underdeveloped compared to those of the more industrialized nations of western Europe. Still, there are connections between the capital and more than 20 major towns. Express trains run from Lisbon, Coimbra (the university city), and Porto. Electric trains, which leave from the Lisbon waterfront, travel along the Costa do Sol (Estoril and Cascais) and on to Queluz and Sintra.

At Lisbon's Santa Apolónia Station, you can make connections for international service and the Northern and Eastern lines. The Rossio Station serves Sintra and the Western line; the Cais do Sodré Station handles service for the Costa do Sol resorts of Estoril and Cascais. Finally, trains leave from the Sul e Sueste Station for the Alentejo and the Algarve. In addition, express trains connect Lisbon to all the major capitals of western Europe, and there's a direct link with Seville.

In summer, express trains depart Lisbon for the Algarve Monday through Saturday. They leave from the Barreiro Station (across the Tagus—take one of the frequently departing ferries). Off-season service runs four times weekly. For information about rail travel in Portugal, phone ✆ **808/208-208** in Lisbon, or check the Portuguese Railways website at www.cp.pt.

Railroad information and tickets for travel between almost any two stations in Europe, including stations throughout Portugal, are available from the representatives of the **Portuguese National Railway,** Rail Europe, Inc., (✆ **800/848-7245** in the U.S.; www.raileurope.com). The telephone representatives sell one-way and round-trip tickets into or out of Portugal, tickets for travel within Portugal, and rail passes for travel within Portugal and the rest of Europe. Couchettes (sleeping cars) can be arranged. See "Getting There," earlier, for information on rail passes.

SENIOR DISCOUNTS The Portuguese National Railway's 50% discount policy applies for people 65 and older. These tickets are good all year.

BY BUS

This is a cheap means of transportation in Portugal. A network of buses links almost all the major towns and cities. Many routes originate in Lisbon. The former national bus company, **Rodoviária Nacional** (✆ **25/894-28-70**), has been privatized but essentially offers the same service as before. In addition, there are local and private regional bus links.

Express coaches between major cities are called *expressos.* Once in most cities and towns, you can take cheap bus rides to nearby villages or sights. Of course, in many towns and all cities, you can take buses to get around within the city.

16 Tips on Accommodations

When you check into a hotel, you'll see the official rates posted in the main lobby and somewhere in your room, perhaps at the bottom of the closet. These rates, dictated by the Directorate of Tourism, are regulated and really are a form of rent control. They include the 13.1% service charge and 17.5% value-added tax (VAT).

If an infraction such as overcharging occurs, you can demand to be given the **Official Complaints Book,** in which you can write your allegations. The hotel manager is obligated to turn your comments over to the Directorate of Tourism. The directorate staff reviews them to see if punitive action should be taken.

The government rates hotels in Portugal from five stars to one. The difference between a five-star hotel and a four-star hotel will not always be apparent to the casual visitor. Often the distinction is based on square footage of bathrooms and other technicalities. When you go below this level, you enter the realm of the second- and third-class hotel. Some can be decent and even excellent places to stay. Third-class hotels are bare-bones accommodations in Portugal.

Coastal hotels, especially those in the Algarve, are required to grant off-season (Nov–Feb) visitors a 15% discount. To attract more off-season business, a number of establishments offer this discount from mid-October through March.

BUDGET TIPS

Try a reservations bureau such as **Accommodations Express** (✆ **800/950-4685** in the U.S.; www.accommodationsexpress.com), **Hotels.Com** (✆ **800/96-HOTEL;** www.hotels.com), or **Quikbook** (✆ **800/789-9887** in the U.S.; www.quikbook.com).

At the inexpensive end, **Hostelling International USA,** 8401 Colesville Rd., Silver Springs, MD 20910 (✆ **202/783-6161;** www.hiayh.org), offers a directory of low-cost accommodations.

Online, try booking your hotel through **Arthur Frommer's Budget Travel** (www.frommers.com), and save up to 50% on the cost of your room. **Microsoft Expedia** (www.expedia.com) features a Travel Agent that will also direct you to affordable lodgings.

PRICES & RATINGS IN THIS GUIDE

Unless otherwise indicated, prices in this guide include service and taxes. Breakfast might or might not be included; individual write-ups reflect various hotel policies about breakfast. All references in Portugal to "including breakfast" refer to continental breakfast of juice, coffee or tea, croissants, butter, and jam. If you stay at a hotel and order bacon and eggs or other extras, you'll likely be billed for them as a la carte items. Parking rates are per day.

POUSADAS

When traveling through the countryside, plot your trips so you'll stop over at the government-owned *pousadas* (tourist inns). The Portuguese government has established these inns in historic buildings, such as convents, palaces, and castles. Often they occupy beautiful physical settings. Generally (but not always), the pousadas are in regions that don't have many suitable hotels—everywhere from Henry the Navigator's Sagres to a feudal castle in the walled city of Obidos. The rates are not low but, for the quality and services offered, are moderate. A guest can't stay more than 5 days because there's usually a waiting list. Special terms are granted to honeymoon couples. For our recommendations, see "The Best Pousadas," in chapter 1.

Travel agents can make reservations at pousadas, or you can contact **Pousadas de Portugal,** Avenida Sta. Joana Princesa 10, 1749 Lisboa (✆ **21/844-20-01;** www.pousadas.pt/).

COUNTRY HOMES

Far more exciting—at least to us—than the pousadas is the chain of farm estates, country homes, and restored manor houses that have opened to the public. These properties are the most highly recommended in this guide, and they offer grand comfort and lots of charm, often in a historic setting.

The best and most extensive network is in the region of Viana do Castelo, where you can sometimes board with the poor but proud Portuguese aristocracy. Many of these manors and farms are called *quintas.* The association **Turismo de Habitação** (Country House Tourism), which mostly operates in the north, has been formed to publicize and link these unique accommodations. In recent years, areas such as the Beiras and Alentejo have been included. Local tourist offices provide directories that include color photographs and maps with directions. All of these properties are privately run, and breakfast is always included. Praça da República, 4990

Ponte de Lima (© **25/874-28-27;** www.solaresdeportugal.pt).

OTHER SPECIAL ACCOMMODATIONS

Tourist inns not run by the government are known as *estalagems.* Often these offer some of the finest accommodations in Portugal; many are decorated in the traditional Portuguese, or *típico,* style and represent top-notch bargains.

The *residência* is a form of boardinghouse, without board. These establishments offer a room and breakfast only. The *pensão* is a boardinghouse that charges the lowest rates in the country. The "deluxe" pensão is a misnomer; the term simply means that the pensão enjoys the highest rating in its category. The accommodation is decidedly not luxurious. A "luxury" pensão is generally the equivalent of a second-class hotel. The boardinghouses are finds for the budget hunter. Many prepare generous portions of good local cuisine. There are both first- and second-class boardinghouses.

A more recent addition to the accommodations scene is the *solare.* Most are spacious country manor houses, formerly property of the Portuguese aristocracy, that are now being restored and opened as guesthouses. Many date from the Age of Exploration, when navigators brought riches back from all over the world and established lavish homes that were passed down to their heirs. The inns are all over the country, but most are along the Costa Verde, between Ponte de Lima and Viana do Castelo.

Information on the solares program is available from the **Portuguese National Tourist Office,** 590 Fifth Ave., 4th Floor, New York, NY 10036 (© **212/354-4403;** fax 212/764-6137; www.portugal.org).

If you prefer to stay on the Costa Verde, you can receive information and assistance from Central Reservations for the houses of the **Delegação de Turismo de Ponte de Lima,** Praça da República, 4990 Ponte de Lima (© **25/894-23-35**). You can arrange to go from one solare to the next through this office.

One of the best associations for arranging stays in private homes is **Privetur,** Rua da Capela, 3850-361, Alkuerubim (© **25/874-39-23;** www.nortenet.pt/org/privetur). It represents manor houses and country homes in all the major tourist districts. Privetur can arrange accommodations in circumstances that are sometimes more personalized than stays in large hotels.

CAMPING & TRAILERS

Portugal provides parks for campers and house trailers (caravans) near beaches and in wooded areas all over the country. For a list of campgrounds throughout the country, contact the **Federação Portuguesa de Campismo** (Portuguese Camping and Caravanning Federation), Avenida Coronel Educardo Gallardo 24 D, 1199 Lisbon (© **21/812-68-90;** www.fpcampismo.pt).

RESERVATIONS

Reservations are essential for peak-season summer travel in Portugal, when many hotels fill with vacationing Europeans. Unless you're incurably spontaneous, you'll probably be better off with some idea of where you'll spend each night, even in low season.

Most hotels require at least a day's deposit before they'll reserve a room. You can usually cancel a room reservation 1 week ahead of time and get a full refund, but check your hotel's policy when you book. It's important that you enclose a prepaid International Reply Coupon with your payment, especially if you're writing to a budget hotel. Better yet, call and speak to a staff member, or send a fax.

If you're booking into a chain hotel, such as Sheraton or Méridien, you can call in North America and easily make reservations over the phone. Toll-free numbers, when available, are included in hotel reviews in this guide.

17 Suggested Itineraries

If You Have 1 Week

Days 1–3 Head for Lisbon, the gateway to Portugal. Count on using the first day for rest time. On the second day, see the highlights of the capital, including St. George's Castle and the major attractions of Belém, such as Jerónimos Monastery. On the third day, while still based in Lisbon, explore the environs. Head first to Quelez Palace, 15km (9⅓ miles) from Lisbon, and then to Sintra, 29km (18 miles) from Lisbon.

Days 4–5 Head to a resort along the Costa do Sol, principally Cascais or Estoril. This sun coast, also called the Coast of Kings, is easy to reach from Lisbon. You can relax in the sun or continue to explore. The most interesting sights are at Guincho, near the westernmost point in continental Europe, and Mafra, which is Portugal's version of Spain's El Escorial.

Day 6 Head south from Lisbon across the Tagus (see chapter 6) to Setúbal, 50km (31 miles) from Lisbon. After exploring the area and visiting Palmela Castle, seek accommodations in and around Setúbal.

Day 7 Time your return to Lisbon to match your flight schedule home.

If You Have 2 Weeks

Days 1–7 Spend the first week as outlined above.

Days 8-10 Journey to the Algarve (see chapter 8); settle into a village, town, or resort; and explore the full length of the coast. Allow a minimum of 3 days and nights. If you stay at Faro, you'll be roughly in the center of the Algarve and can branch out east or west. The coastline stretches 161km (100 miles), but it will be slow moving, regardless of which direction you select.

Day 11 On the 11th day, if you must leave, we recommend that you return to Lisbon by a different route, heading first for Beja, the capital of Baixo Alentejo, 155km (96 miles) north of Faro. After a stopover, you might continue north to Evora, 145km (90 miles) east of Lisbon, where you may want to spend the night. After exploring Evora the next morning, you can drive west to Lisbon.

Days 12–14 From Lisbon, fly to Madeira for a minimum of 3 days to spend time in the sun. Allow a full day for exploring the island, one of the most beautiful in the world. If you prefer to remain on the mainland, you can knock 3 days off the itinerary by skipping Madeira and heading north of Lisbon toward Obidos.

18 Recommended Reading

GENERAL

The Portuguese: The Land and Its People, by Marion Kaplan (Viking), is one of the best surveys of the country. The work covers Portuguese history all the way from the country's Moorish origins to its maritime empire and into the chaotic 20th century. It also gives travel information and discusses politics, the economy, literature, art, and architecture.

A towering achievement, ***Journey to Portugal: In Pursuit of Portugal's History and Culture*** (Harcourt Brace), is a compelling work by the Nobel Prize–winner José Saramago. Saramago traveled across his homeland to get a "new way" of feeling about Portugal's history and culture. From that personal quest, he created this monumental work.

HISTORY

A Concise History of Portugal (Cambridge University Press, by David Birmingham) is far too short at 209 pages to capture the full sweep of Portuguese history, but it is nonetheless a very readable history for those who like at least a brief preview of a country's past before landing there.

Another version of the same subject is ***Portugal: A Companion History*** (Carcanet Press, by José H. Saraiva). It will give you a sweeping saga of the land you're about to visit.

Portugal's role abroad is best presented in ***Portuguese Seaborne Empire*** (Carcanet Press, by Charles Ralph Boxer). Since its initial publication in 1969, this frequently reprinted book has been the best volume for explaining how an unimportant kingdom in western Europe managed to build an empire stretching from China to Brazil.

FICTION & BIOGRAPHY

The epic poem of Portugal, ***O Lusiadas,*** written in 1572 by the premier Portuguese poet Luíz Vaz de Camões, celebrates the Portuguese Age of Discovery. In 1987, Penguin rereleased this timeless classic. The best biography on Camões himself remains Aubrey Bell's ***Luis de Camões*** (Oxford Press).

One of Portugal's most beloved writers, Eça de Queiroz, wrote in the late 19th century. Several of his best-known narratives have been translated into English, notably ***The Maias*** (St. Martin's Press), ***The Illustrious House of Ramires*** (Ohio University Press), ***The Mandarin and Other Stories*** (Ohio University Press), ***The City and the Mountains*** (Ohio University Press), ***The Relic*** (Max Reinhart), ***The Sin of Father Amaro*** (Max Reinhart), and ***Dragon's Teeth*** (Greenwood Press). Queiroz (1845–1900) was the most realistic Portuguese novelist of his time, and his works were much admired by Emile Zola in France. ***The Maias*** is the best known and the best of his works.

The great poet Fernando Pessoa (1888–1935) is second only to Camões in the list of illustrious Portuguese writers. Some of his works have been translated into English. Pessoa is still beloved by the Portuguese, and for decades he appeared on the 100-escudo note before it went out of circulation in 2002.

The Return of the Caravels, by António Lobo Antunes (Grove), is an unusual novel set in 1974. It brings back Portugal's history as an imperial power by "collective memory," as Vasco da Gama, Cabral, and other explorers return to Lisbon, anchoring their small but significant vessels alongside the giant tankers of today.

José Saramago, winner of the Nobel Prize for Literature (see "General," above), remains one of the best novelists of modern-day Portugal. His ***Balthasar and Blimunda*** (Harcourt Brace) is a magical account of a flying machine and the construction of Mafra Palace—it's a delightful read.

The work ***New Portuguese Letters*** by the "Three Marias" (Maria Isabel Barreno, Maria Teresa Horta, and Maria Fátima Velho da Costa), first published in Portugal in 1972, is now available in English (Readers International). The Portuguese government banned and confiscated all copies and arrested its authors on a charge of "outrage to public decency." They were acquitted 2 years later, and the case became a *cause célèbre* for feminist organizations around the world.

WINES

The finest book on the most famous of Portuguese fortified wines, port, is previewed in ***Port and the Douro*** (Faber Books on Wine, by Richard Mayson). This is a comprehensive, articulate, and intriguing work. You learn the history of port from the 4th century up through modern methods of bottling the wine today.

FAST FACTS: Portugal

American Express The entity representing American Express throughout Portugal is **Top Tours.** Its headquarters are in Lisbon at Av. Jose, Lote 1681 Lisboa (✆ **21/723-00-20;** www.topatlantico.com). Branch offices are at Rua Alferes Malheiro 96, 4000 Porto (✆ 22/207-40-20); Rua Judice Biker 26-A, 8500 Portimão (✆ 28/241-75-52); and Av. Infante de Sagres 73, 8125 Quarteira (✆ 28/930-27-26).

Babysitters Check with your hotel's staff for arrangements. Most first-class hotels can provide babysitters from lists that the concierge keeps. Remember to request a babysitter no later than the morning if you're going out that evening. Also request one with at least a minimum knowledge of English, if you and your children do not speak Portuguese.

Business Hours Hours vary throughout the country, but there is a set pattern. Banks generally are open Monday through Friday from 8:30am to 3pm. Currency-exchange offices at airports and rail terminals are open longer hours, and the office at Portela airport outside Lisbon is open 24 hours a day. Most museums open at 10am, close at 5pm, and often close for lunch between 12:30 and 2pm. Larger museums with bigger staffs remain open at midday. Shops are open, in general, Monday through Friday from 9am to 1pm and from 3 to 7pm, and Saturday from 9am to 1pm. Most restaurants serve lunch from noon until 3pm and dinner from 7:30 to 11pm; many close on Sunday. Many nightclubs open at 10pm, but the action doesn't really begin until after midnight and often lasts until between 3 and 5am.

Climate See "When to Go," earlier in this chapter.

Currency See "Money," earlier in this chapter.

Customs See "Visitor Information," earlier in this chapter.

Driving Rules See "Getting Around," earlier in this chapter.

Drugs Illegal drugs are plentiful, although penalties can be severe if you're caught possessing or selling illegal narcotics. Judges tend to throw the book at foreigners caught selling illegal narcotics. Bail for foreigners is rare, and local prosecutors have a high conviction rate. All the U.S., British, and Canadian consulates can do is provide you with a list of local attorneys.

Drugstores The Portuguese government requires selected pharmacies to stay open at all times of the day and night. They do so under a rotation system. Check with your concierge for the locations and hours of the nearest drugstores, called *farmácias de serviço.* In general, pharmacies in Portugal are open Monday through Friday from 9am to 1pm and from 3 to 7pm, and Saturday from 9am to 1pm.

Electricity Voltage is 200 volts AC (50 cycles). Many hardware stores in North America sell the appropriate transformers. The concierge desks of most hotels will lend you a transformer and plug adapters, or tell you where you can buy them nearby. If you have any doubt about whether you have the appropriate transformer, ask at your hotel desk before you try to plug in anything.

Embassies/Consulates If you lose your passport or have some other pressing problem, you'll need to get in touch with your embassy.

- **The Embassy of the United States,** on Avenida das Forças Armadas (Sete Rios), 1600 Lisboa (✆ **21/727-33-00**), is open Monday through Friday from 8am to 12:30pm and from 1:30 to 5pm. If you've lost a passport, the embassy can take photographs for you and help you to obtain the proof of citizenship needed to get a replacement.
- **The Embassy of Canada** is at Avenida da Liberdade 200, EDIT Victoria 4th Floor, 1269 Lisboa (✆ **21/316-46-00**). It's open Monday through Friday from 9am to 12pm and from 2 to 4pm (in July and Aug, the embassy closes at 1pm on Fri).
- **The Embassy of the United Kingdom,** Rua São Bernardo 33, 1249 Lisboa (✆ **21/392-40-00**), is open Monday through Friday from 9am to 11:30pm and from 3 to 4:30pm.
- **The Embassy of the Republic of Ireland,** Rua de Imprensa à Estrêla 1, 1200 Lisboa (✆ **21/392-94-40**), is open Monday through Friday from 9:30am to 12:30pm and from 2:30 to 4:30pm.
- **Australians** and **New Zealanders** should go to the British Embassy (see above).

Emergencies For the **police** (or an ambulance) in Lisbon, telephone ✆ **115.** In case of **fire,** call ✆ **32-22-22** or 60-60-60. For the **Portuguese Red Cross,** call ✆ **61-77-77.** The **national emergency** number in Portugal is ✆ **115.**

Language English is often spoken in the major resorts and at first-class and deluxe hotels; in smaller places, you'll often need the help of a phrase book or dictionary. One of the most helpful is the *Portuguese Phrase Book* (Berlitz).

Legal Aid Contact your local consulate for a list of English-speaking lawyers if you run into trouble with the law. After that, you're at the mercy of the local courts.

Liquor Laws You must be 18 to drink in Portugal. In Lisbon, bars are open until dawn.

Mail While in Portugal, you can have your mail directed to your hotel (or hotels), to the American Express representative, or to *Poste Restante* (General Delivery) in Lisbon. You must present your passport to pick up mail. The general post office in Lisbon is on Praça do Comércio, 1100 Lisbon (✆ **21/346-32-31**); it's open daily from 8am to 10pm.

Maps If you'd like a map before your trip to plan your itinerary, you can obtain one from Rand McNally, Michelin, or AAA. These are sold at bookstores all over the United States. Rand McNally has retail stores in large cities, including 150 E. 52nd St., New York, NY 10022 (✆ **212/758-7488**); and 595 Market St., San Francisco, CA 94105 (✆ 415/777-3131). The U.S. headquarters of Michelin is at P.O. Box 19008, Greenville, SC 29602-9008 (✆ 800/423-0485, or 864/458-5619 in South Carolina).

Passports **For Residents of the United States:** Whether you're applying in person or by mail, you can download passport applications from the U.S. State Department website at **http://travel.state.gov**. For general information, call the **National Passport Agency** (✆ **202/647-0518**). To find your regional passport office, either check the U.S. State Department website or call the **National Passport Information Center** (✆ **900/225-5674**); the fee is 55¢ per minute for automated information and $1.50 per minute for operator-assisted calls.

For Residents of Canada: Passport applications are available at travel agencies throughout Canada or from the central **Passport Office,** Department of Foreign Affairs and International Trade, Ottawa, ON K1A 0G3 (✆ **800/567-6868** in Canada; www.dfait-maeci.gc.ca/passport).

For Residents of the United Kingdom: To pick up an application for a standard 10-year passport (5-yr. passport for children under 16), visit your nearest passport office, major post office, or travel agency. Or, you can contact the **United Kingdom Passport Service** at ✆ **0870/521-0410,** or search its website at www.ukpa.gov.uk.

For Residents of Ireland: You can apply for a 10-year passport at the **Passport Office,** Setanta Centre, Molesworth Street, Dublin 2 (✆ **01/671-1633;** www.irlgov.ie/iveagh). Those under age 18 and over 65 must apply for a 12€ ($14) 3-year passport. You can also apply at 1A South Mall, Cork (✆ **021/272-525**) or at most main post offices.

For Residents of Australia: You can pick up an application from your local post office or any branch of Passports Australia, but you must schedule an interview at the passport office to present your application materials. Call the **Australian Passport Information Service** at ✆ **131-232,** or visit the government website at www.passports.gov.au.

For Residents of New Zealand: You can pick up a passport application at any New Zealand Passports Office or download it from the website. Contact the **Passports Office** at ✆ **0800/225-050** in New Zealand or 04/474-8100, or log on to www.passports.govt.nz.

Pets Pets brought into Portugal must have the approval of the local veterinarian and a health certificate from your home country.

Taxes Since Portugal and neighboring Spain simultaneously joined the Common Market (now the European Union) on January 1, 1986, Portugal has imposed a value-added tax (VAT) on most purchases made within its borders. It ranges from 8% to 30%. Known in Portugal as the IVA, the amount is almost always written into the bottom line of the bill for any purchase a foreign visitor makes. Hotel and restaurant bills are taxed at 17.5%. Car rentals are subject to an additional 17.5% tax (less than in some other European countries).

Such deluxe goods as jewelry, furs, and expensive imported liquors include a 30% built-in tax. Because a scotch and soda in a Portuguese bar carries this high tax, many people have changed their choice of alcohol from scotch to Portuguese brandy and soda or, more prosaically, beer.

To get a VAT refund on purchases that qualify (ask the shopkeeper), present your passport to the salesperson and ask for the special stamped form. Present the form with your purchases at the booth marked for IVA tax refunds at the airport. You'll get your money refunded right at the booth. For VAT refunds, you can also apply to **Global Refund,** 707 St., Stamford, CT 06901 (✆ **800/566-9828** in the U.S.; fax 203/674-8709; www.globalrefund.com).

Telegram/Telex/Fax At most hotels, the receptionist will help you send one of these messages. Otherwise, go to the nearest post office for assistance.

Telephone Portugal Telecom phones accept coins or a prepaid phone card (see below). Calling from a booth with the right change or card allows you to avoid high hotel surcharges. Put coins in a slot at the top of the box while you hold the receiver, and then dial your number after hearing the dial tone. Once a connection is made, the necessary coins will automatically drop. If enough coins are not available, your connection will be broken. A warning tone will sound and a light over the dial will go on if more coins are needed. For long-distance (trunk) calls within the country, dial the city code, followed by the local number. ***Note:*** If you see a city code that begins with a 0, drop this initial 0 and substitute a 2.

At CrediFone locations and at post offices, special phones take prepaid cards sold at post offices.

Telephone calls can also be made at all post offices, which also send telegrams. International calls are made by dialing 00 (double zero), followed by the country code, the area code (not prefaced by 0) and then the local phone number. The country code for the United States and Canada is 1. The country code for Portugal is 351. For further information, see "Telephone Tips," on the inside front cover.

Time Portugal is 6 hours ahead of Eastern Standard Time in the United States. Like most European countries, Portugal has daylight saving time. It moves its clocks ahead an hour in late spring and an hour back in the fall, corresponding roughly to daylight saving time in the United States; exact dates vary.

Tipping Most service personnel expect a good tip rather than a small one, as in the past. Hotels add a service charge (known as *serviço*), which is divided among the entire staff, but individual tipping is also the rule. Tip 1€ ($1.15) to the bellhop for running an errand, 1€ ($1.15) to the doorman who hails you a cab, 1€ ($1.15) to the porter for each piece of luggage carried, 2.50€ ($2.90) to the wine steward if you've dined often at your hotel, and 1.50€ ($1.70) to the chambermaid.

In first-class or deluxe hotels, the concierge will present you with a separate bill for extras, such as charges for bullfight tickets. A gratuity is expected in addition to the charge. The amount will depend on the number of requests you've made.

Figure on tipping about 20% of your taxi fare for short runs. For longer treks—for example, from the airport to Cascais—15% is adequate.

Restaurants and nightclubs include a service charge and government taxes of 17.5%. As in hotels, this money is distributed among the entire staff, so extra tipping is customary. Add about 5% to the bill in a moderately priced restaurant, and up to 10% in a deluxe or first-class establishment. For hat-check in *fado* houses, restaurants, and nightclubs, tip at least 1€ ($1.15). Washroom attendants get .50€ (60¢).

Water Tap water is generally potable throughout Portugal, but bottled water is always safer. Even if the water in Portugal isn't bad, you won't be used to the microbes and can become ill. In rural areas, the water supply might not be purified. Under no circumstances should you swim in or drink from freshwater rivers or streams.

3

Settling into Lisbon

In its golden age, Lisbon gained a reputation as the eighth wonder of the world. Travelers returning from the city boasted that its riches rivaled those of Venice. As one of the greatest maritime centers in history, the Portuguese capital imported exotic wares from the far-flung corners of its empire.

Treasures from Asia—including porcelain, luxurious silks, rubies, pearls, and other rare gems—arrived at Indian seaports on Chinese junks and eventually found their way to Lisbon. The abundance and variety of spices from the East, such as turmeric, ginger, pepper, cumin, and betel, rivaled even Keats's vision of "silken Samarkand."

From the Americas came red dyewood (brazilwood), coffee, gold, diamonds, and other gemstones. The extensive contact signaled a new era in world trade, and Lisbon sat at the center of a great maritime empire, a hub of commerce for Europe, Africa, and Asia.

Today, after a decades-long slumber, there is excitement again in this luminous city. Construction went on around the clock as Lisbon prepared for EXPO '98, which marked the 500th anniversary of Vasco da Gama's journey to India. Lisbon welcomed the world to its doorstep, and the visitors found a brighter, fresher city, as they continue to do today.

The most dramatic change of all was the opening of the Vasco da Gama Bridge spanning the Tagus. Ponte Vasco da Gama speeds access to other areas of Portugal, including Alentejo province, with links to Spain. An entire new suburb being created along the east bank of the Tagus has brought Lisbon a new railway hub, Gare de Oriente. Brash postmodern office buildings and restored medieval facades are just some of the changes that have altered the skyline. Still in place is the Lisbon of old, with its great art and architecture—which is what probably brought you here in the first place.

A BIT OF BACKGROUND Many Lisboans claim unabashedly that Ulysses founded their city. Others, with perhaps a more scholarly bent, maintain that the Phoenicians or the Carthaginians were the original settlers.

The Romans settled in Lisbon in about 205 B.C., later building a fortification on the site of what is now St. George's Castle. The Visigoths captured the city in the 5th century A.D.; in 714, centuries of Moorish domination began. The first king of Portugal, Afonso Henríques, captured Lisbon from the Moors in 1147. But it wasn't until 1256 that Afonso III moved the capital here, deserting Coimbra, now the country's major university city.

The Great Earthquake occurred at 9:40am on All Saints' Day, November 1, 1755. "From Scotland to Asia Minor, people ran out of doors and looked at the sky, and fearfully waited. It was, of course, an earthquake," chronicled *Holiday* magazine. Tidal waves 15m (49 ft.) high swept over Algeciras, Spain. The capitals of Europe shook. Some 22 aftershocks followed. Roofs caved in; hospitals (with more than 1,000 patients), prisons, public buildings, royal palaces, aristocratic town houses, fishers' cottages, churches, and houses of prostitution all were toppled. Overturned candles helped ignite a fire that consumed the once-proud capital in just 6 days, leaving it in gutted, charred shambles. Voltaire described the destruction in Candide: "The sea boiled up in the harbor and smashed the vessels lying at anchor. Whirlwinds of flame and ashes covered the streets and squares, houses collapsed, roofs were thrown onto foundations and the foundations crumbled." All told, 30,000 inhabitants were crushed beneath the tumbling debris.

When the survivors of the initial shocks ran from their burning homes toward the mighty Tagus, they were met with walls of water 12m (39 ft.) high. Estimates vary, but approximately 60,000 drowned or died in the 6-day holocaust.

After the ashes had settled, the Marquês de Pombal, the prime minister, ordered that the dead be buried and the city rebuilt at once. To accomplish that ambitious plan, the king gave him virtually dictatorial powers.

What Pombal ordered constructed was a city of wide, symmetrical boulevards leading into handsome squares dominated by fountains and statuary. Bordering these wide avenues would be black-and-white mosaic sidewalks, the most celebrated in Europe. The mixture of old and "new" (postearthquake) is so harmonious that travelers today consider Lisbon one of the most beautiful cities on Earth. The Tagus, the river flowing through Lisbon, has been called the city's eternal lover.

Seagulls take flight from the harbor, where boats from Africa unload their freight. Pigeons sweep down on Praça do Comércio, also known as Black Horse Square. From the Bairro Alto (Upper City), cable cars run down to the waterfront. Streets bear colorful names or designations, such as *Rua do Açúcar* (Street of Sugar). Fountains abound; one, the *Samaritan,* dates from the 16th century. The boulevards flank new high-rise apartment houses, while in other quarters, laundry hanging from 18th-century houses flaps in the wind. It's a city that gives nicknames to everything, from its districts to its kings. Fernando, who built one of the most characteristic walls around Lisbon, was honored with the appellation "the Beautiful."

Many who have never been to Lisbon know it well from watching World War II spy movies on TV. In the classic film *Casablanca,* Lisbon embodied the passage point to the Americas for refugees stranded in northern Africa. During the war, Lisbon, officially neutral, was a hotbed of intrigue and espionage. It was also a haven for thousands of refugees, including deposed royalty.

LISBON TODAY No longer the provincial town it was in the 1970s, Lisbon today has blossomed into a cosmopolitan city often beset with construction pains. Many of its old structures are simply falling apart and must be either restored or replaced. Some of the formerly clogged streets of the Baixa have been turned into cobblestone pedestrian malls.

Lisbon is growing and evolving, and the city is considerably more sophisticated than it once was, no doubt due in part to Portugal's joining the European Union (EU). The smallest capital of Europe is no longer a backwater at the far corner of Iberia. Some 1.6 million people now live in Lisbon, and many of its citizens, having drifted in from the far corners of the world, don't even speak Portuguese. Lisbon presides over a country with one of the fastest-growing economies in Europe, much of it fueled by investments that have poured in since Portugal joined the EU. Textiles, shoes, clothing, china, and earthenware are among its leading industries.

Sections along Avenida da Liberdade, the main street of Lisbon, at times evoke thoughts of Paris. As in

To Estoril, Sintra, Parque de Monsanto
Auto-Estrada
Av. Eng. D. Pacheco
Av. Joaquim A. d. Aguiar
AMOREIRAS
Praça do Marquês de Pombal
To Zoo, Benfica, Gulbenkian Museum
Rua Joaquim Bonifácio
ESTEFÂNIA
Largo de Santa Bárbara
0 1/10 mile
0 100 meters
Lisbon
PORTUGAL
Church
Information
Railway
Rua das Amoreiras
Rua Silva Carvalho
Campo de Ourique
Rua Dom João V
Rio do Sol ao Rato
Rua Ferr. Borges
Largo do Rato
RATO
Rua de S. Filipe Nery
Rua Rodrigo de Fonseca
Rua Castilho
Rua Braamcamp
Rua Alexandre Herculano
Rua Rosa Araújo
Rua Barata
Av. da Liberdade
Rua Rodrigues Sampaio
Rua de San José
Rue do Passadiço
Rua Luciano Cordeiro
Rua Gomes Freire
Rua da Escola do Exército
Rua dos Anjos
Av. Almirante Reis
Rua Palmira
Paço da Rainha
Rua do Salitre
Rua da Escola
Rua Nova de S. Mamede
Rua de São Bento
Av. Pedro Alvares Cabral
Rua do Cabo
Rua Silva Carvalho
Rua Saraiva
Praça da Alegria
Rua da Fé
Rua Instituto Bacteriologico
R. Renato Baptista
R. d. Moçambique
Rua Maria da Fonte
Rua de S. Lázaro
Jardim Botânico
Rua da Imprensa Nacional
Rua de Alegria
Av. da Liberdade
Rua Damasceno
Rua da Graça
Rua Senhora da Gloria
Jardim de Estrêla
Rua da Estrêla
Rua de S. Bernardo
Rua de Santo Amaro
Rua da Conç. da Gloria
Praça do Principe Real
Rua de S. Marçal
Rua de Gloria
Rua das Taipas
Rua de Pedro V
Rua da Quintinha
Rua da Palma
Rua do Benformoso
Rua S. de Monte
GRAÇA
ESTRÊLA
Calçada da Estrêla
Praça dos Restauradores
Rua de San José
Rua de Cavaleiros
Calç. de San to André
Rua das Olaris
Largo de Graça
Rua Leite de Vasconcelos
To Municipal Museum
Rua Bela Vista
Rua Borges Carneiro
Rua das Francesinhas
Rua Eduardo Coelho
Rua de dos Polais
Rua do Século
Rua S. Boaventura
Rua da Rosa
Rua da Atalaia
Museu St. Roque
Rossio Station
Praça Rossio
Teatro Nacional
Praça da Figueira
Rua da Verónica
Rua da Lapa
Rua du Quelhas
Rua do Meio
Rua S. João
Rua das Praças
LAPA
Av. Dom Carlos I
Calçada do Combro
Calhariz
Rua do Sol
Rua F. Tomás
Rua da Rosa
BAIRRO ALTO
Rua d. Betesga
BAIXA
Rua do Castelo
Rua da Costa
C. da Graça
Rue d. V. do Operário
Rua de Santa Apolónia
Castelo São Jorge
Rua Garcia de Orta
Rua da Madres
Rua da Esperança
R. do Puço
Praça Camões
Rua Garret
Rua do Ouro
Rua Augusta
Rua da Prata
Rua dos Fanqueiros
Rua da Madalena
THE ALFAMA
Rua da Esco las Gerais
Rua dos Remedios
Av. Infante D. Henrique
Santa Apolónia Station
Calçada Marquês de Abrantes
Museu Nacional de Arte Contemporânea
Rua de S. Mamede
Museu de Artes Decorativas
Museu Militar
Rua das Janelas Verdes
Largo de Santos
Rua da Boavista
Rua Dom Luis I
Teatro São Carlos
R. do Limoeiro
Rio Tejo (Tagus River)
Museu Nacional de Arte Antiga
Av. Vinte e Quatro de Julho
Rua de S. Paulo
Rua Vitor Cordon
Rua de S. Julião
Rua do Comércio
Rua C. do Sé
Rua d. Bacaloeiros
Sé (Cathedral)
Av. Infante D. Henrique

Paris, sidewalk portrait painters will sketch your likeness, and artisans will offer you jewelry claiming that it's gold (when you both know it isn't). Handcrafts, from embroidery to leatherwork, are peddled right on the streets as they are in New York.

Consider an off-season visit, especially in the spring or fall, when the city enjoys glorious weather before the hot, humid days of July and August descend. The city isn't overrun with visitors then, and you can wander about and take in its attractions without fear of being trampled.

1 Essentials

ARRIVING

BY PLANE Foreign and domestic flights land at Lisbon's Aeroporto de Lisboa (✆ **21/841-35-00**), about 6.5km (4 miles) from the heart of the city. An AEROBUS runs between the airport and the Cais do Sodré train station every 20 minutes from 7am to 9pm. The fare is 2.45€ ($2.80). It makes 10 intermediate stops, including Praça dos Restauradores and Praça do Comércio. There's no charge for luggage. Taxi passengers line up in a usually well-organized queue at the sidewalk in front of the airport, or you can call **Radiotaxi** at ✆ **21/793-27-56.** The average taxi fare from the airport to central Lisbon is 10€ ($12). Each piece of luggage is 1.50€ ($1.70) extra.

For ticket sales, flight reservations, and information about the city and the country, you can get in touch with the Lisboa personnel of **TAP Air Portugal,** Loja Gare do Oriente, Edificio Estação do Oriente, Avenida de Berlim, 1998 Lisboa(✆ **707/205-700** or 21/841-50-00 for reservations; www.tap-airportugal.pt).

BY TRAIN Most international rail passengers from Madrid and Paris arrive at the Estação da Santa Apolónia, Avenida Infante Dom Henrique, the major terminal. It's by the Tagus near the Alfama district. Two daily trains make the 10-hour run from Madrid to Lisbon. Rail lines from northern and eastern Portugal also arrive at this station. EXPO '98 brought a new, modern terminal to Lisbon. Gare de Oriente at Expo Urbe—connected to the Metro system—opened in 1998 and is the hub for some long-distance and suburban trains, including service to such destinations as Porto, Sintra, the Beiras, Minho, and the Douro. At the Estação do Rossio, between Praça dos Restauradores and Praça de Dom Pedro IV, you can get trains to Sintra. The Estação do Cais do Sodré, just beyond the south end of Rua Alecrim, east of Praça do Comércio, handles trains to Cascais and Estoril on the Costa do Sol. Finally, you can catch a ferry at Sul e Sueste, next to the Praça do Comércio. It runs across the Tagus to the suburb of Barreiro; at the station there, Estação do Barreiro, you can catch a train for the Algarve and Alentejo. For all rail information, at any of the terminals above, call ✆ **808/208-208** between 7am and 11pm daily.

BY BUS Buses from all over Portugal, including the Algarve, arrive at the Rodoviária da Arco do Cego (✆ **21/358-14-81**). If your hotel is in Estoril or Cascais, you can take bus no. 1, which goes on to the Cais do Sodré. At least six buses a day leave for Lagos, a gateway to the Algarve, and nine buses head north every day to Porto. There are 14 daily buses to Coimbra, the university city to the north.

BY CAR International motorists must arrive through Spain, the only nation connected to Portugal by road. You'll have to cross Spanish border points, which usually pose no great difficulty. The roads are moderately well maintained. From Madrid, if you head west, the main road (N620) from Tordesillas goes southwest by way of Salamanca and Ciudad Rodrigo and reaches the Portuguese frontier at Fuentes de Onoro.

If you have a rented car, make sure that your insurance covers Portugal. Drive on the right side of the road; international signs and symbols are used. Most of the 15 border crossings are open daily from 7am to midnight.

VISITOR INFORMATION

The main **tourist office** in Lisbon is at the Palácio da Foz, Praça dos Restauradores (**© 21/346-63-07**), at the Baixa end of Avenida da Liberdade. It's open daily from 9am to 8pm (Metro: Restauradores). It sells the **Lisbon Card,** which provides free city transportation and entrance fees to museums and other attractions, plus discounts on admission to events. For adults, a 1-day pass costs 12€ ($14), a 2-day pass costs 21€ ($24), and a three-day pass costs 27€ ($31). Children 5 to 11 pay 5.70€ ($6.50) for a 1-day pass, 8.55€ ($9.80) for a 2-day pass, and 11.40€ ($13) for a 3-day pass.

CITY LAYOUT

MAIN STREETS & SQUARES Lisbon is the westernmost capital of continental Europe. According to legend, it spreads across seven hills, like Rome. That statement has long been outdated—Lisbon now sprawls across more hills than that. Most of the city lies on the north bank of the Tagus.

No one ever claimed that getting around Lisbon was a breeze. Streets rise and fall across the hills, at times dwindling into mere alleyways. Exploring the city, however, is well worth the effort.

Lisbon is best approached through its gateway, **Praça do Comércio** (Commerce Square), bordering the Tagus. It's one of the most perfectly planned squares in Europe, rivaled only by the piazza dell'Unità d'Italia in Trieste, Italy. Before the 1755 earthquake, Praça do Comércio was known as Terreiro do Paço, the Palace Grounds, because the king and his court lived in now-destroyed buildings on that site. To confuse matters further, English-speaking residents often refer to it as Black Horse Square because of its statue (actually a bronze-green color) of José I.

Today the square is the site of the Stock Exchange and various government ministries. Its center is used as a parking lot, which destroys some of its harmony. In 1908, Carlos I and his elder son, Luís Filipe, were fatally shot here by an assassin. The monarchy held on for another 2 years, but the House of Bragança effectively came to an end that day.

Directly west of the square stands the City Hall, fronting Praça do Município. The building, erected in the late 19th century, was designed by the architect Domingos Parente.

Heading north from Black Horse or Commerce Square, you enter the hustle and bustle of **Praça de Dom Pedro IV,** popularly known as the Rossio. The "drunken" undulation of the sidewalks, with their arabesques of black and white, have led to the appellation "the dizzy praça." Here you can sit sipping strong unblended coffee from the former Portuguese provinces in Africa. The statue on the square is that of the Portuguese-born emperor of Brazil.

Opening onto the Rossio is the **Teatro Nacional de Dona Maria II,** a free-standing building whose facade has been preserved. From 1967 to 1970, workers gutted the interior to rebuild it completely. If you arrive by train, you'll enter the **Estação do Rossio,** whose exuberant Manueline architecture is worth seeing.

Separating the Rossio from Avenida da Liberdade is **Praça dos Restauradores,** named in honor of the Restoration, when the Portuguese chose their own king and freed themselves from 60 years of Spanish rule. An obelisk commemorates the event.

Lisbon's main avenue is **Avenida da Liberdade** (Avenue of Liberty). The handsomely laid-out street dates from 1880. Avenida da Liberdade is like a 1.5km-long (1-mile-long) park, with shade trees, gardens, and center walks for the promenading crowds. Flanking it are fine shops, the headquarters of many major airlines, travel agents, coffeehouses with sidewalk tables, and hotels. The comparable street in Paris is the Champs-Elysées; in Rome, it's via Vittorio Veneto.

At the top of the avenue is Praça do Marquês de Pombal, with a statue erected in honor of the 18th-century prime minister credited with Lisbon's reconstruction in the aftermath of the earthquake.

Proceeding north, you'll enter Parque Eduardo VII, named in honor of the son of Queen Victoria, who paid a state visit to Lisbon. In the park is the Estufa Fria, a greenhouse well worth a visit.

FINDING AN ADDRESS Finding an address in the old quarters of Lisbon is difficult because street numbering at times follows no predictable pattern. When trying to locate an address, always ask for the nearest cross street before setting out. Addresses consist of a street name followed by a number. Sometimes the floor of the building is given as well. For example, Avenida Casal Ribeiro 18 3 means that the building is at number 18 and the address is on the third floor. In Lisbon, the ground floor is not called the first floor as in the United States; what Americans would call the fourth floor is actually the third floor in Portugal. "ESP" after a floor number indicates that you should go left, and "DIR" means turn right.

STREET MAPS Arm yourself with a good city map before setting out. Maps with complete indexes of streets are available at most newsstands and kiosks. Those given away by tourist offices and hotels aren't adequate because they don't show the maze of little streets.

NEIGHBORHOODS IN BRIEF

Baixa The business district of Lisbon, Baixa contains much Pombaline-style architecture. (The term refers to the prime minister who rebuilt Lisbon following the earthquake.) Many major Portuguese banks are headquartered here. Running south, the main street of Baixa separates Praça do Comércio from the Rossio. A triumphal arch leads from the square to Rua Augusta, where there are many clothing stores. The two most important streets of Baixa are **Rua da Prata** (Street of Silver) and **Rua Aurea,** formerly called Rua do Oro (Street of Gold). Silversmiths and goldsmiths are located on these streets.

Chiado If you head west from Baixa, you'll enter this shopping district. From its perch on a hill, it's traversed by **Rua Garrett,** named for the noted romantic writer João Batista de Almeida Garrett (1799–1854). Many of the finest shops in the city, such as the Vista Alegre, a china and porcelain house, are here. One coffeehouse in particular, A Brasileira, has been a traditional gathering spot for the Portuguese literati.

Bairro Alto Continuing your ascent, you'll arrive at the Bairro Alto (Upper City). This sector, reached by trolley car, occupies one of the legendary seven hills of Lisbon. Many of its buildings were left fairly intact by the 1755 earthquake. Containing much of the charm and color of the Alfama, it's the location of some of the finest *fado* (meaning "fate" and describing a type of music) clubs in Lisbon, as well as excellent restaurants and bars. There are also antiques shops.

The Alfama East of Praça do Comércio lies the oldest district, the Alfama. Saved only in part from the devastation of the 1755 earthquake, the Alfama was the Moorish section of the capital. Nowadays it's home in some parts to stevedores, fishermen, and *varinas* (fishwives). Overlooking the Alfama is **Castelo São Jorge,** or St. George's Castle, a visigothic fortification that was later used by the Romans. On the way to the Alfama, on Rua dos Bacalheiros, stands another landmark, the **Casa dos Bicos** (House of the Pointed Stones), an early 16th-century town house whose facade is studded with diamond-shape stones. Be careful of muggers in parts of the Alfama at night.

Belém In the west, on the coastal road to Estoril, is the suburb of Belém. It contains some of the finest monuments in Portugal, several built during the Age of Discovery, near the point where the caravels set out to conquer new worlds. (At Belém, the Tagus reaches the sea.) At one time, before the earthquake, Belém was an aristocratic sector filled with elegant town houses.

Two of the country's principal attractions stand here: the **Mosteiro dos Jerónimos,** a Manueline structure erected in the 16th century, and the **Museu Nacional dos Coches,** the National Coach Museum, the finest of its kind in the world. Belém is Lisbon's land of museums—it also contains the Museu de Arte Popular and the Museu de Marinha.

Cacilhas On the south side of the Tagus, where puce-colored smoke billows from factory stacks, is the left-bank settlement of Cacilhas. Inhabited mainly by the working class, it's often visited by right-bank residents who come here for the seafood restaurants. You can reach the settlement by way of a bridge or a ferryboat from Praça do Comércio.

The most dramatic way to cross the Tagus is on the **Ponte do 25 de Abril.** Completed in 1966, the bridge helped open Portugal south of the Tagus. The bridge is 2.2km (1½ miles) long, and its towers are 190m (623 ft.) high. In 1998, the longest suspension bridge in Europe, **Ponte Vasco da Gama,** opened in time for the EXPO '98. Spanning the Tagus, it stretches for 16km (10 miles). It opens areas to the north of the country and the southern Algarve, and east across the Alentejo plain to southern Spain—all of which are now more accessible. Standing guard on the left bank is a monumental statue of Jesus with arms outstretched.

2 Getting Around

Public transportation is inexpensive but inadequate at times. Yet, considering the hilly terrain and the fact that many of the streets were designed for donkey carts, the system works well. Even the most skilled chauffeurs, however, have been known to scrape the fenders of their clients' rented limousines while maneuvering through the narrow alleyways.

A lot of the city can be covered on foot. However, to get from one point to another—say, from the Alfama to the suburb of Belém—you'll need to use public transportation or your own car.

As Evamarie Doering of Belmont, California, wrote, "In the 15 years since my last visit there, Lisbon has become one of the noisiest cities I've ever visited. Traffic is outrageous; driving is difficult because of the speed and the tendency of the natives to ride 6 inches from your rear bumper. The buses, of which there are a great many, are very noisy, and produce volumes of smoke. Honking of car horns seems to be a national pastime." Her description is, unfortunately, apt.

BY PUBLIC TRANSPORTATION

CARRIS (© **21/361-30-30;** www.carris.pt) operates the network of funiculars, trains, subways, and buses in Lisbon. The company sells a *bilhete de assinatura turístico* (tourist ticket) that's good for 4 days of unlimited travel on its network. It costs 9.95€ ($11). A 1-day pass goes for 2.75€ ($3.15); a 7-day pass costs 14€ ($16). Passes are sold in CARRIS booths, open from 9am to 5pm daily, in most Metro stations and network train stations. You must show a passport to buy a pass.

METRO Lisbon's Metro stations are designated by large M signs. A single ticket costs .65€ (75¢); 10 tickets at one time cost 5.10€ ($5.90). One of the most popular trips—and likely to be jam-packed on *corrida* (bullfight) days—is from Avenida da Republica to Campo Pequeno, the brick building away from the center of the city. Service runs daily from 6:30am to 1am. For more information, call © **21/355-84-57.**

Surprisingly, riding the Lisbon Metro is like visiting an impressive art collection. Paintings, glazed tiles, and sculptures make for an underground museum. You'll see interesting collections of contemporary art, including some works by famous Portuguese artists such as Maria Keil and Maria Helena Vieira da Silva. Stations that display some of the finest art include Cais do Sodré, Baixa/Chiado, Campo Grande, and Marquês de Pombal.

BUS & TRAM These are among the cheapest in Europe. The *eléctricos* (trolley cars, or trams) make the steep run up to the Bairro Alto. The double-decker buses come from London and look as if they need Big Ben in the background to complete the picture. If you're trying to stand on the platform at the back of a jammed bus, you'll need both hands free to hold on.

The basic fare on a bus or eléctrico is 1€ ($1.15) if you buy the ticket from the driver. The transportation system within the city limits is divided into zones ranging from one to five. The fare depends on how many zones you traverse. Buses and eléctricos run daily from 6am to 1am.

At the foot of the Santa Justa Elevator, on Rua Aurea, there's a stand with schedules pinpointing the zigzagging tram and bus routes. Your hotel concierge should have information.

The antediluvian eléctricos, much like San Francisco's cable cars, have become a major tourist attraction. Beginning in 1903, the eléctricos replaced horse-drawn trams. The most interesting ride for sightseers is on eléctrico no. 28, which takes you on a fascinating trip through the most history-rich part of Lisbon.

ELECTRIC TRAIN A smooth-running, modern electric train system connects Lisbon to all the towns and villages along the Portuguese Riviera. There's only one class of seat, and the rides are cheap and generally comfortable. You can board the train at the waterfront Cais do Sodré Station in Lisbon and head up the coast all the way to Cascais.

The electric train does not run to Sintra. For Sintra, you must go to the Estação do Rossio station, opening onto Praça de Dom Pedro IV, or the Rossio, where frequent connections can be made. The one-way fare from Lisbon to Cascais, Estoril, or Sintra is 1.25€ to 2.50€ ($1.45–$2.90) per person.

FUNICULARS Lisbon has a trio of funiculars: the Glória, which goes from Praça dos Restauradores to Rua São Pedro de Alcântara; the Bica, from the Calçada do Combro to Rua do Boavista; and the Lavra, from the eastern side of Avenida da Liberdade to Campo Martires da Pátria. A one-way ticket on any of these costs 1€ ($1.15).

FERRY Long before the bridges across the Tagus were built, reliable ferryboats chugged across the river, connecting the left bank with the right. They still do, and have been rebuilt and remotorized so they're no longer noisy. Many Portuguese who live on the bank opposite Lisbon take the ferry to avoid the heavy bridge traffic during rush hour.

Most boats leave from Cais de Alfândega (Praça do Comércio) and Cais do Sodré, heading for Cacilhas. The trip is worth it for the scenic views alone. Arrivals are at the Estação do Barreiro, where trains leave about every 30 minutes for the Costa Azul and the Algarve. Ferries depart Lisbon throughout the day about every 30 minutes; trip time across the Tagus is 30 minutes. The cost of the continuing train ticket includes the ferry. The separate ferry fare from the center of Lisbon to Cacilhas is 2€ ($2.30).

BY TAXI

Taxis in Lisbon tend to be inexpensive and are a popular means of transport for all but the most economy-minded tourists. They usually are diesel-engine Mercedes. The basic fare is 1.80€ ($2.10) for the first 153m (502 ft.), .05€ (10¢) for each extra 162m (531 ft.), plus 20% from 10pm to 6am. The law allows drivers to tack on another 50% to your bill if your luggage weighs more than 66 pounds. Portuguese tip about 20% of the modest fare. For a Radio Taxi, call ✆ **21/811-90-00.**

Many visitors stay at a Costa do Sol resort hotel, such as the Palácio in Estoril or the Cidadela in Cascais. If you stay there, you'll probably find taxi connections from Lisbon prohibitively expensive. Far preferable for Costa do Sol visitors is the electric train system (see above).

BY CAR

In congested Lisbon, driving is extremely difficult and potentially dangerous—the city has an alarmingly high accident rate. It always feels like rush hour in Lisbon. (Theoretically, rush hours are Mon–Sat 8–10am, 1–2pm, and 4–6pm.) Parking is seemingly impossible. Wait to rent a car until you're making excursions from the capital. If you drive into Lisbon from another town or city, call ahead and ask at your hotel for the nearest garage or other place to park. Leave your vehicle there until you're ready to depart.

CAR RENTALS The major international car-rental companies are represented in Lisbon. There are kiosks at the airport and offices in the center. They include **Avis,** Avenida Praia da Vitória 12C (✆ **21/354-15-60**), open daily from 8am to 7pm; and **Hertz,** Av. Severiano Falcão 7 2685-378 Prior Velho (✆ **21/942-63-00**), open Monday through Friday from 8:30am to 6:30pm, and Saturday from 9am to 6:30pm. **Budget,** rue Castillo 167B (✆ **21/386-05-16**), is open daily from 9am to 7pm.

GASOLINE Lisbon has many garages and gasoline pumps; some are open around the clock.

THE TAGUS BRIDGES The suspension bridge Ponte do 25 de Abril, one of the longest in Europe, connects Lisbon with the district south of the Tagus. The 16km (10-mile) Ponte Vasco da Gama, which opened in 1998, is the longest suspension bridge in Europe. It has greatly relieved overcrowding on the Ponte do 25 de Abril (25th of April Bridge). Tolls are based on the size of the car. You take these bridges to reach Cacilhas and such cities as Setúbal, in the south, and Évora, the old Roman city in the east.

ON FOOT

Central Lisbon is relatively compact, and because of heavy traffic, it's best explored by foot. That's virtually the only way to see such districts as the Alfama. However, when you venture farther afield, such as to Belém, you'll need to depend on public transportation (see above).

FAST FACTS: Lisbon

Your hotel's concierge usually is a reliable source of information. See also "Fast Facts: Portugal," in chapter 2, "Planning Your Trip to Portugal."

Babysitters Most first-class hotels can provide babysitters from lists the concierge keeps. At small establishments, the sitter is likely to be a relative of the proprietor. Rates are low. Remember to request a babysitter early—no later than the morning if you're planning on going out that evening. Also request a sitter with at least a minimum knowledge of English. If your sitter is fluent in English, count yourself lucky.

Currency Exchange There are currency-exchange booths at Santa Apolónia station and at the airport, both open 24 hours a day. ATMs offer the best exchange rates. They pepper the streets of the central Baixa district and are also found less frequently in other parts of the city. The post office (see "Mail," below) will exchange money as well. See also "American Express," in "Fast Facts: Portugal," in chapter 2.

Dentists The reception staff at most hotels maintains lists of local, usually English-speaking dentists who are available for dental emergencies. Some of them will contact a well-recommended dental clinic, **Clinica Medical da Praga d'Espanha,** Rua Dom Luís de Narona 32 (✆ **21/796-74-57**). Some of the staff members speak English.

Doctors See "Hospitals," below.

Drugstores **Farmácia Vall,** Avenida Visconde Valmor 60B (✆ **21/797-30-43**), is centrally located and well stocked.

Emergencies To call the police or an ambulance, telephone ✆ **112.** In case of fire, call ✆ **21/342-22-22.**

Hairdressers/Barbers A recommended hairdresser for women is **Hair,** Rua Castilho 77A (✆ **21/387-78-55**). A sophisticated counterpart for men is **Bengto,** in the Amoreiras shopping center, Travesso das Amoreiras (✆ **21/383-29-29**).

Hospitals In case of a medical emergency, ask at your hotel or call your embassy and ask the staff there to recommend an English-speaking physician. Or try the **British Hospital,** Rua Saraiva de Carvalho 49 (✆ **21/394-31-00**), where the telephone operator, staff, and doctors speak English.

Hot Lines The drug abuse hot line is ✆ **21/726-77-66.** The number for the Lisbon office of Alcoholics Anonymous is ✆ **21/716-29-69.**

Internet Access You can check your e-mail at **Cyber.bica,** Duques de Bragança 7 (✆ **21/322-50-04**), in the Chiado district. Its website is www.cyberbica.com (Metro: Baixa-Chiado.) It's open Monday through Friday from 11am to midnight.

Laundry Keeping your clothes clean can be a problem if you're not staying long in Lisbon. For a self-service laundry, try **Lavatax,** Rua Francisco Sanches 65A (✆ **21/812-33-92**).

Lost Property For items lost on public transportation, inquire at **Secção de Achados da PSP,** Olivais Sul, Praça da Cidade Salazar Lote 180 (✆ **21/853-54-03**), which is open Monday through Friday from 9am to 12:30pm and from 1:30 to 5pm.

Luggage Storage/Lockers These can be found at the **Estação da Santa Apolónia** (✆ **21/888-40-25**), by the river near the Alfama. Lockers cost 3€ ($3.45) for up to 48 hours.

Mail While in Portugal, you can have your mail directed to your hotel (or hotels), to the American Express representative, or to Poste Restante (General Delivery) in Lisbon. You must present your passport to pick up mail. The main post office, Correio Geral, in Lisbon is at Praça do Restauradores, 1100 Lisboa (✆ **21/323-89-71**). It's open Monday through Friday from 8am to 10pm, and Saturday and Sunday 9am to 6pm.

Photographic Needs One of the best places to go for your film needs, including processing, is **Fotosport,** Centro Comercial Amoreiras, Shop no. 1080 (✆ **21/383-21-01**). It's open daily from 10am to 11pm.

Police Call ✆ **112.**

Safety Lisbon used to be one of the safest capitals of Europe, but that hasn't been true for a long time. It's now quite dangerous to walk around at night. Many travelers report being held up at knifepoint. Some bandits operate in pairs or in trios. Not only do they take your money, but they demand your ATM code. One of the robbers holds a victim captive while another withdraws money. (If the number proves to be fake, the robber might return and harm the victim.) During the day, pickpockets galore prey on tourists, aiming for wallets, purses, and cameras. Congested areas are particularly hazardous. Avoid walking at night, especially if you're alone.

Taxes Lisbon imposes no city taxes. However, the national value-added tax (VAT) applies to purchases and services (see "Taxes" under "Fast Facts: Portugal," in chapter 2).

Telegrams/Telex/Fax At most hotels, the receptionist will help you send a telegram. If not, there's a cable dispatch service open 24 hours a day at **Marconi** (the Portuguese Radio Communications Office), Rua de São Julião 131. To send telegrams from any telephone to points outside Portugal, dial ✆ **1582** to reach Marconi. To send telegrams within Portugal (your Portuguese-language skills had better be good), dial ✆ **1583** from any telephone. Most foreign visitors leave the logistics to the hotel concierge. Telexes and faxes can be sent from most hotels, or you can go to the general post office (see "Mail," above).

Telephone You can make a local call in Lisbon in one of the many telephone booths. For most long-distance telephone calls, particularly transatlantic calls, go to the central post office (see "Mail," above). Give an assistant the number, and he or she will make the call for you, billing you at the end. Some phones are equipped for using calling cards, including American Express and Visa. You can also purchase phone cards. See "Telephone" under "Fast Facts: Portugal" in chapter 2. In hotels, local calls are billed directly to your room. Phone debit cards can be used only in public phones in public places. The debit cards are either T.L.P. or CrediFone. Both are sold at the cashier's desks of most hotels and at post offices throughout the country.

Time For the local time in Lisbon, phone ✆ **15.**

Transit Information For airport information, call ✆ **21/841-35-00.** For train information, dial ✆ **808/208-208. TAP Air Portugal** is at Avenida Do Berlin 1998 (✆ **21/841-50-00**).

Weather To find out about the weather, call ✆ **12150** (available only in Portuguese). If you don't speak Portuguese, ask someone at your hotel desk to translate one of the weather reports that appear daily in the leading newspapers.

3 Where to Stay

Lisbon has a much wider range of accommodations than ever before. Once Lisbon hotels were so cheap that they were reason alone to travel to Lisbon. Unfortunately, that's no longer the case. Today hotels such as the Four Seasons Hotel The Ritz Lisbon and the Hotel Tivoli charge virtually the same prices as first-class hotels in other high-priced European capitals.

Most visitors in Lisbon have to decide whether to stay in a hotel in the city proper or at a resort in the neighboring towns of Estoril and Cascais (see chapter 5). Much will depend on your interests. If it's summer and you'd like to have a sea-resort vacation while experiencing Lisbon's cultural attractions, a beach resort might be ideal, even though you'd have to commute into Lisbon. Electric trains run about every 20 minutes, so it's entirely possible to stay on the Costa do Sol and still go sightseeing in Lisbon.

If you're primarily interested in seeing Lisbon's attractions and are pressed for time, you'll probably opt to stay in the city. Also, the off season (Nov–Mar) is not ideal for a sea-resort vacation.

If you can't afford to stay in Lisbon's world-class hotels, you'll find reasonably priced guesthouses—called *pensãos*—in Portugal. Most of these are no-frills accommodations. Often you'll have to share a bathroom, although many have hot and cold running water in a sink in your room. Some of the pensions in Lisbon are centrally located and are a good way to see the sights day and night without shelling out a lot of money for accommodations.

If you arrive without a reservation, begin your search for a room as early in the day as possible. If you arrive late at night, you might have to take what you can get, and pay more than you expected.

Lisbon Accommodations

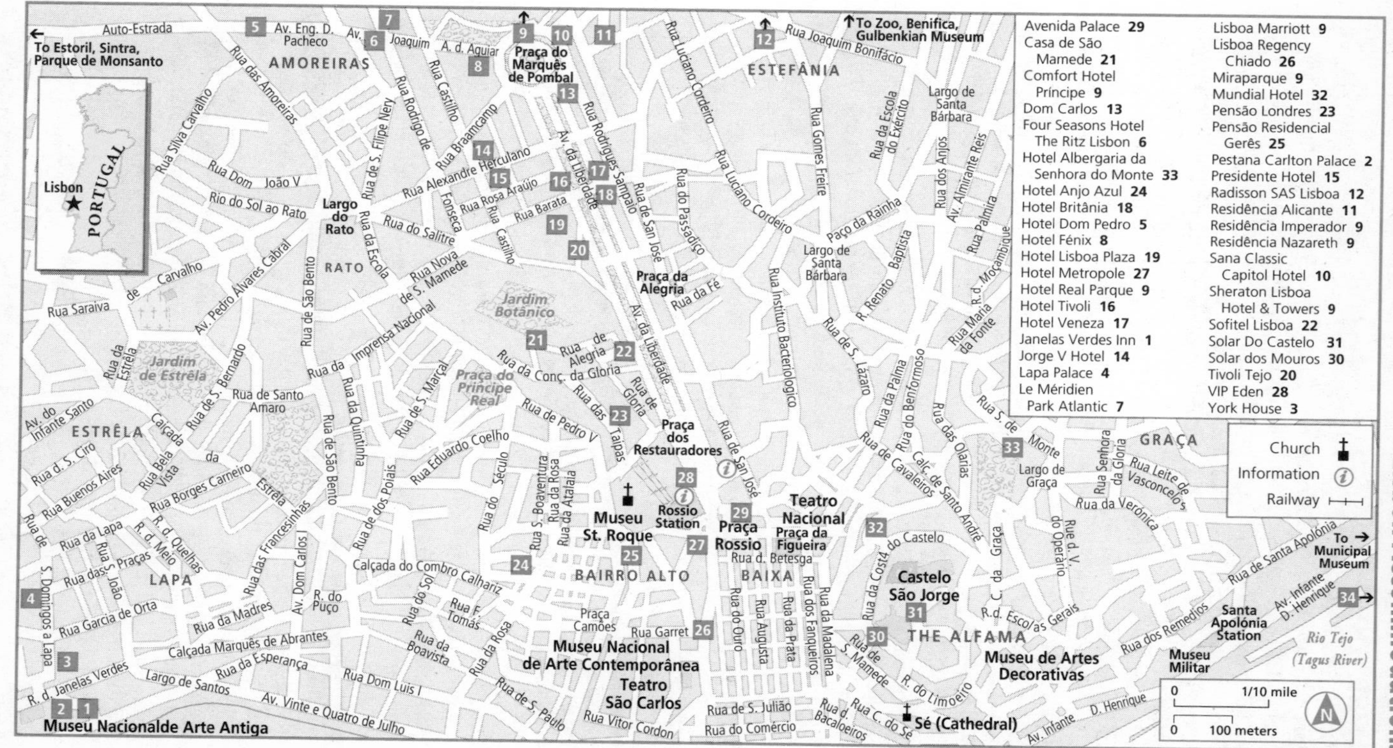

IN THE CENTER

VERY EXPENSIVE

Four Seasons Hotel The Ritz Lisbon ★★★ The 10-floor Ritz, built by the dictator Salazar in the late 1950s, is now operated by Four Seasons. Its suites boast the finest decoration you'll see in any major Portuguese hotel: slender mahogany canopied beds with fringed swags, marquetry desks, satinwood dressing tables, and plush carpeting. Some of the soundproofed, spacious, modern rooms have terraces opening onto Edward VII Park; each boasts a marble bathroom with a double basin and a shower-tub combination. The least desirable rooms are the even-numbered ones facing the street. The odd-numbered accommodations, opening onto views of the park, are the best. Some studios with double beds are rented as singles, attracting business travelers. The fifth floor is reserved for nonsmokers.

Rua Rodrigo de Fonseca 88, 1099-039 Lisboa. ✆ **800/332-3442** in the U.S., or ✆ 21/383-20-20. Fax 21/383-17-83. www.fourseasons.com. 284 units. 380€–415€ ($437–$477) double; from 710€ ($817) suite. AE, DC, MC, V. Free parking. Metro: Rotunda. Bus: 1, 2, 9, or 32. **Amenities:** Restaurant; bar; pool; health spa; sauna; 24-hr. room service; massage; babysitting; laundry service; dry cleaning. *In room:* A/C, TV, minibar, hair dryer, safe.

Hotel Dom Pedro ★★ Rated five stars by the Portuguese government and associated with some of the most glamorous hotels of the Algarve and Madeira, this bastion of luxury is in the central Amoreiras district, across from one of the city's biggest shopping centers. A hypermodern sheathing of reflective glass covers its 21 stories. The interior is as conservative and rich-looking as the exterior is futuristic. The good-size guest rooms are richly furnished, usually with heraldic symbols or medallions woven subtly through the fabrics and wallpapers. Rooms also contain immaculately kept bathrooms with shower-tub combinations. There are 48 nonsmoking rooms for guests and also several rooms for those with limited mobility.

Av. Engenheiro Duarte Pacheco 24, 1070-109 Lisboa. ✆ **21/389-66-00.** Fax 21/389-66-01. www.dompedro.com. 263 units. 300€–332€ ($345–$382) double; from 660€ ($759) suite. AE, DC, MC, V. Parking 15€ ($17). Metro: Marquês de Pombal. **Amenities:** 2 restaurants; 2 bars; car rental; business center; 24-hr. room service; babysitting; laundry; dry cleaning; rooms for those w/limited mobility. *In room:* A/C, TV, dataport, minibar, hair dryer, safe.

Lapa Palace ★★★ In a palace built in 1870 for the count of Valença, this government-rated five-star hotel, purchased by Orient Express in 1998, is the most talked-about accommodation in Lisbon. We never thought we'd see a hotel replace the Four Seasons Hotel The Ritz as the city's premier address, but Lapa has done just that. In 1910, the de Valença family sold the villa and its enormous gardens to a wealthy, untitled family that retained it until 1988. After more than 4 years of renovation, it opened in 1992 amid a flurry of publicity. Its lushly manicured gardens lie close to the Tagus, south of the city center.

All but about 20 of the rooms are in a modern 6-story wing. The spacious guest rooms in both sections contain amply proportioned marble surfaces, reproductions of French and English furniture, and a classic design inspired by a late 18th-century model. The marble bathrooms are among the city's most elegant, often adorned with bas-relief and containing shower-tub combinations and, in some cases, whirlpool baths. Each unit opens onto a balcony. The older rooms have more charm and grace; many of the newer ones open onto panoramic vistas of Lisbon. The public areas have multicolored ceiling frescoes and richly patterned marble floors.

Rua do Pau de Bandeira 4, 1249-021 Lisboa. ✆ **21/394-94-94.** Fax 21/395-06-65. www.orient-expresshotels.com. 109 units. 300€–500€ ($345–$575) double; 575€ ($661) junior suite; from 675€ ($776) suite. Rates include breakfast. AE, DC, MC, V. Free parking. Bus: 13 or 27. **Amenities:** 2 restaurants; bar; pool; health club;

sauna; 24-hr. room service; massage; babysitting; laundry service; dry cleaning. *In room:* A/C, TV, dataport, minibar, hair dryer, safe.

Sheraton Lisboa Hotel & Towers ★★★ Built in 1972, this deluxe hotel is sheltered in a 25-floor skyscraper lying at a traffic-clogged intersection a bit removed from the center of the action, a few blocks north of Praça do Marquês de Pombal. Most of the guests are business travelers. The impressive pink-marble lobby features chandeliers and fancy carpeting. The guest rooms don't match the grandeur of the public spaces, but they're generally spacious. The understated decor includes thick wool carpeting, print fabrics, traditional (if a bit chunky) wood furniture, and excellent beds. The marble bathrooms are a highlight, with shower-tub combinations. Six rooms are available for those with limited mobility. The most desirable rooms are in the tower, opening onto views of the Vasco da Gama bridge, the Tagus, or the city. There's also a private lounge and bar, and you can enjoy drinks on the 26th floor, with a panoramic view of Lisbon and dancing to live music nightly.

Rua Latino Coelho 1, 1069-025 Lisboa. ✆ **800/325-3535** in the U.S., or ✆ 21/357-57-57. Fax 21/354-71-64. www.Sheraton.com/lisboa. 381 units. 320€ ($368) double; from 635€ ($730) suite. AE, DC, MC, V. Parking 12€ ($14). Bus: 1, 36, 44, or 45. **Amenities:** 2 restaurants; 2 bars; pool; health club; sauna; car rental; 24-hr. room service; massage; babysitting; laundry service; dry cleaning. *In room:* A/C, TV, dataport, minibar, hair dryer, safe.

EXPENSIVE

Avenida Palace ★ Built in 1892, Avenida Palace is the grandest old-fashioned hotel in Lisbon, an antiques-filled link to the past. Its extremely convenient location right at the Rossio is terribly noisy, but once inside, it is another world entirely. It underwent a massive overhaul in the late 1990s. Still the grand dame of Lisbon hotels, it retains its 19th-century aura and elegance, with a marble staircase, beautiful salons, and silk brocades. The Belle Epoque–style Palace offers all the modern comforts, especially in its restored guest rooms. They're soundproofed and elegantly furnished, often in 17th- or 18th-century style. The marble bathrooms come equipped with shower-tub combinations.

Rua 1er Dezembro 123, 1200-359 Lisboa. ✆ **21/321-81-00.** Fax 21/342-28-84. hotel.av.palace@mail.telepac.pt. 82 units. 165€–200€ ($190–$230) double; 240€ ($276) junior suite; 350€–375€ ($403–$431) suite. Rates include breakfast. AE, DC, MC, V. Free parking. Metro: Restauradores. Tram: 35. **Amenities:** Breakfast room; bar; lounge; room service (7am–midnight); babysitting; laundry service; dry cleaning. *In room:* A/C, TV, dataport, minibar, hair dryer, safe.

Hotel Lisboa Plaza ★★ Hotel Lisboa Plaza, in the heart of the city, is a charmer. A family-owned and -operated government-rated four-star hotel, it has many appealing Art Nouveau touches, including the facade. The hotel was built in 1953 and has been frequently overhauled and modernized since. A well-known Portuguese designer, Graca Viterbo, decorated it in contemporary classic style. The midsize guest rooms—with well-stocked marble bathrooms with shower-tub combinations—are well styled and comfortable. There are 49 rooms for nonsmoking guests. Seek a unit in the rear, looking out over the botanical gardens. Windows are double-glazed.

Travessa do Salitre 7, Av. da Liberdade, 1269-066 Lisboa. ✆ **21/321-82-18.** Fax 21/347-16-30. www.heritage.pt. 112 units. 148€–225€ ($170–$259) double; 250€–370€ ($288–$426) suite. Children under 13 free in parent's room. AE, DC, MC, V. Parking 9€ ($10) nearby. Metro: Avenida. Bus: 1, 2, 36, or 44. **Amenities:** Restaurant; bar; car rental; 24-hr. room service; babysitting; laundry service; dry cleaning. *In room:* A/C, TV, dataport, minibar, hair dryer, safe.

Hotel Real Parque ★ Always dependable, this 10-story hotel is housed in a modern building and has been rated four stars by the government ever since it opened in 1995. Fairly stylish with up-to-date comforts, it is a choice of both the international business traveler and the vacationer. The hotel is devoid of any real Portuguese flavor and could be in any one of several European cities. It offers small to midsize bedrooms that are good-looking, uncluttered, and tastefully furnished with well-organized private bathrooms with shower-tub combinations. A cosmopolitan crowd patronizes the hotel's drinking and dining facilities. There are 15 nonsmoking rooms and 6 rooms for those with limited mobility.

Av. Luís Bivar 67, 1069-146 Lisboa. ✆ **21/319-90-00.** Fax 21/357-07-50. www.hoteisreal.com. 153 units. 150€–170€ ($173–$200) double; from 240€ ($276) suite. AE, DC, MC, V. Parking 6€ ($7). Metro: São Sebastião. **Amenities:** Restaurant; bar; coffee shop; limited room service; babysitting; laundry service; dry cleaning. *In room:* A/C, TV, minibar, hair dryer.

Hotel Tivoli ★★ In spite of increased competition among upmarket hotels, this enduring favorite continues to hold its own, luring guests with such enticing features as the only hotel pool in central Lisbon. Right on the main boulevard, it has extensive facilities, but its prices are not extravagant, considering the luxuries. The two-story reception lobby has an encircling mezzanine lounge that's almost arena-size, with comfortable islands of furniture arranged on oriental rugs. Adjoining the O Terraço restaurant is a homey salon with a wood-burning fireplace.

The guest rooms contain a mixture of modern and traditional furniture. The first floor is entirely nonsmoking rooms. The larger and best rooms face the front, although those in the rear are quieter. For some reason, rooms ending in the number 50 have the most spacious bathrooms, all of which contain neatly kept shower-tub combinations. There are two rooms for those with limited mobility. Unlike the climate control in many Lisbon hotels, the air-conditioning here actually seems to work. The Tivoli Jardim, next door, is under the same ownership but is inferior to the Hotel Tivoli.

Av. da Liberdade 185, 1269-050 Lisboa Codex. ✆ **21/319-89-00.** Fax 21/319-89-50. www.tivolihotels.com. 329 units. 195€–255€ ($224–$293) double; from 402€ ($462) suite. Rates include continental breakfast. AE, DC, MC, V. Parking 15€ ($17). Metro: Avenida. Bus: 1, 2, 9, or 32. **Amenities:** 2 restaurants; 2 bars; pool; tennis court; health club; solarium; 24-hr. room service; babysitting; laundry service; dry cleaning. *In room:* A/C, TV, dataport, minibar, hair dryer, safe.

Le Méridien Park Atlantic ★ One of the most dramatic major hotels in Lisbon, Le Méridien, which opened in 1985, lies in an 18-floor tower of concrete and mirrored glass. It's across the street from the superior Four Seasons Hotel The Ritz Lisbon. The air-conditioned lobby has lost some of its early glitter, but it's still impressive, with white marble, polished chromium, and mirrors. A symmetrical entrance frames the tile-bottomed fountains, whose splashing water rises to the top of the sunlit atrium. The small to midsize guest rooms are soundproof and tastefully decorated with business travelers in mind. There are two nonsmoking floors. They have thermostats and queen or king beds. The marble bathrooms have robes, shower-tub combinations, and toilet kits. Three rooms are available for those with limited mobility.

Rua Castilho 149, 1099-034 Lisboa. ✆ **21/381-87-00.** Fax 21/389-05-05. www.lemeridien-lisbon.com. 331 units. 127€–350€ ($146–$403) double; from 450€ ($518) suite. AE, DC, MC, V. Parking 12€ ($14). Metro: Rotunda. Bus: 1, 2, 9, or 32. **Amenities:** Restaurant; piano bar; health club; sauna; 24-hr. room service; massage; babysitting; laundry service; dry cleaning. *In room:* A/C, TV, dataport, minibar, hair dryer, safe.

Lisboa Marriott ★ After a 2001 takeover, the Marriott chain now runs this 1970s hotel, which lies a 10-minute taxi ride north of the historic core in the vicinity of the airport and the Gulbenkian Museum. It occupies a panoramic site atop a hill overlooking the city. Part of 2001's massive renovations included the addition of an outdoor pool in the garden, the construction of an all-new health club, and the transformation of each of the bedrooms into the conservatively modern, international decor that's a trademark of most other Marriott hotels. Bathrooms with shower-tub combinations are sheathed in white marble. There are 250 rooms for nonsmoking guests and one floor available for those with limited mobility.

The Marriott compares favorably with the Sofitel Lisboa (see below). The primary difference between the two is location. The Marriott is less convenient to the major sights of Lisbon, but it is in a quieter, more tranquil environment. It has better facilities, including a pool and a health club. The hotel also lies closer to sports facilities, including a full spa, beaches, snorkeling, and golf. If you're interested in outdoor activities, including jaunts to Cascais, Sintra, and Estoril, the Marriott is the better choice for you.

Av. dos Combatentes 45, 1600-042 Lisboa. ✆ **21/723-54-00.** Fax 21/726-42-81. www.marriott.com. 577 units. 250€–290€ ($288–$334) double; from 400€ ($460) suite. Parking 10€ ($12) per night. AE, DC, MC, V. Metro: Cidad Universitária or Santarias. **Amenities:** Restaurant; bar; pool; health club; 24-hr. room service; massage; babysitting; laundry service; dry cleaning. *In room:* A/C, TV, dataport, minibar, hair dryer, safe.

Lisboa Regency Chiado ★ This hotel occupies several floors of an eight-story shopping center that's otherwise devoted to such merchandizing giants as FNAC. Built as a replacement for what burned to the ground during a disastrous fire in 1988, it was designed by prestigious Portugal-born designer Siza Vieira. You'll register within a street-level lobby and then be ushered upstairs to one of the artfully minimalist bedrooms. The best of these have private terraces on a rooftop that blooms with bougainvillea vines and brightly colored wildflowers. The standard bedrooms are midsize, each well furnished in a tasteful modern style with a well-organized private bathroom with a shower-tub combination. Of special note is the hotel's bar, a postmodern oasis of soaring vertical lines, copies of 18th-century antiques, and theatrical panoramas over St. George's Castle.

Rua Nova do Almada 114, 1200-290 Lisboa. ✆ **021/325-61-00.** Fax 21/325-61-61. www.regency-hotels-resorts.com. 40 units. 170€–230€ ($196–$265) double; 255€–325€ ($294–$374) suite. Free parking. AE, DC, MC, V. Metro: Baixa Chiado. **Amenities:** Bar; limited room service. *In room:* A/C, TV, dataport, minibar, hair dryer.

Sofitel Lisboa ★ In the center of one of Lisbon's showcase boulevards, this member of a French-based chain is one of the capital's newest deluxe hotels. With a high-tech edge to its design, the hotel features touches of intimacy. The comfortably appointed and good-size guest rooms offer the standard extras, and accommodations on each of the building's nine floors are outfitted with a different color scheme. Special rooms for business travelers offer extra luxuries. The better units face the front, and some are for nonsmokers. The rooms are well insulated and soundproofed, and contain well-kept bathrooms with shower-tub combinations.

The major difference between the Sofitel and the Marriott, which is of equal rank, is location. The Sofitel is located in the heart of Lisbon on its most prestigious boulevard. This puts you closer to the most important shops and major attractions of the city—it also puts you in a noisy, congested area. But if you will be spending most of your time in the city and aren't too interested in outdoor activities, make it the Sofitel.

Av. da Liberdade 127, 1269-038 Lisboa. ✆ **21/322-83-00.** Fax 21/322-83-10. www.sofitel.com. 176 units. 230€ double ($265); 350€ ($403) suite. AE, DC, MC, V. Metro: Avenida. **Amenities:** Restaurant; bar; 24-hr. room service; babysitting; laundry service; dry cleaning. *In room:* A/C, TV, dataport, minibar, hair dryer, safe.

Tivoli Jardim ★ *Value* This hotel is under the same ownership as its neighbor, the Hotel Tivoli (see above), and is not nearly as prestigious. Nonetheless, it is a most worthy choice. Set behind its more famous namesake, it avoids the traffic noise along Avenida da Liberdade. The modern structure from 1968 is adorned with "cliff-hanging" balconies, two shafts of elevators, and well-styled and attractively furnished midsize bedrooms. Guests of the Jardim share the same facilities as the higher-rated neighbor. There are adequate public lounges where Portuguese businesspeople have found the Jardim ideal for meeting clients in a cathedral-high lobby with its wall of glass through which the Iberian sun pours.

Rua Julio Cesar Machado, 1250–135 Lisboa. ✆ **21/359-10-00.** Fax 21/359-12-45. www.tivolihotels.com. 119 units. 185€ ($213) double. AE, DC, MC, V. Metro: Avenida. Bus: 1, 2, 9, 44, or 45. **Amenities:** 2 restaurants, bar; outdoor pool; room service (7am–midnight); babysitting; laundry service; dry cleaning. *In room:* A/C, TV, dataport, minibar, coffeemaker, hair dryer, safe.

MODERATE

Dom Carlos *Value* This central hotel lies just off Praça do Marquês de Pombal. The reason to stay here is economy: The Dom Carlos charges only a fraction of what its rivals in the neighborhood get. The curvy facade is all glass, lending an outdoorsy feeling reinforced by trees and beds of orange and red canna. The good-size guest rooms are paneled in reddish Portuguese wood; even so, they're rather uninspired and functional. An occasional hand-carved cherub softens the Nordic-inspired furnishings. All units come equipped with well-maintained bathrooms containing shower-tub combinations. The hotel faces a triangular park dedicated to Camilo Castelo Branco, a 19th-century poet. The lobby lounge is satisfactory; more inviting is the mezzanine salon, where sofas and chairs face the park.

Av. Duque de Loulé 121, 1050-089 Lisboa. ✆ **21/351-25-90.** Fax 21/352-07-28. hdcarlos@mail.telepac.pt. 76 units. 118€ ($136) double; 135€ ($157) triple; 150€ ($173) suite. Rates include buffet breakfast. AE, DC, MC, V. Metro: Marquês de Pombal. Bus: 1, 36, 44, or 45. **Amenities:** Restaurant; bar; 24-hr. room service; babysitting; laundry service; dry cleaning. *In room:* A/C, TV, minibar, hair dryer, safe.

Hotel Britânia ★ In its own way, the Britânia is one of the most traditional hotels in Lisbon. The well-known Portuguese architect Cassiano Branco designed the Art Deco building in 1942. Located about a block from Avenida da Liberdade, it boasts a distinguished, loyal clientele and an old-fashioned, almost courtly, staff. In 1995, the six-story hotel was refurbished, making the exceedingly spacious rooms more comfortable. Each has a well-maintained bathroom equipped with a shower-tub combination.

Rua Rodrigues Sampaio 17, 1150-278 Lisboa. ✆ **21/315-50-16.** Fax 21/315-50-21. www.heritage.pt. 30 units. 148€–225€ ($170–$259) double. AE, DC, MC, V. Metro: Avenida. Bus: 1, 2, 11, or 21. **Amenities:** Bar; lounge; 24-hr. room service; laundry service; dry cleaning. *In room:* A/C, TV, dataport, minibar, hair dryer, safe.

Hotel Fénix *Value* A good value for the area, the once-tired Fénix was greatly improved during recent renovations. It enjoys a front-row position on the circular plaza dedicated to an 18th-century prime minister. The location is convenient, but the noise overpowers the double-glazing on the windows. From most of the guest rooms, you can view the trees on the avenue and in Edward VII Park. All the rooms are handsomely decorated; some are quite spacious, but others are too small. All are equipped with neatly kept bathrooms with shower-tub combinations. Four rooms are available for those with limited mobility. Those facing the side street running along the park are your best bets. Only a few suites have balconies, and rooms on the lower floors have no views.

Praça do Marquês de Pombal 8, 1269-133 Lisboa. ✆ **800/44-UTELL** in the U.S., or ✆ 21/386-21-21. Fax 21/386-01-31. www.hotelfenix.pt. 193 units. 164€ ($189) double; 200€ ($230) suite. Rates include continental breakfast. AE, DC, MC, V. Metro: Marquês de Pombal. **Amenities:** Restaurant; bar; room service (7am–10pm); babysitting; laundry service; dry cleaning. *In room:* A/C, TV, dataport, minibar, hair dryer, safe.

Hotel Metropole Originally built around 1900, this is the most centrally located hotel in town, ideal for theater, sightseeing, dining, or business. A narrow flight of marble stairs runs to the lobby. Many 1920s Art Deco appointments adorn the public rooms. The cozy guest rooms, which vary greatly in size, are freshly painted. They contain reproductions of traditional furniture, have firm beds, and come equipped with neatly kept bathrooms with shower-tub combinations. Those in front overlook the noisy, animated square; the rooms in back overlook the congestion of the Barrio Alto.

Rossio 30, 1100-200 Lisboa. ✆ **21/346-91-64.** Fax 21/346-91-66. 36 units. 124€–160€ ($143–$184) double. Rates include buffet breakfast. AE, DC, MC, V. Metro: Rossio. **Amenities:** Bar; room service; babysitting; laundry service; dry cleaning. *In room:* A/C, TV, hair dryer, safe.

Hotel Veneza ★ *Finds* The Veneza, which opened in 1990, occupies one of the few remaining 19th-century palaces that once lined Avenida da Liberdade. A grand staircase leads to the three upper floors. The well-appointed midsize guest rooms are furnished in soothing modern style and are equipped with well-kept bathrooms containing shower-tub combinations. The Veneza has a bar and serves only breakfast. Guests have access to the facilities at the better-equipped Hotel Tivoli (see above).

Av. da Liberdade 189, 1250-141 Lisboa. ✆ **21/352-26-18.** Fax 21/352-66-78. www.3khoteis.com. 37 units. 130€–150€ ($150–$173) double. Rates include continental breakfast. AE, DC, MC, V. Parking 11€ ($13). Metro: Avenida. **Amenities:** Bar; limited room service; laundry service; dry cleaning. *In room:* A/C, TV, minibar, hair dryer, safe.

Janelas Verdes Inn ★★ *Finds* This aristocratic 18th-century mansion near the Museum of Ancient Art was the home of the late Portuguese novelist Eça de Queiroz. It was an annex to York House before becoming a historic hotel. The large, luxurious, marvelously restored rooms have abundant closet space, excellent beds, and generous tile bathrooms equipped with shower-tub combinations. The predominantly red lounge evokes turn-of-the-20th-century Lisbon. The inn has 14 nonsmoking rooms and 1 room for those with limited mobility.

Rua das Janelas Verdes 47, 1200-690 Lisboa. ✆ **21/396-81-43.** Fax 21/396-81-44. www.heritage.pt. 29 units. 165€–245€ ($190–$282) double; 190€–315€ ($219–$362) triple. AE, DC, MC, V. Bus: 27, 40, 49, or 60. **Amenities:** Bar; lounge; 24-hr. room service; babysitting; laundry service; dry cleaning. *In room:* A/C, TV, dataport, hair dryer, safe.

Mundial Hotel One block from the Rossio, the recently expanded Mundial is in the heart of everything. The hotel is high on the list of many European business travelers. The location is both good and bad—the colorful street out front is a bit sleazy, especially at night, but theaters and shops are nearby. The rooms are comfortable, spacious, and restrained in decor. Units in the rear are much quieter than the front rooms, which can be noisy. Seven rooms are available for those with limited mobility. The tiled bathrooms have bidets, shower-tub combinations, and plenty of mirrors and shelf space.

Rua Dom Duarte 4, 1100-198 Lisboa. ✆ **21/884-20-00.** Fax 21/884-21-10. www.hotel-mundial.pt. 262 units. 120€–151€ ($138–$174) double; 180€ ($207) suite. Rates include buffet breakfast. AE, DC, MC, V. Metro: Rossio or Martimonis. **Amenities:** 2 restaurants; bar; car rental; 24-hr. room service; babysitting; laundry service; dry cleaning. *In room:* A/C, TV, minibar, hair dryer, safe.

Sana Classic Capitol Hotel This fine little hostelry is minutes from the top of Avenida da Liberdade and 2 blocks east of Praça do Marquês de Pombal. It's away from the busy boulevards and opens onto a wedge-shape park with weeping willows and oaks. The simply furnished midsize rooms have light-wood furnishings, comfortable beds, and neatly kept bathrooms with shower-tub combinations. They're inviting, although a bit sparse. There are nine rooms for nonsmoking guests. The rooms in the front open onto balconies—and the city's notorious street noise. Some of the units at the rear and side also have balconies, but don't expect panoramas. Try to avoid staying here when a tour group arrives.

Rua Eça de Queiroz 24, 1050-096 Lisboa. ✆ **21/353-68-11.** Fax 21/352-61-65. www.sanahotels.com. 57 units. 70€–110€ ($81–$127) double; from 125€ ($144) suite. Rates include buffet breakfast. AE, DC, MC, V. Free parking. Metro: Rotunda. Bus: 1, 2, 9, or 32. **Amenities:** Restaurant; bar; lounge; 24-hr. room service; babysitting; laundry service; dry cleaning. *In room:* A/C, TV, minibar, hair dryer, safe.

York House ★★ Once a 17th-century convent, York House lies outside the center of traffic-filled Lisbon, attracting those who desire peace and tranquility. It has long been known to the English and to diplomats, artists, writers, poets, and professors. Book well in advance. Near the National Art Gallery, it sits high on a hillside overlooking the Tagus and is surrounded by a garden. A distinguished Lisbon designer selected the tasteful furnishings. Guest rooms vary in size; all have antique beds, bathrooms equipped with shower-tub combinations, and 18th- and 19th-century bric-a-brac. The lack of air-conditioning can be a problem in summer. The public rooms boast inlaid chests, coats of armor, carved ecclesiastical figures, and ornate ceramics. The former monks' dining hall has deep-set windows, large niches for antiques, and—best of all—French-Portuguese cuisine.

Rua das Janelas Verdes 32, 1200-691 Lisboa. ✆ **21/396-24-35.** Fax 21/397-27-93. 34 units. 140€–200€ ($161–$230) double. AE, DC, MC, V. Nearby parking 7€ ($8.05). Bus: 27, 40, 49, 54, or 60. **Amenities:** Restaurant; bar; 24-hr. room service; babysitting; laundry service; dry cleaning. *In room:* A/C, TV, hair dryer, safe.

INEXPENSIVE

Casa de São Mamede ★ *Finds* Built in the 1800s as a private villa for the count of Coruche, this building lies behind the botanical gardens. It became a hotel in 1945. The Marquês family manages the hotel. Although renovated, the high-ceilinged rooms retain an aura of their original slightly dowdy, somewhat frayed charm. All units are well kept and contain private bathrooms with shower-tub combinations. Breakfast is served in a sunny second-floor dining room decorated with antique tiles.

Rua da Escola Politécnica 159, 1250-100 Lisboa. ✆ **21/396-31-66.** Fax 21/395-18-96. 28 units. 80€–95€ ($92–$109) double; 120€ ($138) triple. Rates include continental breakfast. No credit cards. Tram: 24. Bus: 22, 49, or 58. **Amenities:** Breakfast room; lounge; car rental; laundry service; dry cleaning. *In room:* A/C, TV, safe.

Comfort Hotel Príncipe *Kids* Built in 1961, this nondescript place is a favorite with visiting Spanish and Portuguese matadors. Most guest rooms are spacious, and most open onto their own balconies. The rooms come equipped with well-maintained bathrooms with shower-tub combinations. Two floors are available for those with limited mobility. The matadors seem to like the Príncipe's dining room and bar. The hotel's eight floors are accessible by two elevators.

Av. Duque d'Ávila 201, 1050-082 Lisboa. ✆ **21/353-61-51.** Fax 21/353-43-14. www.hotelprincipelisboa.com. 70 units. 90€ ($104) double. Rates include continental breakfast. AE, DC, MC, V. Metro: São Sebastião. Tram: 20. Bus: 41 or 46. **Amenities:** Breakfast room; bar; car rental; 24-hr. room service; babysitting; laundry service; dry cleaning. *In room:* A/C, TV, dataport, hair dryer, safe.

Jorge V Hotel The Jorge V is a neat little hotel with a 1960s design. It boasts a choice location a block off the noisy Avenida da Liberdade. Its facade contains rows of balconies roomy enough for guests to have breakfast or afternoon refreshments. A tiny elevator runs to a variety of aging rooms, which aren't generous in size but are comfortable; all have small tile bathrooms with well-kept showers. There are seven nonsmoking rooms. Guests particularly enjoy the regional-style combination bar and breakfast room.

Rua Mouzinho da Silveira 3, 1250-165 Lisboa. ✆ **21/356-25-25.** Fax 21/315-03-19. www.hoteljorgev.com. 49 units. 79€–92€ ($91–$106) double; 84€–110€ ($97–$106) suite. Rates include continental breakfast. AE, DC, MC, V. Parking 10€ ($12). Metro: Avenida or Marquês de Pombal. **Amenities:** Bar; lounge; limited room service; laundry service; dry cleaning. *In room:* A/C, TV, minibar, hair dryer, safe.

Miraparque Miraparque lies on a secluded, quiet street opposite Edward VII Park. The small guest rooms haven't been called modern since the 1960s, but they're well maintained. All come equipped with tidily kept bathrooms containing shower-tub combinations. The hotel is a little worn but still recommendable because of its central location and low prices. The wood-paneled lounges are furnished in simulated brown leather.

Av. Sidónio Pais 12, 1050-214 Lisboa. ✆ **21/352-42-86.** Fax 21/357-89-20. www.miraparque.com. 100 units. 67€–91€ ($77–$105) double; 82€–115€ ($94–$132) triple. Rates include buffet breakfast. AE, DC, MC, V. Metro: Parque. Bus: 91. **Amenities:** Restaurant; bar; limited room service; laundry service; dry cleaning. *In room:* A/C, TV, minibar, hair dryer, safe.

Pensão Residencial Gerês Just a two-block walk west of Praça do Rossio and convenient to the railway station, this simple pension occupies two floors of a four-story building erected as an apartment house in the 1860s. The small rooms are high-ceilinged and completely unpretentious. Those units with private bathrooms have well-maintained shower-only facilities.

Calçada do Garcia 6, 1150-168 Lisboa. ✆ **21/881-04-97.** Fax 21/888-20-06. 20 units, 16 w/bathroom. 40€–45€ ($46–$52) double w/no bathroom; 50€–60€ ($58–$69) double w/bathroom. AE, DC, MC, V. Metro: Rossio. **Amenities:** Limited room service; laundry service; dry cleaning. *In room:* TV.

Presidente Hotel *Kids* This establishment lies near Avenida da Liberdade on a busy corner. It doesn't deserve a spectacular rating, but it's a decent place to spend the night. Built in the late 1960s, it's recommended for families because the management will add an extra bed to any room for 21€ to 25€ ($24–$29). The guest rooms are small and nicely laid out, each with a built-in chestnut headboard, bed lights, a tiled bathroom with a shower-tub combination, and even a valet stand. The modest-size reception lounges are on three levels, connected by wide marble steps.

Rua Alexandre Herculano 13, 1150-005 Lisboa. ✆ **21/317-35-70.** Fax 21/352-02-72. 59 units. 80€–98€ ($92–$113) double. Rates include buffet breakfast. AE, DC, MC, V. Metro: Marquês de Pombal. Bus: 1, 36, 44, or 45. **Amenities:** Dining room; bar; laundry service; dry cleaning. *In room:* A/C, TV, dataport, minibar, hair dryer, safe.

Residência Alicante This hotel's postwar facade curves around a quiet residential corner in an undistinguished neighborhood. The Alicante is welcoming and safe. You register on the street level with kindly staff members who speak little or no English; a small elevator runs to the four upper floors. Furnishings and room size vary, but most budget-minded visitors find the Alicante an acceptable place to stay. All units are equipped with neatly kept bathrooms with shower-tub combinations. The quieter rooms overlook an interior courtyard.

Av. Duque de Loulé 20, 1050-090 Lisboa. ✆ **21/353-05-14.** Fax 21/352-02-50. 42 units. 60€–70€ ($69–$81) double. Rates include buffet breakfast. AE, DC, MC, V. Metro: Picoas or Marquês de Pombal. Bus: 32, 36, 44, or 45. **Amenities:** Breakfast room; lounge; laundry service; dry cleaning. *In room:* A/C, TV, hair dryer.

Residência Imperador The Portuguese-pinewood entrance of the Residência Imperador is small, even claustrophobic. However, the rooms and the upper lounge are adequate in size. The units are neatly planned, with comfortable beds and simple lines. The decor, however, is dowdy. All units come equipped with neatly kept bathrooms with shower-tub combinations. On the top floor are a public room and a terrace with a glass front, where breakfast is served.

Av. 5 de Outubro 55, 1050-048 Lisboa. ✆ **21/352-48-84.** Fax 21/352-65-37. www.imperador.net. 42 units. 40€–60€ ($46–$69) double; 45€–65€ ($52–$75) triple. Rates include continental breakfast. AE, DC, MC, V. Metro: Saldanha. Bus: 44, 45, or 90. **Amenities:** Breakfast room; bar; room service; laundry service; dry cleaning. *In room:* A/C, TV, hair dryer.

Residência Nazareth You'll recognize this establishment by its dusty-pink facade and its windows, some of which are beneath decorative arches raised in low relief. An elevator runs to the fourth-floor landing, where there's a medieval vaulting. The distressed plaster and wrought-iron lanterns are obvious facsimiles. Even the spacious bar and lounge looks like a vaulted cellar. Some of the basic guest rooms contain platforms, requiring guests to step up or down to the bathroom or to the comfortable bed. All bathrooms are well maintained and have shower-tub combinations.

Av. António Augusto de Aguiar 25, 1050-102 Lisboa. ✆ **21/354-20-16.** Fax 21/356-08-36. 32 units. 48€–55€ ($55–$63) double. Rates include continental breakfast. AE, DC, MC, V. Metro: São Sebastião or Parque. Bus: 46. **Amenities:** Breakfast room; car rental; laundry service; dry cleaning. *In room:* A/C, TV, hair dryer.

VIP Eden ★ *Kids* Awarded a prize as the best renovation project in Lisbon, the former Eden theatre, a landmark Art Deco building in the center of Lisbon, was handsomely reconverted to receive guests. Spacious and well–furnished apartments are rented, housing two in the smaller units and four comfortably in the larger quarters. Apartments open onto a garden or the cityscape. Every apartment, ideal for families, comes with a fully equipped kitchenette, a tiled bathroom with tub and shower, and tasteful furnishings. The biggest treat of all is the rooftop terrace, where breakfast is served until 10:30pm and drinks are served throughout the day and evening until 11pm. The view of Lisbon is spectacular.

Praca dos Restauradores 24, 1250–187 Lisboa. ✆ **21/321-66-00.** Fax 21/321-66-66. www.viphotels.com/uk/vip-eden.htm. 134 units. 89€ ($102) for 2; 129€ ($148) for 4. AE, MC, V. Metro: Restauradores. Bus: 2, 11, 32, 36, 44, 45, or 91. **Amenities:** Breakfast room; bar; outdoor pool; babysitting; laundry service; dry cleaning. *In room:* A/C, TV, dataport, coffeemaker, hair dryer, iron/ironing board, safe.

IN THE ALFAMA

EXPENSIVE

Solar Do Castelo ★★ *Finds* Lying inside the walls of the formidable St. George's Castle, this hotel is reached only on foot because vehicles are off–limits. On the site of the former kitchens of Lisbon's first Royal Palace, this is a converted 18th-century town mansion; a stay here is one of the delights of Lisbon. Some of the medieval architecture remains, such as an old cistern, part of the original palace. Classified as a historic building, the little hotel offers beautifully furnished and atmospheric bedrooms. Although the building is antique, the bedrooms are in a high-quality contemporary design, mixing old elements such as original stone fortifications with contemporary fabrics and furnishings. Each accommodation comes with a balcony overlooking a picture-perfect courtyard.

Rua das Cozinhas 2, 1100-181 Lisboa. ✆ **21/887-09-09.** Fax 21/887-09-07. www.heritage.pt/en/solardocastelo.htm. 14 units. 165€–245€ ($190–$282) double. AE, DC, MC, V. Free parking. Metro: Rossio. Bus: 37. **Amenities:** Breakfast room; bar; 24-hr. room service; babysitting; laundry service; dry cleaning. *In room:* A/C, TV, dataport, hair dryer, safe.

MODERATE

Solar dos Mouros ★ *Finds* One of the most stylish and newest (opened in 2001) small hotels in Lisbon occupies a tangerine-colored, steeply vertical antique building on a quiet street that runs parallel to the base of St. George's Castle. Each of the rooms has a starkly modern, stylishly minimalist decor that might remind you of a photo set from *Architectural Digest.* Each contains at least one boldly abstract painting; some pieces are the work of the hotel's owner, Luis Memos. Rooms feature marble-sheathed bathrooms with tub and shower, hardwood floors, cutting-edge furniture, and lots of space; all of them open onto a starkly contemporary staircase that was added to the building's shell during its complete gutting in 2000. Come here for a location in the heart of the Alfama for a sense of cutting-edge historic restoration and for an insight into hip Europe at its most avant-garde. Breakfast is the only meal served, but the youthful staff will point out nearby restaurants and museums.

Rua Milagre de Santo António 6, 1100-351 Lisboa. ✆ **21/885-49-40.** Fax 021/885-49-45. www.solardosmouros.com. 8 units. 126€–190€ ($145–$219) double. Rates include breakfast. AE, DC, MC, V. Tram: 28. **Amenities:** Breakfast room. *In room:* A/C, TV, minibar, safe.

IN THE BAIRRO ALTO

INEXPENSIVE

Hotel Anjo Azul (Blue Angel) *Finds* This is the only hotel in Lisbon that markets itself to a gay clientele, although heterosexual clients also check in and are welcome. Set on a narrow street in the Bairro Alto, a short walk from such well-recommended gay or mixed bars as Portas Largas and Frágil, it occupies a narrow, much-renovated 18th-century town house that retains many of its original blue and white tiles. Don't expect luxury or even an elevator—just clean but small and exceptionally simple rooms, and a thoughtful and helpful staff well versed in the advantages of the surrounding neighborhood. No meals of any kind are served, there's no bar on-site, and none of the rooms has a private phone or other amenities such as a TV. But the attractive, international, and worldly clientele, many of whom return for second and third visits, don't really seem to mind.

Rua Luz Soriano 75, 1200-246 Lisboa. ✆ and fax **21/347-80-69.** 20 units, 7 w/private shower. 30€–50€ ($35–$58) double w/no bathroom; 40€–60€ ($46–$69) double w/bathroom. AE, MC, V. Metro: Baixa Chiado. Tram: 28. *In room:* No phone.

Pensão Londres Originally a dignified mansion, with high ceilings and ornate moldings, this establishment now functions as a slightly battered, unpretentious hotel. Take the elevator to the second-floor reception area, where the helpful staff will assist you. The small guest rooms contain simple furniture; some (especially on the 3rd and 4th floors) have views of the city. Rooms with bathrooms have neatly kept facilities with mostly shower-tub combinations. The pension is accessible by taking the funicular by the Palácio da Foz in Praça dos Restauradores.

Rua Dom Pedro V 53, 1250-092 Lisboa. ✆ **21/346-22-03.** Fax 21/346-56-82. 40 units, 15 w/bathroom (some w/tub, some w/shower), 8 w/shower and sink only. 40€ ($46) double w/sink only; 56€ ($64) double w/sink and shower only; 67€ ($77) double w/bathroom. Rates include continental breakfast. DC, MC, V. Tram: 28. Bus: 58 or 100. **Amenities:** Breakfast room; lounge. *In room:* TV.

IN THE GRAÇA DISTRICT

MODERATE

Hotel Albergaria da Senhora do Monte ★ *Finds* This unique little hilltop hotel is perched near a belvedere, the Miradouro Senhora do Monte. There's a memorable nighttime view of the city, the Castle of St. George, and the Tagus. The intimate living room features large tufted sofas and oversize tables and lamps. Multilevel corridors lead to the excellent guest rooms, all of which have verandas. The rooms reveal a decorator's touch, especially the gilt-edged door panels, the grass-cloth walls, and the tile bathrooms containing shower-tub combinations with bronze fixtures.

Calçada do Monte 39, 1170-250 Lisboa. ✆ **21/886-60-02.** Fax 21/887-77-83. 28 units. 105€–120€ ($121–$138) double; 150€–175€ ($173–$201) suite. Rates include continental breakfast. AE, DC, MC, V. Metro: Socorro. Tram: 28. Bus: 12, 17, or 35. **Amenities:** Breakfast room; bar; car rental; 24-hr. room service; babysitting; laundry service; dry cleaning. *In room:* A/C, TV, hair dryer.

IN ALTO DE SANTO AMARO

VERY EXPENSIVE

Pestana Carlton Palace ★★★ Set within an upscale residential neighborhood known as Santo Amaro-Ajuda, about 5km (3 miles) west of the commercial core of Lisbon and about 1.5km (1 mile) north of the Alcantara Railway Station, this grand, imperial-looking hotel occupies a villa that was originally built in 1907 by a Portuguese mogul who first made a fortune in cocoa. The hotel's core is one of the best examples of romantic revival architecture in Portugal, combining at least four distinct architectural styles (including what the Portuguese refer to as rocaille baroque and Doña Maria revival) into one shimmering whole. After 11 years of negotiations with Portugal's historic preservation boards, the Pestana hotel chain added two rambling wings and state-of-the-art kitchens and security systems, and opened its doors to a well-heeled clientele that has included Catherine Deneuve and Yasser Arafat. You'll register within an oval, high-ceilinged lobby ringed with stained glass and then walk through impeccably decorated salons that contain many of the Valle Flor family's original antiques. Only four of the bedrooms—each a high-ceilinged suite—lie within the original villa. Most accommodations are elegantly modern, with hardwood trim, trompe l'oeil detailing, upholstered headboards, and hints of the Romantic Revivalism that permeates the hotel's original core. Each unit comes with an elegant and spacious bathroom with a shower-tub combination. There are 88 nonsmoking rooms for guests, and 1 room is available for those with limited mobility.

The palace boasts one of the largest hotel gardens in Lisbon, loaded with botanical specimens from the far corners of what was once the Portuguese empire. There is also a Chinese-inspired garden pavilion.

Rua Jau 54, 1300-314 Lisboa. ✆ **21/361-56-00.** Fax 21/361-56-01. www.pestana.com. 190 units. 150€–350€ ($173–$403) double; 470€–2,200€ ($541–$2,530) suite. Free parking. AE, DC, MC, V. Tram 18. **Amenities:** Restaurant; snack bar; bar; indoor and outdoor pool; health club; Jacuzzi; sauna; car rental; room service; massage; babysitting; laundry service; dry cleaning. *In room:* A/C, TV, dataport, minibar, hair dryer, safe.

AT PARQUE DAS NAÇÕES

EXPENSIVE

Tivoli Tejo ★ Lisbon now has a third Tivoli hotel, this one created at the new Lisbon International Exhibition Centre close to the Vasco de Gama shopping center and about a 5-minute taxi ride from the airport. It is just a 2-minute walk from the splendid new Estaçao do Oriente, a major transportation hub for Lisbon. This hotel has quickly become a landmark in this newly created residential and business neighborhood. Bedrooms are midsize, for the most part, and comfortably and traditionally furnished. The room selection is wide ranging, giving you a choice of double or twin beds and singles or junior or senior suites. The hotel is also one of the best equipped in the area and has many winning features, such as a 16th-floor gourmet restaurant offering a panoramic view over Lisbon and the Tagus River.

Av. D. Joao II, Parque das Nações, 1990-083 Lisboa © **21/891-51-00.** Fax 21/891-53-45. www.tivolihotels.com. 279 units. 190€–280€ ($219–$322) double; from 350€ ($403) suite. AE, MC, V. Parking 8€ ($9.20). Metro: Oriente. Bus: 28. **Amenities:** 2 restaurants; bar; indoor pool; gym/exercise room; 24-hr. room service; babysitting; laundry service; dry cleaning. *In room:* A/C, TV, dataport, minibar, hair dryer, safe.

IN THE CAMPO GRANDE DISTRICT

EXPENSIVE

Radisson SAS Lisboa ★ This is one of the city's most visible hotels, built in the early 1990s. The Radisson/SAS group took it over in 1996, and it appeals mostly to business travelers. Sheathed in pink stone, it rises 12 floors above the Campo Grande residential district, about 3km (1¾ miles) north of the Rossio. The stylish but conservative lobby contains hundreds of slabs of gray-and-white marble. The midsize guest rooms have excellent beds and big windows. They're decorated in an international style, with comfortable, durable furnishings. Fifty-one rooms are available for nonsmoking guests, and two rooms are available for those with limited mobility.

Av. Marechal Craveiro Lopes 390, 1749-009 Lisboa. © **800/333-3333** in the U.S., or © 21/759-96-39. Fax 21/758-69-49. 221 units. 145€–200€ ($167–$230) double; from 230€ ($265) suite. Rates include breakfast. AE, DC, MC, V. Parking: 10€ ($12). Metro: Campo Grande. **Amenities:** Restaurant; bar; health club; room service; babysitting; laundry service; dry cleaning. *In room:* A/C, TV, dataport, minibar, hair dryer, safe.

4 Where to Dine

The explosion of restaurants in Lisbon in the late 20th and early 21st centuries indicates that the Portuguese regard dining just as seriously as Spaniards. High prices have not suppressed their appetites, and residents of the capital are dining out more frequently than in the past.

Plenty of restaurants serve the usual fish and shellfish, and many erstwhile Portuguese colonials from Brazil, and even Mozambique and Goa, have opened restaurants in the capital. The menus in the top establishments remain on par with those of Europe's leading restaurants. In Lisbon, you'll encounter the best of Portuguese cooking mixed with continental classics.

You needn't pay exorbitant prices for top-quality food. Restaurants featuring Portuguese and foreign fare—from beer-and-steak taverns to formal town house dining rooms to cliff-side restaurants with panoramic views—suit all budgets. For the best value, look for the "tourist," or fixed-price menu, which usually includes two or three courses, and sometimes wine, for far less than ordering a la carte. You might also want to consider an evening meal at a fado cafe (see chapter 4). Lisboans tend to eat much later than most American, Canadian, and British visitors, although not as late as their Spanish neighbors. Some restaurants (including Gambrinus, Bachus, and Cervejaria Trindade) stay open very late.

Finds A Picnic in a "Green Lung"

Lisbon has many "green lungs" (public parks) where you can go with picnic fixings. Of these, the most appealing is the **Jardim Botânico,** Rua do Alegria (© **21/362-25-02**), with its ornate iron benches and shrubs and trees from all parts of the world. A good place to stock up is **Pingo Doce,** Rua do 1 de Dezembro 81 (© **21/342-74-95**). To accompany your sandwiches, you'll find a wide selection of cheese and wine, along with fresh fruits and breads. You can also order a roast chicken for 5€ ($5.75) per kilo (2.2 lb.). It's open daily from 8:30am to 8pm (Metro: Rossio).

IN THE CENTER

VERY EXPENSIVE

Gambrinus ★★ SEAFOOD One of the city's premier restaurants, Gambrinus is the top choice for fish and shellfish. It's in the congested heart of the city, off the Rossio near the rail station on a little square behind the National Theater. The dining room is resolutely macho, with leather chairs under a beamed cathedral ceiling, but you can also select a little table beside a fireplace on the raised end of the room.

Gambrinus offers a diverse a la carte menu and specialties of the day. The shades and nuances of the cuisine definitely appeal to the cultivated palate. The soups, especially the shellfish bisque, are good. The most expensive items are shrimp and lobster dishes. However, you might try conch with shellfish thermidor or sea bass *minhota,* cooked in tomato sauce with onions, white wine, and ham. If you don't fancy fish but do like your dishes hot, ask for chicken *piri-piri* (served with blazing chiles). Desserts are elaborate. Coffee with a 30-year-old brandy is the perfect end to a sumptuous meal here.

Rua das Portas de Santo Antão 25. ✆ **21/342-14-66.** Reservations required. Main courses 18€–35€ ($21–$40). AE, MC, V. Daily noon–1:30am. Metro: Rossio.

EXPENSIVE

António Clara ★★ PORTUGUESE/INTERNATIONAL Even if it weren't one of the capital's best restaurants, this exquisite turn-of-the-20th-century Art Nouveau villa would be famous as the former home of one of Portugal's most revered architects, Miguel Ventura Terra (1866–1918), whose photograph hangs amid polished antiques and gilded mirrors, dating from 1890. You might enjoy a before-dinner drink in the 19th-century salon, where griffins snarl from the pink-shaded chandelier. Even the service areas of this house, rarely seen by visitors, display ceiling frescoes. The dining room is one of the loveliest in Lisbon.

The updated classic cooking is guaranteed to please. Most of the flavors are sublime. Meals include such specialties as smoked swordfish, paella for two, chateaubriand béarnaise, monkfish rice, codfish *Margarida da Praça* (baked with tomatoes and onions and served with deep fried sweet potatoes), and beef Wellington. The dishes might be familiar, but only the highest-quality ingredients are used. Seafood dishes change often to reflect the best of market offerings. A well-coordinated group of wine stewards, headwaiters, and attendants makes wine tasting a veritable ceremony. The ground-floor bar, accessible through its own entrance, is perfect for an after-dinner drink. The bar contains an art gallery with frequent shows.

Av. da República 38. ✆ **21/799-42-80.** Reservations required. Main courses 13€–19€ ($15–$22). AE, DC, MC, V. Mon–Sat noon–3pm and 7–10:30pm. Metro: Saldainha.

Café Nobre ★★ MEDITERRANEAN/INTERNATIONAL Set within a 15-minute taxi drive east of Lisbon's commercial core, this restaurant is one of Lisbon's finest. It was built in 1998 as part of massive improvements to what had been an abandoned waterfront and which later flourished as EXPO '98. Today it occupies the top floor of a hypermodern slope-sided building, which is occupied by offices and at least one other restaurant. Flooded with sunlight or moonlight, depending on when you arrive, it has a floor that's sheathed with exotic African hardwood and a highly cooperative staff dressed in nautically inspired uniforms. The effect is equivalent to an ultraformal dining room aboard an upscale ocean liner. Food is artfully presented, with a minimum of pretentiousness. The best

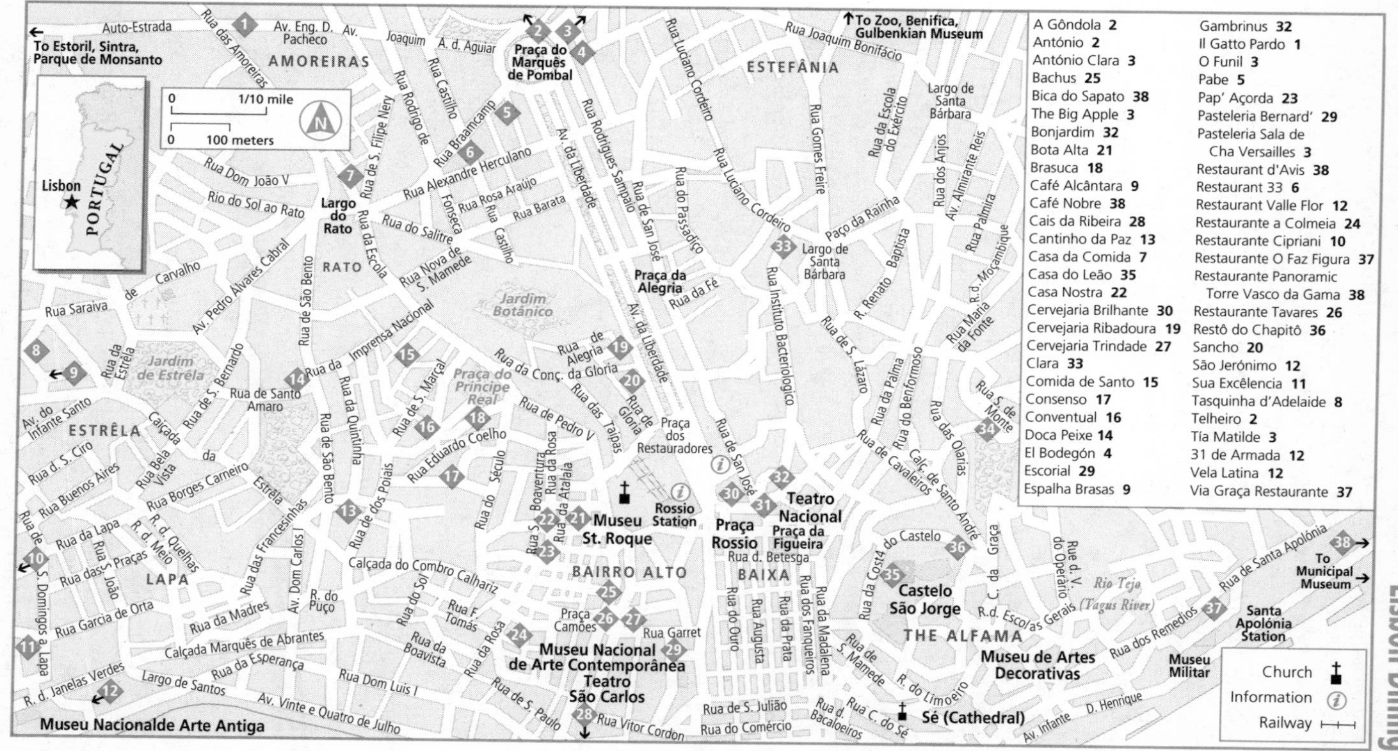
A Gôndola 2
António 2
António Clara 3
Bachus 25
Bica do Sapato 38
The Big Apple 3
Bonjardim 32
Bota Alta 21
Brasuca 18
Café Alcântara 9
Café Nobre 38
Cais da Ribeira 28
Cantinho da Paz 13
Casa da Comida 7
Casa do Leão 35
Casa Nostra 22
Cervejaria Brilhante 30
Cervejaria Ribadoura 19
Cervejaria Trindade 27
Clara 33
Comida de Santo 15
Consenso 17
Conventual 16
Doca Peixe 14
El Bodegón 4
Escorial 29
Espalha Brasas 9
Gambrinus 32
Il Gatto Pardo 1
O Funil 3
Pabe 5
Pap' Açorda 23
Pasteleria Bernard' 29
Pasteleria Sala de Cha Versailles 3
Restaurant d'Avis 38
Restaurant 33 6
Restaurant Valle Flor 12
Restaurante a Colmeia 24
Restaurante Cipriani 10
Restaurante O Faz Figura 37
Restaurante Panoramic Torre Vasco da Gama 38
Restaurante Tavares 26
Restô do Chapitô 36
Sancho 20
São Jerónimo 12
Sua Excêlencia 11
Tasquinha d'Adelaide 8
Telheiro 2
Tía Matilde 3
31 de Armada 12
Vela Latina 12
Via Graça Restaurante 37
Church
Information
Railway
PORTUGAL
Lisbon
0 1/10 mile
0 100 meters
N
To Estoril, Sintra, Parque de Monsanto
To Zoo, Benfica, Gulbenkian Museum
To Municipal Museum
AMOREIRAS
ESTEFÂNIA
RATO
ESTRÊLA
LAPA
BAIRRO ALTO
BAIXA
THE ALFAMA
Praça do Marquês de Pombal
Largo do Rato
Praça da Alegria
Largo de Santa Bárbara
Jardim Botânico
Praça do Príncipe Real
Jardim de Estrêla
Praça dos Restauradores
Museu St. Roque
Rossio Station
Praça Rossio
Teatro Nacional
Praça da Figueira
Castelo São Jorge
Sé (Cathedral)
Museu de Artes Decorativas
Museu Militar
Santa Apolónia Station
Praça Camões
Museu Nacional de Arte Contemporânea
Teatro São Carlos
Museu Nacionalde Arte Antiga
Rio Tejo (Tagus River)
Av. da Liberdade
Rua Rodrigues Sampaio
Rua de São Bento
Rua da Madalena
Rua dos Fanqueiros
Rua da Prata
Rua Augusta
Rua do Ouro
Rua Garret
Rua de S. Julião
Rua do Comércio
Rua Vitor Cordon
Av. Vinte e Quatro de Julho
R. d. Janelas Verdes
Largo de Santos

menu items include many different kinds of fish, usually simply grilled in ways that elicit the natural flavor of the very fresh ingredients.

Edificio Nau, Marina EXPO '98. ✆ **21/893-16-00.** Reservations recommended. Main courses 15€–28€ ($17–$32). AE, DC, MC, V. Mon–Sat noon–4pm and 7:30pm–midnight. Metro: Oriente.

Casa da Comida ★★★ PORTUGUESE/FRENCH Local gourmets tout Casa da Comida as offering some of the finest food in Lisbon. The dining room is handsomely decorated, the bar is done in the French Empire style, and there's a charming walled garden. Specialties include lobster with vegetables, roast kid with herbs, a medley of shellfish, and *faisoa à convento de Alcântara* (stewed pheasant marinated in port wine for a day). The cellar contains an excellent selection of wines. The food is often more imaginative here than at some of the other top-rated choices. The chef is extraordinarily attentive to the quality of his ingredients, and the menu never fails to deliver some delightful surprises.

Travessa de Amoreiras 1 (close to Jardin de Las Amoreiras). ✆ **21/388-53-76.** Reservations required. Main courses 20€–30€ ($23–$35). AE, DC, MC, V. Tues–Fri 1–3pm; Mon–Sat 8–11pm. Metro: Rato.

Clara ★★★ PORTUGUESE/INTERNATIONAL On a hillside amid decaying villas and city squares, this green-tile house owned by Zelia Pimpista contains an elegant restaurant. You can enjoy a drink under the ornate ceiling of the bar. Soft piano music accompanies dinner. At night, an indoor seat—perhaps near the large marble fireplace—is especially appealing. During lunch, however, you might prefer a seat near the garden terrace's plants and fountain. Specialties include tournedos Clara, stuffed rabbit with red-wine sauce, four kinds of pasta, codfish Clara, filet of sole with orange, pheasant with grapes, and Valencian paella. Again, as in too many of Lisbon's top-rated restaurants, these dishes aren't creative and innovative in any way, but they're often prepared flawlessly. As one of the staff told us, "When a dish has stood the test of time, why change it?" Perhaps you'll agree.

Campo dos Mártires da Pátria 49. ✆ **21/885-30-53.** Reservations required. Main courses 17€–22€ ($20–$25). AE, DC, MC, V. Mon–Fri noon–3:30pm and 7–10:30pm, Sat 7–10:30pm. Closed Aug 1–15. Metro: Avenida.

Escorial ★ SPANISH/INTERNATIONAL In the heart of Lisbon's restaurant district, near Praça dos Restauradores, this Spanish-owned restaurant combines classic Spanish dishes with an inviting ambience. The dining room walls are paneled in rosewood, with frosted-globe lighting. You can have a before-dinner drink in the Art Room cocktail lounge, which exhibits work by contemporary Portuguese artists. A menu is printed in English (always look for the course of the day). A selection of the chef's carefully crafted specialties is likely to include barbecued baby goat, beef Stroganoff, paella, mixed shellfish grill, or partridge casserole. In spite of the neighborhood, which grows increasingly sleazy at night, Escorial has stood the test of time and remains an enduring, if not incredibly innovative, favorite. The ingredients are fresh, and the food and service continue to be remarkable for their elegance and professionalism.

Rua das Portas de Santo Antão 47. ✆ **21/346-44-29.** Reservations recommended. Main courses 10€–30€ ($12–$35). AE, DC, MC, V. Daily noon–4pm and 7pm–midnight. Metro: Rossio or Restauradores.

Restaurante Cipriani INTERNATIONAL/PORTUGUESE This is the most upscale and most highly recommended restaurant in Lisbon's major government-rated five-star hotel, the Lapa Palace (reviewed earlier in this chapter). The dignified, elegant dining room has a view of one of the most lavish gardens in this exclusive neighborhood. This restaurant is a favorite with diplomats from the many embassies and consulates nearby. A la carte items available at lunch and dinner vary with the season. They might include fresh salmon fried with sage, lamb chops with mint sauce, a succulent version of a traditional Portuguese *feijoada* (meat stew), and perfectly prepared duck breast baked with pears. This is a perfect spot to retreat to when you want an elegant meal in a refined atmosphere.

In the Lapa Palace Hotel, Rua do Pau de Bandeira 4. ✆ **21/394-94-01.** Reservations recommended. Main courses 17€–29€ ($20–$33). AE, DC, MC, V. Daily 12:30–3:30pm and 7:30–10:30pm. Tram: 25 or 28. Bus: 13 or 17.

Restaurante Tavares ★★★ PORTUGUESE/CONTINENTAL The oldest restaurant in Lisbon, once known for serving the best food in the city, Tavares still surfaces near the top. It serves well-prepared food with flawless service and continues to attract many diplomats and government heads as well as the literati. White- and gold-paneled walls, three chandeliers, and Louis XV armchairs keep the spirit of the 18th century intact. Drinks are served in the petite front salon.

Your meal might begin with *crepes de marisco* (seafood crepes). A main-course selection might be sole in champagne, stuffed crab, clams Bulhão Pato (clams cooked in white wine and garlic), or tournedos Grand Duc. Many continental dishes are scattered throughout the menu, including the classic scallops of veal viennoise. The restaurant nearly always serves such basic Portuguese dishes as sardines and salted codfish. To complete your meal, try the chef's dessert specialty, a high-rise soufflé, followed by a *café filtro* (filtered coffee).

Originally a cafe, Tavares was founded in 1784. When the two Tavares brothers died in the 19th century, six waiters formed a partnership and took it over; it's still owned by a group of waiters, who maintain its high standards.

Rua da Misericórdia 37. ✆ **21/342-11-12.** Reservations required. Main courses 20€–30€ ($23–$35). AE, DC, MC, V. Mon–Fri 12:30–3pm; Sun–Fri 7:30–11pm. Bus: 15.

Sua Excelência ★ *Finds* PORTUGUESE Sua Excelência is the creation of Francisco Queiroz, a travel agent in Angola before settling in Portugal. His restaurant feels like a fashionable drawing room, with colorful tables in intimate Portuguese provincial decor. Some dishes served are uncommon in Portugal, such as Angolan chicken Moamba. Sure-to-please specialties include prawns *piri-piri* (not unreasonably hot), *lulas à moda da casa* (squid stewed in white wine, crème fraîche, and cognac), rollmop sardines, the self-proclaimed best smoked swordfish in Portugal, and clams prepared five different ways. One unusual specialty is "little jacks," a small fish eaten whole, served with a well-flavored paste made from 2-day-old bread. The restaurant is just a block up the hill from the entrance to the National Art Gallery; it could be part of a museum-luncheon adventure, although its ambience is more charming in the evening. Over the years it has remained popular with our readers. We were the first guidebook to discover it, but today it seems to be on everybody's list.

Rua do Conde 34. ✆ **21/390-36-14.** Reservations required. Main courses 13€–19€ ($15–$22). AE, MC, V. Mon–Tues and Thurs–Fri 1–3pm; Thurs–Sun 8–10:30pm. Closed Sept. Bus: 27, 49, or 60. Tram: 25.

MODERATE

A Gôndola ★ ITALIAN/PORTUGUESE A Gôndola serves some of the finest Italian specialties in town. Although the decor isn't particularly inspired, the good food makes the restaurant worth the trip out of the city center. The price makes a full dinner quite a buy, considering what you get. A first-course selection might be Chaves ham with melon and figs, followed by filet of sole meunière or grilled sardines with pimientos. Yet another course—ravioli or cannelloni Roman style or veal cutlet Milanese—follows. The banquet might conclude with fruit or dessert.

The Italian dishes don't compare with the best in Italy, but they're competent and professionally served. The restaurant is convenient to the Gulbenkian Museum. Courtyard seating is available.

Av. de Berna 64. ✆ **21/797-04-26.** Reservations required. Main courses 10€–22€ ($12–$25). Fixed-price lunch 22€ ($25). AE, DC, MC, V. Mon–Sat 12:30–3pm and 7:30–10:30pm. Metro: Praça de Espanha. Bus: 16, 26, 31, or 46.

Bachus ★★ INTERNATIONAL Amusing murals cover the wood-paneled facade of this deluxe restaurant; inside the decor is elaborate and sophisticated. The ambience is a mixture of a private salon in a Russian palace, a turn-of-the-20th-century English club, and a stylized Manhattan bistro. A brass staircase winds around a column of illuminated glass to the dining room. Menu specialties change frequently, depending on what ingredients are available. Full meals might include mixed grill Bachus, chateaubriand with béarnaise, mountain goat, beef Stroganoff, shrimp Bachus, or other daily specials. The chef has a conservative approach, and perhaps because of this, he reportedly rarely gets complaints. The wine list is extensive.

Largo da Trindade 9. ✆ **21/342-28-28.** Reservations recommended. Main courses 15€–20€ ($17–$23). AE, DC, MC, V. Tues–Fri noon–3pm, Tues–Sun 7pm–midnight. Metro: Chiado. Bus: 58.

Conventual ★★ PORTUGUESE Many admirers (including the prime minister of Portugal) rank Conventual as the single finest place to dine out in Lisbon today—even though its prices are about 25% less than those at many of its competitors. Conventual is on one of the loveliest residential squares in town, behind a plain wooden door. Inside you'll see a display of old panels from baroque churches, religious statues, and bric-a-brac. Delectably flavored dishes include creamy coriander soup, stewed partridge in port, duck in rich champagne sauce, grilled monkfish in herb-flavored cream sauce, frog legs in buttery garlic, and—one of our favorites—stewed clams in a sauce of red peppers, onions, and cream.

Praça das Flores 45. ✆ **21/390-91-96.** Reservations required. Main courses 15€–22€ ($17–$25). AE, DC, MC, V. Mon–Fri 12:30–3:30pm and Mon–Sat 7:30–11:30pm. Closed: Aug. Metro: Avenida. Bus: 100.

Doca Peixe ★★ SEAFOOD This restaurant, whose Portuguese name means "Fish Dock," stands virtually under the Ponte do 25 de Abril (25th of April Bridge). The best views of the Tagus are from one of the tables upstairs. The fresh fish served here is among the best quality offered in the markets of Lisbon. Every variety of fish and shellfish seems to be swimming in the small aquarium as you enter. If you don't want your fish charcoal grilled, you can order it cooked in salt or baked. Codfish is a specialty, appearing cooked with clams and flavored with fresh coriander, or you can order the grilled platter of shellfish, one of the true delights. For the meat fancier, there are succulent sirloin steaks, among other winning choices.

Doca de Santo Amaro, Armazem 14. ✆ **21/397-35-65.** Reservations recommended. Main courses 15€–40€ ($17–$46). AE, MC, V. Tues–Sun noon–3pm and 9:30pm–1am. Bus: 15 or 38.

El Bodegón PORTUGUESE/SPANISH/INTERNATIONAL El Bodegón is a first-class restaurant in a recommended hotel. After stopping for an aperitif in the bar, you'll dine in a tavern setting with a beamed ceiling, tile floors, and wood-paneled pillars. You might enjoy delectable quail, partridge, or fresh salmon from the north of Portugal, depending on what's available. You can also order cultivated oysters, which are at their best after October. The specials menu features a different Portuguese dish daily. Among the a la carte selections are perfectly prepared fried squid, Valencian paella, and some Italian dishes. For dessert, try the succulent fresh strawberries from Sintra, if they're featured. Over the years, we've found the fare here reliable and professionally served, but some of our readers find the Iberian dishes too heavy or "too intimidating."

In the Hotel Fénix, Praça do Marquês de Pombal 8. ✆ **21/386-31-55.** Reservations required. Main courses 12€–20€ ($14–$23). AE, DC, MC, V. Daily 7–10am and 12:30–3pm and 7:30–10:30pm. Metro: Rotunda.

Il Gatto Pardo ITALIAN The most appealing and stylish Italian restaurant in Lisbon is distinctly different from the pasta and pizza joints that have filled that niche until now. On the third floor of the hotel (see "Where to Stay," earlier), it has a soothing color scheme of beiges, browns, exposed hardwoods, and leopard skin. Virtually everything was imported from Italy, including many staff members, who prepare ultrafresh seafood and pastas, among other dishes. We're mad for pappardelle seasoned with cubed zucchini and saffron. Risotto with cuttlefish is another winner, as are sea wolf coated with bread crumbs and sautéed, delectable grilled swordfish steak in parsley sauce, and roasted veal cooked in heady Barolo wine. The chef is adept at preparing tender duck breast flavored with honey and vinegar sauce. An outdoor terrace ringed with potted shrubs and vines provides sweeping views over the surrounding district.

In the Hotel Dom Pedro, Av. Engenheiro, Duarte Pacheco. ✆ **21/389-66-00.** Reservations recommended. Main courses 12€–23€ ($14–$26). AE, DC, MC, V. Daily 12:30–3pm and 8–11pm. Metro: Marquês de Pombal.

O Funil *Value* PORTUGUESE O Funil (The Funnel) does *cozinha Portuguesa* (Portuguese cuisine) so well and so inexpensively that a line forms at the door; it's often hard to get a table. The owners serve their own *vinho da casa* (house wine)—try the red Alijo. The kitchen buys good-quality meats and fish fresh daily. The menu offers an array of excellent choices, including filet of fresh fish with rice, strips of cooked codfish flavored with herbs, roast goat with vegetables and roast potatoes, tiger shrimp in a picante sauce, and clams in wine sauce.

Av. Elias Garcia 82A. ✆ **21/796-60-07.** Reservations recommended. Main courses 10€–17€ ($12–$20). AE, MC, V. Tues–Sun noon–3:30pm; Tues–Sat 7–10:30pm. Metro: Campo Pequeno. Bus: 1, 32, 36, 38, 44, or 45.

Pabe PORTUGUESE/INTERNATIONAL Convenient to Praça do Marquês de Pombal, this cozy pub does its best to emulate English establishments. There's soft carpeting, mugs hanging over the long bar, a beamed ceiling, coats of arms, and engravings of hunting scenes around the walls. Two saloon-type doors lead into a wood-paneled dining room, where you can dine on meat specially imported—not from England, but the United States. Chateaubriand for two is among the fanciest dishes. If you prefer local fare, start with shrimp cocktail and then try Portuguese veal liver or *supremo de galinha* (chicken breast with mushrooms). The crowd tends to be a well-groomed Portuguese set, in addition to resident Americans and Brits. The fare, although decent, seems to have no clear sense of direction. Service can be spasmodic, and the staff speaks broken English, at best.

Rua Duque de Palmela 27A. ✆ **21/353-74-84.** Reservations required. Main courses 15€–25€ ($17–$29). AE, DC, MC, V. Daily noon–1am. Metro: Rotunda.

Restaurant 33 ★ *Finds* PORTUGUESE/INTERNATIONAL Restaurant 33 is a treasure. Decorated in a style evocative of an English hunting lodge, it lies near many recommended hotels, including the Four Seasons Hotel The Ritz Lisbon. It specializes in succulent seafood dishes, including shellfish rice served in a crab shell, smoked salmon, and lobster Tour d'Argent; it also features tender, well-flavored pepper steak. One reader from New Rochelle, New York, found her meal here "flawless." A pianist performs during dinner. You can enjoy a glass of port in the small bar at the entrance or in the private garden.

Rua Alexandre Herculano 33A. ✆ **21/354-60-79.** Reservations recommended. Main courses 14€–18€ ($16–$21). AE, DC, MC, V. Mon–Fri noon–3:30pm; Mon–Sat 8–10:30pm. Metro: Marquês Do Pombal. Bus: 6 or 9.

Telheiro PORTUGUESE Telheiro (Portuguese for "the roof") is a bistrolike place not far from the Sheraton Hotel. Under beamed ceilings, you sit on wooden chairs with heart shapes carved out of their backs. Many staff members are from the former Portuguese colony of Angola. Different robust, hearty specialties are featured every day, including gazpacho, cabbage-and-potato soup, mussels, suckling pig, grilled fresh sea bass or sole, and seafood with rice in a casserole. For dessert, try fresh Portuguese fruit. Note that the kitchen makes little concession to "lily-livered" foreign tastes.

Rua Latino Coelho 10A. ✆ **21/353-40-07.** Reservations recommended. Main courses 5€–18€ ($5.75–$21). AE, DC, MC, V. Daily noon–3pm and 7–10:30pm (closed Sat during July and Aug). Bus: 30.

Tía Matilde PORTUGUESE Tía Matilde is a large, busy place in the Praça de Espanha area. The atmosphere is often hectic, but the Portuguese love this restaurant—foreign visitors are rare. You can sample the savory specialties of Ribatejo, including *cabrito assado* (roast mountain goat), *arroz de frango* (chicken with rice), *bacalhau* (codfish) *à Tía Matilde,* and pungent *caldeirada* (fish stew). As one Portuguese father here told his son, "Food like this will make a man out of you."

Rua da Beneficência 77. ✆ **21/797-21-72.** Main courses 10€–25€ ($12–$29). AE, DC, MC, V. Mon–Sat noon–4pm; Mon–Fri 7–10:30pm. Metro: Praça d'Espanha or Palhavã. Bus: 31.

INEXPENSIVE

António PORTUGUESE/INTERNATIONAL Portuguese businesspeople flock to António for its relaxing ambience and good food. It's a refreshing oasis of blue-and-white glazed earthenware tiles, a free-form blue ceiling, and white tablecloths topped with blue linen. The menu is printed in English. You can start with excellent shellfish soup. Fish dishes garnished with vegetables include filets with tomato sauce, and baked sole. *Polvo à lagareira* (octopus with broiled potatoes, olive oil, and garlic) is a justifiably popular specialty. If you prefer fowl or meat, try *frango na prata* (chicken broiled in foil with potatoes) or pork with clams Alentejana style. The owner-manager recommends *açorda de marisco,* a stewlike breaded shellfish-and-egg dish. The dessert list is extensive, even listing a banana split. The chefs still cook exactly as their parents and grandparents did, and that seems to please the mainly local clientele.

Rua Tomás Ribeiro 63. ✆ **21/353-87-80.** Main courses 4.95€–7.60€ ($5.70–$8.75). MC, V. Mon–Sat 7:30am–11pm. Metro: Picoas. Bus: 36, 45, 90, or 101.

The Big Apple *Kids* AMERICAN Dozens of tongue-in-cheek accessories adorn the walls and menu of this American-style eatery on a tree-lined boulevard in a residential neighborhood. You'll find a true Texan's map of the United States (Amarillo appears just south of the Canadian border) and a red-white-and-blue checkerboard awning out front. It's simple and pleasant. Many of the 18 variations of hamburgers constitute a meal in themselves. You can also select from five kinds of dinner crepes and five varieties of temptingly sweet dessert crepes.

Av. Elias Garcia 19B. ✆ **21/797-55-75.** Burgers 5€–6€ ($5.75–$6.90); steaks 6€–11€ ($6.90–$13). AE, DC, MC, V. Mon–Sat noon–3pm and 7–11pm, Sun 7–11pm. Metro: Campo Pequeno.

Bonjardim *Value* *Kids* PORTUGUESE Bonjardim rightly deserves this enthusiastic endorsement of a traveler from Boston: "I was given the names of eight inexpensive restaurants to try in Lisbon during my 5-day stay. I ended up trying only two, as I took the rest of my meals at Bonjardim, sampling a different dish for lunch and dinner every day." The restaurant caters mostly to families, providing wholesome meals that fit most budgets. The operation has been so successful that it has taken over a building across the street, where the same menu is offered. The restaurant is just east of Avenida da Liberdade near the grimy Praça dos Restauradores.

In the main restaurant, the air-conditioned, sun-flooded second-floor dining room is designed in rustic Portuguese style, with a beamed ceiling. The street-floor dining room, with an adjoining bar for before-meal drinks, has walls of decorative tiles. During dinner, the aroma of plump chickens roasting on the charcoal spit is likely to prompt you to try one. An order of this house specialty, *frango no espeto,* is adequate for two, with a side dish of french fries. The cook also bakes hake in the Portuguese style, or try pork fried with clams. For dessert, you can order a cassate. If you want to be daring, order chicken with *piri-piri,* a fiery chile sauce.

Bonjardim also has a self-service cafeteria nearby, at Travessa de Santo Antão II (✆ **21/342-43-89**). It serves Portuguese dishes, including seafood soup; half a roast chicken with trimmings; grilled fish of the day (the chef's specialty); and velvety chocolate mousse.

Travessa de Santo Antão 10. ✆ **21/342-74-24.** Main courses 9€–16€ ($10–$18). AE, DC, MC, V. Daily noon–11pm. Metro: Restauradores.

Cervejaria Brilhante SEAFOOD/PORTUGUESE Lisboans from every walk of life stop here for a stein of beer and *mariscos* (seafood). The tavern is decorated with stone arches, wood-paneled walls, and pictorial tiles of sea life. The front window is packed with an appetizing array of king crabs, oysters, lobsters, baby clams, shrimp, and even barnacles. The price changes every day, depending on the market, and you pay by the kilo. This is hearty, robust eating, although attracting a waiter's attention is a challenge.

Rua das Portas de Santo Antão 105 (opposite the Coliseu). ✆ **21/346-14-07.** Main courses 10€–18€ ($12–$21); tourist menu 14€ ($16). AE, DC, MC, V. Daily noon–midnight. Metro: Rossio. Bus: 1, 2, 36, 44, or 45.

Cervejaria Ribadoura SEAFOOD Cervejaria Ribadoura is one of the typical shellfish-and-beer eateries in central Lisbon, located midway along the city's major boulevard. The decor in this tavern-style restaurant is simple—the emphasis is on the fish. Try the *bacalhau* (codfish) à Bras. You can dine lightly, particularly at lunch, on such plates as a shrimp omelet. Many diners follow their fish with a meat dish. However, only those raised on the most mouth-wilting Indian curries should try the sautéed pork cutlets with *piri-piri,* made with red-hot peppers from Angola. A wedge of Portuguese cheese "from the hills" finishes the meal nicely. Although we've always found fish on our 25-odd visits here, some readers have reported that occasionally the fish market was bare.

Av. da Liberdade 155 (at Rua do Salitre). ✆ **21/354-94-11.** Main courses 8€–26€ ($9.20–$30). AE, DC, MC, V. Daily noon–1:30am. Metro: Avenida. Bus: 1, 2, 44, or 45.

Cervejaria Trindade PORTUGUESE Cervejaria Trindade is a combination German beer hall and Portuguese tavern. In operation since 1836, it's the oldest tavern in Lisbon, owned by the brewers of Sagres beer. It was built on the foundations of the 13th-century Convento dos Frades Tinos, which was destroyed by the 1755 earthquake. Surrounded by walls tiled with Portuguese scenes, you can order tasty little steaks and heaps of crisp french-fried potatoes. Many Portuguese diners prefer *bife na frigideira* (steak with mustard sauce and a fried egg, served in a clay frying pan). The tavern features shellfish; the house specialties are *ameijoas* (clams) à Trindade and giant prawns. A small stein of beer goes nicely with the main courses. For dessert, try a slice of *queijo da serra* (cheese from the mountains) and coffee. Meals are served in the inner courtyard on sunny days.

Rua Nova de Trindade 20C. ✆ **21/342-35-06.** Main courses 10€–15€ ($12–$17). AE, DC, MC, V. Daily noon–2am. Metro: Chiado. Bus: 15, 20, 51, or 100.

Pastelaria Sala de Cha Versailles ★ SANDWICHES/PASTRIES This is the most famous teahouse in Lisbon, and it has been declared part of the "national patrimony." Some patrons reputedly have been coming here since it opened in 1932. In older days the specialty was *Licungo,* the famed black tea of Mozambique; you can still order it, but nowadays many drinkers enjoy English brands. (The Portuguese claim that they introduced the custom of tea-drinking to the English court after Catherine of Bragança married Charles II in 1662.) The decor is rich, with chandeliers, gilt mirrors, stained-glass windows, tall stucco ceilings, and black-and-white marble floors. You can also order milkshakes, mineral water, and fresh orange juice, along with beer and liquor. The wide variety of snacks includes codfish balls and toasted ham-and-cheese sandwiches. Also available is a limited array of platters of simple but wholesome Portuguese fare.

Av. da República 15A. ✆ **21/354-63-40.** Sandwiches 2€ ($2.30); pastries 1€ ($1.15); plats du jour 9.50€–16€ ($11–$18). AE, MC, V. Daily 7:30am–10pm. Metro: Salvanhe.

Restaurante a Colmeia MACROBIOTIC VEGETARIAN On the top floor of a corner building, this center of healthful eating and living offers vegetarian and macrobiotic cuisine. In addition, you'll find a miniature natural-foods shop. The food, although presumably healthful, is rather bland.

Rua da Emenda 110. ✆ **21/347-05-00.** Main courses 4.50€–7€ ($5.20–$8.05) No credit cards. Mon–Fri noon–4pm. Metro: Baixa Chiado. Tram: 28. Bus: 58 or 100.

Sancho PORTUGUESE/INTERNATIONAL Sancho is a cozy rustic-style restaurant with classic Iberian decor—beamed ceiling, fireplace, leather-and-wood chairs, and stucco walls. In summer there's air-conditioning. Fish gratinée soup is a classic way to begin. Shellfish, always expensive, is the specialty. Main dishes are likely to include the chef's special hake or pan-broiled Portuguese steak. If your palate is fireproof, order *churrasco de cabrito ao piri-piri* (goat with pepper sauce). For dessert, sample the crêpes Suzette or perhaps chocolate mousse. This is a longtime (since 1962) local favorite, and the recipes never change. As a waiter said, "As long as we can keep the dining room full every night, why change?"

Travessa da Glória 14 (just off Av. da Liberdade, near Praça dos Restauradores). ✆ **21/346-97-80.** Reservations recommended. Main courses 10€–12€ ($12–$14). AE, DC, MC, V. Mon–Sat noon–3pm and 7–10:30pm. Metro: Avenida or Restauradores.

IN THE BAIRRO ALTO

EXPENSIVE

Tasquinha d'Adelaide ★ *Finds* REGIONAL PORTUGUESE At the western edge of the Bairro Alto, about 2 blocks northeast of the Alcântara subway station and 2 blocks west of the Basilica da Estrêla, this small restaurant is cramped and convivial. It's known for the culinary specialties of Trás-os-Montes, a rugged province in northeast Portugal, and for its homey, unpretentious warmth. Robust specialties include *alheriras fritas com arroz de grelos* (tripe with collard greens and rice) and *lulas grelhadas* (grilled squid served in a black clay casserole). To finish, try Dona Adelaide's *charcade de ovos* (a secret recipe made with egg yolks). Although we like this hearty cooking, the flavors might be too pungent for some palates.

Rua do Patrocinio 70–74. ✆ **21/396-22-39.** Reservations recommended. Main courses 14€–21€ ($16–$24). AE, DC, MC, V. Mon–Sat noon–2am. Closed 7 days in Aug. Metro: Rato. Tram: 25, 28, or 30. Bus: 9, 15, or 28.

MODERATE

Comida de Santo *Finds* BRAZILIAN Opening in the early 1980s, this was the first all-Brazilian restaurant in Lisbon. At the edge of the Barrio Alto, in a century-old former private house, it contains only 12 tables. Recorded Brazilian music plays softly from the bar, lending a New World flavor, and a quintet of oversize panels depicts huge, idealized jungle scenes. The appropriate beginning of any meal is a deceptively potent *caipirinha* (aguardiente cocktail with limes and sugar). Main courses include spicy versions of *feijoada* (meat-and-bean stew), *picanha* (boiled Brazilian beef with salt), *vatapá* (peppery shrimp), and several versions of succulent grilled fish. The place is incredibly popular; reservations are very important.

Calçado Engenheiro Miguel Pais 39. ✆ **21/396-33-39.** Reservations required. Main courses 13€–16€ ($14–$18) AE, DC, MC, V. Daily 12:30–3pm and 7:30pm–1am. Metro: Rato. Bus: 58.

Consenso ★★ PORTUGUESE/CONTINENTAL Set within the cellar of the palace where the Marquês de Pombal (rebuilder of Lisbon after the earthquake of 1755) was born, this restaurant manages to be chic, historically conscious, and trendy all at the same time. It consists of four separate rooms, each with an individualized decor based on air (the bar), fire (trompe l'oeil flames adorn the ceiling, and an iron stove sends warmth into the room), earth, and water—check out their respective color schemes. If you opt for a meal here, you won't be alone: The prime minister of Portugal drops in for meals from time to time, bringing with him one or several of his cabinet ministers. Impeccably prepared menu items include marinated salmon with citrus paté, bacon with dates, grilled monkfish and grouper served with shrimp-studded rice, and monkfish loin in a spicy cream sauce. Veal medallions "à la Consenso" are served with shellfish and shrimp.

Rua da Academia das Ciencias 1–1A. ✆ **21/346-86-11.** Main courses 10€–17€ ($12–$20) AE, DC, MC, V. Tues–Sun 7:30pm–12:30am. Bus: 28, 58, or 100.

Pap' Açorda PORTUGUESE This restaurant is set on a narrow medieval street in the Bairro Alto, a short walk from such popular bars as Portas Largas. Pap' Açorda's facade was originally conceived for a bakery. Today it's high on the list of hip, perpetually fashionable restaurants for the counterculture and media crowd; as such, competition for an available table is stiff. It welcomes one of Lisbon's most colorful collections of people into its dimly lit seashell-pink-and-cream interior. Most visitors order a before-dinner drink at the long, marble-topped bar, which dominates the front of the restaurant. Prospective diners jockey for the attentions of the somewhat blasé maître d'hotel. If you ever get around to dining (and some clients actually prefer to linger at the bar as a social ritual unto itself), you'll be treated to delectable cuisine that includes Spanish-style mussels, shellfish rice, sirloin steak with mushrooms, and a wide array of fish and shellfish dishes. The house specialty, *açorda,* is a traditional dish with coriander, bread, seafood, eggs, garlic, and olive oil.

Rua da Atalaia 57–59. ✆ **21/346-48-11.** Reservations recommended. Main courses 13€–34€ ($14–$39) AE, DC, MC, V. Tues–Sat noon–2:30pm and 8–11pm. Closed first 3 weeks in July. Metro: Chiado.

INEXPENSIVE

Bota Alta PORTUGUESE Bota Alta, at the top of a steep street in the Bairro Alto, boasts a faithful clientele that eagerly crams into its two dining rooms and sometimes stands at the bar waiting for a table. It contains rustic artifacts and lots of original art and photographs. Meals—some familiar to 19th-century diners—might include beefsteak Bota Alta; several preparations of codfish, including *bacalhau real* (fried codfish with port wine and cognac); and a frequently changing array of daily specials, including Hungarian goulash. We still aren't sure why bacalhau is so popular—the Portuguese claim to have as many fish off their coast as there are days on the calendar—but don't leave Portugal without sampling it at least once.

Travessa da Queimada 35–37. ✆ **21/342-79-59.** Reservations required. Main courses 9€–13€ ($10–$15). AE, DC, MC, V. Mon–Fri noon–2:30pm; Mon–Sat 7–10:30pm. Metro: Chiado. Bus: 58 or 100.

Brasuca ★ BRAZILIAN On the edge of the Bairro Alto, near Praça do Principe Real and Largo de Camoes, this is Lisbon's finest Brazilian restaurant. Owner-chef Juca Oliveira presides over the former private mansion, as he has for the past 2 decades. The traditional decor incorporates 19th-century antiques and an open fireplace. The hearty food includes *feijoada,* the traditional Brazilian dish of black beans with meat, rice, and cabbage. Another favorite is *bauru a brasuca,* a tender steak in onion sauce served with cheese and ham. Beef predominates, but the lamb and pork dishes are equally good. Codfish also appears in several tempting ways. Instead of wine, you might decide to try a Brazilian beer.

Rua João Pereira da Rosa 7 (off Rua do Seculo). ✆ **21/322-07-40.** Reservations recommended. Main courses 10€–15€ ($12–$17). AE, DC, MC, V. Tues–Sun noon–3pm and 7–11pm. Closed for lunch in Aug. Metro: Chiado. Tram: 28. Bus: 92.

Cais da Ribeira ★ PORTUGUESE This superb little regional restaurant in a former fish warehouse serves some of the best charcoal-grilled fresh fish in Lisbon. It's a cozy waterfront place with views over the Tagus that uses generations-old recipes. *Caldeirada,* a hearty fishermen's stew, will fortify you for a day. The chef also prepares good-tasting paella for two and tender grilled steaks, sometimes with a peppercorn sauce. Most dishes, except the expensive shellfish, are at the lower end of the price scale.

Cais do Sodré. ✆ **21/342-36-11.** Reservations recommended. Main courses 15€–35€ ($17–$40). AE, DC, MC, V. Wed–Fri and Sun noon–3pm; Tues–Sun 7:30–11pm. Metro: Cais do Sodré.

Cantinho da Paz GOAN This restaurant honors the cuisine of the lost colony of Goa, which the government of India took over in 1961. Many Portuguese Goans brought their spicy cuisine to Lisbon and set up dining rooms, and this is the best of the lot. The curries draw discerning diners, who are richly rewarded with spices and flavors. Our favorite is shrimp curry flavored with coconut and laced with cream. But you might opt for a fiery version made with lamb, fish, or poultry. Veal stew comes with different types and levels of hotness, and succulent medallions of pork are richly flavored with ginger and garlic. The helpful owners speak English.

Rua da Paz 4 (off Rua dos Poiais de São Bento). ✆ **21/396-96-98.** Reservations required. Main courses 10€–22€ ($12–$25). AE, DC, MC, V. Daily 12:30–2:30pm and 7:30–11pm. Tram: 28. Bus: 6 or 49.

Casa Nostra ★ *Finds* ITALIAN Maria Paola Porru, a movie sound engineer whose travels have exposed her to cinematic circles across Europe, rules this hip postmodern hideaway. Behind a century-old, deliberately understated facade, the setting is simple, stylish, and informal. All pastas are homemade on the premises. Accomplished menu items include *fettuccine al mascarpone* (fettuccine with cream cheese), lasagna, spaghetti with Portuguese clams, and several versions of grilled meat. A favorite dessert is Sicilian-style tiramisu, a rich dessert made with ladyfingers, coffee, and mascarpone cream.

Rua de Rosa 84–90 (enter at Travessa de Poco da Cidade 60). ✆ **21/342-59-31.** Reservations recommended. Main courses 6€–15€ ($6.90–$17). AE, MC, V. Tues–Fri 12:30–2:30pm, Tues–Sat 8–11pm; Sun 1–2:30pm. Metro: Chiado. Tram: 28 or 28B.

IN THE CHIADO DISTRICT

INEXPENSIVE

Pastelaria Bernard' SANDWICHES/SNACKS Pastelaria Bernard' is the most fashionable teahouse in Lisbon. Dating from the 1800s, it lies in the heart of the Chiado. In fair weather, there's sidewalk seating. Lunch, served in a back room, is a full meal of such Portuguese specialties as codfish with almonds. Most visitors come here for tea, served with sandwiches and snacks. Desserts, including duchesses (whipped-cream cakes) are justifiably famous. Proper dress is required inside, although visitors in shorts sometimes occupy the outside tables.

Rua Garrett 104. ✆ **21/347-31-33.** Sandwiches 1.50€–2.50€ ($1.75–$2.90) AE, DC, MC, V. Mon–Sat 8am–midnight. Metro: Baixa Chiado.

IN THE GRAÇA DISTRICT

MODERATE

Restaurante O Faz Figura ★ PORTUGUESE/INTERNATIONAL This is one of the best and most attractively decorated dining rooms in Lisbon, and service is faultless. When reserving a table, ask to be seated on the veranda, overlooking the Tagus. You can stop for a before-dinner drink in the "international cocktail bar." Specialties include *feijoada de marisco* (shellfish stew) and *cataplana* (a cooking pot) of fish and seafood. The cuisine is generally very flavorful and occasionally spicy.

Rua do Paraíso 15B. ✆ **21/886-89-81.** Reservations required. Main courses 12€–23€ ($14–$26). AE, DC, MC, V. Mon–Sat 12:30–3pm and 8–10:30pm. Bus: 12, 39, or 46.

Via Graça Restaurante PORTUGUESE In the residential Graça district, a few blocks northeast of the fortifications surrounding Castelo de São Jorge, this restaurant boasts a panoramic view that encompasses the castelo and the Basilica da Estrêla. Flickering candles and attentive service enhance the romantic setting. Dishes aren't inventive, but they're savory and appealing to traditionalists who opt for hearty fare. Specialties of the house include such traditional Portuguese dishes as *pato assado com moscatel* (roast duck with wine from the region of Setúbal) and *linguado com recheio de camarão* (stuffed filet of sole served with shrimp).

Rua Damasceno Monteiro 9B. ✆ **21/887-08-30.** Reservations recommended. Main courses 10€–20€ ($12–$23). AE, DC, MC, V. Mon–Fri 12:30–3:30pm; Mon–Sat 7:30–11pm. Tram: 28.

INEXPENSIVE

Restaurant d'Avis PORTUGUESE/REGIONAL This simple but pleasing restaurant is not associated with the Restaurante Aviz, once an important culinary citadel on Rua Serpa Pinto. This humbler, less expensive competitor was established in the late 1980s as a purveyor of the cuisine of Alentejo to cost-conscious diners. It serves regional dishes such as roast pork with clams, roast baby goat, steaming bowls of *caldo verde* (a fortifying soup made from high-fiber greens and potatoes), and perfectly prepared fresh fish. Don't expect a luxurious setting or anything even vaguely formal—the rustic venue is deliberately unpretentious, and few members of the staff speak English.

Rua de Grilo 98. ✆ **21/868-13-54.** Reservations recommended. Main courses 6.50€–12€ ($7.50–$14). AE, DC, MC, V. Mon–Sat noon–3pm and 7:30–10:30pm. Bus: 18, 39, 42, or 105.

IN THE BELÉM DISTRICT

MODERATE

São Jerónimo PORTUGUESE/INTERNATIONAL You might combine a visit to this lighthearted, elegant restaurant with a trip to the famous monastery of the same name. São Jerónimo sits east of the monastery, behind a big-windowed facade that floods the interior with sunlight. It takes its inspiration from the Roaring Twenties, with French-style decoration; the chairs are by Philippe Starck, and the bar's armchairs are by Le Corbusier. The food is not inspired, but it's usually created from market-fresh ingredients. This place depends on foreign visitors—not wanting to offend the international palate, it sticks to somewhat bland fare.

Rua dos Jerónimos 12. ✆ **21/364-87-97.** Reservations recommended. Main courses 13€–22€ ($15–$25). AE, DC, MC, V. Mon–Fri 12:30–3pm; Mon–Sat 7:30–10:30pm. Bus: 15, 27, 28, or 29.

Vela Latina PORTUGUESE In a verdant park close to the Tagus and the Tower of Belém, this inviting, high-ceilinged restaurant offers well-prepared food, lots of greenery, big windows, and peace. Many visitors opt for lunch here after a visit to the nearby Jerónimos Monastery or the Coach Museum. Specialties include a wide array of classic, well-prepared Portuguese dishes, such as lobster-filled crepes, platters of fresh fish, quail salad, lamb cutlets, and filet of hake with rice. Dessert might be flan, fruit tart, or ice cream. The price of some shellfish dishes can soar.

Doca do Bom Sucesso. ✆ **21/301-71-18.** Main courses 15€–25€ ($17–$29) AE, DC, MC, V. Mon–Sat 12:30–3pm and 8–11pm.

IN THE ALFAMA

Casa do Leão PORTUGUESE/INTERNATIONAL Stop for a midday meal at this restaurant, in a low-slung stone building inside the walls of Saint George's Castle. In the spacious dining room, you'll enjoy a panoramic view of the Alfama and the legendary hills of Lisbon. Your lunch might include roast duck with oranges or grapes, pork chops Saint George style, codfish with cream, or smoked swordfish from Sesimbra. The chefs obviously cook with the international visitor in mind, but what they prepare can be very satisfying. Menus change with the season. We'd like the service to be more attentive, but the hardworking waiters might already be moving at peak capacity.

Castelo de São Jorge. ✆ **21/887-59-62.** Reservations recommended. Main courses 16€–24€ ($18–$28); tourist menu 39€ ($45). AE, DC, MC, V. Daily 12:30–3:30pm and 8:30–10:30pm. Bus: 37.

Restô do Chapitô *Finds* INTERNATIONAL This funky all-purpose rendezvous point occupies the steeply sloping premises of what was built in the 17th century as a women's prison and that functions today as a state-funded school for circus entertainers. Its location, perched on a ledge just below St. George's Castle in the Alfama, encompasses views over all of Lisbon, and its clients include clowns, jugglers, fire-eaters, and stilt-walkers, some or many of whom might be either in costume or practicing their stunts near the outdoor terrace and bar. Come here for drinks, tapas, or a meal, depending on whatever you're in the mood for, and keep moving up and down a labyrinth of indoor and outdoor areas until you find the spot where you feel most comfortable. During the daytime, the crowd is likely to include lots of students; after dark, the age tends to mature a bit, to between 30 and 45. Bruno, the Belgian-born owner, is nonchalant about what the place is exactly. It includes a cafe and bar, a separate tapas bar, at least two different dining areas, and a venue that's conducive to drinks that are consumed in anticipation of moving on to other nocturnal adventures. Menu items are simple, full of flavor, and straightforward, and include steak with a gratin of potatoes and mushroom sauce, breast of duck with orange sauce, smoked salmon, grilled octopus salad, and mango-flavored ice cream.

Rua Costa do Castelo 7. ✆ **21/886-73-34.** Fixed-price menus 18€–21€ ($21–$24). No credit cards. Daily noon–2am whenever school is in session. Between mid-July and mid-Sept, and during other school closings, only Fri 7:30pm–2am and Sat–Sun noon–2am. Tram 28.

IN THE ALCÂNTARA

Café Alcântara FRENCH/PORTUGUESE This is one of the city's most fun dining-and-entertainment complexes. Entertainment is provided by some of the best DJs in Portugal. It lies within the solid walls of a 600-year-old timber warehouse and attracts a hip, attractive, fun-loving young crowd. Today the vast building has forest-green and Bordeaux walls, exposed marble, ceiling fans, plants, and simple wooden tables and chairs. The varied clientele includes resident Brazilian, British, and American expatriates. Chefs make the most of regional foodstuffs and prepare hearty fare that is filled with flavor and plenty of spices—maybe too much for some palates. Menu items include rillettes of salmon, fresh fish, lacquered duck, steak tartare, and a Portuguese platter of the day, which might include fried *bacalhau* (codfish) or a hearty *feijoada,* a bean-and-meat stew inspired by the traditions of Trás-os-Montes.

Rua Maria Luisa Holstein 15. ✆ **21/363-71-76.** Reservations recommended. Main courses 16€–25€ ($18–$29). AE, DC, MC, V. Daily 8pm–1am. Bar daily 9pm–3am. Bus: 20 or 38.

Espalha Brasas *Finds* TAPAS/GRILLS This is our favorite of the many shoulder-to-shoulder restaurants lined up at the Alcântara Docks, although part of your evening's entertainment will involve picking whichever of the 20 or so cheek-by-jowl restaurants you actually prefer. You'll enter a high-ceilinged room whose centerpiece is a weather-beaten wooden statue of a nude male beside stairs leading to an upstairs balcony with additional tables. The setting is comfortably cluttered and amiable, with candlelit tables and a display of whatever fresh seafood and meats can be grilled to your preference. The finest menu items include every imaginable kind of meat or fish, grilled the way you prefer, as well as daily specials that include rice studded with either turbot and prawns or marinated duck meat, baked haunch of pork, and codfish stuffed with prawns and spinach.

Doca de Santa Amaro, Armazem 12. Alcântara. ✆ **21/396-20-59.** Reservations recommended for dinner Fri and Sat nights only. Main courses 9€–22€ ($10–$25). AE, MC, V. Sept–July daily noon–1am; Aug daily 7:30pm–1am. Bus: 57. Tram: 15 and 18.

31 de Armada PORTUGUESE Set directly across the street from the headquarters of the Portuguese navy, this is a well-respected and very traditional restaurant. You'll recognize it by the masses of bougainvillea that cascade over the doorways. Inside, a pair of dining rooms—each interconnected only through the kitchen, but accessible to the street through separate doorways—have beamed ceilings, tiled floors, hardworking and matriarchal-looking waitresses, and an allegiance to the culinary principals of Old Portugal. Your well-prepared meal might begin with soup or a salad, such as cold grilled octopus in vinaigrette, followed with pork or veal cutlets, grilled tuna salads, beefsteaks, and all manner of grilled fish.

Praça de Armada 31. ✆ **21/397-63-30.** Reservations recommended for dinner Fri and Sat night only. Main courses 7€–15€ ($8.05–$17). AE, DC, MC, V. Daily noon–3pm and 7:30–10:30pm. Tram: 15. Bus: 27, 49, or 60.

IN ALTO DE SANTO AMARO

Restaurant Valle Flor ★★ PORTUGUESE This is the most elegant hotel dining room in Lisbon, with a battalion of uniformed staff members and a physical setting that's revered as a national monument. It was designed as part of a cocoa mogul's private villa in 1907, and it contains a pair of dining rooms, each elaborately frescoed, gilded, and adorned with the finest Romantic Revival accessories of their day. Come here for an immersion into old-world glamour and protocol and for food items that are impeccably presented and prepared. The best examples include baby snails nestled inside a potato shell, home-smoked Scottish salmon marinated in port with vermicelli and a lemon-flavored saffron sauce, a casserole of sea bass, turbot and prawns in a white wine sauce, and roasted quail stuffed with white sausage and sautéed turnip greens.

In the Pestana Carlton Palace Hotel, Rua Jau 54. ✆ **21/361-56-00.** Reservations recommended. Main courses 21€–30€ ($24–$35); fixed-price menus 34€ ($39); 8-course tasting menu 58€ ($67). AE, DC, MC, V. Daily 12:30–3pm and 8:30–10:30pm. Tram: 28.

IN SANTA APOLONIA

Bica do Sapato ★★ *Finds* MODERN PORTUGUESE This is the trendiest and hippest restaurant in Lisbon, with a retro-minimalist decor that's calculated to attract what a local commentator described as "the scene-savvy, design-obsessed jet set." Actor John Malkovich, along with four other partners (the most visible of whom is restaurant pro Fernando Fernandes) transformed what had once functioned as a boat factory into a three-part restaurant that packs in enthusiastic scene-setters virtually every night. There's a sushi bar one floor above ground level, and a "cafeteria" that shares its space on street level with the establishment's gastronomic citadel, the restaurant, which is the place we heartily recommend above the other two. Its decor evokes the waiting lounge at a 1960s international airport, but the food takes brilliant liberties with traditional Portuguese cuisine. Stellar examples include seafood broth with grilled red prawns and Asian vegetables; codfish salad in olive oil, served with chick-pea ice cream; a brandade of codfish au gratin, served with sautéed chick peas; and veal knuckle browned in olive oil, with garlic, sautéed potatoes and bay leaves. Especially full of flavor are modernized versions of two old-fashioned Portuguese recipes that many locals remember from their childhoods: leg of kid stuffed with a confit of vegetables, served with new potatoes and turnip greens; and saddle of rabbit stuffed with apples and black sausage, served with rosti spaghetti and braised cabbage.

Av. Infante Don Henrique, Armazém (Warehouse) 8, Cais da Pedra à Bica do Sapato. ✆ **21/881-03-20.** Reservations recommended. Main courses and platters 18€–38€ ($21–$44) in restaurant; 15€–20€ ($17–$22) in cafeteria; 12€–24€ ($14–$27) in sushi bar. AE, DC, MC, V. Restaurant daily noon–2:30pm and 8–11:30pm; cafeteria daily noon–1am; sushi bar daily 7:30pm to 1am. Bus: 9, 35, 39, 46, 59, 104, or 105.

PARQUE DAS NAÇÕES

Restaurante Panoramico Torre Vasco da Gama INTERNATIONAL Come here not only for the grand cuisine, but also for one of the most panoramic views of Lisbon, including the span of the Vasco da Gama Bridge stretching across the Tagus River. The restaurant has been installed atop this landmark built for EXPO '98. The exciting menu borrows freely from whatever recipes or cuisines it wants, and the combinations are often winning, although many savvy diners come here just to order the grilled fish of the day. Many of the dishes are imaginative, as evoked by the filet of black grouper with oyster sauce on spinach with shredded fried leeks.

Torre Vasco da Gama, Parque das Nações. ✆ **21/893-95-50.** Reservations recommended. Main courses 18€–33€ ($21–$38). AE, DC, DISC, V. Tues–Sun 1–2:30pm and 8–10:30pm. Metro: Oriente.

4

Exploring Lisbon

Many visitors use Lisbon as a base for exploring nearby sites, but they often neglect the cultural gems tucked away in the Portuguese capital. One reason Lisbon gets overlooked is that visitors don't budget enough time for it. You need at least 5 days to do justice to the city and its environs. In addition, even Lisbon's principal attractions remain relatively unknown, a blessing for travelers tired of fighting their way to overrun sights elsewhere in Europe.

This chapter guides you to the unknown treasures of the capital. If your time is limited, explore the **National Coach Museum,** the **Jerónimos Monastery,** and the **Alfama** and the **Castle of St. George.** At least two art museums, although not of the caliber of Madrid's Prado, merit attention: the **Museu Nacional de Arte Antiga** and the **Museu da Fundação Calouste Gulbenkian.**

If you have time, visit the **Fundação Ricardo Espírito Santo** and watch reproductions of antiques being made or books being gold-leafed. You could also spend time seeing the gilded royal galleys at the **Naval Museum,** wandering through the fish market, visiting Lisbon's new **aquarium,** or exploring the arts and crafts of Belém's Folk Art Museum.

SUGGESTED ITINERARIES

If You Have 1 Day

Take a stroll through the Alfama (see "Walking Tour 1," later in this chapter), the most interesting district of Lisbon. Visit the 12th-century **Sé** (cathedral), and take in a view of the city and the river Tagus from the **Santa Luzia Belvedere.** Climb up to the **Castelo de São Jorge** (St. George's Castle). Take a taxi or bus to Belém to see the **Mosteiro dos Jerónimos** (Jerónimos Monastery) and the **Torre de Belém.** While at Belém, explore one of the major sights of Lisbon, the **Museu Nacional dos Coches** (National Coach Museum).

If You Have 2 Days

On Day 2, head for Sintra, the single most visited sight in the environs of Lisbon—Byron called it "glorious Eden." You can spend the day exploring the castle and other palaces in the stunning area. Try at least to visit the **Palácio Nacional de Sintra** and the **Palácio Nacional da Pena.** Return to Lisbon for a night at a fado cafe.

If You Have 3 Days

On Day 3, spend a morning at the **Museu da Fundação Calouste Gulbenkian,** one of Europe's artistic treasure troves. Have lunch in the Bairro Alto. In the afternoon, see the **Fundação Ricardo Espírito Santo** (Museum of Decorative Art) and the **Museu Nacional de Arte Antiga** (National Museum of Ancient Art). At the day's end, wander through Parque Eduardo VII.

If You Have 4 Days

On Day 4, take an excursion from Lisbon. (For convenience, consider an organized tour—see listings later

Moments Up, Up & Away

For a splendid rooftop view of Lisbon, take the **Santa Justa elevator** on Rua de Santa Justa. The ornate concoction was built by a Portuguese engineer, Raoul Mesnier de Ponsard, born to French immigrants in Porto in 1849. The elevator goes from Rua Aurea, in the center of the shopping district near Rossio Square, to the panoramic viewing platform. It operates daily from 7am to 11pm. A ticket costs 1€ ($1.15), and children under 4 ride free (Metro: Rossio).

in this chapter.) Visit the fishing village of **Nazaré** and the walled city of **Óbidos.** Those interested in Roman Catholic sights might also want to include a visit to the shrine at **Fátima,** although seeing this on the same day would be hectic.

If You Have 5 Days

On the final day, slow your pace a bit with a morning at the beach at **Estoril** on Portugal's Costa do Sol. Then continue along the coast to **Cascais** for lunch. After lunch, wander around the old fishing village, now a major resort. Go to **Guincho,** 6.5km (4 miles) along the coast from Cascais, which is near the westernmost point on the European continent and has panoramic views.

1 The Top Attractions: The Alfama, Belém & Museums

The Lisbon of bygone days lives on in the **Alfama** ★★, the most emblematic quarter of the city. The wall built by the Visigoths and incorporated into some of the old houses is a reminder of its ancient past. In east Lisbon, the Alfama was the Saracen sector centuries before its conquest by the Christians.

The devastating 1755 earthquake spared some of the buildings, and the Alfama has retained much of its original charm. You'll see narrow cobblestone streets, cages of canaries, strings of garlic and pepper adorning old taverns, and street markets. Houses are so close together that in many places it's impossible to stretch your arms wide. The poet Frederico de Brito dramatically expressed that proximity: "Your house is so close to mine! In the starry night's bliss, to exchange a tender kiss, our lips easily meet, high across the narrow street."

Stevedores, fishmongers, and sailors still occupy the Alfama. In the street markets, you can wander in a maze of brightly colored vegetables from the countryside, bananas from Madeira, pineapples from the Azores, and assorted fish. Armies of cats prowl in search of rats. Occasionally, a black-shawled widow, stooping over a brazier, grilling sardines in front of her house, will toss a fish head to a passing feline.

Aristocrats once lived in the Alfama; a handful still do, but their memory is perpetuated mostly by the noble coats of arms fading on the fronts of some 16th-century houses. The best-known aristocratic mansion is the one formerly occupied by the count of Arcos, the last viceroy of Brazil. Constructed in the 16th century and spared, in part, from the earthquake, it lies on Largo da Salvador.

As you explore, you'll be rewarded with a perspective of the contrasting styles of the Alfama, from a simple tile-roofed fishmonger's abode to a festively decorated baroque church. One of the best views is from the belvedere of **Largo das Portas do Sol,** near the Museum of Decorative Art. It's a balcony opening onto the sea, overlooking the typical houses as they sweep down to the Tagus.

One of the oldest churches in Lisbon is **Santo Estevão** (St. Stephen), on Largo de Santo Estevão, originally constructed in the 13th century. The present marble structure dates from the 1700s. One of the most dramatic **views** ★ of the Alfama is possible from the southwestern corner of Largo de Santo Estevão. Also of medieval origin is the Church of São Miguel (St. Michael), on Largo de São Miguel, deep in the Alfama on a palm-tree-shaded square. Reconstructed after the 1755 earthquake, the interior is richly decorated with 18th-century gilt and trompe l'oeil walls.

Rua da Judiaria is another poignant reminder of the past. It was settled largely by Jewish refugees fleeing Spain to escape the Inquisition.

At night, the neighborhood's spirit changes. Street lanterns cast patterns against medieval walls, and the plaintive voice of the *fadista* (fado singers) rings out until the early morning hours. Although the Bairro Alto is the city's traditional fado quarter, the cafes of the Alfama also reverberate with these nostalgic sounds.

For specific routes through the Alfama, refer to the walking tour later in this chapter. The Alfama is best explored by day; it can be dangerous to wander around the area at night.

Castelo de São Jorge ★★ Locals speak of Saint George's Castle as the cradle of their city, and it might have been where the Portuguese capital began. Its occupation is believed to have predated the Romans—the hilltop was used as a fortress to guard the Tagus and its settlement below. Beginning in the 5th century A.D., the site was a visigothic fortification; it fell to the Saracens in the early 8th century. Many of the existing walls were erected during the centuries of Moorish domination. The Moors held power until 1147, the year Afonso Henríques chased them out and extended his kingdom south. Even before Lisbon became the capital of the newly emerging nation, the site was used as a royal palace.

For the finest **view** ★★ of the Tagus and the Alfama, walk the esplanades and climb the ramparts of the old castle. The castle's name commemorates an Anglo-Portuguese pact dating from as early as 1371. (George is the patron saint of England.) Portugal and England have been traditional allies, although their relationship was strained in 1961 when India, a member of the Commonwealth of Nations, seized the Portuguese overseas territories of Goa, Diu, and Damão.

Huddling close to the protection of the moated castle is a sector that appears almost medieval. At the entrance, visitors pause at the Castle Belvedere. The Portuguese refer to this spot as their "ancient window." It overlooks the Alfama, the mountains of Monsanto and Sintra, Ponte do 25 de Abril, Praça do Comércio, and the tile roofs of the Portuguese capital. In the square stands a heroic statue—sword in one hand, shield in the other—of the first king, Afonso Henríques.

Inside the castle grounds you can stroll through olive, pine, and cork trees, all graced by the appearance of a peacock. Swans with white bodies and black necks glide in a silence shattered only by the piercing scream of the rare white peacock.

Rua da Costa do Castelo. ✆ **21/887-72-44.** Free admission. Apr–Sept daily 9am–9pm; Oct–Mar daily 9am–6pm. Bus: 37. Tram: 12 or 28.

Sé (Cathedral) ★ Even official tourist brochures admit that this cathedral is not very rich. Characterized by twin towers flanking its entrance, it represents an architectural wedding of Romanesque and Gothic style. The facade is severe enough to resemble a medieval fortress. At one point, the Saracens reportedly used the site of the present Sé as a mosque. When the city was captured early in the 12th century by Christian crusaders, led by Portugal's first king, Afonso

Henríques, the structure was rebuilt. The Sé then became the first church in Lisbon. The earthquakes of 1344 and 1755 damaged the structure.

Beyond the rough exterior are many treasures, including the font where St. Anthony of Padua is said to have been christened in 1195. A notable feature is the 14th-century gothic chapel of Bartholomeu Joanes. Other items of interest are a crib by Machado de Castro (the 18th-century Portuguese sculptor responsible for the equestrian statue on Praça do Comércio), the 14th-century sarcophagus of Lopo Fernandes Pacheco, and the original nave and aisles.

A visit to the sacristy and cloister requires a guide. The cloister, built in the 14th century by King Dinis, is of ogival construction, with garlands, a Romanesque wrought-iron grille ★, and tombs with inscription stones. In the sacristy are marbles, relics, valuable images, and pieces of ecclesiastical treasure from the 15th and 16th centuries. In the morning, the stained-glass reflections on the floor evoke a Monet painting.

Largo da Sé. ✆ **21/886-67-52.** Admission: Cathedral free; cloister 1.50€ ($1.75). Tues–Sat 9am–7pm; Sun–Mon 9am–5pm. Tram: 28 (Graça). Bus: 37.

Santo António de Lisboa St. Anthony of Padua, an itinerant Franciscan monk who became the patron saint of Portugal, was born in 1195 in a house that once stood here. The 1755 earthquake destroyed the original church, and Mateus Vicente designed the present building in the 18th century.

In the crypt, a guide will show you the spot where the saint was reputedly born. (He's buried in Padua, Italy.) The devout come to this little church to light candles under his picture. He's known as a protector of young brides and has a special connection with the children of Lisbon. To raise money to erect the altar at the church, the children of the Alfama built miniature altars with a representation of the patron saint. June 12 is St. Anthony's Day, a time of merrymaking, heavy eating, and drinking. In the morning there are street fires and singing, followed by St. Anthony's Feast on the following day.

Largo de Santo António de Sé. ✆ **21/886-04-47.** Free admission. Daily 7:30am–7:30pm. Metro: Rossio. Bus: 37.

BELÉM ★

At Belém, where the Tagus (*Tejo* in Portuguese) meets the sea, the Portuguese caravels that charted the areas unknown to the Western world set out: Vasco da Gama to India, Ferdinand Magellan to circumnavigate the globe, and Bartholomeu Dias to round the Cape of Good Hope.

Belém emerged from the Restelo, the point of land from which the ships set sail across the so-called Sea of Darkness. The district flourished as riches, especially spices, poured into Portugal. Great monuments, including the **Belém Tower** and **Jerónimos Monastery,** were built and embellished in the Manueline style.

In time, the royal family established a summer palace here. Much of the district's character emerged when wealthy Lisboans began moving out of the city center and building town houses here. For many years Belém was a separate municipality. Eventually it was incorporated into Lisbon as a parish. Nowadays it's a magnet for visitors to its many museums. For most tourists, the primary sight is the Torre de Belém.

Torre de Belém ★★ The quadrangular Tower of Belém is a monument to Portugal's Age of Discovery. Erected between 1515 and 1520, the Manueline-style tower is Portugal's classic landmark and often serves as a symbol of the country. A monument to Portugal's great military and naval past, the tower stands on or near the spot where the caravels once set out across the sea.

Its architect, Francisco de Arruda, blended Gothic and Moorish elements, using such architectural details as twisting ropes carved of stone. The coat of arms of Manuel I rests above the loggia, and balconies grace three sides of the monument. Along the balustrade of the loggias, stone crosses represent the Portuguese crusaders.

The richness of the facade fades once you cross the drawbridge and enter the Renaissance-style doorway. Gothic severity reigns. There are a few antiques, including a 16th-century throne graced with finials and an inset paneled with pierced Gothic tracery. If you scale the steps leading to the ramparts, you'll be rewarded with a panorama of boats along the Tagus and pastel-washed, tile-roofed old villas in the hills beyond.

Facing the Tower of Belém is a monument commemorating the first Portuguese to cross the Atlantic by airplane (not nonstop). The date was March 30, 1922, and the flight took the pilot Gago Coutinho and the navigator Sacadura Cabral from Lisbon to Rio de Janeiro.

At the center of Praça do Império at Belém is the Fonte Luminosa (the Luminous Fountain). The patterns of the water jets, estimated at more than 70 original designs, make an evening show lasting nearly an hour.

Praça do Império, Avenida de Brasília. ✆ **21/362-00-34.** Admission 3€ ($2.70) adults, 1.50€ ($1.35) children, free for seniors (65 and over), Sun free until 2pm. Tues–Sun 10am–5pm. Tram: 15 or 17. Bus: 27, 28, 43, 49, or 51.

Padrão dos Descobrimentos ★ Like the prow of a caravel from the Age of Discovery, the Memorial to the Discoveries stands on the Tagus, looking ready to strike out across the Sea of Darkness. Notable explorers, chiefly Vasco da Gama, are immortalized in stone along the ramps.

At the point where the two ramps meet is a representation of Henry the Navigator, whose genius opened up new worlds. The memorial was unveiled in 1960, and one of the stone figures is that of a kneeling Philippa of Lancaster, Henry's English mother. Other figures in the frieze symbolize the crusaders (represented by a man holding a flag with a cross), navigators, monks, cartographers, and cosmographers. At the top of the prow is the coat of arms of Portugal at the time of Manuel the Fortunate. On the floor in front of the memorial lies a map of the world in multicolored marble, with the dates of the discoveries set in metal.

Praça da Boa Esperança, Avenida de Brasília. ✆ **21/303-19-50.** Admission 1.90€ ($2.20). July–Aug Tues–Sun 9:30am–9pm; Sept–June Tues–Sun 9:30am–5pm. Tram: 15. Bus: 15, 27, 28, 43, or 49.

Mosteiro dos Jerónimos ★★ In an expansive mood, Manuel I, the Fortunate, ordered this monastery built to commemorate Vasco da Gama's voyage to India and to give thanks to the Virgin Mary for its success. Manueline, the style of architecture that bears the king's name, combines flamboyant Gothic and Moorish influences with elements of the nascent Renaissance. Henry the Navigator originally built a small chapel dedicated to St. Mary on this spot. Today this former chapel is the Gothic and Renaissance **Igreja de Santa Maria** ★★, marked by a statue of Prince Henry the Navigator. The church is known for its deeply carved stonework depicting such scenes as the life of St. Jerome. The church's interior is rich in beautiful stonework, particularly evocative in its **network vaulting** ★ over the nave and aisles.

The west door of the church leads to the **Cloisters** ★★★, which represent the apex of Manueline art. The stone sculpture here is fantastically intricate. The two-story cloisters have groined vaulting on their ground level. The recessed upper floor is not as exuberant but is more delicate and lacelike in character. The

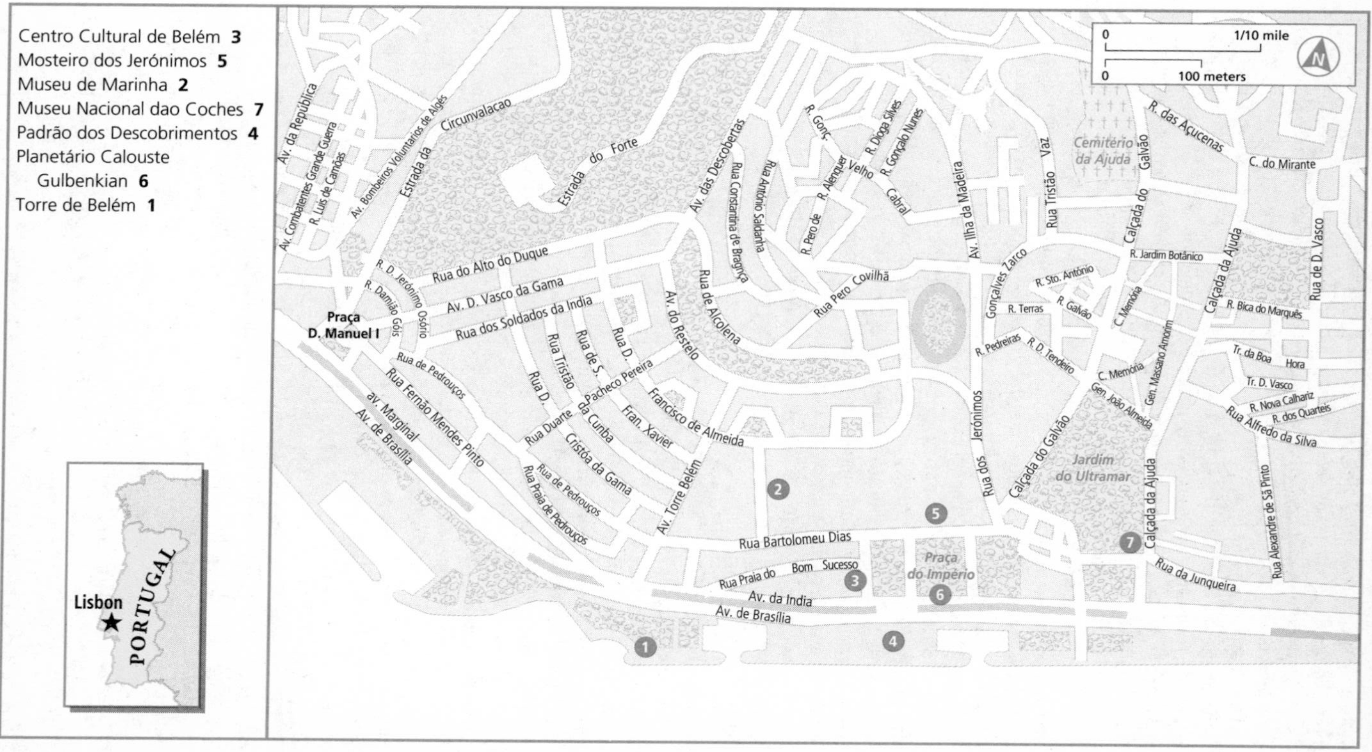
Centro Cultural de Belém 3
Mosteiro dos Jerónimos 5
Museu de Marinha 2
Museu Nacional dao Coches 7
Padrão dos Descobrimentos 4
Planetário Calouste Gulbenkian 6
Torre de Belém 1
PORTUGAL
Lisbon
0 1/10 mile
0 100 meters
Praça D. Manuel I
Praça do Império
Jardim do Ultramar
Cemitério da Ajuda
Av. de Brasília
Av. da India
Rua Bartolomeu Dias
Rua Praia do Bom Sucesso
Av. Torre Belém
Rua dos Jerónimos
Calçada do Galvão
Calçada da Ajuda
Rua da Junqueira
Rua Alexandre de Sá Pinto
Rua Alfredo da Silva
Rua de D. Vasco
C. do Mirante
R. das Açucenas
Rua Tristão Vaz
Av. Ilha da Madeira
Gonçalves Zarco
Rua Pero Covilhã
Rua António Saldanha
Rua Constantina de Bragnça
Av. das Descobertas
Rua de Alcolena
Av. do Restelo
Estrada do Forte
Estrada da Circunvalacao
Rua do Alto do Duque
Av. D. Vasco da Gama
Rua dos Soldados da India
Rua Fernão Mendes Pinto
av. Marginal
Av. Bombeiros Voluntarios de Algés
R. Luis de Camões
Av. Combatentes Grande Guerra
Av. da República

monastery was founded in 1502, partially financed by the spice trade that grew following the discovery of the route to India. The 1755 earthquake damaged but didn't destroy the monastery. It has undergone extensive restoration, some of it ill conceived.

The church encloses a trio of naves noted for their fragile-looking pillars. Some of the ceilings, like those in the monks' refectory, have a ribbed barrel vault. The "palm tree" in the sacristy is also exceptional.

Many of the greatest figures in Portuguese history are said to be entombed at the monastery; the most famous is Vasco da Gama. The Portuguese also maintain that Luís Vaz de Camões, author of the epic *Os Lusíadas* (The Lusiads), in which he glorified the triumphs of his compatriots, is buried here. Both tombs rest on the backs of lions. Camões's epic poetry is said to have inspired a young Portuguese king, Sebastião, to dreams of glory. The foolish king—devoutly, even fanatically, religious—was killed at Alcácer-Kibir, Morocco, in a 1578 crusade against the Muslims. Those refusing to believe that the king was dead formed a cult known as Sebastianism; it rose to minor influence, and four men tried to assert their claim to the Portuguese throne. Each maintained steadfastly, even to death, that he was King Sebastião. Sebastião's remains were reputedly entombed in a 16th-century marble shrine built in the Mannerist style. The romantic poet Herculano (1800–54) is also buried at Jerónimos, as is the famed poet Fernando Pessoa.

Praça do Império. ✆ **21/362-00-34.** Admission: Church free; cloisters 3€ ($3.45) adults, free for seniors 65 and over and children under 12. May–Sept Tues–Sun 10am–6pm; Oct–Apr Tues–Sun 10am–5pm. Tram: 15. Bus: 27, 28, 29, 43, or 49.

Museu de Marinha (Maritime Museum) ★★ The Maritime Museum, one of the most important in Europe, evokes the glory that characterized Portugal's domination of the high seas. Appropriately, it's installed in the west wing of the Mosteiro dos Jerónimos. These royal galleys re-create an age of opulence that never shied away from excess. Dragons' heads drip with gilt; sea monsters coil with abandon. Assembling a large crew was no problem for kings and queens in those days. Queen Maria I ordered a magnificent galley built for the 1785 marriage of her son and successor, Crown Prince João, to the Spanish Princess Carlota Joaquina Bourbon. Eighty dummy oarsmen, elaborately attired in scarlet-and-mustard-colored waistcoats, represent the crew.

The museum contains hundreds of models of 15th- to 19th-century sailing ships, 20th-century warships, merchant marine vessels, fishing boats, river craft, and pleasure boats. In a section devoted to the East is a pearl-inlaid replica of a dragon boat used in maritime and fluvial corteges. A full range of Portuguese naval uniforms is on display, from one worn at a Mozambique military outpost in 1896 to a uniform worn as recently as 1961. In a special room is a model of the queen's stateroom on the royal yacht of Carlos I, the Bragança king who was assassinated at Praça do Comércio in 1908. It was on this craft that his son, Manuel II; his wife; and the queen mother, Amélia, escaped to Gibraltar following the collapse of the Portuguese monarchy in 1910. The Maritime Museum also honors some early Portuguese aviators.

Praça do Império. ✆ **21/362-00-19.** Admission 3€ ($3.45) adults, 1.50€ ($1.75) students and children ages 6–17, free for seniors (65 and over) and children under 6. Apr–Sept Tues–Sun 10am–6pm; Oct–Mar Tues–Sun 10am–5pm. Bus: 27, 28, 29, 43, 49, or 51.

Museu Nacional dos Coches (National Coach Museum) ★★ Visited by more tourists than any other attraction in Lisbon, the National Coach Museum is the finest of its type in the world. Founded by Amélia, wife of Carlos I, it's housed in a former 18th-century riding academy connected to the Belém Royal Palace. The coaches stand in a former horse ring; most date from the 17th to the 19th centuries. Drawing the most interest is a trio of opulently gilded baroque carriages used by the Portuguese ambassador to the Vatican at the time of Pope Clement XI (1716). Also on display is a 17th-century coach in which the Spanish Hapsburg king, Phillip II, journeyed from Madrid to Lisbon to see his new possession.

Praça de Afonso de Albuquerque. ✆ **21/361-08-50.** Admission 3€ ($3.45) adults, 1.50€ ($1.75) students 14–25, free for children under 14. Tues–Sun 10am–5:30pm. Closed holidays. Tram: 15. Bus: 14, 27, 28, 29, 43, 49, or 51.

Centro Cultural de Belém This center occasionally functions as a showcase for temporary exhibitions of Portuguese art. Although it is mostly devoted to conventions, the center also functions at least part of the time as a concert hall, a temporary art museum, or a catchall venue. Events staged here, widely publicized in local newspapers, might include classical concerts and film festivals, in addition to industrial conventions. There is an inexpensive cafeteria and a handful of shops on the premises. The building was constructed in the early 1990s as a convention hall for the meetings that brought Portugal membership in the European Union.

Praça do Império. ✆ **21/361-24-00.** Admission to center free; varies for temporary exhibitions. Daily 10am–7pm. Tram: 15. Bus: 27, 28, 29, or 43.

TWO MORE TOP MUSEUMS

Most major Lisbon museums are at Belém, but two major attractions are in the city proper: the National Art Gallery and the Gulbenkian Center for Arts and Culture.

Museu Nacional de Arte Antiga ★★★ The National Museum of Ancient Art houses the country's greatest collection of paintings. It occupies two connected buildings—a 17th-century palace and an added edifice that was built on the site of the old Carmelite Convent of Santo Alberto. The convent's chapel was preserved and is a good example of the integration of ornamental arts, with gilded carved wood, glazed tiles, and sculpture of the 17th and 18th centuries.

The museum has many notable paintings, including the **polyptych** ★★★ from St. Vincent's monastery attributed to Nuno Gonçalves between 1460 and 1470. There are 60 portraits of leading figures of Portuguese history. Other outstanding works are Hieronymus Bosch's triptych ***The Temptation of St. Anthony*** ★★★, Hans Memling's *Mother and Child,* Albrecht Dürer's *St. Jerome,* and paintings by Velázquez, Poussin, and Courbet. Especially noteworthy is the *12 Apostles,* by Zurbarán. Paintings from the 15th through the 19th centuries trace the development of Portuguese art.

The museum also exhibits a remarkable collection of gold- and silversmiths' works, both Portuguese and foreign. Among these is the cross from Alcobaça and the monstrance of Belém, constructed with the first gold brought from India by Vasco da Gama. Another exceptional example is the 18th-century French silver tableware ordered by José I. Diverse objects from Benin, India, Persia, China, and Japan were culled from the proceeds of Portuguese expansion overseas. Two excellent pairs of **screens** ★★ depict the Portuguese relationship with Japan in the 17th century. Flemish tapestries, a rich assemblage of church vestments, Italian polychrome ceramics, and sculptures are also on display.

Rua das Janelas Verdes 95. ✆ **21/391-28-00.** Admission 3€ ($3.45) adults, 1.50€ ($1.75) students, free for children under 14. Tues 2–6pm, Wed–Sun 10am–6pm. Tram: 15 or 18. Bus: 7, 27, 40, 49, or 60.

Finds Secrets of Lisbon

The places below provide a view of Lisbon not often seen by the casual visitors passing through the city.

The Markets The big market of **Ribeira Nova** is as close as you can get to the heart of Lisbon. Behind the Cais do Sodré train station, an enormous roof shelters a collection of stalls offering the produce used in Lisbon's fine restaurants. Foodstuffs arrive each morning in wicker baskets bulging with oversize carrots, cabbages big enough to be shrubbery, and stalks of bananas. Some of the freshly plucked produce arrives by donkey, some by truck, and some balanced on the heads of Lisboan women in the Mediterranean fashion. The rich soil produces the juiciest peaches and the most aromatic tomatoes.

At the market, women festively clad in voluminous skirts and calico aprons preside over the mounds of vegetables, fruit, and fish. On cue, the vendors begin howling about the value of their wares, stopping only to pose for an occasional snapshot. Fishing boats dock at dawn with their catch. The fishermen deposit the cod, squid, bass, hake, and swordfish on long marble counters. The *varinas* (fishwives) balance wicker baskets of the fresh catch on their heads and climb the cobblestone streets of the Alfama or the Bairro Alto to sell fish from door to door.

Estufa Fria (The Greenhouse) The Estufa Fria is in the handsome Parque Eduardo VII (✆ **21/388-22-78**), named after Queen Victoria's son to commemorate his three trips to Lisbon. Against a background of streams and rocks, tropical plants grow in such profusion that the place resembles a rain forest. The park lies at the top of Avenida da Liberdade, crowned by a statue of the Marquês de Pombal with his "house pet," a lion. There's a 1.20€ ($1.40) fee to enter the greenhouse, which

Museu da Fundação Calouste Gulbenkian ★★★ Opened in 1969, this museum, part of the Fundação Calouste Gulbenkian, houses what one critic called one of the world's finest private art collections. It belonged to the Armenian oil tycoon Calouste Gulbenkian, who died in 1955. The modern, multimillion-dollar center is in a former private estate that belonged to the count of Vilalva.

The collection covers Egyptian, Greek, and Roman antiquities; a remarkable assemblage of Islamic art, including ceramics and textiles from Turkey and Persia; Syrian glass, books, bindings, and miniatures; and Chinese vases, Japanese prints, and lacquerware. The European displays include **medieval illuminated manuscripts and ivories** ★, 15th- to 19th-century paintings and sculpture, Renaissance tapestries and medals, important collections of 18th-century French decorative works, French Impressionist paintings, René Lalique jewelry, and glassware.

In a move requiring great skill in negotiation, Gulbenkian managed to buy art from the Hermitage in St. Petersburg. Among his most notable acquisitions are two Rembrandts: *Portrait of an Old Man* and *Alexander the Great.* Two other well-known paintings are *Portrait of Hélène Fourment,* by Peter Paul Rubens, and *Portrait of Madame Claude Monet,* by Pierre-Auguste Renoir. In addition, we is open daily June to September 9am to 6pm and October to May 9am to 5pm. Metro: Rotunda. Bus: 2, 11, 12, 27, 32, 38, 44, 45, or 83.

Cemitério dos Ingleses (British Cemetery) The British Cemetery lies up Rua da Estrêla at one end of the Estrêla Gardens. It's famous as the burial place of Henry Fielding, the novelist and dramatist who's best known for *Tom Jones.* Fielding went to Lisbon in 1754 to try to recover his health; his posthumous tract *Journal of a Voyage to Lisbon* tells the story of that trip. He reached Lisbon in August and died 2 months later. A monument honoring him was erected in 1830. Ring the bell for entry. Bus: 9, 20, 27, or 38.

Aqueduto das Aguas Livres (Aguas Livres Aqueduct) An outstanding baroque monument, this aqueduct runs from the Aguas Livres River in Caneças to the Casa da Agua reservoir in Amoreiras. The aqueduct, built under João V in the early 18th century, stretches for about 18km (11 miles) and is visible from the highway (N7) that leads to Sintra and Estoril. Part of it lies underground; some of the 109 stone arches are visible above ground. The best view is of the 14 arches stretching across the valley of Alcântara from Serafina to the Campolide hills.

Jardim Botânico (Botanical Garden) ★ Connected with the National Costume Museum is the Parque do Monteiro-Mor, Largo Julio de Castilho, Lumiar. It's one of Lisbon's most beautiful botanical gardens. A restaurant (✆ **21/759-03-18**) lies on the park grounds. The park is open Tuesday through Sunday from 10am to 6pm. Admission is 1.25€ ($1.45) and free for children under 10. It's free to all Sunday morning. A combination ticket with the National Costume Museum costs 3€ ($3.45) for adults and 1.25€ ($1.45) for children 11 to 14. Bus: 1, 3, 4, or 36.

suggest that you seek out Mary Cassatt's *The Stocking.* The French sculptor Jean-Antoine Houdon is represented by a statue of Diana. Silver made by François-Thomas Germain, once used by Catherine the Great, is here, as is one piece by Thomas Germain, the father.

As a cultural center, the Gulbenkian Foundation sponsors plays, films, ballets, and concerts, as well as a rotating exhibition of works by leading modern Portuguese and foreign artists.

Av. de Berna 45. ✆ **21/782-30-00.** Admission 3€ ($3.45), free for seniors (65 and over) and students and teachers. Free to all Sun. Wed–Sun 10am–6pm. Metro: Sebastião. Bus: 16, 26, 31, 41, 46, or 56.

2 More Attractions

THE BAIRRO ALTO ★

Like the Alfama, the Bairro Alto (Upper City) preserves the characteristics of the Lisbon of yore. In location and population, it once was the heart of the city. Many of its buildings survived the 1755 earthquake. Today it's home to some of the finest fado cafes in Lisbon, making it a center of nightlife. It's also a fascinating place to visit during the day, when its charming, narrow cobblestone streets and alleys lined with ancient buildings can be appreciated in the warm light coming off the sea.

Originally called Vila Nova de Andrade, the area was started in 1513 when the Andrade family bought part of the huge Santa Catarina and then sold the land as construction plots. Early buyers were carpenters, merchants, and ship caulkers. Some of them immediately resold their land to aristocrats, and little by little noble families moved to the quarter. The Jesuits followed, moving from their modest College of Mouraria to new headquarters at the Monastery of São Roque, where the *Misericórdia* (social assistance to the poor) of Lisbon proceeds today. The Bairro Alto gradually became a working-class section. Today the quarter is also the domain of journalists—most of the big newspapers' plants are here. Writers and artists have been drawn here to live and work, attracted by the ambience and the good local cuisine.

The area is resoundingly colorful. From the windows and balconies, streamers of laundry hang out to dry, and there are cages of canaries, parrots, parakeets, and other birds. In the morning, housewives hit the food markets, following the cries of the *varinas* (fishmongers) and other vendors. Women lounge in doorways or lean on windowsills to watch the world go by.

This area comes alive at night, luring visitors and natives with fado, food, dance clubs, and small bars. Lisbon's taverns, the *tascas,* abound, together with more deluxe eateries. Victorian lanterns light the streets, and people stroll leisurely.

CHURCHES

"If you want to see all of the churches of Lisbon, you'd better be prepared to stay here for a few months," a guide once told a tourist. True enough, the string of churches seems endless. What follows is a selection of the most interesting.

Panteão Nacional When a builder starts to work on a Portuguese house, the owner will often say, "Don't take as long as St. Engrácia." Construction on this Portuguese baroque church, Igreja de Santa Engrácia, began in 1682; it resisted the 1755 earthquake but wasn't completed until 1966. The building, with its four square towers, is pristine and cold, and the state has fittingly turned it into a neoclassical National Pantheon containing memorial tombs to heads of state.

Memorials honor Henry the Navigator; Luís Vaz de Camões, the country's greatest poet; Pedro Álvares Cabral, "discoverer" of Brazil; Afonso de Albuquerque, viceroy of India; Nuno Álvares Pereira, warrior and saint; and, of course, Vasco da Gama. Entombed in the National Pantheon are presidents of Portugal and several writers: Almeida Garrett, the 19th-century literary figure; João de Deus, a lyric poet; and Guerra Junquiero, also a poet.

Ask the guards to take you to the terrace for a beautiful view of the river. A visit to the pantheon can be combined with a shopping trip to the Flea Market (walk down Campo de Santa Clara, heading toward the river).

Largo de Santa Clara. ✆ **21/885-48-20.** Admission 2€ ($2.30), 1€ ($1.15) children 11–14, free for children under 11. Free to all Sun after 2pm. Tues–Sun 10am–5pm. Closed holidays. Tram: 28. Bus: 9, 39 or 46.

Igreja da São Vicente de Fora In this Renaissance church, the greatest names and some forgotten wives of the House of Bragança were laid to rest. It's more like a pantheon than a church. Originally a 12th-century convent, the church was erected between 1582 and 1627. At that time, it lay outside the walls of Lisbon (hence the name St. Vincent Outside the Walls). On the morning of the 1755 earthquake, the cupola fell in.

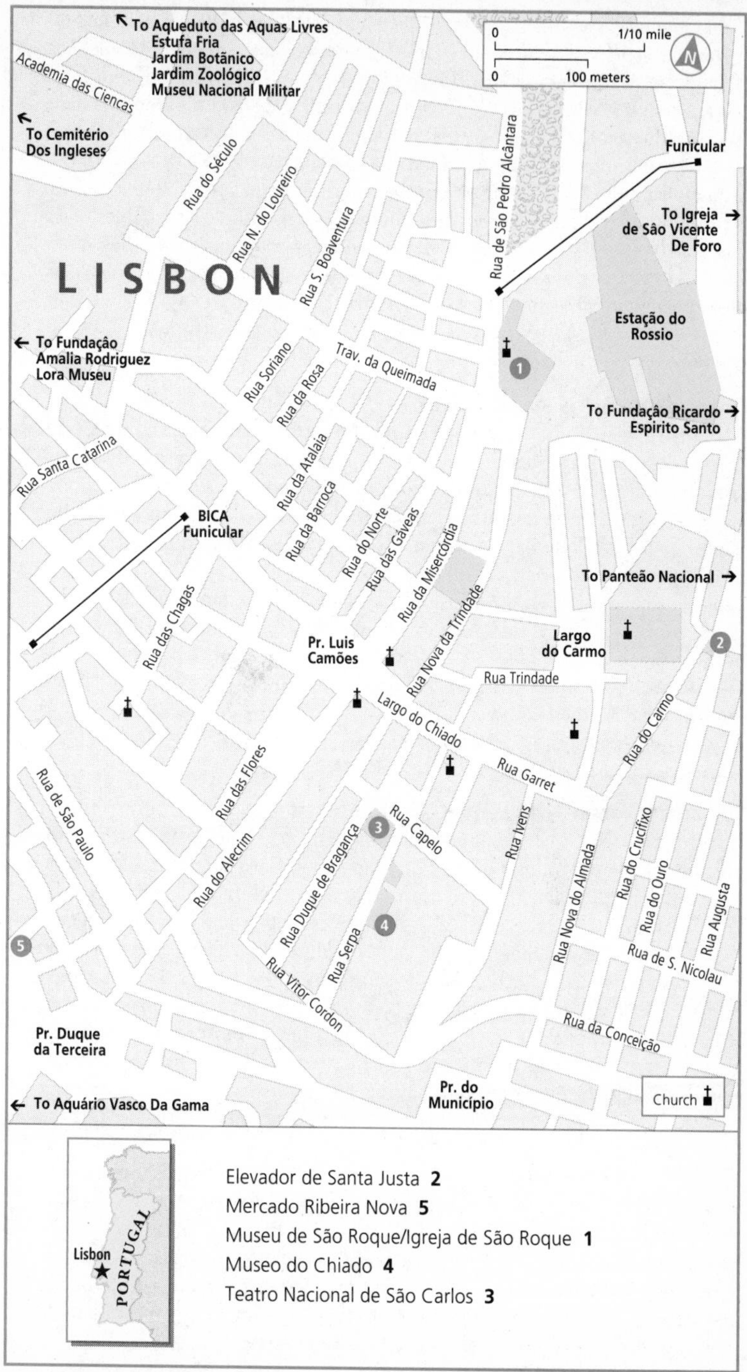
To Aqueduto das Aquas Livres
Estufa Fria
Jardim Botânico
Jardim Zoológico
Museu Nacional Militar
Academia das Ciencas
To Cemitério Dos Ingleses
0 1/10 mile
0 100 meters
N
Funicular
To Igreja de São Vicente De Foro
Rua do Século
Rua N. do Loureiro
Rua S. Boaventura
Rua de São Pedro Alcântara
LISBON
Estação do Rossio
To Fundaçâo Amalia Rodriguez Lora Museu
Rua Soriano
Rua da Rosa
Trav. da Queimada
To Fundaçâo Ricardo Espirito Santo
Rua Santa Catarina
Rua da Atalaia
Rua da Barroca
Rua do Norte
Rua das Gáveas
Rua da Misercórdia
BICA Funicular
To Panteão Nacional
Rua das Chagas
Rua Nova da Trindade
Pr. Luis Camões
Largo do Carmo
Rua Trindade
Largo do Chiado
Rua do Carmo
Rua Garret
Rua de São Paulo
Rua das Flores
Rua Capelo
Rua Ivens
Rua do Alecrim
Rua Duque de Bragança
Rua Nova do Almada
Rua do Crucifixo
Rua do Ouro
Rua Augusta
Rua Serpa
Rua de S. Nicolau
Rua Vitor Cordon
Rua da Conceição
Pr. Duque da Terceira
Pr. do Município
To Aquário Vasco Da Gama
Church
Lisbon
PORTUGAL
Elevador de Santa Justa 2
Mercado Ribeira Nova 5
Museu de São Roque/Igreja de São Roque 1
Museo do Chiado 4
Teatro Nacional de São Carlos 3

The Braganças assumed power in 1640 and ruled until 1910, when the Portuguese monarchy collapsed and Manuel II and the queen mother, Amélia, fled to England. Manuel II died in 1932, and his body was returned to Portugal for burial. Amélia, the last queen of Portugal, died in 1951 and is entombed here, as are her husband, Carlos I (the painter king), and her son, Prince Luís Felipe; both were killed by an assassin at Praça do Comércio in 1908.

Aside from the royal tombs, one of the most important reasons for visiting St. Vincent is to see its spectacular tiles, some of which illustrate the fables of La Fontaine. While we suspect that no one has officially counted them, their number is placed at 1 million. Look for the curious ivory statue of Jesus, carved in the former Portuguese province of Goa in the 18th century.

Largo de São Vicente. ✆ **21/882-44-00.** Free admission. Daily 9am–12:30pm and 3–6pm. Tram: 28. Bus: 12 or 28.

MUSEUMS & AN AQUARIUM

Centro de Arte Moderna ★ Around the corner from the entrance to the Calouste Gulbenkian Museum (see "The Top Attractions," earlier in this chapter), the Center of Modern Art is Lisbon's first major permanent exhibition center of modern Portuguese art. The center shares parklike grounds with the Gulbenkian Foundation and was, like the Gulbenkian Museum, a legacy of the late Armenian oil magnate.

It's housed in a British-designed complex of clean lines and dramatically proportioned geometric forms with a Henry Moore sculpture in front. The museum owns some 10,000 items, including the works of such modern Portuguese artists as Souza-Cardoso, Almada, Paula Rego, João Cutileiro, Costa Pinheiro, and Vieira da Silva.

Rua Dr. Nicolau de Bettencourt. ✆ **21/782-30-00.** Admission 3€ ($3.45), free for children under 10. Free to all Sun. Wed–Sun 10am–6pm. Metro: Praça d'Espagna. Bus: 16, 26, 31, 46, or 56.

Fundação Amalia Rodriguez Casa Museu *Finds* Fado diva Amalia Rodriguez (1920–99) is credited more than any other singer in history with touching the nerve endings of the Portuguese soul. Born in Lisbon into a large and very poor family, her musical expressions of *saudade* (nostalgia provoked by a sense of loss) have been defined as the musical expression of the Portuguese soul. Hers is the music most likely to be heard in traditional bars, and hers is the voice most immediately recognizable to most Portuguese. After her death, which was considered a national tragedy, her body was buried with pomp and circumstance in the National Pantheon alongside the country's most prominent statesmen and writers. Today, on the street where she used to live (Rua São Bento), you'll see hundreds of stencils proclaiming it as Rua Amalia.

Her ochre-color town house, not far from the Portuguese Parliament, is the headquarters of a charitable foundation established in her name. In July 2001, it was reconfigured as a testimonial to her life and accomplishments, and instantly became a pilgrimage site for her fans, evoking huge controversies about how she would (and should) be remembered within Portuguese history. You'll be issued a number when you first arrive and then be escorted on a multilingual (Portuguese, French, and English) guided tour of what used to be her home. Come here for a view of videotapes of some of her performances, especially those from the 1950s and 1960s. Tours last about 30 minutes each.

Rua de São Bento 193. ✆ **21/397-18-96.** Admission 5€ ($5.75) per person, free for children under 5. Tues–Sun 10am–1pm and 2–6pm. Bus 6, 49, or 100.

Fundaçao Ricardo do Espírito Santo Silva ★★ *Finds* Few other sites in Lisbon offer as comprehensive an overview of the 18th-century Portuguese aesthetic as this one. The setting is the 17th-century Azurara Palace, which was acquired in 1947 by the museum's namesake and benefactor. In 1953, his collection was bequeathed to a private foundation that, after his death, continued to amass hundreds of the country's finest antiques, art objects, silverware, and paintings. These are proudly displayed over four floors of the stately looking building within a labyrinth of rooms and hallways that evoke 18th-century life in a hyper-upscale home. There's a bookstore and coffee shop on the premises, and a battalion of attentive guards protect the lavish art objects inside as if they were their own. Anyone interested in the decorative arts in general and the Portuguese Empire in particular will find this collection fascinating.

Largo das Portas do Sol 2. ✆ **21/881-46-37.** Admission 5€ ($5.75), 2€ ($2.30) children 12–18, free for children under 12. Tues–Sun 10am–5pm. Tram 12 or 28. Bus: 37.

Museu do Chiado Housed in the former Convento de São Francisco, the Chiado museum was designed by the French architect Jean-Michel Wilmotte. It replaced the Museum of Contemporary Art. The permanent collection of post-1850 art and sculpture extends to 1950 and crosses the artistic bridge from Romanticism to Postnaturalism. Some excellent examples of Modernism in Portugal are on display. The museum also houses frequently changing contemporary exhibitions devoted to art, sculpture, photography, and mixed media.

Rua Serpa Pinto 4. ✆ **21/343-21-48.** Admission 3€ ($3.45). Tues 2–6pm; Wed–Sun 10am–6pm. Metro: Chiado. Tram: 28. Bus: 58 or 100.

Museu Nacional Militar The National Military Museum sits in front of the Santa Apolónia Station, not far from Terreiro do Paço and Castelo de São Jorge. It's on the site of a shipyard built during the reign of Manuel I (1495–1521). During the reign of João III, a new foundry for artillery was erected; it was also used for making gunpowder and storing arms to equip the Portuguese fleet. A fire damaged the buildings in 1726, and the 1755 earthquake destroyed them completely. Rebuilt on the orders of José I, the complex was designated as the Royal Army Arsenal. The museum, originally called the Artillery Museum, was created in 1851. Today the facility exhibits not only arms, but also paintings, sculpture, tiles, and examples of architecture.

The museum boasts one of the world's best collections of historical artillery. Bronze cannons of various periods include one from Diu, weighing 20 tons and bearing Arabic inscriptions. Some iron pieces date from the 14th century. Light weapons, such as guns, pistols, and swords, are displayed in cases.

Largo do Museu de Artilharia. ✆ **21/884-25-69.** Admission 2.50€ ($2.90) adults, 1€ ($1.15) children. Tues–Sun 10am–6pm. Bus: 9, 35, 39, 45, 46, 59, or 105.

Museu de São Roque/Igreja de São Roque ★ The Jesuits, who at one time were so powerful they virtually governed Portugal, founded St. Roque Church in the late 16th century. Beneath its painted wood ceiling, the church contains a celebrated chapel by Luigi Vanvitelli honoring John the Baptist. The chapel, ordered by the Bragança king João V in 1741, was assembled in Rome from such precious materials as alabaster and lapis lazuli, and then dismantled, shipped to Lisbon, and reassembled. The marble mosaics look like a painting. You can also visit the sacristy, rich in paintings illustrating scenes from the lives of saints pertaining to the Society of Jesus.

The St. Roque Museum inside the church merits a visit chiefly for its collection of baroque silver. A pair of bronze-and-silver torch holders, weighing about 380kg (838 lb.), is among the most elaborate in Europe. The 18th-century gold embroidery is a rare treasure, as are the vestments. The paintings, mainly from the 16th century, include one of a double-chinned Catherine of Austria and another of the wedding ceremony of Manuel I. Look for a remarkable 15th-century Virgin (with Child) of the Plague and a polished 18th-century conch shell that served as a baptismal font.

Largo Trindade Coelho. ✆ **21/323-53-80.** Admission 1€ ($1.15), free for seniors and children under 10. Free to all Sun. Tues–Sun 10am–5pm. Metro: Chiado. Bus: 28.

Oceanario de Lisboa ★★ This world-class aquarium is the most enduring and impressive achievement of EXPO '98. Marketed as the second-biggest aquarium in the world (the largest is in Osaka, Japan), it's in a stone-and-glass building whose centerpiece is a 5-million-liter (1.3-million-gal.) holding tank. Its waters consist of four distinct ecosystems that replicate the Atlantic, Pacific, Indian, and Antarctic oceans. Each is supplemented with above-ground portions on which birds, amphibians, and reptiles flourish. Look for otters in the Pacific waters, penguins in the Antarctic section, trees and flowers that might remind you of Polynesia in the Indian Ocean division, and puffins, terns, and seagulls in the Atlantic subdivision. Don't underestimate the national pride associated with this huge facility: Most Portuguese view it as a latter-day reminder of their former mastery of the seas.

Esplanada d. Carlos I. ✆ **21/891-70-02.** Admission 9€ ($10) adults, 4.60€ ($5.30) students and children under 13. Daily 10am–7pm. Metro: Estação do Oriente.

3 Especially for Kids

Jardim Zoológico de Lisboa ★★ The Zoological Garden, with a collection of some 2,000 animals, occupies a flower-filled setting in the 26-hectare (64-acre) Park of Laranjeiras. It's about a 10-minute subway ride from the Rossio. There are also a small tram and rowboats.

Estada de Benfica 58. ✆ **21/723-29-00.** Zoo admission 11€ ($13) adults, 8.30€ ($9.55) children 3–8, free for children 2 and under. Daily 10am–8pm. Metro: Mardim Zoologico. Bus: 15, 16, 16C, 26, 31, 46, 58, 63, or 68.

Planetário Calouste Gulbenkian An annex of the Maritime Museum, the Calouste Gulbenkian Planetarium is open to the public all year, with astronomical shows throughout the day (check with the planetarium for current schedules).

Praça do Império, Belém. ✆ **21/362-00-02.** Admission 3€ ($3.45) adults, 1.50€ ($1.75) children 10–18, free for seniors and children 6–9. Children under 6 not admitted (except for Sun morning). Tues–Sun 10am–6pm. Bus: 29, 43, or 49.

Aquário Vasco da Gama The Vasco da Gama Aquarium, on N6, near Algés on the Cascais railway line, has been in operation since 1898. Live exhibits include the eared seals pavilion and a vast number of tanks that hold fish and other sea creatures from all over the world. A large portion of the exhibits consist of zoological material brought back from oceanographic expeditions by Carlos I. They include preserved marine invertebrates, water birds, fish, mammals, and some of the king's laboratory equipment.

Rua Direita do Dafundo. ✆ **21/419-63-37.** Admission 3€ ($3.45) adults, 1.50€ ($1.75) children 7–17, free for children under 7. Daily 10am–6pm. Metro: Algés. Bus: 29 or 51.

4 City Strolls

Lisbon is a walker's delight; the city's principal neighborhoods abound with major sights and quiet glimpses into daily life.

WALKING TOUR 1 THE ALFAMA

Start: Take a taxi to Largo do Salvador.
Finish: Miradouro de Santa Luzia.
Time: 2 hours, or more if you add sightseeing time.
Best Times: Any sunny day.
Worst Times: Twilight or after dark.

The streets of the Alfama are best traversed on foot; at times you must walk up steep stone stairs. Once aristocratic, this fabled section has fallen into decay. Parts of it allow the visitor a rare opportunity to wander back in time. Be aware that the Alfama can be dangerous at night.

A good point to begin your tour is:

1 Largo do Salvador

Here you'll see a 16th-century mansion that once belonged to the count of Arcos.

From here, turn down Rua da Regueira to:

2 Beco do Carneiro, the "cul-de-sac of rams"

This lane is impossibly narrow. Families live in houses that are, at most, just 1.2m (4 ft.) apart.

At the end of the alley, circle back using the flight of steps to your left to:

3 Largo de Santo Estevão

This square was named after the church on the site.

Round the church and, from the back, use the flight of steps to proceed to the:

4 Pátio das Flores

The Pátio das Flores has some of the most delightful little houses in the Alfama, adorned with characteristic Portuguese *azulejos* (tiles).

Walk down the steps to Rua dos Remédios, cutting right to:

5 Largo do Chafariz de Dentro

Here you might see housewives drawing water from a fountain—many apartments don't have running water.

From the square, connect with:

6 Rua de São Pedro

This is perhaps the most animated street in the Alfama. As you stroll the streets, you'll probably attract a trail of boisterous children.

You'll pass some local taverns; venture inside to sample a glass of *vinho verde* (green wine). Stepping out onto the narrow street again, you might cross paths with an old fisherman with nets draped over his shoulder as he heads to the sea.

Rua de São Pedro leads into:

7 Largo de São Rafael

The Largo de São Rafael might convince you that the 17th century never ended. You pass a *leitaria* (dairy) that sells milk by the bottle; cows used to be kept right inside.

Off the square is:

8 Rua da Judiaria

Many Jews settled here after escaping the Inquisition in Spain.

Walking Tour: The Alfama

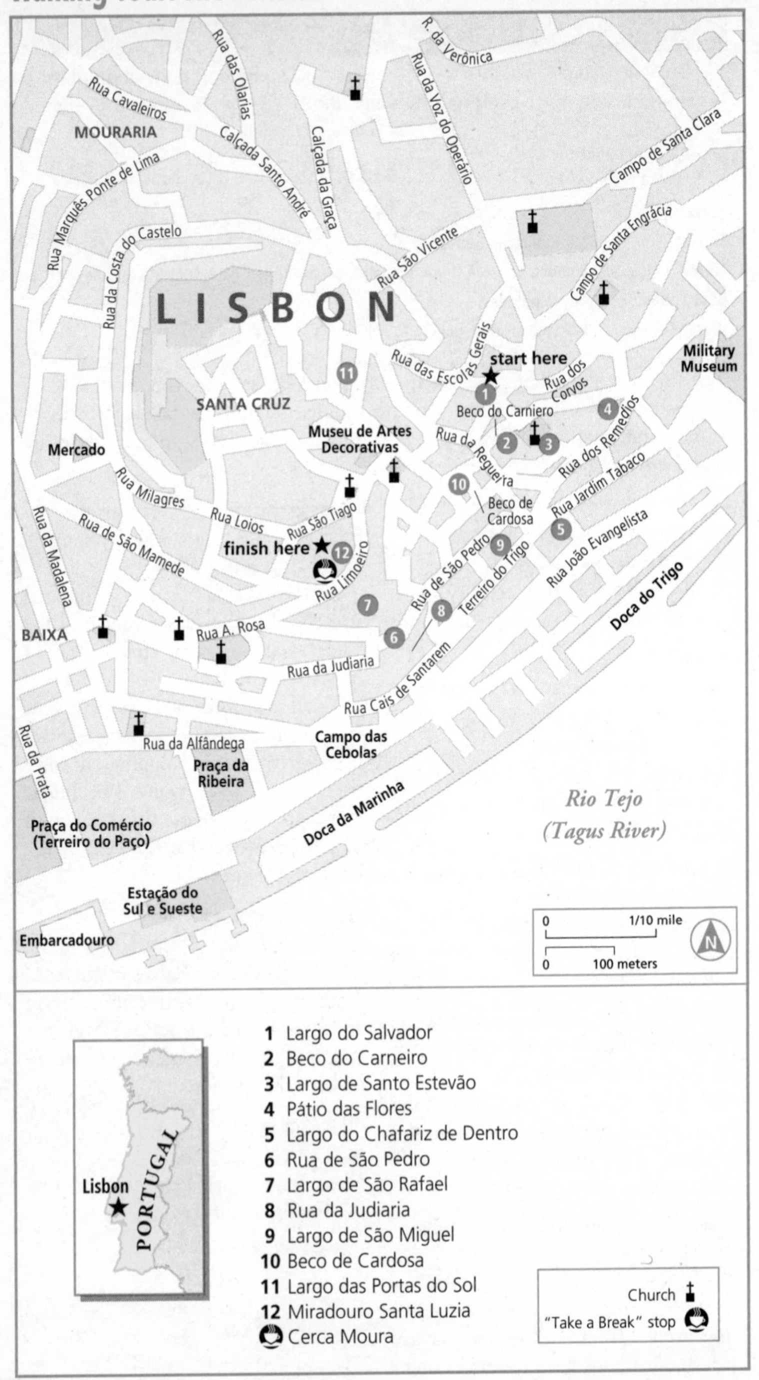

Go back to Largo de São Rafael, crossing to rejoin Rua de São Pedro. Walk down the street to the intersection, forking left. You enter:

9 Largo de São Miguel

Take a moment to enjoy the richly baroque church on this square.

From here, walk up Rua de São Miguel, cutting left into:

10 Beco de Cardosa

Many fishermen and their *varinas* (fishwives) still live here. They often decorate their homes' wrought-iron balconies with flowers.

At the end of the alley, you connect with Beco Santa Helena, which leads up several flights of stairs to:

11 Largo das Portas do Sol

On this square is the Fundação Ricardo Espirito Santo, a museum of decorative art (see "More Attractions," earlier in this chapter).

TAKE A BREAK
At the Miradouro de Santa Luzia are several tiny **cafes** and **bars** with outside seating. Visitors from all over the world come here to order coffee and refreshments and take in the view of the shipping activity on the Tagus. These establishments are virtually all the same, but we recommend **Cerca Moura,** Largo das Portas do Sol 4 (✆ **21/887-48-59**), which offers the finest menu of snacks and drinks in the area and affords a breathtaking view.

Continue south down Rua Limoeiro until you reach one of the Alfama's most fabled belvederes:

12 Miradouro de Santa Luzia

The belvedere overlooks the houses of the Alfama as they sweep down in a jumbled pile to the Tagus.

WALKING TOUR 2 BAIXA, THE CENTER & THE CHIADO

Start:	Praça do Comércio.
Finish:	Elevador de Santa Justa.
Time:	3 hours.
Best Times:	Any sunny day except Sunday.
Worst Times:	Monday to Saturday from 7:30 to 9am and 5 to 7pm; Sunday, when shops are closed.

The best place to begin this tour is:

1 Praça do Comércio (also known as Terreiro do Paço)

This is at the waterfront end of Baixa. The House of Bragança ended here with the assassination of Carlos I and his elder son, Luís Filipe, in 1908. Regrettably, employees in the surrounding government buildings now use the Praça as a parking lot. The Marquês de Pombal designed the square when he rebuilt Lisbon following the 1755 earthquake. The equestrian statue is of Dom José, the Portuguese king at the time of the earthquake.

From the square, head west along Avenida Ribeira das Naus until you reach:

2 Cais do Sodré, the train station

As you walk, you can enjoy views of the Tagus. At Cais do Sodré, you'll come to an open-air produce market on the waterfront behind the station. The Ribeiro fish market takes place in a domed building on the right daily (except Sun) starting at dawn. *Varinas* (fishwives) carry away huge baskets of the catch of the day, which they deftly balance on their heads.

Return to Praça do Comércio, but this time take a street away from the river, going east along Rua do Arsenal until you reach the northwest corner of the square. After all that walking, especially if it's a hot day, you might need to:

TAKE A BREAK
Café Martinho da Arcada, Praça do Comércio 3 (© **21/ 887-92-59**), has been the haunt of the literati since 1782, attracting such greats as the Portuguese poet Fernando Pessoa. The old restaurant has gone up-market, but it adjoins a cafe and bar, often called the best cafe in Portugal. If you're here for lunch, ask for a savory kettle of fish, called *cataplana,* or clam stew served in the style of the Algarve. It's open Monday through Saturday from 7am to 11pm.

After dining, head north along:

3 Rua Augusta

This is one of Baixa's best-known shopping streets. Leather stores and bookshops, embroidery outlets, and even home-furnishings stores line the bustling street. Many of the cross streets are closed to traffic, making window-shopping more enjoyable. The glittering jewelry stores you'll see often have some good buys in gold and silver. The many delis display vast offerings of Portuguese wine and cheese, along with endless arrays of the pastries Lisboans are so fond of.

The western part of this grid of streets is known as the **Chiado.** It's the city's most sophisticated shopping district. In 1988, a devastating fire swept the area, destroying many shops, particularly those on the periphery of Rua Garrett. The area has bounced back with vigor.

Rua Augusta leads into the:

4 Rossio (formally called Praça de Dom Pedro IV)

The principal square of Baixa, it dates from the 1200s. During the Inquisition, it was the setting of many an auto-da-fé, during which Lisboans turned out to witness the torture and death of an "infidel," often a Jew. This was the heart of Pombaline Lisbon as the marquês rebuilt it following the 1755 earthquake. Neoclassical buildings from the 1700s and 1800s line the square, which has an array of cafes and souvenir shops. The 1840 Teatro Nacional de Dona Maria II sits on the north side of the square, occupying the former Palace of the Inquisition. The statue on its facade is of Gil Vicente, the Shakespeare of Portugal, credited with the creation of the Portuguese theater.

Crowds cluster around two baroque fountains at either end of the Rossio. The bronze statue on a column is of Pedro IV, for whom the square is named. (He was also crowned king of Brazil as Pedro I.) Dozens of flower stalls soften the square's tawdry, overly commercial atmosphere.

TAKE A BREAK
The **Café Nicola,** Praça de Dom Pedro IV 24–25 (© **21/ 346-05-79**), dates from 1777. It gained fame as a gathering place of the Portuguese literati in the 19th century. Though somewhat short on charm, it's the most popular cafe in Lisbon. Pastries, endless cups of coffee, and meals can be consumed indoors or out. It's open Monday through Saturday from 8am to 8pm.

From the Rossio, proceed to the northwest corner of the square and walk onto the satellite square, Praça da Camara. If you continue north, you'll reach the beginning of:

5 Avenida da Liberdade

This is Lisbon's main thoroughfare, laid out in 1879. More than 90m (295 ft.) wide, the avenue runs north for 1.5km (1 mile), cutting through the heart of the city. It has long been hailed as the most splendid boulevard of Lisbon, although many of the Art Deco and Belle Epoque mansions that once lined it are gone. Its sidewalks are tessellated in black and white. This is the heart of Lisbon's cinema district; you'll also pass airline offices, travel agencies, and other businesses.

Walking Tour: Baixa, the Center & the Chiado

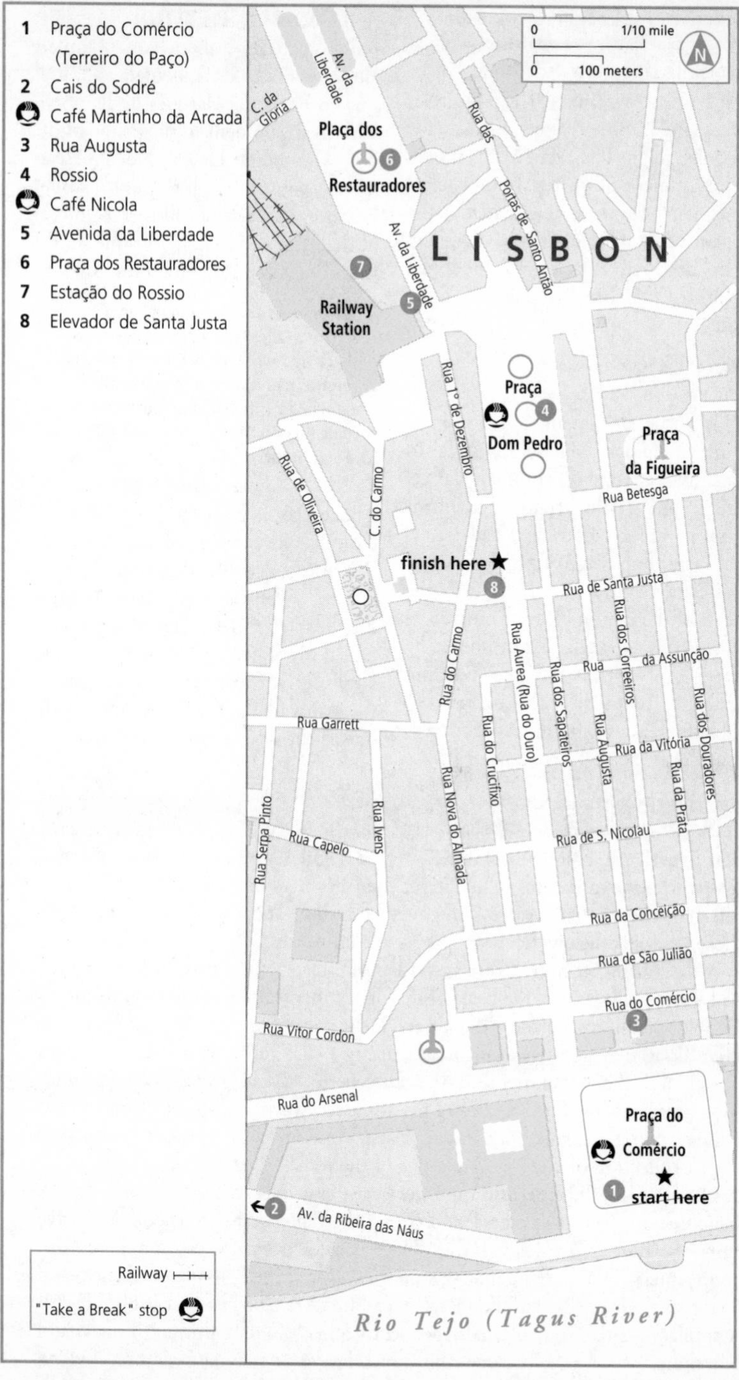

An open-air esplanade lies in the center. Almost immediately you come to:

6 Praça dos Restauradores

This square was named for the men who, in 1640, revolted against the Spanish reign. The event led to the reestablishment of Portugal's independence. An obelisk in the center of the square commemorates the uprising. The deep-red Palácio Foz, now the Ministry of Information, is also on the square.

West of the square is the:

7 Estação do Rossio

This is the city's main rail terminus. Built in mock Manueline style to resemble a lavishly adorned palace, this is one of the strangest architectural complexes housing a rail terminal in Europe. Trains from Sintra and the Estremadura pull right into the heart of the city and leave from a platform that's an escalator ride above the street-level entrances. The bustling station abounds with businesses, including souvenir shops and currency-exchange offices.

A POSSIBLE DETOUR At this point, you can walk 1.5km (1 mile) along Avenida da Liberdade all the way to Praça do Marquês de Pombal, with its monument to the prime minister who rebuilt Lisbon. North of the square, you can stroll through Parque Eduardo VII. If you'd like to see more of the heart of Lisbon, continue south from Praça dos Restauradores.

If you choose to walk south again along Avenida da Liberdade, retrace your steps to Praça de Dom João da Câmara. Instead of returning to Rossio, continue south along Rua do 1 de Dezembro, which will become Rua do Carmo. This street will lead you to the:

8 Elevador de Santa Justa

The elevator, built in 1902, is in a Gothic-style tower at the junction of Rua Aurea and Rua de Santa Justa. It is often falsely attributed to Alexandre-Gustave Eiffel, who designed the fabled tower of Paris. In no more than a minute, it whisks you from Baixa to the Bairro Alto. You're rewarded with one of the city's grand panoramas.

5 Organized Tours

Star Travel, Av. Duque De Loulé 74 (© **21/330-12-00**), is popular with visitors who want to see the sights or get their bearings in and around the city. It offers seven different year-round tours of Lisbon and its environs, including those described below. Reservations are recommended.

A daily half-day tour, **"Touristic Lisbon"** starts with a drive down Avenida da Liberdade to Rossio, the heart of the city. It then climbs uphill to St. George's Castle for a glimpse of the old quarters, including the ancient Alfama district. A drive along the Tagus River includes stops in Black Horse Square and at Belém Tower and the Monument to the Discoveries. Next comes the Jerónimos Monastery, where you can admire the stone lacework. Except on Monday and holidays, the tour concludes at the Coach Museum, which houses the nation's largest collection of coaches. The price of the tour is 25€ ($29).

Offered daily, **"Lisbon and the Blue Coast"** is a full-day tour that includes the same sites as "Touristic Lisbon" and crosses the Tagus in the afternoon. You drive along the Blue Coast through the "Three Castles" region of Sesimbra, Setúbal, and Palmela. The route includes a stop for coffee at the Pousada do Castelo and a visit to a wine cellar and handcrafts center at Azeitão. The cost is 65€ ($75). A similar half-day tour offered April to October Monday through Friday, and November to March Tuesday and Thursday, is "Arrábida/Sesimbra," which includes the same stops as the afternoon of the "Blue Coast" tour, with an additional stop in the nature preserve on Arrábida Mountain. The cost is 47€ ($54).

For a different view, take the **"Lisbon by Night"** tour, offered on Monday, Wednesday, and Friday evenings. Reservations are required. It includes the same city stops as the other tours and then delves into the old quarter of Alcântara. The evening concludes with dinner and drinks at a restaurant featuring entertainment by a *fadista* (fado singer). The price of the tour is 58€ ($67) with two drinks at the restaurant, or 71€ ($82) for dinner and drinks. A nighttime offering on Tuesday, Thursday, or Saturday, the **"Casino Estoril"** tour has the same itinerary as "Lisbon by Night" but concludes with dinner and an international show at the casino in the coastal resort of Estoril. The cost is 68€ ($78) with two drinks at the casino, or 87€ ($100) with dinner.

If you'd rather see the beaches, sign up for the **"Costa do Estoril/Sintra"** tour. It explores the coast at Estoril and Cascais but also stops at the cliffs of Boca do Inferno and the westernmost point in Europe, Cabo da Roca. You then cross Sintra Mountain to conclude at the Vila Palace. It costs 45€ ($52).

Another venture into Lisbon's surroundings, the **"Cascais/Mafra/Sintra/Estoril/Queluz"** tour, strikes out daily for a full day that includes visiting the sumptuous 18th-century rooms of the Queluz Palace (closed Tues) and the basilica in Mafra. After lunch in the seaside resort of Ericeira, it continues with the Pena palace in Sintra and passage through the resorts of Guincho, Cascais, and Estoril. The price is 70€ ($81) with lunch and 60€ ($69) without lunch.

6 Outdoor & Recreational Activities

Lisbon itself has very few sports facilities. Most outdoor activities, such as watersports, fishing, and scuba diving, take place on the Costa do Sol, north of the city.

If you want to lie on the beach, you can take the train from Lisbon to the Costa do Sol; the main resorts there are Estoril and Cascais (see chapter 5).

FISHING Head for Sesimbra (see chapter 6), south of Lisbon, where local fishers take visitors out on boats looking for "the big one." Fees can be negotiated.

FITNESS CENTERS Some hotels recommended in chapter 3 allow nonguests to use their health clubs for a fee. It's always best to call in advance. Outside of the hotels, a worthwhile fitness club is **Gynasium Academia de Fitness,** Rua Domingo Sequeira 42C (✆ **21/396-20-98**), costing 6€ ($6.90) for one-time use of its facilities. It's open Monday through Friday from 8am to 10pm, and Saturday from 10am to 6pm (bus: no. 58).

GOLF The best courses lie along the Costa do Sol and Estoril Coast. The closest course to Lisbon (but not the best) is at the **Lisboa Sports Club,** Casal da Carregueira, near Belas (✆ **21/432-14-74**). It's about a 25-minute drive from the center; allow more time if traffic is heavy. A former playground for the Portuguese royal family, the **Penha Longa Golf Club,** Quinta da Penha Longa, is at Linhó, near Sintra (✆ **21/924-90-31**), 32km (20 miles) northwest of Lisbon. Designed by Robert Trent Jones Jr. in 1992, the resort is open to members and guests of the **Caesar Park Penha Longa,** Estate da Logoa Azul, Linhó, 2710 Sintra (✆ **21/924-90-11;** fax 21/924-90-07). Serious golfers should consider a stay at this 177-room Westin hotel overlooking the golf course. For 18 holes, greens fees range from 82€ to 104€ ($94–$120).

JOGGING We used to recommend Parque Eduardo VII as the best place for jogging, but joggers there have recently been the victims of muggings. Daytime jogging in the park is risky enough, but nighttime jogging is unwise. Some joggers head for the Estádio Nacional (National Stadium), on the northern outskirts of the city on the road to Estoril. A track worn smooth by joggers winds through pinewoods. It is also unsafe at night. You might prefer to jog along the Tagus between Ponte do 25 de Abril (the major suspension bridge) and Belém, heading north. Another possibility (but likely to be congested) is the median strip of the main street of Lisbon, Avenida da Liberdade, from Praça do Marquês de Pombal toward Baixa.

SWIMMING Options include the **Piscina do Campo Grande,** Campo Grande (✆ **21/795-79-45**); the **Piscina dos Olivais,** Avenida Dr. Francisco Luís Gomes (✆ **21/855-14-70**), about 5km (3 miles) northeast of Lisbon, which charges 1.80€ ($2.05) for adults and children; and the **Piscina do Areiro,** Avenida de Roma (✆ **21/848-67-94**), which charges 1.35€ ($1.55) for adults and .90€ ($1.05) for children.

TENNIS Public tennis courts are available at **Campo Grande Estádio do 1 de Maio,** at Alvalade. To play, inquire at the main tourist office in Lisbon. Real tennis buffs head for either the **Club de Tenis de Estoril** at Estoril or the **Quinta da Marinha at Cascais.**

7 Spectator Sports

The following activities are accessible from the city center.

BULLFIGHTING Bullfighting was once the sport of Portuguese noblemen. Unlike in neighboring Spain, the bull is not killed—a prohibition the Marquês de Pombal instituted in the 18th century, after the son of the duke of Arcos was killed in the sport. Much ceremony and pageantry attend the drama: The major actors are elegantly costumed cavaleiros, who charge the bull on horseback, and *maços de forçado,* who grapple with the bull. Many find this face-to-face combat the most exciting component of the bullfight.

Warning: Bullfights are not spectacles fit for every taste. Even though the animal is not killed, many spectators find the event nauseating and object to the notion that it's a beautiful art form. The spears that jab the bull's neck draw blood, of course, making the animal visibly weaker. One reader wrote to us, "The animals are frightened, confused, and badgered before they are mercifully allowed to exit. What sport!"

The bullfighting season in Lisbon runs from Easter until mid-July. Lisbon's 8,500-seat **Praça de Touros Campo Pequeno,** at Campo Pequeno, Avenida da République (✆ **21/293-24-42;** Metro: Campo Pequeno), is the largest ring in the country, but at the time of this writing, it was closed for renovations, with an anticipated reopening due sometime during 2004. In the meanwhile, bullfight aficionados must commute to Montiijo, an industrial town on the Sétubal peninsula, across the Tagus from Lisbon. Here, in Montiijo, bullfights on a much smaller scale are presented on a somewhat erratic basis with the **Praça de Touros Montijo** (✆ **21/231-06-32**).

The details of each *tourada* and the names of the stars who will appear are usually announced well in advance of each event. Your hotel concierge can usually help you arrange tickets, or try **Agência de Bilhetes para Espectáculos Públicos,** Praça dos Restauradores (✆ **21/346-11-89**). Tickets generally cost 25€ to 60€ ($29–$69), depending on whether they're in the sun or the shade.

SOCCER The Portuguese love football (known to Americans as soccer). Nothing—not even politics, boiled codfish, or fado—excites them more. When favorite teams are playing, soccer has a following of startling passion and hysteria. "It's better than sex," one fan told us, although his wife disagreed. It's also a way for pickpockets to earn a living. They work the intent crowds, lifting wallets during intense moments.

Lisbon has a trio of teams that play almost every Sunday, but the season stretches only from September to May. You'll miss out if you visit in the summer. Try to arrive at least an hour before the match is scheduled to begin; pregame entertainment ranges from marching bands to fireworks.

The best-known team is Benfica, which holds matches in northwest Lisbon at the new and gigantic **Estádio da Luz,** Avenida General Norton Matos (© **21/862-70-00**). One of the largest sports stadiums in Europe, it evokes memories of the legendary Eusebio, who led his team to five European championship finals in the 1960s. All young soccer players in Lisbon grow up with dreams of becoming the next Eusebio.

The **Sporting Clube de Portugal** plays at the **Estádio do José Alvalade** (© **21/758-56-71**), in the north of the city, near Campo Grande. The third team is Belém's **Belenenses,** which plays at the Estádio do Rastelo (© **21/301-04-61**). The team might not be as good or nearly as famous as Benfica, but don't tell that to a loyal fan during the heat of the game.

Tickets vary in price depending on the event but average 20€ to 30€ ($23–$35). You can buy them on the day of the game at all three stadiums. However, when Benfica plays Sporting, tickets usually sell out; buy them in advance at the booth in Praça dos Restauradores. Tickets also go fast when FC Porto, from the northern city of Porto, Lisbon's main rival, is in town to play Benfica or Sporting.

8 Lisbon Shopping: From Antiques to Wine

Portuguese handcrafts often exhibit exotic influences, in large part because of the artisans' versatility and their skill in absorbing other styles. Portugal's vast history as a seafaring nation also surely has something to do with it. The best place to see their work is in Lisbon, where shopkeepers and their buyers hunt out unusual items from all over Portugal, including the Madeira Islands and the Azores.

SHOPPING AREAS Shops operate all over the city, but **Baixa,** in downtown Lisbon, is the major area for browsing. **Rua Aurea** (Street of Gold, the location of the major jewelry shops), **Rua da Prata** (Street of Silver), and **Rua Augusta** are Lisbon's three principal shopping streets. The Baixa shopping district lies between the Rossio and the river Tagus. **Rua Garrett,** in the Chiado, is where you'll find many of the more up-market shops.

Antiques lovers gravitate to Rua **Dom Pedro V** in the Bairro Alto. Other streets with antiques stores include Rua da Misericórdia, Rua de São Pedro de Alcântara, Rua da Escola Politécnica, and Rua do Alecrim.

HOURS, SHIPPING & TAXES Most stores open between 9 and 10am, close at noon for lunch, reopen at 2pm, and close for the day at 7pm. However, many shopkeepers take lunch from 1 to 3pm, so check before making the trip. On Saturday, many stores open from 9 or 10am to 1pm; on Sunday, most stores in Lisbon and elsewhere in Portugal are closed. If the open hours of an individual place listed below differ from the norm, we give the specific hours.

Many establishments will crate and ship bulky objects. Any especially large item, such as a piece of furniture, should be sent by ship. Every antiques dealer in Lisbon has lists of reputable maritime shippers. For most small and medium-size shipments, air freight isn't much more expensive than sending the items by ship. TAP, the Portuguese airline, has a separate toll-free U.S. number for cargo inquiries (✆ **800/221-7370** or 718/656-7455). Once in Lisbon, you can contact TAP to make air-shipping arrangements for larger purchases by calling the Lisbon cargo department offices at ✆ **21/841-52-74** or 21/841-67-94. It's open Monday through Friday from 8:30am to 7:30pm.

Remember that all your air-cargo shipments will need to clear Customs in the United States, Canada, or your home country. This involves some additional paperwork and perhaps a trip to the airport near where you live. It's usually best to hire a commercial Customs broker to do the work for you.

Value-added tax (called **IVA** in Portugal) ranges from 8% for basics, such as books and food, to 17% for luxury goods and for most of the things a foreign visitor would want or need during a holiday in Portugal. The tax is already factored into the sales price of virtually every good and service you're likely to come across, making payment seem relatively painless.

Foreigners traveling in Portugal with valid passports can obtain a refund for the value of the tax they pay on purchases in stores that display a government-approved tax-free logo, provided that they spend more than 61€ ($70) in any one store. Ask before you make the purchase whether the store is equipped for the mechanics of arranging refunds on the tax (again, it's factored into the price), and then ask the staff to fill out a **Tax Free Check.** When you leave Portugal, you exchange the check for cash at the airport or frontier.

Note that the IVA you'll pay in the semiautonomous regions of the Azores and Madeira, ranging from 4% to 12%, is less than that on the Portuguese mainland. Other than that, tax refunds work the same.

When you leave Portugal, show your passport and purchases (which you must carry by hand, not check with your luggage) to the Portuguese Customs officials. If everything is in order, your Tax Free Checks will be stamped and you can redeem them at a Tax Refund counter for cash. There are Tax Refund offices at the airport and the Lisbon harbor.

BEST BUYS Regardless of where it's made—from the Azores to the remote northeast province of Trás-os-Montes—merchandise from all over Portugal ends up in Lisbon stores. But if you're going to a particular province, try to shop locally, where prices are often about 20% less than those in Lisbon. A general exception is the fabled handmade **embroideries** from Madeira; prices there are about the same as in Lisbon.

Products made of **cork,** which range from place mats to cigarette boxes, are good buys. Collectors seek out **decorative glazed tiles.** You also might find good buys in Lisbon in **porcelain** and **china,** in **fishermen's sweaters** from the north, and in **fado recordings.**

Intricately woven lightweight **baskets** make attractive, practical gifts. It's best to shop for handmade **lace** in Vila do Conde, outside Porto, where you get a better buy; many Lisbon outlets carry the lace as well.

Pottery is one of the best buys in Portugal, and pottery covered with brightly colored roosters from Barcelos is legendary. In fact, the rooster has become the virtual symbol of Portugal. Blue-and-white pottery is made in Coimbra and often in Alcobaça. Our favorite items come from Caldas da Rainha. They include yellow-and-green dishes in the shape of vegetables (especially cabbage), fruit, animals, and even leaves. Vila Real is known for its black pottery, and Aceiro is known for polychrome pottery. Some red-clay pots from the Alentejo region in the southeast are based on designs that go back to the Etruscans. **Atlantis crystal** is another good buy. **Suede** and **leather,** as in Spain, are also good buys. In the Algarve, handsome **lanterns, fire screens,** and even **outdoor furniture** are constructed from metal—mainly copper, brass, and tin.

The best buy in Portugal, **gold,** is strictly regulated by the government. Jewelers must put a minimum of 19.2 karats into the jewelry they sell. **Filigree jewelry** in gold and silver is popular in Lisbon and elsewhere in Portugal. The art of ornamental openwork made of fine gold or silver wire dates to ancient times. The most expensive items—often objets d'art—are fashioned from 19¼-karat gold. Filigree is often used in depictions of caravels. Less expensive trinkets are often made of sterling silver, sometimes dipped in 24-karat gold.

Portugal is also famous for **Arraiolos carpets,** fine woolen rugs that have earned an international reputation. You can visit the little town of Arraiolos, in Alentejo. According to legend, Moorish craftsmen expelled from Lisbon in the early 16th century first made the rugs. The patterns were said to imitate Persian designs. Some Arraiolos carpets eventually find their way into museums.

SHOPPING A TO Z

ANTIQUES

Along both sides of the narrow **Rua de São José** in the Graça District are treasure troves of shops packed with antiques from all over the world. Antiques dealers from the United States come here to survey the wares. You'll find ornate spool and carved beds, high-back chairs, tables, wardrobes with ornate carving, brass plaques, copper pans, silver candelabra, crystal sconces, chandeliers, and a wide selection of wooden figures, silver boxes, porcelain plates, and bowls. But don't count on getting spectacular bargains.

Cavalo de Pau Set across the street from the Portuguese Parliament, on the street where fado diva Amalia Rodriguez used to live, this is a genuinely charming store that's loaded with antiques from Portugal and art objects from around the world. Look for elaborate baskets, sculptures, antique furniture, and gift items handcrafted in places like Brazil, Indonesia, Mozambique, and France, with an articulate sales staff that's ready, willing, and able to describe the provenance of each piece. Rua de São Bento 164. ✆ **21/396-66-05.** Tram: 28.

Santos & Marcos, Lda, Antiguidades This shop, a few steps from the Praça do Principe Real, stocks a noteworthy collection of 18th- and 19th-century paintings, furniture, and sculpture, some of it ecclesiastical in nature and some of it very unusual. The best pieces require permission from a government agency to leave the country; other less valuable pieces can be exported without hindrance. Rua Don Pedro V. ✆ **21/342-63-67.** Tram: 28.

Solar Rua Dom Pedro V is another street lined with antiques shops; this is our favorite. It's stocked with antique tiles salvaged from some of Portugal's historic buildings and manor houses. The condition of the tiles varies. Many date from the 15th century. The store also sells 18th- and 19th-century Portuguese ceramics and antique Portuguese furniture from different eras in varying price ranges. Rua Dom Pedro V 68–70. ✆ **21/346-55-22.** Metro: Restauradores. Bus: 58 or 100.

ART GALLERIES

EuroArte Many members of Iberia's emerging community of young painters exhibit here, and many others hope to. EuroArte's focus on contemporary art is roughly equivalent to that of the Galeria Yela (see below). Look for trends (often short-lived) and sometimes genuine value if you catch artists on the road to fame. Rua Rodrigo de Fonseca 107. ✆ **21/385-40-69.** Metro: Marquês de Pombal. Bus: 2 or 12.

Galeria 111 Operated by Manuel and Arlete de Brito since 1964, Galeria 111 is one of Lisbon's major art galleries. The wide-ranging exhibitions of sculpture, painting, and graphics include work by leading contemporary Portuguese artists. The gallery also sells drawings, etchings, silk screens, lithographs, art books, and postcards. It's closed August 4 to September 4. Campo Grande 113. ✆ **21/797-74-18.** Metro: Entre Campus. Bus: 1, 36, 38, or 88.

Galeria Sesimbra Near the Ritz Hotel, this is one of the city's leading art galleries, operated by one of the most distinguished art dealers in Iberia. It sells the finest Portuguese painting, sculpture, and ceramics. A moderately liberal purveyor of fine contemporary artwork, the gallery avoids displaying artists who might strike some buyers as too experimental and bizarre. The focus is on evocative pieces that appeal to the traditional tastes of upscale clientele. The work is mainly by Portuguese artists, plus foreign artists "who have lived in Portugal long enough to get a feeling for the country." The best-known works are Agulha tapestries, whose controlled variation of stitching makes them more desirable than those made on looms. Former U.S. President Jimmy Carter owns an Agulha tapestry. Rua Castilho 77. ✆ **21/387-02-91.** Metro: Marquês de Pombal. Bus: 2, 11, or 58.

Galeria Yela This showcase near the Ritz Hotel prides itself on its cutting-edge expositions of emerging Iberian artists. The EuroArte gallery (see above) is its only rival on the contemporary-art scene. Look for acrylics, drawings, and engravings, most of them avant garde in their focus and inspiration. Rua Rodrigo de Fonseca 103. ✆ **21/388-03-99.** Metro: Marquês de Pombal.

BASKETS

One of the best selections of Portuguese baskets is at the **Feira da Ladra** (see "Markets," below). Another good outlet is **Centro do Turismo e Artesanato** (see "Pottery & Ceramics," below).

BOOKS

Livraria Bertrand You'll find a good selection at Livraria Bertrand, which has the latest bestsellers (Grisham and the like), along with some English-language magazines, travel guides, and maps of Lisbon and Portugal. Rua Garrett 75. ✆ **21/346-86-46.** Metro: Chiado.

Livraria Britanic This shop across from the British Institute in the Bairro Alto stocks the best selection of English-language books in Lisbon. Livraria Britanic has a good collection of popular novels in English, along with reprints of some classics. Rua Luís Fernandes 14–16. ✆ **21/342-84-72.** Metro: Rato. Bus: 58 or 100.

Tabacaria Mónaco This narrow *tabacaria* (magazine and tobacco shop) opened in 1893 and has kept its original Art Nouveau look. Tiles from Rafael Bordalo Pinheiro and an adobe painting by Rosendo Carmalheira adorn the interior. You'll find a selection of international periodicals, guidebooks, and maps. Rossio 21. ✆ **21/346-81-91.** Metro: Rossio. Tram: 12, 20, or 28.

CHINA & GLASSWARE

Vista Alegre This company, founded in 1824, turns out some of the finest porcelain dinner services in the country. It also carries objets d'art and limited editions for collectors, and a range of practical day-to-day tableware. The government presents Vista Alegre pieces to European heads of state when they visit. Largo do Chiado 23. ✆ **21/346-14-01.** Metro: Chiado. Tram: 28.

CORK PRODUCTS

Casa das Cortiças For typically Portuguese souvenirs, try Casa das Cortiças. "Mr. Cork," the original owner, became somewhat of a legend in Lisbon for offering "everything conceivable" that could be made of cork (of which Portugal controls a hefty part of the world market). He's long gone, but the store carries on. A surprising number of items are made from cork, including a chess set and a checkers board. Rua da Escola Politécnica 4–6. ✆ **21/342-58-58.** Metro: Rato. Bus: 58.

CRYSTAL

Deposito da Mainha Grande This unpretentious store offers glass items created in the century-old Marinha Grande factory. The merchandise includes traditional *bico de Jacpues* (thick, patterned glass) service glasses, dishes, water pitchers, and salt and pepper shakers, as well as modern colored glass services. Other items include Atlantis crystal services and Vista Alegre porcelain. Atlantis crystal from Marinha Grande is renowned in Portugal, and there are some good buys here. You can purchase full services or individual pieces. Another branch is down the road at Rua de São Bento 418–420 (✆ 21/396-30-96). Rua de São Bento 234–242. ✆ **21/396-32-34.** Metro: Rato Bus: 6, 49, or 100.

EMBROIDERY

Casa Bordados da Madeira In the same building as the Hotel Avenida Palace, this establishment offers handmade embroideries from Madeira, Viana, and Lixa e Prado. If you want to place an order, the staff will mail it to you. In the winter, the store sells thick fisher's sweaters from Póvoa do Varzim. Rua do 1 de Dezembro 137. ✆ **21/342-14-47.** Metro: Restauradores. Bus: 1, 2, 36, or 44.

Casa Regional da Ilha Verde This shop in the Chiado specializes in handmade items, especially embroideries from the Azores—that's why it's called the Regional House of the Green Island. Each piece carries a made-by-hand guarantee. Some of the designs on the linen placemats with napkins have been in use for centuries. You can get some good buys here. Rua Paiva de Andrade 4. ✆ **21/342-59-74.** Metro: Chiado. Tram: 28.

Madeira House Madeira House specializes in high-quality regional cottons, linens, and gift items. Its other location in Lisbon is at Avenida da Liberdade 159 (✆ 21/315-15-58). Rua Augusta 131–135. ✆ **21/342-68-13.** Metro: Chiado. Tram: 28.

Príncipe Real Príncipe Real specializes in linens elegant enough to grace the tables of monarchs, including that of the late Princess Grace of Monaco. Owned by Cristina Castro and her son, Victor Castro, this store is one of the last that does artistic manual embroidery by order. It produces some of Europe's finest tablecloths and sheets in cotton, linen, and organdy. The owner-designer sells to famous names (the Rockefellers, Michael Douglas, the Kennedys, and many members of European royalty), but the merchandise is not beyond the means of the middle-class tourist. The shop's factory handles custom orders quickly and professionally. It employs 80 skilled workers who can execute a linen pattern to match a client's favorite porcelain or one of Cristina Castro's original designs. Rua da Escola Politécnica 12–14. ✆ **21/346-59-45.** Metro: Rato or Chiado. Bus: 58.

Teresa Alecrim This store bears the name of the owner, who creates refined embroideries in the style of Laura Ashley. You'll see sheets, pillowcases, towels, and bedcovers in plain and patterned cotton, plus monogrammed damask cotton hand towels. Rua Nova do Almada 76. ✆ **21/346-30-69.** Metro: Chiado. Tram: 28 or 28B. Bus: 2.

FADO RECORDINGS

Valentim de Carvalho This large, modern store carries a comprehensive roster of recordings by the country's most popular fado artists. If you want an introduction to Portugal's most enduring musical form, names to look for include Amalia Rodriguez, Nuno Câmara Pereira, Carlos Ducarmo, and Carlos Paredes. The Fado Capital series of CDs showcases at least three lesser-known *fadistas* on each recording.

Valentim de Carvalho carries books about the music world and English-language books in addition to music. On the ground floor, you'll find fado compact discs and LPs, Portuguese folk music, contemporary rock, and recordings by international artists in musical styles from classical to punk rock. Rua Ventu du Jesus Caraças 17. ✆ **21/324-97-50.** Metro: Baxia Chiado.

FASHION

Ana Salazar An internationally known name in fashion, Ana Salazar is the most avant-garde Portuguese designer of women's clothes. Known for her stretch fabrics, Salazar designs clothes that critics have called "body-conscious yet wearable." In addition to her main store, she has a branch at Avenida de Roma 16E (✆ 21/848-67-99). Rua do Carmo 87. ✆ **21/347-22-89.** Metro: Rossio. Bus: 21.

Laurenço y Santos One of Lisbon's most prominent menswear stores, Laurenço y Santos is a place where a concierge at a grand hotel might refer a well-dressed guest who needs to augment his wardrobe with anything from a business suit to a golf outfit. Praça dos Restauradores 47. ✆ **21/346-25-70.** Metro: Restauradores.

Rosa y Peixeira This is another prominent Lisbon store, similar to Laurenço y Santos, with a variety of men's clothing. Av. da Liberdade 204. ✆ **21/311-03-50.** Metro: Avenida.

LEATHER & SUEDE

Buckles & Company In a mirrored, wood-paneled setting, this store specializes in high-quality leather jackets, bags, and shoes, as well as women's clothing by national and foreign makers. The staff is knowledgeable. The store is accessible by train from Cais do Sodré. Benovo Comercial do Vestuareo Alea cascais, Estrada Nacional 9 (N9), near Estoril. ✆ **21/460-25-62.**

MARKETS

Feira da Ladra You can experience the fun of haggling for bargains. The open-air street market resembles the flea markets of Madrid and Paris. Nearly everything you can imagine is for sale. Vendors peddle their wares on Tuesday and Saturday; for the finest pickings, go in the morning. The market is about a 5-minute walk from the waterfront in the Alfama district. Start your browsing at Campo de Santa Clara. Portable stalls and individual displays climb the hilly street.

METALS

Casa Maciel Ltda Founded in 1810 as a specialized tinker shop that created the city's best lanterns and original cake molds, this house has distinguished itself in numerous national and international contests. You can select from the in-house patterns or have the artisans create pieces from your designs; the store will also ship items. Rua da Misericórdia 63–65. ✆ **21/342-24-51.** Metro: Chiado. Tram: 28. Bus: 10, 24, 29, or 30.

PORCELAIN

Many stores in Lisbon sell Portuguese porcelain—notably the landmark **Fábrica Viúva Lamego** (see "Tiles," below). **Deposito da Marinha Grande** (see "Crystal," above) carries a good selection of Vista Alegre porcelain.

POTTERY & CERAMICS

Centro do Turismo e Artesanato Here you'll find handcrafts, including pottery, ceramics, baskets, and embroidery. The good selection of pottery and ceramics includes items from all over Portugal. Worthwhile ceramic objects begin at around 7.50€ ($8.65) each, and some less significant objects (ashtrays, small vases, and the like) might begin at around 3.75€ ($4.30). The extensive clothing selection includes a Póvoa do Varzim sweater for between 25€ and 45€ ($29–$52) and a fisher's plaid shirt for 45€ ($52). The shop also stocks Portuguese wines and liqueurs ranging from 7.50€ to 100€ ($8.65–$115). Rua Castilho 61B. ✆ **21/386-38-30.** Metro: Rotunda. Tram: 25 or 26. Bus: 20, 22, 27, or 49.

SILVER, GOLD & FILIGREE

Joalharia do Carmo Nearly a century old, this is one of the best shops in Lisbon for filigree work. It stocks everything from simple, elegant pendants to models of fully rigged caravels fashioned entirely from thin strands of gold or silver (or both) woven together. All the silver pieces are handmade. Precious or semiprecious stones adorn some gold items. You'll also see platinum pieces, often in stunning designs. For the simplest items, such as bangles and earrings, prices start at around 25€ ($29), but most of the inventory is more valuable. Rua do Carmo 87B. ✆ **21/342-42-00.** Metro: Chiado. Bus: 21, 31, 36, or 41.

W. A. Sarmento At the foot of the Santa Justa elevator, W. A. Sarmento has been in the hands of the same family for well over a century. They are the most distinguished silver- and goldsmiths in Portugal, specializing in lacy filigree jewelry, including charm bracelets. The shop has been Lisboans' favorite place to buy treasured confirmation and graduation gifts, and its clientele includes Costa do Sol aristocracy as well as movie stars and diplomats. Rua Aurea 251. ✆ **21/347-07-83.** Metro: Chiado. Tram: 28 or 28B. Bus: 1, 21, 31, or 36.

SWEATERS

The vendors at the **Feira da Ladra** marketplace (see "Markets," above) sell a wide selection of Portuguese sweaters. You can also check out the selection at **Centro do Turismo e Artesanato** (see "Pottery & Ceramics," above). **Casa Bordados da Madeira** (see "Embroidery," above) carries a fine selection of Nazaré-style fisher's sweaters.

Casa do Turista This centrally located store stocks more than 2,000 handmade items from throughout Portugal. Regional clothing and accessories include sweaters from Póvoa do Varzim and traditional scarves from Minho. (The fabled fisher's sweaters of Nazaré are much more likely to be made in Póvoa do Varzim than in Nazaré.) Other items for sale include embroidered hand towels and napkins, tablecloths, ceramics, and straw baskets. Av. da Liberdade 159. ✆ **21/315-15-58.** Metro: Avenida. Bus: 1, 41, 42, 45, 44, or 46.

TILES

Fábrica Viúva Lamego Founded in 1879, this shop offers contemporary tiles—mostly reproductions of old Portuguese motifs—and pottery, including an interesting selection of bird and animal motifs. When you reach the store, you'll know you're at the right place: Its facade is decorated with colorful glazed tiles. Largo do Intendente 25. ✆ **21/885-24-08.** Metro: Intendente. Tram: 28. Bus: 8.

Sant'Anna Founded in 1741 in the Chiado district, Sant'Anna is Portugal's leading ceramic center. It's famous for its glazed tiles. You can also visit the factory at Calçada da Boa Hora 96 (✆ **21/363-82-92**), but you must telephone ahead for an appointment. The artisans who create some of the handmade designs are among the finest in Europe, and many of them employ designs in use since the Middle Ages. Rua do Alecrim 95–97. ✆ **21/342-25-37.** Metro: Estação do Cais do Sodré or Chiado. Tram: 28.

9 Lisbon After Dark

If you have only 1 night in Lisbon, spend it at a fado club. The nostalgic sounds of fado, Portuguese "songs of sorrow," are at their best in Lisbon—the capital attracts the greatest *fadistas* (fado singers) in the world. Fado is high art in Portugal, so don't plan to carry on a private conversation during a show—it's bad form. Most of the authentic fado clubs cluster in the Bairro Alto and in the Alfama, between St. George's Castle and the docks. You can "fado hop" between the two quarters. If you're visiting the Alfama, have the taxi driver let you off at **Largo do Chafariz,** a small plaza a block from the harbor; in the Bairro Alto, get off at **Largo de São Roque.** Most of the places we recommend lie only a short walk away.

Moments Fado: The Music of Longing

The *saudade* (Portuguese for "longing" or "nostalgia") that infuses the country's literature is most evident in fado. The traditional songs express Portugal's sad, romantic mood. The traditional performers are women (*fadistas*), often accompanied by a guitar and a viola.

Experiencing the nostalgic sounds of fado is essential to apprehending the Portuguese soul. Fado is Portugal's most vivid art form; no visit to the country is complete without at least 1 night spent in a local tavern listening to this traditional folk music.

A rough translation of *fado* is "fate," from the Latin *fatum* (prophecy). Fado songs usually tell of unrequited love, jealousy, or a longing for days gone by. The music, as is often said, evokes a "life commanded by the Oracle, which nothing can change."

Fado became famous in the 19th century when Maria Severa, the beautiful daughter of a gypsy, took Lisbon by storm. She sang her way into the hearts of the people of Lisbon—especially the count of Vimioso, an outstanding bullfighter. Present-day fadistas wear a black-fringed shawl in her memory.

The most famous 20th-century exponent of fado was Amalia Rodriguez, who was introduced to American audiences in the 1950s at the New York club La Vie en Rose. Born into a simple Lisbon family, she was discovered while walking barefoot and selling flowers on the Lisbon docks near the Alfama. For many she is the most famous Portuguese figure since Vasco da Gama. Swathed in black, sparing of gestures and excess ornamentation, Rodriguez almost single-handedly executed the transformation of fado into an international form of poetic expression.

Fado outshines all other nighttime entertainment in Lisbon. For a change of pace and more information about nighttime attractions, go to the tourist office (see "Visitor Information," in chapter 3) which maintains a list of events. Another helpful source is the **Agência de Bilhetes para Espectáculos Públicos** in Praça dos Restauradores (✆ **21/346-11-89**). It's open daily from 9am to 9:30pm; go in person instead of trying to call. The agency sells tickets to most theaters and cinemas.

Also consult a copy of ***What's On in Lisbon*** or ***Your Companion in Portugal,*** available at most newsstands. You might also consult *Sete,* a weekly magazine with entertainment listings, or the free monthly guides *Agenda Cultural* and *LISBOaem.* Your hotel concierge is also a good bet for information because one of his or her duties is reserving seats. The local newspaper, *Diário de Noticias,* carries all cultural listings, but only in Portuguese.

By the standards of the United States and Canada, "the party" in Lisbon begins late. Many bars don't even open until 10 or 11pm, and very few savvy young Portuguese would set foot in a club before 1am. The Bairro Alto, with some 150 restaurants and bars, is the most happening place after dark.

THE PERFORMING ARTS

CLASSICAL MUSIC

Museu da Fundação Calouste Gulbenkian From October through June, concerts, recitals, and occasionally ballet performances take place here; sometimes there are also jazz concerts. Av. de Berna 45. ✆ **21/782-30-00.** Metro: Sebastião. Bus: 26, 31, 46, or 56.

OPERA & BALLET

Teatro Nacional de São Carlos The Teatro Nacional de São Carlos attracts opera and ballet aficionados from all over Europe. Top companies from around the world perform at the 18th-century theater. The season begins in mid-September and extends through July. There are no special discounts. Rua Serpa Pinto 9. ✆ **21/325-30-30.** Tickets 25€–63€ ($29–$72). Box office Mon-Fri 1–7pm. Tram: 6, 28, or 28B. Bus: 46.

THEATER

Teatro Nacional de Dona Maria II At the most famous theater in Portugal, the season usually begins in the autumn and lasts through spring. It presents a repertoire of both Portuguese and foreign plays, with performances strictly in Portuguese. Praça de Dom Pedro IV. ✆ **21/342-22-10.** Tickets 2.50€–15€ ($2.90–$17) 50% discount for students up to 25 years old with valid ID. Metro: Rossio. Bus: 21, 31, 36, or 41.

THE CLUB & MUSIC SCENE

FADO CLUBS

In the clubs listed below, it isn't necessary to have dinner; you can just have a drink. However, you often have to pay a minimum consumption charge. The music begins between 9 and 10pm, but it's better to arrive after 11pm. Many clubs stay open until 3am; others stay open until dawn.

Adega Machado This spot has passed the test of time and is one of the country's favorite fado clubs. Alternating with such modern-day *fadistas* as the critically acclaimed Marina Rosa are folk dancers whirling, clapping, and singing native songs in colorful costumes. Dinner is a la carte, and the cuisine is mostly Portuguese, with a number of regional dishes. Expect to spend 25€ to 30€ ($29–$35) for a complete meal. The dinner hour starts at 8pm, music begins at

9:15pm, and the doors don't close until 3am. It's open Tuesday through Sunday. Rua do Norte 91. ✆ **21/347-05-50.** Cover (including 2 drinks) 16€ ($18). AE, DC, MC, V. Bus: 58 or 100.

A Severa Good food and the careful selection of *fadistas* make this a perennial favorite. Every night, top male and female singers appear, accompanied by guitar and viola music, alternating with folk dancers. In a niche, you'll spot a statue honoring the club's namesake, Maria Severa, the legendary 19th-century gypsy fadista. As difficult or as unsettling as it might be to imagine, before Richard Nixon became U.S. president, he came here with his wife, Patricia, and led a congalike line between tables while warbling the refrain, "Severa . . . Severa . . . Severa." After midnight, tourists seem to recede a bit in favor of loyal habitués, who request and sometimes join in on their favorite fado number (though not usually forming Nixonian conga lines).

The kitchen turns out regional dishes based on recipes from the north of Portugal. Expect to spend at least 35€ ($40) per person for a meal with wine. It's open daily from 8pm to 3:30am. Rua das Gaveas 51. ✆ **21/346-40-06.** Cover (including 2 drinks) 18€ ($20). AE, DC, MC, V. Bus: 20 or 24.

Luso In a vaulted network of 17th-century stables, Luso is one of the most famous and enduring fado clubs of the Bairro Alto. Despite a recent trend toward the touristy, it still exerts a folkloric appeal, as it has since it was transformed into a restaurant with music in the 1930s. The entertainment and regional food are presented most nights to some 160 patrons. Full dinners are served, costing from 35€ ($40). It's open Monday through Saturday from 8pm to 2am; the show runs from 9pm to 2am. Travessa da Queimada 10. ✆ **21/342-22-81.** Cover (including 2 drinks) 20€ ($23). AE, DC, MC, V. Bus: 58 or 100.

Parreirinha da Alfama Every *fadista* worth her shawl seems to have sung at this old-time cafe, just a minute's walk from the docks of the Alfama. It's fado only here, not folk dancing, and the place has survived more or less unchanged since its establishment in the early 1950s. In the first part of the program, fadistas get the popular songs out of the way and then settle into their more classic favorites. You can order a good regional dinner for around 25€ ($29), although many visitors opt to come here just to drink. It's open daily from 8:30pm to 1am; music begins at 9:30pm. The atmosphere is a lot more convivial after around 10:30pm, when local stars (who include such luminaries and divas as Lina Maria) have warmed up the crowd a bit. Beco do Espírito Santo 1. ✆ **21/886-82-09.** Cover (credited toward drinks) 10€ ($12). AE, MC, V. Bus: 9, 39, or 46.

COFFEEHOUSES

To the Portuguese, the coffeehouse is an institution, a democratic parlor where they can drop in for their favorite libation, abandon their worries, relax, smoke, read the paper, write a letter, or chat with friends about tomorrow's football match.

The coffeehouse in Portugal, however, is now but a shade of its former self. The older and more colorful places, filled with turn-of-the-century charm, are rapidly yielding to chrome and plastic.

One of the oldest surviving coffeehouses in Lisbon, **A Brasileira,** Rua Garrett 120 (✆ **21/346-95-41;** Metro: Rossio), lies in the Chiado district. It has done virtually nothing to change the opulent but faded Art Nouveau decor that has prevailed since it became a fashionable rendezvous in 1905. Once a gathering place of Lisbon's literati, it was the favored social spot of the Portuguese poet

Moments Port Wine Tasting

Solar do Vinho do Porto (✆ 21/347-57-07) is devoted exclusively to the drinking and enjoyment of port in all its glory and varieties. A quasi-governmental arm of the Port Wine Institute established the bar a few years after World War II as a low-key merchandizing tool. In a 300-year-old setting near the Glória funicular and the fado clubs of the Bairro Alto, it exudes Iberian atmosphere. The *lista de vinhos* includes more than 200 types of port wine in an amazing variety of sweet, dry, red, and white. A glass of wine costs 1€ to 23€ ($1.15–$26). Open Monday through Saturday from 2pm to midnight, it's located at Rua de São Pedro de Alcântara 45 (Metro: Restauradores; bus: 58 or 100.)

Bocage of Setúbal, whose works are read by high school students throughout Portugal. He was involved in an incident that has since been elevated into Lisbon legend: When accosted by a bandit who asked him where he was going, he is said to have replied, "I am going to the Brasileira, but if you shoot me I am going to another world." Patrons sit at small tables on chairs made of tooled leather, amid mirrored walls and marble pilasters. A statue of the great Portuguese poet Fernando Pessoa sits on a chair amid the customers. At a table, sandwiches run 2.20€ to 2.50€ ($2.55–$2.90), pastries are 1.25€ to 2.50€ ($1.45–$2.90), a demitasse costs 1€ to 2€ ($1.15–$2.30), and bottled beer goes for 1.75€ to 2.50€ ($2–$2.90). Prices are a bit lower at the bar, but you'll probably want to linger a while—we recommend sitting down to recover from the congestion and heat. It's open daily from 8am to midnight and accepts cash only.

Although lacking A Brasileira's tradition and style, the **Pastelaria Suiça,** on the south corner of Praça de Dom Pedro IV in the Baixa (✆ **21/321-40-90**), is a sprawling cafe-pastelaria. It stretches all the way back to the adjoining Praça da Figueira. This house draws more visitors than any other cafe in Lisbon. The outdoor tables fill first, especially in fair weather. In addition to serving an array of coffee and tea, the pastelaria is known for its tempting pastries baked on-site. The atmosphere is boisterous, and the place is generally mobbed. It's open daily from 7am to 9pm.

Another possibility is **Versailles,** Avenida da República 15 (✆ **21/354-63-40**), long known as the grande dame of Lisbon coffeehouses. It's also an ideal place for afternoon tea, in a faded but elegant 60-year-old setting of chandeliers, gilt mirrors, and high ceilings. As an old-fashioned and formal touch, immaculately attired waiters serve customers from silver-plated tea services. In addition to coffee and tea, the house specialty is hot chocolate. The homemade cakes and pastries are delectable. (They're baked on-site.) It's open daily from 7am to 10pm.

DANCE CLUBS & LIVE MUSIC

The Bar of the Café Alcântara Although this establishment draws most of its business from its sophisticated restaurant (see the Café Alcântara in "Where to Dine," in chapter 3), many club-hoppers come here only for the bar. It's in a former factory and warehouse beside the river, decorated with accessories that evoke a railway car in turn-of-the-20th-century Paris. The patrons—Americans, Portuguese, English, Germans, and Brazilians—aren't shy about striking up dialogues with attractive newcomers. Draft beer in the bar begins at 2.50€ ($2.90);

imported whisky sells for 6€ ($6.90) and up. Expect lots of deliberately provocative outrageousness, gay customers mingling with straights, and sometimes one of the highest percentages of flamboyant drag queens in Lisbon. It's open nightly from 8pm to 3am. Rua Maria Luisa Holstein 15. ✆ **21/363-71-76.** No cover. Bus: 12 or 18.

Blues Café You'll probably like this place (as we do), even though it has very little to do with blues music and doesn't even remotely resemble a cafe. It's in a publike space on the river; an eagle's-nest balcony circles around one floor. Docks (see below) is next door, and there's a restaurant that serves late-night platters of uncomplicated Portuguese food. Rather than blues, the patrons, usually in their 20s to early 30s, prefer the latest hip-hop and garage music. Beer costs 3€ to 4.50€ ($3.45–$5.20) a bottle. It's open Monday through Thursday from 8:30pm to 4am, and Friday and Saturday from 8:30pm to 6am. Rua Cintura do Puerto do Lisboa 3-4. ✆ **21/395-70-85.** Cover 50€ ($57) if full; otherwise free. Tram: 15.

Docks As its name implies, this place is on the Tagus, with windows overlooking the river. Sophisticated and stylish, with one of the most beautiful interiors in the neighborhood, it attracts a 30-something clientele. The club has vaguely nautical decor and one busy floor that's ringed, amphitheater-style, with a circular mezzanine overlooking the action below. Beer costs around 3€ ($3.45) a bottle, and recorded music plays in ways that sometimes gets people up and dancing. It's open Tuesday through Saturday from 11:30pm to 6am. Av. do 24 de Julio, at Centro Mare. ✆ **21/395-08-56.** Cover 15€ ($17) if full; otherwise free. Tram: 15.

Kapital Next to the docks of the Tagus, this dance club and bar appeals to one of the widest socioeconomic ranges of Portuguese society. You're likely to find surprisingly elite patrons rubbing elbows with regular folks. Detractors claim that Kapital is for people with money or for rich wannabes; still, it can be a whole lot of fun, especially if you limit your visit to a single night so that the novelty doesn't wear off. In the animated dance floor on the ground level, the music is loud, sometimes experimental, danceable, and up-to-date. The second floor contains a central bar surrounded by rows of comfortable chairs and sofas; the third floor has another dance floor with predominantly 1980s dance music. The cover charge varies widely depending on whether the doorman thinks you're cool, well-dressed, or rich-looking enough. It's open Tuesday through Saturday from 11:30pm till dawn; Tuesday night is least crowded. Av. do 24 de Julio 68. ✆ **21/395-71-01.** Cover 5€–50€ ($5.75–$58). Tram: 15. Bus: 6, 28, 43, 49, or 60.

Lux Popular, free-form, and hip, this two-story warehouse contains a labyrinth of interconnected spaces, each of which is likely to feature a radically different scene from the one in the room that's immediately adjacent. Set on the banks of the Tagus, a short walk from the Santa Apolónia railway station, it attracts and amuses counterculture hipsters with theatrical lighting, deep sofas, cutting-edge music, and some highly unusual accessories—one of them is an enormous chandelier composed entirely of steel wire and tampons. Expect this and other forms of offbeat humor, and an ambience that might remind you of a be-in from the 1960s. The upstairs bar, where a DJ spins records, is open daily from 10pm to 6am. The more manic, street-level dance floor is open Thursday through Saturday from 1am to 7am. Entrance to both areas is free before midnight; after that, there is a 12€ ($14) cover, although there might be a doorman with a velvet rope/barrier keeping out rowdies on weekends. Ave. Infante Don Henrique, Armazen (Warehouse) A, Cais da Pedra a Sta. Apolónia. ✆ **21/882-08-90.** Bus: 9, 39, or 46.

Plateau Near the Kapital (see above), this is a 1-story nightclub with a confetti-colored decor and a mixed clientele. The elite mingle with everyday folk who are just looking for love and good music. What you see is what you get—comfortable seating, cooperative bartenders skilled at mixing anything you can think of, and an appealing mixture of rock 'n' roll, garage, hip-hop, and, on rare occasions, even reggae. Surprisingly, the place is less dance oriented than you might think—many patrons come to watch and listen, not to boogie. It's open Tuesday through Saturday from midnight to 4:30am. Escadinhas da Praia 7. ✆ **21/396-51-16.** Cover 5€ ($5.75). Tram: 15.

THE BAR SCENE

Bachus This restaurant offers one of the capital's most convivial watering spots. Surrounded by oriental carpets, bronze statues, intimate lighting, and polite uniformed waiters, you can hobnob with some of the most glamorous people in Lisbon. Late-night candlelit suppers are served in the bar. The array of drinks is international; prices start at 3.50€ ($4.05). It's open Monday through Saturday from noon to 3:30am. Largo da Trindade 9. ✆ **21/342-28-28.** Bus: 58 or 100.

Bar do Rio Set directly on a battered-looking quay on the Tagus within what used to be a warehouse, a short walk past grimy piers from the Cais do Sodré railway station, this is a fashionable nightspot that's known as a cutting-edge hideaway for ultra-late-night hipsters. You'll recognize it by its lemon-yellow entrance and by bright lights that make it a landmark in this otherwise dimly lit neighborhood. Some of the DJs who organize the music featured here have become minor celebrities within the counterculture world of late-night Lisbon. It's open Wednesday through Sunday from 11pm to at least 4am. Cais do Sodré 7, Armazém A. ✆ **21/342-95-23.** Cover: 5€ ($5.75). Bus: 44 or 45.

Bora-Bora A Polynesian bar might seem out of place in Lisbon, but the theme draws packs of locals who are tired of a constant diet of Iberian folklore. As you might expect from an urban bar with a Hawaiian theme, Bora-Bora specializes in imaginative variations on fruity, flaming, and rum-laced drinks. The couches are comfortable and inviting, angled for views of the Polynesian art that lines the walls. Beer costs 4€ ($4.60); mixed drinks are 6€ ($6.90) and up. It's open Friday and Saturday from 9pm to 3am. Rua da Madalena 201. ✆ **21/887-20-43.** Metro: Rossio. Tram: 12 or 28.

Indochina Best defined as a "night bar," Indochina doesn't try to compete with other clubs that emphasize danceable, recently released music. The comfortable seats invariably encourage conversation among patrons both gay and straight. The atmosphere is generally calmer, gentler, and softer than the hard-edged danceteria modes of some nearby competitors. There's an Asian restaurant on the premises, but most people come here just to drink and judge who's looking the most chic. It's open Thursday through Saturday from 11:30pm till dawn. Rua Cintura Do Porto do Lisboa, Armazen H. ✆ **21/395-58-75.** Cover 15€ ($17). Tram: 15.

Panorama Bar The Panorama Bar occupies the top floor of one of Portugal's tallest buildings, the 30-story Lisboa Sheraton. The view (day or night) is of the old and new cities of Lisbon, the mighty Tagus, and many of the towns on the river's far bank. The cosmopolitan decor incorporates chiseled stone and stained glass. You'll pay 8.50€ to 10€ ($9.80–$12) for a whisky and soda. It's open daily from 6pm to 2am. In the Lisboa Sheraton Hotel, Rua Latino Coelho 1. ✆ **21/357-57-57.** Metro: Picoas. Bus: 1, 2, 9, or 32.

Pavilhão Chines The mother of all flea market bars, this mostly heterosexual watering hole in the Bairro Alto contains a collection of kitsch that alone is worth the trek here. Replicas of everyone from Buddha to Popeye decorate the joint, along with bronze cupids, Toby tankards, baubles and beads, and enough Victoriana to fill half the attics of London. It's a lively venue open Monday through Friday from 5pm to 2am, and Saturday from 6pm to 2am. Dom Pedro V. 89. ✆ **21/342-47-29.** Metro: Rato.

Portas Largas This bar, retaining many of its original accessories, originated many years ago as an old-fashioned Portuguese *tasca* (tavern). Today, attracting clients of all sexual persuasions, it's the busiest and most animated bar in a neighborhood that's loaded with viable competitors. It sits at the junction of two narrow, bar-studded streets (Rua da Atalaia and the Travessa da Queimada) in the Bairro Alto and enjoys sweeping views out over the nightlife scene that unfolds around it. You'll find a mixture of gay and straight people from Portugal and the rest of Europe, several hundred of whom usually spill out onto the impossibly narrow sidewalks on warm nights. Expect lots of good-looking gay men, as well as attractive women (straight and gay) dressed for whatever dance or disco venue they expect to pursue later in the evening. It's open daily from 7pm to 3:30am. Rua da Atalaia 105. ✆ **21/346-63-79.** Metro: Baixa Chiado. Tram: 28.

Procópio Bar A longtime favorite of journalists, politicians, and foreign actors, the once-innovative Procópio has become a tried-and-true staple among Lisbon's watering holes. Guests sit on tufted red velvet, surrounded by stained and painted glass and ornate brass hardware. Mixed drinks cost 5€ ($5.75) and up; beer costs 3€ ($3.45) and up. Procópio might easily become your favorite bar, if you can find it. It lies just off Rua de João Penha, which is off the landmark Praça das Amoreiras. It's open Monday through Saturday from 6pm to 3am. Alto de São Francisco 21. ✆ **21/385-28-51.** Closed Aug 11–Sept 8. Metro: Rato. Bus: 9.

GAY & LESBIAN BARS & CLUBS

Although this ultra-Catholic country remains one of the most closeted in Western Europe, at least eight gay nightspots have sprung up in the district known as Príncipe Real. With each passing year, the gay presence in Lisbon becomes more visible. You might begin your night crawl at either of the first two establishments listed below.

Agua no Bico At the eastern edge of the Bairro Alto, this bar and dance club combines aspects of an English pub with the futuristic trappings of a gay club. It's marked by a discreet brass plaque on a steeply sloping street lined with 18th-century villas. The young crowd sometimes remains after the "official" 2am closing for all-male porn flicks. Beer prices start at 2€ ($2.30); whisky and soda goes for 3.50€ ($4.05) or more. We recommend that you take a taxi here because public transport in this neighborhood is difficult at night. A medieval folk tale inspired the name (Water in the Beak). If you're curious, ask one of the handsome bartenders to recite the original story. It's open nightly from 9pm to 2am. Rua de São Marçal 170. ✆ **21/347-28-30.** No cover. Bus: 15, 58, or 100.

Bar 106 Set midway between the also-recommended Finalmente and Agua non Bico, a short walk from them both, this is a popular bar, rendezvous point, and watering hole for gay men, most of whom arrive here after around 10pm. Expect a simple, restrained decor, a busy bar area, and enough space to allow subgroups and cliques of like-minded friends to form quickly and easily. It's open nightly from 9pm till 2am. Rua de São Marçal 106. ✆ **21/342-73-73.** Tram: 28 or 100.

Finalmente Club This is the dance club that many gay men in Lisbon end up at after an evening of drinking and talking in other bars around the Bairro Alto. There's a hard-working, hard-drinking bar area; a crowded dance floor; lots of bodies of all shapes and sizes; and a small stage upon which drag shows allow local *artistes* to strut their stuff and emulate—among others—Carmen look-alikes from Sevilla. A stringent security system requires that you ring a bell before an attendant will let you in. It's open daily from 1am to between 3 and 6am, depending on business. Rua de Palmeira 38. ✆ **21/347-99-23.** Cover: 5€ ($4.50), including first drink. Bus: 100.

Frágil Don't expect a sign that indicates the location of this place: All you'll see are some blue neon lights and a vigilant doorman. Frágil devotes itself to counterculture music, gay men and women, and a scattering of heterosexuals who appreciate the cutting-edge music and permissive context. Technically, the place opens nightly at 11pm, but don't expect a crowd until at least midnight—and a mob by around 3am. Closing is around 6am the following morning. Rua da Atalaia 126–128. ✆ **21/346-95-78.** Cover 8€–75€ ($9.20–$86). Bus: 58 or 100.

Memorial Bar In the narrow streets of the Bairro Alto, the Memorial Bar is well known to the city's lesbian community. Around 60% of its patrons are women—the remainder are gay men. Twice a week (days vary), the joint features live entertainment—including comedy, cross-dressing shticks, or live Portuguese musicians. A beer costs 2.50€ ($2.90). It's open Tuesday through Sunday from 11pm to 4am. (Dance music begins at midnight.) Rua Gustavo de Matos Sequeira 42A. ✆ **21/396-88-91.** Cover 5€ ($5.75). Bus: 58 or 100.

Queens This nightclub, in a cavernous, industrial-looking building near the Tagus, is larger than any of its nearby competitors. The sophisticated sound system floods the enormous dance floor with late-breaking music. Most of the crowd is male and under 35. It's open Monday through Saturday from 11pm till 6am. Rua de Cintura do Porto de Lisboa, Armazém (Warehouse) 8, Naves A&B, Doca de Alcântara Norte. ✆ **21/395-58-70.** Cover 10€ ($12). Tram: 14 or 15.

Trumps Of the several bars recommended within this nightlife section, this is the one with the most whimsical staff and the most erratic opening hours. Known to local English-speaking wits as Tramps, it's positioned near (but not in) the Bairro Alto. Several bars are scattered throughout its two levels, along with an active dance floor and lots of cruising options within its shadowy corners. Lesbians make up about a quarter of the crowd, but most of the patrons here are gay males. In theory, this place is open Thursday through Saturday from 11:30pm to 6am, but because of some recent problems, even that isn't terribly reliable. ***Our advice:*** Hang out at Finalmente, Portas Largas, or Frágil, and ask one of the regular patrons there about the opening hours and ongoing viability of Trumps. Rua da Imprensa Nacional 104B. ✆ **21/397-10-59.** Cover (credited toward drinks) 10€ ($12). Bus: 58.

5

Estoril, Cascais & Sintra

Lured by Guincho (near the westernmost point in continental Europe), the Boca do Inferno (Mouth of Hell), and Lord Byron's "glorious Eden" at Sintra, many travelers spend much of their time in the area around Lisbon. You could spend a day drinking in the wonders of the library at the monastery-palace of Mafra (Portugal's El Escorial), dining in the pretty pink rococo palace at Queluz, or enjoying seafood at the Atlantic beach resort of Ericeira.

However, the main draw in the area is the Costa do Sol. The string of beach resorts, including Estoril and Cascais, forms the Portuguese Riviera on the northern bank of the mouth of the Tagus. If you arrive in Lisbon when the sun is shining and the air is balmy, consider heading straight for the shore. Estoril is so near to Lisbon that darting in and out of the capital to see the sights or visit the fado clubs is easy. An inexpensive electric train leaves from the Cais do Sodré station in Lisbon frequently throughout the day and evening; its run ends in Cascais.

Although the beachfront strip of the Costa do Sol is justifiably famous, it's generally recommended that you swim in the pools (indoor or outdoor) at the resort hotels. For the most part, the waters along the coast are polluted and, therefore, not recommended for swimming. Despite this, the beaches are still great for getting a suntan.

The sun coast is sometimes known as A Costa dos Reis, the Coast of Kings because it's a magnet for deposed royalty—exiled kings, pretenders, marquesses from Italy, princesses from Russia, and baronesses from Germany. Some live simply, as did the late Princess Elena of Romania (Magda Lupescu), a virtual recluse in an unpretentious villa. Others insist on a rigid court atmosphere, as did Umberto, who was king of Italy for 1 month in 1946 and then was forced into exile. Other nobles who settled here include Princess Elena of Romania; Don Juan, the count of Barcelona, who lost the Spanish throne in 1969 when his son, Don Juan Carlos, was named successor by Generalissimo Franco; Joanna, the former queen of Bulgaria; and the Infanta Dona Maria Adelaide de Bragança, sister of the pretender to the Portuguese throne.

Despite the heavy concentration of royals, the Riviera is a microcosm of Portugal. Take a ride out on the train, even if you don't plan to stay here. You'll pass pastel-washed houses with red-tile roofs and facades of antique blue-and-white tiles; miles of modern apartment dwellings; rows of canna, pine, mimosa, and eucalyptus; swimming pools; and, in the background, green hills studded with villas, chalets, and new homes.

Lisbon is the aerial gateway for the Costa do Sol and Sintra. Once in Lisbon, you can drive or take public transportation.

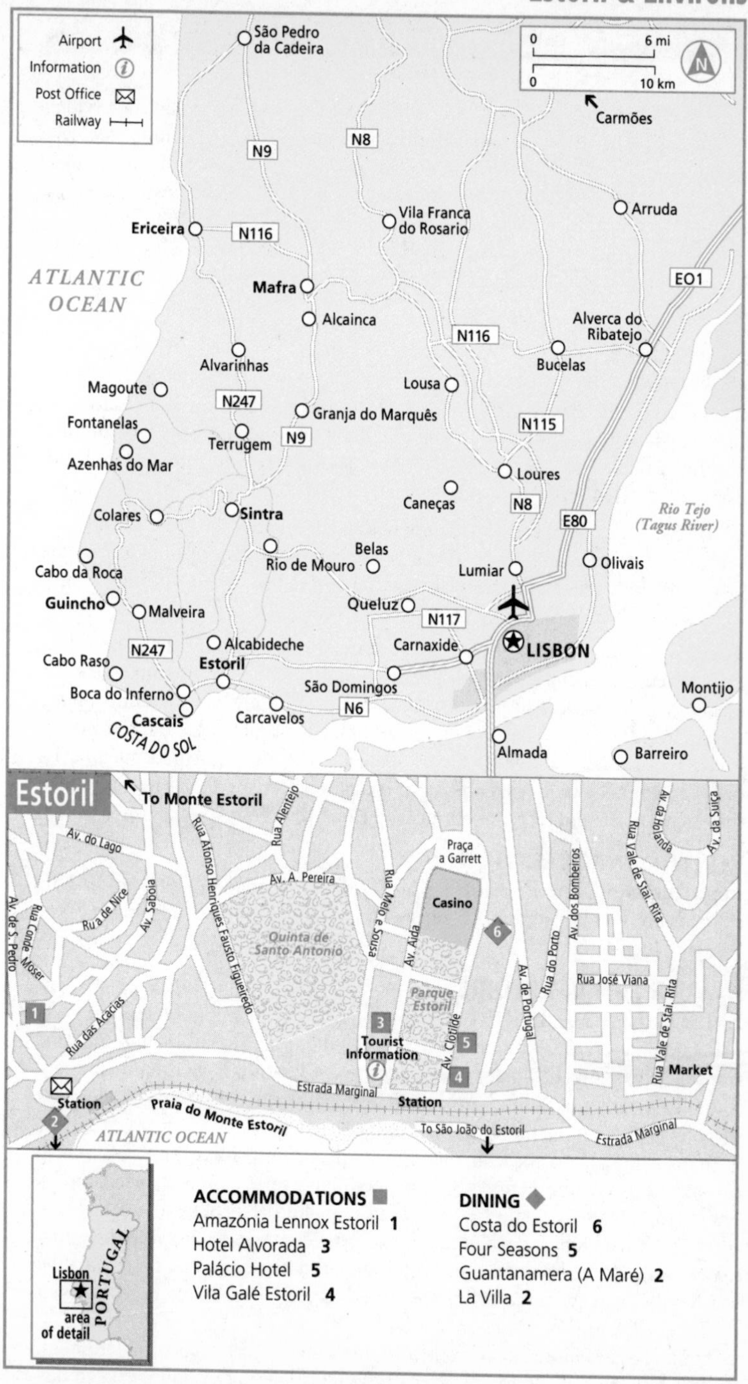

Airport
Information
Post Office
Railway
0 6 mi
0 10 km
N
Carmões
São Pedro da Cadeira
N9
N8
Ericeira
N116
Vila Franca do Rosario
Arruda
ATLANTIC OCEAN
Mafra
Alcainca
EO1
N116
Alverca do Ribatejo
Alvarinhas
Bucelas
Magoute
N247
Lousa
Granja do Marquês
Fontanelas
N115
Terrugem
N9
Azenhas do Mar
Loures
Caneças
N8
Colares
Sintra
E80
Rio Tejo (Tagus River)
Belas
Cabo da Roca
Rio de Mouro
Lumiar
Olivais
Guincho
Malveira
Queluz
N117
Alcabideche
Carnaxide
LISBON
Cabo Raso
N247
Estoril
São Domingos
Montijo
Boca do Inferno
Cascais
Carcavelos
N6
COSTA DO SOL
Almada
Barreiro
Estoril
To Monte Estoril
Av. do Lago
Rua Alentejo
Rua Afonso Henriques Fausto Figueiredo
Praça a Garrett
Av. da Holanda
Av. da Suiça
Rua Vale de Stai. Rita
Av. dos Bombeiros
Av. A. Pereira
Rua Melo e Sousa
Casino
Rua de Nice
Av. Saboia
Av. de S. Pedro
Rua Conde Moser
Quinta de Santo Antonio
Av. Aida
Av. de Portugal
Rua do Porto
Rua José Viana
Rua Vale de Stai. Rita
Parque Estoril
Rua das Acacias
Tourist Information
Av. Clotilde
Market
Estrada Marginal
Station
Station
Praia do Monte Estoril
ATLANTIC OCEAN
To São João do Estoril
Estrada Marginal
Lisbon
area of detail
PORTUGAL
ACCOMMODATIONS
Amazónia Lennox Estoril 1
Hotel Alvorada 3
Palácio Hotel 5
Vila Galé Estoril 4
DINING
Costa do Estoril 6
Four Seasons 5
Guantanamera (A Maré) 2
La Villa 2

1 Estoril: Playground of Royalty ★

13km (8 miles) S of Sintra, 24km (15 miles) W of Lisbon

This chic resort with its beautiful beaches along the Portuguese Riviera has long basked in its reputation as a playground of monarchs. Fading countesses arrive at the railway station, monarchs in exile drop in at the Palácio Hotel for dinner, and the sons of deposed dictators sunbathe by the pool. Today's Estoril was the creation of Fausto Figueiredo, who built the deluxe Palácio in 1930. The casino opened in the late 1960s. During World War II, as Nazi troops advanced across Europe, many collapsed courts fled to Estoril to wait out the war in a neutral country.

ESSENTIALS

ARRIVING

BY TRAIN Electric trains leave from the waterfront Cais do Sodré station in Lisbon. The round-trip fare is 2.50€ ($2.90), and departures are every 20 minutes for the half-hour trip. Trains operate daily from 7am to 1am. For information, call ✆ **21/486-41-65.**

BY BUS Buses from Lisbon are impractical, considering the low cost and convenience of the frequent trains. But if you're coming to Estoril from Sintra, the bus is your best bet; about a dozen buses a day make the 1-hour run. The round-trip fare is 2.30€ ($2.65).

BY CAR From Lisbon, head west on Route 6; try to avoid driving on weekends, when there's considerable traffic in both directions. Driving time depends on traffic, which tends to be heavy almost day and night. It's lightest Monday through Friday from 10am to 4pm. Rush hours are brutal, as is the rush to the beach on Saturday and Sunday before 10am and the rush back to Lisbon on Saturday and Sunday between 4 and 6pm. It might be easier on your nerves to take the electric train and forget about driving along the coast.

VISITOR INFORMATION

Junta Turismo Costa do Estoril is at Arcadas do Parque (✆ **21/466-38-13**), across from the train station. It's open Monday through Saturday 9am to 7pm, Sunday 10am to 6pm.

HAVING FUN IN ESTORIL

EXPLORING THE RESORT Parque Estoril, in the center of town, is a well-manicured landscape. At night, when it's floodlit, you can stroll amid the subtropical vegetation. The palm trees studding the grounds have prompted many to call it "a corner of Africa." At the top of the park sits the casino, which offers gambling, international floor shows, dancing, and movies.

Across the railroad tracks is the beach, where some of the most fashionable people in Europe sun themselves on peppermint-striped canvas chairs along the Praia Estoril Tamariz. The beach is sandy, unlike the pebbly strand at Nice. Although it is a lovely stretch of sand, we don't recommend going into the water, which is almost too polluted for swimming. You can enjoy the sands and the beach scene, but for actual swimming, head to one of the many hotel pools in the area.

Tamariz draws more gay patrons than any other beach in Portugal, although the beach in general has a little bit of everything. The gay section is easy to discern; as one beach buff said, "It's easy. Just gravitate to the section with the most pumped-up bodies."

To the east is São João do Estoril, which also has a regrettably polluted beach but many handsome private villas. Most visitors go there to dine and dance.

OUTDOOR ACTIVITIES Other than the beach, the big activity here is golf. A fixture in Estoril since 1940, **Clube de Golf do Estoril,** Avenida da República (✆ **21/468-01-76**), lies in the foothills of Sintra, a 3-minute drive from the casino at Estoril. The course, one of the finest in Europe, has played host to international championship matches. The club has a 9-hole course and an 18-hole course. Monday through Friday, nonmembers can play 18 holes for 51€ ($59). Saturday and Sunday are reserved for members of the club or guests of the Palácio Hotel (see below), who pay 16€ ($18) Monday through Friday and 30€ ($35) on weekends.

The most modern complex of tennis courts in town, shared by most of the city's major resorts, is the **Clube de Tenis do Estoril,** Avenida Conte de Barcelona (✆ **21/466-27-70**). It offers more than 20 tennis courts, including most of the newest in town, and charges between 7€ ($8.05) and 10€ ($12) per person per hour for play. Within a short walk of the Palácio Hotel, it's open daily from 9am till dusk.

SHOPPING Other than the upscale hotel boutiques that sell scarves and poolside accessories, Estoril does not abound with shopping options. Most dedicated consumers head for the markets of Lisbon or for the large-scale shopping center in Cascais (see "Cascais," later in this chapter), a 10-minute drive from Estoril.

In July and August, the resort sponsors an open-air handcrafts fair, the Feira do Artesanato, near the casino. It's worth a visit even if you're staying in Cascais. The fair runs nightly from around 5pm until midnight. In addition to good regional specialties, the stalls sell handcrafts and art, including ceramics, from all parts of Portugal. You can also drive 6.5km (4 miles) southeast of Estoril to the town of Carcavelos, which has a busy market on Thursday from 7am to 5pm. You'll see local arts and crafts along with more mundane items such as food and clothing. You can also reach Carcavelos by train from Estoril; it's best to go in the morning.

WHERE TO STAY

EXPENSIVE

Palácio Hotel ★★★ The Palácio Hotel is legendary as a retreat for exiled royalty and a center of espionage during World War II. At its 1930 debut, the Palácio received the honeymooning Japanese crown prince and his bride. Umberto, the deposed king of Italy, and Don Juan, the count of Barcelona, followed. During World War II, when people escaped from Nazi-occupied Europe with little more than a case of jewels and the clothes on their back, the hotel accepted diamonds, rubies, and gold instead of money.

The reception rooms are Pompeiian, with sienna-colored marble pillars, bold bands of orange, and handmade carpets. The intimate salons are ideal for a tête-à-tête. The large guest rooms are traditional, with fine Regency-style furnishings, walk-in closets, and luxurious bathrooms with bidets, heated towel racks, and shower-tub combinations. Single rooms facing the rear are the smallest but also the quietest. The hotel opens onto the side of Estoril Park, which is capped by the casino. The beach is a short walk away.

Rua do Parque, 2769-504 Estoril. ✆ **21/464-80-00.** Fax 21/464-81-59. 162 units. 250€–300€ ($288–$345) double; from 300€ ($345) junior suite. Rates include breakfast. AE, DC, MC, V. Free parking. **Amenities:** 2 restaurants; bar; pool; golf course nearby; sauna; valet; salon; 24-hr. room service; babysitting; laundry service. *In room:* A/C, TV, minibar, hair dryer, safe.

MODERATE

Amazónia Lennox Estoril ★★ *Finds* Partially because of its emphasis on golf, this hillside hotel seems a lot like a corner of Scotland. It's located about 2km (1¼ miles) from the Clube de Golf do Estoril course. Near the bar, there's even a map of the golf course at St. Andrews, close to autographed photos of the many championship golfers who have stayed here. The gardens make this place one of the town's prime attractions.

The midsize accommodations are comfortable and attractive. The most desirable and spacious are in the main building, a former private home. All the rooms have balconies and are equipped with bathrooms containing shower-tub combinations. Suites are equipped with kitchenettes.

Rua Eng. Álvaro Pedro Sousa 5, 2765 Estoril. ✆ **21/468-04-24.** Fax 21/467-08-59. 32 units. 85€–134€ ($98–$154) double; 114€–165€ ($131–$190) suite. Rates include buffet breakfast. AE, DC, MC, V. Free parking. **Amenities:** Restaurant; bar; pool; limited room service; babysitting; laundry service; dry cleaning. *In room:* A/C, TV, dataport, minibar, hair dryer, safe.

Hotel Alvorada This hotel, which opened its doors in 1969, is fully renovated but still merely functional. It provides pousada-style accommodations on a small scale. The hotel stands opposite the casino and the Parque Estoril, just a 3-minute walk from the beach. It's recommended for its well-maintained but unstylish midsize guest rooms, each of which have balconies. Renovations in the mid-1990s paid special attention to the bathrooms, all of which contain shower-tub combinations. The top-floor solarium offers a panoramic view of the sea. Only breakfast is served.

Rua de Lisboa 3, 2765-240 Estoril. ✆ **21/464-98-60.** Fax 21/468-72-50. www.hotelalvorada.com. 53 units. 56€–99€ ($64–$114) double; 72€–132€ ($82–$152) triple. Rates include continental breakfast. AE, DC, MC, V. Free parking. **Amenities:** Breakfast room; bar; limited room service; babysitting; laundry service; 1 room for those w/limited mobility. *In room:* A/C, TV, dataport, hair dryer.

Vila Galé Estoril ★ Built in the late 1950s next door to the far more glamorous Palácio (see above), this hotel rises seven floors with walls of soaring glass. About half the rooms boast good-size balconies overlooking the water and the casino. Only a minute or so from the sea and the electric train station, it's in the center of Estoril's boutique district.

Expansion of the hotel and much-needed guest room renovations were completed in 1996. Both new and old rooms feature stylish modern stained-wood furniture and a neatly kept bathroom equipped with a shower-tub combination.

Av. Marginal, 2766-901 Estoril. ✆ **21/464-84-00.** Fax 21/464-84-32. www.vilagale.pt. 126 units. 103€–142€ ($118–$163) double. Rates include breakfast. AE, DC, MC, V. Parking 3.75€ ($4.30). **Amenities:** Restaurant; bar; outdoor pool; golf and tennis nearby; Turkish bath; concierge; tour desk; car rental desk; 24-hr. room service; babysitting; laundry service; dry cleaning, 1 room for those w/limited mobility. *In room:* A/C, TV, dataport, minibar, hair dryer.

NEARBY PLACES TO STAY

A satellite of Estoril, Monte Estoril is less than 1km (¾ mile) west, on the road to Cascais. Built across the slope of a hill, it opens onto a vista of Cascais Bay and the Atlantic beyond.

EXPENSIVE

Estoril Eden ★ *Kids* The government-rated four-star Estoril Eden is a great place for families because it offers apartments. Built in 1985, the white-walled tower sits on a rocky knoll above the road paralleling the edge of the sea. The soundproof, moderately sized apartments are decently decorated. Each has a kitchenette, firm beds, neatly kept bathrooms with shower-tub combinations, and a balcony with a sea view. The decor is a bit worn.

Av. Sabóia 209, Monte Estoril, 2769-502 Estoril. ✆ **21/466-76-00.** Fax 21/466-76-01. www.hotel-estoril-eden.pt. 162 apts. 75€–150€ ($86–$173) apt for 2. Rates include breakfast. AE, DC, MC, V. Parking 8.50€ ($9.80). **Amenities:** Restaurant; bar; outdoor and indoor pools; health club; sauna; solarium; free summer entertainment program for kids; 24-hour concierge; babysitting; laundry service; rooms for those w/limited mobility. *In room:* A/C, TV, dataport, kitchenette, hair dryer, safe.

Grande Hotel A grand hotel has stood on this site since 1895; the present building is a reconstruction. Just a few minutes up from the beach, it offers seven floors of spacious, well-furnished rooms, about half of which have balconies large enough for breakfast or sunbathing. All come equipped with well-maintained bathrooms containing shower-tub combinations. The public rooms are inviting, with a fireplace and groupings of casual furnishings. The guest rooms are furnished in contemporary style, with modern headboards and Nordic-style chairs. Both business travelers and beach buffs frequent this hotel.

Av. Sabóia 488, Monte Estoril, 2765-277 Estoril. ✆ **21/464-97-00.** Fax 21/468-48-34. www.grandehotelmonteestoril.com. 73 units. 65€–110€ ($75–$127) double. Children under 11 half-price in parent's room. Rates include buffet breakfast. AE, DC, MC, V. Free parking. **Amenities:** Restaurant; bar; pool; limited room service; babysitting; laundry service; 1 room for those w/limited mobility. *In room:* A/C, TV, minibar, safe.

INEXPENSIVE

Saboia Hotel You'll find comfortable 1970s-style accommodations in this white-and-cream-colored tower jutting skyward from a neighborhood of 19th-century villas above town. In the late 1990s, the six-floor hotel got a completely new look following renovations. Each small to midsize guest room contains a well-kept bathroom equipped with shower-tub combination.

Rua Belmonte 1, Monte Estoril, 2765-398 Estoril. ✆ **21/468-11-22.** Fax 21/468-11-17. 48 units. 55€–100€ ($63–$115) double. Rates include buffet breakfast. AE, DC, MC, V. Free parking. **Amenities:** Snack bar; bar; pool; babysitting; laundry service. *In room:* A/C, TV, minibar, hair dryer, safe.

WHERE TO DINE

EXPENSIVE

Four Seasons ★★★ INTERNATIONAL For fine food, go to the Four Seasons, whose connection with one of Portugal's most famous hotels gives it immediate cachet. But even on its own merit, it is one of the finest—and one of the most expensive—restaurants in Estoril.

The menus and the service at the Four Seasons reflect the seasons, changing four times a year. Other than the handful of intimate tables set on the upper mezzanine, the elaborately decorated tables cluster around a beautiful but purely decorative Iberian kitchen. The quiet, the candles, and the rich colors invite comparison to an elegant 19th-century Russian home. However, the discreet charm and polite manners of the well-trained staff are distinctively Portuguese.

The international cuisine is superb. For an appetizer, you might select three-cheese crepes, lobster bisque, or chilled mussel soup. To follow, try sole meunière, medallions of grouper with seaweed and salmon roe, flamed shrimp amira, or a parrillada of lobster, shrimp, mussels, and clams for two. Meat dishes include beef and veal stuffed with shrimp, medallions of venison with chestnuts, and wild boar cutlets with pineapple. The fixed-price menu includes soup or appetizer, a main course, dessert, mineral water, and coffee. Wine can be added for a supplement of 6.50€ ($7.50).

In the Palácio Hotel, Rua do Parque. ✆ **21/464-80-00.** Reservations required. Main courses 10€–45€ ($12–$52); fixed-price menu 32€ ($37). AE, DC, MC, V. Daily 1–3pm and 7:30–10:30pm.

MODERATE

Costa do Estoril ★ PORTUGUESE This highly respected restaurant stands next to the casino and serves a large variety of excellent, fresh grilled fish. The most popular and most frequently ordered fish is codfish, so-called "faithful friend" to the Portuguese. But there are many other delights as well, including grouper, dorado, and fresh sardines. You can also order a limited selection of the other dishes. The chefs insist on using fresh ingredients, the service is impeccable, and the welcome is warm—all making for a winning combination. The bar, open daily from 1pm to 6am, is popular with guests from the casino.

Av. Amaral. ✆ **21/468-18-17.** Reservations recommended. Main courses 7€–25€ ($8.05–$29). AE, DC, MC, V. Tues–Sun noon–3:30pm and 7:15–11pm.

Guantanamera (A Maré) *Finds* PORTUGUESE/CUBAN Prominently positioned on the main strip interconnecting Estoril with Cascais, this ochre-colored restaurant occupies what was originally built as a private villa for a mysteriously deposed countess around the turn of the century. Since then, it has been much modernized with a big neon sign, lots of plants, and a modern kitchen—although some vestiges of its original romantic flair are still visible. The cuisine includes many of the grilled meats and fish you've come to associate with Portuguese cuisine, as well as a roster of Cuban specialties such as roasted pork and grouper, accompanied with ample portions of *platanos* (plantains), rice, beans, and avocados.

Alamedo Columbano 6, Monte Estoril. ✆ **021/468-55-70.** Reservations recommended. Main courses 10€–22€ ($12–$25); set menus 9€ ($10). AE, DC, MC, V. Daily noon–3pm and 7–11pm.

La Villa MEDITERRANEAN Although it doesn't equal such a deluxe citadel as the Four Seasons, this well-run restaurant is one of the leading dining rooms along the Estoril coast. The restaurant is installed in a palace from the 18th-century and opens onto the local beach, Praia do Tamariz. Prepare yourself for some fine dining, beginning with one of the featured pasta and rice dishes, perhaps shrimp with garlicky *aïoli* sauce or spaghetti vongole with coriander-flavored clams. Count on a fresh grilled fish of the day, perhaps sea bass. The latter is also served under a potato crust. One winning dish is braised black pork filet served with a wild Moroccan rice in a light curry sauce, or roast breast of duck with a medley of tempura-style spring vegetables. The chef is also known for his desserts, including an exotic selection of homemade sorbets, or you can order a Belgian chocolate soufflé.

Praia do Estoril 3. ✆ **21/468-00-33.** Reservations recommended. Main courses 15€–22€ ($17–$25). AE, DC, MC, V. Tues-Sun 1–3pm and 8pm–midnight.

ESTORIL AFTER DARK

GAMBLING An alcohol-stoked crawl through the upscale bars of such hotels as the Palácio might provide insights into the glamour of this pocket of Portugal. If you're looking for something more formal, check out the **Estoril Casino,** in the Parque Estoril, Praça José Teodoro dos Santos (✆ **21/466-77-00**). There's a cover charge of 4€ ($4.60) for entrance into the section with the gaming tables (roulette, French *banque, chemin de fer,* blackjack, and craps); you can gamble to your heart's content every day between 3pm and 3am. You must present a passport, driver's license, or other form of photo ID, and you must be 18 or over. A jacket is required. Entrance to the separate slot-machine room is free and

requires no ID. Built in the late 1950s, the casino rises from a formally landscaped garden on a hilltop near the town center. Glass walls enclose an inner courtyard with fountains and tiled paths.

CLUBS & BARS The casino is the venue for the region's splashiest and most colorful cabaret act, **Salão Preto e Prata,** in the Estoril Casino, Parque Estoril, Praça José Teodoro dos Santos (✆ **21/466-77-00**). We usually skip the dinner offered here and pay a cover charge of 15€ ($17), which includes the first two drinks. Shows begin at 11pm, and most spectators who aren't dining show up at around 10:30pm for views of leggy, feathered, and bejeweled dancers strutting around in billowing trains and bespangled bras. Food is served in the 700-seat theater or in a 150-seat satellite restaurant, Wunderbar. Dinner, including access to the show, costs 52€ to 62€ ($60–$71) per person.

For a more regional watering hole, try a fast pick-me-up at the raffish-looking **Forte Velho** (Old Fort), Estrada Marginal, São João do Estoril (✆ **21/468-13-37**). It isn't the most fashionable club in the region, but its location within the 500-year-old walls of a once-powerful fort adds an undeniable allure. You'll find a high-energy crowd of under-30s on weekends, and a more varied age range on weeknights. There's a cover charge of 5€ ($5.75), a beer costs around 3€ ($3.45), and whiskey costs 5€ ($5.75).

Looking to rub elbows with some of the Costa do Sol's corps of English-speaking expatriates enjoying their gin and tonics? Head for the long-established premises of **Ray's Cocktail Bar & Lounge,** Av. Sabóia 425, Monte Estoril (✆ **21/468-01-06**). The eclectic, kitschy, colonial decor seems to celebrate English-speaking, hard-drinking communities throughout the world. Mixed-drink prices start at 4€ ($4.60); beer costs at least 1.25€ to 2€ ($1.45–$2.30). It's open Monday through Saturday from 6pm to 2am.

Many foreign visitors, especially expatriate Brits, flock to the **English Bar,** Av. Sabóia 9 in Monte Estoril (✆ **21/468-04-13**), to catch the sunset over the Bay of Cascais. Behind its mock-Elizabethan facade, this popular gathering place serves pub snacks and the town's best selection of brew.

2 Cascais ★★

6.5km (4 miles) W of Estoril, 61km (38 miles) W of Lisbon

In the 1930s, Cascais was a tiny fishing village that attracted artists and writers to its little cottages. But it was once known as a royal village because it enjoyed the patronage of Portugal's ruling family. When the monarchy died, the military replaced it. Gen. António de Fragoso Carmona, president of Portugal until 1951, once occupied the 17th-century fort guarding the Portuguese Riviera.

To say Cascais is growing would be an understatement: It's exploding! Apartment houses, new hotels, and the finest restaurants along the Costa do Sol draw a never-ending stream of visitors every year.

However, the life of the simple fisher folk goes on. Auctions, called *lotas,* of the latest catch still take place on the main square. In the small harbor, rainbow-colored fishing boats share space with pleasure craft owned by an international set that flocks to Cascais from early spring until autumn.

The town's tie with the sea is old. If you speak Portuguese, chat up any of the local fishers. They'll tell you that one of their own, Afonso Sanches, discovered America in 1482. Legend has it that Columbus learned of his accidental find, stole the secret, and enjoyed the subsequent acclaim.

ESSENTIALS

ARRIVING

BY TRAIN The round-trip fare from Lisbon's Cais do Sodre to either Estoril (the second-to-last stop) or Cascais (the end of the line) costs 2.50€ ($2.90). Trains arrive from and depart from Lisbon at intervals of every 20 minutes. Service is daily from 5:30am to 1:30am. For information, call ✆ **021/888-40-25** in Lisbon, or ✆ **21/881-62-42** in Cascais or Estoril.

BY BUS Buses from Lisbon are impractical, considering the low cost and convenience of the frequent trains. But if you're coming to Cascais from Sintra, the bus is your best bet; about a dozen buses a day make the 1-hour run. The round-trip fare is 2.30€ ($2.65).

BY CAR From Estoril (see "Estoril," earlier in this chapter), continue west along Route 6 for another 6.5km (4 miles).

VISITOR INFORMATION

Cascais Tourist Office is at Av. Combatentes da Grande Guerra 25, 2750-326 Cascais (✆ **21/486-82-04**). Between October and May, the tourist office is open Monday through Saturday from 9am to 7pm, and Sunday from 10am to 6pm. In summer (June–Sept), it's open Monday through Saturday from 9am to 8pm, and Sunday from 10am to 6pm.

HAVING FUN IN CASCAIS

EXPLORING THE TOWN Many visitors, both foreign and domestic, clog the roads to Cascais on summer Sundays, when there are bullfights at the **Monumental de Cascais,** a ring outside the "city" center (see "Spectator Sports," in chapter 4).

When you're not at the beach, a good place to relax is the sprawling **Parque do Marechal Carmona,** open daily from 9am to 8pm. It lies at the southern tip of the resort, near the water. Here you'll find a shallow lake, a cafe, and a small zoo. Chairs and tables are set out under shade trees if you'd like to picnic.

The most important church is the **Igreja de Nossa Senhora da Assunção** (Church of Our Lady of the Assumption), on Largo da Assunção (✆ **21/484-74-80**), a leafy square toward the western edge of town. It's open daily from 9am to 1pm and 5 to 8pm. Paintings by Josefa de Obidos, a 17th-century artist, fill the nave. They're unusual because women rarely attained such artistic posts in those days. The hand-painted *azulejos* (tiles) date from 1720 and 1748. The beautiful altar dates from the end of the 16th century.

Cascais also has some minor museums, including the **Museu do Mar** (Museum of the Sea), Rua Julio Pereira de Melo (✆ **21/486-13-77**). The museum displays fishing artifacts, including equipment and model boats. Folkloric apparel worn by residents in the 1800s is also on exhibit. Old photographs and paintings re-create the Cascais of long ago. The museum is open November to April Tuesday through Sunday from 10am to 5pm, and May to October 10am to 9pm; admission is 1.50€ ($1.75).

Another museum is the **Museu do Conde de Castro Guimarães,** Estrada da Boca do Inferno (✆ **21/482-54-07**). On the grounds of the Parque do Marechal Carmona, it occupies the former 19th-century home of a family whose last surviving member died in 1927. The museum offers a rare glimpse into life in the 18th and 19th centuries, with ceramics, antiques, artwork, silver ewers, samovars, and Indo-Portuguese embroidered shawls—you name it. It's open Tuesday through Sunday from 10am to 12:30pm and 2 to 5pm; admission is

1.54€ ($1.75) and free for children under 18. Guided tours are on the hour between 10am and 5pm.

The most popular excursion outside Cascais is to **Boca do Inferno** ★ (Mouth of Hell). Thundering waves sweep in with such power that they've carved a wide hole resembling a mouth, or *boca,* into the cliffs. However, if you should arrive when the sea is calm, you'll wonder why it's called a cauldron. The Mouth of Hell can be a windswept roar if you don't stumble over too many souvenir hawkers. Take the highway toward Guincho and then turn left toward the sea.

OUTDOOR ACTIVITIES Most visitors are content with the trio of fair beaches here. Lying on the lovely, sandy beach here is a fine way to spend the day. Fortunately, the waters of Cascais are no longer polluted as they were in the late '90s, and swimmers have returned.

The best year-round center for horseback riding is **Quinta da Marinha** (✆ **21/486-90-84**), 4km (2½ miles) west of Cascais. Call for directions and information.

The best golf course at Cascais is at the **Clube de Golfe da Marinha,** Quinta da Marinha (✆ **21/486-01-80** or 21/486-01-00), which was carved out of sprawling woodlands of umbrella pines. The master himself, Robert Trent Jones Sr., designed the 18-hole course, the showcase of an upscale residential resort complex that stretches over some 131 hectares (324 acres). Windblown dunes and sea-lashed outcroppings are part of the backdrop along its 6,120m (20,074 ft.). The 18th hole, facing a deep rocky gorge, is the most challenging. Weekday greens fees are 65€ ($75), or 36€ ($41) after 4pm; on weekends, the fees are 60€ ($69) until 4pm and then 41€ ($47).

SHOPPING As a prominent beachfront resort, Cascais offers lots of simple kiosks selling sunglasses and beachwear. The region's densest concentration of stores catering to united Europe's definition of the good life is nearby. The sprawling shopping center **Shopping Cascais,** Estrada de Sintra (✆ **21/460-00-53** for information), is beside highway 5A, the road between Cascais and Sintra. Some locals refer to it as the Shopping Center of Cascais, dropping the English-language term easily. It contains two floors and more than 100 boutiques, with special emphasis on housewares, home furnishings and accessories, and clothing.

Tear Linhos, Rua da Saudade 6 (✆ **21/484-43-36**), is our favorite emporium for hand-embroideries in all of Cascais, with a selection of sheets, tableware, and women's nightgowns. The owners also believe that a well-dressed child is a well-behaved child; as a consequence, the store carries some of the most charming children's clothes in Cascais.

If you're in the mood for more folkloric, less overtly commercial settings, you might want to ignore the megamall. Wander instead through the warren of small ceramics shops that surround Cascais's church, or walk along the town's most commercialized street, **Rua da Raita,** an all-pedestrian walkway in the town center.

The most intriguing shopping possibilities are at the markets. Head north of the center along Rua Mercado, off Avenida do 25 be Abril, on Wednesday or Saturday morning, and you'll find a fruit and vegetable market (along with a lot of other items). Another sprawling market operates at the bullring, **Praça de Touros,** on Avenida Pedro Álvares, west of the center, on the first and third Sunday of each month.

WHERE TO STAY

Advance reservations are necessary in July and August.

VERY EXPENSIVE

Albatroz ★★★ After many decades, this monument to aristocratic glamour still reigns undisputed as the most elegant and sought-after hotel on the Costa do Sol. Today, although confronted with stiff competition from newer hotels that are almost as charming, it continues to hold its reputation as a lodging for the quietly rich. Don't expect glitziness: The property is small-scale and restrained, although in the opinion of some, a tad pretentious and even a wee bit stuffy. Its centerpiece is a pair of interconnected beach houses, one of which was originally built in 1793 for the Duke of Loulé and acquired during the 19th century as a holiday home for the Count and Countess de Foz. In the 20th century, it became an inn. In 1983, a series of additions and alterations eventually engulfed the original villas, even though you can still see traces of the original architecture, especially in the foyer to the much-heralded restaurant. Today you'll find airy, open spaces, contemporary tile-work, and low-slung furniture that's in keeping with its image as an upscale beach hotel. In 2000, the hotel acquired a neighboring neo-Romantic villa, which at great expense was converted into a conference center with six extremely upscale suites. Units in the building's ivy-draped main core vary in size, and all are extremely comfortable, albeit, for the most part, blandly conservative and uncontroversial in their decor. All units contain elegant bathrooms with shower-tub combinations.

Rua Frederico Arouça 100, 2750-353 Cascais. ✆ **21/484-73-80.** Fax 21/484-48-27. www.albatrozhotel.pt. 46 units. Nov–Mar 175€–265€ ($201–$305) double; 295€–325€ ($340–$374) suite. Apr–May and Aug–Oct 230€–340€ ($265–$391) double, 490€ ($564) suite; Jun-July 300€–450€ ($345–$518) double, 600€ ($690) suite. Extra bed in any season 68€ ($61). AE, DC, MC, V. **Amenities:** Restaurant; bar; pool; valet, 24-hr. room service; babysitting; laundry service, 1 room for those w/limited mobility. *In room:* A/C, TV, dataport, minibar, hair dryer, safe.

EXPENSIVE

Estalagem Villa Albatroz ★★ *Finds* Set in the geographic heart of Cascais, a very short walk from city hall and the bandstand where midsummer civic concerts are held, this hotel was originally built in the 19th century as the beach house of the Dukes of Palmela. In the late 1990s, it was acquired by the owners of the also-recommended Hotel Albatroz and reconfigured as a small-scale boutique hotel. Its prices are consistently about 15% less than those at the Albatroz, which tends to attract a younger, less formal clientele. Overall, the aura is airy, bemused, and breezy. Rooms are smaller than those at the Albatroz and not quite as grand as you might expect. Each unit comes with a shower-tub combination. Overall, the experience is comfortable and convenient, particularly because of the hotel's superb location and thoughtful staff.

Rua Fernandes Tomás 1, 2750-353 Cascais. ✆ **21/486-34-10.** Fax 21/484-46-80. 11 units. Nov–Mar 143€–212€ ($165–$244) double; 233€ ($268) suite. Apr–Oct 187€–255€ ($215–$293) double; 365€ ($420) suite. Extra bed 30€–60€ ($35–$69). AE, DC, MC, V. **Amenities:** Restaurant; bar; 24-hr. room service. *In room:* A/C, TV, minibar, hair dryer, safe.

Farol Design Hotel ★★ *Finds* The region's newest government-rated five-star hotel opened in 2002 and became an instant hit with a chic crowd. Enjoying a scenic waterfront location a 10-minute walk from the center of town, this is a completely remodeled 19th-century mansion that has been handsomely converted, making it the most stylish boutique hotel along the Costa del Sol. Furnishings are tasteful—sometimes elegant—and there are extra-special features such as hydromassage in each tiled bathroom. Bedrooms have parquet floors and dark-wood furnishings, and the blankets and fabrics, including the draperies, are beautifully color coordinated. All in white, the building rises four stories, housing mainly midsize to spacious bedrooms. You never have to leave at night because there is a first-class restaurant serving international food, along with two fashionable bars and a well-attended dance club for the young and beautiful.

Avenida Rei Humberto II de Italia 7, 2750-461 Cascais. ✆ **21/482-34-90.** Fax 21/484-14-47. www.cascais.org. 34 units. 125€–235€ ($144–$270) double; 150€–280€ ($173–$322) junior suite. **Amenities:** Restaurant; bar; outdoor pool; limited room service; massage; babysitting; laundry service; dry cleaning. *In room:* A/C, TV, dataport, minibar, coffeemaker, hair dryer, safe.

Village Cascais ★★ In the historic quarter of Cascais, this stunningly modern hotel doesn't quite challenge the Albatroz, but it is nonetheless a first-class citadel of charm and comfort. The balconied hotel, surrounded by palaces and the Parque de Candarinha, offers beautifully furnished bedrooms, including 70 suites, each with a beehive-shape balcony overlooking the sea or mountains. Some accommodations are set aside for nonsmokers. In terms of prestige, comfort, and desirability, this hotel is no. 2 at the resort. The hotel is also one of the best equipped in the area, known for its pools and bar and restaurant facilities.

Rua Frei Nicolau de Oliveira, Parque da Candarinha, 2750-641 Cascais. ✆ **21/482-60-00.** Fax 21/483-73-19. www.vilagale.pt. 233 units. 90€–184€ ($104–$212) double, 177€–239€ ($204–$275) suite. Free parking. **Amenities:** Restaurant; 2 bars; 2 pools; sauna; 24-hr. room service; massage; babysitting; laundry service; dry cleaning. *In room:* A/C, TV, dataport, minibar, coffeemaker, hair dryer, safe.

MODERATE

Hotel Baia One of the most appealing things about this well-managed, government-rated three-star hotel is its location directly above the town's fishing port, adjacent to town hall, within a short walk of five-star hotels whose accommodations cost a whole lot more. Originally built in the 1960s, it was extensively renovated in the mid-1990s, enlarged, and modernized. Today its five floors contain contemporary furnishings, a clean and simple decor, and tidy bathrooms with tub and shower.

Av. Marginal, 2754-509 Cascais. ✆ **21/483-10-33.** Fax 21/483-10-95. www.portugalvirtual.pt/hotelbaia. 113 units. 65€–115€ ($75–$132) double; 105€–160€ ($121–$184) suite. Rates include breakfast. AE, DC, MC, V. **Amenities:** Restaurant; snack bar; bar; pool; terrace; solarium; rooms for those w/limited mobility. *In room:* A/C, TV.

INEXPENSIVE

Albergaria Valbom Built in 1973, this hotel offers an indistinct white-concrete facade with recessed balconies. It is battered but acceptable, and the staff is helpful and polite. Conservatively decorated guest rooms surround the sun-washed TV lounge. Some of the rooms have TVs. The quieter accommodations look out over the back. All units come with well-maintained bathrooms, most of which contain shower-tub combinations. The Valbom lies on a drab commercial-residential street close to the center of Cascais, near the rail station.

Av. Valbom 14, 2750-508 Cascais. ✆ **21/486-58-01.** Fax 21/486-58-05. 40 units. 35€–63€ ($40–$72) double. Rates include breakfast. AE, DC, MC, V. Free parking. **Amenities:** Breakfast room; babysitting; laundry service. *In room:* A/C.

Casa da Pérgola ★★ *Value* Built in the 18th century, this elegant villa behind a garden offers one of the most charming, tranquil interiors in Cascais. In the center of town, it stands in a neighborhood filled with restaurants and shops. The manager/owner is Patricia Gonçalves. It was her childhood home, and today she maintains it as if it were still her private domain. Her genteel staff proudly displays a collection of antique furniture and blue-and-white tiles that surround the elegant ground-floor parlor and second-floor sitting room. Each small accommodation is well furnished, with excellent beds and well-maintained bathrooms that mostly contain shower-tub combinations. Reserve in advance. Although it's technically closed from mid-December through late January, the hotel will open during that time for any party that reserves five or more rooms.

Av. Valbom 13, 2750-508 Cascais. ✆ **21/484-00-40.** Fax 21/483-47-91. www.ciberguia.pt/casa-da-pergola. 11 units. 100€–115€ ($115–$132) double. Rates include breakfast. No credit cards. Closed Dec 15–Feb 1. **Amenities:** Breakfast room; laundry service. *In room:* A/C, TV, hair dryer, safe.

Solar Dom Carlos *Value* If you're saving money and your expectations aren't too high, this little back-street inn is most inviting. Once the mansion of a local aristocrat, it dates from the 1500s. An original chapel from the nobleman's home remains intact. The place is immaculately kept and makes heavy use of tiled floors. The comfortably furnished rooms are often large and have good beds but not a lot of other luxuries. Bathrooms are well kept and come equipped with shower-tub combinations. The inn also has a private garden.

Rua Latina Coelho, 2750-408 Cascais. ✆ **21/482-81-15.** Fax 21/486-51-55. 18 units. 40€–65€ ($46–$75). Rates include breakfast. AE, DC, MC, V. Free parking. **Amenities:** Breakfast room; babysitting; laundry service. *In room:* TV, safe.

WHERE TO DINE

After Lisbon, sprawling Cascais offers the second-highest concentration of quality restaurants. Even if you're based in the capital, consider a trip to Cascais for seafood.

EXPENSIVE

Restaurant Albatroz ★★★ PORTUGUESE/INTERNATIONAL One of the finest places to dine along the Costa do Sol, this elegantly decorated restaurant is part of the most famous hotel on the coast (see "Where to Stay," above). From its windows, you'll have a sweeping view of one of the Costa do Sol's most popular beaches. Its summer-style decor is inviting year-round. The room is not grand or stuffy, but the service is rather formal. Diners' attire is probably best described as "neat casual."

Begin with an aperitif on the covered terrace. Afterward, you'll be ushered into a glistening dining room that serves some of the finest Portuguese and international cuisine in Cascais. Your options might include poached salmon, partridge stew, chateaubriand, or a savory version of stuffed sole with shellfish. There are also daily fresh fish specials; one especially succulent offering is monkfish with sea clams. For dessert, choices range from crêpes Suzette to iced soufflé. There's a wide selection of Portuguese and international wines.

In the Hotel Albatroz, Rua Frederico Arouca 100. ✆ **21/484-73-80.** Reservations required. Main courses 17€–38€ ($20–$44). AE, DC, MC, V. Daily 12:30–3pm and 7:30–10pm.

Visconde da Luz ★ PORTUGUESE/SEAFOOD This well-known restaurant sits in a low-slung bungalow at the edge of a park in the center of Cascais. The view encompasses rows of lime trees and towering sycamores where flocks of birds congregate at dusk (be warned if you're walking underneath). The decor is modernized Art Nouveau. The uniformed staff is polite and eager. The Portuguese food is well prepared with fresh ingredients. A meal might include fried sole, shellfish, pork with clams, seafood curry, or clams in garlic sauce, finished off with almond cake. Many seafood choices are sold by the kilogram (2.2 lb.), a generous portion that can easily feed two.

In the Jardim Visconde da Luz. ✆ **21/484-74-10.** Reservations required. Main courses 15€–30€ ($17–$35). AE, DC, MC, V. Tues–Sun noon–4pm and 7pm–midnight.

MODERATE

Beira Mar ★★ PORTUGUESE Cozy and crowded, with an outdoor terrace that spills onto a traffic-free plaza in front, this is the best restaurant in the center of Cascais. Established in the 1950s, with present management in place since 1973, it evokes a relatively simple seafront tavern, except that the food and service are a lot better than that cliché might imply. Within sight of a well-scrubbed kitchen, you'll enjoy such menu items as a savory *sopa de marisco* (shellfish soup), filet of whitefish with shellfish rice, baked sea bass in a salt crust, or whitefish crowned with a banana. Grilled sole and several kinds of shellfish round out the menu.

Rua das Flores 6. ✆ **021/482-73-80.** Reservations recommended. Main courses 14€–25€ ($16–$29). AE, DC, MC, V. Wed–Mon noon–3pm and 7–11pm.

Eduardo's PORTUGUESE/BELGIAN Rustically decorated with regional artifacts, this provincial restaurant occupies the street level of a postwar apartment building in the center of Cascais. It's named after its Belgian-born owner, Edouard de Beukelaer, who turns out savory Portuguese and Belgian meals. The well-prepared food might include filet steaks, braised filet of turbot, crayfish in butter sauce with capers, and veal liver. Nothing very imaginative is served, but everything is decently prepared.

Largo das Grutas 3. ✆ **21/483-19-01.** Reservations recommended. Main courses 9€–28€ ($10–$32); fixed-price menu 21€ ($19). AE, DC, MC, V. Thurs–Tues noon–3pm and 7–11pm.

O Pipas PORTUGUESE/INTERNATIONAL This is a well-established Portuguese tavern, with a location on an all-pedestrian street in the heart of the resort, a narrow outdoor terrace (where prices of food and drink are about 10% more expensive than inside) and an interior decor that has lots of dark wood trim and tones of navy blue and white. This is not a particularly cutting-edge place (and doesn't try to be), and the recorded *musak* that's played can be moderately annoying. But food is well prepared and includes roasted pork with clams, duck with orange sauce, grilled sardines, a creamy version of vegetable soup, and grilled lamb chops.

Rua das Flores 18. ✆ **21/486-45-01.** Reservations recommended. Main courses 8€–30€ ($9.20–$35), AE, DC, MC, V. Tues–Sun noon–3:30pm and 7–11:30pm.

Reijos ★ *Finds* PORTUGUESE This place is likely to be crowded, so in high season you'll have to wait for a table or abandon all hope—this intimate, informal bistro is that good. The menu combines fine American and Portuguese foods, with pleasing results. Tony and Maria José Brito run this successful enterprise.

Justifiably popular items include grilled lobster with butter sauce, shrimp curry, and filet mignon. Two dishes from Macau are prepared at your table: beef with garden peppers, and shrimp and cucumbers. Fresh seafood includes sole, sea bass, grouper, fresh salmon, and *bacalhau a Reijos* (oven-baked dry codfish with cheese sauce). Unlike many European restaurants, Reijos serves fresh vegetables with its main dishes at no extra cost. The service is excellent.

Rua Frederico Arouca 35. ✆ **21/483-03-11.** Reservations required for dinner. Main courses 12€–25€ ($14–$29). AE, DC, MC, V. Mon–Sat 12:30–3:30pm and 7–11pm. Closed Dec 15–Dec 30.

Restaurante o Batel ★ PORTUGUESE/INTERNATIONAL O Batel fronts the fish market. Styled as a country inn, it's semirustic, with rough white walls and beamed ceilings. The reasonable prices and hearty regional cuisine explain its popularity. The fixed-price menu includes soup, a main course, dessert, and your choice of mineral water, coffee, or half a bottle of wine. Lobster Thermidor and lobster stewed in cognac (both priced daily) are the house specialties. For something less expensive, we recommend succulent Cascais sole with banana, clams with cream, or savory mixed shellfish with rice. For an appetizer, try the prawn cocktail. Desserts include pineapple with Madeira wine.

Travessa das Flores 4. ✆ **21/483-02-15.** Reservations required. Main courses 9€–30€ ($10–$35). AE, DC, MC, V. Tues–Sun noon–4pm and 6:30pm–midnight.

INEXPENSIVE

Brasserie de l'Entrecôte *Value* STEAKS At first glance, this restaurant resembles the kind of turn-of-the-century brasserie you'd find in central France, with mahogany paneling, polished brass, and apron-clad staff members. A glance at the menu, however, quickly reveals that this is a French brasserie with a twist: The only available choice is *entrecôte* (steak) with french fries, accompanied with a salad and your choice of sauces. But despite the limited menu, the place is crowded, especially in high season. You can order, for a supplement, any of five kinds of dessert that include tarts, sorbets (lime or mango), and fruit salads, as well as wines from a savvy list of mostly Portuguese vintages. But overall, if you don't mind the limited menu, the place is one of the most cost-effective in Cascais for the presentation of satisfyingly generous meals at rock-bottom prices in a good-looking setting.

Marina de Cascais, Loja 43. ✆ **21/481-81-96.** Reservations recommended only for dinner on weekends. Two-course fixed-price menu 14€ ($16); supplement for dessert 3.35€ ($3.85) extra. AE, DC, MC, V. Daily 12:30–3:30pm and 8pm–midnight.

Dom Manolo *Value* PORTUGUESE In the center of Cascais—in fact, on its main street—this Spanish-operated restaurant and grill looks like an Iberian tavern. The kitchen dishes out reasonably priced, tasty, uncomplicated regional fare. It attracts more local residents than fancy foreign visitors. The perfectly cooked spit-roasted chicken, with french fries or a salad, is a favorite. Other good choices are the savory grilled sardines, any shrimp dish, and most definitely the fresh catch of the day. For dessert, there's velvety flan.

Av. Marginal 13. ✆ **21/483-11-26.** Main courses 5€–10€ ($5.75–$12). No credit cards. Daily 10am–11:30pm. Closed Jan.

John Bull/Britannia Restaurant ENGLISH/PORTUGUESE/AMERICAN This centrally located pub and restaurant shows its English roots in both the black-and-white timbered Elizabethan facade and the John Bull Pub. The street-level room has dark wooden paneling, oak beams, a fireplace, rough-hewn stools and tables, and pewter pots. Pints of hand-pumped ales and lagers are popular with those who want only to drink and talk. Hungry customers head upstairs to the Britannia Restaurant, where the menu features English, American, and Portuguese dishes. Popular items include cottage pie, Southern fried chicken, T-bone steaks, and local seafood. The food is solid and reliable—nothing more.

Largo Luís de Camões 4A. ✆ **21/483-33-19.** Main courses 6€–15€ ($6.90–$17). AE, DC, MC, V. Daily 12:30–3:30pm and 7:30–11:30pm.

CASCAIS AFTER DARK

Nightlife in this burgeoning resort incorporates old-fashioned fado and glittery urban-style dance clubs.

Bally Bally Pub This replica of a wood-sheathed English pub is one of the town's most central and most likable bars. Despite the kind of Victorian bric-a-brac you might expect in London, there's something unmistakably Latino about the place, including the salsa and merengue that's played as background music. During July and August, it's open daily from 8pm to 4am. The rest of the year, it's open daily from 8pm to 3:30am. Rua Marques Leal Pancada 16A. ✆ **21/486-87-17.**

Baluarte Bar Spacious, streamlined, and airy, this is the bar that many employees of local hotels and restaurants drop into when their work day is finished. It evokes the kind of hip, youth-oriented place that you might expect within the Bairro Alto of Lisbon, except that it occupies the street level of a condominium complex directly across the street from the town's most central beach, the Praia do Peixe. Although it's associated with a restaurant directly above it, most clients come here just for a drink and a dialogue with their friends, and never actually climb the stairs for a meal. It's open daily from 4:30pm to 4am. Av. Don Carlos I, no. 6 (Marginal). ✆ **21/486-51-57.**

Coconuts If you're looking for a bona-fide dance club with mobs of horny and sometimes manic heterosexuals from throughout Europe, this is the place. The setting is a sprawling and much-weathered seafront pavilion, open to the breezes, on the western edge of town, about a 12-minute walk from the center. There's a stage for live entertainment, a busy dance floor, an active bar area, and lots of testosterone- and estrogen-driven dialogues between visitors from virtually everywhere. The scene sometimes spills out of the pavilion onto a lawn. In some cases, it's even carried into the bar (a congenially battered turn-of-the-20th-century salon) of a nearby hotel, the Estalagem do Farol, which is owned by the same investors. The entire complex opens nightly at 11pm, entertainment begins at midnight, and closing occurs sometime between 4 and 6am, depending on business. Whereas single women pay a cover charge of 13€ ($14), a cover charge of 25€ ($29) is somewhat arbitrarily applied to both single men and men with dates. Every Monday, single women enter free and are treated to at least three free drinks. Av. Real Humberto II de Italia. ✆ **21/483-01-73.**

Ferdi's Bar This German-owned bar is offhanded, charming, and fun—the kind of place where the staff at other bars around Cascais head after their shifts. Some of its fans refer to it as more of a lifestyle choice than a bar, since so many friendships (and romances) have been formed within this cozy, one-story Iberian cottage. It's a short uphill walk from City Hall. It's open Thursday to Saturday from 11pm till 4am. Rua Afonso Sanches 36. ✆ **21/483-57-84.**

O'Neill's Irish Pub Set within a few steps of Cascais's town hall, this is a genuine Irish pub with a rowdy permissiveness. Amid dark paneling and etched mirrors, you'll hear live Irish music (Wed–Sat beginning at 11pm) and can order snack items that include chili and full Irish breakfasts. It's open daily from noon to 2am. Rua Afonso Sanches 8. ✆ **21/486-82-30.**

3 Guincho ★

6.5km (4 miles) N of Cascais, 9.5km (6 miles) N of Estoril

The word *guincho* is best translated as "caterwaul," the cry that swallows make while darting along the air currents over the wild sea. The swallows stay at

Guincho year-round. Sometimes at night, the sea, driven into a frenzy, howls like a wailing banshee—and that, too, is *guincho.*

The town lies near the westernmost point on the European continent, known to the Portuguese as **Cabo da Roca** ★. The beaches are spacious and sandy, the sunshine is incandescent, and the nearby promontories, jutting into white-tipped Atlantic waves, are spectacular. Wooded hills back the windswept dunes, and to the east, the Serra de Sintra is silhouetted on the distant horizon.

ESSENTIALS

ARRIVING

BY BUS From the train station at Cascais, buses leave for the Praia do Guincho every hour. The trip takes 20 minutes.

BY CAR From Cascais, continue west along Route 247.

VISITOR INFORMATION

The nearest tourist office is in Cascais (see earlier).

TREACHEROUS BEACHES & SEAFOOD FEASTS

Praia do Guincho draws large beach crowds. The undertow is treacherous, so it's wise to keep in mind the advice of Jennings Parrott, writing in the *International Herald Tribune:* "If you are caught up by the current, don't fight it. Don't panic. The wind forces it to circle, so you will be brought back to shore." A local fisherman, however, advises that you take a box lunch along. According to him, "Sometimes it takes several days to make the circle."

One of the primary reasons for coming to Guincho is to sample its seafood restaurants (see "Where to Dine," below). You can try the crayfish-size box-jaw lobsters known as *bruxas,* which in Portuguese means "sorcerer," "wizard," "witch doctor," and even "nocturnal moth." To eat like the Portuguese, you must also sample the barnacles, called *percêbes.* (Many foreign visitors fail to comprehend their popularity.) The fresh lobsters and crabs are cultivated in nearby shellfish beds, which are fascinating sights in themselves.

WHERE TO STAY

EXPENSIVE

Hotel Fortaleza do Guincho ★★★ Designated as a Relais & Châteaux hotel in 2001, this is one of the grandest and most prestigious hotels in the region. It originated in the 17th century within a few hundred feet of the westernmost point in Europe, when an army of stonecutters built one of the most forbidding fortresses along the coast. The twin towers that flank the vaguely Moorish facade still stand sentinel over a sun-bleached terrain of sand and rock.

You enter the hotel through an enclosed, once-fortified courtyard, where there's a well that used to provide water for the garrison. The public rooms contain all the antique trappings of an aristocratic private home. In cold weather, a fire might blaze in a granite-framed fireplace, illuminating the thick carpets and the century-old furniture.

Tips Danger on the Surf

Praia do Guincho is peppered with blue flags, which mean "dangerous waters, treacherous surf, swim at your own risk." There is no place to rent sailboards, but windsurfers show up here from other parts of Europe, bringing their own sailboards and taking their lives into their own hands.

Each small but luxuriously furnished guest room is behind a thick pine door heavily banded with iron under a vaulted stone ceiling. Most rooms overlook the savagely beautiful coastline. Some beds are set in alcoves. The marble bathrooms are supplied with robes and neatly kept shower-tub combinations. There are also three small but elegant suites, some with their own fireplaces.

Estrada do Guincho, 2750-642 Cascais. ✆ **21/487-04-91.** Fax 21/487-04-31. www.guinchotel.pt. 27 units. 165€–330€ ($190–$380) double; 295€–385€ ($340–$443) suite. Rates include buffet breakfast. AE, DC, MC, V. Free parking. **Amenities:** Restaurant; bar; limited room service; babysitting; laundry. *In room:* A/C, TV, minibar, hair dryer, safe.

MODERATE

Estalagem Senhora da Guia ★★ *Finds* Returning to their native Portugal after a sojourn in Brazil, the Ornellas family now runs this gem. They turned the former country villa of the Sagres brewery family into one of the loveliest hotels in the region. The 1970 house has thick walls, high ceilings, and elaborately crafted moldings that give the impression of a much older building.

A trio of multilingual siblings restored the house to its former glory. The elegant midsize guest rooms and suites contain reproductions of 18th-century Portuguese antiques, thick carpets, louvered shutters, and spacious modern bathrooms with shower-tub combinations. Because the villa sits on a bluff above the sea, the views are panoramic.

Estrada do Guincho, 2750-642 Cascais. ✆ **21/486-92-39.** Fax 21/486-92-27. www.senhoradaguia.com. 43 units. 125€–250€ ($144–$288) double; 170€–330€ ($196–$380) suite. Rates include buffet breakfast. Children 2–12 30€–40€ ($35–$46) in parent's room. AE, DC, MC, V. Free parking. **Amenities:** Restaurant; 2 bars; pool; concierge; limited room service; babysitting; laundry service. *In room:* A/C, TV, minibar, hair dryer, safe.

WHERE TO DINE

VERY EXPENSIVE

Restaurant Fortaleza do Guincho ★★ FRENCH/CONTINENTAL No other restaurant along the coast between Cascais and Guincho can compete with the sheer drama and majesty of this one. Set directly atop jagged rocks a few feet from the surf, it's part of what was once a military outpost for the Portuguese monarchs, built on this isolated site in the 17th century. In 2001, the restaurant was designated as a Relais & Châteaux establishment, thanks partly to its devoted allegiance to the tenets of modern French cuisine. A disciple (Marc Leouedec) of one of eastern France's most celebrated chefs (Antoine Westermann, owner of Beureheisl in Alsace) was installed as the hard-working director of the kitchens. Since then, the site has been acknowledged as the most gastronomically sophisticated in the region, with a world-class cuisine and impeccable service. Menu items change with the seasons and the inspiration of the chef but are likely to include shellfish soup with basil and saffron sauce, roasted monkfish in a red wine sauce with a confit of garlic and onions, pigeon and duck foie gras wrapped in cabbage and served with steamed celeriac, and shoulder of lamb in an herb and salt crust with thyme-flavored potatoes. An especially appealing dessert is fresh pineapple with vanilla, pineapple sorbet, and lemon-flavored biscuit.

In the Hotel Fortaleza do Guincho, Praia do Guincho. ✆ **021/487-04-91.** Reservations recommended. Main courses 18€–39€ ($21–$45). 3-course fixed-price menus 38€ ($44); 4-course fixed-price menu 53€ ($61). AE, DC, MC, V. Daily 12:30–3pm and 7–10:30pm.

MODERATE

Monte-Mar ★ *Finds* PORTUGUESE/SEAFOOD One of the most appealing restaurants in the region around Cascais occupies a low-slung seafront pavilion set above jagged rocks and a savagely beautiful landscape about 5km (3 miles) west of Cascais, beside the highway leading to Guincho. It contains two sun-flooded, contemporary-looking dining rooms separated by a busy, open-to-view kitchen. The entire structure is ringed with wide balconies. This has been a much-respected staple in Cascais for nearly a decade, thanks to an attentive staff and a policy of buying very fresh fish at least once (and usually twice) a day. Don't be fooled by what looks like a drainage ditch for storm water between the restaurant and the nearby sea. Beneath it are massive holding tanks that are likely to have contained some of the specialties that later appear at your table. All the seafood is beautifully prepared and served. But if you're unsure of what to order, consider sea bass or golden bream baked in a salt crust (usually prepared for two diners at a time). Or, opt for the time-tested dish on which this place has built its reputation: deep-fried filets of hake served with tartar sauce and new potatoes or rice. Buttery and firm-fleshed, it's one of the most delicious—and artfully simple—dishes in the region.

Oitavos, Estrada do Guincho. ✆ **21/486-92-70.** Reservations recommended. Main courses 15€–25€ ($17–$29). Tues–Sat noon–4pm and 7–11pm.

Restaurante Porto de Santa Maria ★★★ PORTUGUESE If you drive to this isolated windswept bluff, 8km (5 miles) west of Cascais, you won't be alone. This restaurant is one of the most appealing of its type along the coast, making it quite popular. It serves some of the best seafood in the area, worth the ride out from Lisbon. A doorman ushers you into the low-lying seafront building whose large windows take in views of the occasionally treacherous surf.

Lobster tanks bubble energetically near the entrance, and a trussed wooden ceiling holds up a contemporary piece of design. The polite staff serves every conceivable form of succulent shellfish, priced by the gram, as well as such house specialties as grilled sole. *Arroz de mariscos* (shellfish rice) is the most popular specialty—and justifiably so. Try the rondelles of pungent sheep's milk cheese that await you on the table.

Estrada do Guincho. ✆ **21/487-10-36** or 21/487-02-40. Regular main courses 10€–30€ ($12–$35). AE, DC, MC, V. Tues–Sun noon–5pm and 7–11pm.

4 Queluz

15km (9 miles) NW of Lisbon

Queluz, only 20 minutes from Lisbon, makes a great excursion from the capital or en route to Sintra. The Queluz Palace (see "Exploring the Palace," below), in its pink rococo glory, offers storybook Portuguese charm.

ESSENTIALS

ARRIVING

BY TRAIN From the Estação do Rossio in Lisbon, take the Sintra line to Queluz. Departures during the day are every 15 minutes. The trip takes 30 minutes. A one-way ticket costs 1€ ($1.15). Call ✆ **808/208-208** for schedules. At Queluz, turn left and follow the signs for less than 1km (¾ mile) to the palace.

BY CAR From Lisbon, head west along the express highway (A1), which becomes Route 249. Turn off at the exit for Queluz. It usually takes 20 minutes.

VISITOR INFORMATION

You can ask for information at the tourist office in Sintra (see below).

Exploring the Palace

Palácio Nacional de Queluz ★★, Largo do Palácio, 2745-191 Queluz (✆ **21/434-38-60**), on the highway from Lisbon to Sintra, shimmers in the sunlight. It's a brilliant example of the rococo in Portugal. Pedro III ordered its construction in 1747, and the work dragged on until 1787. The architect Mateus Vicente de Oliveira was later joined by the French decorator-designer Jean-Baptiste Robillion, who was largely responsible for planning the garden and lakeside setting.

Pedro III had adapted an old hunting pavilion that once belonged to the Marquis Castelo Rodrigo but later came into the possession of the Portuguese royal family. Pedro III liked it so much that he decided to make it his summer residence. What you'll see today is not what the palace was like in the 18th century; during the French invasions, almost all of its belongings were transported to Brazil with the royal family. A 1934 fire destroyed a great deal of Queluz, but tasteful and sensitive reconstruction restored the lighthearted aura of the 18th century.

Blossoming mauve petunias and red geraniums highlight the topiary effects, with closely trimmed vines and sculptured box hedges. Fountain pools on which lilies float are lined with blue tiles and reflect the muted facade, the statuary, and the finely cut balustrades.

Inside you can wander through the queen's dressing room, lined with painted panels depicting a children's romp; the Don Quixote Chamber (Dom Pedro was born here and returned from Brazil to die in the same bed); the Music Room, complete with a French *grande pianoforte* and an 18th-century English harpsichord; and the mirrored throne room adorned with crystal chandeliers. The Portuguese still hold state banquets here.

Festooning the palace are all the eclectic props of the rococo era. You'll see the inevitable chinoiserie panels from Macau, Florentine marbles from quarries once worked on by Michelangelo, Iberian and Flemish tapestries, Empire antiques, Delft indigo-blue ceramics, 18th-century Hepplewhite armchairs, Austrian porcelains, Rabat carpets, Portuguese Chippendale furnishings, and Brazilian jacaranda wood pieces—all of exquisite quality. When they visited Portugal, Presidents Eisenhower, Carter, and Reagan stayed in the 30-chambered Pavilion of Dona Maria I, as did Elizabeth II and the prince and princess of Wales. These fabled chambers are said to have reverberated with the rantings of the grief-stricken monarch Maria I, who reputedly had to be strapped to her bed at times. Before becoming mentally ill, she was an intelligent, brave woman who did a great job as ruler of her country in a troubled time.

The palace is open Wednesday through Monday from 10am to 5pm. It's closed on holidays. Admission is 3€ ($3.45), free for children under 14.

WHERE TO STAY

Pousada Dona Maria ★★★ Uniquely located, this is one of the gems of Portugal's network of pousadas. This building's function during the 17th century was to house the staff that maintained the Palace of Queluz, which rises in stately majesty across the road. The pousada is graced with an ornate clock tower that evokes an oversize ornament in the garden of a stately English home. In addition to the pousada's comfortable midsize guest rooms and well-managed dining room, the premises contain touches of complicated Manueline stonework. The 17th-century theater holds occasional concerts. The high-ceilinged rooms are severely dignified and contain fine beds and neatly kept bathrooms equipped with shower-tub combinations.

Largo do Palácio, 2745 Queluz. ✆ **800/223-1356** for reservations in the U.S., or ✆ 21/435-61-58. Fax 21/435-61-89. 26 units. 112€–173€ ($129–$199) double; 135€–213€ ($155–$245) suite. Rates include breakfast. AE, DC, MC, V. From Sintra, take highway IC-19 and follow signs to Queluz. Free parking. **Amenities:** Restaurant; bar; room service; laundry service. *In room:* A/C, TV, minibar, hair dryer, safe.

WHERE TO DINE

Cozinha Velha (The Old Kitchen) ★★★ PORTUGUESE/INTERNATIONAL If you have only two or three meals in the Lisbon area, take one at the Cozinha Velha. Once it was the kitchen of the palace, built in the grand style; it has since been converted into a colorful dining room favored by those seeking a gourmet dinner in a romantic setting.

The dining room is like a small chapel, with high stone arches, a freestanding fireplace, and marble columns. Along one side is a 6m (20-ft.) marble table laden with baskets of fruit and vases of flowers. You sit on ladder-back chairs surrounded by shiny copper, oil paintings, and torchières. The innovative handling of regional ingredients pleases most diners, and the cooking uses spices, herbs, and textures well. We recommend the hors d'oeuvres for two, followed by a main course such as black grouper medallions with prawn béchamel, poached sole Cozinha Velha, fried goat with mashed turnip sprouts, or pepper steak with spinach mousse. For dessert, try the crepes Cozinha Velha with champagne sorbet.

Palácio Nacional de Queluz, Largo do Palácio. ✆ **21/435-02-32.** Reservations required. Main courses 20€–26€ ($23–$30). AE, DC, MC, V. Daily 12:30–3pm and 7:30–10pm.

5 Sintra: Byron's "Glorious Eden" ★★★

29km (18 miles) NW of Lisbon

Writers have sung Sintra's praises ever since Portugal's national poet, Luís Vaz de Camões, proclaimed its glory in *Os Lusíadas* (The Lusiads). Lord Byron called it "glorious Eden" when he and John Cam Hobhouse included Sintra in their 1809 grand tour. English romantics thrilled to its description in Byron's autobiographical *Childe Harold's Pilgrimage.*

Picture a town on a hillside, with decaying birthday-cake villas covered with tiles coming loose in the damp mist. Luxuriant vegetation covers the town: camellias for melancholic romantics, ferns behind which lizards dart, pink and purple bougainvillea over garden trelliswork, red geraniums on wrought-iron balconies, eucalyptus branches fluttering in the wind, lemon trees in groves, and honey-sweet mimosa scenting the air. But take heed—some who visit Sintra fall under its spell and stay forever.

Sintra is one of the oldest towns in the country. When the crusaders captured it in 1147, they fought bitterly against the Moors firmly entrenched in their hilltop castle, the ruins of which remain today.

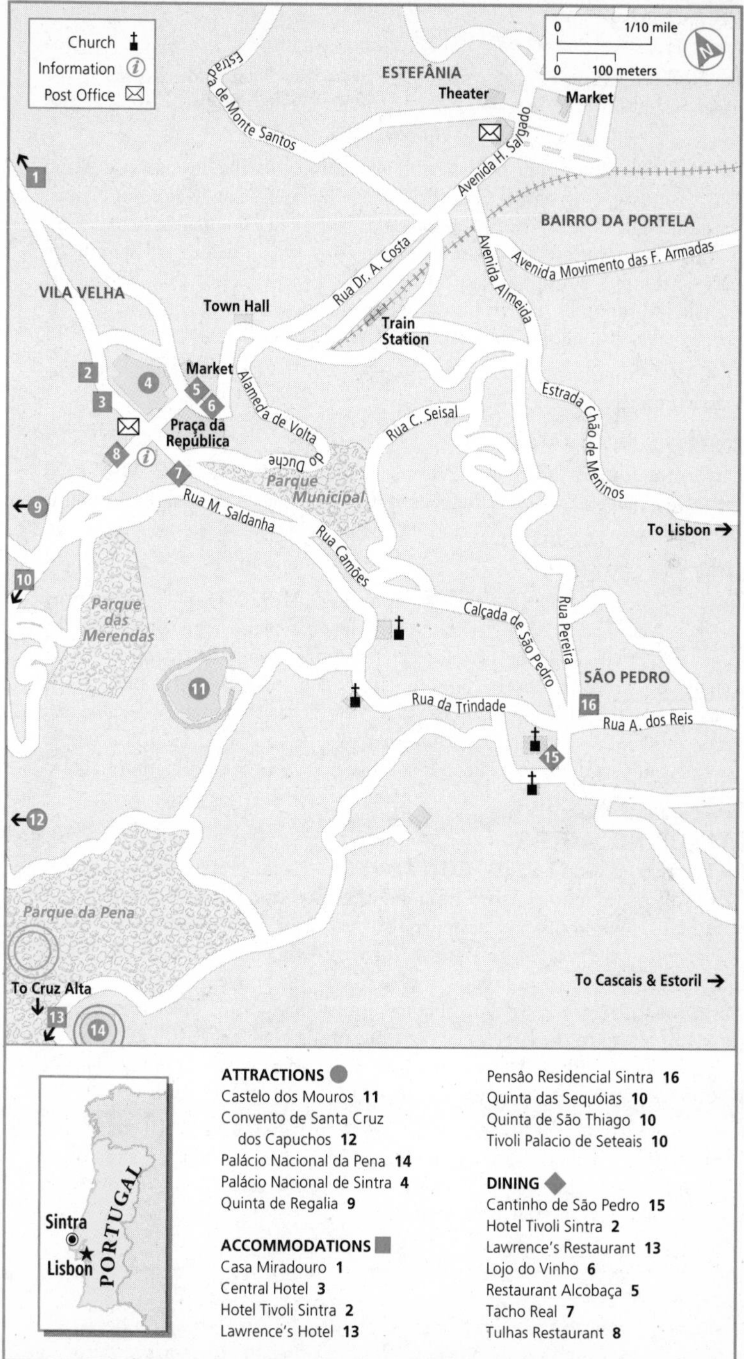
Church
Information
Post Office
0 1/10 mile
0 100 meters
ESTEFÂNIA
Theater
Market
Estrada de Monte Santos
Avenida H. Sargado
BAIRRO DA PORTELA
Avenida Movimento das F. Armadas
Avenida Almeida
Rua Dr. A. Costa
VILA VELHA
Town Hall
Train Station
Market
Praça da República
Alameda de Volta do Duche
Parque Municipal
Rua C. Seisal
Estrada Chão de Meninos
To Lisbon
Rua M. Saldanha
Rua Camões
Parque das Merendas
Calçada de São Pedro
Rua Pereira
SÃO PEDRO
Rua da Trindade
Rua A. dos Reis
Parque da Pena
To Cruz Alta
To Cascais & Estoril
Sintra
Lisbon
PORTUGAL
ATTRACTIONS
Castelo dos Mouros 11
Convento de Santa Cruz dos Capuchos 12
Palácio Nacional da Pena 14
Palácio Nacional de Sintra 4
Quinta de Regalia 9
ACCOMMODATIONS
Casa Miradouro 1
Central Hotel 3
Hotel Tivoli Sintra 2
Lawrence's Hotel 13
Pensâo Residencial Sintra 16
Quinta das Sequóias 10
Quinta de São Thiago 10
Tivoli Palacio de Seteais 10
DINING
Cantinho de São Pedro 15
Hotel Tivoli Sintra 2
Lawrence's Restaurant 13
Lojo do Vinho 6
Restaurant Alcobaça 5
Tacho Real 7
Tulhas Restaurant 8

ESSENTIALS

ARRIVING

BY TRAIN Sintra is a 45-minute ride from the Estação do Rossio at the Rossio in Lisbon. A train leaves every 15 minutes. The round-trip fare is 2.50€ ($2.90). For information, call ✆ **808/208-208.**

BY BUS The bus from Lisbon is not recommended because service is too slow. Visitors staying on the Costa do Sol can make bus connections at Cascais or Estoril. The Sintra depot is on Avenida Dr. Miguel Bombarda, across from the main train station. Departures from in front of the Estoril rail station are every 45 minutes during the day. A one-way ticket costs 2.40€ ($2.75), and the trip takes 40 minutes. Eleven buses a day run between Sintra and Cascais. The journey takes 1 hour, and the round-trip fare is 2.50€ ($2.90).

BY CAR From Lisbon, head west along A1, which becomes Route 249 on its eastern approach to Sintra.

VISITOR INFORMATION

The **Sintra Tourist Office** is at Praça da República 23 (✆ **21/923-11-57**). It's open daily 9am to 7pm from October to May, and daily 9am to 8pm from June to September.

SPECIAL EVENTS

From June to early August, the Sintra Festival (✆ **21/910-71-17**) attracts many music lovers. The program consists entirely of a piano repertoire from the romantic period, with the best interpreters from today's international music scene. The concerts, about eight in all, usually take place in the region's churches, palaces (Palácio da Vila, Palácio da Pena, and Palácio de Queluz), parks, and country estates. Each concert costs 20€ to 25€ ($23–$29), but the price depends on the event. The tourist office (see "Visitor Information," above) will furnish details.

EXPLORING SINTRA

PALACES, CASTLES & CONVENTS

Many organized tours depart from both Lisbon and Sintra. However, this approach allows no time for personal discovery, a must in Sintra.

Horse-drawn carriages are available for rent between the town and Serra de Sintra. The 45-minute tour costs 25€ ($29) for up to five passengers. It's well worth the price for a most agreeable trip under shady trees. The carriages start from and return to the large square in front of the National Palace of Sintra.

If you arrive in Sintra by train, you'll have to either take a taxi to the sights or trek up the long, lush hill to the national palace—a very long walk.

Palácio Nacional de Sintra ★★★ A royal palace until 1910, the Sintra National Palace was last inhabited by Queen Maria Pía, the Italian grandmother of Manuel II, the last king of Portugal. Much of the palace was constructed in the days of the first Manuel, the Fortunate.

Crime Watch

Warning: Don't leave valuables in unguarded cars in Sintra, and beware of pickpockets and purse-snatchers. Not only does the town attract virtually every tourist in Portugal, but it also attracts those who prey on them. While violence is not generally a problem, theft is.

Tips Getting to the Palace

If you're not driving, you can take a 20-minute taxi or bus ride; the bus departs from Sintra's main square from May to September. Many visitors have a taxi wait for them. If you walk, be warned that the arduous 2.5km (1½-mile) climb from the square takes about 2 hours even if you're in good shape.

Long before the arrival of the crusaders under Afonso Henríques, this was a summer palace of Moorish sultans. The original palace was torn down, and the Moorish style of architecture was incorporated into latter-day versions. The structure is now a conglomeration of styles, with Gothic and Manueline predominant. The glazed earthenware tiles lining many of the chambers are among the most beautiful in Portugal.

The Swan Room was a favorite of João I, one of the founding kings of Portugal, father of Henry the Navigator and husband of Philippa of Lancaster. The Room of the Sirens or Mermaids is one of the most elegant in the palace. The Heraldic or Stag Room holds coats of arms of aristocratic Portuguese families, and hunting scenes. In most of the rooms, wide windows look out onto attractive views of the Sintra mountain range. Tile-fronted stoves are in the Old Kitchen, where feasts were held in bygone days. The palace is rich in paintings and Iberian and Flemish tapestries, but perhaps you can best appreciate the place as you wander into a tree- and plant-shaded patio and listen to the water gurgling in a fountain.

As you approach the palace, you can buy a ticket at the kiosk on your left. The palace opens onto the central town square. Outside, two conical chimney towers form the most distinctive landmark on the Sintra skyline.

Largo da Rainha Dona Amélia. ✆ **21/910-68-40.** Admission 3€ ($3.45) adults, 1.50€ ($1.75) children 14–25, free for children under 14. Thurs–Tues 10am–1pm and 2–5pm.

Palácio Nacional de Pena ★★ Pena perches above Sintra on a plateau about 450m (1,476 ft.) above sea level. Part of the fun of visiting the castle is the ride up the verdant, winding road through the Parque das Merendas.

The inspiration behind this castle in the sky was Ferdinand of Saxe-Coburg-Gotha, the husband of Maria II. Ferdinand called on a fellow German, Baron Eschwege, to help him build his fantasy. You can see a sculpture of the baron if you look out from the Pena toward a huge rock across the way.

In the early 16th century, Manuel the Fortunate ordered a monastery for the Jerónimos monks built on these lofty grounds. Today you can visit a preserved cloister and small ogival chapel.

The palace's last royal occupant was Queen Amélia. One morning in 1910, she clearly saw that the monarchy in Portugal was ending. Having lost her husband and her soldier-son to an assassin 2 years before, she was determined not to lose her second son, Manuel II. Gathering her most precious possessions, she fled to Mafra, where her son waited. She did not see the Pena palace again until 1945, when she returned to Portugal under much more favorable conditions. Pena has remained much as Amélia left it, making it a rare record of European royal life in the halcyon days preceding World War I.

Pena Park was designed and planted for more than 4 years, beginning in 1846. Ferdinand was the force behind the landscaping. He built one of the most spectacular parks in Portugal, known for the scope of its shrub and tree life. For an eye-opening vista of the park and the palace, you can make the ascent to Cruz Alta. Admission to the park is free.

Estrada de Pena. ✆ **21/923-73-00.** Admission 5€ ($5.75), 3.50€ ($4.05) children 6–17, free for children 5 and under. Oct–May Tues–Sun 10am–5pm; June–Sept Tues–Sun 10am–6:30pm. Last admission half-hour before closing.

Castelo dos Mouros ★ The Castle of the Moors was built sometime between the 8th and 9th centuries in a position 412m (1,351 ft.) above sea level. In 1147, Scandinavian crusaders besieged and captured it from its Moorish occupants. Ferdinand of Saxe-Coburg-Gotha, the royal consort responsible for Pena palace (see above), attempted to restore the castle in the 19th century. He was relatively unsuccessful.

From the parking area, a guide will send you in the right direction. From the royal tower, the view of Sintra, its palace and castle, and the Atlantic coast is panoramic.

Calçada dos Clérigos. ✆ **21/923-73-00.** 3€ ($3.45) adult, 2€ ($2.30) seniors and children 6–17, free for children under 6. Daily June–Sept 9am–8pm; Oct–May 9am–7pm. From Pena palace (10-min. walk), follow signs to the castelo.

Convento de Santa Cruz dos Capuchos ★ In 1560, Dom Álvaro de Castro ordered that this unusually structured convent be built for the Capuchins. The construction used cork so extensively that the building is sometimes known as the cork monastery.

The convent is in a secluded area 7.25km (4½ miles) from Sintra. You walk up a moss-covered path and ring the bell, and a guide appears to show you around the miniature cells. Today the convent seems forlorn and forgotten. Even when it was in use, it probably wasn't noted for its liveliness. The Capuchins who lived here, perhaps eight in all, had a penchant for the most painstakingly detailed work. For example, they lined the monastery walls with cork-bark tiles and seashells. They also carved a chapel out of rock, using cork for insulation. Outside there's an altar fresco in honor of St. Francis of Assisi. In 1834, the monks suddenly abandoned the convent, most likely to escape the crowded, primitive conditions in which the harsh environment forced them to live.

There's no bus service; if you're not driving, take a taxi from Sintra's main square.

Estrada de Pena. ✆ **21/923-73-00.** Admission 3€ ($3.45). Daily June–Sept 9am–8pm; Oct–May 9am–6pm.

Quinta de Regaleiga Classified as a World Heritage Site by UNESCO, this *quinta* (manor house) in the old quarter was built at the turn of the 20th century. It incorporates architectural elements of the Gothic, Manueline, and Renaissance styles. You can take a tour of the property, which is filled with antiques and artifacts. The building's turrets afford panoramic views of the countryside. After touring the house, visitors can stroll through the surrounding park.

Rua Visconde de Monserrate. ✆ **21/910-66-50.** Admission 10€ ($12) adults, 5€ ($5.75) children 8–14, free for children under 8. Daily 10am–6pm.

HAVING FUN IN SINTRA

OUTDOOR ACTIVITIES The best golf course is the **Estoril-Sol Golf Club,** Estrada da Lagoa Azul, outside Sintra (✆ **21/923-24-61**). At the foot of the Sintra mountain range, the course lies some 32km (20 miles) from Lisbon. The Palácio Nacional da Pena looms overhead, and the course occupies a forest setting with acacias and pines. It's fairly short, stretching 4,429m (14,527 ft.)

and offering only 9 holes. A 9-hole round costs 24€ ($28) Monday through Friday, 31€ ($36) Saturday and Sunday, and 17€ ($20) after 4pm Monday through Friday. It's open Monday through Friday 8 am to 7 pm, and Saturday and Sunday 8am to 8pm.

SHOPPING Folkloric, history-rich Sintra has been a repository of salable Portuguese charm since the dawn of modern tourism. As you wander through its cobblestone streets and alleyways, you'll find many intriguing outlets for handmade folk art from the region and the rest of Portugal.

The best shops include the **Sintra Bazar,** Praça da República 37 (✆ **21/924-82-40**), where seven or eight different merchants maintain individual boutiques selling creative handcrafts. On the same street is **A Esquina,** Praça da República 20 (✆ **21/923-34-27**). It carries many hand-painted ceramics, some of which are reproductions of designs that originated between the 15th and 18th centuries. **Almorábida,** Rua Visconde de Monserrate 12–14 (✆ **21/924-05-39**), in front of Sintra Palace, sells Arraiolos carpets, lace, and intricately hammered copperware. A worthy antiques shop close to the town center is **Henríque Teixera,** Rua Consiglieri Pedroso 2 (✆ **21/923-10-43**). It carries sometimes dauntingly expensive furniture and accessories, including an exceptional collection of antique brass and bronze hardware.

Casa Branca, Rua Consiglieri Pedroso 12 (✆ **21/923-05-28**), is the shop for linens. A recent client included U.S. Secretary of State Madeleine Albright, who binge-shopped here for what we were told was more than 30,000€ ($34,500) worth of bed- and tableware. Inventories include embroideries from Madeira, the Azores, and the north of Portugal. Nightdresses and negligees, some of them with rich embroideries on silk or cotton, are particularly beautiful, often with provocatively flimsy décolletage.

Violeta, Rua das Padarias 19 (✆ **21/923-40-95**), stocks hand-embroidered linen tablecloths, towels, sheets, and bedspreads.

WHERE TO STAY

VERY EXPENSIVE

Tivoli Palácio de Seteais ★★★ This is one of the most luxurious palaces at which you can lodge in all of Portugal. Lord Byron worked on *Childe Harold's Pilgrimage* in the front garden of this palace, which later became a hotel. Seteais looks older than it is—a Dutch Gildmeester built it in the late 18th century. The fifth marquês de Marialva, who sponsored many receptions and galas for the aristocrats of his day, later took over and restored the palace.

The hotel lies at the end of a long driveway. An arched entryway dominates the formal stone architecture. The palace is on the crest of a hill; most of its drawing rooms, galleries, and chambers overlook the formal terraces, flower garden, and vista toward the sea. A long hall and a staircase with white-and-gilt balustrades and columns lead to the lower-level dining room, drinking lounge, and garden terraces. The library and adjoining music room are furnished with period pieces. The main drawing room contains antiques and a fine mural extending around the cove and onto the ceiling.

There are only 30 units; and advance reservations are necessary. The beautiful, spacious rooms are furnished with antiques or tasteful reproductions. All contain immaculately kept bathrooms with shower-tub combinations.

Rua Barbosa do Bocage 8, Seteais, 2710-517 Sintra. ✆ **21/923-32-00.** Fax 21/923-42-77. www.tivolihotels.com/tivoli/www/E/hoteis/seteais/descricao.asp. 30 units. 240€–285€ ($276–$328) double; 375€ ($431) suite. Rates include breakfast. AE, DC, MC, V. **Amenities:** Restaurant; bar; pool; tennis courts; concierge; limited room service; babysitting; laundry service. *In room:* TV, minibar, hair dryer, safe.

MODERATE

Hotel Tivoli Sintra ★ This is the finest hotel in the center of Sintra and a favorite with groups. The modern, airy Tivoli Sintra opened in 1981. It lies only a few doors from the Central Hotel (see below) and the National Palace, and offers an abundance of modern conveniences, including a garage. The spacious guest rooms are comfortably furnished, with large beds and big easy-chairs. All units are also equipped with well-maintained bathrooms containing shower-tub combinations. The balconies and the public rooms look out onto a wooded hill with views of Sintra's *quintas* (manor houses). The sight, according to a reader from Berkeley, California, "could have inspired mad Ludwig of Bavaria or at least Walt Disney." The hotel has a restaurant with panoramic views of Monserrate.

Praça da República, 2710-616 Sintra. ✆ **21/923-35-05.** Fax 21/923-72-45. www.tivolihotels.com. 76 units. 115€–135€ ($132–$155) double; 150€–185€ ($173–$213) suite. Rates include breakfast. AE, DC, MC, V. Free parking. **Amenities:** Restaurant; bar; car rental desk; business center; limited room service; laundry service; dry cleaning; nonsmoking rooms; 1 room for those w/limited mobility. *In room:* A/C, TV, minibar, hair dryer, safe.

Lawrence's Hotel ★★ *Finds* Lawrence's Hotel boasts a pedigree that's older than that of any other hotel in Iberia. It originated in the 1760s, when an eccentric but formidable English innkeeper (Jane Lawrence) established the hotel. Its fortunes were assured in 1809, when Lord Byron stayed here for a 12-day visit and publicized the virtues of Sintra and the hotel in his writings. In 1999, after more than 30 years as a derelict shell, the hotel was renovated, enlarged, and reopened under the supervision of the Dutch-born Bos (Jan and Coreen) family. After millions of dollars of expenditures, the hotel is now one of the most desirable inns in Portugal. It occupies a low-slung yellow building a short walk uphill from the center of town, on the road that leads to the Pena Palace. Because of the sloping terrain on which it sits, you enter from the street onto the third floor of a six-story building with a tasteful, completely unglitzy decor and the most recent in electronics and security devices. Bedrooms are airily furnished with tasteful replicas of 19th century furniture, in a spirit of thrift that emulates that of a discreetly upscale private home. Some units have private terraces, and all have a combination shower-tub. Many of this hotel's famous visitors (Bill Clinton, Madeleine Albright, Tony Blair, and the president of Portugal) have also eaten in the hotel's restaurant, which is described separately below.

Rua Consigliéri Pedroso 38–40, 2710-550 Sintra. ✆ **21/910-55-00.** Fax 21/910-55-05. lawrences_hotel@email.com. 16 units. 171€–264€ ($197–$304) double; 299€–395€ ($344–$454) suites. Extra bed 34€–39€ ($39–$45) per person. Rates include breakfast. AE, DC, MC, V. **Amenities:** Restaurant; bar; concierge. *In room:* A/C, TV, hair dryer, safe.

Quinta das Sequóias ★★ *Finds* Standing on 16 hectares (40 acres) of wooded grounds, this beautiful 19th-century manor house lies less than 1km (¾ mile) below the Palacio de Seteais (see above). The manor house was originally built as a rural annex of a much larger palace (the Palácio do Relogio) in Sintra's center. The generally spacious nonsmoking rooms have high ceilings and formal 19th-century furniture. All units come equipped with neatly kept bathrooms containing shower-tub combinations. On the premises is a verdant English-style garden. Within a 16km (10-mile) walk from the main house are an archaeological dig, where Roman coins and artifacts from the Bronze Age have been unearthed, and bubbling springs whose pure waters were noted by historians during the 15th century. If you give notice at breakfast, dinner can be prepared.

Apdo. 1004, 2710-801 Sintra. ✆ **21/910-60-65.** Fax 21/910-60-65. www.quintadasequoias.com. 6 units. 120€–145€ ($138–$167) double. Rates include buffet breakfast. AE, DC, MC, V. Closed 2 weeks in Jan. Free parking. From Sintra, take the road signposted for Montserrate and then fork left at signpost for hotel. **Amenities:** Dining room; bar; pool; sauna; room service; laundry service.

Quinta de São Thiago ★ Visited by Lord Byron in 1809, Quinta de São Thiago is one of the most desirable places to stay in the Sintra area. Reached on a rough road, it edges up the side of a mountain in a woodland setting. Its origins as a *quinta* (manor house) go back to the 1500s. It has been refurbished and handsomely furnished with antiques. Many of the units open onto views of the Valley of Colares and the water beyond. The pool offers views of Monserrate and the Atlantic coastline.

In the finest British tradition, tea is offered in the parlor, which was transformed from the original kitchen. Dances are held in summer in the music room, and summertime buffets are true occasions. The midsize guest rooms are comfortably furnished and attractively decorated, with neatly kept bathrooms with modern plumbing and shower-tub combinations.

Estrada de Monserrate, 2710-610 Sintra. ✆ **21/923-29-23.** Fax 21/923-43-29. 9 units. 110€ ($126) double; 165€ ($190) suite. Rates include buffet breakfast. No credit cards. Free parking. **Amenities:** Dining room; bar; tennis court; laundry service.

INEXPENSIVE

Casa Miradouro ★★ *Finds* At the edge of Sintra, this candy-striped house is a snug, cozy retreat. From its 1894 construction until 1987, it belonged to several generations of a family that included important figures in the Portuguese army. In 1993, Swiss-born Frederic Kneubühl bought it, renovated it, and filled it with a practical mixture of modern and late-19th-century furniture. It's now a well-managed, attractively indulgent B&B. About .5km (⅓ mile) north of Sintra, it boasts a small garden, very few amenities other than the owner's genteel goodwill, and a facade that art historians have defined as Iberian chalet style. The excellently maintained rooms are most inviting, with provincial carpets, tile floors, wrought-iron bedsteads, and neatly kept bathrooms equipped with showers. Views from upper-floor rooms include the Pena Palace and, on clear days, the faraway Atlantic.

Rua Sotto Mayor 55, 2710-801 Sintra. ✆ **21/923-59-00.** Fax 21/924-18-36. www.casa-miradouro.com. 6 units. 104€–122€ ($120–$140) double. Rates include breakfast. AE, MC, V. Closed Jan 6–Feb 22. From the Hotel Tivoli Sintra (see above), take Rua Sotto Mayor for .4km (¼ mile). **Amenities:** Breakfast room; bar; babysitting; laundry service. *In room:* No phone.

Central Hotel *Value* This charming but slightly tarnished family-owned and -operated village inn offers personalized accommodations and good food. The hotel opens onto the main square, facing the National Palace; accommodations fronting the square are noisy. The facade is inviting, with decorative blue-and-white tiles and an awning-covered front veranda with dining tables. The interior, especially the small guest rooms, is English in style. Each room is furnished individually with such fine pieces as polished wood and inlaid desks. Nearly all the tiled bathrooms are equipped with shower-tub combinations and are well designed and decorated in cheerful colors.

The Central's restaurant offers seating on the veranda overlooking the village or in one of the large interior rooms.

Praça da República, 2710-616 Sintra. ✆ **21/923-09-64.** 10 units. 50€–75€ ($58–$86) double; 65€–85€ ($75–$98) triple. Rates include breakfast. MC, V. **Amenities:** Restaurant; bar; room service; laundry service.

Pensão Residencial Sintra In São Pedro, a verdant suburb of Sintra, this is an 1850s stone house commissioned by its former occupant, Viscount Tojal. Shortly after World War II, the German-born parents of the present owner, Susana Rosner Fragoso, bought the house and transformed it into a dignified *pensão* (boarding house). The pastel-colored midsize rooms contain simple but comfortable furniture from the 1950s and '60s. All units contain well-maintained bathrooms equipped with shower-tub combinations.

Travessa dos Avelares 12, 2710-506 Sintra. ✆ and fax **21/923-07-38.** 15 units. 45€–85€ ($52–$98) double. Rates include buffet breakfast. MC, V. Free parking. From Sintra, take a bus marked São Pedro or Mirasintra. **Amenities:** Breakfast room; bar; pool; limited room service; laundry service; rooms for those w/limited mobility. *In room:* TV.

WHERE TO DINE

MODERATE

Cantinho de São Pedro ★ PORTUGUESE/FRENCH Less than 2km (1¼ mile) southeast of Sintra, in São Pedro de Sintra, this is one of the hillside village's finest dining choices. It's right off the main square, Praça Dom Fernando II, where the *Feira da Sintra* (Sintra Fair) is staged every second and fourth Sunday of the month. Dating from the time of the Christian Reconquest, the fair is one of the oldest in the country. Look for the *pratos do dia* (daily specials), or save your appetite for the tasty specialties. They include velvety crepes stuffed with fresh lobster, and meltingly tender beefsteak in green pepper sauce. On a recent visit, we enjoyed salmon and shrimp au gratin. Pork with clams in the style of the province of Alentejo remains the eternal and justifiably popular favorite.

Praça Dom Fernando II 18 (at Lojas do Picadeiro). ✆ **21/923-02-67.** Reservations recommended. Main courses 14€–27€ ($16–$31); 18€ ($21) tourist menu. AE, DC, MC, V. Daily noon–3pm and 7:30–10pm.

Hotel Tivoli Sintra ★ PORTUGUESE/INTERNATIONAL Because this restaurant is within the concrete-and-glass walls of the town center's most desirable hotel, many visitors might overlook the Tivoli Sintra as a dining spot. That would be too bad—it serves some of the finest food in town. Staffed by a battalion of uniformed waiters, the room has a shimmering metallic ceiling, dark paneling, and floor-to-ceiling windows on one side. The daily menu is likely to include such carefully crafted dishes as tournedos Rossini, fish soup, and filet of turbot with mushrooms and garlic.

Praça da República. ✆ **21/923-35-05.** Reservations recommended. Main courses 13€–17€ ($15–$20); fixed-price menu 21€ ($24). AE, DC, MC, V. Daily 12:30–3pm and 7:30–10pm.

Lawrence's Restaurant ★ INTERNATIONAL The owners of this restaurant describe it as the main focus of the hotel that contains it, occupying more of their attention than the hotel itself. Outfitted in a tasteful interpretation of a late-19th-century decor, it has welcomed diners that have included presidents, statesmen, diplomats, and actors, all of whom seem to appreciate the superb cuisine and graceful service. The menu changes frequently, but it's likely to include a sophisticated version of fish soup; black tagliolini with grilled octopus, squid ink, and fresh sweet basil; house-style codfish; and grilled filet of sea bass with a confit of leeks. Meat items include a roasted spit that contains both venison and white veal, and a roasted magret of duck served with Roösti potatoes and wild berry sauce. Dessert might be a theatrical version of flambéed crepes prepared directly at tableside.

In Lawrence's Hotel, Rua Consigliéri Pedroso 38–40. ✆ **21/910-55-00.** Reservations recommended. Main courses 13€–42€ ($15–$48). AE, DC, MC, V. Daily 12:30–2:30pm and 7:30–9:45pm.

Tacho Real ★★ PORTUGUESE/FRENCH Lisboans come in from the city to enjoy the well-prepared meals at this chic, elegant, and stylish restaurant. It's set at the top of a steep flight of cobble-covered steps and ramps that lead uphill, after a huff-and-puff short walk from the Praça da República below. The kitchen deftly handles fish and meat dishes, and some succulent poultry dishes also appear on the menu. Two popular house specialties are fish filet with shrimp sauce and rice, and filet steak with cream sauce and mushrooms. We always like the bubbling fish stew. The fixed-price menu is a bargain that includes soup, a main course, dessert, coffee, and half a bottle of wine. Service is efficient and polite, and English is spoken.

Rua da Ferraria 4. ✆ **21/923-52-77.** Reservations recommended. Main courses 8€–19€ ($9.20–$22); fixed-price menu 12€ ($14). AE, DC, MC, V. Thurs–Tues noon–3pm and 7:30–10:30pm.

INEXPENSIVE

Lojo do Vinho SNACKS/WINE Set directly on the town's main square, this establishment combines aspects of both a restaurant and a wine shop. No one will mind if you browse the inventory of wine and port from throughout the country. But if you're hungry, you can sit at any of several low-slung tables and enjoy wine by the glass with some simple snacks. These might include a selection of Portuguese cheese, sausages, olives, or smoked ham. Additional bottles are on display in the slightly claustrophobic setting. Overall, it's a fine way to acquaint yourself with ethnic Portuguese wines in a setting that evokes a medieval wine cellar.

Praça da República 3. ✆ **21/924-44-10.** Snacks, platters, and sandwiches 4€–16€ ($4.60–$18); glasses of wine 2.50€–18€ ($2.90–$21). AE, DC, MC, V. Daily 9am–10:30pm.

Restaurant Alcobaça PORTUGUESE Popular with English visitors, this shop-size restaurant occupies two floors of a centrally located building on a steep, narrow pedestrian street. You can get one of the cheapest meals in town here. The Alcobaça serves typical Portuguese cuisine, including flavorful monkfish rice, tasty roast sardines, *caldo verde* (a soup with ham hock, greens, and potatoes), hake filet with rice, octopus, Alcobaça chicken, and succulent pork with clams. It's the kind of robust food beloved by locals.

Rua das Padarias 7, 9, and 11. ✆ **21/923-16-51.** Reservations recommended. Main courses 5€–11€ ($5.75–$13); fixed-price menu 10€ ($12). AE, MC, V. Daily noon–4pm and 7–10:30pm.

Tulhas Restaurant PORTUGUESE This restaurant, decorated with tiles and wood, is between the tourism office and San Martin Church. Specialties of the house are codfish in cream sauce with potatoes, roasted lamb or duck with rice, steak *au poivre* (pepper steak with pepper sauce), and veal Madeira. You'll find better food elsewhere, but the quality of the meat and fish is good, and the chefs present platters with perfectly balanced flavors.

Gil Vicente 4. ✆ **21/923-23-78.** Main courses 7€–17€ ($8.05–$20). AE, DC, MC, V. Thurs–Tues noon–3:30pm and 7–10pm.

SINTRA AFTER DARK

Sintra is not a party town; the most intriguing soirées are private. A worthy bar in the center of town, where you might meet people from any country in Europe, is **Adega das Caves,** Praça da República 2–10 (✆ **21/923-08-48**). The establishment is a restaurant that does a busy lunch trade. After dark, it mellows into a likable bar and bodega, specializing in beer and Portuguese wine. It's open every day till around 2am. A nearby competitor is the **Taverna dos Trovadores,** São Pedro (✆ **21/923-35-48**), which lies in the center of the tiny hamlet of São

Pedro, less than 2km (1¼ miles) south from the center of Sintra. Popular and convivial, it incorporates aspects of an old-fashioned *tasca* (tavern) with a modern singles bar and it features recorded and (on rare occasions) live music, a long drink list, and a cross-section of residents from throughout the region.

6 Ericeira ★

21km (13 miles) NW of Sintra, 50km (31 miles) NW of Lisbon

This fishing port is nestled on the Atlantic shore. Whitewashed houses accented with pastel-painted corners and window frames line its narrow streets. To the east rise the mountains of Sintra.

The sea gives life to Ericeira, as it has for some 700 years. Fishermen still pluck their food from it. The beach lures streams of visitors every summer, giving a much-needed boost to the local economy. Along the coast, cliffside nurseries called *serrações* breed lobsters. Lobster is the house specialty at every restaurant in Ericeira.

In 1584, Mateus Alvares arrived in Ericeira from the Azores, claiming to be King Sebastião, who had reportedly been killed on the battlefields of North Africa. Alvares and about two dozen of his chief supporters were executed after their defeat by the soldiers of Philip II of Spain, but today he is regarded as the king of Ericeira. In October 1910, the fleeing Manuel II and his mother, Amélia, set sail from the Ericeira harbor to a life of exile in England.

ESSENTIALS

ARRIVING

There is no direct rail service to Ericeira.

BY BUS Mafrense buses from both Sintra and Lisbon serve Ericeira. One bus per hour leaves Lisbon's Largo Martim Moniz for the 1¼-hour trip. A one-way ticket costs 4€ ($4.60). From Sintra, there's one bus per hour. The trip takes 1 hour and costs 3.90€ ($4.50) one-way.

BY CAR From Sintra (see earlier), continue northwest along Route 247.

VISITOR INFORMATION

The **Ericeira Tourist Office** is at Largo de Santa Marta (✆ **26/186-31-22**). It's open Sunday through Friday, 9:30am to 7pm, and Saturday 9:30am to 10pm.

EXPLORING THE TOWN

For such a small place, Ericeira has quite a few sights of religious and historic interest. The **Church of São Pedro** (St. Peter) and the **Misericórdia** (charitable institution) both contain rare 17th- and 18th-century paintings. The **Hermitage of São Sebastião,** with its Moorish designs, would seem more fitting in North Africa. There's one more hermitage, honoring St. Anthony.

The crescent-shape, sandy **Praia do Sol,** the favorite beach of Portuguese and foreign visitors, attracts many travelers. There are three other good beaches: **Ribeira Beach, North Beach,** and **St. Sebastian Beach.** All are suitable for swimming, unlike the beaches at Estoril and Cascais.

A NEARBY ATTRACTION

Palácio Nacional de Mafra ★★ This palace is a work of extraordinary discipline, grandeur, and majesty. At the peak of its 13-year construction, it reputedly employed 50,000; a small town was built just to house the workers. Its master model was El Escorial, the Daedalian maze constructed by Philip II outside

Madrid. Mafra's might not be as impressive or as labyrinthine, but the diversity of its contents is amazing. Its 880 rooms housed 300 friars who could look through 4,500 doorways and windows.

The summer residence of kings, Mafra, 40km (25 miles) northwest of Lisbon, was home to the banished queen Carlota Joaquina. In addition to having a love of painting, Carlos I, the Bragança king assassinated at Praça do Comércio in 1908, was an avid hunter. In one room he had chandeliers made out of antlers and upholstery of animal skins. His son, who ruled for 2 years as Manuel II, spent his last night on Portuguese soil at Mafra before fleeing to England with his mother, Amélia.

Two towers hold more than 110 chimes, made in Antwerp, Belgium, that can be heard for up to 24km (15 miles) when they're played at Sunday recital. The towers flank a basilica, capped by a dome that has been compared to that of St. Paul's in London. The church contains an assortment of chapels, 11 in all, expertly crafted with detailed jasper reredos, bas-reliefs, and marble statues from Italy. The monastery holds the pride of Mafra, a 40,000-volume library with tomes hundreds of years old—many gold-leafed. Viewed by some more favorably than the world-famous library at Coimbra, the room is a study in gilded light. The collection of elaborately decorated vestments in the Museum of Religious Art is outstanding.

Following the omnipresent red Sintra marble, you enter the monks' pharmacy, hospital, and infirmary. Later you can explore the spacious kitchens and the penitents' cells with the flagellation devices used by the monks. You can wander through the audience room with trompe l'oeil ceilings, Maria I's sewing room, and Carlos's music room.

2640 Mafra. ✆ **26/181-75-50.** Admission 3€ ($3.45) adults, 1.50€ ($1.75) seniors (65 and over), students, and children under 15. Wed–Mon 10am–4:30pm. Bus: Mafrense bus from Lisbon.

WHERE TO STAY

Hotel Vilazul ★ *Value* The town's leading hotel also serves the best cuisine in its restaurant, O Poco. Rooms are simply furnished but comfortable, and some have small private balconies. All rooms come with neatly kept bathrooms with shower-tub combinations. On the third floor of the hotel is a pleasant TV lounge with a panoramic view over the south side of Ericeira.

Calçada da Baleia 10, 2655-238 Ericeira. ✆ **26/186-00-00.** Fax 26/186-29-27. 21 units. 50€–72.50€ ($58–$84) double. Rates include breakfast. AE, DC, MC. V. Free parking. **Amenities:** Restaurant; 2 bars; laundry service. *In room:* A/C, TV, safe.

Pedro o Pescador The resort's second-best choice is a relatively modest inn that attracts a devoted clientele from Lisbon. Though relatively lean on amenities, the immaculate rooms are comfortably furnished, each with a private shower-only bathroom, and the owners are friendly. Call ahead to see if the restaurant, once a well-known destination, will be open when you visit.

Rua Dr. Eduardo Burnay 22, 2655-370 Ericeira. ✆ **26/186-40-32.** Fax 26/186-23-21. hotelpedropescador@oninet.pt. 25 units. 35€–65€ ($40–$75) double. Rates include buffet breakfast. AE, DC, MC, V. Free parking. **Amenities:** Breakfast room; bar; limited room service. *In room:* TV.

WHERE TO DINE

O Barco PORTUGUESE This is the port's best independent restaurant outside the hotels. The kitchen takes full advantage of the ocean's riches but also brings in fresh meat and poultry supplies from neighboring farms. You'll be courteously welcomed into an unpretentious dining room. As you sit back enjoying an aperitif, you can study the specialties of the day offered on the limited but choice menu. Codfish invariably appears. We recently enjoyed a plate of codfish baked and served with creamy potatoes and fresh vegetables. The most delectable main course on the menu is a platter of savory shrimps in a tangy garlic sauce. Grilled beef is the favorite meat course. Desserts are often luscious, especially in summer when made with fresh fruit from nearby orchards.

Rua Capitão João Lopés. ✆ **26/186-31-22.** Reservations not required. Main courses 8.50€–16€ ($9.80–$18). AE, DC, MC, V. Fri–Wed noon–3pm and 7–10pm. Closed Nov 20–27.

O Porco INTERNATIONAL/PORTUGUESE The town's leading hotel is also the site of one of its best restaurants. The decor is rather formal, vaguely English country house in motif. With the sea at their doorstep, the chefs turn to the ocean for their specialties. Their best dish is Pescado a la Sal. The cooks bake a fish in salt to seal its natural juices. When the salt is peeled away, the fish is both pleasantly aromatic and juciy. You can also order the fresh catch of the day, grilled as you like it. Meat and poultry dishes, especially a tasty chicken Cordon Bleu (ham and cheese) served with potatoes and a mixed salad, are well prepared. Vegetables—often from the nearby countryside—are fresh and not overcooked, and the pastries are made fresh daily.

Calçada de Baleia 10. ✆ **26/186-00-00.** Reservations not required. Main courses 8€–14€ ($9.20–$16). AE, DC, MC, V. Apr–Sept daily noon–3pm and 9–11pm; Oct–Mar daily noon–3pm and 9–10pm.

6

South of the Tagus

Historically cut off from Lisbon, this narrow isthmus south of the Tagus is wild and rugged as well as lush. In different places, the strip of land plummets toward the sea, stretches along miles of sandy beaches, and rolls through groves heavy with the odors of ripening oranges. With craggy cliffs and coves in the background, the crystalline Atlantic is ideal for swimming, skin-diving, or fishing for tuna, swordfish, and bass.

The area has enjoyed an upsurge of interest since the construction of the Ponte do 25 de Abril, a long suspension bridge that makes it possible to cross the Tagus in minutes—though traditionalists prefer taking the ferry from Praça do Comércio in Lisbon and docking in Cacilhas. Whichever way of crossing you prefer, once you get to Lisbon's left bank, good roads will help you head rapidly through pine groves to the apex of the triangle known as The Land of the Three Castles: Sesimbra, Setúbal, and Palmela.

The land south of the Tagus River retains vivid reminders of its past, reflected in its Moorish architecture, Roman ruins and roads, Phoenician imprints, and Spanish fortresses. The region's proximity to Lisbon (Setúbal is only 40km/25 miles southeast of the capital) makes it perfect for a 1-day excursion. Though train travel is very limited, the area has an extensive network of ferry connections as well as bus services from Lisbon. You'll find driving to be the ideal way to explore the district at your leisure. Otherwise, you can take a bus from Lisbon to the beaches at Caparica in about 45 minutes.

If you take a ferry from Lisbon's Praça do Comércio to Cacilhas, you can catch a bus there for the beaches of Caparica. If you're visiting the peninsula by bus, use Setúbal as your hub; from there you can take local buses to Palmela and Sesimbra.

In summer, a narrow-gauge railway runs for 8km (5 miles) along the Costa da Caparica, making 20 stops at beaches along the way. If you go by rail to the peninsula, service is from Lisbon to Setúbal. From there, you must rely on buses to visit the fishing villages along the southern coast.

1 Azeitão

15km (9⅓ miles) NW of Setúbal, 25km (16 miles) SE of Lisbon

This sleepy village lies in the heart of ***quinta*** country. In its most meager manifestation, a quinta is a simple farmhouse surrounded by land. At its best, it's a mansion of great architectural style filled with art. Azeitão boasts some of the finest quintas in the country. The village makes a good base for trekkers, especially those who want to scale the limestone Serra de Arrábida. For others, long walks through scented pinewoods or silvery olive groves will suffice. To cap off your day, try some Azeitão cheese and a bottle of local muscatel wine.

Azeitão is also home to one of the region's biggest ceramics factories: **São Simão Arte** (✆ **21/218-31-35**). The factory outlet sells its products at prices that are somewhat less than in equivalent retail shops.

ESSENTIALS

ARRIVING

Because the village is not served by public transportation, you'll need a car. After crossing one of the bridges across the Tagus, continue south along the old road to Setúbal (N10) until you see the turnoff for the village of Azeitão.

VISITING THE QUINTAS

Quinta de Bacalhoa ★ Manuel I reputedly introduced the concept of quintas in the early 16th century when he built the Quinta de Bacalhoa. Eventually, the quinta fell into disrepair and vandals carted off many of its decorations, specifically the antique tiles.

An American woman bought the mansion before World War II and worked for years to restore it to its original condition. Some architectural critics have suggested that the palace is the first example of the Renaissance in Portugal.

Bacalhoa is a private villa, but the gardens are open to the public on request when you arrive, for a small fee. The quinta's farmland is devoted to vineyards owned by J. M. da Fonseca, International-Vinhos, Ltda., makers of Lancers wine. There are two J. M. da Fonseca wineries .75km (½ mile) apart: the "mother house," as it's called, and a newer plant.

The original winery and warehouses are in the center of Azeitão, as is the classic 19th-century house (also a quinta) that was the Fonseca family home. A little museum and public reception room on the ground floor of the house are open to visitors. This museum (consisting mainly of unimportant antique paintings, plus a scattering of artifacts related to the history of wine-making at the quinta) is worth visiting only if you are already there viewing the gardens. The century-old Fonseca wineries have made their product from grapes grown on the slopes of the Arrábida Mountains since the early 19th century. The top product is a muscatel called Setúbal, rarely sent abroad but considered delectable by wine connoisseurs.

Vila Fresca de Azeitão. ✆ **21/218-00-11.** Admission 10€ ($12) adults; free for children under 13. Gardens Tues–Sat 9:30am–1pm and 2–5:30pm.

WHERE TO STAY & DINE

INEXPENSIVE

Quinta das Torres ★ *Finds* A 16th-century baronial mansion of deteriorating elegance, Quinta das Torres is still intact for those who want to step back in time. Each guest room is unique; they range from smaller chambers to a ballroom-size suite dominated by princess-style brass beds. Some units have high shuttered windows, time-mellowed tile floors, antique furnishings, and niches with saints or Madonnas. The bungalows, which sleep four and have kitchenettes, ensure privacy. All units are equipped with well-maintained bathrooms containing shower-tub combinations.

The dining room (also open to those who aren't guests) has a tall stone fireplace where log fires burn on chilly evenings, plus elaborate scenic tiles depicting *The Rape of the Sabine Women* and *The Siege of Troy.* The chef specializes in a cuisine of the region, which is rich in sauces and strong in flavors. *Bacalao* (dried codfish) is cooked to a golden-brown perfection. Tender cutlets of accord-fed pork meat are sautéed and served with the fresh vegetable of the season. A special dish, when it appears on the menu, is a delectable roasted pheasant.

Estrada Nacional 10, Azeitão 2925-601. ✆ **21/218-00-01.** Fax 21/219-06-07. 10 units, 2 bungalows. 65€–100€ ($75–$115) double; 85€–167€ ($98–$192) bungalow. Rates include breakfast. AE, DC, MC, V. Free parking. **Amenities:** Restaurant; bar; pool; room service; laundry. *In room:* TV, kitchenette (in bungalow), hair dryer.

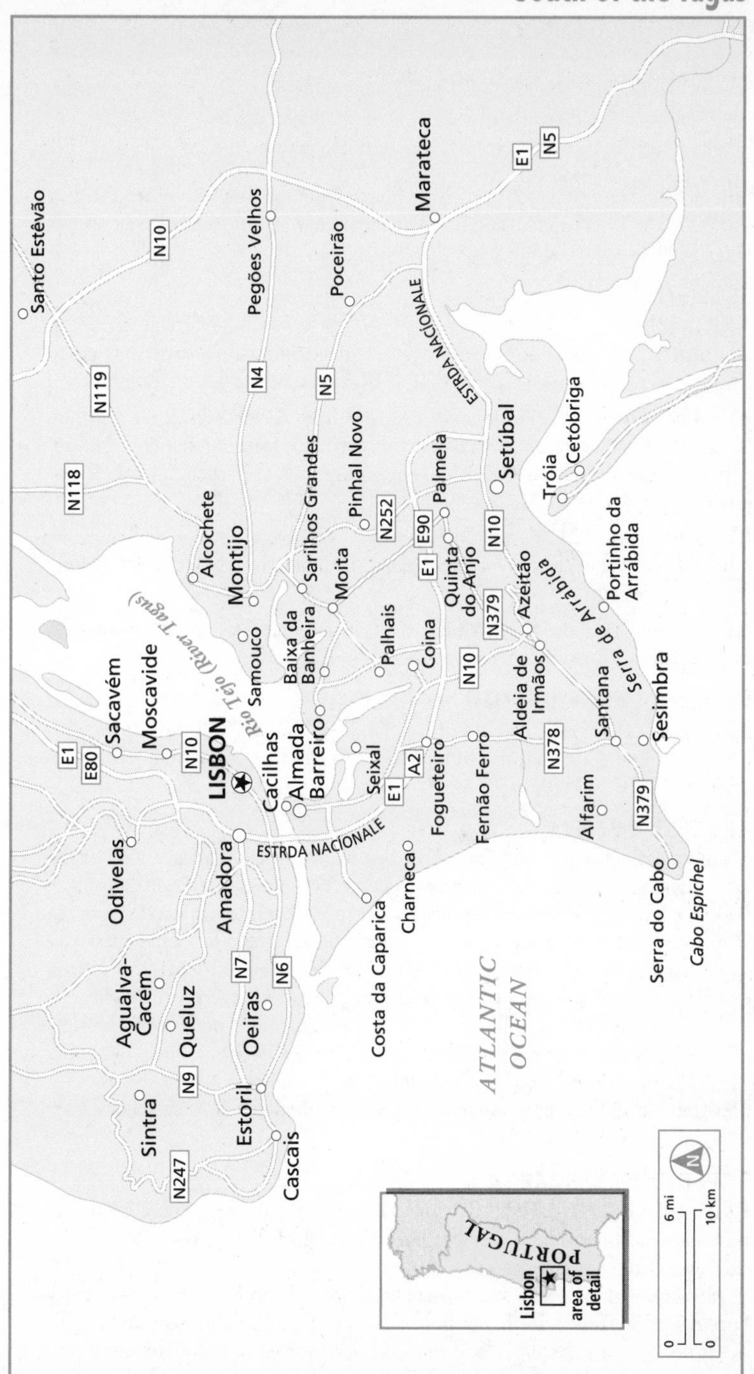
Santo Estêvão
N10
Pegões Velhos
Marateca
E1
N5
Poceirão
ESTRDA NACÍONALE
N119
N4
N5
Setúbal
Cetóbriga
Tróia
N118
Alcochete
Montijo
Sarilhos Grandes
Pinhal Novo
N252
Palmela
E90
E1
Quinta do Anjo
N10
Portinho da Arrábida
Rio Tejo (River Tagus)
Samouco
Baixa da Banheira
Moita
Palhais
Coina
N379
Azeitão
Serra de Arrábida
Sacavém
Moscavide
LISBON
Cacilhas
Almada
Barreiro
Seixal
N10
Aldeia de Irmãos
Santana
Sesimbra
E1
E80
N10
A2
Fogueteiro
Fernão Ferro
N378
Alfarim
N379
Odivelas
Amadora
ESTRDA NACÍONALE
E1
Costa da Caparica
Charneca
Serra do Cabo
Cabo Espichel
Agualva-Cacém
Queluz
N7
N6
Oeiras
ATLANTIC OCEAN
N9
Sintra
Estoril
Cascais
N247
PORTUGAL
Lisbon
area of detail
0
6 mi
0
10 km
N

2 Sesimbra

26km (16 miles) SW of Setúbal, 43km (27 miles) S of Lisbon

Among the Portuguese, Sesimbra used to be a closely guarded secret. It was justifiably considered one of the most unspoiled fishing villages in the country. Today signs of rapid growth are apparent. However, fishermen still go about the time-honored task of plucking their livelihood from the Atlantic. When the fleet comes in, the day's catch is auctioned at the harbor (Porto Abrigo). Sesimbra is also a popular sport-fishing center.

ESSENTIALS

ARRIVING

BY TRAIN From Lisbon, the bus is a better choice. Rail passengers go to Setúbal by train and then have to double back on a bus to get to Sesimbra.

BY BUS Buses to Sesimbra leave regularly from Lisbon's Praça de Espanha (Metro: Palhavã) and from Cacilhas, across the Tagus from the center of Lisbon. The 1-hour trip costs 3.10€ ($3.55). For information and schedules, call **Transportes sul do Tejo** (© **21/223-30-71**).

BY CAR From Lisbon, cross the Ponte do 25 de Abril bridge and continue southwest on the expressway to Setúbal. At the junction of N378, head directly south into Sesimbra.

BY FERRY Take the ferry to Cacilhas from the Praça do Comércio wharf in Lisbon (Metro: Rossio). Then take a bus from Cacilhas.

VISITOR INFORMATION

The tourist office is on Largo da Marinha 26-27 (© **21/228-85-00**). June to September hours are 9am to 8pm; October to May, it's open from 9:30am to 12:30pm and 2 to 7:30pm.

SPECIAL EVENTS

Sesimbra has many fairs and festivals during which the town attracts a lot of visitors, making accommodations hard to come by unless reservations are made well in advance. Each year, in February or early March (dates vary), Sesimbra stages ***Cegadas,*** which are a series of street theater presentations. Unless you speak Portuguese, it's more interesting for the casual visitor to attend the **Festa dos Pescadores** (or festival of the fishermen) celebrated every year on May 4. This is the most exciting, biggest, and best festival, but hotels are impossibly crowded in early May because of it. From June 23 to 30 annually, Sesimbra stages the **Festival of the Popular Saints,** which is an exciting event—even for non-Catholics. The town is gaily decorated with paper flowers, parades are staged, and there is live music.

EXPLORING SESIMBRA

EXPLORING THE AREA The most intriguing sight in Sesimbra is the picturesque (and often photographed) **harbor** ★, which lies against the foot of a cliff, away from the city center.

Farther down the beach, beyond the boat-clogged harbor, is the 17th-century **Fortress of St. Teodosio.** It was built to fortify the region against pirates. The site is not open to the public and must be viewed from outside. However, even though the fortress can't be visited, this is the town's most scenic walk, taking you along the old port with dramatic views of the sea on one side and colorful cliffs on the other.

A walk along the ruined battlements of the five-towered **Castle of Sesimbra** reduces the village to a miniature. The castle encloses a 12th-century church, the oldest in Sesimbra. The site is open daily from 7am to 7pm. Admission is free.

From Sesimbra, you can head west to the headland of **Cabo Espichel,** with views of arcaded pilgrim hospices dating from the 1700s. The baroque interior (gilded wood and sculpture) of a pilgrimage church, the **Santuário da Nossa Senhora do Cabo,** can be inspected daily from 9am to 1pm and 3 to 6pm. Admission is free. Later, walk to the edge of the cliffs behind the church for a panoramic view of the sea. At the southern end of the Arrábida Mountain chain, this pilgrimage site has been popular since the 13th century. Modern sculpture now stands in the forlorn setting. There's no guardrail, and it's a sheer drop of more than 100m (328 ft.) to the ocean waters, so be very careful. From Sesimbra, six buses a day make the 30-minute journey to this southwestern cape.

OUTDOOR ACTIVITIES Sesimbra's popularity stems from its position on a long, lovely sandy **beach.** The beach is overpopulated in summer, often by Lisbons, but the unpolluted water is ideal for swimming.

Sesimbra is also a center for **fishing.** The locals are famous for their swordfish catches, and many will take visitors out in their boats for a negotiated fee. Inquire at the tourist office (see "Visitor Information," above) about making arrangements.

SHOPPING **Avenida da Liberdade,** in the heart of town, is lined with all kinds of souvenir shops. The ceramics outlet at Azeitão (see above) is just 15km (9⅓ miles) from the center of town, along the road to Setúbal.

WHERE TO STAY

MODERATE

Hotel do Mar ★★ One of the most unusual self-contained beach-resort hotels south of the Tagus, Hotel do Mar spreads from a high cliff to the water below. The main lobby houses a glassed-in tropical bird aviary, and the passageways are like art galleries, with contemporary paintings and ceramic plaques and sculpture. All the airy guest rooms have private terraces, with views of the ocean and gardens sweeping down the hillside. Some bathrooms are very small, but all contain shower-tub combinations. Suites vary widely in size, facilities, and price. Less expensive suites are comfortable standard accommodations; the more expensive deluxe unit features a pool and Jacuzzi. Breakfast is served on a flower-filled terrace. The wood-paneled restaurant overlooks the sea.

Rua General Humberto Delgado 10, 2970-68 Sesimbra. ✆ **21/228-83-00.** Fax 21/223-38-88. www.hoteldomar.pt. 168 units. 120€–145€ ($138–$167) double; 125€–215€ ($144–$247) suite. Rates include breakfast. AE, DC, MC, V. Free parking. **Amenities:** Restaurant; bar; 2 pools; 2 tennis courts; sauna; concierge; limited room service; laundry service. *In room:* A/C, TV, dataport, hair dryer, safe.

Sana Park Sesimbra ★ A modern balconied hotel, this is the second-best choice in this resort. Completely modernized and up-to-date, it offers comfortably and tastefully furnished bedrooms, with some of the accommodations set aside for nonsmokers or those with limited mobility. A government-rated four-star hotel, Sana Park offers many rooms with views. In facilities, it is one of the better-equipped hotels in the area, especially with its pool, exercise room, and sauna. The food is good, especially the fresh fish brought in by the local fishermen.

Av. 25 de Abril, 2970 Sesimbra. ✆ **21/228-90-00.** Fax 21/228-90-01. www.sanahotels.com/sesimbra.html. 100 units. 85€–120€ ($98–$138) double, 220€–230€ ($253–$265) suite. Rates include breakfast. AE, DC, MC, V. 24-hr. parking 9.50€ ($11). **Amenities:** Restaurant; bar; indoor pool; gym/exercise room; 24-hr. room

The Best Beaches: Where the Locals Sun

The beaches along the Costa da Caparica, on the left bank of the Tagus, across from the center of Lisbon, are not as polluted as those along the more fashionable Costa do Sol (Estoril and Cascais). Surprisingly, foreigners still flock to the Costa do Sol, leaving much of the Costa da Caparica to locals.

The *costa,* on the west side of the Setúbal peninsula, stretches for some 9km (5½ miles) and abounds with sandy beaches and coves. Rocky outcroppings and clear, placid lagoons characterize these beaches. The farther you go from the little resort of Caparica, the better and more beautiful the beaches become.

A narrow-gauge railway serves the coast, making 20 stops over 8km (5 miles). Each white-sand beach along the way has a different allure. In general, families of all age groups are attracted to the beaches along the first eight stops. Beginning at stop 9, gay visitors become more prominent. As you travel the greater length of Costa da Caparica, the beaches become less crowded, and in the final southern stretches, nudists are often seen.

To reach the beach strip by public transport, you can take a ferry from Lisbon to Cacilhas, on the other side of Tagus. They leave every 15 minutes from Praça do Comércio's Terminal Fluvial (Metro: Rossio). You then board a bus marked CAPARICA at the station next door to the ferry terminal. The trip to the beaches takes about 45 minutes. The narrow-gauge train runs from June to September, and the bus from Cacilhas stops at the rail terminus, where you can connect with the little train.

The Setúbal peninsula has many other wonderful beaches. There are sandy beaches at Sesimbra (see section 2 of this chapter), but they are likely to be overcrowded from June to August.

The most alluring beach strip is across the mouth of the Sado at Tróia (p. 185), a major resort with some utterly charmless apartment complexes. Ferries leave from Setúbal harbor every 45 minutes throughout the day. Trip time is 15 minutes. The ocean side of the promontory at Tróia is less filled with beach buffs and is less polluted.

Many little hidden beaches lie west of Setúbal at the foothills of the Serra de Arrábida mountain range. For example, at Portinho da Arrábida (p. 183), the bay makes a perfect curve, forming sand beaches and opening onto clear waters.

service; babysitting; laundry service; dry cleaning; rooms for those w/ limited mobility. *In room:* A/C, TV, dataport, minibar, hair dryer, safe.

WHERE TO DINE

MODERATE

Restaurante Ribamar ★ PORTUGUESE/INTERNATIONAL This restaurant serves some of the best Portuguese cooking in the area. It specializes in seafood fresh from local waters. The building is a short stroll from the beach, with a view of the bay from most of the indoor and outdoor seating. The chef's specialty is a delectable platter of mixed fish and shellfish for two, flavored with herbs, steamed in wine, and served cold with fresh lemon, if you wish. Swordfish caught in local waters is another favorite. The reasonable fixed-price menu includes soup, a main course, dessert, wine, and coffee.

Av. dos Náufragos 29. © **21/223-48-53.** Reservations recommended. Main courses 15€–18€ ($17–$21); fixed-price menus 22€–30€ ($25–$35). AE, DC, MC, V. Daily noon–4pm and 7–11pm.

SESIMBRA AFTER DARK

If you're looking for a quiet hideaway for a few rounds, consider either the **De Facto Bar,** Avenida dos Náufragos (© **21/223-42-14**), open daily from 6pm, or its immediate neighbor, **Bar Inglês,** Avenidados Náufragos 33–34 (© **21/223-56-11**), open daily from 3pm to 4am.

3 Portinho da Arrábida

13km (8 miles) SW of Setúbal, 37km (23 miles) SE of Lisbon

The fishing village of Portinho da Arrábida, a favorite with vacationing Lisbon families, is at the foot of the **Serra de Arrábida** ★. If you drive here in July and August, watch out. There's virtually no parking, and the road should be one-way but isn't—you can wait for hours to get back up the hill. In addition, the walk down and back could qualify you for the Olympics. Try to park on a wider road above the port, and then negotiate the hordes of summer visitors on foot.

There's really no place to stay in Portinho. Your best bet is to return to Sesimbra or to drive on to Setúbal for the night.

Exploring the Mountains

The limestone, whale-backed Serra de Arrábida stretches for about 36km (22 miles), beginning at Palmela and rolling to a dramatic end at Cabo Espichel on the Atlantic. The Portuguese government has wisely set aside 10,800 hectares (26,677 acres) as a sanctuary between Sesimbra and Setúbal to protect the area from developers and to safeguard the local scenery and architecture.

At times, the cliffs and bluffs are so high that it seems you have to peer through clouds to see the purple waters of the Atlantic below. More than 1,000 species of plant life have been recorded, including holm oaks, sweet bay, pines, laurel, juniper, cypress, araucaria, magnolia, lavender, myrtle, and pimpernels. Our favorite time to visit is in late March or the beginning of April (around Easter), when wildflowers—everything from coral-pink peonies to Spanish bluebells—cover the mountains.

Numerous sandy coves lie at the foot of the Serra de Arrábida's limestone cliffs. One of the finest beaches is **Praia de Galapos.** Another popular beach is **Praia de Figuerinha,** between Portinha da Arrábida and Setúbal, known for sport fishing, windsurfing, and sailing. The *serra* (mountain) abounds with caves and grottoes. The best known is **Lapa de Santa Margarida,** of which Hans Christian Andersen wrote, "It is a veritable church hewn out of the living rock, with a fantastic vault, organ pipes, columns, and altars."

ESSENTIALS

ARRIVING

BY BUS Because of an inadequate road, there is no bus service between Sesimbra and Portinho da Arrábida.

BY CAR From Sesimbra, continue along N379 toward Setúbal, forking right at the turnoff for Portinho da Arrábida. But first, see the warning about parking, above. Portinho makes a good lunch stop for motorists exploring the foothills of the Serra de Arrábida.

VISITOR INFORMATION

The nearest tourist offices are at Setúbal (✆ **26/553-91-20**) or Sesimbra (✆ **21/223-57-43**), but they offer little help to visitors to Portinho.

WHERE TO DINE

MODERATE

Restaurante Beira-Mar PORTUGUESE A meal at this airy restaurant can be your reward for the trek down the hill. The most sought-after warm-weather tables are on a concrete balcony, a few feet above the port's still waters, near the many fishing vessels. Full, hearty, and robust meals include choices like superb pork with clams, tender roast chicken, savory fish stew, grilled sardines, several preparations of codfish, grilled sole, shellfish rice, and several regional wines. On overcrowded weekends, you might have trouble attracting the waiter's attention—if you can even find a table.

Portinho da Arrábida. ✆ **21/218-05-44.** Main courses 5€–18€ ($5.75–$21). May–Sept daily noon–9:30pm; Jan–Apr and Oct–Nov Thurs–Tues noon–9:30pm. Closed Dec 15–Jan 15.

4 Setúbal ★

40km (25 miles) SE of Lisbon

On the right bank of the Sado River lies one of Portugal's largest and oldest cities, said to have been founded by Noah's grandson. Motorists often include it on their itineraries because of the exceptional inn, the **Pousada de São Filipe,** in a late 16th-century fort overlooking the sea (see "Where to Stay," below).

Setúbal, the center of Portugal's sardine industry, is known for the local production of the most exquisite muscatel wine in the world. Orange groves, orchards, vineyards, and outstanding beaches such as the popular Praia da Figuerinha all lie near Setúbal. The white pyramidal mounds dotting the landscape are deposits of sea salt drying in the sun, another major commercial asset of this seaside community.

Many artists and writers have come from Setúbal, most notably the 18th-century Portuguese poet Manuel Maria Barbosa du Bocage, forerunner of the Romantics. At Praça do Bocage, a monument honors him.

ESSENTIALS

ARRIVING

BY TRAIN The trip from Lisbon takes 1½ hours, and a one-way ticket costs 2.10€ ($2.40). For more information and schedules, call ✆ **808/208-208.**

BY BUS Buses from Lisbon arrive every hour or two, depending on the time of day. The trip takes an hour, and a one-way ticket costs 3.10€ ($3.55). For more information and schedules, call ✆ **265/52-50-51.**

Peninsula de Tróia

Tróia is a long, sandy peninsula across the Sado River estuary. It's accessible by ferry from Setúbal. The pine-studded strip of land is the site of one of Portugal's largest tourist enterprises: the **Tróia Tourist Complex,** Torralta C.I.F. 7570-789 Carvallal, Grandola (✆ **26/549-90-00**), with high-rise apartment-hotels and a par-72, 6,374m (20,907 ft.), 18-hole golf course designed by Robert Trent Jones. Other sporting facilities include seawater swimming pools, watersports facilities, playgrounds for children, and about a dozen tennis courts. You can rent bicycles to tour the island or go horseback riding. Additionally, the beaches are some of the best south of Lisbon, and the waters are unpolluted.

You can rent an apartment on the island if you'd like a seaside holiday. Further information is available from **Torralta-CIF,** S.A., Avenida Duque de Loulé 24, 1098 Lisboa Codex (✆ **21/330-12-00**).

Cetóbriga, on the peninsula, contains ruins of a thriving Roman port. Excavations began in the mid–19th century. The city, dating from the 3rd and 4th centuries, was destroyed by the ocean, but traces of villas, bathing pools, a fresco-decorated temple, and a place for salt preservation of fish have been unearthed. Cetóbriga's ruins are about 2.5km (1½ miles) from the site of the present tourist development of Tróia but are worth seeing only if you have time. Otherwise, the simple foundations of long-gone buildings are too minor to merit a special visit.

To reach Tróia from Setúbal, buy a ticket from **Transsado,** Doca do Comércio (✆ **26/549-40-35**), off Avenida Luisa Todi at the eastern sector of the waterfront. At least 36 ferries run throughout the day. The trip takes 15 minutes and costs 1€ ($1.15) for adults and children. Taking a car costs 5€ ($5.75) each way. For information, call ✆ **26/523-51-01.**

BY CAR After crossing one of the Tagus bridges from Lisbon, follow the signs to Setúbal along the express highway, A2, until you see the turnoff for Setúbal. The old road (N10) to Setúbal is much slower.

VISITOR INFORMATION

The **Setúbal Tourist Office** is at Traversa Frai Gaspar 10 (✆ **26/553-91-20**). The office is open June to September Monday through Saturday from 9am to 7pm and Saturday and Sunday from 9am to 5pm. From October to May, hours are Monday through Friday from 9am to 12:30pm and 2 to 6pm.

EXPLORING SETÚBAL

Igreja de Jesús ★ This church is a late-15th-century example of the Manueline style of architecture. Of particular interest are the main chapel, the ornate decorations on the principal doorway, and the Arrábida marble columns. Hans Christian Andersen called the monument "one of the most beautiful small churches that I have ever seen." The church has been extensively restored; the latest wholesale renovation took place in 1969 and 1970.

Praça Miguel Bombarda (off Av. do 22 de Dezembro). ✆ **26/553-78-90.** Suggested donation 1€ ($1.15). Tues–Sat 9am–1pm and 1:30–5:30pm. Bus: 1, 4, 7, 10, or 12.

Museu da Setúbal Adjoining the Ingreja de Jesús, this unpretentious town museum houses some early 16th-century Portuguese paintings, as well as Spanish and Flemish works and contemporary art. The museum is also rich in antique *azulejos* (hand-painted tiles) and has a large antique coin collection, plus artifacts found from archeological digs in the area. Don't miss the collection of ecclesiastical gold and silver, especially a Gothic processional cross in crystal and gilt from the 15th century. If you have an hour or so, this museum is well worth a visit.
Rua Balneário Paula Borba. ✆ **26/553-78-90.** Free admission. Tues–Sat 9am–noon and 1:30–5:30pm. Bus: 1, 4, 7, 10, or 12.

OUTDOOR ACTIVITIES The playground of Setúbal is the Peninsula of Tróia (see above), site of some excellent white-sand beaches. Parts of the lonely, rocky stretches of land between Lisbon and Setúbal have undergone massive upgrades, making way for some of Europe's best golf courses to emerge.

Portugal's most acclaimed golf course is the **Aroeira Clube de Golf,** Herdade de Aroeira, Fonte da Telha, 2825 Monte de Caparica, Aroeira (✆ **21/297-91-00**). Designed as a 364-hectare (899-acre) "golf estate" in the early 1970s by the English architect Frank Pennink, it's a par-72, 6,040m (19,811-ft.) course. International golf magazines have hailed the layout as one of the finest in Europe. Low, rocky cliffs and a network of lakes separate the long, lush fairways and copses of pine trees from the surging Atlantic. Advance reservations are essential. Greens fees for 18 holes run 45€ to 62€ ($52–$71), depending on the time and day. Golf clubs can be rented for 40€ ($46), and an electric cart costs 18€ ($21) for 18 holes. To reach the club from Lisbon (a 25km/15½-mile ride, which takes about 35 min.), take one of the bridges over the Tagus. Drive south for 32km (20 miles), and exit the highway at Costa da Caparica. From Setúbal (a 40km/25-mile ride, which takes about 1 hr.), take highway N10 northwest to Lisbon and exit at Foguateiro.

If the Aroeira course is booked, you can schedule a round at another course in the region. **The Clube de Golf Perú** is near the hamlet of Negreiros (✆ **21/213-43-00**). From Setúbal, take Estrada Nacionale 10 for about 19km (12 miles), following signs to Lisbon. Reservations are required. Another, less prestigious, option is the **Clube de Golf Montado,** in the hamlet of Montado (✆ **26/570-81-50**). From Setúbal, drive 10km (6½ miles) south along the Estrada Nacionale, following signs to Alentejo and Algarve. Greens fees are comparable to those at the Aroeira, but professionals don't consider either of those newcomers as exciting.

SHOPPING Setúbal offers enough outlets for local handcrafts to keep any devoted shopper busy for at least a full afternoon.

Fortuna (✆ **21/287-10-68**), a ceramics factory and technical school, dominates the hamlet of **Quinta do Anjo,** 6.5km (4 miles) northeast of Setúbal. To reach it, follow signs to Palmela. **São Simão Arte** (✆ **21/218-02-64**), a leading competitor, manufactures ceramics that are glazed and painted fancifully with renditions of flowers, vines, and woodland animals, some of them mythical. The store is the focal point of the hamlet of **Azeitão,** 15km (9⅓ miles) northwest of Setúbal. Both offer factory tours and ample shopping opportunities.

WHERE TO STAY

EXPENSIVE

Estalagem Do Sado ★★ Although lacking the history and ambience of the Pousada de São Filipe (see below), this hotel is even better rated with superior amenities and facilities. Its older four-story section, containing a series of nine junior suites, is housed in a pink-painted structure with sections built in 1963 and 1993. Other more modern rooms were added in a new wing. All of the accommodations open onto a small balcony overlooking cityscapes. Some of the bedrooms are in a very contemporary style, whereas others are more classical. If you want smaller rooms reeking of atmosphere, check into the older section; if you seek spacious and modern, then head for the newer wing. The on-site restaurant has the most panoramic view of any place in Setúbal, including the hills of Sierre de Arrabida in the background.

Rua Irene Lisboa 1 and 3, 2900-028 Setúbal. ✆ **26/554-28-00.** Fax 26/444-28-28. www.estalagemdosado.com. 66 units. 110€–145€ ($127–$167) double, 140€–260€ ($161–$299) suite. Rates include breakfast. AE, DC, MC, V. Free parking. **Amenities:** Restaurant; bar; room service (10:30am–1am); babysitting; laundry service; dry cleaning. *In room:* A/C, TV, dataport, minibar, hair dryer, safe.

Pousada de São Filipe ★★ This fortress-castle, on a hilltop overlooking the town and the harbor, dates from the 17th century. It's the work of Italian architect Philipe Terzl. The road leading to the pousada winds up a mountain and passes through a stone arch and past towers to the belvedere. The walls of the chapel and the public rooms contain tile dados depicting scenes from the life of São Filipe and the life of the Virgin Mary. They're dated 1736 and signed by Policarpo de Oliveira Bernardes.

Guest rooms that once housed soldiers and the governor have been tastefully furnished with antiques and reproductions of 16th- and 17th-century pieces. Guns and ammunition have given way to soft beds and ornate Portuguese-crafted headboards. All units are equipped with neatly kept bathrooms containing shower-tub combinations. The hotel is flooded with what seems like miles of plant-filled corridors.

If you're not driving, take a taxi from Setúbal—the walk is too long for most people.

Castelo de São Filipe, 2900-300 Setúbal. ✆ **26/552-38-44.** Fax 26/553-25-38. www.pousadas.pt. 16 units. 112€–200€ ($129–$230) double; 135€–222€ ($155–$255) suite. Rates include breakfast. AE, DC, MC, V. Free parking. **Amenities:** Restaurant; bar; room service; laundry service. *In room:* A/C, TV, minibar, hair dryer.

MODERATE

Hotel Bonfim ★ This 10-story government-rated 4-star hotel in the center of Setúbal is one of the most modern and international in town. It rises from the eastern edge of the inner city's largest park, a short walk inland from the sea, and offers views that its management wryly compares to those overlooking Central Park in New York. It opened in 1993 and has well-furnished midsize rooms, each with a shower-tub combination. Two rooms are available for those with limited mobility.

Av. Alexandre Herculano 58, 2900-206 Setúbal. ✆ **26/555-07-00.** Fax 26/553-48-58. www.hotelbonfim.com. 100 units. 85€–94€ ($98–$108) double; 117€–145€ ($135–$167) suite. Rates include breakfast. AE, DC, MC, V. Free parking. **Amenities:** Breakfast room; bar; laundry service; 2 rooms for those w/limited mobility. *In room:* A/C, TV, dataport, minibar, hair dryer.

INEXPENSIVE

Residencial Setúbalense About a minute's walk north of Setúbal's central plaza, Largo da Misericórdia, this is a family-run hotel that opened in the early 1990s. The carefully restored 3-story building was erected 200 years ago as a substantial private home. The midsize rooms have high ceilings and streamlined modern furniture, including neatly kept bathrooms with shower-tub combinations.

Rua Major Afonso Pala 17, 2900-127 Setúbal. ✆ **26/552-57-90.** Fax 26/552-57-89. 24 units. 37€–47€ ($43–$54) double. Rates include breakfast. AE, DC, MC, V. Free parking. **Amenities:** Breakfast room; bar; limited room service; laundry service. *In room:* TV, hair dryer, fan.

WHERE TO DINE

MODERATE

Restaurante Bocage PORTUGUESE Old Portugal comes alive behind the faded facade of this town house, on a corner of the traffic-free main square. You'll dine under 1950s-era ceiling fans and a coffered white ceiling. Most patrons order a fruity muscatel to accompany their fresh fish. This hearty tavern is no place for those with dainty tastes—the almost exclusively local clientele comes here for regional Portuguese cookery, including *lulas de caldeirada* (squid stew). A taste of muscatel brandy traditionally tops off a meal.

Rua da Marqueza do Faial 8–10. ✆ **26/552-25-13.** Main courses 9€–13€ ($10–$15). AE, DC, MC, V. Wed–Mon noon–3:30pm; Wed–Sun 7–10pm.

INEXPENSIVE

O Beco PORTUGUESE This is one of the leading restaurants in the city. The dining rooms are decorated with old ovens and regional artifacts. The service is efficient, the food robust and full of flavor, and the portions humongous. Shellfish soup is the classic opener. Pork chops are the acorn-sweetened variety from Alentejo; other good choices include special beefsteak, *pato com arrozca a antiga* (baked duck and rice), paella, and *cozido,* a Portuguese stew. *Cabrito* (goat) is a Sunday special. A typical dessert is orange tart.

Largo da Misericórdia 24. ✆ **26/552-46-17.** Main courses 8€–13€ ($9.20–$15). AE, DC, MC, V. Daily noon–4pm; Wed–Sun 7–10:30pm. Bus: 2, 7, 8, or 20.

SETUBAL AFTER DARK

The densest concentration of nightlife options lies near the western terminus of Avenida Luisa Todi, the road leading west to a string of beaches. The most intriguing is **Scandall,** Avenida Luisa Todi (no phone). A series of rooms with elaborately vaulted ceilings (which long ago sheltered a convent) offer several bars and musical atmospheres. Although most of the place seems designed for talking and drinking, one room functions as a dance club. It's open daily from 11pm till dawn.

Another rich concentration of nightlife options is in the seafront village of **Albarquel,** less than 2km (about 1¼ miles) west of Setúbal. Try the late-night eatery **Restaurant All-Barquel,** Praia de Albarquel (✆ **26/522-19-46**), which caters to night owls of all ages. **Cosopas,** Rua Regimento Infantaria 14 (✆ **26/523-76-75**), is an offbeat little bar and diner near the market square. It fills with local workers during the day, but at night the crowd grows younger and more fun, when lots of *vinho verde* (green wine) is consumed. You can drop in for a full meal—try the grilled squid—or perhaps a sandwich and certainly a drink. It's open Monday through Friday from 8am to 9pm, and Saturday from 8am to 1am.

5 Palmela

8km (5 miles) N of Setúbal, 32km (20 miles) SE of Lisbon

The village of Palmela lies in the heart of wine country, the foothills of the Arrábida Mountains. It's famous for its fortress, which offers one of the best views in Portugal from an elevation of 366m (1,200 ft.). From this vantage point, you can see over sienna-hued valleys and vineyards flush with grapes to the capital in the north and to the estuary of the Sado to the south.

ESSENTIALS

ARRIVING

There is no bus or train service to Palmela.

BY CAR From Lisbon, cross the Ponte do 25 de Abril bridge and head south along E1. Exit at the cutoff marked Palmela. From Setúbal, continue north along A2 to the same exit.

VISITOR INFORMATION

The local tourist office (✆ **21/233-21-22**) is at the Castelo de Palmela (see below). The office is open Monday through Friday from 10am to 12:30pm and 2 to 7pm, and Saturday from 10am to 1pm and 3 to 7pm.

WHERE TO STAY & DINE

EXPENSIVE

Castelo de Palmela Pousada ★★★ This is one of the last remaining segments of the 12th-century castle. It was built as a monastery within the castle walls in 1482, on orders of João I and dedicated to St. James. Its use as a pousada kept it from falling into ruin, and the skillful, unobtrusive conversion preserved the classic look and feel of a cloister. On the crest of a hill, the pousada is traditional in design; a huge square building opens onto a large courtyard, and the lower-level arches have been glassed in and furnished with lounge chairs.

Most of the guest rooms have been opened up, enlarged, and brought glamorously up-to-date. They're furnished in Portuguese style with hand-carved pieces and fine fabrics, and most of the rooms open onto nice views. All units are equipped with well-maintained bathrooms with shower-tub combinations. Near the dining room is a comfortable drawing room with a noteworthy washbasin that the monks once used for their ablutions. There are two rooms for nonsmoking guests

2950 Palmela. ✆ **21/235-12-26.** Fax 21/233-04-40. enatur@mail.telepac.pt. 28 units. 125€–200€ ($144–$230) double; 168€–222€ ($193–$255) suite. Rates include breakfast. AE, DC, MC, V. Free parking. **Amenities:** Restaurant; bar; limited room service; babysitting; laundry service. *In room:* A/C, TV, minibar, hair dryer.

INEXPENSIVE

Quinta do Patricio ★ *Finds* The oldest part of this charming, family-run bed-and-breakfast hotel is its stone-sided windmill. Built in 1798, it's now the establishment's most comfortable accommodation. Other rooms are in the main house, a short walk away through a nice garden. Don't expect a conventional, international feel: Life here is slow, revolving around the pleasant garden and tastefully decorated public areas. The simple guest rooms are small, comfortable, and well maintained, with neatly kept bathrooms equipped with shower-tub combinations. Breakfast is the only meal served. The quinta lies about .4km (¼ mile) west of the center of town.

Estrada do Castelo de São Felipe, 2900-300 Setúbal. ✆ **26/555-04-75.** Fax 26/523-38-17. 3 units. 75€–85€ ($86–$98) double or apt. Rates include breakfast. AE, MC, V. Free parking. **Amenities:** Breakfast room; pool; laundry. *In room:* No phone.

Exploring the Castle

Castelo de Palmela ★ occupies a position that has long been a strategic point for securing control of the lands south of the Tagus. From Palmela, Afonso Henríques, the first king of Portugal, drove out the Moors and established his new nation's domination of the district. In its day, the 12th-century fortress was a splendid example of medieval military architecture.

7

Estremadura

Estremadura is a land of contrasts. The Atlantic crashes upon the southern coast, but farther up, it can hardly muster a ripple in the snug cover of São Martinho do Porto. East of the flat seascapes of the west are two mountain ranges. But the presence of the nearby sea is evident throughout Estremadura. Even in the many examples of Manueline architecture, especially at Batalha, the tie with the sea remains unbroken. Its nautical designs—ropes, cables, armillary spheres, and seascape effects—reflect Portugal's essential connection to the sea.

Estremadura contains lovely towns as old as Portuguese nationhood whose beauty has not been diminished by time. Despite the name (which means "extremities"), the region is neither extremely harsh nor especially remote. Rather, it is in many ways the spiritual heart of Portugal. Its isolation derives more from the slow, erratic, and sometimes undependable public transportation, which makes the region best suited to a driving tour.

1 Óbidos ★★

93km (58 miles) N of Lisbon, 7km (4½ miles) S of Caldas da Rainha

The poet king Dinis and his saintly wife, Isabella of Aragón, once passed by the walls of this medieval village and noted its beauty. The queen likened the village to a jewel-studded crown. Eager to please, Dinis made her a present of the village. He established a tradition: Instead of precious stones, Portuguese royal bridegrooms presented Óbidos to their spouses.

Entered through a tile-coated gatehouse, the town is definitely a trip back in time. The **medieval city** ★★ rises on a sugarloaf hill above a valley of vineyards. Its golden towers, crenellated battlements, and ramparts (which afford views of Estremadura) contrast with gleaming white houses and the rolling countryside, where windmills clack in the breeze.

ESSENTIALS

ARRIVING

BY TRAIN From the Estação do Rossio station in Lisbon (Metro: Rossio), commuter trains run to Cacém, where you can change trains for Óbidos. About 11 trains a day make the approximately 2-hour run; the one-way fare is 5.10€ ($5.85). For information and schedules, call ✆ **808/208-208.**

BY BUS There are bus connections from Lisbon, but the train is easier. Buses leave from Avenida Casal Ribeiro in Lisbon for the 75-minute trip to Caldas da Rainha, where you transfer to another bus to Óbidos. The one-way fare is 5.20€ ($6). About six buses a day make the 20-minute trip from Caldas da Rainha to Óbidos. For information, call ✆ **26/283-10-67.**

BY CAR From Lisbon, N8 runs north to Óbidos via Torres Vedras. This trip takes about an hour. You can also take highway A8.

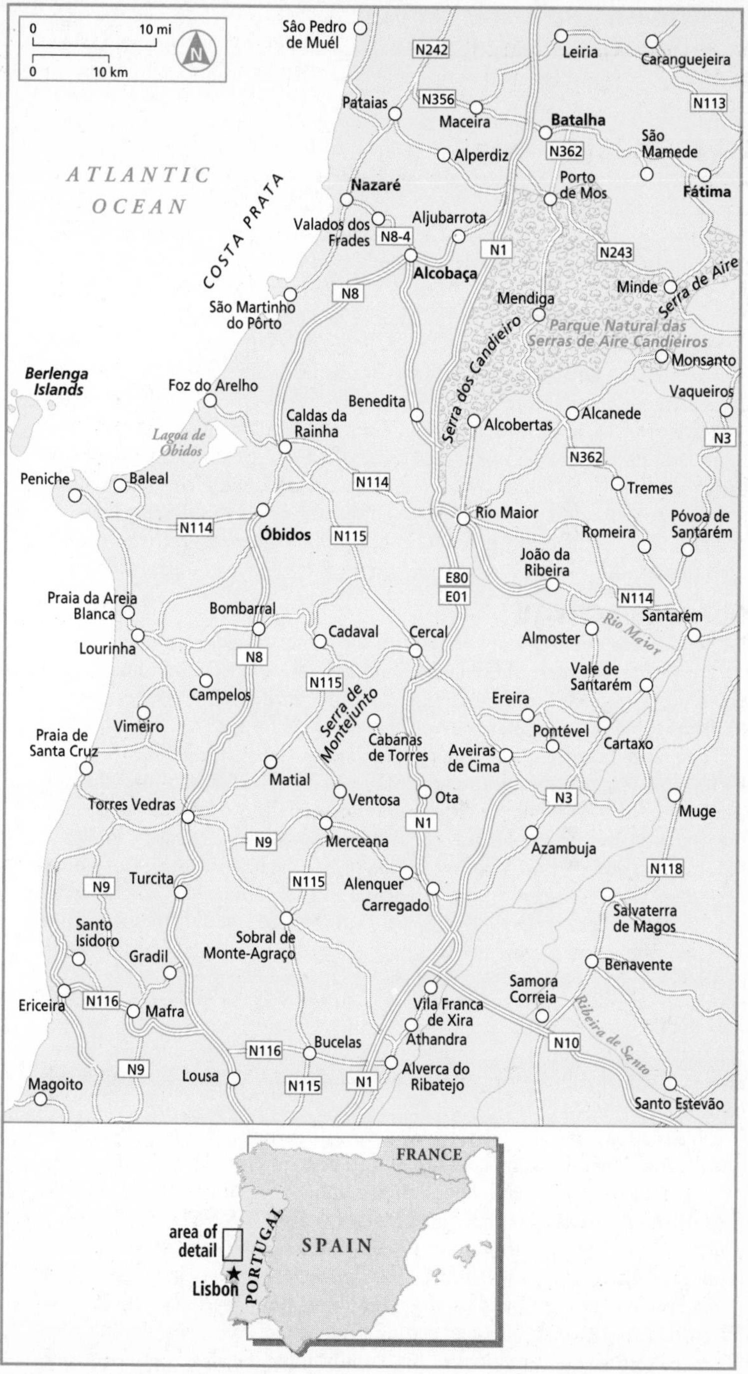
0 10 mi
0 10 km
N
ATLANTIC OCEAN
COSTA PRATA
Berlenga Islands
Lagoa de Óbidos
São Pedro de Muél
N242
Leiria
Caranguejeira
Pataias
N356
Maceira
N113
Batalha
São Mamede
Alperdiz
N362
Porto de Mos
Fátima
Nazaré
Valados dos Frades
N8-4
Aljubarrota
N1
N243
Alcobaça
Serra de Aire
Minde
N8
Mendiga
São Martinho do Pôrto
Parque Natural das Serras de Aire Candieiros
Monsanto
Serra dos Candieiro
Vaqueiros
Foz do Arelho
Benedita
Caldas da Rainha
Alcobertas
Alcanede
N3
N362
Peniche
Baleal
N114
Tremes
Rio Maior
Póvoa de Santarém
N114
Óbidos
N115
Romeira
João da Ribeira
E80
E01
N114
Praia da Areia Blanca
Bombarral
Santarém
Rio Maior
Lourinha
Cadaval
Cercal
Almoster
N8
Campelos
N115
Vale de Santarém
Serra de Montejunto
Ereira
Vimeiro
Pontével
Cartaxo
Praia de Santa Cruz
Cabanas de Torres
Aveiras de Cima
Matial
Ventosa
Ota
N3
Muge
Torres Vedras
N1
N9
Merceana
Azambuja
N118
N9
Turcita
N115
Alenquer
Carregado
Salvaterra de Magos
Santo Isidoro
Sobral de Monte-Agraço
Gradil
Benavente
Samora Correia
Ericeira
N116
Mafra
Vila Franca de Xira
Athandra
Ribeira de Santo
N10
N116
Bucelas
N9
Lousa
Alverca do Ribatejo
Magoito
N115
N1
Santo Estevão
FRANCE
SPAIN
PORTUGAL
area of detail
Lisbon

VISITOR INFORMATION

You'll find the **Óbidos Tourist Office** on Porta DeVilla (© **26/295-92-31**). It's open May to September daily from 9:30am to 7:30pm, and October to April daily from 9:30am to 6pm.

EXPLORING THE TOWN

In the Renaissance church **Igreja de Santa Maria,** blue-and-white *azulejos* (tiles) line its **interior** ★. Look for the Renaissance **tomb** ★ and the paintings of Josefa of Óbidos, a 17th-century artist. The church lies to the right of the post office in the central square. It's open daily from 9:30am to 12:30pm and 4:30 to 7pm April to September, and from 9:30am to 12:30pm and 2:30 to 6pm October to March. Admission is free. For information, call © **26/295-96-33.**

The other major attraction in Óbidos is the *castelo* (part of which is now a tourist inn; see "Where to Stay," below). The castle suffered severe damage in the 1755 earthquake but was restored. It's one of Portugal's greatest medieval castles, with a host of Manueline architectural elements. In 1148, Dom Afonso Henríques and his troops, disguised, incredibly, as cherry trees, captured the castle from the Moors. The Moors were driven from the land, and Henríques went on to become the founding father of Portugal; he was proclaimed its first king.

The main entrance to Óbidos is a much-photographed gate, the narrow, zigzag **Porta da Villa.** Be sure to watch your car mirrors as you pass through it.

OUTDOOR ACTIVITIES

Ideal for general sunning and swimming is the beach at Lagoa de Óbidos, northwest of Óbidos and west of Caldas da Rainha. Windsurfers can be rented on the beach here, although surfers generally prefer the beach at Peniche, southwest of Lagoa de Óbidos, because the waves are better there for surfing.

The one golf course in the region, the **Vimeiro Golf Club,** is allied with the **Hotel Golf Mar,** at Torres Vedras (© **26/198-41-57**), which towers over the cliff. The course has 9 holes, all relatively narrow and well defined by trees and shrubs; the river is an ever-present hazard. The first-class hotel, the best sports complex in the area, also offers tennis, three swimming pools (one heated), horseback riding, fishing, great views, access to several beaches, and a recommended restaurant, all for a reasonable price. (Doubles are 76€–98€/$87–$113). The thermal spa of Vimeiro, with its curative waters, is close by. The course is 34km (21 miles) south of Óbidos, and greens fees are 25€ ($29) for 9 holes.

SHOPPING

Save some time for browsing through the **shops** and searching out thick woven fabrics, regional rugs (both hand- and machine-made), raffia and handmade bags, and local lace.

Óbidos is one of the most folkloric towns in Portugal; dozens of boutiques line the town's main street, **Rua Direita** ★. These stores are loaded with ceramics, embroideries, wine, and woodcarvings. Individual outlets of note include the **Oficina do Barro,** Praça de Santa Maria (© **26/295-92-31**), which is associated with the town's tourist office. It maintains a studio (open to visitors) that produces delicate ceramics—usually glazed in white—that resemble the texture of a woven basket. Nearby is **Espaço Oppidum,** Rua Direita (© **26/295-96-53**), which does a masterful job of glazing antique terra-cotta roof tiles and etching them with artists' renditions of birds and wildlife. Finally, **Loja dos Arcos,** Rua Direita (© **26/295-98-33**), sells wine, leather, and ceramics that are usually a bit more interesting than the wares at equivalent shops nearby.

WHERE TO STAY

EXPENSIVE

Pousada do Castelo ★★ This Manueline-trimmed stone palace is one of the most heavily booked in the country, so rooms should be reserved as far in advance as possible. Rooms vary in size, but most of them are quite comfortable and well furnished with reproduction furniture inspired by the 16th and 17th centuries. Deep-set windows have tiny ledges where you can look out onto views of the countryside. Homemade quilts or fabrics cover the beds, and the bathrooms, a bit small, are covered with hand-painted *azulejos* (tiles). The cuisine and service are the finest in Óbidos.

Paço Real (Apdo. 18), 2510-999 Óbidos. ✆ **26/295-50-80.** Fax 26/295-91-48. www.pousadas.pt. 9 units. 149€–201€ ($171–$231) double; from 185€–237€ ($213–$273) suite. Rates include breakfast. AE, DC, MC, V. Free parking. **Amenities:** Restaurant; bar; laundry service. *In room:* A/C, TV, minibar, safe.

MODERATE

Casa de S. Thiago do Castelo ★ *Value* It's like staying at a private home. You get comfort and tranquility in an intimate atmosphere in this manorial guesthouse placed inside the walls near the castle. Walls are covered with authentic Portuguese *azulejos,* and all the bedrooms are midsize, each with a new private bathroom. Fellow guests meet in the living rooms with a fireplace. Breakfast is taken in the courtyard, and you get personalized hospitality here.

Largo de S. Tiago, 2510 Obidos. ✆ or fax **262/959-587.** 8 units. 80€–95€ ($92–$109) double. Ages 10 and under free. Rates include breakfast. AE, DC, MC, V. **Amenities:** Breakfast room. *In room:* TV.

Estalagem do Convento ★ This is the second-finest accommodation in Óbidos. The inn, installed in a former nunnery, is handsomely decorated in a rustic Iberian style. Bedrooms are small but well furnished, mainly with reproductions of furnishings from the 17th and 18th centuries. Housekeeping is top-notch here, and the little tiled bathrooms come with immaculately clean shower-tub combinations.

Rua Dom João de Ornelas, 2510 Óbidos. ✆ **26/295-92-16.** Fax 26/295-91-59. www.estalagemdoconvento.com. 31 units. 55€–84€ ($63–$97) double; 77€–123€ ($89–$141) suite. Rates include breakfast. AE, MC, V. Free parking. **Amenities:** Restaurant; bar; limited room service; laundry service. *In room:* TV, minibar, hair dryer, safe.

INEXPENSIVE

Albergaria Josefa d'Óbidos *Finds* This is a flower-bedecked inn that lies outside the old town's fortifications. It was constructed in 1983 in the traditional style. The inn lies on a hillside that overlooks the main gate into Óbidos. The guest rooms range from small to midsize and are furnished with 18th-century reproductions of regional furniture. Each unit comes with a tiny neatly kept bathroom covered with hand-painted tiles and equipped with a shower-tub combination. The restaurant, in the classic style of an old-fashioned Portuguese tavern, serves excellent regional and international cuisine with an emphasis on fish. Main courses cost 10€ to 22€ ($12–$25), and the restaurant is open for lunch and dinner.

Rua Dom João de Ornelas, 2510 Óbidos. ✆ **26/295-92-28.** Fax 26/295-95-33. 34 units. 48€–65€ ($55–$75) double; 89€–100€ ($103–$115) suite. Rates include breakfast. AE, DC, MC. Free parking. **Amenities:** Restaurant; bar; room service. *In room:* A/C, TV, minibar (in suite), hair dryer, safe.

Albergaria Rainha Santa Isabel *Value* On a narrow cobblestone street running through the center of town, this building, once a private home, is many centuries old. Blue, white, and yellow tiles cover the high-ceilinged lobby. There's a comfortable bar area filled with leather sofas and Victorian-style chairs.

The Beaches of Estremadura

Take your pick from the ribbonlike string of beaches that stretches almost continuously along the coast of Estremadura. Some 240km (149 miles) of sand extend all the way to its northern edge, just south of the beach resort of **Figueira da Foz.**

Many of Estremadura's beaches are uncrowded and filled with powdery sand bordering crystal-clear waters. Others, especially those near industrial wastelands, are much less desirable and might be polluted. Look for beaches flying a blue banner, which indicates that the European Union has granted its seal of approval to the beach's hygiene and safety.

One of our favorites is the seaside village of **São Martinho do Porto,** 116km (72 miles) north of Lisbon and a short run south of overcrowded Nazaré. This resort nestles between pine-covered foothills and the ocean, and its waters are calm and clear. Another good beach, north of Nazaré, is at **São Pedro de Muél,** 135km (84 miles) north of Lisbon. It has a 55-room resort hotel, **Mar e Sol,** Avenida da Liberdade 1 (**© 24/459-00-00**), where you can take a room or a meal. Rooms range from 55€ to 75€ ($63–$86) for a double, and the rates include breakfast. The chefs here serve an excellent regional cuisine for lunch and dinner, focused mainly on locally caught fish. Main courses cost 7.50€ to 13€ ($8.65–$15).

Another place worth seeking out is the town of **Peniche,** 92km (57 miles) north of Lisbon. This fishing port stands high on a peninsula, with wide, sandy beaches at the foot of rocky cliffs. It doesn't always have the cleanest water (compared to other uncrowded, remote places), but it is nevertheless a family favorite. When you tire of the beach, you can explore **Cabo Carvoeiro** on the peninsula, about 4.75km (3 miles) east of Peniche. It offers panoramic views of the surf smashing against the wild rock formations hundreds of feet below the road. Or, you can go to the large water-park complex, **Peniche Sportagua,** Avenida Monsenhor Basto (**© 26/278-91-25**), where there are water slides and swimming pools for adults and separate ones for children, plus snack bars and dining places. Admission is 9€ ($10) for adults, 7€ ($8.05) for children 5 to 11, and free for children under 5. Hours are daily 10am to 7pm from mid-July to mid-September.

Other less frequented but good beaches are at **Pedrogão, Baleal, Consolação, Porto Covo, Porto Dinheiro,** and **Santa Cruz.** All are signposted from the highway.

Many of the most popular beaches, those with the most facilities, are frequented for their sands. They might not have blue flags, depending on conditions, when you visit. These include **Milfontes, Foz do Arelho,** and **Nazaré.** When red flags are up, beach buffs don't go into the water but still flock to the sands for sunning. We recommend these beaches always for sunning, but only for swimming when blue flags are flying.

An elevator runs to the simply furnished but immaculate guest rooms, containing well-maintained bathrooms with shower-tub combinations. Most guests deposit their luggage at the reception desk before parking for free on the square in front of the village church nearby.

Rua Direita, 2510 Óbidos. ✆ **26/295-93-23.** Fax 26/295-91-15. 20 units. 70€–78€ ($80–$89) double. Rates include breakfast. AE, DC, MC, V. **Amenities:** Breakfast room; bar; room service; laundry service. *In room:* A/C, TV, minibar, safe.

WHERE TO DINE

MODERATE

Most visitors to Óbidos like to dine at the Pousada do Castelo (see "Where to Stay," above). However, you get far better value, less formality, and more local color at one of the typical little restaurants inside or outside the city's walls.

Café/Restaurante 1 de Dezembro PORTUGUESE This snack bar and restaurant is known for its reliable *pratos do día* (plates of the day), made with market-fresh ingredients. You can drop in for something quick to eat at just about any time. The format is friendly, simple, and convenient.

Largo São Pedro. ✆ **26/295-92-98.** Main courses 9€–10€ ($10–$12). MC, V. Mon–Sat 8am–midnight.

Restaurante Alcaide ★ *Value* REGIONAL PORTUGUESE A local favorite inside the city walls, this spot is known for its tasty regional dishes and good, inexpensive wines. Appetizers that might tempt here include a delectable Iberian smoked ham. From here, you can go on to such excellent fish dishes as grouper filet gratin or one of the meat specialties, such as escalopes of veal in a tangy Madeira sauce. The chef also prepares a tender and well-flavored Portuguese beefsteak and small pork tournedos with *fines herbes,* another specialty.

Rua Direita 60. ✆ **26/295-92-20.** Reservations recommended. Main courses 10€–15€ ($12–$17). AE, DC, MC, V. Thurs–Tues 12:30–3pm and 7:30–10pm. Closed last 2 weeks in Nov and last 2 weeks in March.

Restaurante Dom João V REGIONAL PORTUGUESE Less than 1km (½ mile) west of the center of Óbidos, this restaurant specializes in the regional cuisine of Estremadura, accompanied by good Portuguese wines. You can look into the kitchen and make your own selection if you find the menu confusing. The food is not fancy, but it's tasty and offers good value. Parking is possible, an important plus in Óbidos.

Largo da Igreja Senhor da Pedra. ✆ **26/295-91-34.** Main courses 7€–15€ ($8.05–$17). MC, V. Daily noon–4pm and 7–11pm.

NEARBY PLACES TO STAY & DINE

MODERATE

Quinta da Cortiçada ★ *Finds* This is one of the most formal and elegant manor houses in the area. On 90 hectares (222 acres) of field, park, and forest, it's a distinguished compound of buildings surrounded by emerald lawns and a circular pool. Antiques fill the public rooms and the comfortably furnished midsize guest rooms. All come equipped with neatly kept bathrooms containing shower-tub combinations. The chef specializes in the regional cuisine of Estremadura, along with a sampling of continental dishes. Fresh local ingredients are used whenever available, and there is always an abundance of seafood. The Quinta lends bikes to guests who want to explore the park on which it sits.

Outeiro da Cortiçada, 2040-511 Riomaior. ✆ **24/347-00-00.** Fax 24/347-00-09. www.quintacorticada.com. 9 units. 88€–113€ ($101–$130) double; 106€–131€ ($122–$151) suite. Rates include breakfast. AE, DC,

A Side Trip to Caldas da Rainha

The rheumatic sister-queen of Manuel the Fortunate, Leonor, discovered the therapeutic value of the springs here on a trip to Óbidos. The town has been a spa ever since.

Leonor returned to Caldas da Rainha again and again, and constructed a hospital and an adjoining church. The chapel, **Nossa Senhora do Pópulo,** was built in the early 16th century in the Manueline style, then at its apex. The spa, which was particularly popular in the 19th century, lies some 95km (59 miles) north of Lisbon. It's usually visited after Óbidos, 6.5km (4 miles) away. It's worth the 30 minutes or so needed to explore the interior of the church: The walls are entirely covered in beautiful hand-painted *azulejos.* The outstanding artistic treasure of the church is a **triptych** ★ of the Crucifixion, which lies above the triumphal arch of the church.

Caldas da Rainha is also noted for its ceramics. Many roadside stands charge far lower prices than you'd pay in Lisbon. The best selections are in the showrooms of factories, notably **Secla,** Rua São João de Deus (✆ **26/284-21-51**).

MC, V. Free parking. From Óbidos, take N114 39km (24 miles) SE to the hamlet of Riomaior; then look for signs. **Amenities:** Restaurant; bar; pool; tennis courts; free use of bicycles; 24-hr. room service; babysitting; laundry service; nonsmoking rooms. *In room:* A/C, TV, hair dryer.

INEXPENSIVE

Quinta da Ferraria ★ This is a rustic and charming small inn constructed in 1992 from a century-old run-down compound of farm buildings. Surrounded by 80 hectares (198 acres) of rolling fields and orchards, it's less formal than the Quinta da Cortiçada, which appeals to those who appreciate authenticity and lack of pretension. Guest rooms are well maintained, and all come equipped with a tidily kept bathroom with a shower-tub combination.

Ribeira de São João, 2040-511 Riomaior. ✆ **24/394-50-01.** Fax 24/394-56-96. 12 units, 2 apts. 81€–98€ ($93–$113) double; 89€–114€ ($102–$131) suite; 120€–146€ ($138–$168) apt. Double and suite rates include breakfast. AE, MC, V. Free parking. From Óbidos, take N114 39km (24 miles) SE to the hamlet of Riomaior; then look for signs. **Amenities:** Restaurant; bar; pool; tennis court; bike rental; 24-hr. room service; babysitting; laundry service. *In room:* A/C, TV, dataport.

2 Alcobaça ★★

108km (67 miles) N of Lisbon, 16km (10 miles) NE of Caldas da Rainha

The main attraction in Alcobaça is its stately monastery. Also explore the nearby market, said to sell the best fruit in Portugal. The peaches, grown in surrounding orchards originally planted by the Cistercian monks, are especially succulent. Many stalls also sell the blue-and-white pottery typical of Alcobaça.

ESSENTIALS

ARRIVING

BY TRAIN Trains depart from Lisbon's Estação do Rossio station (Metro: Rossio) for the 2-hour trip to Valado dos Frades, the nearest railway station

(5km/3 miles) to both Nazaré and Alcobaça. For information and schedules, call © **808/208-208.** About 14 buses per day make the short run from the train station at Valado dos Frades to Alcobaça; a one-way ticket is .80€ (90¢). From Lisbon to Valado dos Frades, the cost ranges from 5.50€ to 8€ ($6.35–$9.20).

BY BUS About 15 buses a day connect Nazaré with Alcobaça; a one-way ticket costs 1.35€ ($1.55), and the trip takes about 20 minutes. For information, call © **262/55-11-72.** From Lisbon, there are four *expressos* a day to Alcobaça. The trip takes 2 hours and costs 7.80€ ($8.95) one-way.

BY CAR From Caldas da Rainha, continue northeast along N8.

VISITOR INFORMATION

The **Alcobaça Tourist Office** is on Praça do 25 de Abril (© **26/258-23-77**). It's open May to September daily from 10am to 1pm and 3 to 7pm, and October to April daily 10am to 1pm and 2 to 6pm.

EXPLORING THE TOWN

VISITING THE MONASTARY In the Middle Ages, the Cistercian **Mosteiro de Santa Maria (St. Mary Monastery)** ★★ was one of the richest and most prestigious in Europe. Begun in 1178, it was founded to honor a vow made by Portugal's first king, Afonso Henríques, before he faced the Moors at Santarém. Alcobaça, at the confluence of the Alcoa and Baça Rivers, was built to show his spiritual indebtedness to St. Bernard of Clairvaux, who inspired (some say goaded) many Crusaders into battle against the infidel.

Today, in spite of its baroque facade and latter-day overlay, the monastery is a monument to simplicity and majesty. Above the 98m-long (321-ft.-long) nave, quadripartite vaulting is supported on transverse arches. These rest on towering pillars and columns. The aisles, too, have stunning vertical lines and are practically as tall as the nave itself.

The transept shelters the **Gothic tombs** ★★ of two star-crossed lovers, the Romeo and Juliet of Portuguese history. Though damaged, their sarcophagi are the greatest pieces of sculpture from 14th-century Portugal. The artist is unknown.

The Cloisters of Silence, with their delicate arches, were favored by Dinis, the poet-king. He sparked a thriving literary colony at the monastery, where the monks were busily engaged in translating ecclesiastical writings. Aside from the tombs and cloisters, the curiosity is the kitchen, through which a branch of the Alcoa River was routed. As in most Cistercian monasteries, the flowing brook was instrumental for sanitation purposes. Chroniclers have suggested that the friars fished for their dinner in the brook and later washed their dishes in it.

Finally, in the 18th-century Salon of Kings are niches with sculptures of some Portuguese rulers. The empty niches, left waiting for the rulers who were never sculptured, lend a melancholic air. The tiles in the room depict, in part, Afonso Henríques's triumph over the Moors.

516 Mosteiro Alcobaça. © **26/250-51-20.** Admission 3€ ($3.45). Daily Apr–Sept 9am–7pm; Oct–Mar 9am–5pm.

SHOPPING You'll find a dozen or so handcraft and ceramics shops lining the square in front of the monastery. One of the best outlets is **Casa Artisate Egarafeira** (© **26/259-01-20**), which sells antiques, ceramics, and regional wine, among other offerings.

Finds Off the Beaten Path: Nature in the Raw

The area around Alcobaça contains two of the least discovered but most dramatic havens for nature in Portugal: a national park and an offshore island that's ideal for scuba diving.

Parque Natural das Serras de Aire e Candieiros straddles the border between Estremadura and Ribatejo, almost halfway between Lisbon and Coimbra. Encompassing more than 30,000 hectares (74,100 acres) of moors and scrubland, the rocky landscape is sparsely settled. A center for hikers is the small hamlet of **Minde,** where women weave patchwork rugs that are well known in the region. Take along plenty of supplies (water, lunch, sunscreen, and so on) for a day's hike in the wilderness.

In this rocky landscape, farmers barely eke out a living. They gather local stones to build their shelters, and they get energy from windmills. If you'd rather drive than hike through the area, take N362, which runs for some 45km (28 miles) from Batalha in the north to Santarém in the south.

The other great area of natural beauty is **Berlenga Island** ★★. A granite rock in the Atlantic, Berlenga is an island hideaway and nature preserve. Eleven kilometers (7 miles) out in the ocean west of Peniche, a medieval fortress once stood guard over the Portuguese coastline from this island. Berlenga is the largest island in a little archipelago made up of three groups of rocky rises known as the Farilhões, the Estelas, and the Forcades.

The medieval fortress on Berlenga, **Forte de São João Batista,** was destroyed in 1666 when 28 Portuguese tried to withstand a force of 1,500 Spaniards who bombarded it from 15 ships. Rebuilt toward the end of the 17th century, it now houses a hostel. You can take a stairway from the fortress to the lighthouse, stopping along the way to

WHERE TO STAY

MODERATE

Challet Fonte Nova ★ *Finds* A majestic iron gate dating from the 19th century guards the entrance to this traditional chaletlike structure. Once a private mansion, this is now an inn of charm and grace, consisting of three floors plus a basement that has been turned into a saloon with a pool table and bar. It is the second-highest-rated accommodation in town. Bedrooms vary in size and dimensions, but all are comfortable, with excellent maintenance and midsize private bathrooms with tubs.

Rua da Fonte Nova, 2461-601 Alcobaça. ✆ **26/259-83-00.** Fax 26/259-84-30. www.challetfontenova.pt. 10 units. 110€ ($127) double. Rates include breakfast. AE, MC, V. Free parking. **Amenities:** Bar. *In room:* A/C, TV, hair dryer.

INEXPENSIVE

Hotel Santa Maria ★ The most attractive modern hotel in town is ideally located in a quiet but central part of the historic city, on a sloping street just above the plaza in front of the monastery. Guest rooms are small and a bit look over the panorama of the archipelago. A cobblestone walk from the top of the lighthouse site takes you down to a little bay with fishermen's cottages along a beach.

At the hostel (✆ **26/278-25-50**), you can arrange for a boat trip around the island. The hostel also accepts overnight guests from June to September 21, charging 8.50€ ($9.80) per night in a double, though some dorm accommodations are also available. Be warned in advance that this is the most rawboned hostel in all of Portugal. It has antiquated shared bathroom facilities, and you must bring your own food and cooking equipment, linens, and flashlight. You must also be willing to make your own bed, cook your own meals, and even clean the place—there is no maid service. The hostel's canteen stocks only very basic foodstuffs. If you need something special, bring it from the mainland. The reception area at the hostel is open Monday through Friday from 10am to 11pm.

To the south of the hostel you can see the **Furado Grande,** a long marine tunnel that leads to a creek walled in by the granite cliffs. Under the fortress is a cave the locals call the **blue grotto,** but its pool is really closer to emerald green. The clear waters of the grotto and the island itself make Berlenga a mecca for snorkelers and scuba divers. Local waters contain an array of fish, including bream, red mullet, and sea bass. To reach the island, head first for Peniche, 92km (57 miles) north of Lisbon. A ferry makes two trips a day to the island in July and August; the first leaves at 9:30am. A same-day round-trip ticket costs 17€ ($20). From September to June, there's one ferry a day that leaves at 10am and returns at 6pm. This boat ride is rough: If you're prone to getting seasick, take the proper precautions.

cramped, but filled with polished paneling cut into geometrical shapes. They contain comfortable contemporary chairs, and some have views and balconies over the monastery and square. All contain neatly kept bathrooms equipped with shower-tub combinations. If parking is a problem, the hotel will open its garage for free.

Rua Francisco Zagalo 20-22, 2460-041 Alcobaça. ✆ **26/259-73-95.** Fax 26/259-01-61. 76 units. 45€ ($52) double; 55€ ($63) suite. Rates include breakfast. AE, MC, V. Free parking. **Amenities:** Breakfast room; bar; 24-hr. room service; babysitting; laundry service; rooms for those w/limited mobility. *In room:* A/C, TV, minibar, hair dryer (on request).

WHERE TO DINE

INEXPENSIVE

Trindade PORTUGUESE/ALENTEJO The most popular restaurant in town opens onto a side of the monastery fronting a tree-shaded square. Trindade has both full restaurant service and a snack bar. Your tasty meal is likely to include shellfish soup, roast rabbit, or the fresh fish of the day. Tender roast chicken is also available. The food is hearty and full of flavor, but the place is often overrun with international religious pilgrims and is a popular hangout for locals.

Praça do Dom Afonso Henríques 22. ✆ **26/258-23-97**. Main courses 7€–11€ ($8.05–$13). AE, MC, V. Daily 9:30am–11pm. Closed first 2 weeks of Oct.

ALCOBAÇA AFTER DARK

The town's only dance club, **Sunset** (✆ **26/259-70-17**), dominates the center of Fervença, about 1.5km (1 mile) west of Alcobaça. This is where just about everyone ends up late at night before staggering off to bed. From the center of town, follow the signs to Nazaré. It's open Friday through Saturday from 11pm until at least 6am; it's open daily in August.

3 Nazaré ★★

132km (82 miles) N of Lisbon, 13km (8 miles) NW of Alcobaça

The inhabitants of Portugal's most famous fishing village live in a unique, tradition-bound world that tourists threaten to overthrow. Many residents have never left their village, except perhaps to make the pilgrimage to nearby Fátima. The people remain insular, even as their village blossoms into a big summer resort.

Nazaré is probably best experienced in the off season; chances are that you won't really get to see it in summer. You'll be too busy looking for a parking place (good luck) or elbowing your way onto the beach. The crowds who come to visit the "most picturesque fishing village in Portugal," coupled with widespread high-rise construction, have made people wonder what happened to the fishing village. Amazingly, it's still here—you just have to look for it.

ESSENTIALS

ARRIVING

BY TRAIN There's no direct link to Lisbon. Nine trains per day run from Lisbon to Valado dos Frades; the 3-hour trip costs 5.50€ to 8€ ($6.35–$9.20) one-way. For information, call ✆ **808/208-208.** Buses (see below) run from Valado dos Frades to Nazaré.

BY BUS About a dozen buses a day make the short run between Nazaré and Valado dos Frades. A one-way ticket costs .90€ ($1.05). Eight express buses per day arrive from Lisbon. The trip takes 2 hours (1 hr. less than the train) and costs 7.30€ ($8.40) one-way. For information, call ✆ **96/744-98-68.**

BY CAR From Alcobaça (see above), continue northwest along N8-5 for about 13km (8 miles). From Lisbon, take highway A-8.

VISITOR INFORMATION

The **Nazaré Tourist Office** is on Avenida da República (✆ **26/256-11-94**). It's open daily, but hours vary depending on the time of year, so you should call ahead.

EXPLORING THE RESORT

PEOPLE-WATCHING Don't expect stunning architecture or historic sights—the big attractions in Nazaré are the people and their fabled boats. The villagers' clothes are patchwork quilts of sun-faded colors. The rugged men don rough woolen shirts and trousers, patched in kaleidoscopic rainbow hues resembling tartan, as well as long woolen stocking caps, in the dangling ends of which they keep their prized possessions—a favorite pipe or a crucifix. The women walk about mostly barefoot wearing embroidered, handmade blouses and pleated skirts of patched tartan woolens.

The fishing boats are Phoenician in design: slender, elongated, and boldly colored. On the high, knifelike prows, you'll often see crudely shaped eyes painted on the vessels—eyes supposedly imbued with the magical power to search the deep for fish and to avert storms. Even so, the boats sport lanterns for the dangerous job of fishing after dark. During the gusty days of winter or at high tide, the boats are hauled into a modern harbor about 10 minutes from the city's center. If you want to look at a boat, one of the locals will lead you—for a price.

Nazaré consists of two sections: the fishing quarter and the **Sítio** ★, the almost exclusively residential upper town. Near the beach you'll find handcraft shops, markets, restaurants, hotels, and boardinghouses. The main square opens directly onto the sea, and narrow streets lead to the smaller squares, evoking a medina in a Moorish village. At the farthest point from the cliff and square are the vegetable and fish markets, where auctions are held.

Jutting out over the sea, the promontory of the Sítio is a sheer drop to the ocean and the beach below. It's accessible by either a funicular or a goat-steep cobblestone pathway. The Virgin Mary supposedly appeared here in 1182: A young horseback-riding nobleman, Faus Roupinho, was pursuing a wild deer near the precipice, which was shrouded in mist. The fog lifted suddenly to reveal the Virgin and the chasm below. In honor of this miracle, the nobleman built the **Chapel of Memory.** Today, near the spot, you can go inside the 18th-century structure honoring the event. The tiny chapel is known for its *azulejos,* or hand-painted tiles, that cover its facade, roof, and interior. Many of the tiles depict the legend of Fraus Roupinho. A staircase leads down into a small crypt, and here, in a recess, is what is said to be the hoof-print left by Roupinho's horse as it came to a screeching halt at the edge of the cliff, saving its rider's life. The panoramic view of Nazaré and the Atlantic coast is one of the great seascapes in Estremadura.

SHOPPING Few other towns in Portugal are so promising—and so disappointing. Perhaps it's the sheer volume of merchandise in the crammed boutiques, all featuring much-the-same wares. The residents of tourist-conscious Nazaré long ago lost their enthusiasm for their ubiquitous, rough-textured fisher's sweaters, which seem to spill over shelves of virtually every boutique in town. The robust *varinas* (fishwives) of Nazaré gave up knitting long ago in favor of more modern commercial pursuits, such as running snack bars, souvenir shops, and postcard kiosks. Most of the knitwear you'll see here is imported from less prosperous communities in Portugal's far north.

WHERE TO STAY

Although Nazaré is one of the most popular destinations in Portugal, for some reason it has never had a first-rate hotel. Note that Beira-Mar (see "Where to Dine," below) also offers accommodations.

MODERATE

Hotel Mar Bravo Considerably improved in recent years, this place is now a government-rated four-star inn. The small guest rooms are comfortably furnished, and modern facilities such as private bathrooms with shower-tub combinations have been added. The location on the main square in front of the beach is ideal only if you like lots of tourists.

Praça Sousa Oliveira 70-71, 2450-159 Nazaré. ✆ **26/256-91-60.** Fax 26/256-91-69. www.marbravo.com. 16 units. 70€–120€ ($81–$138) double. Rates include breakfast. AE, DC, MC, V. Parking 8€ ($9.20). **Amenities:** 2 restaurants; bar; TV lounge; room service; babysitting; laundry service. *In room:* A/C, TV.

Hotel Praia ★ The leading hotel in town (though the competition is not compelling) is the Praia (literally, "Beach"). Built in the late 1960s, when the world's tourists were discovering Nazaré, the six-floor hotel is decorated in a modern but uninspired style. It's about a 3-minute walk from the sandy beach where the fishing boats and bathing cabins lie. Remodeled in the '90s, the midsize rooms are reasonably comfortable and well maintained. All units contain well-kept bathrooms equipped with shower-tub combinations. This is the only hotel in town that comes even close to being ranked as first class. All the other accommodations are either a bit second rate or just simple boardinghouses.

Av. Vieira Guimarães 39, 2450-110 Nazaré. ✆ **26/256-14-23.** Fax 26/256-14-36. 40 units. 70€–140€ ($81–$161) double; 130€–145€ ($150–$167) suite. Rates include breakfast. AE, DC, MC, V. Parking 10€ ($12). **Amenities:** Restaurant; bar; 24-hr. room service; laundry service; rooms for those w/limited mobility. *In room:* A/C, TV, safe.

INEXPENSIVE

Da Nazaré Hotel da Nazaré is the runner-up to the Praia (see above). This hotel doesn't please everybody, yet many patrons count themselves lucky if they can get a room because doing so is almost impossible in July and August. The hotel is on a busy and noisy street set back from the water, about a 3-minute walk from the promenade. It opens onto a tiny plaza, and many of the front guest rooms have private balconies. The small, simply furnished rooms have good beds and well-kept bathrooms with shower-tub combinations. A rooftop sun terrace has views of Nazaré and the cliff-top Sítio.

The best feature of this hotel is its fourth and fifth floors, which contain a restaurant and bar. The dining room opens onto windowed walls peering out over the village housetops, the rugged cliffs, and the harbor.

Largo Afonso Zuquete, 2450-065 Nazaré. ✆ **26/256-90-30.** Fax 26/256-90-38. 52 units. 59€–86€ ($68–$99) double; 92€–110€ ($106–$127) suite. Rates include breakfast. AE, DC, MC, V. Free parking. **Amenities:** Restaurant; bar; 24-hr. room service; laundry service. *In room:* A/C, TV, minibar, hair dryer, safe.

Pensão-Restaurante Ribamar ★ This genuine old-fashioned village inn is right on the water, and most of its small guest rooms open onto balconies. A twisting stairway in the rear leads to the old-style rooms. Each immaculate room is individually decorated and comfortable, equipped with good beds and a well-kept bathroom containing a shower-tub combination.

Rua Gomes Freire 9, 2450-222 Nazaré. ✆ **26/255-11-58.** Fax 26/256-22-24. 25 units. 25€–90€ ($28–$104) double; 95€–124€ ($109–$143) suite. AE, DC, MC, V. Parking 5€–10€ ($5.75–$12). **Amenities:** Restaurant; bar. *In room:* TV, safe.

WHERE TO DINE

MODERATE

Mar Bravo PORTUGUESE One of the busiest of the dozens of overpriced restaurants in this bustling village is Mar Bravo, on the corner of the square overlooking the ocean. A complete and consistently pleasing meal consists of soup followed by a fish or meat dish and bread. An English-language menu lists a la carte specialties such as classic bass caprice, fish stew Nazaréna, lobster stew, and grilled pork. Dessert might be a soufflé, fruit salad, or pudding. Upstairs is a second dining room, with an ocean view.

Praça Sousa Oliveira 71. ✆ **26/256-91-60.** Reservations recommended. Regular main courses 7€–18€ ($8.05–$21); seafood main courses 15€–45€ ($17–$52). AE, DC, MC, V. Daily noon–10pm.

NAZARÉ AFTER DARK

Many bars and bodegas line the main boulevards of Nazaré. You'll find dozens of establishments along such main arteries as Avenida da República and Avenida Marginale. Bar-hop as energetically as you please, but do stop at our favorite,

Bar Gaibota, Avenida Marginal (✆ **26/256-22-85**). The owners speak English, and no one will wince if you order a martini, though most patrons drink Portuguese wines.

4 Batalha

118km (73 miles) N of Lisbon

Batalha merits a visit for only one reason: to see the monastery. Most visitors choose to stay in Fátima or Nazaré, which have more hotels and restaurants. However, there are places to sleep and eat in Batalha.

ESSENTIALS

ARRIVING

BY TRAIN There's no direct rail link to Lisbon. Trains run to the junction at Valado dos Frades, and buses continue from there to Batalha. For rail schedules, call ✆ **808/208-208.** Tickets cost 5.40€ to 7.85€ ($6.20–$9.05).

BY BUS From Nazaré (see above), seven buses a day make the 1-hour trip to Batalha, with a change at Alcobaça; one-way tickets cost 2.25€ ($2.05). From Lisbon, there are six *expresso* buses a day; the trip lasts 2 hours and costs 7.80€ ($8.95) one-way.

BY CAR From Alcobaça (see earlier), continue northeast along N8 for about 20 minutes.

VISITOR INFORMATION

The **Batalha Tourist Office** is on Praça Mouzinho de Albuquerque (✆ **24/476-51-80**). If you're traveling by bus, the tourist office keeps detailed schedules of the best connections to surrounding towns. It's open daily from 10am to 1pm and 3 to 7pm.

VISITING THE MONASTERY

Mosteiro de Santa Maria da Vitória ★★★ In 1385, João I vowed on the plains of Aljubarrota that if his underequipped and outnumbered army defeated the invading Castilians, he would commemorate his spiritual indebtedness to the Virgin Mary. The result is the magnificent Monastery of the Virgin Mary, designed in splendid Gothic and Manueline style.

The **western porch** ★, ornamented by a tangled mass of Gothic sculpture of saints and other figures, sits beneath a stained-glass window of blue, mauve, and amber. The windows are of exceptional beauty and are best enjoyed on a sunny day. As windows were damaged over the centuries, various artisans have replaced them in their original 16th-century Manueline detail.

In the **Founder's Chapel** ★, João I and his English queen, Philippa of Lancaster (daughter of John of Gaunt), lie in peaceful repose, their hands entwined on their stone effigies beneath an exquisite octagonal lantern. Prince Henry the Navigator's tomb is near that of his parents. His fame eclipsed theirs even though he never sat on the throne. The **Royal Cloisters** ★★★ reveal the beginnings of the nautically oriented Manueline architecture.

The magnum opus of the monastery is the **Chapter House** ★★, a square chamber whose **vaulting** ★★★ is an unparalleled example of the Gothic style, bare of supporting pillars.

Sentinels and the glow of an eternal flame guard the two tombs of Portugal's Unknown Soldiers from World War I. In one part of the quadrangle is the Unknown Soldiers Museum, which houses gifts to the fallen warriors from the people of Portugal and other countries. Beyond the crypt are the remains of the old wine cellars. You can visit the crypts daily from 9am to 5pm, but you might not want to unless you're a crypt aficionado. These consist of a series of dank and gloomy ancient tombs, but no notable treasures.

Stunning filigree designs ornament the coral-stone entrance to the seven unfinished chapels ★★. The *capelas,* under a "sky ceiling," are part of one of the finest examples of the Manueline style, a true stone extravaganza. Construction was abandoned so workers for Manuel I could help build his monastery at Belém.

Outside, in the forecourt, stands a heroic statue to Nuno Alvares, who fought with João I on the plains of Aljubarrota. It was unveiled in 1968.

Praça Moozinho de Obuquerque. ✆ **24/476-54-97.** Admission 3€ ($3.45), free for children under 14. Daily Oct–Mar 9am–5pm; Apr–Sept 9am–6pm.

WHERE TO STAY & DINE

MODERATE

Mestre Afonso Domingues Pousada This pousada fills a big accommodations gap in this part of the country. It stands right across the square from the monastery. Guests can relax in well-kept modern comfort, if not great style. The good-size rooms are well furnished, with comfortable beds. All units are also equipped with well-maintained bathrooms containing shower-tub combinations. The staff is helpful and friendly. And the restaurant here serves the finest cuisine in town to nonguests as well as guests, although that is no great compliment because Batalaha is hardly a gourmet citadel.

Largo do Mestre Afonso Domingues, 2440-102 Batalha. ✆ **24/476-52-60.** Fax 24/476-52-47. www.pousadas.com. 21 units. 85€–118€ ($98–$136) double; 92€–164€ ($106–$189) suite. Rates include breakfast. AE, DC, MC, V. Free parking. **Amenities:** Restaurant; bar; limited room service; laundry service; 1 room for those w/limited mobility. *In room:* A/C, TV, minibar, hair dryer, safe.

5 Fátima

142km (88 miles) N of Lisbon, 58km (36 miles) E of Nazaré

Fátima is a world-famous pilgrimage site because of reported sightings of the Virgin Mary in the early 20th century. The terrain around the village is wild, almost primitive, with an aura of barren desolation hanging over the countryside. However, when religious pilgrims flock to the town twice a year, its desolation quickly turns to fervent drama.

ESSENTIALS

ARRIVING

BY TRAIN Four trains run daily from Lisbon to Chão de Maças, 20km (13 miles) outside Fátima. A ticket costs 7.50€ ($8.65), and the trip takes 1 hour and 10 minutes. For information and schedules, call ✆ **808/208-208.** Buses await passengers at Chão de Maças and run into Fátima, taking 30 minutes and costing 2.20€ ($2.55) one-way.

BY BUS On bus schedules, Fátima is often listed as Cova da Iria, which leads to a lot of confusion. Cova da Iria is less than 1km (⅔ mile) from Fátima and is the focus of pilgrimages and the site of the alleged religious miracles. About three buses a day connect Fátima with Batalha. The trip takes 40 minutes and costs 2.10€ ($2.40) one-way. Fifteen buses a day arrive from Lisbon. The 1½-hour trip costs 7.80€ ($8.95) one-way. For information and schedules, call ✆ **808/208-208.**

BY CAR From Batalha (see above), continue east along Route 356 for 15km (9¼ miles).

VISITOR INFORMATION

The **tourist office** is on Avenida Dom José Alves Correia da Silva (✆ **24/953-11-39**) and is open daily from 10am to 1pm and 3 to 7pm.

EXPLORING THE TOWN

A PILGRIMAGE TO FÁTIMA On May 13 and October 13, pilgrims overrun the town, causing the roads leading to Fátima to be choked with pilgrims in donkey carts, on bicycles, or in cars beginning on the 12th of each month. Many also approach on foot; some even "walk" on their knees in penance. Once in Fátima, they camp out until day breaks. In the central square, which is larger than St. Peter's in Rome, a statue of the Madonna passes through the crowd between about 10am and 12:30pm. When it does, some 75,000 handkerchiefs flutter in the breeze.

Then as many as are able crowd in to visit a small slanted-roof shed known as the **Chapel of the Apparitions.** Inside stands a single white column marking the spot where a small holm oak once grew. An image of the Virgin Mary reputedly appeared over this oak on May 13, 1917, when she is said to have spoken to three shepherd children. That oak long ago disappeared, torn to pieces by souvenir collectors. The original chapel constructed here was dynamited on the night of March 6, 1922, by skeptics who suspected the church of staging the so-called miracle.

While World War I dragged on, three devout children—Lúcia de Jesús and her cousins, Jacinta and Francisco Marto—claimed that they saw the first appearance of "a lady" on the tableland of Cova da Iria. Her coming had been foreshadowed in 1916 by what they would later cite as "an angel of peace," who is said to have appeared before them.

Attempts were made to suppress their story, but it spread quickly. During the July appearance, the lady was reported to have revealed three secrets to them, one of which prefigured the coming of World War II; another was connected with Russia's "rejection of God." The final secret, a "sealed message" recorded by Lúcia, was opened by church officials in 1960, but the contents of that message, according to a Vatican spokesperson, are known only to the pope. Acting on orders from the Portuguese government, the mayor of a nearby town threw the children into jail and threatened them with torture, even death in burning oil. Still, they would not be intimidated and stuck to their story. The lady reportedly made six appearances between May and the final one on October 13, 1917, when the children were joined by an estimated 70,000 people who witnessed the famous Miracle of the Sun. The day had begun with pouring rain and driving winds. Observers from all over the world testified that at noon "the sky opened up" and the sun seemed to spin out of its axis and hurtle toward the Earth. Many at the site feared the Last Judgment was upon them. Others later reported that they thought the scorching sun was crashing into the Earth and would consume it in flames. Many agreed that a major miracle of modern times had occurred. Only the children reported seeing Our Lady, however.

Both Francisco and Jacinta died in the influenza epidemic that swept Europe after World War I. Lúcia became a Carmelite nun in a convent in the university city of Coimbra. She returned to Fátima in 1967 to mark the 50th anniversary of the apparition, and the pope flew in from Rome.

A cold, pristine white basilica in the neoclassic style was erected at one end of the wide square. If you want to go inside, you might be stopped by a guard if you're not suitably dressed. Women are asked not to enter wearing slacks or "other masculine attire." Men wearing shorts are also excluded.

SHOPPING Many of the souvenirs you'll find in Fátima are religious in nature. If you're interested in an even-handed mixture of religious and secular objects, head for the town's biggest gift shop, **Centro Comercial Fatima,** Estrada de Leira (✆ **24/953-23-75**). The staggering inventory is piled to the ceiling. If you're looking for devotional statues or a less controversial example of regional porcelain, you'll find it here, 450m (1,476 ft.) from the town's main religious sanctuary. There's another well-stocked gift shop in the **Pax Hotel,** Rua Francisco Marto (✆ **24/953-94-00**).

WHERE TO STAY

On the days of the major pilgrimages, it's just about impossible to secure a room unless you've reserved months in advance.

INEXPENSIVE

Hotel Cinquentenário This balconied structure, on a corner lot a short walk east of the sanctuary, offers comfortable but small accommodations. Patterned carpets and wallpaper make the interior warmly agreeable. Each guest room has a firm bed and well-maintained plumbing; most units contain shower-tub combinations.

Rua Francisco Marto 175, 2495-448 Fátima. ✆ **24/953-04-00.** Fax 24/953-29-92. hotel.cinquentenario@ip.pt. 150 units. 65€–75€ ($75–$86) double; 97€ ($112) suite. Rates include continental breakfast. AE, DC, MC, V. Free parking. **Amenities:** Restaurant; coffee shop; bar; laundry service; rooms for those w/limited mobility. *In room:* A/C, TV, dataport, safe.

Hotel de Fátima ★ Hotel de Fátima is the leading accommodation of a fairly standard but ordinary lot (which are clean, comfortable, and decently run, but not luxurious or architecturally distinguished in any way). Many of the midsize rooms overlook the sanctuary. The best rooms are in the newer 45-room addition. All units contain neatly kept bathrooms equipped with shower-tub combinations. This is the only hotel in town that can be rated as first class.

Rua João Paulo II, 2495-308 Fátima. ✆ **24/953-33-51.** Fax 24/953-26-91. www.hotelfatima.com. 126 units. 70€–83€ ($81–$95) double; 95€–122€ ($109–$140) suite. Rates include buffet breakfast. AE, DC, MC, V. Parking 2.50€ ($2.90) in garage, free outside. **Amenities:** Restaurant; bar; 24-hr. room service; laundry service; rooms for those w/limited mobility. *In room:* A/C, TV, minibar.

Hotel Dom Gonçalo This modern Best Western hotel sits in a large garden at the entrance to town, only 365m (1,197 ft.) from the Sanctuary of Our Lady of Fátima. The small to midsize guest rooms are among the town's finest, although Hotel de Fátima probably has the edge. All are comfortably and attractively furnished, with firm beds and rather uninspired decor. The bathrooms are small but well maintained, with shower-tub combinations and recently renewed plumbing.

Rua Jacinta Marto 100, 2495-450 Fátima. ✆ **800/582-1234** in the U.S., or 24/953-93-30. Fax 24/953-93-35. www.bestwestern.com. 42 units. 72€–80€ ($83–$92) double; 99€–110€ ($114–$127) suite. Rates include breakfast. AE, DC, MC, V. Free parking. **Amenities:** Restaurant; bar; 24-hr. room service; babysitting; laundry service; nonsmoking rooms. *In room:* A/C, TV, dataport, minibar, hair dryer.

Hotel Santa Maria This comfortable modern hotel is on a quiet side street just a few steps east of the park surrounding the sanctuary. Each modern room, attended by a well-trained staff, contains a balcony, a firm bed, and a well-maintained bathroom with a shower-tub combination. The small accommodations are plain but entirely acceptable.

Rua de Santo António, 2495-430 Fátima. ✆ **24/953-01-10.** Fax 24/953-01-19. www.hotelsantamaria.com. 180 units. 60€–75€ ($69–$86) double; from 90€–150€ ($104–$173) suite. Rates include continental breakfast. AE, MC, V. Free parking. **Amenities:** Restaurant; bar; limited room service; laundry service; rooms for those w/limited mobility. *In room:* A/C, TV, hair dryer.

Hotel São José On one of the busiest streets in Fátima, within walking distance of the sanctuary, this modern balconied hotel is large and urban. It has a uniformed staff, a marble-floor lobby, and comfortable midsize rooms. This hotel seems to have a bit more style than some of its more spartan competitors. Each guest room has a firm bed and a shower-tub combination with smoothly functioning plumbing.

Av. Dom José Alves Correia da Silva, 2495-402 Fátima. ✆ **24/953-01-20.** Fax 24/953-01-19. 76 units. 57€–75€ ($66–$86) double; 110€ ($127) suite. Rates include breakfast. AE, MC, V. Free parking. **Amenities:** Restaurant; 2 bars; room service; laundry service. *In room:* A/C, TV, hair dryer.

Hotel Três Pastorinhos The Hotel of the Three Shepherd Children, a government-rated three-star establishment, offers modern facilities in a setting as sparse as a convent. Its newest guest rooms open onto private balconies that overlook the sanctuary. All units are equipped with well-maintained bathrooms containing shower-tub combinations.

Rua João Paulo II, 2495 Fátima. ✆ **24/953-99-00.** Fax 24/953-99-50. www.hotel3pastorinhos.pt. 92 units. 57€ ($66) double; 85€ ($98) suite. Rates include continental breakfast. AE, DC, MC, V. Free parking. **Amenities:** Restaurant; bar; limited room service; laundry service. *In room:* A/C, TV, hair dryer, safe.

WHERE TO DINE

MODERATE

Grelha PORTUGUESE/GRILLS If you don't want to eat at a hotel, try Grelha, one of the best of a meager selection. It's 275m (902 ft.) from the sanctuary at Fátima. Grelha offers regional specialties but is known for its grills, especially steaks and fish. Grilled codfish is an especially good choice. In the cooler months, the fireplace is an attraction, and the bar is busy year-round.

Rua Jacinta Marto 78. ✆ **24/953-16-33.** Main courses 6.75€–12€ ($7.75–$14). AE, DC, MC, V. Fri–Wed noon–3pm and 7–10:30pm. Closed 2 weeks in Nov (dates vary).

Tía Alice ★ PORTUGUESE This simple, rustic restaurant offers copious portions of food inspired by the rural traditions of Estremadura. It's the finest dining choice in the area, though that's not saying a lot. Specialties include broad-bean soups, roast lamb with rosemary and garlic, fried hake with green sauce, chicken, Portuguese sausages, and grilled lamb or pork chops.

Rua do Adro. ✆ **24/953-17-37.** Reservations required. Main courses 145€–18€ ($17–$21); fixed-price menu 25€ ($29). AE, MC, V. Tues–Sun noon–3pm; Tues–Sat 7:30–10pm. Closed July.

FÁTIMA AFTER DARK

As you might expect of a destination for religious pilgrimages, Fátima is early to rise (in many cases, for morning mass) and early to bed. Cafes in town tend to be locked tight after around 10pm, so religion-weary residents who want to escape drive 2km (1¼ mile) south of town along Estrada de Minde. Here you'll find two music bars that are much more attuned to human frailties than the ecclesiastical monuments in the core. They are **Teles,** Estrada de Minde (no phone), and its neighbor, **Bar Truao,** Estrada de Minde (✆ **24/952-15-42**). Both are open Friday and Saturday night from midnight to 4am. The 5€ to 8€ ($5.75–$9.20) cover charge at either place includes the first drink.

8

The Algarve

In the ancient Moorish town of Xelb (today called Silves), a handsome and sensitive vizier once lived. During one of his sojourns into northern lands, he fell in love with a beautiful Nordic princess. After they married, he brought her back to the Algarve. Soon the young princess began to pine for the snow-covered hills and valleys of her native land. The vizier decreed that thousands of almond trees would be planted throughout his realm. Since that day, pale-white almond blossoms have blanketed the Algarve in late January and early February. The young princess lived happily ever after in her vizier's sun-drenched kingdom, with its sweet-smelling artificial winters—or so the story goes.

The maritime province of the Algarve, often called the Garden of Portugal, is the southwesternmost part of Europe. Its coastline stretches 160km (99 miles) from Henry the Navigator's Cape St. Vincent to the border town of Vila Real de Santo António, fronting once-hostile Spain. The varied coastline contains sluggish estuaries, sheltered lagoons, low-lying areas where clucking marsh hens nest, long sandy spits, and promontories jutting out into the white-capped aquamarine foam.

Called Al-Gharb by the Moors, the land south of the *serras* (mountains) of Monchique and Caldeirão remains a spectacular anomaly that seems more like a transplanted section of the North African coastline than a piece of Europe. The temperature averages around 15°C (60°F) in winter and 23°C (74°F) in summer. The countryside abounds in vegetation: almonds, lemons, oranges, carobs, pomegranates, and figs.

Even though most of the towns and villages of the Algarve are more than 240km (149 miles) from Lisbon, the great 1755 earthquake shook this area. Entire communities were wiped out; however, many Moorish and even Roman ruins remain. In the fret-cut chimneys, mosquelike cupolas, and cubist houses, a distinct Oriental flavor prevails. Phoenicians, Greeks, Romans, Visigoths, Moors, and Christians all touched this land.

However, much of the historic flavor is gone forever, swallowed by a sea of dreary high-rise apartment blocks surrounding most towns. Years ago, Portuguese officials, looking in horror at what happened to Spain's Costa del Sol, promised more limited and controlled development so that they wouldn't make "Spain's mistake." That promise, in our opinion, has not been kept.

Algarvian beaches are some of the best in Portugal. Their quality has led to the tourist boom across the southern coastline, making it a formidable rival of Lisbon's Costa do Sol and Spain's Costa del Sol. There are literally hundreds of beaches, many with public showers and watersports equipment available for rent. Not all beaches are suitable for swimming because some have sloping seabeds or swift currents—heed local warnings.

Since around 1965, vast stretches of coastal terrain have been bulldozed,

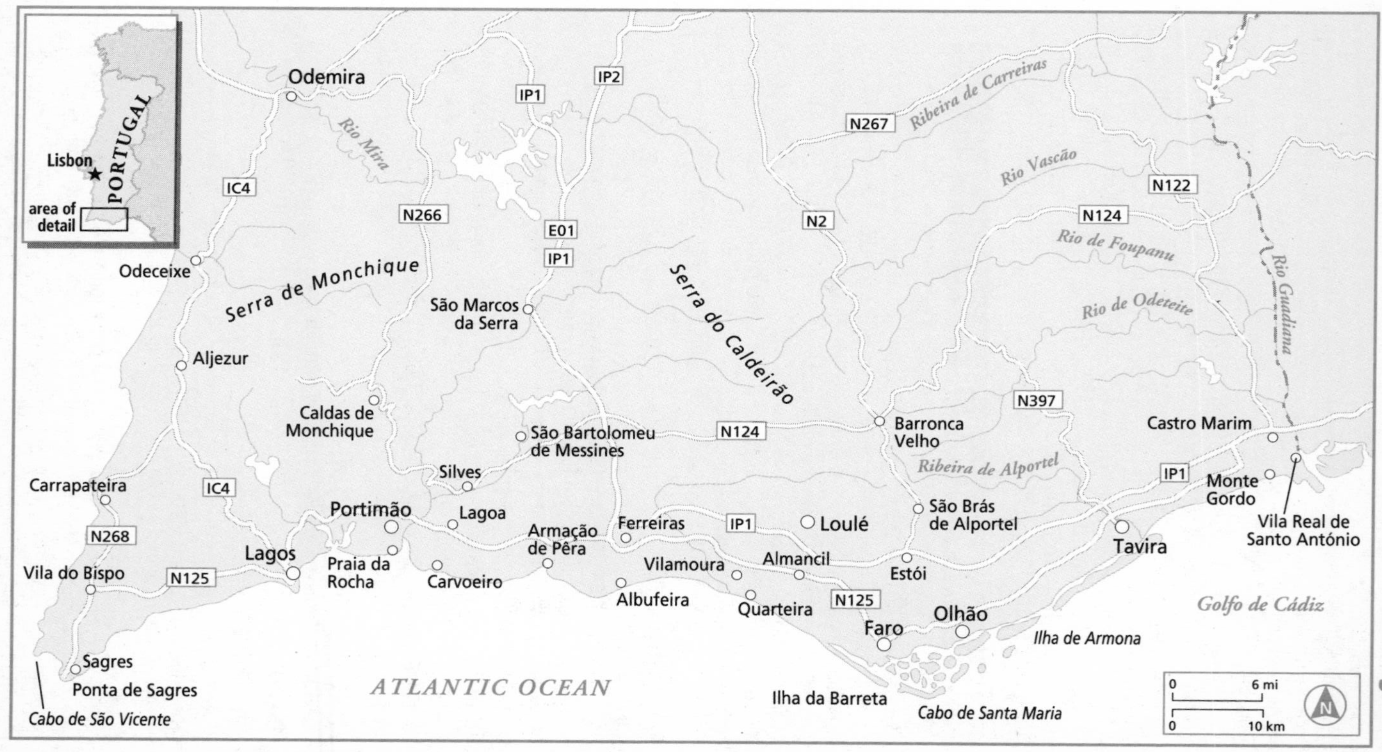
PORTUGAL
Lisbon
area of detail
Odemira
IP1
IP2
N267
Ribeira de Carreiras
Rio Mira
Rio Vascão
IC4
N122
N266
N2
N124
E01
IP1
Rio de Foupanu
Odeceixe
Serra de Monchique
São Marcos da Serra
Serra do Caldeirão
Rio de Odeteite
Rio Guadiana
Aljezur
Caldas de Monchique
N397
São Bartolomeu de Messines
N124
Barronca Velho
Castro Marim
Ribeira de Alportel
Silves
IP1
Carrapateira
IC4
Monte Gordo
Portimão
Lagoa
Ferreiras
IP1
Loulé
São Brás de Alportel
Vila Real de Santo António
N268
Armação de Pêra
Lagos
Tavira
Praia da Rocha
Almancil
Vila do Bispo
N125
Vilamoura
Estói
Carvoeiro
Albufeira
N125
Quarteira
Golfo de Cádiz
Faro
Olhão
Ilha de Armona
Sagres
Ponta de Sagres
ATLANTIC OCEAN
Ilha da Barreta
Cabo de Santa Maria
Cabo de São Vicente
0
6 mi
0
10 km

landscaped, irrigated, and reconfigured into golf courses. Many are associated with real-estate developments or major resorts, such as the 800-hectare (1,976-acre) Quinta do Lago, where retirement villas nestle amid vegetation at the edges of the fairways. Most are open to qualified golfers who inquire in advance.

Many former fishing villages—now summer resorts—dot the Algarvian coast: Carvoeiro, Albufeira, Olhão, Portimão. The sea is the source of life, as it always has been. The village marketplaces sell esparto mats, copper, pottery, and almond and fig sweets, sometimes shaped like birds and fish. Through the narrow streets comes the fast sound of little accordions pumping out the rhythmical *corridinho.*

For motorists, the big news is that the final 62km (39-mile) stretch of A2 is open, linking Lisbon and the Algarve with more efficient access than ever. The road took a decade to complete and cost $375 million.

1 Sagres: "The End of the World" ★

280km (174 miles) S of Lisbon, 34km (21 miles) W of Lagos, 114km (71 miles) W of Faro

At the extreme southwestern corner of Europe—once called *o fim do mundo* (the end of the world)—Sagres is a rocky escarpment jutting into the Atlantic Ocean. From here, Henry the Navigator, the Infante of Sagres, launched Portugal and the rest of Europe on the seas of exploration. Here he established his school of navigation, where Magellan, Diaz, Cabral, and Vasco da Gama apprenticed. A virtual ascetic, Henry brought together the best navigators, cartographers, geographers, scholars, sailors, and builders; infused them with his rigorous devotion; and methodically set Portuguese caravels upon the Sea of Darkness.

ESSENTIALS

ARRIVING

BY FERRY & TRAIN From Lisbon's Praça do Comércio, you can take a ferry across the Tagus to Barreiro. From there, take the Southern Line Railway to Lagos. For information and schedules, call © **21/888-40-25.** From Lagos, buses go to Sagres.

BY BUS Ten Rodoviária buses (© **28/276-29-44**) run hourly from Lagos to Sagres each day. The trip time is 1 hour, and a one-way ticket costs 2.60€ ($3).

BY CAR From Lagos, drive west on Route 125 to Vila do Bispo, and then head south along Route 268 to Sagres.

VISITOR INFORMATION

The **Sagres Tourist Office,** Plaza da Republica, Sagres (© **28/262-00-03**), is open Tuesday through Saturday from 10am to 12:30pm and 1:30 to 6:30pm.

EXPLORING SAGRES

Both the cape and Sagres offer a view of the sunset. In the ancient world, the cape was the last explored point, although in time the Phoenicians pushed beyond it. Many mariners thought that when the sun sank beyond the cape, it plunged over the edge of the world.

Today, at the reconstructed site of Henry's windswept fortress on Europe's Land's End (named after the narrowing westernmost tip of Cornwall, England), you can see a huge stone compass dial. Henry supposedly used the Venta de Rosa in his naval studies at Sagres. Housed in the **Fortaleza de Sagres** is a small museum of minor interest that documents some of the area's history. It's open Tuesday through Sunday from 10am to noon and 2 to 6pm. Admission is

2€ ($2.30). At a simple chapel, restored in 1960, sailors are said to have prayed for help before setting out into uncharted waters. The chapel is closed to the public.

About 5km (3 miles) away is the promontory of **Cabo de São Vicente** ★★. It got its name because, according to legend, the body of St. Vincent arrived mysteriously here on a boat guided by ravens. (Others claim that the body of the patron saint, murdered at Valencia, Spain, washed up on Lisbon's shore.) A lighthouse, the second most powerful in Europe, beams illumination 100km (62 miles) across the ocean. To reach the cape, you can take a bus Monday through Friday only leaving from Rua Comandante Matos near the tourist office. Trip time is 10 minutes, and departures are at 11:15am, 12:30pm, and 4:15pm; a one-way ticket costs 1€ ($1.15). You can also contact Turinfo (see below), which offers 2-hour boat rides to the tip of Cabo de São Vicente for sightseeing (no fishing) for 18€ ($21) per person every afternoon, weather permitting, at 2pm.

OUTDOOR ACTIVITIES

BEACHES Many beaches fringe the peninsula; some attract nude bathers. Mareta, at the bottom of the road leading from the center of town toward the water, is the best and most popular. East of town is Tonel, also a good sandy beach. The beaches west of town, Praia de Baleeira and Praia de Martinhal, are better for windsurfing than for swimming.

EXPLORING If you'd like to rent a bike to explore the cape, go to **Turinfo,** Praça da República, Sagres (✆ **28/262-00-03**). The charge is 6€ ($6.90) for 4 hours and 9.50€ ($11) for a full day. Turinfo's Jeep tours of the natural preserve of the cape, including lunch, cost 38€ ($44).

FISHING Between October and January you'll be assured of a prolific catch, and at times you can walk down to almost any beach and hire a local fisherman to take you out for a half day. Just about every large-scale hotel along the Algarve will arrange a fishing trip for you.

WHERE TO STAY

MODERATE

Hotel da Baleeira In a ship's-bow position, Hotel da Baleeira is designed like a first-class *baleeira* (whaleboat) and spread out above the fishing port, lying 50m (164 ft.) from a good beach. The largest hotel on this land projection, it offers guest rooms with sea-view balconies and a private beach. The number of its rooms has nearly doubled in recent years; the older ones are quite small, and some have linoleum floors. The bathrooms are also tiny and equipped with shower-tub combinations.

Sítio da Baleeira, Sagres, 8650 Vila do Bispo. ✆ **28/262-42-12.** Fax 28/262-44-25. www.sagres.net/sagres/baleeira/index.htm. 122 units. 60€–122€ ($69–$140) double. Rates include breakfast. AE, DC, MC, V. Free parking. **Amenities:** Restaurant; snack bar; bar; saltwater pool; tennis court; car rental; room service; babysitting; laundry service. *In room:* TV, safe.

Pousada do Infante ★★ Pousada do Infante, the best address in Sagres, seems like a monastery built by ascetic monks who wanted to commune with nature. You'll be charmed by the rugged beauty of the rocky cliffs, the pounding surf, and the sense of the ocean's infinity. Built in 1960, the glistening white government-owned tourist inn spreads along the edge of a cliff that projects rather daringly over the sea. It boasts a long colonnade of arches with an extended stone terrace set with garden furniture, plus a second floor of accommodations with private balconies. Each midsize guest room is furnished with traditional pieces. Rooms 1 to 12 are the most desirable. All are equipped with neatly kept bathrooms containing shower-tub combinations.

The public rooms are generously proportioned, gleaming with marble and decorated with fine tapestries depicting the exploits of Henry the Navigator. Large velvet couches flank the fireplace. An official annex, the Fortaleza do Belixe (see "Where to Dine," below), offers less luxurious rooms.

Ponta da Atalaia, 8650-385 Sagres. © **28/262-02-40.** Fax 28/262-42-25. www.pousadas.pt. 39 units. Sun–Thurs 97€–139€ ($112–$160) double, Fri–Sat 107€–152€ ($123–$175) double; Sun–Thurs 135€–184€ ($155–$212) suite, Fri–Sat 148€–204€ ($170–$235) suite. Rates include breakfast. AE, DC, MC, V. Free parking. **Amenities:** Restaurant; bar; tennis court; riding stables; car rental; limited room service; babysitting; laundry service. *In room:* A/C, TV, minibar, hair dryer, safe.

WHERE TO DINE

Fortaleza do Beliche ★ PORTUGUESE/INTERNATIONAL This establishment occupies the much-restored remnants of a medieval fortress built around the heyday of Henry the Navigator. It's on a sandy, rocky stretch of the coastal road between Sagres and the southwesternmost tip of Portugal, Cabo de São Vicente. All four dining rooms enjoy partial, or angled, views of the nearby sea, but one offers a wider panorama. The menu offerings are simple, straightforward, and flavorful. They include *caldo verde* (soup with ham hocks, greens, and potatoes); tasty fish soup; fried or grilled squid; grilled swordfish; well-prepared but uncomplicated versions of veal, pork, and beef; and whatever fresh fish is available from the local market.

In addition to its restaurant, the establishment maintains four guest rooms, each with TV and telephone. Doubles cost 90€ ($104) Sunday through Thursday and 102€ ($117) Friday and Saturday, including breakfast. The place is an official annex of the more expensive, more luxurious Pousada do Infante (see "Where to Stay," above). Parking is free.

Fortaleza do Beliche, Vila do Bispo, 8650 Sagres. © **28/262-41-24.** Main courses 10€–14€ ($12–$16); fixed-price menu 22€ ($25). AE, MC, V. Daily 1–2:30pm and 7:30–9:30pm. Closed Nov 15–Feb 15. From Sagres, drive W for 5km (3 miles) along the coastal road, following signs to Cabo de São Vicente.

SAGRES AFTER DARK

The best of the many nightspots in the town's historic core include the **Bar Dromedário,** Rua Comandante Meteoso (© **28/262-42-19**), and the **A Rosa dos Ventos (Pink Wind) Bar,** Praça da República (© **28/262-44-80**). Folks from all over Europe talk, relax, and drink beer, wine, or sangría.

2 Lagos ★

34km (21 miles) E of Sagres, 69km (43 miles) W of Faro, 264km (164 miles) S of Lisbon, 13km (8 miles) W of Portimão

Lagos, known to the Lusitanians and Romans as Locobriga and to the Moors as Zawaia, became a shipyard of caravels during the time of Henry the Navigator. Edged by the Costa do Ouro (Golden Coast), the Bay of Sagres was at one point in its epic history big enough to allow 407 warships to maneuver with ease.

An ancient port city (one historian traced its origins to the Carthaginians, 3 centuries before the birth of Christ), Lagos was well known by the sailors of Admiral Nelson's fleet. From Liverpool to Manchester to Plymouth, the sailors spoke wistfully of the beautiful green-eyed, olive-skinned women of the Algarve. Eagerly they sailed into port, looking forward to carousing and drinking.

Actually, not that much has changed since Nelson's day. Few go to Lagos wanting to know its history; rather, the mission is to drink deeply of the pleasures of table and beach. In winter, the almond blossoms match the whitecaps on the water, and the weather is often warm enough for sunbathing. In town, the flea market sprawls through narrow streets.

Less than 2km (1¼ mile) down the coast, the hustle and bustle of market day is forgotten as the rocky headland of the **Ponta da Piedade** ★★ (Point of Piety) appears. This spot is the most beautiful on the entire coast. Amid the colorful cliffs and secret grottoes carved by the waves are the most flamboyant examples of Manueline architecture.

Much of Lagos was razed in the 1755 earthquake, and it lost its position as the capital of the Algarve. Today only the ruins of its fortifications remain. However, traces of the old linger on the back streets.

ESSENTIALS

ARRIVING

BY FERRY & TRAIN From Lisbon, take the ferry from Praça do Comércio across the Tagus to Barreiro. From there, the **Southern Line Railway** runs to Lagos. Five trains a day arrive from Lisbon. The trip takes 5½ hours and costs at least 14€ ($16) one-way. For more information and schedules, call ✆ **808/208-208.**

BY BUS Eight buses a day make the run between Lisbon and Lagos. The trip takes 4 hours and costs 15€ ($17) each way. Call ✆ **28/276-29-44** for schedules.

BY CAR If you're coming from Lisbon, after leaving Sines, take Route 120 southeast toward Lagos and follow the signs into the city. From Sagres, take N268 northeast to the junction with N125, which will lead you east to Lagos.

VISITOR INFORMATION

The **Lagos Tourist Office,** Sitio de São Joao, Lãgos (✆ **28/276-30-31**), is open daily from 9:30am to 1pm and 2 to 5:30pm.

EXPLORING THE TOWN

Igreja de Santo António ★ The 18th-century Church of St. Anthony sits just off the waterfront. The altar is decorated with some of Portugal's most notable baroque **gilt carvings** ★, created with gold imported from Brazil. Begun in the 17th century, they were damaged in the earthquake but subsequently restored. What you see today represents the work of many artisans—each, at times, apparently pursuing a different theme.

Rua General Alberto Carlos Silveira. ✆ **28/276-23-01.** Free admission. Tues–Sun 9:30am–12:30pm and 2–5pm.

Museu Municipal Dr. José Formosinho The Municipal Museum contains replicas of the fret-cut chimneys of the Algarve, three-dimensional cork carvings, 16th-century vestments, ceramics, 17th-century embroidery, ecclesiastical sculpture, a painting gallery, weapons, minerals, and a numismatic collection. An oddity is a sort of believe-it-or-not section displaying, among other things, an eight-legged calf. In the archaeological wing are Neolithic artifacts, Roman mosaics found at Boca do Rio near Budens, fragments of statuary and columns, and other remains of antiquity from excavations along the Algarve.

Rua General Alberto Carlos Silveira. ✆ **28/276-23-01.** Admission 2€ ($2.30), children 11–14 1€ ($1.15). Tues–Sun 9:30am–noon and 2–5pm. Closed holidays.

Antigo Mercado de Escravos The Old Customs House stands as a painful reminder of the Age of Exploration. The arcaded slave market, the only one of its kind in Europe, looks peaceful today, but under its four Romanesque arches, captives were once sold to the highest bidders. The house opens onto the tranquil main square dominated by a statue of Henry the Navigator.

Praça do Infante Dom Henríques. Free admission. Daily 24 hours.

OUTDOOR ACTIVITIES

BEACHES Some of the best beaches—including Praia de Dona Ana, the most appealing—are near Lagos, south of the city. Follow signs to the Hotel Golfinho. If you go all the way to the southernmost point, Ponta da Piedade, you'll pass some pretty cove beaches set against a backdrop of rock formations. Steps are sometimes carved into the cliffs to make for easier access. Although it's crowded in summer, another good white-sand beach is at the 2.5km-long (1½-mile-long) Meia Praia (Half Beach), across the river from the center of town.

DIVING One of the Algarve's most highly recommended outlets for scuba diving is **Blue Ocean Divers,** Estrada de Porto de Mos (Motel Ancora) (✆ **28/278-27-18**), one of the region's few fully licensed and insured scuba outfits. It pays special attention to safety, and its staff focuses on the coastline between Lagos and Sagres, site of numerous underwater caves and (mostly) 20th-century shipwrecks at depths of between 12m (39 ft.) and 35m (115 ft.) beneath the high-tide level. One dive with full equipment costs 40€ ($46); a PADI scuba course of 3 days and two dives costs 220€ ($253).

GOLF **Palmares,** Meia Praia, 8600 Lagos (✆ **28/276-29-61**), is not a particularly prestigious or championship-level course—it's "medium" in both difficulty and desirability. Frank Pennink designed it in 1975 on land with many differences in altitude. Some fairways require driving a ball across railroad tracks, over small ravines, or around palm groves. Its landscaping suggests North Africa, partly because of its hundreds of palms and almond trees. The view from the 17th green is exceptionally dramatic. Par is 71. Greens fees are 48€ to 75€ ($55–$86), depending on the season. The course lies on the eastern outskirts of Lagos, less than 1km (¾ mile) from the center. To reach it from the heart of town, follow signs toward Meia Praia.

Another course is **Parque da Floresta,** Budens, Vale do Poço, 8650 Vila do Bispo (✆ **28/269-00-00**). One of the few important Algarvian courses west of Lagos, it's just inland from the fishing hamlet of Salema. Designed by the Spanish architect Pepe Gancedo and built as the centerpiece of a complex of holiday villas completed in 1987, the par-72 course offers sweeping views; we find it to be more scenic and more challenging than the Palmares course. Some shots must be driven over vineyards, and others over ravines, creeks, and gardens. Critics of the course have cited its rough grading and rocky terrain. Some of these drawbacks are offset by a clubhouse with a sweeping view over the Portuguese coast. Greens fees are 24€ to 42€ ($28–$48) for 9 holes, and 40€ to 70€ ($46–$81) for 18. To reach the course from the center of Lagos, drive about 15km (9⅓ miles) west, following road signs toward Sagres and Parque da Floresta.

Go to www.algarvegolf.net for more information on courses in the Algarve region.

SHOPPING

Foremost among the many handcrafts dealers is **Algife,** Rua Portes de Portugal 911 (✆ **28/276-14-56**), a purveyor of pottery, hand-blown glass and more formal leaded crystal, china, and all kinds of housewares. Even more appealing is **Casa des Verges,** Rua do 25 de Abril 77 (© **28/276-00-28**). It sells wickerwork, leather ware, crystal, china, pottery, and kitchen accessories. Note the Algarvian blankets, woven on hand-operated looms in colorful patterns with antecedents in the Moorish era.

A jewelry shop where silver and gold filigrees seem somehow finer and more delicately wrought than anywhere else in town is **Ouraivesaria Lagos,** Rua do 25 de Abril 6 (© **28/276-27-72**). Also look here for antique coins, silver candelabras, spoons with the royal crest of Lagos or of Portugal, and silver plates.

A worthy bookshop filled with books in Portuguese and English, as well as postcards and periodicals, is **Loja do Livro,** Rua Dr. Joaquim Telo 3 (© **28/276-73-47**).

A final choice is **Terra Cotta,** Praça Luís de Camões (© **28/276-33-74**). You'll find pottery from Spain, art objects from Portugal, and inlaid wood and artfully ornate brass and copper from Morocco, Tunisia, Egypt, and Greece.

WHERE TO STAY

EXPENSIVE

Romantik Hotel Vivenda Miranda ★★★ *Finds* A real discovery, this small, Moorish-style hotel towers on a cliff overlooking the coast, 2.8km (1¾ miles) south of Lagos near the beach of Praia do Porto de Mos. Surrounded by exotic gardens and terraces, the inn opens onto the most panoramic views of any hotel in the area. Midsize to spacious bedrooms are stylish and exceedingly comfortable, with first-class tiled bathrooms, mainly with shower-tub combinations (some with shower only). This is the kind of hotel that would be ideal for a honeymoon or romantic getaway. The cuisine is so good that you might want to stay in at night enjoying a gourmet dinner with organic produce along with an excellent selection of regional wines.

Porto de Mos, 8600-282 Lagos. © **28/276-32-22.** Fax 28/276-03-42. 28 units. 134€–184€ ($154–$212) double; 174€–245€ ($200–$282) suite. **Amenities:** Restaurant; bar; outdoor pool; room service; babysitting. *In room:* TV, minibar, hair dryer, safe.

Tivoli Lagos ★ A 20th-century castle of Moorish and Portuguese design, Tivoli Lagos lies within its own ramparts and moats—okay, a swimming pool and a paddling pool. It's at the eastern side of the old town, far removed from the beach. This first-class hotel spreads over 1.2 hilltop hectares (3 acres) overlooking Lagos; no matter which room you're assigned, you'll have a view, even if it's of a sun-trap courtyard with semitropical greenery. The main room has a hacienda atmosphere, with white-plaster walls enlivened by sunny colors. The surrounding area is rather unappetizing.

Some of the midsize guest rooms have ground-level patios, but most are on the upper six floors and have a 1960s feel. All units are equipped with well-maintained bathrooms containing shower-tub combinations. Many rooms open onto a wedge-shape balcony where you can eat breakfast. A 31-room wing, complete with pool and health club, was added in 1989. The hotel owns the Duna Beach Club on Meia Praia beach, which has a saltwater pool, a restaurant, and three tennis courts; guests have free membership during their stay. A private motor coach makes regular trips to the beach club, 5 minutes from the hotel. Arrangements can be made for golf at the nearby Palmares course (where guests get a 10%–20% discount on greens fees), skin diving and sportfishing in the waters along the coast, horseback riding, and sailing in the bay.

Rua Antonio Crisógono Santos, 8600-678 Lagos. ✆ **28/279-00-79.** Fax 28/279-03-45. www.tivolihotels.com. 324 units. 63€–165€ ($72–$190) double; 88€–218€ ($101–$251) suite. Rates include breakfast. AE, DC, MC, V. Free parking outside, 5€ ($5.75) in garage. **Amenities:** 3 restaurants; 2 bars; 3 pools; 3 tennis courts; health club; game room; 24-hr. room service; babysitting; laundry service; dry cleaning. *In room:* A/C, TV, minibar, hair dryer, safe.

MODERATE

Albergaria Marina Rio The second-best place in town, this government-rated four-star hotel is in the center of town opposite the Lagos marina. Its small to midsize guest rooms are nicely decorated, and many open onto views of the sea. All have neatly kept bathrooms with shower-tub combinations. On the top floor is a sun terrace overlooking the Bay of Lagos. In summer, a courtesy bus takes guests to the beaches and golfers to the course at Palmares. A major problem here is that tour agents from Germany often book all the rooms en masse.

Av. dos Descobrimentos (Apdo. 388), 8600-645 Lagos. ✆ **28/276-98-59.** Fax 28/276-99-60. www.marinario.com. 36 units. 41€–90€ ($47–$104) double. Rates include buffet breakfast. AE, MC, V. Free parking on street, 4.50€ ($5.20) in garage. **Amenities:** Breakfast room; bar; pool; babysitting. *In room:* A/C, TV, dataport, hair dryer, safe.

Hotel Aqua Meia Praia This first-class hotel, 4km (2½ miles) northeast of Lagos, is for those who want sand, sun, and good food rather than exciting decor. The hotel stands at a point where a hill begins its rise from the sea. Surrounded by private gardens, it regrettably fronts railway tracks, but also a 6.5km-long (4-mile-long), wide, sandy beach. Guests linger in the informal garden under olive and palm trees. The midsize guest rooms have balconies with partitions for sunbathing; they were recently renovated. The furnishings are uncluttered and functional. The place is comfortable, the beds are firm, and the bathrooms are neatly kept with shower-tub combinations. The best units have sea views.

Meia Praia, 8600-315 Lagos. ✆ **28/277-00-00.** Fax 28/276-20-08. www.hotelaquameiapraia.com. 66 units. 55€–130€ ($63–$150) double. Rates include breakfast. AE, DC, MC, V. Free parking. **Amenities:** Restaurant; bar; lounge; 2 pools; minigolf course; 2 tennis courts; laundry service. *In room:* TV, safe.

INEXPENSIVE

Casa de São Gonçalo da Lagos ★ *Finds* This pink villa with fancy iron balconies dates to the 18th century. At the core of Lagos, close to restaurants and shops, the antiques-filled home is almost an undiscovered gem. Most of the public lounges and guest rooms turn, in the Iberian fashion, to the inward peace of a sun-filled patio. Surrounded by bougainvillea climbing balconies, guests order breakfast while sitting under a fringed parasol and enjoying the splashing of the fountain. Furnishings include hand-embroidered linens, period mahogany tables, chests with brass handles, ornate beds from Angola, and even crystal chandeliers. The street-level rooms can be very noisy. During the house's restoration in 1982, it gained modern luxuries, including well-maintained bathrooms that, for the most part, contain shower-tub combinations.

Rua Cândido dos Reis 73, 8600-315 Lagos. ✆ **28/276-21-71.** Fax 28/276-39-27. 13 units. 50€–70€ ($58–$81) double. Rates include breakfast. AE. Closed Nov–Mar. Limited free parking on street. **Amenities:** Breakfast room; bar. *In room:* A/C in some rooms.

WHERE TO DINE

MODERATE

A Lagosteira PORTUGUESE A Lagosteira has long been a mecca for knowledgeable diners. Its decor is simple, and there's a small bar on one side.

From the a la carte menu, the best openers for a big meal are classic Algarvian fish soup and savory clams Lagosteira style. After the fishy beginning, you might happily move on to a tender sirloin steak grilled over an open fire. Lobster is also a specialty. The selection of vintage wines complements the food.

Rua do 1 de Maio 20. ✆ **28/276-24-86.** Reservations recommended. Main courses 7€–14€ ($8–$16). AE, DC, MC, V. Mon–Fri 12:30–3pm and daily 6:30–11pm. Closed Jan 10–Feb 10.

Don Sebastião ★ PORTUGUESE This rustically decorated tavern on the main pedestrian street is one of the finest dining choices in Lagos. Portuguese-owned and -operated, it offers a varied menu of local specialties. Options include lip-smacking pork chops with figs, succulent shellfish dishes like clams and shrimp cooked with savory spices, and grills. Live lobsters are kept on the premises. One of the best selections of Portuguese vintage wines in town accompanies the filling, tasty meals. In summer, outdoor dining is available.

Rua do 25 de Abril 20. ✆ **28/276-27-95.** Reservations recommended. Main courses 7€–25€ ($8–$29). Daily noon–10pm. Closed Dec 24–26 and Dec 31–Jan 2.

O Galeão INTERNATIONAL Hidden on a back street, the air-conditioned Galeão offers a wide range of dishes, and you can watch the action through an exposed kitchen, which gets very busy in season. Meats are savory; fish dishes are fresh from the sea and tasty. Seafood options include king prawns and garlic, gratinée of seafood, sole meunière with almonds, lobster Thermidor, or salmon trout in champagne sauce. You can also order meat dishes, such as savory pork medallions in curry sauce and tender sirloin steak.

Rua de Laranjeira 1. ✆ **28/276-39-09.** Reservations recommended. Main courses 7€–12€ ($8–$14). AE, DC, MC, V. Mon–Sat 12:30–3pm and 7–11pm. Closed Nov 27–Dec 27.

O Trovador INTERNATIONAL Marion (she's German) and Dave (he's English) run O Trovador. It's especially inviting in the off season, when you can sit in comfortable chairs placed around a log-burning fireplace. But at any time of year, you get a pleasant atmosphere, good service, and competently prepared food. The restaurant is behind the Hotel de Lagos (follow the signs from Rua Vasco da Gama). Among the well-recommended appetizers are homemade duck-liver paté, succulent octopus cocktail, fish paté, and escargots. Shellfish dishes incorporate local herbs and spices. Main courses include beef casserole cooked in black beer, Portuguese swordfish, and duck roasted with orange sauce. The desserts are all good, but we especially like the homemade cheesecake, coupe Trovador (ice cream), and Marion's famous lemon crunch cake.

Largo do Convento da Senhora de Glória 29. ✆ **28/276-31-52.** Reservations recommended. Main courses 8€–17€ ($9–$20). MC, V. Tues–Sat 7–10:30pm. Closed Dec–Jan.

LAGOS AFTER DARK

You'll find hints of big-city life in Lagos and a devoted cadre of night owls. Two bars land at the top of everybody's list of favorite hangouts. The first is the **Bar Amuras,** Marinha de Lagos 2 (✆ **28/279-20-95**), which presents live music almost nightly. Views from the nautically inspired interior take in the boats in the nearby marina. Equally popular is the unpretentious yet cosmopolitan **Bar Mullens,** Rua Cândido dos Reis 86 (no phone). Its mock-medieval decor and big mirrors have witnessed the arrival of every sociable bar-hopper in town. The most popular and best-known dance club inside the city limits is **Phoenix,** Rua do 5 de Outubro 11 (no phone). Filled with energetic dancers in their 20s and 30s, it's open every night from 11pm till around 4am.

3 Portimão

18km (11 miles) E of Lagos, 61km (38 miles) W of Faro, 290km (180 miles) SE of Lisbon

Portimão is perfect if you want to stay in a bustling fishing port rather than a hotel perched right on the beach. Since the 1930s, **Praia da Rocha** ★★, 3km (1¾ miles) away, has snared sun-loving traffic. Today it's challenged by Praia dos Três Irmãos, but tourists still flock to Portimão in the summer.

The aroma of the noble Portuguese sardine permeates every street. Portimão is the leading fish-canning center in the Algarve. For a change of pace, this town, on an arm of the Arcade River, makes a good stopover for its fine dining. Stroll through its gardens and its shops (especially noted for their pottery), drink wine in the cafes, and roam down to the quays to see sardines roasting on braziers. The routine activity of the Algarvians is what gives the town its charm.

ESSENTIALS

ARRIVING

BY TRAIN From Lagos (see earlier), trains on the Algarve Line run frequently throughout the day to Portimão. The trip takes 15 minutes and costs 1€ to 1.50€ ($1.15–$1.75). For information and schedules, phone ✆ **21/888-40-25.**

BY BUS An express bus from Lisbon makes the 4½-hour trip and costs 15€ ($17). A bus runs from the beach at Portimao, 3km (1¾ miles) away. For **information** and schedules, call ✆ **21/314-77-10.**

BY CAR The main highway across the southern coast, Route 125, makes a wide arch north on its eastern run to Portimão.

VISITOR INFORMATION

At Praia da Rocha, the **tourist office** (✆ **28/241-91-32**) is on Avenida Tomás Cabreiro and is open daily from 9:30am to 5pm.

EXPLORING THE TOWN

Although it lacks great monuments and museums, Portimão is worth exploring. Just wander through its colorful streets, stopping at any sight that interests you. The once-colorful fishing boats used to unload their catch here at the port but have moved to a terminal across the river. High-rise buildings ring the area, but the core of the old town is still intact.

Try to be in Portimão for lunch. Of course, you can dine at a restaurant, but it's even more fun to walk down to the harborside, where you can find a table at one of the low-cost eateries. The specialty is charcoal-grilled sardines, which taste like nothing you get from a can. They make an inexpensive meal accompanied by chewy, freshly baked bread; a salad; and a carafe of regional wine.

If you're in town in August, stay for the **Sardine Festival** (dates vary), where the glory that is the Portuguese sardine is honored, lauded, and, finally, devoured.

If you'd like to go sightseeing, you can visit **Ferragudo,** a satellite of Portimão, 5km (3 miles) east and accessible by bridge. The beach area here is being developed rapidly but remains largely unspoiled. The sandy beach lies to the south, and kiosks rent sailboards and sell seafood from a number of waterside restaurants. In the center you can see the ruins of the **Castelo de São João,** which was constructed to defend Portimão from English, Spanish, and Dutch raids. There's no need to return to Portimão for lunch. Try **A Lanterna,** Parchal (✆ **28/241-44-29**), which you'll see on the main highway over the bridge from Portimão.

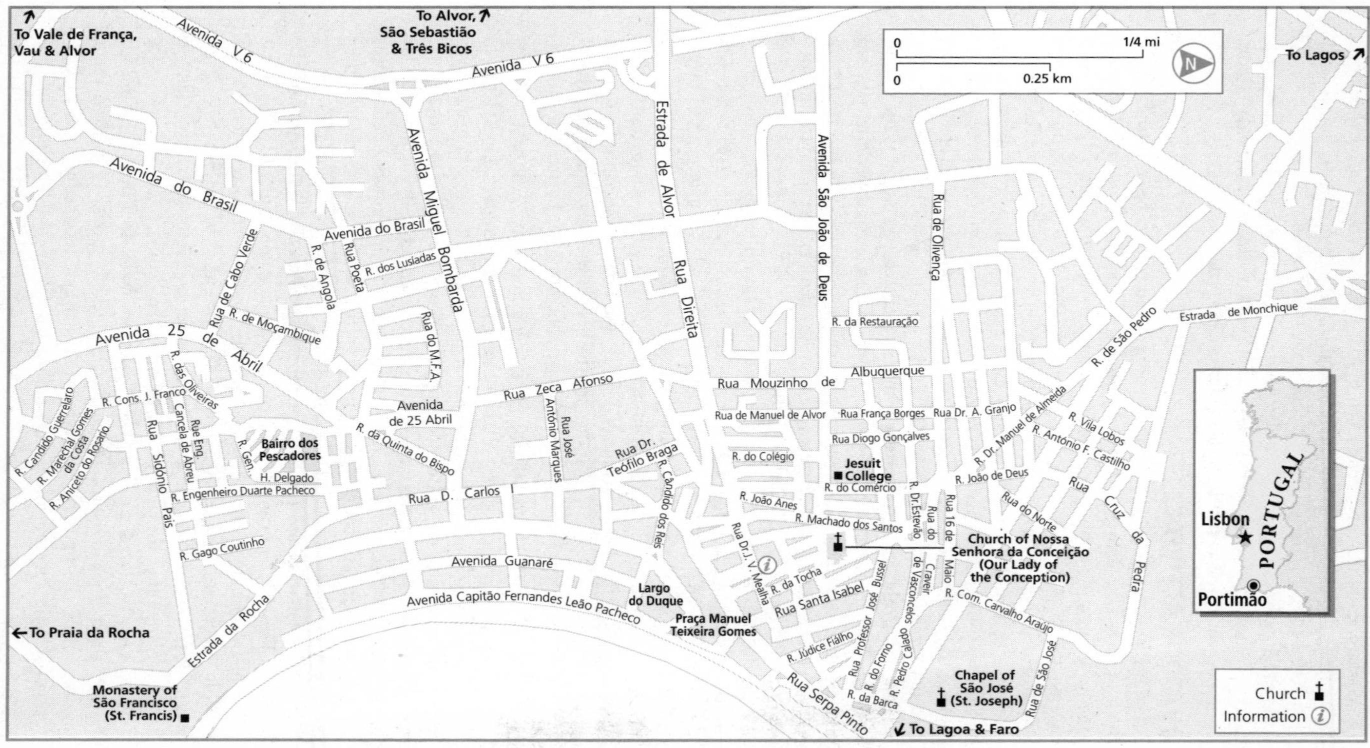
To Vale de França, Vau & Alvor
To Alvor, São Sebastião & Três Bicos
To Lagos
0 1/4 mi
0 0.25 km
N
Avenida V 6
Avenida V 6
Avenida do Brasil
Avenida do Brasil
Avenida Miguel Bombarda
Estrada de Alvor
Rua Direita
Avenida São João de Deus
Rua de Olivença
R. de Angola
Rua Poeta
R. dos Lusíadas
Rua de Cabo Verde
R. de Moçambique
Rua do M.F.A.
Avenida 25 de Abril
R. das Oliveiras
R. Cons. J. Franco
Rua Sidónio Pais
Rue Eng. Cancela de Abreu
R. Cândido Guerreiro
R. Marechal Gomes da Costa
R. Aniceto do Rosário
Bairro dos Pescadores
R. Gen. H. Delgado
R. Engenheiro Duarte Pacheco
R. Gago Coutinho
Avenida de 25 Abril
R. da Quinta do Bispo
Rua Zeca Afonso
Rua José António Marques
Rua D. Carlos I
Rua Dr. Teófilo Braga
R. Cândido dos Reis
Avenida Guanaré
Avenida Capitão Fernandes Leão Pacheco
Largo do Duque
Praça Manuel Teixeira Gomes
Estrada da Rocha
To Praia da Rocha
Monastery of São Francisco (St. Francis)
R. da Restauração
Rua Mouzinho de Albuquerque
Rua de Manuel de Alvor
Rua França Borges
Rua Dr. A. Granjo
Rua Diogo Gonçalves
R. do Colégio
Jesuit College
R. do Comércio
R. João Anes
R. Machado dos Santos
Rua Dr. J. V. Mealha
R. da Tocha
Rua Santa Isabel
R. Júdice Fialho
Rua Professor José Bussel
R. do Forno
R. Pedro Calado
R. da Barca
Rua Serpa Pinto
R. Dr. Estevão
Rua do Craveir de Vasconcelos
Rua 16 de Maio
Church of Nossa Senhora da Conceição (Our Lady of the Conception)
R. João de Deus
R. Dr. Manuel de Almeida
R. Vila Lobos
R. António F. Castilho
Rua do Norte
Rua Cruz da Pedra
R. de São Pedro
Estrada de Monchique
R. Com. Carvalho Araújo
Rua de São José
Chapel of São José (St. Joseph)
To Lagoa & Faro
Lisbon
PORTUGAL
Portimão
Church
Information

The cooks prepare the most savory fish soup in the area and an array of seafood dishes from the catch the fishermen brought in that morning. It's open daily from 7 to 11pm. Meals cost around 27€ ($31) per person.

At Praia da Rocha, 3km (1¾ miles) south of Portimão, you can explore the ruins of the 16th-century **Fortaleza de Santa Catarina,** Avenida Tomás Cabreira, which was constructed for defensive purposes.

OUTDOOR ACTIVITIES

BEACHES Even those staying in Portimão head for the beach first thing in the morning. The favorite is **Praia da Rocha,** a creamy yellow strand that has long been the most popular seaside resort on the Algarve. English voyagers discovered the beauty of its rock formations around 1935. At the outbreak of World War II there were only two small hotels and a few villas on the Red Coast, most built by wealthy Portuguese. Nowadays, Praia da Rocha is booming. At the end of the mussel-encrusted cliff, where the Arcade flows into the sea, lie the ruins of the Fortress of Santa Catarina. The location offers views of Portimão's satellite, Ferragudo, and of the bay.

Although **Praia dos Três Irmãos** is more expensive, you might want to visit its beach, 5km (3 miles) southwest of Portimão. From Portimão's center you can take a public bus; they run frequently throughout the day. The bus is marked PRAIA DOS TRÊS IRMÃOS. Departures are from the main bus terminal in Portimão at Largo do Duque (✆ **28/241-81-20**).

Praia dos Três Irmãos has 15km (9⅓ miles) of burnished golden sand, interrupted only by an occasional crag riddled with arched passageways. This beach has been discovered by skin divers who explore its undersea grottoes and caves.

Nearby is the whitewashed fishing village of Alvor, where Portuguese and Moorish arts and traditions have mingled since the Arab occupation ended. Alvor was a favorite coastal haunt of João II, and now summer hordes descend on the long strip of sandy beach. It's not the best in the area, but at least you'll have plenty of space. Alvor is accessible by public bus from Portimão's center.

GOLF **Penina** (✆ **28/242-02-00**) is 5km (3 miles) west of the center of Portimão, farther west than many of the other great golf courses. Completed in 1966, it was one of the first courses in the Algarve and the universally acknowledged masterpiece of the British designer Sir Henry Cotton. It replaced a network of marshy rice paddies on level terrain that critics said was unsuited for anything except wetlands. The solution involved planting groves of eucalyptus (350,000 trees in all), which grew quickly in the muddy soil. Eventually they dried it out enough for the designer to bulldoze dozens of water traps and a labyrinth of fairways and greens. The course wraps around a luxury hotel (Le Méridien Penina). You can play the main championship course (18 holes, par 73), and two 9-hole satellite courses, Academy and Resort. Greens fees for the 18-hole course are 60€ to 70€ ($69–$81); for either of the 9-hole courses, they're 35€ ($40). To reach it from the center of Portimão, follow signs to Lagos, turning off at the signpost for Le Méridien Penina.

Amid tawny-colored rocks and arid hillocks, **Vale de Pinta** (✆ **28/234-09-00**), Praia do Carvoeiro, sends players through groves of twisted olive, almond, carob, and fig trees. Views from the fairways, designed in 1992 by Californian Ronald Fream, sweep over the low masses of the Monchique mountains, close to the beach resort of Carvoeiro. Experts say it offers some of the most varied challenges in Portuguese golf. Clusters of "voracious" bunkers, barrier walls of beige-colored rocks assembled without mortar, and abrupt changes in elevation complicate the course. Par is 72. Greens fees are 50€ to 90€ ($58–$104). From Portimão, drive 14km (8⅔ miles) east on N125, following signs to Lagoa and Vale de Pinta/Pestana Golf.

Visit www.algarvegolf.net for more information on courses in the Algarve region.

WINDSURFING & WATER-SKIING There are fewer reputable schools along the Algarve than you might imagine. The one that's always recommended for both professionalism and longevity (it was established in 1981) is the **Algarve Windsurfing School,** Praia Grande, Ferragudo (✆ **28/246-11-15**). It's on the beach, about 3km (1¾ miles) east of Portimão, in a compound that contains a tropical-style bar and lots of rental chaises. You can windsurf to your heart's content, thanks to gusts blowing up from the Sahara. A 4-hour communal lesson costs 85€ ($98), plus a 50€ ($58) deposit, and a 1-hour private lesson is 25€ ($29). Windsurfers rent for 15€ ($17). The entire outfit shuts down between late October and mid-March.

SHOPPING

The fishers unload their boats by tossing up wicker baskets full of freshly caught fish Monday through Saturday between 9:30 and 10:30am. Fish, fruit, and vegetable markets are held every morning (except Sun) until 2pm in the market building and open square. On the first Monday of every month, a gigantic daylong regional market sells local artifacts, pottery, wicker, and even snake oil. Boutiques offering the Algarve's best selection of sweaters, porcelain, and pottery abound.

You'll find modern, pan-European commercialism in this once-sleepy fishing village—most noticeably on such busy shopping streets as **Rua Comerciale** and **Rua Vasco da Gama.** Goods include hand-knit sweaters, hand-painted porcelains, and tons of pottery from factories and individual artisans throughout Portugal. Some of the best of it is available from two connected stores, **Aquarius I** and **II** (Plaza do Republica 42 and 46; ✆ **28/242-66-73**). Look for knitwear, ceramics, pottery, leatherwear, and woodcarvings. **Gaby's,** Rua Direita 5 (✆ **28/241-19-88**), specializes in linens, cottons, sheets, and bedspreads.

WHERE TO STAY

Hotels are limited in the center of Portimão, but Praia da Rocha has one of the largest concentrations on the Algarve. Praia dos Três Irmãos, though less developed, is the challenger to Praia da Rocha. In summer, don't even consider arriving at one of these beachfront establishments without a reservation.

CENTRAL PORTIMÃO

Inexpensive

Albergaria Miradouro Albergaria Miradouro benefits from a central location on a quiet square opposite an ornate Manueline church. Its modern facade is banded with concrete balconies. A few of the no-frills guest rooms, which are rather small, contain terraces. Furnishings are meager, but the beds are reasonably comfortable. All units have well-maintained bathrooms equipped with shower-tub combinations and decent plumbing. Here you're likely to meet an array of European backpackers eager to converse and share travelers' tales. Motorists can usually find a parking space in the square just opposite.

Rua Machado Santos 13, 8500-581 Portimão. ✆ and fax **28/242-30-11.** 32 units. 25€–50€ ($29–$58) double. No credit cards. Free parking. **Amenities:** Breakfast room. *In room:* TV, safe.

Hotel Globo ★ Despite its location in the heart of the old town, the Globo is contemporary. A first-class hotel, it's recommended for its good design. Snug modern balconies overlook the tile rooftops crusted with moss. In 1967, the owner and manager imported an architect to turn his inn into a top-notch hotel. Each midsize guest room exhibits good taste in layout and furnishings: matching ebony panels on the wardrobes, built-in headboards, and marble desks. Each unit also has a well-maintained bathroom with a shower-tub combination.

On the ground floor is an uncluttered, attractive lounge with an adjoining bar. Crowning the top floor is a dining room, open for breakfast only. Its four glass walls permit unblocked views of the harbor, ocean, or mountains.

Rua do 5 de Outubro 26, 8500-581 Portimão. ✆ **28/241-63-50.** Fax 28/248-31-42. 71 units. 65€–80€ ($75–$92) double; 95€–125€ ($109–$144) suite. Rates include breakfast. AE, DC, MC, V. Limited free parking in front of hotel. **Amenities:** Breakfast room; billiards room; limited room service; laundry service. *In room:* TV.

PRAIA DA ROCHA

Expensive

Algarve Hotel Casino ★★★ The leading hotel at the resort is strictly for those who love glitter and glamour and don't object to the prices. With a vast staff at your beck and call, you'll be well provided for in this elongated block of rooms poised securely on the top ledge of a cliff.

The midsize to spacious guest rooms have white walls, colored ceilings, intricate tile floors, mirrored entryways, indirect lighting, balconies with garden furniture, and bathrooms with separate shower-tub combinations. Many are vaguely Moorish in design, and many have terraces opening onto the sea. The Yachting, Oriental, Presidential, and Miradouro suites are decorative tours de force. There are 24 nonsmoking rooms and 10 rooms for those with limited mobility.

Av. Tomás Cabreira, Praia da Rocha, 8500-802 Portimão. ✆ **28/240-20-00.** Fax 28/240-20-99. www.solverde.pt. 209 units. 117€–264€ ($135–$304) double; 183€–488€ ($210–$561) suite. Rates include breakfast. AE, DC, MC, V. Free parking on street, 5€ ($5.75) in garage. **Amenities:** 3 restaurants; 5 bars; 2 pools; 2 tennis courts; sauna; watersports; salon; barber shop; boutiques; 24-hr. room service; babysitting; laundry; dry cleaning; 10 rooms for those w/limited mobility. *In room:* A/C, TV, dataport, minibar, hair dryer, safe.

Bela Vista ★ *Finds* Bela Vista is an old Moorish-style mansion built in 1916 as a wealthy family's summer home. It has a minaret-type tower at one end and a statue of the Virgin set into one of the building's corners. Since 1934, it has been a special kind of hotel, ideal for those who respond to the architecture of the past; you'll need to make a reservation way in advance. The guest rooms facing the sea, the former master bedrooms, are the most desirable. All come with neatly kept bathrooms equipped with shower-tub combinations. Decorations vary from crystal sconces to an inset tile shrine to the Virgin Mary. The hotel is on the ocean, atop its own palisade, with access to a sandy cove where you can swim. The villa is white with a terra-cotta tile roof, a landmark for fishermen bringing in their boats at sundown. It's flanked by the owner's home and a simple cliff-edge annex shaded by palm trees.

The attractive structure and its decorations have been preserved, but the public lounges contain plastic furniture. The entry hallway has a winding staircase and an abundance of 19th-century blue-and-white tiles depicting allegorical scenes from Portuguese history. Guests gather around a baronial fireplace.

Av. Tomás Cabreira, Praia da Rocha, 8500-802 Portimão. ✆ **28/245-04-80.** Fax 28/241-53-69. 14 units. 50€–115€ ($58–$132) double; 75€–170€ ($86–$196) suite. Rates include breakfast. AE, DC, MC, V. Free parking. **Amenities:** Breakfast room; bar; limited room service; laundry service. *In room:* TV, minibar, safe.

Moderate

Júpiter Júpiter occupies the most prominent street corner in this bustling summer resort. Boutiques fill the wraparound arcade, and in the spacious lobby guests relax, sometimes with drinks, on comfortable couches. The midsize guest rooms are comfortably modern but uninspired. They have balconies with views of the river or the sea. All units also contain well-maintained bathrooms with shower-tub combinations. The hotel is just across from a wide beach. The Blexus dance club provides late-night diversion beneath a metallic ceiling.

Av. Tomás Cabreira, Praia da Rocha, 8500-802 Portimão. ✆ **28/241-50-41.** Fax 28/241-53-19. www.hoteljupiter.com. 180 units. 48€–152€ ($55–$175) double; 90€–152€ ($104–$175) suite. AE, DC, MC, V. **Amenities:** Restaurant; bar; pool; room service (7am-midnight); babysitting; laundry service. *In room:* A/C, TV, dataport, minibar, hair dryer, safe.

Inexpensive

Pensão Tursol This simple but charming hotel lies behind a garden rich with flowering vines and shrubs. You'll find it on a street running parallel to the main road beside the beach, in a quiet part of the resort not far from the center. Guest rooms are small but offer reasonable comfort and have neatly kept bathrooms with shower-tub combinations. The staff is helpful. When the weather is fair, the windows are thrown open for a better view of the surrounding landscape.

Rua Antonio Feu, Praia da Rocha, 8500-805 Portimão. ✆ **28/242-40-46.** 22 units. 35€–55€ ($40–$63) double. Rates include breakfast. No credit cards. Closed Dec–Feb. Free parking. **Amenities:** Breakfast room; TV lounge. *In room:* No phone.

Residencial Sol *Value* Partly because of its location near the noisy main street, the painted concrete facade of this establishment appears somewhat bleak. In this case, however, appearances are deceiving. The small to midsize guest rooms offer some of the tidiest, least pretentious, most attractive accommodations in town. Each unit is designed for two and contains a neatly kept bathroom with shower-tub combination. The accommodations in back are quieter, but the front units (some with terrace) look across the traffic toward a bougainvillea-filled park.

Av. Tomás Cabreira 10, Praia da Rocha, 8500-802 Portimão. ✆ **28/242-40-71.** Fax 28/241-99-44. 30 units. 42€–45€ ($48–$52) double. Rates include breakfast. AE, DC, MC, V. Closed Nov–Mar. Free parking. **Amenities:** Breakfast room; TV lounge; laundry service. *In room:* No phone.

PRAIA DOS TRÊS IRMÃOS

Expensive

Le Méridien Penina Golf Hotel ★★★ This was the first deluxe hotel to be built on the Algarve. Located between Portimão and Lagos, it's now a Le Méridien property and has serious competition from the other luxury hotels. Fans of golf (see "Outdoor Activities," above) remain loyal to the Penina, however. It's a big sporting mecca and stands next to the Algarve's major casino. Besides the golf courses, the hotel has a private beach with its own snack bar and changing cabins, reached by a shuttle bus.

Most of the guest rooms contain picture windows and honeycomb balconies with views of the course and pool, or vistas of the Monchique hills. The standard rooms are furnished pleasantly, combining traditional pieces with Portuguese provincial spool beds. All rooms are spacious, with neatly kept bathrooms containing shower-tub combinations and good-size beds. The so-called attic rooms have the most charm, with French doors opening onto terraces. On the fourth floor are some duplexes, often preferred by families. The hotel has 24 nonsmoking rooms and 24 rooms for those with limited mobility.

Estrada Nacional 125, 8501-952 Portimão. ✆ **800/225-5843** in the U.S. or 28/242-02-00. Fax 28/242-03-00. www.lemeridien-penina.com. 196 units. 145€–325€ ($167–$374) double; 275€–715€ ($316–$822) suite. 1 child 3–11 free in parent's room. Rates include breakfast. AE, DC, MC, V. Free parking. **Amenities:** 4 restaurants; 2 bars; pool; 3 golf courses; 6 tennis courts; sauna; watersports; nursery for children; salon; room service; babysitting; laundry service. *In room:* A/C, TV, dataport, minibar, hair dryer, safe.

Pastana Alvor Prair Hotel ★★★ "You'll feel as if you're loved the moment you walk in the door," said a visitor from the Midwest. This citadel of hedonism, built in 1968 and constantly renewed (its last renovation was May 2003), has more joie de vivre than any other hotel on the Algarve. Its location, building, good-size guest rooms, decor, service, and food are ideal. The luxury hotel on a landscaped crest is so well appointed that you might never stray from the premises. Many of the guest and public rooms face the ocean, the gardens, and the free-form Olympic-size pool. Gentle walks and an elevator lead down the palisade to the sandy beach and the rugged rocks that rise out of the water. Inside, a wide domed airborne staircase leads to a lower level, which encircles a Japanese garden and lily pond.

Accommodations vary from a cowhide-decorated room evoking Arizona's Valley of the Sun to typical Portuguese-style rooms with rustic furnishings. Most contain oversize beds, plenty of storage space, long desk-and-chest combinations, and well-designed bathrooms with double basins and shower-tub combinations. Many rooms have private balconies where guests can have breakfast facing the Bay of Lagos. Avoid rooms in the rear with so-so views, small balconies, and Murphy beds.

Praia dos Três Irmãos, Alvor, 8501-904 Portimão. ✆ **28/240-09-00.** Fax 28/240-09-99. www.pestana.com. 198 units. 239€–299€ ($275–$344) double; 381€–449€ ($438–$516) suite. Rates include buffet breakfast. AE, DC, MC, V. Free parking. **Amenities:** 3 restaurants; 2 bars; 3 pools; 7 tennis courts; health club; sauna; solarium; water-skiing; horseback riding; salon; 24-hr. room service; babysitting; laundry service. *In room:* A/C, TV, dataport, minibar, hair dryer, safe.

Pestana Delfim Hotel ★★ The developers of this haven chose their site wisely; it's near the beach Três Irmãos, on a scrub-covered hillside whose sands offer a sweeping view of the coastline and its dozens of high-rises. With a central tower and identical wings splayed like a boomerang in flight, the hotel is one of the region's most dramatic modern buildings. In spite of the proximity of the beach, many guests prefer the parasol-ringed pool, which encloses a swim-up bar. Each well-furnished, midsize guest room has a private terrace. All units have well-maintained bathrooms containing shower-tub combinations.

Praia dos Três Irmãos, 8501-904 Alvor. ✆ **28/240-08-00.** Fax 28/240-08-99. www.pestana.com. 312 units. 62€–199€ ($71–$229) double; 110€–299€ ($127–$344) suite. Rates include buffet breakfast. AE, DC, MC, V. Free parking. **Amenities:** 2 restaurants; bar; pool; gym; Jacuzzi; sauna; 24-hr. room service; babysitting; laundry service. *In room:* A/C, TV, dataport, minibar (in suites), hair dryer, safe.

WHERE TO DINE

If you're sightseeing in Portimão, you might want to seek out a restaurant here; otherwise, most people dine along the beaches, especially those at Praia da Rocha and Praia dos Três Irmãos. All the major hotels have at least one deluxe or first-class restaurant. There's a wide selection catering to a range of budgets.

CENTRAL PORTIMÃO

Kibom ★ *Finds* PORTUGUESE/SEAFOOD Some of the best-tasting and freshest seafood in the area is served at this restaurant, and a few of the chef's recipes have been entered in national competitions. The restaurant is located in a simple Algarvian house with a rustic decor. Guests dine at wooden tables, enjoying the affordable food and the bountiful selection of regional Portuguese wines. Ingredients are fresh, and the food is well flavored and served in plentiful proportions. Codfish is the local favorite, and it's prepared in a number of delectable ways. The *cataplana* (seafood casserole) is among the finest along the coast, a savory kettle of fish that often features lobster. Seafood rice remains a justifiably popular favorite.

Rua Damião Faria e Castro. ✆ **28/241-46-23.** Reservations recommended. Main courses 7€–21€ ($8–$24), AE, DC, MC, V. Mon–Sat noon–4pm and 6–10:30pm. Closed Nov 15–Dec 15.

O Bicho Restaurant ★ *Finds* ALGARVIAN O Bicho is one of the best places in the Algarve to order *cataplana,* a typical regional dish of clams, pork, green peppers, tomatoes, and spices, including hot pepper, garlic, and bay leaf. It's cooked in a special copper pot, also called cataplana, that steams the mixture under a tight lid. Other inviting choices include oysters and grilled seafood, but they don't seem to equal the cataplana. This simple place is popular with both locals and discerning visitors.

Largo Gil Eanes 12. ✆ **28/242-29-77.** Reservations recommended. Main courses 5€–18€ ($5.75–$21). AE, DC, MC, V. Mon–Sat noon–3pm and 6:30–11pm.

PRAIA DA ROCHA

Bamboo Garden ★ *Finds* CHINESE Bamboo Garden, which has a classic Asian decor, serves some of the best Chinese food on the coast. The large menu includes everything from squid chop suey to prawns with hot sauce. After deciding on a soup or an appetizer (try the spring roll), guests can select from various categories, including chicken, beef, squid, and prawns. You might, for example, try fried duck with soybean sauce or chicken with almonds from the Algarve. Peking duck is the chef's specialty. This air-conditioned spot is a safe haven for reliable food when you've overdosed on Portuguese codfish.

Edificio Lamego, Loja 1, av. Tomás Cabreira. ✆ **28/248-30-83.** Reservations recommended. Main courses 5€–13€ ($5.75–$15). DC, MC, V. Daily 12:30–3pm and 6–11:30pm.

Safari ★ *Finds* PORTUGUESE/ANGOLAN Safari is a Portuguese-run restaurant with a "taste of Africa" in its cuisine; the former Portuguese colony of Angola inspired many of its savory specialties. The name also suggests a faux-African tourist trap, but this place isn't. Safari offers good value and is known for its commendable fresh fish and seafood. Many guests in neighboring hotels escape their board requirements just to sample the good home-cooked meals. On summer weekends you might hear live Brazilian or African music. The fare includes steak, curries, and shrimp, and such delectable dishes as swordfish steak in pepper sauce, charcoal-grilled fresh fish, and *bacalhau a Safari* (fried codfish with olive oil, garlic, and peppers, served with homemade potato chips). It's customary to begin with a bowl of savory fish soup. The building stands on a cliff overlooking the beach and has a glass-enclosed terrace.

Rua António Feu. ✆ **28/242-35-40.** Reservations recommended. Main courses 6.25€–15€ ($7.20–$17); fixed-price menus 12€–15€ ($14–$17) and 17€ ($20). AE, DC, MC, V. Daily noon–midnight. Closed Dec.

Titanic ★★ INTERNATIONAL Complete with gilt and crystal, the 100-seat air-conditioned Titanic is the most elegant restaurant in town. Its open kitchen serves the best food in Praia da Rocha, including shellfish and flambé dishes. Despite the name, it's not on—or in, thank goodness—the water, but in a modern residential complex. You can dine very well here on such appealing dishes as the fish of the day, pork filet with mushrooms, prawns *a la plancha* (grilled), Chinese fondue, or excellent sole Algarve. Service is among the best at the resort.

In the Edifício Colúmbia, Rua Eng. Francisco Bivar. ✆ **28/242-23-71.** Reservations recommended, especially in summer. Main courses 9€–24€ ($10–$28). AE, DC, MC, V. Daily 7–midnight. Closed Nov 27–Dec 27.

PRAIA DOS TRÊS IRMÃOS

Harira/O Almofariz/Sale & Pepe MOROCCAN/PORTUGUESE/ITALIAN To satisfy changing modern tastes, this hotel operates restaurants featuring three different cuisines. The menu changes every day, with the chefs in each restaurant featuring their particular country's finest dishes. All rely on first-rate, market-fresh ingredients.

The Moroccan restaurant, Harira, is known for its couscous and lamb dishes. Sale & Pepe, the Italian option, presents succulent pastas and flavorful meat dishes. The Portuguese restaurant, O Almofariz, serves dishes from around the country; its Algarvian specialties shine. The first-rate service and the prices are the same in all three restaurants.

In the Alvor Praia Hotel, Praia dos Três Irmãos. ✆ **28/240-09-00.** Reservations required. Main courses 10€–20€ ($12–$23). AE, DC, MC, V. Daily 7:30–10pm.

O Búzio ★ INTERNATIONAL Restaurante O Búzio stands at the end of a road encircling a resort development dotted with private condos and exotic shrubbery. In summer, so many cars line the narrow blacktop road that you'll probably need to park near the resort's entrance and then walk downhill to the restaurant.

Dinner is served in a room whose blue curtains reflect the shimmering ocean at the bottom of the cliffs. Your meal might include excellent fish soup, refreshing gazpacho, or *carre de borrego Serra de Estrêla* (gratinée of roast rack of lamb with garlic, butter, and mustard). Other good choices are Italian pasta dishes, boiled or grilled fish of the day, flavorful pepper steak, and lamb kebabs with saffron-flavored rice. There's seating for 50 inside and for almost as many on the sea-view terrace. There's an extensive wine cellar.

Aldeamento da Prainha, Praia dos Três Irmãos. ✆ **28/245-87-72.** Reservations recommended. Main courses 9.25€–21€ ($11–$24). AE, DC, MC, V. Daily 7–10:30pm. Closed Dec. 15–Jan 7.

PORCHES

O Leão de Porches FRENCH/BELGIAN O Leão de Porches lies in a small village a 3-minute drive from Lagoa. The menu crackles with good-tasting dishes, beginning with an appetizer such as lobster soup with cognac. The seafood pasta is the most exciting alternative in that category, and meat and poultry dishes include "the classics," such as breast of duck with orange sauce, fried rack of lamb in a honey-flavored thyme sauce, and even an old-fashioned dish rarely seen on menus—rabbit stew with dates. Two kinds of the "catch of the day" appear on the menu and can be prepared more or less to your specifications

Rua da Igreja-Porches, 8400 Porches, Lagoa. N25. ✆ **28/238-13-84.** Reservations required. Main courses 13€–25€ ($15–$29). MC, V. Thurs–Tues 6:30–10pm. Closed Jan. From Lagoa, take N25 toward Faro.

PORTIMÃO AFTER DARK

The town center has about a dozen *tascas* (taverns) and bodegas, but you might be happier with the glossier after-dark venues in internationally minded Praia da Rocha. Many bars and pubs, as well as the resort's casino (see below), line Avenida Tomás Cabreira. Depending on your mood, you might enjoy popping in and out of several of them—a ritual akin to a London pub-crawl. The most active and intriguing hangouts include **Farmer's Bar,** Rua do Mar (✆ **28/242-57-20**), which serves wine, beer, and cocktails. It's open daily from 10am to 4am. A 5-minute walk uphill from the harbor front, **Mariners,** Rua Santa

Finds Monchique: Escape to the Cool Mountains

The Monchique range of hills is the Algarve at its coolest and highest. The rocky peak of the range, some 900m (2,952 ft.) high, looks down on forested slopes and green valleys, burgeoning with orange groves, Indian corn, heather, mimosa, rosemary, oleander bushes, and cork-oak, chestnut, pine, and eucalyptus trees. Icy water springs from the volcanic rock that makes up the range, flowing down to the foothills.

The largest town in the borough, also named Monchique, lies on the east side of Mount Fóia, 26km (16 miles) north of Portimão. The town was once engaged in the manufacture of wooden casks and barrels and the making of oakum and rough cloth. The Manueline-style parish church, with its interesting radiated door facing, dates from the 16th century. Colorful decorated tiles and carved woodwork grace the interior, along with a statue of Our Lady of the Immaculate Conception, an 18th-century work attributed to Machado de Castro. The convent of Nossa Senhora do Desterro is in ruins, but you can look at the curious tiled fountain and the impressive old magnolia tree on its grounds.

Caldas de Monchique was discovered in Roman days and turned into a spa. The waters, from springs in volcanic rock, are still considered good treatment for respiratory disorders, accompanied as they are by the clear air of the highlands.

Nearly 13km (8 miles) from the town of Monchique, Alferce, nestled among trees and mountains, has traces of an ancient fortification. There's also an important handicraft center here. In the opposite direction, about 13km (8 miles) west of Monchique, is Fóia, the highest point in the Algarve. From here you have splendid views of the hills and the sea.

A small inn in the town of Monchique, the **Estalagem Abrigo de Montanha,** 8550-257 Monchique (✆ **28/291-21-31;** fax 28/291-36-60), is in a botanical garden. With all the blooming camellias, rhododendrons, mimosa, banana palms, and arbutus, plus the tinkling waterfalls, you'd never believe the hot Algarve coast was in the same province. The inn has 15 doubles and two suites. Rates are 65€ to 87€ ($75–$100) for a double or 82€ to 109€ ($94–$125) for a suite, including breakfast. On chilly evenings, guests gather before a fireplace in the lounge.

Isabel 28 (✆ **28/242-58-48**), is a popular watering spot, open daily from noon to 10pm. This is a 4-century-old stone house with a patio and garden. Foodstuff is served here along with the good brew and regional wines. Danceaholics and devoted night owls appreciate the shenanigans at **Disco Babylonia,** Avenida Tomás Cabreira (✆ **28/241-68-38**), and its nearby competitor, **Disco Horago,** Avenida Tomás Cabreira (✆ **28/242-63-77**). Both get going after midnight every night in high season and remain open till the last person staggers off the next morning. The cover charge is 10€ ($12).

Casino Praia da Rocha is on the glittering premises of the five-star Hotel Algarve Casino, Avenida Tomás Cabreira (✆ **28/240-20-00**). Its gaming tables and slot machines open every night at 4pm and shut down at 3am, or later if business warrants. Its entertainment highlight is the cabaret show, featuring lots of dancers in spangles and feathers, magicians, and a master of ceremonies telling not-very-subtle jokes. Dinner, served beginning at 8pm, precedes the show and costs 36€ ($41). If you skip dinner, the entrance fee of 10€ ($12) includes the first drink. Show time is 10pm. Also look for other forms of entertainment, such as live concerts or fado.

4 Silves ★

6.5km (4 miles) N of Lagoa, 11km ($6\frac{3}{4}$ miles) NE of Carvoeiro

When you pass through its Moorish-inspired entrance, you'll quickly realize that Silves is unlike other towns and villages of the Algarve. It lives in the past, recalling its heyday when it was known as Xelb. It was the seat of Muslim culture in the south before it fell to the Crusaders. Christian warriors and earthquakes have been rough on Silves.

The Castle of Silves, crowning the hilltop, has held on, although it has seen better days. Once the blood of the Muslims, staging their last stand in Silves, "flowed like red wine," as one Portuguese historian wrote. The cries and screams of women and children resounded over the walls. Nowadays the only sound you're likely to hear is the loud rock music coming from the gatekeeper's house. Silves is most often visited on a day trip from one of the beach towns to the south.

ESSENTIALS

ARRIVING

BY TRAIN Trains from Faro serve the Silves train station, 1.75km (1 mile) from the center of the town. For information, call ✆ **808/208-208.**

BY BUS The bus station is on Rua da Cruz de Palmeira; EVA (✆ **28/244-23-38**) runs eight buses a day from Portimão. Trip time is 45 minutes.

BY CAR Coming east or west along Route 125, the main road traversing the Algarve, you arrive at the town of Lagoa (not to be confused with Lagos). From there, head north to Silves along Route 124.

VISITOR INFORMATION

The **tourist office** (✆ **28/244-22-55**) is located on Rua 25 de Abril and is open Monday through Friday from 9:30am to 12:30pm and 2 to 5pm.

EXPLORING THE TOWN

The red-sandstone **Castelo dos Mouros** ★ might date from the 9th century. From its ramparts you can look out on the saffron-colored, mossy tile roofs of the village houses down the narrow cobblestone streets where roosters strut and scrappy dogs sleep peacefully in the doorways. Inside the walls, the government has planted a flower garden with golden chrysanthemums and scarlet poinsettias. In the fortress, water rushes through a huge cistern and a deep well made of sandstone. Below are dungeon chambers and labyrinthine tunnels where the last of the Moors hid out before the Crusaders found them and sent them to their deaths. The site is open daily from 9am to 5:30pm. Admission is 1.25€ ($1.45) and free for children 11 and under.

The 13th-century former **Cathedral of Silves** ★, on Rua de Sé, was built in the Gothic style. It is one of the most outstanding religious monuments in the Algarve. The aisles and nave are beautiful in their simplicity. The flamboyant Gothic style of both the chancel and the transept dates from a later period. The Christian architects who originally constructed the cathedral might have torn down an old mosque to do so. Many of the tombs here are believed to be the graves of Crusaders who took the town in 1244. It's open daily from 8:30am to

1pm and 2:30 to 5:30pm, and until 6pm from June to September. Admission is free, but donations are welcome.

The best artifacts found in the area are on display at the **Museu Arqueologia,** Rua das Portas de Loulé (✆ **28/244-48-32**), a short walk from the Sé. The museum's major sight is an ancient Arab water cistern preserved as part of a 9m-deep (30-ft.-deep) well. Admission is 1.50€ ($1.75). It's open Monday through Saturday from 9am to 6pm.

Outside the main part of town, on the road to Enxerim, near an orange grove, a lonely open-air pavilion shelters a 15th-century stone lacework cross. This ecclesiastical artwork, **Cruz de Portugal,** is two-faced, depicting a *pietà* (the face of Christ is destroyed) on one side and the crucifixion on the other. It has been declared a national monument of incalculable value. A guide isn't really necessary, but if you'd like, one of the local boys will serve as your guide for a modest fee.

WHERE TO STAY

Colina dos Mouros ★ *Finds* On the outskirts of town, this modern inn at last provides a decent place to stay in the historic town of Silves. Only a short walk from the historic core, the well-managed and well-furnished hotel offers midsize to spacious bedrooms that are comfortably and immaculately kept, mostly with shower-tub combinations. You approach the hotel across a Roman bridge spanning the River Arade. Enveloped by gardens, the hotel is completely refurbished. The building opens onto views of the rooftops of Silves and its major monuments. Beaches can be reached in just a short drive from the inn.

Pocinho Santo 8300-999 Silves. ✆ **28/244-04-20.** Fax 28/244-04-26. www.eurosun.com/colimou.htm. 55 units. 35€–80€ ($40–$92) double. Rates include breakfast. AE, MC, V. **Amenities:** Restaurant; 2 bars; swimming pool; children's pool; laundry service; 1 room for those w/limited mobility. *In room:* A/C, TV, hair dryer, safe.

WHERE TO DINE

Ladeira PORTUGUESE This small, rustic restaurant is known to almost everyone in its neighborhood on the western outskirts of Silves. Steak Ladeira and mixed-fish cataplana are the two best specialties; also featured are grilled fish and regional dishes. If you call in advance, someone will explain the restaurant's location, often in great detail. In season, game such as succulent partridge or rabbit is likely to be on the menu.

Ladeira de São Pedro. ✆ **28/244-28-70.** Main courses 6€–16€ ($7–$18); tourist menu 8€ ($9.20). AE, MC, V. Mon–Sat noon–3pm and 7–10pm.

Rui I PORTUGUESE Rui I prides itself on seating more customers than any other restaurant in town. The availability of certain dishes varies according to what fish is fresh. The house specialty is shellfish rice, a highly recommended herb-laden stew. Other palate-pleasing choices include grilled filet of beef, savory rack of lamb, swordfish, and a choice of traditional desserts. This is competent, hearty cooking—nothing more.

Rua Comendador Vilarim 27. ✆ **28/244-26-82.** Main courses 6€–25€ ($6.90–$29). AE, MC, V. Wed–Mon noon–2am.

5 Albufeira ★

37km (23 miles) W of Faro, 325km (202 miles) SE of Lisbon

This cliff-side town, formerly a fishing village, is the St. Tropez of the Algarve. The lazy life, sunshine, and beaches make it a haven for young people and artists, although the old-timers still regard the invasion that began in the late

1960s with some ambivalence. That development turned Albufeira into the largest resort in the region. Some residents open the doors of their cottages to those seeking a place to stay. Travelers with less money often sleep in tents.

ESSENTIALS

ARRIVING

BY TRAIN Trains run between Albufeira and Faro (see later), which has good connections to Lisbon. For schedule information, call ✆ **28/957-26-91.** The train station lies 6.5km (4 miles) from the center. Buses from the station to the resort run every 30 minutes; the fare is 1€ ($1.15) one-way.

BY BUS Buses run between Albufeira and Faro every hour. Trip time is 1 hour, and a one-way ticket costs 3.30€ ($3.80). Seven buses per day make the 1-hour trip from Portimão to Albufeira. It costs 3.50€ ($3.15) one-way. For information and schedules, call ✆ **28/958-97-55.**

BY CAR From east or west, take the main coastal route, N125. Albufeira also lies near the point where the express highway from the north, N264, feeds into the Algarve. The town is well signposted in all directions. Take Route 595 to reach Albufeira and the water.

VISITOR INFORMATION

The **Tourist Information Office** is at Rua do 5 de Outubro (✆ **28/958-52-79**). From July to September, hours are daily from 9:30am to 7pm; October to June, they're from 10am to 5:30pm.

EXPLORING THE TOWN

With steep streets and villas staggered up and down the hillside, Albufeira resembles a North African seaside community. The big, bustling resort town rises above a sickle-shape beach that shines in the bright sunlight. A rocky, grottoed bluff separates the strip used by sunbathers from the working beach, where brightly painted fishing boats are drawn up on the sand. Access to the beach is through a tunneled rock passageway.

After walking Albufeira's often hot but intriguing streets, you can escape and cool off at **Zoo Marine,** N125, Guia (✆ **28/956-03-00;** www.zoomarine.com), 6.5km (4 miles) northwest. It's a popular water park, with rides, swimming pools, gardens, and even sea lion and dolphin shows. It's open daily from 10am to 6pm. Admission is 18€ ($21) for adults and 11€ ($13) for children 10 and under.

OUTDOOR ACTIVITIES

BEACHES Some of the best beaches—but also the most crowded—are near Albufeira. They include Falesia, Olhos d'Agua, and Praia da Oura. Albufeira, originally discovered by the British, is now the busiest resort on the Algarve. To avoid the crowds on Albufeira's main beaches, head west for 4km (2½ miles) on a local road to São Rafael and Praia da Galé. You might also go east to the beach at Olhos d'Agua.

GOLF Many pros consider the extremely well-maintained **Pine Cliffs** course, Pinhal do Concelho, 8200 Albufeira (✆ **28/950-01-00**), relaxing but not boring. It has only 9 holes scattered over a relatively compact area. Opened in 1990, its fairways meander beside copper-colored cliffs that drop 75m (246 ft.) down to a sandy beach. Par is 33. Greens fees are 33€ to 63€ ($38–$72) for Sheraton Algarve guests (see below), and 43€ to 80€ ($50–$92) for nonguests. The course lies 6.5km (4 miles) west of Vilamoura and less than 5km (3 miles) east of Albufeira. To reach it from Albufeira, follow signs to the hamlet of Olhof Agua, where more signs direct you to the Sheraton and Pine Cliffs.

Visit www.algarvegolf.net for more information on courses in the Algarve region.

SHOPPING

One of the busiest resorts along the Algarve, Albufeira maintains an almost alarming roster of seafront kiosks, many selling fun-in-the-sun products of dubious (or, at best, transient) value. The main shopping areas are along Rua do 5 de Outubro and Praça Duarte de Pacheco. An even denser collection of merchandise is on display in the town's largest shopping plaza, **Modelo Shopping Center,** Rua de Munícipio, about .5km (⅓ mile) north of the town center. Most of the independently operated shops inside are open daily from 10am to 10pm. Although Albufeira produces limited amounts of ceramics, you'll find a wide selection of pottery and glazed terra cotta from throughout Portugal at the **Infante Dom Henrique House,** Rua Cândido do Reis 30 (✆ **28/951-32-67**). Also look for woven baskets and woodcarvings.

WHERE TO STAY

The town has many accommodations. However, many establishments charge rates more suited to the middle-of-the-road traveler than to the young people who favor the place.

EXPENSIVE

Clube Mediterraneo de Balaia ★ On 16 hectares (40 acres) of sun-drenched scrubland about 6.5km (4 miles) east of Albufeira, this all-inclusive high-rise resort is one of the most stable in the Club Med empire. Favored by vacationers from northern Europe, it encompasses a shoreline of rugged rock formations indented with a private beach and a series of coves for surf swimming. The small accommodations have twin beds, two safes, and piped-in music. They're decorated in understated, uncluttered style, with private balconies or terraces. All units here have well-kept bathrooms equipped with shower-tub combinations. Many vacationers here appreciate the nearby golf course; others opt to participate in semiorganized sports. Meals are usually consumed at communal tables; there are many lunchtime buffets and copious amounts of local wine.

Praia Maria Luisa, 8200-854 Albufeira. ✆ **800/CLUB-MED** in the U.S. or ✆ 28/951-05-00. Fax 28/958-71-79. 412 units. 150€–362€ ($56–$235) double. Rates include full board and use of most sports facilities. Children 4–12 45€–108€ ($52–$124) in parent's room. AE, DC, MC, V. **Amenities:** 3 restaurants; 2 bars; pool; 9-hole golf course; health club; sauna; 24-hr. room service; laundry service; nonsmoking rooms available; 2 rooms for those w/ limited mobility. *In room:* A/C, TV, dataport, minibar, hair dryer, safe.

Hotel Montechoro ★ The leading choice at Montechoro, just more than 3km (1¾ miles) northeast of the center of Albufeira, looks like a hotel you might encounter in North Africa. It's a fully equipped, self-contained, government-rated four-star resort complex, with such ample facilities that you might get lost—which is just as well because the one thing it lacks is a beach. The spacious rooms afford views of the countryside and are generally done in modern style, with excellent beds and tidily kept bathrooms equipped with shower-tub combinations.

Rua Alexandre O'Neill (Apdo. 928), 8201-912 Albufeira. ✆ **28/958-94-23.** Fax 28/958-99-47. hotel@grupomontechoro.com. 362 units. 83€–171€ ($95–$197) double; 124€–256€ ($143–$294) suite. Rates include buffet breakfast. AE, DC, MC, V. Free parking. **Amenities:** 2 restaurants; 2 bars; pool; 8 tennis courts;

2 squash courts; sauna; car rental; 24-hr. room service; babysitting; laundry service; dry cleaning. *In room:* A/C, TV, dataport, hair dryer, safe.

MODERATE

Villa Galé Cerro Alagoa ★★ A sort of South Seas ambience predominates at this fine resort. Most guests are from Northern Europe, and they find this a relaxing environment to soak up the sun. A large, sprawling property, it lies near the sandy beach of Albufeira and is also within an easy commute of several other Algarvian beaches, both east and west. Each room has a balcony to soak up the view; comfortable, durable furnishings; and tiled bathrooms with a shower-tub combination. You can also dine in style here; the chefs are fond of presenting theme evenings, and there is great variety of cuisines. Nonguests often drop in here to patronize the Dog & Duck Pub, a British-style bar featuring live music and karaoke. The hotel is one of the best equipped in leisure facilities (see below).

Rua do Municipio, 8200-916 Albufeira. ✆ **28/958-31-00.** Fax 28/958-31-99. www.portugalvirtual.pt/_lodging/algarve/cerro.alagoa/. 310 units. 85€–170€ ($98–$196) double; 124€–328€ ($143–$377) suite. Rates include breakfast. AE, DC, MC, V. **Amenities:** Restaurant; 2 bars; indoor and outdoor pools; gym; Jacuzzi; sauna; game room; 24-hr. room service; massage; laundry service; dry cleaning. *In room:* A/C, TV, minibar, safe.

INEXPENSIVE

Apartamentos Albufeira Jardim This establishment is especially popular with northern Europeans, Spaniards, and North Americans who want to linger a while before resuming their tours of the Algarve. On a hill high above Albufeira, it opened in the 1970s as Jardim I. In the late 1980s it gained another section, Jardim II, a 5-minute walk away. The older section is larger and has gardens that are a bit more mature.

The attractively furnished, good-size units are in four- and five-story buildings. Each apartment has a balcony with a view of the faraway ocean and the town. All rooms are equipped with well-maintained bathrooms containing shower-tub combinations. Guests usually prepare breakfast (which is not included in the rates) in their rooms. A minibus makes frequent runs from the apartments to the beach, a 10-minute drive away.

Cerro da Piedade, 8200-916 Albufeira. ✆ **28/957-00-70.** Fax 28/957-00-71. www.albufeira-jardim.com. 460 apts. 29€–101€ ($33–$116) 1-bedroom apt; 40.54€–162.10€ ($47–$186) 2-bedroom apt. AE, DC, MC, V. Free parking. **Amenities:** 2 restaurants; 2 coffee shops; 2 bars; 5 pools; 3 tennis courts; car rental; babysitting; laundry service. *In room:* Kitchenette, safe.

Aparthotel Auramar One of the resort's largest hotels sits about 1.5km (1 mile) east of the center, in large gardens on a low cliff overlooking a sandy beach. Built in 1974, it resembles a series of fortresses facing the ocean. The complex consists of a quartet of three-, four-, and five-story buildings separated by wide stretches of greenery. Self-contained kitchenettes make the guest rooms suitable for vacationers who prefer to eat in occasionally. Each unit has living-room furnishings, a terrace or balcony, an excellent bed, and a neatly kept bathroom with a shower-tub combination.

Praia dos Aveiros, Areias de São Albufeira, 8200-777 Albufeira. ✆ **28/959-91-00.** Fax 28/959-91-99. 287 units. 52€–102€ ($60–$117) double. Extra bed 19€–23€ ($22–$26). Rates include breakfast. AE, DC, MC, V. Free parking. **Amenities:** Restaurant; bar; snack bar; 2 pools; 2 tennis courts; gym; sauna; laundry service. *In room:* A/C, TV, safe.

Estalagem do Cerro ★ *Finds* Estalagem do Cerro, built in 1964, captures Algarvian charm without neglecting modern amenities. This Inn of the Craggy Hill is at the top of a hill overlooking Albufeira's bay, about a 10-minute walk from the beach. A similar Moorish style unites an older, regional-style building and a more modern structure. The tastefully furnished midsize guest rooms have verandas overlooking the sea, pool, or garden. All units also have neatly kept bathrooms with shower-tub combinations. Two rooms are available for those with limited mobility, and 10 of the units are large enough for families —ideal for couples with their children.

Rua Samora Barros Cerro de Piedade, 8200-320 Albufeira. ✆ **28/958-61-91.** Fax 28/958-61-94. www.docerro.com. 95 units. 60€–130€ ($69–$150) double; 170€ ($196) suite. AE, DC, MC, V. Limited free parking on street. **Amenities:** 2 restaurants; 2 bars; pool; gym; Jacuzzi; sauna; Turkish bath; salon; room service; massage room; babysitting; laundry service. *In room:* A/C, TV, minibar, hair dryer, safe.

Hotel BoaVista Built in the Algarvian style, the Residence of the Good View sits high above the sea outside the center, some 450m (1,476 ft.) from a good beach. The units open onto balconies, some of which afford views over orange-tile-roofed whitewashed cottages to the bay below. Traditional wicker-wood decor matches the carpets and ceramics, and bathrooms contain shower-tub combinations.

Rua Samora Barros 20, Albufeira. ✆ **28/958-91-75.** Fax 28/958-91-80. www.hotelboavista.pt. 85 units. 57€–133€ ($66–$153) double; 101€–230€ ($116–$265) suite. Rates include breakfast. AE, DC, MC, V. Limited free parking on street. **Amenities:** 2 restaurants; 2 bars; pool; sauna; car rental; room service; babysitting; laundry service. *In room:* A/C, TV, minibar, safe.

Hotel Rocamar You might think that this cubistic hotel looks like an updated version of a Moorish castle, a well-ordered assemblage of building blocks, or the partially excavated side of a stone quarry. Built in 1974, it was enlarged in 1991. It rises six stories above the tawny cliffs that slope down to one of the most inviting beaches on the Algarve. Many of its windows and all of its balconies benefit from the view. The hotel is a 5-minute walk from the town's attractions. Rooms are simple and sun-washed yet comfortable, with neatly kept bathrooms with shower-tub combinations.

Largo Jacinto d'Ayet 7, 8200-071 Albufeira. ✆ **28/954-02-80.** Fax 28/954-02-81. www.hotel-rocamar.com. 91 units. 50€–100€ ($58–$115) double. Rates include breakfast. AE, DC, MC, V. Limited free parking on street. **Amenities:** Restaurant; bar; 24-hr. room service; laundry service. *In room:* A/C, TV, safe.

Hotel Sol e Mar This government-rated four-star hotel occupies a prime location in the heart of Albufeira above the beach. It dates from 1969 and was enlarged in 1975. The two-story entrance on the upper palisade can be deceiving—when you walk across the spacious sun-filled lounges to the picture windows and look down, you'll see a six-story drop. Hugging the cliff are midsize guest rooms and a wide stone terrace with garden furniture and parasols. On a lower level is a sandy beach. The guests are a Continental crowd with a sprinkling of Americans. All units have private balconies, wooden headboards, locally painted seascapes, slim-line armchairs, and plenty of wardrobe space. Each also comes equipped with a well-maintained bathroom containing a shower-tub combination.

Rua Bernardino de Sousa, 8200-071 Albufeira. ✆ **28/958-00-80.** Fax 28/958-70-36. www.manorhouses.com/hotels/solemar.html. 74 units. 70€–120€ ($81–$138) double. Rates include breakfast. AE, DC, MC, V. **Amenities:** 2 restaurants; 2 bars; pool; snack bar; 24-hr. room service; laundry service. *In room:* A/C, TV, hair dryer (on request), safe.

WHERE TO STAY NEARBY

PRAIA DA FALÉSIA

Sheraton Algarve ★★★ Opened in 1992, this government-rated five-star hotel is laid out like an Algarve village, with no building rising higher than three floors. About 8km (5 miles) east of Albufeira, the Sheraton was designed to blend tastefully into its oceanfront location. Its wings ramble through a subtropical garden dotted with copses of the site's original pine trees. Conceived as a complete resort incorporating a 9-hole golf course, the hotel caters to an international clientele. Accommodations range from midsize to spacious and open onto land, garden, or sea views. Each is traditionally furnished with luxurious pieces, including quality beds and shower-tub combinations with state-of-the-art plumbing.

Praia da Falésia (P.O. Box 644), 8200-909 Albufeira. ✆ **800/325-3535** in the U.S., or ✆ 28/950-01-00. Fax 28/950-19-50. www.pinecliffs.com. 215 units. 327€–384€ ($376–$442) double; 408€–504€ ($470–$580) suite. Rates include breakfast. AE, DC, MC, V. Free parking. **Amenities:** 4 restaurants; 3 bars; 3 pools; golf course; 4 tennis courts; health club; Jacuzzi; sauna; car rental; business center; salon; 24-hr. room service; massage; babysitting; laundry service; dry cleaning. *In room:* A/C, TV, dataport, minibar, hair dryer, safe.

PRAIA DA GALÉ

Hotel Villa Joya ★★★ The most luxurious and intimate inn in the Algarve, the Villa Joya is especially favored by Germans (ex-chancellor Willy Brandt came here just before his death). The establishment lies 15km (9⅓ miles) west of Albufeira in a residential neighborhood dotted with other dwellings, but within the confines of its large gardens, visitors can easily imagine themselves in the open countryside. A footpath leads down to the beach. Every accommodation has a view of the sea and a private bathroom equipped with a shower-tub combination. In the 1980s, the hotel was converted from a Moroccan-inspired private villa built during the 1970s.

Praia da Galé (Apdo. Postal 120), 8200-917 Albufeira. ✆ **28/959-17-95.** Fax 28/959-12-01. 17 units. 350€–400€ ($403–$460) double; 750€–1,000€ ($863–$1,150) suite. Rates include half-board. AE, DC, MC, V. Closed Nov 10–Mar 1. Free parking. **Amenities:** Restaurant; bar; pool; nearby tennis; sauna; room service; babysitting; laundry service. *In room:* Minibar, hair dryer, safe.

WHERE TO DINE

EXPENSIVE

O Cabaz da Praia ★ FRENCH/PORTUGUESE The Beach Basket, near the Hotel Sol e Mar, sits on a colorful little square near the Church of São Sebastião. In a former fishermen's cottage, the restaurant has an inviting ambience and good food. It has a large, sheltered terrace and a view over the main Albufeira beach. Main courses, including such justifiable favorites as cassoulet of seafood, salade océane, monkfish with mango sauce, and beef filet with garlic and white-wine sauce, are served with a selection of fresh vegetables. The restaurant is renowned for its lemon meringue pie and soufflés.

Praça Miguel Bombarda 7. ✆ **28/951-21-37.** Reservations recommended. Main courses 19€–24€ ($22–$28). AE, MC, V. Fri–Wed noon–2pm and 7:30–11pm.

MODERATE

Alfredo PORTUGUESE/ITALIAN Just a minute's stroll from the market square, Alfredo is in a century-old building that looks as if it has always been an inn. It's full of atmosphere, with crude wooden tables and chairs made for leisurely drinking. The second-floor restaurant is a heavily beamed room with a marble slab floor and simple wooden tables. Ceiling fans create a cooling breeze, and the partially visible kitchen provides all the entertainment many diners require. Your menu includes regional specialties such as tuna salad, cataplana clams, bream, and swordfish, as well as tournedos with mushrooms and Portuguese-style steak. The house wine, Portas do Sado, is available by the glass.

Rua do 5 de Outubro 9–11. ✆ **28/951-20-59.** Reservations required. Main courses 6€–13€ ($6.90–$15). AE, DC, MC, V. Daily noon–11pm.

A Ruína ★ PORTUGUESE This restaurant sits opposite the fish market, overlooking the main beach. From the arcaded dining room, with its long candlelit wooden tables, you can watch the fishers mending their nets. Another cavelike room has more tables and a bar. The decor is unpretentious, and the reasonably priced seafood is fresh. A bowl of flavorful soup will get you going; then it's on to one of the fish specialties, such as grilled fresh tuna. The fish stew, *caldeirada,* is the chef's specialty and our favorite dish. Desserts are usually custard and mousse.

Cais Herculano, Albufeiria. ✆ **28/951-20-94.** Reservations recommended. Main courses 15€–25€ ($17–$29). AE, DC, MC, V. Daily 12:30–3pm and 7–11pm.

Café Doris GERMAN/PORTUGUESE This is a German-operated rotisserie-crêperie-restaurant. It turns out well-prepared crepes, home-baked cakes, and ice cream in many flavors, as well as heartier fare. Rich-tasting goulash-meat soup is always offered as an appetizer, as is savory goat stew. You might move on to roast pork with onion sauce, monkfish with rice curry, or a good steak with cream sauce, herbs, lyonnaise potatoes, and a salad. Doris has an unusual selection of hot drinks, including coffee Algarve (with Medronho).

Av. Dr. Francisco Sá Carneiro, Areias de São João. ✆ **28/951-24-55.** Reservations required in summer. Main courses 5€–12€ ($5.75–$14). MC, V. Open daily 9am–1am. Closed Nov–Feb.

La Cigale PORTUGUESE/FRENCH La Cigale stands right on the beach, 7.25km (4½ miles) from Albufeira; its terrace makes it a romantic choice at night. Its atmosphere reflects the mood of the sunny southern coast of Europe—and, fortunately, the food matches the atmosphere. The wine list is fairly distinguished, in keeping with the impressive menu. The amiable management works efficiently. Specialties include clams a la Cigale, shellfish rice, steak with pepper sauce, sea bass, and a daily selection of fresh-caught fish.

Prada Olhos d'Agua. ✆ **28/950-16-37.** Reservations required. Main courses 15€–30€ ($17–$35). AE, MC, V. Daily noon–3pm and 7–11pm.

INEXPENSIVE

Fernando *Value* PORTUGUESE Fernando, with its large terrace and pleasant indoor dining room, serves tempting, economical fare. We always go here for the fish of the day. You can count on good soup, usually fish based. If you're tired of fish, the chef will fix you a simple steak or a Portuguese specialty such as clams with pork. Several varieties of tempting kebabs are also available. Desserts aren't anything special.

In the Hotel Sol e Mar, Rua Bernardino de Sousa. ✆ **28/951-21-16.** Main courses 11€–15€ ($12–$17). AE, DC, MC, V. Daily noon–midnight.

ALBUFEIRA AFTER DARK

You can have a lot of fun in this hard-drinking, fun-in-the-sun town, discovering your own favorite tucked-away bar. To get rolling, you might begin at the **Falan Bar,** Rua São Gonçalo de Lagos (no phone), or the nearby **Fastnet Bar,** Rua Cândido dos Reis 10 (✆ **28/958-91-16**), where no one will object if you jump to your feet and begin to dance. A few storefronts away is the **Classic Bar,** Rua Cândido dos Reis 8 (✆ **28/951-20-75**), a folksy, comfortably battered place that's almost completely devoid of pretension. The bars are usually open until 3 or 4am, depending on business. Dancing, anyone? The hottest dance club in town is **Kiss,** Montechoro (✆ **28/951-56-39**), which draws the most energetic dance enthusiasts in town every night from 11pm to 6am. The cover charge is 10€ ($9).

6 Quarteira

23km (14 miles) W of Faro, 307km (190 miles) SE of Lisbon

This once-sleepy fishing village between Albufeira and Faro used to be known only to a handful of artists who amused the local fisherfolk. Now, with the invasion of outsiders, the traditional way of life has been upset. A sea of high-rise buildings has swallowed Quarteira, and the place is now a bustling, overgrown resort. The big attraction is one of the Algarve's longest beaches. In summer it's filled with vacationing Portuguese and other Europeans who supply a much-needed boost to the local economy.

Golfers who don't want to pay the high rates at Vale do Lobo or Vilamoura (both of which have 18-hole courses) can stay inexpensively in Quarteira (see "Where to Stay," below). The courses are only a 10-minute drive away, and Quarteira lies about 11km (6¾ miles) from the Faro airport.

The largest concentration of quality hotels and restaurants is not in Quarteira or even Praia de Quarteira, but in the satellite of Vilamoura, west of Quarteira. Buses run between Quarteira and Vilamoura frequently throughout the day. Tourist information is available in Quarteira (see below).

At a central point on the Algarve coast, only 18km (11 miles) west of Faro airport, Vilamoura is an expansive land-development project, the largest private tourist "urbanization" in Europe. Although the remains of a Roman villa were discovered when builders were working on the local marina, the history of Vilamoura is yet to be written. Plans call for a city larger than Faro and an interior lake linked with the bay and ocean by two canals. There's already a marina that can hold 1,000 pleasure boats. Vilamoura is now filled with "holiday villages" and apartment complexes.

ESSENTIALS

ARRIVING

BY BUS If you're dependent on public transportation, take a plane, bus, or train from Lisbon to Faro (see "Faro," later in this chapter), and then catch one of the buses that runs frequently between Faro and Quarteira. Call EVA (✆ **28/938-91-43**) for schedules and information.

BY CAR From Albufeira, head east along Route 125; from Faro, go west on Route 125. Signposts point to the little secondary road that runs south to Quarteira, which is the center for exploring the more extensive tourist developments along Praia de Quarteira and Vilamoura.

VISITOR INFORMATION

The **tourist information office** is at Avenida Infante Sagres, Prago do Mar (✆ **28/938-92-09**). It's open October to May Tuesday through Thursday from 9:30am to 1pm and 2 to 5:30pm, and Friday through Monday 9am to 1pm and 2 to 5:30pm. June to September, it's open Tuesday through Thursday from 9:30am to 7pm, and Friday through Monday from 9am to 1pm and 2 to 5:30pm.

HAVING FUN IN QUARTEIRA

OUTDOOR ACTIVITIES

Sports are a main attraction here. There are 18-hole golf courses, watersports, tennis courts, a riding center, and yachting. Shops and other tourist facilities, including restaurants and bars, also provide pleasant diversions.

BOATING Marinas have been tucked into virtually every navigable cove along the Algarve, and most contain a handful of sailboats or motorboats that can be rented, with or without a skipper, to qualified sailors. ***Note:*** Before you can rent, you must present accreditation or some certificate from a yacht club proving your seaworthiness.

Algariate operates a boat-charter business from the 100-berth Marina de Vilamoura, 8125 Quarteira (✆ **28/938-99-33**). Algariate was established in 1993 and is one of the largest yacht and motorboat charterers in the Algarve. Boats up to 14m (46 ft.) in length are available. Without a crew, they rent for 2,050€ to 3,140€ ($2,358–$3,611) per week, depending on size and season. Clients often use Vilamoura as a point of origin for visits to Madeira, North Africa, or the southern coast of Spain. If you prefer to have someone else worry about navigation, you can sail on the Atlantico Limitado (✆ **28/931-29-41**), which departs from the Vilamoura Marina at least once a day, depending on business, for 3-hour cruises toward Albufeira. The cost is 18€ ($21) per person. A full-day cruise lasting about 7 hours costs 35€ ($40), with lunch included.

GOLF **Vila Sol,** Alto do Semino, Vilamoura, 8125 Quarteira (✆ **28/930-05-05**), has the best fairways and the boldest and most inventive contours of any golf course in the Algarve. Designed by the English architect Donald Steel, it opened in 1991 as part of a 147-hectare (363-acre) residential estate. Steele took great care in allowing the terrain's natural contours to determine the layout of the fairways and the impeccable greens. Although it hasn't been around long, Vila Sol has twice played host to the Portuguese Open. Golfers especially praise the configuration of holes 6, 8, and 14, which incorporate ponds, creek beds, and pine groves in nerve-wracking order. Par is 72. Greens fees are 35€ to 115€ ($40–$132). From Quarteira, drive east for about 5km (3 miles), following signs to Estrada Nacional 125, and turn off where signs point to Vila Sol.

Vilamoura has three famous courses, each with its own clubhouse, managed and owned by the same investors. They're 4km (2½ miles) east of Quarteira and are carefully signposted from the center of town. Discounts on greens fees are offered to the guests of five nearby hotels according to a complicated, frequently changing system of hierarchies and commercial agreements.

The most famous and most sought-after of Vilamoura's trio of golf courses is the **Vilamoura Old Course,** 8125 Vilamoura, sometimes referred to as Vilamoura I (✆ **28/931-03-90** for information). Noted English architect Frank Pennink laid out the course in 1969, long before American tastes in golf influenced Portugal. In design, texture, and conception, it's the most English of southern Portugal's golf courses, and it's invariably cited for its beauty, its lushness, and the maturity of its trees and shrubbery. Although some holes are almost annoyingly difficult (four of them are par 5), the course is among the most consistently crowded on the Algarve. Par is 73. Greens fees are 110€ ($127).

Adjacent to the Old Course are a pair of newer, less popular par-72 courses that nonetheless provide challenging golf for those who prefer different terrain. The first is the **Pinhal Golf Course,** 8125 Vilamoura, also known as Vilamoura II (✆ **28/931-03-90**), which opened in the early 1970s. It's noted for the challenging placement of its many copses of pine trees. Greens fees run 37€ to 75€ ($43–$86), depending on the season and the time of day. Nearby is the newest of the three courses, the **Laguna Golf Course,** 8125 Vilamoura, or Vilamoura III (✆ **28/931-03-90**). Known for its labyrinth of water traps and lakes, it opened in the late 1980s. Greens fees run 35€ to 53€ ($40–$60), depending on the season and the time of day. Tee times during the midday heat are less expensive than those in the early morning.

Visit www.algarvegolf.net for more information on courses in the Algarve region.

TENNIS The English influence in southern Portugal is so strong that no self-respecting resort would be built without at least one tennis court. The **Vilamoura Tennis Centre,** 8125 Vilamoura (© **28/931-21-25**), has 12. They're open to suitably dressed players for 10€ ($12) per hour. Hours are daily from 10am to 6:30pm. After 6:30pm, there is an extra 5€ ($5.75) charge per hour. Tennis racquets rent for 5€ ($5.75), and three tennis balls rent for 2€ ($2.30) per hour.

WHERE TO STAY

Vilamoura is a better place to use as a base than Praia de Quarteira, whose less attractive accommodations are often filled with tour groups.

PRAIA DE QUARTEIRA

Atis Hotel High-rise apartment blocks line this street so completely that it resembles Manhattan. Fortunately, many of the Atis Hotel's balconied, tastefully decorated rooms look out over the beach, 50m (164 ft) away. Though small, rooms are comfortable, with well-maintained bathrooms equipped with shower-tub combinations. A fence separates the tiny outdoor pool from the sidewalk; many guests prefer to swim at the beach.

Av. Francisco Sá Carneiro, 8125-145 Quarteria. © **28/938-97-71.** Fax 28/938-97-74. www.lunahoteis.com. 97 units. 38€–85€ ($44–$98) double. Rates include breakfast. AE, DC, MC, V. **Amenities:** Restaurant; bar; pool; TV room; room service; babysitting; laundry service. *In room:* A/C, TV, safe.

Hotel Dom José Hotel Dom José is sometimes completely booked, often by vacationers from Britain who consider its amenities considerably better than its three-star status dictates. At its tallest point, the hotel has eight balconied stories; the outlying wings are shorter. The double rooms are small and plain but comfortably furnished, with neatly kept bathrooms containing shower-tub combinations. A low wall separates the pool from the town's portside promenade. The public rooms fill every evening as guests enjoy drinks, live music, and the air-conditioned sea view. In another corner of the ground floor, a lattice-covered room contains a wide-screen TV.

Av. Infante do Sagres 141-143, 8125-157 Quarteira. © **28/930-27-50.** Fax 28/930-27-55. hoteldomjose@mail.telepac.pt. 146 units. 58€–108€ ($67–$124) double. Rates include breakfast. AE, DC, MC, V. Parking 5€ ($5.75). **Amenities:** Restaurant; 2 bars; pool; babysitting; laundry service. *In room:* A/C, TV, hair dryer, safe.

Hotel Zodiaco *Kids* At a location only 400m (1,312 ft.) from Forte Novo Beach, this is an economical choice. Its bedrooms, though lackluster, are well maintained and comfortable. Most of them are midsize, with tiled bathrooms that have tubs and showers. For those who want to lodge in the center of Quarteira itself, the Zodiaco ranks just under the Atis. This is a modern structure that is like a miniresort. Its kindergarten makes it popular with families.

Fonte Santa, 8125-298 Quarteira. © **28/938-14-20.** Fax 28/938-14-25. www.hotel-zodiaco.com. 60 units. 37€–90€ ($43–$104) double. Rates include breakfast. AE, DC, MC, V. **Amenities:** Restaurant; bar; pool; tennis court; limited room service; babysitting; day care; 1 room is available for those w/ limited mobility. *In room:* A/C, TV, dataport, safe.

VILAMOURA

Expensive

Hotel Atlantis Vilamoura ★★ This is one of the most stylish hotels in town, near four of the best golf courses on the Algarve. Pointed arches accent the facade, adding Moorish flair. Removed from the congested section of Vilamoura, the contemporary building boasts gleaming marble, coffered wooden ceilings, and polished mirrors. The good-size guest rooms are well furnished, often with silk wall coverings and bright fabrics. Each has a sea-view veranda. The bathrooms tend to be small but are equipped with shower-tub combinations.

Av. Oceano Atlantico, 8125-401 Quarteira. ✆ **28/938-16-00.** Fax 28/938-99-62. www.graopara.pt. 310 units. 106€–217€ ($122–$250) double; 164€–329€ ($189–$378) suite. Rates include buffet breakfast. AE, DC, MC, V. Free parking. **Amenities:** 2 restaurants; 2 bars; 4 pools; 3 tennis courts; health club; sauna; room service; massage; babysitting; laundry service; nonsmoking rooms; rooms for those w/ limited mobility. *In room:* A/C, TV, dataport, minibar, hair dryer, safe.

Tivoli Marinotel Vilamoura ★★★ The government-rated five-star Marinotel is one of the finest deluxe hotels on the Algarve, standing in the midst of 30,000 sq. m (322,917 sq. ft.) of landscaped gardens with direct access to a splendid private beach. The hotel is popular with well-heeled Portuguese and international visitors. During the slower winter months, it accommodates conventions.

The massive, rectangular hotel sits next to the Vilamoura marina. Each well-furnished guest room has a view of the marina or the ocean, but views from floors 8 and 9 are the most panoramic. All units contain well-kept bathrooms equipped with shower-tub combinations. The high-ceilinged interior, with a huge lounge with space for 500, is decorated in traditional and modern designs, although the lobby is brassy and garish.

Marina de Vilamoura, 8125-901 Quarteira. ✆ **28/930-33-03.** Fax 28/930-33-45. www.tivolihotels.com. 389 units. 144€–301€ ($166–$346) double; 220€–472€ ($253–$543) suite. Rates include buffet breakfast. AE, DC, MC, V. Free parking. **Amenities:** 2 restaurants; 2 bars; 3 pools; 2 tennis courts; health club; Jacuzzi; sauna; room service; babysitting; laundry. *In room:* A/C, TV, minibar, hair dryer, safe.

Moderate

Dom Pedro Golf Hotel ★★ This 10-story hotel offers first-class comfort in the tourist whirl of Vilamoura. It's close to the casino and a short walk from the sands. The public rooms are sleekly styled. The midsize guest rooms are pleasantly furnished and carpeted, with private terraces, but the overall effect is uninspired. All units have neatly kept bathrooms with shower-tub combinations. The hotel is a favorite with touring groups from England and Scandinavia. The house band provides nightly entertainment, and there's a casino in front of the hotel. Deep-sea fishing and horseback riding can be arranged, and guests receive a 15% to 20% discount on greens fees at various area golf courses.

Rua Atlantico, Quarteira 8125-478, Vilamoura. ✆ **28/930-07-00.** Fax 28/930-07-01. www.dompedro.com. 263 units. 85€–274€ ($98–$315) double; 153€–342€ ($176–$393) suite. Rates include breakfast. AE, DC, MC, V. Free parking. **Amenities:** 2 restaurants; 2 bars; 3 pools; 3 tennis courts; sauna; limited room service; babysitting; laundry service; 100 nonsmoking rooms; 18 rooms for those w/ limited mobility. *In room:* A/C, TV, dataport, minibar, hair dryer, safe.

WHERE TO DINE

PRAIA DE QUARTEIRA

Piteu ★ PORTUGUESE/SEAFOOD It's worth the detour from your hotel dining room to have a meal at this typically Portuguese restaurant. The cooks always select an array of the best fresh fish from the catch of the day. Live seafood in tanks is also a feature, so you know what you're getting is fresh. For appetizers, perhaps start with king prawns fried with garlic and hot peppers, or Algarvian clams with garlic and a wine sauce. We prefer to make our main course selection from the grilled fish, although you can always order an excellent mixed fish stew nightly. There is also a selection of grilled meat. Entertainment, such as fado and Portuguese guitarists, is often presented.

Av. Doutor Francisco Sa Carneiro, Torre 20. ✆ **28/931-58-02.** Reservations recommended. Main courses 3.75€–8€ ($4.30–$9.20). AE, MC, V. Daily noon–3pm and 6–11pm.

Restaurante O Pescador ALGARVIAN/INTERNATIONAL O Pescador (The Fisherman) is an unpretentious spot across the parking lot from the fish market, just west of the straw market. Although it's low-key, it serves some of the best seafood in the area. Beneath a lattice-accented wooden ceiling, diners enjoy polite service and fresh fish and vegetables. A display case contains some of the ingredients that go into the meals. The simple fare is typically Portuguese; options include fresh squid, grilled gray mullet, grilled prawns, fresh hake, steak, and grilled filet of pork. The fish dishes are far better than the meat selections.

Largo das Cortés Reais. ✆ **28/931-47-55.** Main courses 5€–16€ ($5.75–$18). AE, MC, V. Fri–Wed 1–3pm and 7–10pm. Closed Dec 16–Jan 15.

VILAMOURA

Grill Sirius ★ PORTUGUESE/INTERNATIONAL The most exclusive and expensive dining spot in the Tivoli Marinotel Vilamoura (reviewed separately, above) is the Grill Sirius, on the main floor. It's the most elegant drinking and dining establishment in Vilamoura and consistently serves the best food in town. A grand piano on a dais separates the restaurant from the chic Bar Castor. Live music filters into both areas. The stylish bar offers a large variety of drinks daily from 10:30am to 1am.

Overlooking the marina under high ceilings, Grill Sirius is sophisticated but not fussy. The chefs prepare splendid Portuguese and international dishes, and the service is formal. You might begin with assorted smoked fish and follow with a seafood specialty, such as divinely smooth lobster cassoulet, turbot in seafood sauce, sea bass flambé with fennel, stuffed trout, or excellent filet of sole. Meat dishes use only the finest cuts—rack of lamb, T-bone steak, and tournedos stuffed with shrimp and scallops and served with béarnaise.

In the Vilamoura Marinotel, Vilamoura, 8125-901 Quarteira. ✆ **28/930-33-03.** Reservations recommended. Main courses 18€–30€ ($21–$35). In summer, only buffet served 31€ ($36). AE, DC, MC, V. Daily 12:30–2:30pm and 7:30–10pm.

QUARTEIRA AFTER DARK

Much of the tourist expansion in this region has occurred outside the immediate confines of Quarteira, so you're likely to find only a handful of sleepy bodegas and *tascas* (taverns) inside the city limits. Most cater to locals and serve beer and wine. One of the most internationally conscious is the **Jazz Bar,** Avenida Infante do Sagres 133 (✆ **28/938-88-64**). It occasionally presents live entertainment by Portuguese and northern European musicians beginning around 10:30pm. Don't expect big-city gloss; the ambience is small-scale and folksy.

Glossier diversions are the norm in the massive marina and tourist developments of nearby Vilamoura. Foremost among these is the **Casino de Vilamoura,** Vilamoura, 8125 Quarteira (✆ **28/931-00-00**), one of the finest nightspots in the Algarve. Its most appealing feature is a gambling salon that offers roulette, blackjack, French banque, and baccarat. It's open every day from

7pm to 3am. To enter, you must present a passport or photo ID and pay 2.50€ ($2.90). A separate, less glamorous slot-machine salon at the casino, open daily from 4pm to 4am, doesn't charge admission.

The casino's 600-seat supper club serves meals nightly starting at 8:30pm; one of the Algarve's splashiest floor shows and cabaret revues begins at 10:30pm. A fixed-price meal costs 36€ ($41), including the show. You must make a reservation at the supper club. The show alone costs 13€ ($15), which includes one drink. Physically part of the casino, but with a separate entrance and separate staff, is Vilamoura's most action-oriented dance club, **Black Jack** (✆ **28/930-29-99**). Every danceaholic in the region comes to get down and boogie. It's open nightly from 11:30pm to 6am. The cover charge is 30€ ($35) and includes the first drink. The casino and its facilities are open every night except December 24 and 25.

7 Almancil

13km (8 miles) W of Faro, 306km (190 miles) SE of Lisbon

Almancil is a small market town of little tourist interest, but it's a center for two of the most exclusive tourist developments along the Algarve. **Vale do Lobo** lies 6.5km (4 miles) southeast of Almancil, and **Quinta do Lago** is less than 10km (6¼ miles) southeast of town.

The name *Vale do Lobo* (Valley of the Wolf) suggests a forlorn spot, but in reality the vale is the site of a golf course designed by Henry Cotton, the British champion. It's west of Faro, about a 20-minute drive from the Faro airport. Some holes are by the sea, which results in many an anxious moment as shots hook out over the water. The property includes a 9-hole course, a 9-hole par-three course, a putting green, and a driving range. The tennis center is among the best in Europe.

Quinta do Lago, one of the most elegant "tourist estates" on the Algarve, also has superb facilities. The pine-covered beachfront property has been a favored retreat of movie stars and European presidents. The resort's 27 superb holes of golf are also a potent lure. This is true luxury—at quite a price.

ESSENTIALS

ARRIVING

BY TRAIN Faro, the gateway to the eastern Algarve, makes the best transportation hub for Almancil and its resorts. Go to Faro by train (see section 8, "Faro") and then take a bus the rest of the way.

BY BUS Almancil is a major stop for buses to the western Algarve. About 17 a day run from Faro to Albufeira, with a stop at Almancil. For more information, call ✆ **28/989-97-00** or 28/930-18-23.

BY CAR From Faro, head west along Route 125; from Albufeira or Portimão, continue east along Route 125.

VISITOR INFORMATION

There is no tourist office. Some information is available in Loulé at the **Edifício do Castelo** (✆ **28/946-39-00**) or at the tourist office in Quanteira (see "Visitor Information" under "Quanteira," earlier in this chapter).

OUTDOOR ACTIVITIES

GOLF One of the most deceptive golf courses on the Algarve, **Pinheiros Altos,** Quinta do Lago, 8135 Almancil (✆ **28/935-99-10**), has contours that even professionals say are far more difficult than they appear at first glance. American architect Ronald Fream designed the 100 hectares (247 acres), which abut the wetland refuge of the Rio Formosa National Park. Umbrella pines and dozens of small lakes dot the course. Par is 73. Greens fees are 35€ ($40) for 9 holes and 70€ ($81) for 18 holes. Pinheiros Altos lies about 5km (3 miles) south of Almancil. From Almancil, follow the signs to Quinta do Lago and Pinheiros Altos.

The namesake course of the massive development, **Quinta do Lago,** Quinta do Lago, 8135 Almancil (© **28/939-07-00**), consists of two 18-hole golf courses, Quinta do Lago and Rio Formosa. Together they cover more than 240 hectares (593 acres) of sandy terrain that abuts the Rio Formosa Wildlife Sanctuary. Very few long drives here are over open water; instead, the fairways undulate through cork forests and groves of pine trees, sometimes with abrupt changes in elevation. Greens fees are 75€ ($86) for 9 holes and 150€ ($173) for 18 holes. The courses are 6km (3¾ miles) south of Almancil. From Almancil, follow signs to Quinta do Lago.

Of the four golf courses at the massive Quinta do Lago development, the par-72 **San Lorenzo** (São Lourenço) course, Quinta do Lago, Almancil, 8100 Loulé (© **28/939-65-22**), is the most interesting and challenging. San Lorenzo opened in 1988 at the edge of the grassy wetlands of the Rio Formosa Nature Reserve. American golf designers William (Rocky) Roquemore and Joe Lee created it. The most panoramic hole is the sixth; the most frustrating is the eighth. Many long drives, especially those aimed at the 17th and 18th holes, soar over a saltwater lagoon. Priority tee times go to guests of the Granada organization's Dona Filipa and Penina Hotel, but others may play when the course is not too busy. Greens fees are 75€ ($86) for 9 holes and 150€ ($173) for 18 holes. From Almancil, drive 8km (5 miles) south, following signs to Quinta do Lago.

Vale do Lobo course, Vale do Lobo, 8135 Almancil (© **28/939-39-39**), technically isn't part of the Quinta do Lago complex. Because it was established in 1968, before any of its nearby competitors, it played an important role in launching southern Portugal's image as a golfer's mecca. Designed by the British golfer Henry Cotton, it contains four distinct 9-hole segments. All four include runs that stretch over rocks and arid hills, often within view of olive and almond groves, the Atlantic, and the high-rise hotels of nearby Vilamoura and Quarteira. Some long shots require driving golf balls over two ravines, where variable winds and bunkers that have been called "ravenous" make things particularly difficult. Greens fees, depending on the day of the week and other factors, range from 55€ to 69€ ($63–$79) for 9 holes to 115€ to 135€ ($132–$155) for 18 holes. From Almancil, drive 4km (2½ miles) south of town, following signs to Vale do Lobo.

Visit www.algarvegolf.net for more information on courses in the Algarve region.

HORSEBACK RIDING One of the most well-established riding stables in the area is Quinta do Lago at Edificio Pinheiros Altos Casa Teft, Almancil (© **28/939-60-99**). Reservations are recommended. The riding trails pass through the forest, beside golf courses, and even, in some cases, beside a beach. Rides cost 30€ ($35) for 1 hour and 50€ ($58) for 2 hours. Private lessons are 35€ ($40) per hour, and a pony walk is 15€ ($17) per hour.

WHERE TO STAY

VALE DO LOBO

Le Méridien Dona Filipa ★★★ *Kids* A citadel of ostentatious living, Dona Filipa is a deluxe golf hotel with such touches as gold-painted palms holding up the ceiling. The grounds are impressive, embracing 180 hectares (445 acres) of rugged coastline with steep cliffs, inlets, and sandy bays. The hotel's exterior is comparatively uninspired, but Duarte Pinto Coelho lavished the interior with green silk banquettes, marble fireplaces, Portuguese ceramic lamps, and old prints over baroque-style love seats. The midsize to spacious guest rooms are handsomely decorated with antiques, rustic accessories, and handmade rugs. Most have balconies and twin beds. Bathrooms have dual basins, shower-tub combinations, and robes.

Vale do Lobo, 8135-901 Almancil. ✆ **28/935-72-00.** Fax 28/935-72-00. www.lemeridien-donafilipa.com. 154 units. 296€–414€ ($340–$476) double; 446€–626€ ($513–$720) junior suite; 610€–930€ ($702–$1,070) deluxe suite. Rates include breakfast. AE, DC, MC, V. Free parking. **Amenities:** 2 restaurants; bar; 2 pools; golf nearby; 3 tennis courts; "village" for children; salon; 24-hr. room service; babysitting; laundry service. *In room:* A/C, TV, dataport, minibar, hair dryer, safe.

QUINTA DO LAGO

Quinta do Lago ★★★ A pocket of the high life since 1986, Quinta do Lago is a sprawling 800-hectare (1,976-acre) estate that contains some private plots beside the Ria Formosa estuary. The hotel is an investment by Prince Faisal of Saudi Arabia, who has wisely turned over management to the Orient Express hotel chain. Its riding center and 27-hole golf course are among the best in Europe.

The estate's contemporary Mediterranean-style buildings rise three to six floors. The luxurious hotel rooms overlook a saltwater lake and feature modern comforts. Decorated with thick carpeting and pastel fabrics, the guest rooms are generally spacious, with tile or marble bathrooms equipped with shower-tub combinations. Rooms are decorated with contemporary art and light-wood furniture, and the balconies open onto views of the estuary.

Quinta do Lago, 8135-024 Almancil. ✆ **800/223-6800** in the U.S., or 28/935-03-50. Fax 28/939-49-05. www.quintadolagohotel.com. 141 units. 190€–510€ ($219–$587) double; 295€–565€ ($339–$650) junior suite. Rates include breakfast. AE, DC, MC, V. Free parking. **Amenities:** 2 restaurants; bar; 2 pools; 2 tennis courts; health club; sauna; concierge; car rental; business center; 24-hr. room service; massage; babysitting; laundry service; 70 nonsmoking rooms; 2 rooms for those w/ limited mobility. *In room:* A/C, TV, dataport, minibar, hair dryer, safe.

WHERE TO DINE

Casa Velha ★★★ FRENCH Casa Velha, an excellent dining choice, is not part of the nearby Quinta do Lago resort. On a hillside behind its massive neighbor, it overlooks the resort's lake from the premises of a century-old farmhouse that has functioned as a restaurant since the early 1960s. The cuisine is mainly French, with a scattering of Portuguese and international dishes. Start with foie gras or marinated lobster salad. Specialties include a salad of chicken livers and gizzards with leeks and vinaigrette, and lobster salad flavored with an infusion of vanilla. Other choices are carefully flavored preparations of sea bass, filet of sole, and breast of duck with 12 spices.

Quinta do Lago. ✆ **28/939-49-83.** Reservations recommended. Main courses 15€–28€ ($17–$32). AE, MC, V. Mon–Sat 7:30–10:30pm.

Ermitage ★★★ *Finds* INTERNATIONAL This Dutch-Swiss collaboration is a favorite in the region. About 3km (1¾ miles) from Almancil, it occupies an 18th-century stone *quinta* (farmhouse) that's surrounded by gardens and flowering vines. In the cozy dining room, fireplaces add warmth in winter; an outdoor terrace is very popular during warm weather. The restaurant attracts a cosmopolitan clientele from throughout Europe. Starters include goose-liver terrine with blackberry sauce, and shrimp- and spinach-stuffed ravioli surrounded by four other homemade pastas and sauces, all artfully arranged on an oversize platter. Delightful main courses, which change with the season and the inspiration of the chef, might include grilled fish of the day with herb-flavored hollandaise sauce, or filet of monkfish with prawn-and-curry sauce. Everybody's favorite dessert is a walnut-flavored parfait with freshly made ice cream and mocha sauce. The restaurant is run by the Dutch-born team of Willemina Gilhooley, the manager, and her husband, Vincent, the chef.

Estrada Almancil-Vale do Lobo. ✆ **28/939-43-29.** Reservations recommended. Main courses 26€–32€ ($30–$37); fixed-price menus 65€ ($75). AE, MC, V. Tues–Sun 7–10:30pm. Closed 2 weeks in Jan and 3 weeks in Dec. Drive about 3km (1¾ miles) from Almancil, following signs to Vale do Lobo.

Henrique Leis ★★★ FRENCH/INTERNATIONAL In Vale Formoso, lying 3km (1¾ miles) from Almancil, is one of the region's most outstanding restaurants, fully the equal of São Gabriel and Ermitage, which gives Almancil the most unprecedented possibility of offering its visitors three Michelin-starred restaurants. The restaurant takes its name from Chef Henrique Leis, who is a whiz in the kitchen, turning out one sumptuous platter after another and winning a devoted following with his top-class dining and elegant, tranquil surroundings. The restaurant looks like it belongs on some chalet-studded hillside in Switzerland. The cuisine is vivid and modern, including such appetizers as a fresh goose foie gras prepared two different ways, or scallop and langoustine supreme with a boletus sabayon. The quail salad with foie gras and truffles from the Périgord region adds divine taste and a touch of class. Signature main courses include breast of barberry duck with caramelized apples and passion fruit, and a piccata of veal tenderloin with a light sabayon of two mustards and honey. Fish depends on the catch of the day and is always very fresh.

Vale Formosa. ✆ **28/939-34-38.** Reservations required. Main courses 25€–30€ ($29–$35). AE, MC, V. Mon–Sat 7–10pm. Closed Nov 15–Dec 25.

Mr. Freddie's INTERNATIONAL On the Almacil to Vale do Lobo highway, this restaurant with its outdoor terrace and beautifully set tables is increasingly known for its excellent cuisine and refined service. The market-fresh specialties keep satisfied diners—both expats living in the area and temporary visitors—coming back for more. Whether you opt for the roast duck or the pepper steak—or our recommendation, the fresh fish—all your platters will be accompanied by the season's freshest and best vegetables. Golfers in the area are especially fond of this one, enjoying a selection of cold starters—none better than the smoked swordfish with horseradish sauce or one of the hot starters such as sautéed clams delicately flavored with coriander and seasoned with fresh lemon and olive oil. We have taken particular delight in the filet of pork with apple slices and honey, and the roast rack of lamb in a rosemary and mustard sauce. Desserts are old-fashioned. Remember a banana split and a peach melba?

Escanxinas—Estrada de Vale do Lobo. ✆ **28/939-36-51.** Reservations recommended. Main courses 13€–30€ ($14–$35). AE, DC, MC, V. Mon–Sat 7–10:30pm. Closed Dec. 25–Jan 1.

Pequeno Mundo ★ FRENCH In Almancil itself, this is the most tranquil and elegant—and, in fact, the best overall—choice for dining. It's a delightful house with a lovely courtyard that is romantic on a summer night. Reached by following a signposted, rough dirt track, Pequeno Mundo was converted from an old farmhouse. The finely tuned cuisine makes the trip worthwhile. The chef's specialty is chateaubriand, and it's the best we've had on the coast, served with a perfectly made Béarnaise sauce and accompanied by sautéed potatoes. Alternately, you can also order a tender filet steak in a green pepper sauce or a filet of lamb with fresh vegetables. The fish stew is the best in the area, and the fresh fish of the day can be prepared "as you like it." Service is formal and refined, making this a worthy choice in every way.

Pereiras-Oeste. ✆ **28/939-98-66.** Reservations required. Main courses 15€–43€ ($17–$50). AE, MC, V. Mon–Sat 7:30–10:30pm. Closed Nov 15–Dec 25.

São Gabriel ★★★ SWISS/CONTINENTAL A classic, elegant restaurant, this deluxe choice lies directly southeast of the center of Almancil. Gourmets drive for miles around to sample the food and wine at this refined dining room, which also features a summer terrace. The actual dishes served depend on the time of the year and the mood of the chef. You might encounter lamb perfectly roasted in an old oven, tender duck flavored with port wine, or roasted veal cutlets with Swiss-style "hash browns." The cuisine is remarkably well crafted, though not daringly original. You are, however, assured of the freshest of ingredients and a changing array of tempting desserts.

Estrada da Quinta do Lago. ✆ **28/939-45-21.** Reservations required. Main courses 22€–36€ ($25–$41). AE, MC, V. Thurs–Tues 7–10:30pm. Closed Dec–Feb 15.

8 Faro ★

258km (160 miles) SE of Setúbal, 309km (192 miles) SE of Lisbon

Once loved by the Romans and later by the Moors, Faro is the provincial capital of the Algarve. In this bustling little city of some 30,000 permanent residents, you can sit at a cafe, sample the wine, and watch yesterday and today collide as old men leading donkeys brush past German backpackers in shorts. Faro is a hodgepodge of life and activity: It has been rumbled, sacked, and "quaked" by everybody from Mother Nature to the Earl of Essex (Elizabeth I's favorite).

Since Afonso III drove out the Moors for the last time in 1266, Faro has been Portuguese. On its outskirts, an international airport brings in thousands of visitors every summer. The airport has done more than anything else to increase tourism not only to Faro, but also to the entire Algarve.

Many visitors use Faro only as an arrival point, rushing through en route to a beach resort. Those who stick around will enjoy the local charm and color, exemplified by the tranquil fishing harbor. A great deal of antique charm is gone, thanks to the Earl of Essex, who sacked the town, and the 1755 earthquake. Remnants of medieval walls and some historic buildings stand in the Cidade Velha, or Old Town, which can be entered through the Arco da Vila, a gate from the 18th century.

ESSENTIALS

ARRIVING

BY PLANE Jet service makes it possible to reach Faro from Lisbon in 30 minutes. For flight information, call the **Faro airport** (✆ **28/980-08-01** or 28/980-08-00). You can take bus nos. 14 or 16 from the airport to the railway station in Faro for 1.10€ ($1.25). The bus operates every 35 minutes daily from 7:10am to 7:45pm.

BY TRAIN Trains arrive from Lisbon five times a day. The trip takes 5 hours and costs 14€ ($16) one-way. For rail information in Faro, call the train station at Largo da Estação (✆ **28/980-30-89**). For information in Lisbon, dial ✆ **808/208-208.**

BY BUS Buses arrive every 5 hours from Lisbon. The journey takes 3½ hours. The bus station is on Avenida da República 5 (✆ **28/989-97-61**); a one-way ticket costs 15€ ($17).

BY CAR From the west, Route 125 runs into Faro and beyond. From the Spanish border, pick up N125 west.

VISITOR INFORMATION

The **tourist office** is at Rua da Misericórdia 8–12 (✆ **28/980-36-04**) or at the airport ✆ **28/981-85-82.** At the tourist office, you can pick up a copy of *The Algarve Guide to Walks,* which will direct you on nature trails in the area. It's open daily 9:30am to 5:30pm October through April, and 9:30am to 7:30pm May through September.

EXPLORING THE TOWN

The most bizarre attraction in Faro is the **Capela d'Ossos (Chapel of Bones).** Enter through a courtyard from the rear of the **Igreja de Nossa Senhora do Monte do Carmo do Faro,** Largo do Carmo (✆ **28/982-44-90**). Erected in the 19th century, the chapel is completely lined with human skulls (an estimated 1,245) and bones. It's open daily May to September 10am to 1pm and 3 to 6pm; and October to April Monday through Friday 10am to 1pm and 3 to 5pm, and Saturday 10am to 1pm. Entrance is free to the church and .75€ (85¢) to the chapel.

The church, built in 1713, contains a gilded baroque altar. Its facade is also baroque, with a bell tower rising from each side. Topping the belfries are gilded, mosquelike cupolas connected by a balustraded railing. The upper-level windows are latticed and framed with gold; statues stand in niches on either side of the main portal.

Other religious monuments include the old **Sé** (cathedral), on Largo da Sé (✆ **28/980-66-32**). Built in the Gothic and Renaissance styles, it stands on a site originally occupied by a Muslim mosque. Although the cathedral has a Gothic tower, it's better known for its tiles, which date from the 17th and 18th centuries. The highlight is the Capela do Rosário, on the right. It contains the oldest and most beautiful tiles, along with sculptures of two Nubians bearing lamps and a red chinoiserie organ. Admission is free. The beautiful cloisters are the most idyllic spot in Faro. The cathedral is open Monday through Friday from 10am to noon, Saturday at 5pm for services, and Sunday from 8am to 1pm for services.

Igreja de São Francisco, Largo de São Francisco (✆ **28/982-36-96**), is the other church of note. Its facade doesn't even begin to hint at the baroque richness inside. Panels of glazed earthenware tiles in milk-white and Dutch blue depict the life of the patron saint, St. Francis. One chapel is richly gilded. Open hours are Monday through Friday from 8 to 9:30am and 5:30 to 7pm (but in the sleepy Algarve, you might sometimes find it closed).

If it's a rainy day, three minor museums might hold some interest. The municipal museum, or **Museu Municipal,** Praça Afonso III 14 (✆ **28/989-74-00**), is in a former 16th-century convent, the Convento de Nossa Senhora da Assunção. Even if you aren't particularly interested in the exhibits, the two-story cloister is worth a visit. Many artifacts dating from the Roman settlement of the area are on display. Some of the Roman statues are from excavations at Milreu. The museum is open Tuesday through Friday from 10am to 6pm. Admission is 2€ ($2.30) for adults, 1€ ($1.15) for those 13 to 18 years old, and free to those 12 and under.

The dockside **Museu Maritimo,** Rua Communidade Luisada (✆ **28/989-49-90**), displays models of local fishing craft and of the boats that carried Vasco da Gama and his men to India in 1497. There are replicas of a boat the Portuguese used to sail up the Congo River in 1492 and of a vessel that bested the entire Turkish navy in 1717. It's open Monday through Friday from 2:30 to 4:30pm. Admission is 1€ ($1.15).

Finally, the **Museu Ethnografico Regional,** Plaça da Liberdade 2 (✆ **28/982-76-10**), is a museum devoted to the region's folkloric culture. The focus is on the fishing industry; crafts and reconstructions of regional interiors are also on display. In photographs you can see rather sad, nostalgic pictures of Algarvian fishing villages before they were surrounded by high-rise developments. The museum is open Monday through Friday from 9am to 12:30pm and 2 to 5:30pm. Admission is 1.50€ ($1.75).

OUTDOOR ACTIVITIES Most visitors don't come to Faro to look at churches or museums, regardless of how interesting they are. Bus no. 16, leaving from the terminal, runs to Praia de Faro; the one-way fare is 1€ ($1.15). A bridge also connects the mainland and the beach, about 6km (3½ miles) from the town center. At the shore, you can water-ski, fish, or just rent a deck chair and umbrella and lounge in the sun.

SHOPPING Most of the shopping outlets in Faro are on Rua Santo António or its neighbor, Rua Francisco Gomes, in the heart of town. Check out **Carminho,** Rua Santo António 29 (✆ **28/982-65-22**), a well-recommended outlet for handcrafts and, to a lesser extent, traditional clothing. If you're interested in wandering like a local resident amid stands and booths piled high with the produce of southern Portugal, consider a trek through the **Mercado de Faro,** Largo do Mercado, in the town center. It's open daily from 6:30am to 1:30pm.

WHERE TO STAY

Eva ★ Eva dominates the harbor like a fortress. It's a modern, eight-story hotel that occupies an entire side of the yacht-clogged harbor. There are direct sea views from most of the midsize guest rooms, which are furnished in a restrained, even austere style. The better rooms have large balconies and open onto the water. All units are equipped with well-maintained bathrooms containing shower-tub combinations. Three rooms are available for those with limited mobility. Eva's best features are its penthouse restaurant and rooftop pool, supported on 16 posts, with sun terraces and a bar.

Av. da República, 8000-078 Faro. ✆ **28/900-10-00.** Fax 28/900-10-02. 148 units. 90€–133€ ($104–$153) double; 133€–213€ ($153–$245) suite. Rates include breakfast. AE, DC, MC, V. Limited free parking available on street. **Amenities:** 2 restaurants; 3 bars; pool; salon; 24-hr. room service; babysitting; laundry service. *In room:* A/C, TV, minibar, hair dryer, safe.

Residencial Algarve ★ *Value* In a building that opened in 1999, this is Faro's best hotel deal. The inn was created from an 1880s private dwelling that once belonged to a rich seafarer. When the present owner took over the premises, the building had deteriorated to the point that it had to be demolished. The reconstruction, however, honored the original architectural style. Some of the original hand-painted tiles have been preserved in glass cabinets in the foyer. Lying only a short walk from the historic core of Faro, the inn is most inviting. All the midsize to spacious bedrooms are well furnished and comfortable, with up-to-date amenities and all new bathrooms that rival those of many a first-class hotel. Some have bathtubs; others have a shower.

Rua Infante Dom Henrique 52, 8000-363 Faro. © **28/989-57-00.** Fax 28/989-57-03. www.residencialalgarve.com/facil_eng.htm. 18 units. 45€–70€ ($52–$81) double; 53€–83€ ($61–$95) triple. Rates include breakfast. AE, MC, V. **Amenities:** Bar; babysitting; laundry service; dry cleaning. *In room:* A/C, TV, minibar, hair dryer.

WHERE TO DINE

Adega Nortenha *Value* PORTUGUESE It's hardly a deluxe choice, but if you gravitate to simple regional food served at an affordable price, check out this little eatery. It offers one of the town's best food values. Fresh tuna steak is a delicious choice, as is the roast lamb, which is herb-flavored and perfumed with garlic. A mixture of bits of seafood cooked with chunks of pork makes for a savory cataplana casserole. The service is friendly and efficient, and locals swear by this one. The decoration is in the typical Algarvian style with a balcony.

Praça Ferreira de Almeida 25. © **28/982-27-09.** Main courses 5.50€–11€ ($6.35–$12). AE, DC, MC, V. Daily noon–3pm and 7–10pm.

Dois Irmãos PORTUGUESE This popular bistro, founded in 1925, offers a no-nonsense atmosphere and has many devotees. The menu is as modest as the establishment and its prices, but you get a good choice of fresh grilled fish and shellfish dishes. Ignore the paper napkins and concentrate on the fine kettle of fish before you. Clams in savory sauce are a justifiable favorite, and sole is regularly featured—but, of course, everything depends on the catch of the day. Service is slow but amiable.

Largo do Terreiro do Bispo 13–15. © **28/982-33-37.** Reservations recommended. Main courses 10€–20€ ($12–$23). AE, DC, MC, V. Daily noon–4pm and 6–11pm.

FARO AFTER DARK

What Bourbon Street is to New Orleans, **Rua do Prior** is to Faro. In the heart of town, adjacent to the Faro Hotel, it's chock-a-block with dozens of night cafes, pubs (English and otherwise), and dance clubs that rock from around 10:30pm till dawn. Head to this street anytime after noon for insights into the hard-drinking, hard-driving nature of this hot southern town. For a specific bar of good quality, head for **Upa Upa Café & Bar,** Rua Conselheiro Bivar 51 (© **28/980-78-32**), which draws a medley of visitors and locals to its popular precincts. Tables overflow onto the spacious patio. It's open daily from 9pm to 4am.

EASY EXCURSIONS FROM FARO

Some of the most interesting towns in the Algarve surround the capital. Exploring any one takes a half day.

LOULÉ This market town 15km (9⅓ miles) north of Faro lies in the heart of the Algarve's chimney district. If you think chimneys can't excite you, you haven't seen the ones here. The fret-cut plaster towers rise from many of the cottages and houses (and even the occasional doghouse).

Bus service is good during the day; about 40 buses arrive from various parts of the Algarve, mainly Faro. Five trains per day arrive from Faro at the Loulé rail station, about 5km (3 miles) from the center of town. There are bus connections to the center of town from the station, or you can take a taxi.

The **Loulé Tourist Information Office** is in the Edifício do Castelo (© **28/946-39-00**). It's open October to May Monday through Friday from 9:30am to 5:30pm, and Saturday from 9:30am to 3:30pm; and June to September Monday through Friday from 9:30am to 7pm, and Saturday 9:30am to 3:30pm.

Loulé and the villages around it are known for their handcrafts. They produce work in palm fronds and esparto, such as handbags, baskets, mats, and hats.

Loulé artisans also make copper articles, bright harnesses, delicate wrought-iron pieces, clogs, cloth shoes and slippers, tinware, and pottery. Products are displayed in workshops at the foot of the walls of an old fortress and in other showrooms, particularly those along Rua do 9 de Abril.

In Loulé, you might want to visit the Gothic-style **Igreja Matriz,** or parish church, Largo do Matriz 19 (✆ **28/941-51-67**). It was given to the town in the late 13th century. It's open Monday through Friday from 9 to 10:30am, Saturday 10 to 11:30am, and Sunday noon to 1:30pm.

The remains of the **Moorish castelo** are at Largo Dom Pedro I (✆ **28/941-50-00**). The ruins house a historical museum and are open Monday through Friday from 9am to 5:30pm, and Saturday from 10am to 2pm. Admission is 1€ ($1.15).

For meals, try the Portuguese cuisine at **O Avenida,** Avenida José da Costa Mealha 13 (✆ **28/946-21-06**), on the main street close to the traffic circle. It's one of the finest restaurants in the Algarve. The specialty is shellfish cooked cataplana style. You can also order beefsteak à Avenida or sole meunière. The restaurant is open Monday through Saturday from noon to 3:30pm and 7 to 10pm; it's closed for most of November. Meal prices start at 8€ to 15€ ($9.20–$17). Occasional live entertainment is featured. O Avenida accepts most major credit cards.

SÃO BRÁS DE ALPORTEL Traveling north from Faro, you'll pass through groves of figs, almonds, and oranges, and through pine woods where resin collects in wooden cups on the tree trunks. After 20km (12½ miles) you'll come upon isolated São Brás de Alportel, one of the most charming and least-known spots on the Algarve. Far from the crowded beaches, this town attracts those in search of pure air, peace, and quiet. It's a bucolic setting filled with flowers pushing through nutmeg-colored soil. Northeast of Loulé, the whitewashed, tile-roofed town livens up only on market days. Like its neighbor, Faro, it's noted for its perforated plaster chimneys. The area at the foot of the Serra do Caldeirão has been described as one vast garden.

Pousada de São Brás ★, Estrada de Lisboa (N2), 8150-054 São Brás de Alportel (✆ **28/984-23-05**), is a change of pace from seaside accommodations. The government-owned hilltop villa has fret-cut limestone chimneys and a crow's-nest view of the surrounding countryside. It's approached through a fig orchard.

Many visitors come to the pousada just for lunch or dinner (served daily 12:30–3pm and 7:30–10pm), returning to the coastline at night, but a knowing few remain for the evening. In the dining room, rustic mountain-tavern chairs and tables rest on hand-woven rugs. The 22€ ($25) table d'hôte dinner offers soup, a fish course, a meat dish, vegetables, and dessert. The cuisine is plain but good. After dinner, you might want to retire to the sitting room to watch the embers of the evening's fire die down. The 22 guest rooms contain private bathrooms and phones. Doubles cost 140€ ($161) Friday and Saturday, and 130€ ($150) Sunday through Thursday, including breakfast. Amenities include an outdoor swimming pool, laundry service, and room service (until 10pm). Parking is free, and most major credit cards are accepted.

OLHÃO This is the Algarve's famous cubist town, long beloved by painters. In its heart, white blocks stacked one upon the other, with flat red-tile roofs and exterior stairways on the stark walls, evoke the Casbahs of North Africa. The cubist buildings are found only at the core. The rest of Olhão has almost disappeared under the onslaught of modern commercialism.

While you're here, try to attend the fish market near the waterfront when a *lota,* or auction, is underway. Olhão is also known for its "bullfights of the sea," in which fishers wrestle with struggling tuna trapped in nets en route to the smelly warehouses along the harbor.

If you're here at lunchtime, go to one of the inexpensive markets along the waterfront. At **Casa de Pasto O Bote,** Avenida do 5 de Outubro 122 (✆ **28/972-11-83**), you can select your food from trays of fresh fish. Your choice is then grilled to your specifications. Meal prices start at 10€ ($12). It's open Monday through Saturday from noon to 3pm and 7 to 10pm.

For the best view, climb **Cabeça Hill,** with grottos punctured by stalagmites and stalactites, or St. Michael's Mount, offering a panorama of the Casbahlike Baretta. Finally, to reach one of the most idyllic beaches on the Algarve, take a 10-minute motorboat ride to the Ilha de Armona, a nautical mile away. Ferries run hourly in summer; the round-trip fare is 2€ ($2.30). Olhão is 8km (5 miles) east of Faro.

TAVIRA A gem 31km (19 miles) east of Faro, Tavira is approached through green fields studded with almond and carob trees. Sometimes called the Venice of the Algarve, Tavira lies on the banks of the Ségua and Gilão Rivers, which meet under a seven-arched Roman bridge. In the town square, palms and pepper trees rustle under the cool arches of the arcade. In spite of modern encroachments, Tavira is festive looking. Floridly decorated chimneys top many of the houses, some of which are graced with emerald-green tiles and wrought-iron balconies capped by finials. Fretwork adorns many doorways. The liveliest action centers are the fruit and vegetable market on the river esplanade.

The **Tavira Tourist Office** is on Rua da Galeria (✆ **28/132-25-11**). Tavira has frequent bus connections with Faro throughout the day. It's open June to September Tuesday through Friday from 9:30am to 7:30pm, and Saturday 9:30am to 1pm and 2 to 5:30pm; and October to May Monday through Friday 9:30am to 1pm and 2 to 5:30pm.

Climb the stepped street off Rua da Liberdade, and you can explore the battlemented walls of a castle once known to the Moors. From here you'll have the best view of the town's church spires; across the river delta, you can see the ocean. The castle is open Monday through Friday from 8am to 5:30pm, and Saturday and Sunday from 10am to 7pm. Admission is free.

A tuna-fishing center, Tavira is cut off from the sea by an elongated spit of sand. The **Ilha de Tavira** begins west of Cacela and runs all the way past the fishing village of Fuzeta. On this sandbar, accessible by motorboat, are two beaches: the Praia de Tavira and the Praia de Fuzeta. Some people prefer the beach at the tiny village of Santa Luzia, about 3km (1¾ miles) from the heart of town.

If you're here for lunch, try the **Restaurante Imperial,** Rua José Pires Padinha 22 (✆ **28/132-23-06**). A small, air-conditioned place off the main square, it serves regional food, including shellfish, shellfish rice, garlic-flavored pork, roast chicken, fresh tuna, and other Portuguese dishes, accompanied by vegetables and good local wines. A favorite dish is pork and clams with french fries, topped off with a rich egg-and-almond dessert. Meals cost 7€ to 14€ ($8.05–$16) or more, including wine. Food is served daily from noon to 3:30pm and 7 to 11pm. American Express, MasterCard, and Visa are accepted.

ESTÓI & MILREU A little village some 8km (5 miles) northeast of Faro, Estói is still mainly unspoiled by tourists. Buses run to the area from Faro. Visitors are objects of some curiosity, stared at by old women sheltered behind the curtains of their little houses and followed by begging children. Sometimes you see women washing their clothing in a public trough. Garden walls are decaying here, and the cottages are worn by time and the weather.

The principal sight in Estói is the **Palácio do Visconde de Estói.** The villa, with its salmon-pink baroque facade, has been described as a cross between Versailles and the water gardens of the Villa d'Este near Rome. It was built in the late 18th century for Francisco José de Moura Coutinho; José Francisco da Silva rescued it from near ruin between 1893 and 1909. A palm-lined walk leads to terraced gardens with orange trees along the balusters.

The villa is not open to the public, but the grounds can be visited Tuesday to Saturday from 10am to 5pm. To enter, ring a bell at the iron gates outside the palm-lined walk, and a caretaker will guide you to the gardens. There's no entrance fee, but tip the caretaker.

Monte do Casal ★★, Cerro de Lobo-Estoi, 8005-436 Faro (✆ **28/999-15-03**), is a country house from the 18th century that offers one of the most sedate and charming places to stay in the region. Totally renovated, the British-owned inn lies on 3 hectares (7½ acres) of grounds planted with olive, fruit, and almond trees along with bougainvillea climbing white walls. The well-manicured garden contains a swimming pool. The spacious and comfortably furnished bedrooms, with shower-tub combinations, have terraces with panoramic views of the countryside. This inn represents gracious Algarvian living at its best. In the regional-style dining room, an excellent French cuisine is served nightly in a setting that was originally part of an old farmhouse. Guests meet and mingle in the spacious drawing room with luxurious furnishings, a bookcase, oil paintings, and a fireplace. Doubles cost 134€ to 248€ ($154–$285); suites cost 180€ to 288€ ($207–$331). It's closed November 21 to February 7.

9 Vila Real de Santo António

314km (195 miles) SE of Lisbon, 85km (53 miles) E of Faro, 50km (31 miles) W of Huelva, Spain

Twenty years after the Marquês de Pombal rebuilt Lisbon, which had been destroyed in the great 1755 earthquake, he sent architects and builders to Vila Real de Santo António. They re-established this frontier town on the bank opposite Spain in only 5 months. Pombal's motivation was jealousy of Spain. Much has changed, but **Praça de Pombal** remains. An obelisk stands in the center of the square, which is paved with inlays of black-and-white tiles radiating like sunrays and is filled with orange trees. Separated from its Iberian neighbor by the Guadiana River, Vila Real de Santo António has car-ferry service between Portugal and Ayamonte, Spain.

ESSENTIALS

ARRIVING

BY TRAIN The bus (see below) is a better option for travelers from Faro. Eighteen trains per day arrive from Faro. The trip takes 1 hour and 20 minutes and costs 1.50€ ($1.75) one-way. Four trains make the 4½-hour trip from Lagos; a one-way ticket costs 5.25€ ($4.75). The station is located on Rua dos Caminho de Serro; for information and schedules, call ✆ **808/208-208.** To make connections with trains from Spain (1 hr. ahead of Portuguese time in summer), take a ferry from Vila Real de Santo António to Ayamonte (for ferry information, see below). From Ayamonte, buses from the main square will deliver you to the station at Huelva or Sevilla.

BY BUS From Faro to Vila Real, the bus is better than the train. Buses run each day to the Vila Real bus station on Avenida da República. They take 1 hour and 45 minutes and cost 3.50€ ($4.05) one-way. Eight buses make the 4-hour journey from Lagos, which costs 5.50€ ($6.35) one-way. For information and schedules, call ✆ **28/151-18-07.**

BY FERRY In summer, ferries run between Ayamonte, Spain, and Vila Real daily from 9am to 7pm. The fare is 1.20€ ($1.40) per passenger or 4€ ($4.60) per car. Ferries depart from the station on Avenida da República; call ✆ **28/154-31-52** for more information.

VISITOR INFORMATION

The **tourist office** is on Avenida Infante Dom Henríque, 8900 Monte Gordo (✆ **28/154-44-95**). It's open Monday through Friday from 9:30am to 5:30pm October through April, and Tuesday through Thursday 9:30am to 7pm and Friday through Monday 9:30am to 5:30pm May through September.

EXPLORING THE TOWN

Vila Real de Santo António is a great example of 18th-century town planning. A long esplanade, Avenida da República, follows the river, and from its northern extremity you can view the Spanish town across the way. Gaily painted horse-drawn carriages take you sightseeing past the shipyards and the lighthouse.

You can visit the **Museu de Manuel Cabanas,** Rua Doctor Teofilo Braga, Central Cultural de Volla Real do San António (✆ **28/151-00-45**). On the main square of town, it contains regional ethnographical artifacts, plus some paintings and antique engravings. From mid-July to mid-September it's open daily 4pm to midnight, and Monday through Friday 10am to 1pm and 3 to 7pm the rest of the year. Admission is free.

A 5km (3-mile) drive north on the road to Mertola (N122) will take you to the gull-gray castle-fortress of **Castro Marim.** This formidable structure is a legacy of the border wars between Spain and Portugal. The ramparts and walls stand watch over the territory across the river. Afonso III, who expelled the Moors from this region, founded the original fortress, which was razed by the 1755 earthquake. Inside the walls are the ruins of the Igreja de São Tiago, dedicated to St. James.

Southwest of Vila Real is the emerging resort of **Monte Gordo,** which has the second-greatest concentration of hotels in the eastern Algarve (after Faro). Monte Gordo, 4km (2½ miles) southwest of Vila Real at the mouth of the Guadiana River, is the last in a long line of Algarvian resorts. Its wide, steep beach, **Praia de Monte Gordo,** is one of the finest on Portugal's southern coast. This beach, backed by pine-studded lowlands, has the highest average water temperature in Portugal.

Sadly, what was once a sleepy little fishing village has succumbed to high-rises. Nowadays the *varinas* (fishermen's wives) urge their sons to work in the hotels instead of the sea, fishing for tips instead of tuna.

WHERE TO STAY

Although Vila Real has hotels, most visitors prefer to stay at the beach at Monte Gordo (see below).

VILA REAL

Hotel Apolo This hotel lies on the western edge of town. Near the beach and the river, it attracts vacationers as well as travelers who don't want to cross the

Spanish border at night. The hotel is a marginal choice, with a spacious marble-floored lobby leading into a large bar scattered with comfortable sofas and flooded with sunlight. Each small, simply furnished guest room has a private balcony and a neatly kept bathroom equipped with a shower-tub combination. It's not the classiest stopover on the Algarve, but it's certainly adequate for an overnight stay.

Av. dos Bombeiros Portugueses, 8900-209 Vila Real de Santo António. ✆ **28/151-24-48.** Fax 28/151-24-50. www.apolo-hotel.com. 42 units. 41€–100€ ($47–$115) double. Rates include breakfast. AE, DC, MC, V. Free parking. **Amenities:** Bar; pool; laundry. *In room:* A/C, TV, hair dryer, safe.

Hotel Guadiana ★ This is the best hotel in town (which isn't saying a lot), installed in a mansion classified as a national historic monument. The core was built in 1916, and after falling into disrepair, the hotel was renovated in 1992. Close to the river and the Spanish border, this is an ideal base for exploring the town, Santo António beach, and the beach attractions of the resort of Monte Gordo. Despite the renovations, the government-rated three-star hotel retains an aura of Portuguese tradition. Tiles line some walls. The small to midsize guest rooms are traditional and old-fashioned in decor, but they have modern luxuries such as well-maintained bathrooms with shower-tub combinations. Breakfast is the only meal served, but there's a cozy bar.

Av. da República 94, 8900-206 Vila Real de Santo António. ✆ **28/151-14-82.** Fax 28/151-14-78. 35 units. 45€–75€ ($52–$86) double. Rates include breakfast. AE, DC, MC, V. Free parking. **Amenities:** Breakfast room; bar; laundry. *In room:* A/C, TV, safe.

MONTE GORDO

Casablanca Inn ★ *Finds* Casablanca Inn is not directly on the beach, but its location on a flower-dotted downtown park makes up for it. The owner designed it to look like something you might find in a wealthy part of Morocco. There's a lush flower garden and a series of recessed arched balconies, and the design might be suitable for an updated version of the film classic *Casablanca.* The lobby bar is called Rick's and is covered with movie photos. Each midsize guest room contains a terrace and neatly kept bathrooms with shower-tub combinations.

Rua 7, Monte Gordo, 8900-474 Vila Real de Santo António. ✆ **28/151-14-44.** Fax 28/151-19-99. 42 units. 57€–104€ ($66–$120) double. Rates include breakfast. AE, DC, MC, V. Limited free parking on street. **Amenities:** Restaurant; bar; pool; laundry. *In room:* A/C, TV, safe.

Hotel Alcázar ★ This hotel is the best in town, but don't get your hopes up too high. Curved expanses of white balconies punctuate its palm-fringed brick facade. A free-form pool is built on terraces into the retaining walls that shelter it from the wind and extend the high season far into autumn. The vaguely Arab-style interior design incorporates many arches and vaults that create niches that are imaginatively lit at night. Each rather austere midsize room contains its own sun terrace. Beds, usually twins, are excellent. All units contain neatly kept bathrooms with shower-tub combinations.

Rua de Ceuta 9, Monte Gordo, 8900-474 Vila Real de Santo António. ✆ **28/151-01-40.** Fax 28/151-01-49. 119 units. 48€–104€ ($55–$120) double; 60€–124€ ($69–$143) suite. Rates include breakfast. AE, DC, MC, V. **Amenities:** Restaurant; bar; pool; tennis court; room service; laundry service. *In room:* A/C, TV, safe.

Hotel dos Navegadores The sign in front of this large hotel is so discreet that you might mistake it for an apartment house. The establishment is popular with vacationing Portuguese and British families, who congregate under the dome covering the atrium's swimming pool, near the reception desk. You'll find a bar that serves fruit-laden drinks, and semitropical plants throughout the public rooms. About three quarters of the guest rooms have private balconies. The hotel remains a group tour favorite. Rooms are comfortable but standard, without any flair. All units are equipped with well-maintained bathrooms containing shower-tub combinations. The beach is a 5-minute walk away.

Monte Gordo, 8900-474 Vila Real de Santo António. ✆ **28/151-08-60.** Fax 28/151-08-79. www.navaotel.com. 344 units. 64€–160€ ($74–$184) double; 88€–210€ ($101–$242) suite. Rates include breakfast. AE, DC, MC, V. Free parking. **Amenities:** Restaurant; 3 bars; pool; gym; sauna; salon; 24-hr. room service; laundry service. *In room:* A/C, TV, dataport, minibar, hair dryer, safe (only in suites).

Hotel Vasco da Gama The entrepreneurs here know what their northern guests seek: lots of sunbathing and swimming. Although the hotel sits on a long, wide sandy beach, it also offers an Olympic-size pool with a high-dive board and about .5 hectares (1¼ acres) of flagstone sun terrace. All the spartan, rather small guest rooms are furnished conservatively and come equipped with neatly kept bathrooms containing shower-tub combinations. Glass doors open onto balconies.

Av. Infante Dom Henríque, Monte Gordo, 8900-412 Vila Real de Santo António. ✆ **28/151-09-00.** Fax 28/151-09-01. 182 units. 54€–153€ ($62–$176) double; 64€–164€ ($74–$189) triple. Rates include breakfast. AE, DC, MC, V. Free parking. **Amenities:** Restaurant; bar; snack bar; pool; room service; babysitting; laundry service. *In room:* A/C, TV, minibar, hair dryer, safe.

WHERE TO DINE

Edmundo PORTUGUESE The most popular restaurant in Vila Real, Edmundo overlooks the river and Spain across the water—try to get a sidewalk table. It's a longtime favorite with Spaniards who visit the Algarve for the day. The people who run this place are friendly and justifiably proud of their local cuisine, especially fresh fish. You might begin with shrimp cocktail and then follow with fried sole, crayfish, or delightful sautéed red mullet. Meat dishes such as lamb cutlets and veal filet are also available.

Av. da República 55. ✆ **28/154-46-89.** Reservations recommended. Main courses 6€–12€ ($6.90–$14). AE, DC, MC, V. Mon–Sat noon–3pm; daily 7–10pm.

9

Alentejo & Ribatejo

The adjoining provinces of Alentejo and Ribatejo constitute the heartland of Portugal. Ribatejo is a land of bull-breeding pastures; Alentejo is a plain of fire and ice.

Ribatejo is river country; the Tagus, coming from Spain, overflows its banks in winter. The region is famed for bluegrass, Arabian horses, and black bulls. Its most striking feature, however, is human: *campinos,* the region's sturdy horsemen. They harness the Arabian pride of their horses and discover the intangible quality of bravery in the bulls. Whether visiting the château of the Templars, which rises smack in the middle of the Tagus at Almourol, or attending an exciting *festa brava,* when horses and bulls rumble through the streets of Vila Franca de Xira, you'll marvel at the passion of the people. Ribatejo's *fadistas* (fado singers) have long been noted for their remarkable intensity.

The cork-producing plains of Alentejo (which means "beyond the Tagus") make up the largest province in Portugal. It's so large that the government has divided it into the northern Alto Alentejo (the capital of which is Évora) and southern Baixo Alentejo (whose capital is Beja).

Locals in Alentejo insulate themselves in tiny-windowed, whitewashed houses—warm in the cold winters and cool during the scorching summers. This is the least populated of Portuguese provinces, with seemingly endless fields of wheat. It's the world's largest producer of cork, whose trees can be stripped only once every 9 years.

In winter the men make a dramatic sight, outfitted in characteristic long brown coats with two short-tiered capes, often with red-fox collars. The women are more colorful, especially when they're working in the rice paddies or wheat fields. Their short skirts and patterned undergarments allow them to wade barefooted into the paddies. On top of knitted cowls, with mere slits for the eyes, women wear brimmed felt hats usually studded with flowers.

Although dusty Alentejo is mostly a region of inland plains, it also has an Atlantic coast. It stretches from the mouth of the Sado River all the way to the border of the Algarve, just south of Zambujeira do Mar Carvalhal. This stretch of beach is the least crowded and least developed in Portugal. Towering rock cliffs punctuate much of the coastline south of Lisbon, interrupted by the occasional sandy cove and tranquil bay. Regrettably, there isn't much protection from the often-fierce waves and winds that rush in from the Atlantic; the waters are generally too chilly for most tastes.

Driving is the best way to see the region because there are numerous towns to see and excursions to take from the major cities. There is public transportation, but often you'll have a long, tiresome wait between connections. Both provinces lie virtually on Lisbon's doorstep—in fact, suburbs of the capital lie on their edges.

If you've just explored the Algarve (see chapter 8), you'll find Alentejo within striking distance. The best route to take into Alentejo from the south is IP-1 from Albufeira.

1 Tomar ★★

65km (40 miles) N of Santarém, 137km (85 miles) NE of Lisbon

Divided by the Nabão River, historic Tomar was bound to the fate of the notorious quasi-religious order of the Knights Templar. In the 12th century, the powerful, wealthy monks established the beginnings of the Convento de Cristo on a tree-studded hill overlooking the town. Originally a monastery, it evolved into a kind of grand headquarters for the Templars. The knights, who swore a vow of chastity, had fought ferociously at Santarém against the Moors. As their military might grew, they built a massive walled castle at Tomar in 1160. The ruins—primarily the walls—can be seen today.

By 1314, the Templars had amassed both great riches and many enemies; the pope was urged to suppress their power. King Dinis allowed them to regroup their forces under the new aegis of the Order of Christ. Henry the Navigator became the most famous of the grand masters, using much of their money to subsidize his explorations.

ESSENTIALS

ARRIVING

BY TRAIN The train station (✆ **24/931-28-15**) is on Avenida Combatentes da Grande Guerra, at the southern edge of town. Nine trains arrive daily from Lisbon; the trip takes 2 hours and costs 5.60€ ($6.45) one-way. From Porto, five trains daily make the 4-hour trip, which costs 11.50€ ($13.25) one-way.

BY BUS The bus station is on Avenida Combatentes da Grande Guerra (✆ **96/894-35-50**), next to the train station. Four buses a day arrive from Lisbon. The 2-hour trip costs 7.50€ ($8.65) one-way.

BY CAR From Santarém, continue northeast along Route 3 and then cut east at the junction of N110. When you reach Route 110, head north. To reach Santarém from Lisbon, go north on E1.

VISITOR INFORMATION

The **Tomar Tourist Office** is on Avenida Dr. Cândido Madureira (✆ **24/932-24-27**). It's open daily 10am to 1pm, and 2 to 6pm October through April, and daily 10am to 8pm May through September.

EXPLORING THE TOWN

Convento da Ordem de Cristo ★★ From its inception in 1160, the Convent of the Order of Christ monastery experienced 5 centuries of inspired builders, including Manuel I (the Fortunate). It also fell victim to destroyers, notably in 1810, when Napoléon's overzealous troops turned it into a barracks. What remains on the top of the hill is one of Portugal's most brilliant architectural accomplishments.

The portal of the Templars Church, in the Manueline style, depicts everything from leaves to chubby cherubs. Inside is an **octagonal church** ★ with eight columns, said to have been modeled after the Temple of the Holy Sepulchre at Jerusalem. The mosquelike effect links Christian and Muslim cultures, as in the Mezquita in Córdoba, Spain. The author Howard La Fay called it "a muted echo of Byzantium in scarlet and dull gold." The damage the French

0
30 mi
0
30 km
N
Castelo Branco
Tomar
N18
Castelo de Vide
N118
Marvão
Abrantes
Leiria
Portalegre
Santarém
Chouto
Ponte de Sor
Alburqueque →
N80
Almeirim
Cartaxo
E01
Rio Tejo
(Tagus River)
Montargil
Badajoz
(Spain)→
Estremoz
Vila Franca
de Xira
Coruche
Elvas
E90
Borba
N10
Vila
Viçosa
Arraiolos
N18
Vendas
Novas
N4
Évora
E90
E01
Rio Guadiana
Setúbal
E01
N5
Reguengos de
Monsaraz
Alcácer
do Sal
Alcáçovas
Viana do Alentejo
Rio Sado
ATLANTIC
OCEAN
Vidigueira
Grândola
N18
Moura
Beja
Santiago do Cacém
Serpa
Sines
FRANCE
PORTUGAL
SPAIN
Lisbon
area of
detail

troops inflicted is very evident. On the other side, the church is in the Manueline style with rosettes. Throughout, you'll see the Templars insignia.

The monastery's eight cloisters embrace a variety of styles. The most notable, a two-tiered structure dating from the 12th century, exhibits perfect symmetry, the almost severe academic use of the classical form that distinguishes the Palladian school. A guide will also take you on a brief tour of a dormitory where the monks lived in austere cells.

The monastery possesses some of the greatest Manueline stonework in Portugal. A fine example is the grotesque **west window** ★★★ of the chapter house. At first the forms emanating from the window might confuse you, but closer inspection reveals a meticulous symbolic and literal depiction of Portugal's sea lore and power. Knots and ropes, mariners and the tools of their craft, silken sails wafting in stone and re-created coral seascapes—all are delicately interwoven in this chef d'oeuvre of the whole movement.

Atop a hill overlooking the old town. ✆ **24/931-34-81.** Admission 3€ ($3.45) adults, 1.50€ ($1.75) children 14–25, free for children under 14. Daily June–Sept 9am–6pm; Oct–May 9:15am–12:30pm and 2–5pm.

Capela de Nossa Senhora da Conceição On the way up the hill to see the monastery, you can stop off at this chapel, crowned by small cupolas and jutting out over the town. Reached through an avenue of trees, it was built in the Renaissance style in the mid–16th century. The interior is a forest of white Corinthian pillars.

Between the old town and the Convento da Ordem de Cristo. ✆ **24/932-24-27.** Free admission. Daily 9am–6pm.

Igreja de São João Baptista In the heart of town is this 15th-century church, built by Manuel I. It contains black-and-white diamond mosaics and a white-and-gold baroque altar; a chapel to the right is faced with antique tiles. In and around the church are the narrow cobblestone streets of Tomar, where shops sell dried codfish, and wrought-iron balconies are decorated with birdcages and flowerpots.

Praça da República. ✆ **24/931-26-11.** Free admission. Daily 9:30am–6pm.

Museu Luso-Hebraico This Portuguese-Hebrew museum lies in the heart of the old Jewish ghetto. The building was the Sinogoga de Tomar—the oldest Jewish house of worship in Portugal, dating from the mid-1400s. A Jewish community worshipped here until 1496, when the Catholic hierarchy ordered its members to convert or get out of town. In time, the synagogue assumed many roles: Christian chapel, prison, warehouse, even hayloft. Today it enjoys national monument status. Samuel Schwartz, a German who devoted part of his life to restoring it, bought the building in 1923. He donated it to the Portuguese state in 1939. In return, Schwartz and his wife were awarded citizenship and protection during World War II. The museum exhibits many 15th-century tombs with Hebrew inscriptions, along with Jewish artifacts donated from around the globe. A recent excavation unearthed a mikvah, or ritual purification bath.

Rua Dr. Joaquim Jaquinto 73. ✆ **24/932-26-96.** Free admission; donations accepted. Daily 10am–1pm.

SHOPPING

Shopkeepers in Tomar work hard to acquire premises on the town's main shopping thoroughfare, Rua Serpa Pinto, an avenue known locally as *Corre Doura,* which refers to a medieval horse race that used to take place along this street in the 12th century. You'll find lots of outlets for folkloric goods, pottery, copperware, and wrought iron. One of the best is **Artlandica,** Convento de São Francisco, Rua de São Francisco (✆ **24/932-33-55**).

WHERE TO STAY

MODERATE

Estalagem de Santa Iria ★ *Finds* Although not as swanky as Dos Templários, this inn of charm and grace is like a grand country villa, filled with regional touches in both architecture and decor. Hallways with arches lead to the small to midsize bedrooms, which are furnished with regional artifacts and wood furnishings, along with shiny and well-kept bathrooms. Decoration is minimalist, with plaster walls painted white. Families are also fond of the inn, and the staff provides extra beds in the rooms for children ages 4 to 12 years. In business since the mid–20th century, the colonial-style, two-story inn lies in the center. Its on-site restaurant is a popular place with both locals and visitors, specializing in market-fresh regional produce.

Parque do Mouchão, 2300-586 Tomar. ✆ **24/931-33-26.** Fax 24/932-12-38. 14 units. 53€–85€ ($61–$98) double, 82€–125€ ($94–$144) suite. Rates include breakfast. AE, DC, MC, V. **Amenities:** Restaurant; bar; laundry service. *In room:* TV.

Hotel dos Templários ★★★ This large government-rated four-star hotel on the banks of the Rio Nabão seems incongruous in such a small town—it was expanded in 1994 to make it the largest hotel in the district. Five local businessmen created the hotel in 1967, but they would hardly recognize the place today. The midsize guest rooms, although ordinary, are quite agreeable, especially those in the new wing. Many open onto views of the Convent of Christ. All are well furnished and equipped, with neatly kept bathrooms containing shower-tub combinations. The public areas, including the lounges and the terrace-view dining room, are spacious. The hotel has wide sun terraces and a greenhouse.

Largo Cândido dos Reis 1, 2300-909 Tomar. ✆ **24/931-01-00.** Fax 24/932-21-91. www.hoteldostemplarios.pt. 178 units. 74€–105€ ($85–$121) double; 127€–162€ ($146–$186) suite. Rates include breakfast. Children ages 5–12 get 50% discount in parent's room. AE, DC, MC, V. Free parking. **Amenities:** Restaurant; bar; 2 pools; tennis courts; gym; health club; sauna; salon; limited room service; babysitting; laundry service; 1 room for those w/limited mobility. *In room:* A/C, TV, dataport, minibar, hair dryer, safe.

INEXPENSIVE

Hotel Residencial Trovador *Value* Rooms here are clean and comfortable, with conservatively patterned wallpaper and good beds. All units come equipped with well-maintained bathrooms containing mostly shower-tub combinations. Breakfast is the only meal served. The hotel is close to the bus station and the commercial center of town, in a drab neighborhood of apartment buildings.

Rua 10 d'Agosto, 2300-553 Tomar. ✆ **24/932-25-67.** Fax 24/932-21-94. 30 units. 40€–46€ ($46–$53) double. Rates include breakfast. AE, DC, MC, V. Free parking. **Amenities:** Breakfast room; 24-hr. room service; laundry service. *In room:* A/C, TV.

A PLACE TO STAY & DINE NEARBY

Pousada de São Pedro ★★ Built in the 1950s, this pousada 15km (9⅓ miles) southeast of Tomar is one of the country's most unusual pousadas. The flagstone-covered terrace in back affords a close-up view of Portugal's version of Hoover Dam. It curves gracefully against a wall of water, upon which local residents sail, swim, and sun themselves.

The pousada has a scattering of Portuguese antiques, some of them ecclesiastical, in its stone-trimmed hallways. The tidy, unpretentious rooms are small,

Finds Travel Secrets of the Portuguese Plains

Certain towns in the region—such as Évora—are on the main tourist circuit, but both Alentejo and Ribatejo have an abundance of small towns and villages intriguing to the traveler with the time and desire to seek them out. Our favorites:

SERPA Still languishing in the Middle Ages, Serpa is a walled town with defensive towers. It was incorporated into the kingdom of Portugal in 1295, after having belonged to the Infante of Serpa, Dom Fernando, brother of Dom Sancho II. Overlooking the vast Alentejo plain, Serpa is a town of narrow streets and latticed windows, famous for the cheese that bears its name, for pork sausage, and for sweets. Silvery olive trees surround the approaches to the town, and the whiteness of the buildings contrasts with the red-brown of the plains. The wild beauties of the river Guadiana, endless fields of grain, and cork-oak groves mark the landscape. In the town, you can see unique painted furniture, an archaeological museum, and several ancient churches. Serpa has become a lunch stop or rest stop for travelers on the way to and from Spain; many motorists spend the night at the hilltop pousada.

MONSARAZ The old fortified town of Monsaraz lies 51km (32 miles) east of Évora en route to Spain. It's a village of antique whitewashed houses, with cobblestone lanes and many reminders of the Moors who held out here until they were conquered in 1166. Some of the women still wear traditional garb: men's hats on shawl-covered heads and men's pants under their skirts. The custom derives from a need for protection from the sun. Monsaraz overlooks the Guadiana Valley, which forms the border between Spain and Portugal.

The walled town can easily be visited from Évora in an afternoon. As you scale the ramparts, you're rewarded with a view over what looks like a cross between a bullring and a Greek theater. The highlight of a

with neatly kept bathrooms equipped with shower-tub combinations. Following a major fire in the early 1990s, a new annex added seven units. The public rooms are more alluring than the guest rooms.

Castelo de Bode, 2300-909 Tomar. ✆ **24/938-11-75.** Fax 24/938-11-76. www.pousadas.pt. 25 units. 92€–188€ ($106–$216) double; 114€–169€ ($131–$194) suite. Rates include continental breakfast. AE, DC, MC, V. Free parking. **Amenities:** Restaurant; bar; laundry service, nonsmoking rooms. *In room:* A/C, TV, minibar, hair dryer.

WHERE TO DINE

Bella Vista ★ PORTUGUESE This restaurant, in a 150-year-old stone-sided house in the town center, has belonged to three generations of the Sousa family. The patriarch, Eugenio, founded it in 1975 and still operates it from a perch in its busy kitchens. From your table you're likely to have a pleasant view over the old town and a small canal. There's a rustic, cozy indoor dining area, plus seating on an outdoor terrace ringed with flowering shrubs. Menu items are simple but plentiful, and prices are affordable. The cook usually makes a fresh visit is the main street, Rua Direita. It contains the most distinguished architecture, wrought-iron grilles, balconies, and outside staircases.

BORBA On the way to Borba, you'll pass quarries filled with black, white, and multicolored deposits. In the village, marble reigns. Many cottages have marble door trimmings and facings, and the women kneel to scrub their doorways, a source of special pride. On Rua São Bartolomeu sits a church dedicated to São Bartolomeu. It displays a groined ceiling; walls lined with blue, white, and gold *azulejos* (decorative tiles); and an altar in black-and-white marble. The richly decorated ceiling is painted with four major medallions. As Portuguese churches go, this one isn't remarkable. But there are eight nearby antiques shops (amazing for such a small town) filled with interesting items. Borba is also a big wine center, and you might want to sample the local brew at a cafe, or perhaps at the pousada at Elvas.

MARVÃO This ancient walled hill town, close to Castelo de Vide, is well preserved and is visited chiefly for its spectacular views. Just less than 6.5km (4 miles) from the Spanish frontier, the once-fortified medieval stronghold retains a rich flavor of the Middle Ages. Those with limited time who can explore only one border town in Portugal should make it this one—it's that panoramic. You get to Marvão by following a road around the promontory on which the little town stands, past the Church of Our Lady of the Star, the curtain walls, watchtowers, and parapets. Arcaded passageways, balconied houses with wrought-iron grillwork and Manueline windows, and a number of churches can be seen along the hilly streets. The castle, built in the 13th century, stands at the western part of the rocky outcropping. From the parapet, you'll have a panoramic view of the surrounding country—all the way to the Spanish mountains in the east, and a vast sweep of Portuguese mountain ranges.

pot of *caldo verde* (soup with ham hocks, greens, and potatoes) every day, and shellfish soup is generally available. Main courses include several variations of Portuguese codfish, savory roast goat, grilled filet of sole, aromatic roast pork, and several versions of succulent chicken, including one with curry. Wines are unpretentious, plentiful, and inexpensive.

Rua Marquês de Pombal and Rua Fonte do Choupo. ✆ **24/931-28-70.** Reservations recommended. Main courses 6.50€–13€ ($7.50–$15); fixed-price menu 12€ ($13). No credit cards. Mon and Wed–Sun noon–3pm; Wed–Sun 7–9:30pm. Closed Nov for 2 weeks.

TOMAR AFTER DARK

Despite Tomar's small size and emphasis on folklore, there are lots of outlets for drinking and barhopping with gregarious locals. You'll find *tascas* (taverns) and bars scattered throughout the town's historic core. Two of the most charming and convivial are the **Bar Akiakopus,** Rua de São João 28 (✆ **24/932-38-00**), and the **Quinta Bar,** Quinta do Falcão 26 (✆ **24/938-17-67**). People between the ages of 20 and 45 hang out and listen to live music. Also worth ducking into for at least one drink is **Casablanca,** Rua de São João (© **24/931-47-57**), a mellow, quiet hangout with, as you might have guessed, a Moroccan theme.

2 Estremoz ★

46km (28 miles) NE of Évora, 174km (108 miles) E of Lisbon, 12km (7½ miles) W of Borba

Rising from the plain like a pyramid of salt set out to dry in the sun, fortified Estremoz is in the center of the marble-quarry region of Alentejo. Cottages and mansions alike use the abundant marble in their construction and trim.

ESSENTIALS

ARRIVING

BY TRAIN There is no train service to Estremoz.

BY BUS The bus station is at Rossio Marquês de Pombal (© **26/832-22-82**). Three buses arrive daily from Évora, 1 hour away; five buses a day arrive from Portalegre, 1½ hours away.

BY CAR From Évora (see below), head northeast along Route 18.

VISITOR INFORMATION

The **Estremoz Tourist Office** is at Largo da Republique 26 (© **26/833-35-41**). It's open daily from 9:30am to 12:30pm and 2 to 6pm.

EXPLORING THE TOWN

With enough promenading soldiers to man a garrison, the open quadrangle in the center of the Lower Town is called the **Rossio Marquês de Pombal.** The **Town Hall,** with its twin bell towers, opens onto this square. It has a grand stairway whose walls are lined with antique blue-and-white tiles, depicting hunting, pastoral, and historical scenes.

In the 16th-century **Igreja de Santa Maria (Church of St. Mary),** you'll see pictures by Portuguese primitive painters. The church formed part of the ancient fortress. It is open Tuesday through Sunday from 9:30am to noon and 3 to 5pm. Admission is free.

Another church worth a stop is .6km (less than ½ mile) south of the town on the road to Bencatel. The **Igreja de Nossa Senhora dos Mártires (Church of Our Lady of the Martyrs)** has beautiful tiles and an entrance marked by a Manueline arch. Dating from 1844, the church has a nave chevet after the French Gothic style of architecture.

Castelo da Rainha Santa Isabel From the ramparts of the Castle of Queen Saint Isabel, which dates from the 13th-century reign of Dinis, the plains of Alentejo spread out before you. Although one 75-year-old British lady reportedly walked it, the route to the top is best covered by car. Drive to the top of the Upper Town and stop on Largo de Dom Dinis. The stones of the castle, the cradle of the town's past, were decaying so badly that the city leaders pressed for its restoration in 1970. It was turned into a luxurious pousada (see "Where to Stay," below), the best place in town to stay or dine.

The castle's imposing keep, attached to a palace, dominates the central plaza. Dinis's wife, Isabella, died in the castle and was unofficially proclaimed a saint by her local followers. Also opening onto the marble-and-stone-paved Largo are two modest chapels and a church. As in medieval days, soldiers still walk the ramparts, guarding the fortress. There is no admission. Nonguests can visit Tuesday through Sunday 10:30am to noon and 3 to 5pm.

Largo de Dom Dinis. No phone for sightseeing information. (See "Where to Stay," below, for hotel reservation information.)

Museu Rural da Casa do Povo de Santa Maria de Estremoz The Rural Museum, open for guided tours, displays the life of people of the Alentejo through models and crafts. The 18th-century-style building is part of the property of the Convento das Maltezas de São João da Penitência, today the Misericórdia (national charity organization).

Rossio Marquês de Pombal. ✆ **26/833-35-41.** Admission 1€ ($1.15), free for children under 12. Mon–Sat 10am–12:30pm and 2–5:30pm.

SHOPPING

The town's most famous product is a type of traditional earthenware water jug. Known as a *moringue,* it has two spouts, one handle, and sometimes a decorative crest that's stamped into the wet clay before it's fired. At least half a dozen street merchants sell the jugs in the town's main square, **Rossio Marquês de Pombal.** Stylish reminders of Portugal's agrarian past, they're associated with love and marriage. (Housewives traditionally carried water in them to workers in the fields.) Some are simple; others are glazed in bright colors.

At **Artesanato,** Avenida de São António (no phone), you'll find hundreds of terra-cotta figurines, another of the town's specialties. Each represents an archetype from the Alentejo workforce, and the designs include artfully naive depictions of washerwomen, sausage makers, carpenters, priests, and broom makers. Artesanato also sells some of the region's other handcrafts, including metalwork, wood carvings, and weavings.

WHERE TO STAY

EXPENSIVE

Pousada da Rainha Santa Isabel ★★★ This is one of the best of the government-owned tourist inns; reserve months in advance. In the old castle dominating the town and overlooking the battlements and the Estremoz plain, it's a deluxe establishment. Gold leaf, marble, velvet, and satin mingle with 17th- and 18th-century reproductions of furniture and decorations in the guest rooms and corridors. The accommodations range from former monks' cells to sumptuous suites with canopied beds. Ten excellent rooms are in a modern addition, all with well-maintained bathrooms equipped with shower-tub combinations. Dom Manuel received Vasco da Gama in the salon of this castle before the explorer left for India. In 1698, a terrible explosion and fire destroyed the royal residence, which then underwent several alterations. It became an armory, then a barracks, and then an industrial school. Its transformation into a castle-pousada has restored it as a historic monument. Comfort and style fit delightfully in this historical framework.

Largo de Dom Dinis, 7100-509 Estremoz. ✆ **26/833-20-75.** Fax 26/833-20-79. www.pousadas.pt. 33 units. 149€–195€ ($171–$224) double; 204€–293€ ($235–$337) suite. Rates include continental breakfast. AE, DC, MC, V. Free parking. **Amenities:** Restaurant; bar; pool; limited room service; laundry service. *In room:* A/C, TV, minibar, hair dryer, safe.

MODERATE

Estalgem Páteo dos Solares ★ *Finds* A 10-minute walk from the center, this charming inn opened in 2001. It doesn't challenge the Pousada, but many visitors can't get into that hotel because of its popularity. This Estalagem is a viable second choice, especially because of its evocative atmosphere of old Portugal and its large collection of century-old Portuguese tiles. The manor house is rather pristine architecturally on its exterior, but it warms considerably once you're inside. Each bedroom is modernized but traditionally furnished—for example, some have a fireplace and a hydromassage. All bedrooms are fully comfortable and well maintained. The hotel is set in well-kept gardens with an outdoor pool and tennis court. The on-site restaurant is known for its regional specialties.

Rua Brito Capelo, Largo do Castelo, 7100-509 Estremoz. ✆ **26/833-84-00.** Fax 26/833-84-19. www.inn-portugal.com/inns/estpateo.html. 41 units. 150€–181€ ($172–$208) double. Rates include breakfast. AE, DC, MC, V. **Amenities:** Restaurant; bar; pool; tennis court; limited room service; babysitting; laundry service; nonsmoking rooms; rooms for those w/limited mobility. *In room:* A/C, TV, dataport, minibar, hair dryer, safe.

INEXPENSIVE

Monte Dos Pensamentos ★ *Finds* A real discovery, this antique manorial house lies 2km (1¼ mile) from Estremoz in a setting of orange trees and olive groves. The staff will instantly link you to the area, renting mountain bikes and directing you to a stable if you want to go horseback riding 8km (5 miles) away. This is a good place to catch up on some R&R during your tour of Portugal, relaxing in the citrus grove with its swimming pool. Dark-wood furnishings rest on terra cotta floors throughout, and the style is vaguely colonial. Hand-painted ceramics along with a big collection of dolls and local artifacts create somewhat the aura of a museum. In cooler weather, guests enjoy a blazing fireplace in the lounge. The little inn rents a double or suite in the main house and two well-equipped apartments on the grounds, each with kitchenette and fireplace (one of these units is air-conditioned).

Estrada Estação do Ameixial, 7100 Estremoz. ✆ **26/833-31-66.** Fax 26/833-24-09. http://home.online.no/~nancys/portugal/stay/planicies/estremoz. 5 units. 60€ ($69) double; 70€ ($81) suite; 75€ ($86) apt. No credit cards. **Amenities:** Pool. *In room:* A/C, TV, kitchenette in apt.

WHERE TO DINE

Pousada da Rainha Santa Isabel ★ PORTUGUESE/INTERNATIONAL The finest cuisine in town is served at this classic restaurant with vaulted ceilings. The best regional foodstuffs from the countryside are incorporated into a menu of perfectly seasoned and well-prepared dishes. The traditional tomato soup, an Alentejo classic, is served along with another classic, fried pork flavored with bits of fresh clams. Local trout filets are grilled with mint that's grown along the riverbanks. Meat dishes, such as grilled lamb cutlets flavored with fresh rosemary, are another winning combination, as is the selection of regional smoked meats from Alentejo. In such a provincial capital, the extensive menu comes as a surprise, especially in its array of products, from Iranian caviar to foie gras from the Landes region of France.

A selection of fresh desserts and pastries is made daily, and the wine cellar is the best in the city.

Largo D. Diniz, Castelo de Estremoz. ✆ **26/833-20-75.** Reservations recommended. Main courses 13€–26€ ($14–$30); 3-course fixed-price menu 25€ ($29). AE, MC, DC, V. Daily 12:30–3pm and 7:30–10pm.

ESTREMOZ AFTER DARK

There aren't any noteworthy dance clubs in Estremoz, so local residents seek out centrally located pubs. Foremost among these is **Ze's Pub,** Largo General Graça 78 (✆ **26/832-31-39**). Patrons between 20 and 50 mingle gracefully over pints of beer, wine, and whiskey. A slightly younger crowd congregates at the **Reguengo Bar,** Rua Serpa Pinto 128 (✆ **26/833-33-78**), usually to the sound of recorded hits from throughout Europe and the Americas.

3 Elvas ★★

11km (7 miles) W of Badajoz, Spain, 223km (138 miles) E of Lisbon

The "city of plums," Elvas is characterized by narrow cobblestone streets (pedestrians have to duck into doorways to allow automobiles to inch by) and crenellated fortifications. The Moors held the town until 1226. Later Spanish troops frequently assaulted and besieged it. It finally fell in the 1801 War of the Oranges, which ended with a peace treaty signed at Badajoz. Elvas remained part of Portugal, but its neighbor, Olivença, became Spanish. The Elvas ramparts are an outstanding example of 17th-century fortifications, with gates, curtain walls, moats, bastions, and sloping banks around them.

Lining the steep, hilly streets are tightly packed gold- and oyster-colored cottages with tile roofs. Many of the house doors are just 1.5m (5 ft.). In the tiny windows are numerous canary cages and flowering geraniums. The four-tier **Aqueduto da Amoreira,** built between 1498 and 1622, transports water into Elvas from about 8km (5 miles) southwest of the town.

ESSENTIALS

ARRIVING

BY TRAIN The train station is at Fontainhas (© **26/862-28-16**), about 3km (2 miles) north of the city. Local buses connect the station to Praça da República, in the center. Four trains a day make the 5½-hour trip from Lisbon. The one-way fare is 10€ ($12). From Badajoz, Spain, there is one train per day. The trip takes 20 minutes, and the fare is 4€ ($4.60) each way.

BY BUS The bus station is at Praça 25 do Abril (© **26/862-28-75**). Four buses per day make the 4-hour trip from Lisbon. The one-way fare is 11€ ($12). Two buses daily make the 2-hour trip from Évora. The one-way fare is 8.50€ ($9.80). From Badajoz, there are frequent buses throughout the day. The ride lasts 20 minutes.

BY CAR From Estremoz (see section 2, "Estremoz"), continue east toward Spain along Route 4.

VISITOR INFORMATION

The **Elvas Tourist Office** is on Praça da República (© **26/862-22-36**). It's open Monday through Friday from 9am to 6pm, and Saturday and Sunday from 10am to 5pm.

EXPLORING THE TOWN In **Praça Dom Sancho II,** named in honor of the king who reconstructed the town, stands the **Sé** (cathedral). Under a cone-shape dome, it's a forbidding fortresslike building decorated with gargoyles, turrets, and a florid Manueline portal. The cathedral opens onto a black-and-white diamond square. It's open daily from 9am to 12:30pm and 2 to 5pm. A short walk up the hill to the right of the cathedral leads to **Largo de Santa Clara** ★, a small plaza that holds an odd Manueline pillory with four wrought-iron dragon heads.

On the south side of Largo de Santa Clara is the **Igreja de Nossa Senhora de Consolação** ★ (Church of Our Lady of Consolation), a 16th-century octagonal Renaissance building with a cupola lined in 17th-century *azulejos* (tiles). It's open Tuesday through Sunday from 9am to 12:30pm and 2 to 5pm.

The **castelo** (castle), Praça da República, built by the Moors and strengthened by Christian rulers in the 14th and 16th centuries, offers a panoramic view of the town, its fortifications, and the surrounding countryside. It's open daily from 9:30am to 1pm and 3 to 6pm. (It closes at 5:30pm Oct 10–Apr.)

SHOPPING The abundant folklore of this small town might whet your appetite for souvenirs. Take a stroll along the town's best shopping streets, **Rua de Alchemin** and **Rua de Olivença.** Rustic artifacts appear on all sides, allowing you to choose your favorites. If you want to target your destinations in advance, consider the handcrafts at **Alchemin,** Rua de Alchemin, or any of the merchandise at the town's leading clothier, **Rente,** Rua de Alchemin (✆ **26/862-92-73**).

WHERE TO STAY

MODERATE

Estalagem Quinta de Santo António ★★ *Finds* This once private Quinta, dating from 1668, now receives paying guests. This is one of the finest examples of Alentejo architecture in the region, and the property is enveloped by a beautiful garden. The interior was faithfully restored and decorated with antique furniture. The bedrooms are generally spacious and exceedingly comfortable, with well-maintained bathrooms with tubs. The on-site restaurant, A Quinta, is known locally for its superb cuisine of the Alentejo school. Activities on site or nearby include horseback riding, biking, and motorboat rides.

Carretera de Barbacena, Aptdo. 206, 7350-903 Elvas. ✆ **26/862-84-06.** Fax 26/862-50-50. http://inn-portugal.com/inns/estqtasant.html. 69€–100€ ($79–$115) double; 90€–133€ ($104–$153) suite. Rates include breakfast. AE, DC, MC, V. 6.5km (4 miles) NE of Elvas along Estrada de Portalegre. **Amenities:** Restaurant; bar; pool; babysitting; laundry service; dry cleaning; 1 room for those w/limited mobility. *In room:* A/C, TV, safe.

Pousada de Santa Luzia ★★ A major link in the government-inn circuit is the Pousada de Santa Luzia, a hacienda-style building just outside the city walls. It sits at the edge of a busy highway (Estrada N4), about a 5-minute walk east of the town center. Fully renovated in the '90s, with typical Alentejo hand-painted furniture, it was built in 1942 as a private hotel (which failed). The bone-white stucco villa faces the fortifications. The ground floor holds a living room, an L-shape dining salon, and a bar, all opening through thick arches onto a Moorish courtyard with a fountain, a lily pond, and orange trees.

There are some guest rooms on the upper floor, and you can also stay in the nearby annex, a villa with a two-story entrance hall and an ornate staircase. All rooms are comfortable and cozily furnished, with good beds. Each unit has a well-maintained bathroom equipped with a shower-tub combination. Because the hotel is small, getting a room without a reservation might be difficult.

Av. de Badajoz, 7350-097 Elvas. ✆ **26/863-74-70.** Fax 26/862-21-27. www.pousadas.pt. 25 units. 80€–130€ ($92–$150) double. Rates include breakfast. AE, DC, MC, V. Free parking. **Amenities:** Restaurant; bar; pool; tennis court; room service; laundry service; nonsmoking rooms. *In room:* A/C, TV, minibar, hair dryer.

INEXPENSIVE

Hotel Dom Luís This well-run hotel—the largest in town—offers the best amenities in Elvas. Rooms have modern furnishings; some, however, are showing wear and tear. All units are equipped with a tidy bathroom with a shower, tub, or both.

Av. de Badajoz-estrada N4, 7350-903 Elvas. ✆ **26/862-27-56.** Fax 26/862-07-33. 90 units. 49€–59€ ($56–$68) double. Rates include breakfast. AE, DC, MC, V. Free parking. **Amenities:** Restaurant; bar; limited room service; laundry service. *In room:* A/C, TV, minibar, hair dryer, safe.

WHERE TO DINE

Estalagem Don Quixote ★ *Finds* PORTUGUESE/FRENCH The most adventurous dining choice around Elvas lies about 2.5km (1½ miles) to the west. The isolated compound is the focus of many a culinary pilgrimage. The place is very busy on weekends, especially with Spaniards, who create a holiday feeling with lots of convivial chatter. You can order a drink in the leather-upholstered English-style bar near the entrance and then move on to the dining room, decorated in traditional Iberian style. Rows of fresh fish arranged on ice behind glass grace the entrance to the sprawling dining room. Specialties include shellfish rice, grilled sole, grilled swordfish, roast pork, beefsteak Alentejano, and at least five kinds of shellfish. The fare is interesting and skillfully prepared, although never scaling any gastronomic peaks. Service takes a nosedive when the place is full.

Estrada 4, Pedras Negras. ✆ **26/862-20-14.** Reservations recommended. Main courses 11€–27€ ($12–$31); tourist menu 15€ ($17). AE, DC, MC, V. Mon–Sat noon–4pm and 7pm–midnight, Sun noon–4pm.

ELVAS AFTER DARK

Don't expect the diversions and distractions of Lisbon—sleepy Elvas simply doesn't have them. Instead, consider a stroll through the town's historic core, looking for likable *tascas* (bars). Or, head less than 1km (about ¾ mile) west of town to the **Albergaria Jardim,** Estrada Nacionale 4 (✆ **26/862-10-50**). Local residents who come to drink and socialize fill the handsome pub. A generally lively place is the **Player Bar,** Barrio de Santa Onofre Alves (✆ **26/862-86-45**).

4 Évora ★★★

102km (63 miles) SW of Badajoz, Spain, 155km (96 miles) E of Lisbon

The capital of Alto Alentejo, Évora, a designated UNESCO World Heritage Site, is a historical curio. Considering its size and location, it's also something of an architectural phenomenon. Its builders freely adapted whatever styles they desired, from Mudejar to Manueline to Roman to rococo. Évora, once enclosed behind medieval walls, lives up to its reputation as a living museum. Sixteenth- and seventeenth-century houses, many with tile patios, fill nearly every street. Cobblestones, labyrinthine streets, arcades, squares with bubbling fountains, whitewashed houses, and a profuse display of Moorish-inspired arches characterize the town.

Many conquerors passed through Évora, and several left behind architectural remains. The Romans at the time of Julius Caesar knew the town as Liberalitas Julia. Its heyday was during the 16th-century reign of João III, when it became the Montmartre of Portugal; avant-garde artists, including the playwright Gil Vicente, congregated under the aegis of royalty.

Évora today is a sleepy provincial capital, perhaps rather self-consciously aware of its attractions. One local historian recommended to an American couple that they see at least 59 monuments. Rest assured that you could capture the essence of the town by seeing only a fraction of that. Évora is a popular day trip from Lisbon, but it's a long trek, which doesn't leave enough time to enjoy the town thoroughly.

ESSENTIALS

ARRIVING

BY TRAIN The train station (✆ **26/670-21-25** for information) lies less than 1km (¾ mile) from the center of town. Five trains per day arrive from Lisbon; the trip takes 3 hours and costs 8.05€ ($9.25) one-way. One train arrives from Faro, in the Algarve; the trip takes 6 hours and costs 11€ ($12) one-way. There are also four trains per day from Beja (see section 5). The trip takes 1½ hours, and the one-way fare is 5.80€ ($6.65).

BY BUS **Rodoviária Nacional,** Avenida Tulio Sbanca (✆ **26/676-94-10**), provides bus service for the area. Three buses a day arrive from Lisbon; the trip takes 1 hour and 45 minutes and costs 9.80€ ($11) one-way. Three daily buses make the 5-hour trip from Faro, in the Algarve. The cost is 12€ ($14) one-way. Seven buses a day connect Beja with Évora; the trip takes 1 hour and 15 minutes and costs 7.50€ ($8.65) one-way.

BY CAR From Beja (see section 5, below), continue north along Route 18.

VISITOR INFORMATION

The **Évora Tourist Information Office** is at Praça do Giraldo 71 (✆ **26/673-00-30**). It's open daily from 9am to 12:30pm and 2 to 5pm.

SPECIAL EVENTS

Évora's major festival is the **Feira de São João,** a folkloric and musical extravaganza. All the handcrafts of the area, including fine ceramics, are on display, and hundreds of people from the Alentejo region come into the city. The event, which takes place over the last 10 days of June, celebrates the arrival of summer. Food stalls sell regional specialties, and regional dances are presented. The tourist office (see "Visitor Information," above) will supply more details.

EXPLORING THE TOWN

Templo de Diana ★ The major monument in Évora is the Temple of Diana, directly in front of the government-owned pousada (see "Where to Stay," below). Dating from the 1st or 2nd century A.D., it's a light, graceful structure with 14 granite Corinthian columns topped by marble capitals. Although it is said to have been dedicated to the goddess, no one has actually proved it. The temple withstood the 1755 earthquake, and there's evidence that it was once used as a slaughterhouse. Walk through the garden for a view of the Roman aqueduct and the surrounding countryside.

Largo do Conde de Vila Flor. No phone. Free admission. Daily 24 hr.

Sé (Cathedral) ★★ The cathedral of Évora was built in the Roman-Gothic style between 1186 and 1204. The bulky structure was notably restored and redesigned over the centuries. Two square towers, both topped by cones, flank the stone facade; one is surrounded by satellite spires. The **interior** ★ consists of a nave and two aisles. The 18th-century main altar, of pink, black, and white marble, is the finest in town. At the sculptured work *The Lady of Mothers,* young women pray for fertility.

The museum houses treasures from the church, the most notable of which is a 13th-century Virgin carved out of ivory. It opens to reveal a collection of scenes from her life. A reliquary is studded with 1,426 precious stones, including sapphires, rubies, diamonds, and emeralds. The most valuable item is a piece of wood said to have come from the True Cross.

Largo Marquês de Mariak (Largo de Sé). ✆ **26/675-93-30.** Admission to Cathedral free; to museum 3€ ($3.45) adults, free for children under 12. June–Aug Tues–Sun 9am–5pm; Sept–May Tues–Sun 9am–noon and 2–5pm.

Igreja Real de São Francisco The Church of St. Francis contains a chapel that's probably unlike any you've seen: The chancel walls and central pillars of the ghoulish 16th-century *Capela dos Ossos* (Chapel of Bones) are lined with human skulls and other parts of skeletons. Legend has it that the bones came either from soldiers who died in a big battle or from plague victims. Over the door is a sign that addresses visitors' own mortality: OUR BONES THAT STAY HERE

ARE WAITING FOR YOURS! The church was built in the Gothic style with Manueline influences between 1460 and 1510.

Rua da República. ✆ **26/670-45-21.** Admission 1€ ($1.15). Daily 8:30am–1pm and 2:30–6pm.

Igreja de Nossa Senhora de Graça The Church of Our Lady of Grace is notable chiefly for its baroque facade, with huge classical nudes over the pillars. Above each group of lazing stone giants is a sphere with a flame—pieces of sculpture often compared to works by Michelangelo. The church was built in Évora's heyday, during the reign of João III. Columns and large stone rosettes flank the central window shaft, and ponderous neoclassic columns support the lower level. The church can be viewed only from the outside.

Largo da Graça. No phone.

Universidade de Évora You might want to visit the ancient University of Évora. In 1559, during the town's cultural flowering, the university was constructed and placed under the tutelage of the Jesuits. It flourished until the Jesuit-hating marquês de Pombal closed it in the 18th century. The compound wasn't used as a university again until 1975.

The double-tiered baroque structure surrounds a large quadrangle. Marble pillars support the arches, and brazilwood makes up the ceilings. Blue-and-white tiles line the inner courtyard. Other azulejo representations, depicting women, wild animals, angels, cherubs, and costumed men, contrast with the austere elegance of the classrooms and the elongated refectory.

Largo do Colégio. ✆ **26/674-08-00.** Free admission. Mon–Fri 8am–7pm (w/permission).

Igreja de São João Evangelista ★ The Gothic-Mudejar Church of St. John the Evangelist, facing the Temple of Diana and next door to the government-owned pousada, is connected to the palace built by the dukes of Cadaval. Although it's one of the undisputed gems of Évora, it's seemingly little visited. It deserves to be better known: It contains a collection of 18th-century tiles, and a guide will show you a macabre sight—an old cistern filled with neatly stacked bones removed from tombs. In the chapel's sacristy are some paintings, including a ghastly rendition of Africans slaughtering a Christian missionary. A curiosity is a painting of a pope that has moving eyes and moving feet. In addition, you can see part of the wall that once encircled Évora.

Largo do Conde de Vila Flor. ✆ **26/670-47-14.** Admission 3€ ($3.45). Tues–Sun 10am–noon and 2–6pm.

SHOPPING

Most of the interesting shops in Évora are on **Rua do 5 de Outubro,** which leads from a point near the cathedral to the perimeter of the historic town. A particularly well-stocked shop is **Baiginho,** Rua do 5 de Outubro 44 (✆ **26/670-91-09**). Beyond that, your best bet is wandering and window-shopping in the neighborhood around the cathedral.

WHERE TO STAY

EXPENSIVE

Pousada dos Lóios ★★★ One of the most splendid government-owned tourist inns in Portugal is the Pousada dos Lóios, now under UNESCO protection. It occupies the Lóios Monastery, built in 1485 on the site of the old Évora Castle, which was destroyed during a riot in 1384. A powerful noble, Don Rodrigo Afonso de Melo, founded the monastery and carried on his back two baskets of soil and the first stone for the foundation ceremony. João II, IV, and

V visited the monastery. Official Inquisition reports were kept in the chapter room, which features 16th-century doorways in Moorish-Portuguese style. After the 1755 earthquake, extensive work was done to repair and preserve the structure. Over the years it was used as a telegraph station, a primary school, an army barracks, and offices. The 1965 opening of the pousada made possible the architectural restoration of the monastery. Its position in the center of Évora, between the cathedral and the ghostlike Roman Temple of Diana, is unrivaled.

The white-and-gold salon (once a private chapel) boasts an ornate Pompeii-style decor and frescoes and is decorated with antique furnishings, hand-woven draperies, crystal chandeliers and sconces, and painted medallion portraits. All the guest rooms are furnished in traditional provincial style, with antique reproductions. Because the rooms used to be monks' cells, they are rather small. Make sure you duck at the doorway, and ask for one of the tranquil interior rooms. All units have well-maintained bathrooms with shower-tub combinations.

Largo Conde de Vila Flor, 7000-804 Évora. ✆ **26/673-00-70.** Fax 26/670-72-48. 32 units. 149€–195€ ($171–$224) double; 204€–293€ ($235–$337) suite. Rates include breakfast. AE, DC, MC, V. Free parking. **Amenities:** Restaurant; bar; pool; 24-hr. room service; laundry service; nonsmoking rooms. *In room:* A/C, TV, dataport, minibar, hair dryer, safe.

MODERATE

Hotel da Cartuxa ★ Next to a 14th-century city wall, this modern hotel lies between the Alconchel and Raimundo gates in the most ancient part of Évora. Although the two-story hotel is contemporary and up-to-date in all ways, it manages to evoke a warm, cozy, regional ambience. The inn has furnished its public rooms with antiques gathered from the province. The beautifully furnished bedrooms are well maintained, with neatly kept tiled bathrooms, mainly with tubs. The on-site restaurant serves a notable provincial cuisine. Guests can enjoy jumping in the hotel pool on a hot day or taking an evening walk in the garden.

Travessa da Palmeira 4, 7000-546 Elvora. ✆ **26/673-93-00.** Fax 26/673-93-05. www.hoteldacartuxa.com. 91 units. 115€–150€ ($132–$173) double; from 190€–210€ ($219–$242) suite. AE, DC, MC, V. **Amenities:** Restaurant; bar; pool; limited room service; babysitting; laundry service; dry cleaning. *In room:* A/C, TV, high-speed Internet service, minibar, hair dryer, safe.

INEXPENSIVE

Albergaria do Calvário This is a former olive-processing plant that was renovated and turned into this well-run little hotel in 1998. It's about a 5-minute walk from the historic center. Next to the Convento do Calvário (a convent that's closed to the public), the hotel is attractively furnished, with good beds and tidy appointments, including new private bathrooms equipped with shower-tub combinations. Neoclassic and rustic reproductions of antiques are used extensively. Breakfast is served in your room or on the Esplanade Terraces.

Traversa dos Lagares 3, 7000-565 Évora. ✆ **26/674-59-30.** Fax 26/674-59-39. www.softline.pt/calvario. 23 units. 90€–120€ ($104–$138) double; 110€–120€ ($127–$138) suite. Rates include breakfast. AE, DC, MC, V. Free parking. **Amenities:** Breakfast room; bar; TV lounge; limited room service; laundry service; 1 room for those w/limited mobility. *In room:* A/C, TV, minibar, hair dryer, safe.

Albergaria Solar de Monfalm ★ *Finds* This is a delightful guesthouse with a touch of grandeur: A stone staircase leads up to a plant-lined entrance decorated with tiles. The hosts, the Serrabulhos, have improved the building by making the small to midsize guest rooms more comfortable while keeping the original antique atmosphere. The rooms, all in the main building, are well maintained, traditional, and quite pleasant. All come with neatly kept bathrooms, most of which contain shower-tub combinations. You can sit on the terrace nursing a drink and peering through the cloisterlike mullioned veranda.

Largo da Misericórdia 1, 7000-646 Évora. © **26/675-00-00.** Fax 26/674-23-67. www.monfalimtur.pt. 26 units. 65€–80€ ($75–$92) double. Rates include breakfast. AE, MC, V. Parking 3€ ($3.45). **Amenities:** Breakfast room; cafe; 1 room for those w/limited mobility. *In room:* A/C, TV, minibar, hair dryer, safe.

Albergaria Vitória In a somewhat inconvenient location near the beltway surrounding the old city, this modern concrete-walled hotel juts above a dusty neighborhood of villas. It's usually reached by taxi. The Albergaria sits on the southeastern edge of the city, less than 1km (about ¾ mile) from the cathedral, but it can be a handy address in summer when all the central hotels are full. Built in 1985, it contains motel-like bedrooms, with balconies and good beds and well-maintained bathrooms with shower-tub combinations.

Rua Diana de Lis 5, 7000 Évora. © **26/670-71-74.** Fax 26/670-09-74. albergariavitoria@ip.pt. 48 units. 60€–71€ ($69–$82) double; from 82€–98€ ($94–$113) suite. Rates include breakfast. AE, DC, MC, V. Limited free parking on street. **Amenities:** Restaurant; bar; limited room service; laundry service; 1 room for those w/limited mobility. *In room:* A/C, TV, hair dryer.

Riviera This small inn sits beside the cobblestones of one of the most charming streets in town, about two blocks downhill from the cathedral. Designed as a private villa, it retains many handcrafted details from the original building, including stone window frames, ornate iron balustrades, and the blue-and-yellow tiles of its foyer. Its small guest rooms are quite comfortable, with good beds, but are not very tastefully decorated. Each unit is equipped with a small bathroom with a private shower.

Rua do 5 de Outubro 49, 7000 Évora. © **26/673-72-10.** Fax 26/673-72-12. 21 units. 58€–68€ ($66–$78) double. Rates include breakfast. AE, DC, MC, V. Limited free parking on street. **Amenities:** Breakfast room. *In room:* A/C, TV, minibar, safe.

WHERE TO DINE

Cozinha de São Humberto ★ ALENTEJAN Évora's most atmospheric restaurant is hidden away on a narrow side street leading down from Praça do Giraldo. Rustic decorations include old pots, blunderbusses, standing lamps, a grandfather clock, and kettles hanging from the ceiling. Seating is in rush chairs or on divans. In warm weather, you can enjoy gazpacho Alentejana, followed by fried fish with tomato and garlic, or pork Évora style (a meal in itself), topped off by regional cheese. The chefs elevate local dishes to another level with the use of seasonings and market-fresh ingredients. A bottle of Borba wine is a good complement to most meals.

Rua da Moeda 39. © **26/670-42-51.** Reservations required. Main courses 11€–16€ ($12–$18). AE, DC, MC, V. Fri–Wed noon–4pm and 7–10pm.

Fialho ★ ALENTEJAN Fialho, which has flourished on this site since the end of World War II, is Évora's most traditional restaurant. Its entrance is unprepossessing, but the interior is warmly decorated in the style of a Portuguese tavern. Although Évora is inland, Fialho serves good shellfish dishes, including *sopa de Cacão* (regional shark soup), along with such fare as succulent pork with baby clams in savory sauce, and partridge stew. In season, a whole partridge might be available. The air-conditioned restaurant seats 90. The staff is particularly proud of the lavish array of local wines, one of the most comprehensive cellars in the district.

Travessa do Mascarenhas 14. © **26/670-30-79.** Reservations recommended. Main courses 12€–17€ ($14–$20). AE, DC, MC, V. Tues–Sun 12:30–4pm and 7pm–midnight. Closed Sept 1–21 and Dec 24–31.

Guião ★ REGIONAL PORTUGUESE Guião is a regional tavern that's widely considered one of Évora's top four restaurants. It lies just off the main square, Praça do Giraldo. It's charmingly decorated with antique blue-and-white tiles. The family-run tavern offers local wines and Portuguese specialties. The hearty, robust meals are filling, if not exceptional. A typical bill of fare includes grilled squid, grilled fish, swordfish steak, and clams with pork Alentejo style. The kitchen also prepares partridge in season.

Rua da República 81. ✆ **26/670-30-71.** Main courses 7.50€–12€ ($8.65–$13); tourist menu 15€ ($17). AE, DC, MC, V. Tues–Sat noon–3:30pm and 7–10:30pm; Sun noon–3:30pm. Closed 2 weeks in July.

ÉVORA AFTER DARK

The town's historic core contains a few sleepy-looking bars, any of which might strike your fancy as part of an after-dark pub-crawl. The bar of the **Pousada dos Lóios,** Largo Conde de Vila Flor (✆ **26/673-00-70**), is a dignified option for a drink in a historic setting.

If you want to mingle and dance with the city's high-energy Lisbon wannabes, head for **Praxis Discoteca,** Rua Valdevinos, 21A (no phone), which attracts both young locals and visitors to its precincts off Rua 5 de Outurbro. It imposes a 10€ ($12) cover, but entrance includes your first two beers. It's open Monday through Saturday from 10pm to 6am. The most frequented bar in town is **Jonas,** Rua Serpa Pintas 67 (✆ **26/482-16-47**), down off Praça Fraldo. On two levels, this bar attracts mostly a young crowd in their 20s and 30s. It doesn't really get going until after midnight. The drink of choice is a Brazilian *calprinnhas,* costing 2.50€ ($2.90). It's open Monday through Saturday 10:30pm to 3am.

5 Beja ★

187km (116 miles) SE of Lisbon, 76km (47 miles) S of Évora

Julius Caesar founded Beja, which was once known as Pax Julia. The capital of Baixo Alentejo, the town rises like a pyramid above the surrounding fields of swaying wheat.

Beja's fame rests on what many authorities believe to be a literary hoax. In the mid–17th century, in the Convent of the Conceição, a young nun named Soror Mariana Alcoforado is said to have fallen in love with a French military officer. The officer, identified as the chevalier de Chamilly, reputedly seduced her and then left Beja forever.

The girl's outpouring of grief and anguish found literary release in *Lettres Portugaises,* published in Paris in 1669. The letters created a sensation and endured as an epistolary classic. In 1926, F. C. Green wrote *Who Was the Author of the Lettres Portugaises?,* claiming that their true writer was the comte de Guilleragues. However, a modern Portuguese study has put forth evidence that the *Lettres Portugaises* were, in fact, written by a nun named Sister Alcoforado.

ESSENTIALS

ARRIVING

BY TRAIN Three trains a day make the 3-hour journey from Lisbon. The one-way fare is 8.55€ ($9.85). Four daily trains arrive from Évora. The journey takes an hour and costs 5.80€ ($6.65) one-way. From the Algarve (see chapter 8), four trains a day leave from Faro. The trip takes 3½ hours and costs 8€ ($9.20) one-way. For information, call ✆ **28/432-61-35.**

BY BUS Eight *expressos* (express buses) per day make the 3-hour run between Lisbon and Beja; the one-way fare is 9.80€ ($11). Four buses a day come from Évora. The 1-hour trip costs 7.50€ ($8.65) one-way. Four buses a day run from Faro; it's a 3½-hour trip and costs 10€ ($12) one-way. For schedules, call ✆ **28/431-36-20.**

BY CAR From Albufeira in the Algarve, take IP-1 north to the junction with Route 263, which heads northeast into Beja.

VISITOR INFORMATION

The **Beja Tourist Office** is at Rua Capitão João Francisco de Sousa 25 (✆ **28/431-19-13**). The office is open Saturday from 10am to 1pm and 2 to 6pm.

EXPLORING THE TOWN

Museu Rainha Dona Leonor ★ The Queen Leonor Museum (founded in 1927–28) occupies three buildings on a broad plaza in the center of Beja: the Convento da Conceição and the Churches of Santo Amaro and São Sebastião. The main building was a convent founded in 1459 by the parents of the Portuguese king Manuel I. Favored by royal protection, it became one of the richest and most important convents of that time. The Convento da Conceição is famous throughout the world because of a single nun, Mariana Alcoforado. She is said to have written the *Lettres Portugaises,* love letters to the French chevalier de Chamilly, at the convent in the 17th century.

Some of the building's most important features are the surviving pieces of the ancient convent. They are the church, with its baroque decoration, and the cloister and chapter house, which present one of the area's most impressive collections of 15th- to 18th-century Spanish and Portuguese tiles. Also on display are statuary and silverwork belonging to the convent and a good collection of Spanish, Portuguese, and Dutch paintings from the 15th to 18th centuries. The *Escudela de Pero de Faria,* a piece of 1541 Chinese porcelain, is especially unique. The first-floor permanent archaeological exhibition features artifacts from the Beja region.

The Santo Amaro church is one of the oldest churches of Beja and rests on what could be an early Christian foundation. It houses the most important visigothic collection (from Beja and its surroundings) in Portugal.

The Church of São Sebastião is a small temple of no great architectural interest. It houses part of the museum's collection of architectural goods from Roman to modern times. It's not open to the public; access is by special request.

Largo da Conceição. ✆ **28/432-33-51.** Admission 2€ ($2.30), 1€ ($1.15) students, free for children under 15. Tues–Sun 9:30am–12:30pm and 2–5:15pm.

Castelo de Beja Beja castle, which King Dinis built in the early 14th century on the ruins of a Roman fortress, crowns the town. Although some of its turreted walls have been restored, the defensive towers—save for a long marble keep—are gone. Traditionally the final stronghold in the castle's fortifications, the old keep appears to be battling the weather and gold fungi. The walls are overgrown with ivy, the final encroachment on its former glory. From the keep you can enjoy a view of the provincial capital and the outlying fields.

Largo Dr. Lima Faleiro ✆ **28/431-18-00.** Admission 1.25€ ($1.45), .65€ (75¢) children under 18. June–Sept Tues–Sun 10am–1pm and 2–6pm; Oct–May Tues–Sun 9am–noon and 1–4pm. From the center, walk along Rua de Aresta Branco, following signposts.

SHOPPING

Beja is known for handcrafts, including charming hammered copper, in the form of serving dishes and home accessories, as well as the many forms of pottery and wood carvings you might see in other parts of Ribatejo and Alentejo. **Rua Capital João Francisco de Sousa,** in the town center, is lined with all manner of shops. An interesting shop specializing in handcrafts from near Beja and elsewhere in Portugal is **Arabe,** Artes Infiel, Plaça da Republica (✆ **28/432-95-45**).

WHERE TO STAY

MODERATE

Pousada do Convento de São Francisco ★★★ In the historic heart of a town that sorely needed another hotel, this is a government-owned conversion of a 13th-century Franciscan monastery. São Francisco opened for business in 1994. From the end of World War II until the 1980s, it had functioned as an army barracks and training camp. Government architects attempted to retain some of the building's severe medieval lines with limited success because of serious deterioration. Rooms are generally spacious and attractively furnished, with good beds and excellent bathrooms with shower-tub combinations. There's a garden on the premises with a modest but interesting chapel.

Largo do Nuno Álvarez Pereira, 7801-901 Beja. ✆ **28/431-35-80.** Fax 28/432-91-43. 35 units. 112€–173€ ($129–$199) double; 135€–287€ ($155–$330) suite. Rates include breakfast. AE, DC, MC, V. Free parking. **Amenities:** Restaurant; bar; pool; tennis courts; 24-hr. room service; laundry service; nonsmoking rooms; rooms for those w/limited mobility. *In room:* A/C, TV, dataport, minibar, hair dryer.

INEXPENSIVE

Hotel Melius *Value* This is the town's newest and best-recommended independent hotel, although not as good as the pousada (see above). Opened in 1995, it lies on the southern outskirts of town beside the main road to the Algarve. The government-rated three-star, four-story hotel provides services that had been sorely lacking. The midsize guest rooms, though bland, are comfortable and well maintained, with good beds. All units are also equipped with tidily kept bathrooms containing shower-tub combinations.

Av. Fialhu Almeida, 7800-395 Beja. ✆ **28/432-18-22.** Fax 28/432-18-25. 60 units. 63€ ($72) double; 80€ ($92) suite. Rates include breakfast. AE, DC, MC, V. Parking 1.50€ ($1.75). **Amenities:** Breakfast room; bar; gym; sauna; limited room service; laundry service; rooms for those w/limited mobility. *In room:* A/C, TV, hair dryer.

Residencial Cristina This is the largest hostelry in town and the third-best place to stay (after the Melius and the pousada). It's a five-story building on a main shopping street. The helpful management rents small, simply furnished guest rooms that, although recently restored, remain rather austere. All units have well-maintained bathrooms with shower-tub combinations. Everything is immaculately kept. Breakfast is the only meal served.

Rua de Mértola 71, 7800 Beja. ✆ **28/432-30-35.** Fax 28/432-04-60. 32 units. 52€ ($60) double; 62€ ($71) suite. AE, DC, MC, V. **Amenities:** Breakfast room; bar; laundry service. *In room:* A/C, TV.

Residêncial Santa Bárbara *Value* This is a little oasis in a town that has few suitable accommodations. The hotel is a shiny-clean, well-kept bandbox building. It's small in scale, with only a whisper of a reception lobby and elevator. There are two street-level lounges. The smallish guest rooms are compact but adequate, with good beds and neatly kept bathrooms that mostly contain shower-tub combinations.

Rua de Mértola 56, 7800 Beja. ✆ **28/431-22-80.** Fax 28/431-22-89. www.residencialsantabarbara.pa.net.pt. 26 units. 40€–45€ ($46–$52) double. Rates include breakfast. AE, MC, V. **Amenities:** Breakfast room; bar; limited room service; laundry service; nonsmoking rooms. *In room:* A/C, TV.

WHERE TO DINE

Esquina PORTUGUESE Esquina serves well-seasoned food based on old-fashioned culinary traditions. The restaurant lies at the edge of town, a 5-minute walk from the tourist office. The setting isn't historic, but the service is warm. The fare includes soups, roast pork with clams (the chef's specialty), grilled cuts of beef, and chicken served with vegetables and savory broth. Dessert might be flan or fruit tart.

Rua Infante do Henríque 26. ✆ **28/438-92-38.** Main courses 6€–9.50€ ($6.90–$11); tourist menu 13€ ($14). AE, MC, V. Mon–Sat noon–3pm and 7–10pm.

Luís da Rocha REGIONAL PORTUGUESE At Luís da Rocha, on the same street as the tourist office, you can sit downstairs in the cafe or go upstairs to a spacious neon-lit dining room. Although the whole town seems to congregate for coffee and pastries here, many visitors find Esquina (see above) more appealing. You might begin with one of the cream soups, prepared fresh daily, and then follow with boiled or fried fish, or pork with clams Alentejo style. In the words of one staff member, "It's the cooking of the people here—we don't get fancy for tourists."

Rua Capitão João Francisco de Sousa 63. ✆ **28/432-31-79.** Main courses 5.50€–12€ ($6.35–$14). AE, DC, MC, V. Daily noon–3:30pm and 7–11pm. Closed Sun May–Sept.

Os Infantes ALENTEJANA With its antique decor, this long-established local favorite is moving into its third decade of pleasing the palates of local foodies. In the heart of Beja, it invites with its immaculate white tablecloths, its wooden chairs, its whitewashed stucco walls so typical of Alentejo, and its domed ceiling built of brick. Recipes are time-tested and old favorites. The fish soup in Alentejana is the best in town, and the cooks are good with almost anything involving *bacalhau* (dried codfish). They also do beefsteak in winning ways and are known for their well-flavored pork dishes; the meat comes from pigs who eat a diet of acorns, giving the meat a rich, nutty taste. You wash it all down with the house wines.

Rua dos Infantes 14. ✆ **28/433-27-89.** Reservations recommended. Main courses 13€–25€ ($15–$29). AE, DC, MC, V. Thurs–Tues noon–3pm and 7:30–10:30pm. Closed 1st week of Jan.

BEJA AFTER DARK

The town has a worthy roster of pubs and bars. Leading destinations include **Barrote,** Rua Genente Valadim (✆ **28/432-09-79**), a laid-back pub. Also appealing is the **Cockpit,** Rua Aferidores (no phone). It attracts music fans, mostly under 35, who congregate within earshot of live or recorded music, including punk rock.

6 Vila Nova de Milfontes

32km (20 miles) SW of Santiago do Cacém, 186km (115 miles) S of Lisbon

A good stopover in lower Alentejo as you're heading south to the Algarve is the little beach town of Vila Nova de Milfontes. At the wide mouth of the Mira River, the sleepy resort is attracting more visitors because of the soft white-sand beaches that line both sides of the river. There are no other attractions and nothing to do here but relax, or perhaps search for antiques.

The castle that once protected the area from Moroccan and Algerian pirates has been restored and is now an inn. After a day on the beach, you can head south to even more beaches.

ESSENTIALS

ARRIVING

BY TRAIN There is no train service from Lisbon.

BY BUS Five express buses a day make the trip from Lisbon. It takes 4 hours and costs 11€ ($13) one-way. For schedules, call ✆ **808/208-208** in Lisbon.

BY CAR Chances are, you'll drive south from Setúbal (see chapter 6). Continue along N261 in the direction of Sines, and then follow N120-1 until you see the cut-off heading west in Vila Nova de Milfontes.

VISITOR INFORMATION

The **tourist office** is on Rua António Mantas (✆ **28/399-65-99**). It's open daily from 10am to 1pm and 2 to 6pm.

WHERE TO STAY

EXPENSIVE

Castelo de Milefontes ★ *Finds* In a castle dating from the 17th century is the area's most charming inn, which was renovated in 1998. High on a hill "guarding" the resort, the castle has panoramic views of the sea. It's about a 3-minute walk from the center. The well-appointed midsize to spacious rooms contain old-fashioned furniture or antiques. The beds are excellent, and the bathrooms are well maintained and contain showers. The cuisine is well prepared, with an emphasis on fresh seafood. This is one of the best stopovers on the drive from Lisbon to the Algarve.

Castelo de Milefontes, 7645-234 Vila Nova de Milfontes. ✆ **28/399-82-31.** Fax 28/399-71-22. 7 units. 155€–166€ ($178–$191) double. Rates include breakfast and dinner. No credit cards. Free parking. **Amenities:** Restaurant; bar; laundry service. *In room:* Hair dryer.

INEXPENSIVE

Casa dos Arcos In the center of the resort, a 5-minute walk from the beach, this is a simple pension that was renovated in 1996. The small to midsize guest rooms were modernized with neatly kept bathrooms that, for the most part, contain shower-tub combinations. There is no grandeur or pretense here—the place provides an adequate stopover for the night, nothing more.

Rua do Cais, 7645-236 Vila Nova de Milfontes. ✆ **28/399-62-64.** Fax 28/399-71-56. 25 units. 35€–55€ ($40–$63) double. Rates include breakfast. No credit cards. Free parking. **Amenities:** Breakfast room. *In room:* A/C, TV.

WHERE TO DINE

Restaurante O Pescador ★ PORTUGUESE O Moura, as it's known locally, is the best *marisqueira* (seafood restaurant) at the resort. Even the town residents, who certainly know their fish, swear by it. Monkfish with rice is a savory offering, as is the kettle of *caldeirada,* a succulent seafood stew. The place is air-conditioned, and the welcome is friendly. The owners, Mr. and Mrs. Moura, used to be fishmongers, and they know their product well. Don't expect much in the way of decor—people come here just for the fish.

Largo da Praça 18. ✆ **28/399-63-38.** Reservations recommended. Main courses 5€–22€ ($5.75–$25). AE, MC, V. Daily 9am–midnight. Closed Oct 15–31.

10

Coimbra & the Beiras

Encompassing the university city of Coimbra, the three provinces of the Beiras are the quintessence of Portugal. *Beira* is Portuguese for "edge" or "border"; the provinces are Beira Litoral (coastal), Beira Baixa (low), and Beira Alta (high). The region embraces the Serra de Estrêla, Portugal's highest mountains—a haven for skiers in winter and a cool retreat in summer. The granite soil produced by the great mountain ranges blankets the rocky slopes of the Dão and Mondego river valleys and is responsible for producing the region's wine, ruby-red or lemon-yellow Dão.

The famed resort of **Figueira da Foz** draws the most beach devotees and is overcrowded in summer. However, you can take your pick of other beaches, from **Praia de Leirosa** in the south all the way to the northern tip at **Praia de Espinho.** Unlike those in the Algarve, the beaches along the Atlantic coast have powerful surf and potentially dangerous undertows, plus much cooler water. Check local conditions before going into the water. A yellow or red flag indicates that the water isn't safe for swimming (sometimes because of pollution).

Anglers from all over the world fly in to fish the waters in the **Serra de Estrêla National Park** and the Vouga River. More casual fishing is done along the Beira Litoral beach strip, with its many rocky outcroppings. Bream, sole, and sea bass are the major catches. Ocean fishing doesn't require a permit, but fishing in freshwater streams and rivers does. Regional tourist offices will give you information about permits.

1 Leiria

32km (20 miles) N of Alcobaça, 129km (80 miles) N of Lisbon

On the road to Coimbra, Leiria rests on the banks of the Liz and spreads over the surrounding hills. Though the modern-day town is industrial, it's still an inviting stop, with its hilltop castle, old quarter, and cathedral. Leiria is also the center of an area rich in handcrafts, like hand-blown glassware. Its folklore is comparable to that of neighboring Ribatejo. This city of 105,000 is an important transportation hub and a convenient point for exploring Nazaré or Fátima (see chapter 7) or the Atlantic coast beaches.

ESSENTIALS

ARRIVING

BY TRAIN Leiria is 3½ hours from Lisbon. At least six trains a day make the journey; a one-way ticket is 7.50€ ($8.65). For train information and schedules, call ✆ **24/488-20-27.**

BY BUS Eight express buses from Lisbon make the 1-hour run to Leiria. A one-way ticket costs 7.80€ ($8.95). You can also take 1 of 10 daily buses from

Coimbra (see section 3 in this chapter); the 1-hour trip costs 7€ ($8.05) one-way. For information and schedules, call ✆ **808/200-370.**

BY CAR Head north from Lisbon on the express highway A1.

VISITOR INFORMATION

The **Leiria Tourist Office** is at Jardim Luís de Camões (✆ **24/482-37-73**). The office is open Monday through Friday from 9am to 12:30pm and 2 to 5:30pm.

WHAT TO SEE & DO IN LEIRIA

EXPLORING THE TOWN From any point in town, you can see the great **Castelo de Leiria** ★ (✆ **24/481-39-82**), once occupied by Dinis, the poet-king, and his wife, known as St. Isabella. The imposing castle has been extensively restored. The castle church, like the palace, is Gothic. From an arched balcony there's a great **view** ★ of the city and its surroundings. The Moors had a stronghold on this hill while they were taking possession of the major part of the Iberian peninsula. Portugal's first king, Afonso Henríques, took the fortress in the 12th century and twice recovered it after the Moors had retaken it.

Admission to the fortress is 1.40€ ($1.60); the museum admission is 2.70€ ($3.10). It's open daily April to October from 9am to 6:30pm, and November to March from 9am to 5pm. For more information, ask at the tourist office (see above). You can drive right to the castle's front door. On the way, you might visit the **Igreja de São Pedro,** Largo de São Pedro, which dates from the 12th century.

Around Leiria is one of the oldest state forests in the world. In about 1300, Dinis began the systematic planting of the **Pinhal do Rei,** with trees brought from the Landes area in France. He hoped to curb the spread of sand dunes, which ocean gusts were extending deep into the heartland. The forest, still maintained today, provided timber used to build the caravels to explore the Sea of Darkness.

OUTDOOR ACTIVITIES If you'd like to combine sightseeing with some beach life, head to **São Pedro de Moel,** 23km (14 miles) west of Leiria and 135km (84 miles) north of Lisbon. Take N242 west of Leiria to the glass-manufacturing center of Marinha Grande, and then take N242 the rest of the way (9km/5½ miles) to the ocean. São Pedro de Moel, perched on a cliff above the Atlantic, is known for its bracing ocean breezes. New villas have sprung up, yet the old quarter retains its cobblestone streets. The white-sand beaches run up to the village's gray-walled ramparts, and the scattered rocks offshore create controlled conditions, rolling breakers, and rippling surf. On a palisade above the beach at the residential edge of the village is a good hotel, the **Mar e Sol,** Avenida da Liberdade 1, 2430-501 Marinha Grande (✆ **24/459-00-00;** fax 24/459-00-19). A double room is 50€ to 70€ ($58–$81), including breakfast.

SHOPPING For such a small town, Leiria has a large number of shopping centers, called ***centros comerciales.*** We usually prefer to wander the streets of the historic core, looking for bargains and unusual handcrafts on **praça Rodrigues Lobo** and the many narrow medieval streets radiating from it.

WHERE TO STAY

MODERATE

Hotel Eurosol e Eurosol Jardim ★ This is the best hotel in town; two contemporary midrise towers compete to dominate the skyline, with the stone castle

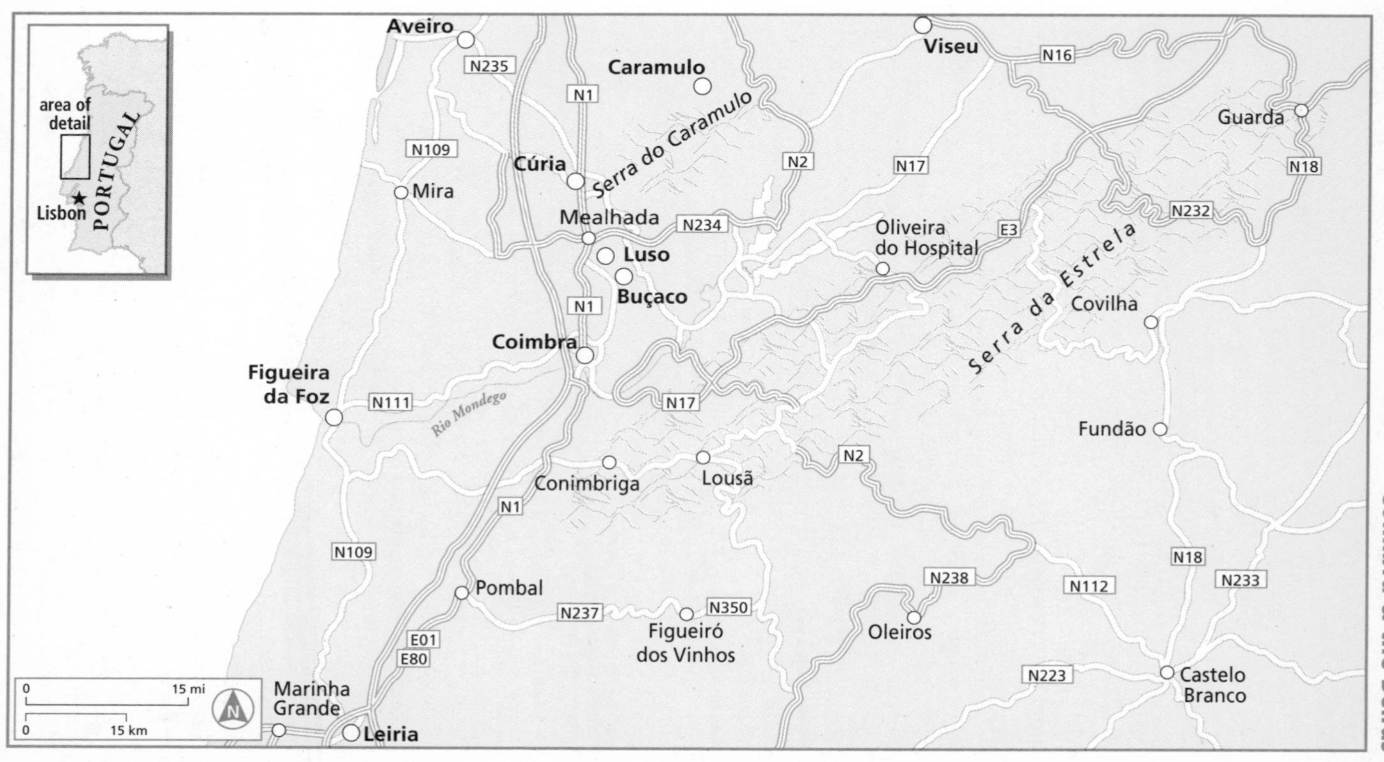
Aveiro
Caramulo
Viseu
Guarda
Serra do Caramulo
Cúria
Mira
Mealhada
Luso
Buçaco
Oliveira do Hospital
Serra da Estrela
Covilha
Coimbra
Figueira da Foz
Rio Mondego
Fundão
Conimbriga
Lousã
Pombal
Figueiró dos Vinhos
Oleiros
Castelo Branco
Marinha Grande
Leiria
N235
N1
N109
N2
N17
N16
N18
N234
N232
E3
N111
N2
N1
N109
N238
N112
N233
N237
N350
E01
E80
N223
area of detail
Lisbon
PORTUGAL
0
15 mi
15 km

crowning the opposite hill. The midsize rooms, well liked by business travelers, are equivalent to those in any first-class hotel in the north. They're all smart yet simple, with views, built-in headboards, and wood-paneled wardrobe walls. All units have neatly kept bathrooms with shower-tub combinations.

The hotel is the social hub of Leiria, attracting patrons to its rooftop lounge bar and dining room.

Rua Dom José Alves Correia da Silva, 2414-010 Leiria. ✆ **24/484-98-49.** Fax 24/484-98-40. www.eurosol.pt. 134 units. 75€ ($86) double; 98€–120€ ($113–$138) suite. AE, DC, MC, V. Free parking. **Amenities:** Restaurant; 2 bars; pool; health club; sauna; limited room service; laundry service; nonsmoking rooms. *In room:* A/C, TV, minibar, safe.

INEXPENSIVE

Hotel São Francisco This affordable inn sits on the top floor of a nine-story building on the north side of town, a short walk from the river. Some of the well-maintained but small rooms offer panoramic views of Leiria. All have patterned wallpaper, functional leatherette furniture, and well-kept bathrooms with shower-tub combinations. Breakfast is the only meal served.

Rua de São Francisco 26, 2430 Leiria. ✆ **24/482-31-10.** Fax 24/481-26-77. 18 units. 40€ ($46) double. Rates include breakfast. AE, DC, MC, V. Limited free parking on street. **Amenities:** Breakfast room. *In room:* A/C, TV, minibar, hair dryer.

Hotel São Luís *Value* This is the best budget hotel in Leiria. Ranked two stars by the government, it's spotless, and some of the rooms are very spacious. Units are equipped with well-maintained bathrooms with shower-tub combinations. You don't get a lot of frills, but you do get comfort and convenience at a good price. The hotel serves a good breakfast (the only meal available).

Rua Henríque Sommer, 2410-089 Leiria. ✆ **24/484-83-70.** Fax 24/484-83-79. 48 units. 45€ ($52) double; 62€ ($71) suite. Rates include breakfast. AE, DC, MC, V. Limited free parking on street. **Amenities:** Breakfast room; bar. *In room:* A/C, TV.

WHERE TO DINE

O Casarão PORTUGUESE The discerning palates of Leiria drive 5km (3 miles) south of the town to the village of Azoia, located at the signposted turnoff to the port of Nazare. Chef José Rodrigues prepares some of the finest regional fare in the area. Over the years, Rodrigues has gathered some once-secret and ancient recipes from monasteries in the region. Adapting them to modern standards, he prepares an unusual repertoire of dishes, including such specialties as *bolo pinão,* a cake made of ground pine nuts. Of course, he's also an expert at more common dishes and offers a wide selection of fish, depending on the catch of the day. Two local favorites are codfish cooked with potatoes and rice studded with bites of seafood. We recently enjoyed an excellent sole with tiny roasted potatoes. Surrounded by gardens, the dining room is in a large rustic home decorated with regional artifacts in a style typical of the region.

Cruzamiento de Azoia. ✆ **24/487-10-80.** Reservations recommended. Main courses 10€–16€ ($12–$18). AE, DC, MC, V. Tues–Sun noon–3pm and 7–10:30pm. Closed 1 week in July.

Reis PORTUGUESE/SEAFOOD In spite of its simplicity, this is the best independent restaurant in Leiria. Its faithful devotees like its basic but good food and reasonable prices. The chef specializes in grills, along with such regional fare as hearty soups, excellent fresh fish, and well-seasoned meats. Portions are large. In winter, a fireplace makes the Reis more inviting.

Rua Wenceslau de Morais 17. ✆ **24/482-28-34.** Main courses 5.50€–8.75€ ($6.35–$10). AE, DC, MC, V. Mon–Sat noon–3pm and 7–10pm.

LEIRIA AFTER DARK

Despite its modest size, Leiria has plenty of nightlife, both high energy and laid back. We usually begin with a promenade along **Largo Cândido dos Reis,** which is lined with small *tascas* (taverns). If you're looking for something more substantial, try the well-upholstered **Eurosol Bar,** in the Hotel Eurosol, Rua Dom José Alves Correia da Silva (© **24/484-98-49**). In a setting lined with unusual art, you can drink or flirt (or both) to your heart's content. Finally, look for one of the most diverse crowds in town at the **Yellow Bar,** Rua João Pereira 103 (© **24/482-70-82**).

2 Figueira da Foz ★

129km (80 miles) S of Porto, 201km (125 miles) N of Lisbon, 40km (25 miles) W of Coimbra

North of Cascais and Estoril, at the mouth of the Mondego River, Figueira da Foz is the best-known and oldest resort on Iberia's Atlantic coast. Its name means "Fig Tree at the Mouth of the River," but how it got that name is long forgotten. Aside from its sunny climate, the resort's most outstanding feature is the golden-sand beach that stretches for more than 3km (2 miles).

ESSENTIALS

ARRIVING

BY TRAIN Trains arrive at Largo da Estação (© **23/342-83-16**), near the bridge. Thirteen trains per day arrive from Coimbra (see below). The cost of the 1-hour trip is 1.55€ ($1.80) one-way. Twelve trains per day make the 3-hour trip from Lisbon. A one-way ticket costs 9.50€ ($11).

BY BUS The bus station is the **Terminal Rodoviária,** Rua Erois do Ultramar (© **23/342-30-95**). Three buses a day arrive from Lisbon; the trip takes 3 hours and costs 9.80€ ($11) one-way.

BY CAR From Leiria (see above), continue north along Route 109.

VISITOR INFORMATION

The **Figueira da Foz Tourist Office** is on Avenida do 25 de Abril (© **23/340-28-20**) and is open daily from 9am to 8pm. In summer, it's open until midnight.

WHAT TO SEE & DO IN FIGUEIRA DA FOZ

EXPLORING THE TOWN Most visitors don't come to Figueira to look at museums, but the **Casa do Paço** ★, Largo Prof. Vitar Guerra 4 (no phone), is exceptional. It contains one of the world's greatest collections of Delft tiles, numbering almost 7,000; most depict warriors with gaudy plumage. The *casa* was once the palace of Conde Bispo de Coimbra, Dom João de Melo, who came here in the 19th century when royalty frequented Figueira. It's at the head office of the Associação Comerciale e Industriale, a minute's walk from the main esplanade that runs along the beach. The museum is open Monday through Friday from 9:30am to 12:30pm and 2 to 5pm. Admission is free.

The casino (see below) owns one of the sightseeing oddities of the resort, **Palácio Sotto Mayor,** Rua Joaquim Sotto Mayor (© **23/340-84-00**), which was once one of the grandest private manors in town, for decades owned by one of Portugal's most prominent families. Local rumors claim the property was seized by the casino to pay off a massive gambling debt. Today a visit here will give you a rare look into a luxurious private villa filled with antiques and paintings. Admission is 11€ ($13) to see the show at 11pm. It is open only in July and August daily from 3pm to 3am. You don't have to pay an admission for the slot machine area.

About 3km (2 miles) north of Figueira da Foz, bypassed by new construction and sitting placidly on a ridge near the sea, is **Buarcos,** a fishing village far removed from casinos and overpopulated beaches. From its central square to its stone seawalls, it remains unspoiled. Take Avenida do Brasil north from Figueira da Foz to get to Buarcos.

OUTDOOR ACTIVITIES Figueira da Foz is on a wide, sandy **beach,** on a site first occupied by the Lusitanians. In July and August, the beach is usually packed body to body. Those who don't like sand and surf can swim in a **pool** sandwiched between the Grande Hotel da Figueira and the Estalagem da Piscina on the main esplanade.

You can also trek into the **Serra da Boa Viagem,** a range of hills whose summit is a favorite vantage point for photographers and sightseers. **Bullfights** are popular in season; the old-style bullring operates from mid-July to September.

Near Figueira da Foz, the **Quiaios Lakes** are ideal for sailing and windsurfing. (For information, contact the tourist office in Figueira da Foz; see above.) Another good center for windsurfing is the bay at **Buarcos,** adjoining Figueira da Foz. You can rent most windsurfing equipment at kiosks right on the beaches.

SHOPPING If you're looking for handcrafts, head for **Shangrira,** Rua Dr. Calado (no phone), or **Chafariz,** Rua do Estendal 34 (© **23/342-06-86**). They carry terra cotta, glazed porcelain, and some carved wood, leatherwork, and incised or burnished copper and brass. Looking for gold or silver filigree? Try the **Ourivesaria Ouro Nobre,** Pracetta Dr Joaquin Lopez Feteira 11 (© **23/342-39-52**), for one of the town's most appealing selections.

WHERE TO STAY

Ibis Hotel *Value* Just a 5-minute stroll from the sandy beach, this is a midsize, efficiently run, affordable, and functional hotel. It's dependable but hardly dramatic, with a chain format and streamlined but standard bedrooms. The structure itself has more character than most cookie-cutter Ibis hotels because it was created out of a vastly restored stone house that was erected during World War I. Bedrooms are medium in size and comfortably though blandly furnished, each with a small bathroom with a shower-tub combination.

Rua da Liberdade 20, 3080-168 Figueira da Foz. © **23/342-20-51.** Fax 23/342-07-56. 47 units. 39€–57€ ($45–$66) double. AE, DC, MC, V. **Amenities:** Bar; pool nearby; laundry service; dry cleaning; nonsmoking rooms; 1 room for those w/limited mobility. *In room:* A/C, TV, dataport.

Mercure Figueira da Foz ★★ This 1950s-era hotel, on the seafront promenade overlooking the ocean, is the leading choice in town. The hotel's interior is a world of marble and glass, more like that of a big-city hotel than a resort. A few of the midsize rooms on the sea have glass-enclosed balconies; most have open balconies. The private bathrooms are well maintained and equipped with shower-tub combinations. The hotel is open all year, though it's sleepy here in January.

Av. do 25 de Abril 22, 3080-086 Figueira da Foz. © **23/340-39-00.** Fax 23/340-39-01. 102 units. 85€–105€ ($98–$121) double; 175€ ($201) suite. Rates include continental breakfast. AE, DC, MC, V. Parking 3.25€ ($3.75). **Amenities:** Restaurant; bar; pool nearby; heath club nearby; limited room service; laundry. *In room:* A/C, TV, minibar, hair dryer, safe.

Pensão Esplanada Across from a sandy beach, this little boarding house is in a building that dates from the turn of the 20th century, although the establishment itself is only 20 years old. This recommendation is strictly for the frugal traveler who wants a Portuguese seaside holiday on a slim purse. Frankly, the place has creaky joints, and the rooms are not at the peak of their glory, although they are scrubbed daily and maintenance is good. In rooms with private bathroom, some units have tubs; others have showers. Hallway bathrooms are generally adequate unless the hotel is operating at its peak capacity. At least no one complains when it comes time to pay the bill.

Rua Engenheiro Silva 86, 3080-086 Figueira da Foz. ✆ **23/342-21-15.** Fax 23/342-98-71. 19 units, 10 w/bathroom. 40€–60€ ($46–$69) double. Rates include breakfast. No credit cards. Free parking. **Amenities:** Breakfast room. *In room:* TV.

WHERE TO DINE

O Peleiro ★ *Finds* PORTUGUESE Unless you're dining at your hotel, such as the Mercure, you'll find that Figueira da Foz is not known for its restaurants. In-the-know foodies journey to the tranquil little village of Paião, 10km (6¼ miles) from Figueira for some fine dining in a building that used to be a tannery. Here the proprietor, Henrique, will welcome you into his establishment, which has been winning customers for more than 2 decades. The decor is in the classic Portuguese style, with terra-cotta floors and dark-wood furnishings placed under low ceilings. The rich bounty of the countryside shows up in the kitchen, where palate-pleasing dishes are turned out, including the fresh fish of the day, which can be broiled, grilled, or fried. Other specialties, each worthy, is roast *cabrito* or kid; a savory rice dish studded with prawns; or a mixed grill. Veal is grilled to perfection, as is zesty herb-flavored pork. Everything is backed up by a good choice of regional wines.

Largo Alvideiro, Paião. ✆ **23/394-01-59.** Reservations recommended. Main courses 13€–20€ ($14–$23). AE, MC, V. Mon–Sat noon–4pm and 7pm–midnight. Closed 2 weeks in May and 2 weeks in Sept.

FIGUEIRA DA FOZ AFTER DARK

Built in 1886, the **Grande Casino Peninsular,** Rua Dr. Calado 1 (✆ **23/340-84-00**), features shows, dancing, a nightclub, and gambling salons. Games of chance include blackjack, American and Continental roulette, and an old Continental game known as French Table (played with three dice). Admission, including one drink, is 11€ ($13) per person; expect to pay 4€ to 6€ ($4.60–$6.90) and up for beverages. An a la carte meal averages 24€ ($28); the food is standard nightclub chow. The casino show begins at 11pm, and the club is open daily from 5pm to 3am.

You'll find many evocative, peaceful, or sleepy bars on Travesso São Lourenço. One of the most appealing is the **Bar Dom Copo,** Rua São Lourenço (✆ **23/342-68-17**). Karaoke is presented on Sunday according to an oft-changing schedule and adds to the place's reputation as one of the most consistently popular bars in town. If you want to go dancing, three good dance clubs await: **Pessidonio,** Condados Tavarede (✆ **23/343-56-37**); **Beach Club,** Esplanade Dr. Silva Guimarães (no phone); and perhaps the busiest and most amusing, **Bergantim,** Rua Dr. António Lopez Guimarães (✆ **23/342-38-85**). They don't get animated until after 10:30pm. Admission is around 5€ ($5.75), including the first drink.

3 Coimbra ★★

118km (73 miles) S of Porto, 198km (123 miles) N of Lisbon

Coimbra, known as Portugal's most romantic city, was the inspiration for the song "April in Portugal." On the weather-washed right bank of the muddy Mondego, Coimbra is also the educational center of the country. Dinis I originally founded its university at Lisbon in 1290. Over the years, the university moved back and forth between Lisbon and Coimbra, but in 1537 it settled here for good. Many of the country's leaders were educated here, including Dr. António Salazar, dictator from 1932 to 1968. Coimbra is at its best when the university is in session. Students still wear black capes; their briefcases bear colored ribbons denoting the school they attend. Yellow, for example, stands for medicine.

This city of medieval churches is also filled with youthful energy. Noisy cafeterias, raucous bars, and such events as crew races lend a certain joie de vivre to the cityscape.

The students of Coimbra band together in "republics" that usually rent cramped buildings in the old quarter. The republic isn't very democratic, run as it is on a strict seniority basis.

ESSENTIALS

ARRIVING

BY TRAIN Coimbra has two train stations: **Estação Coimbra-A,** Largo das Ameias, and **Estação Coimbra-B,** 5km (3 miles) west of central Coimbra. For information, call (✆ **23/983-49-98**). Coimbra-B station is mainly for trains coming from cities outside the region, but regional trains serve both stations. Frequent shuttles connect the two. The train ride takes 5 minutes and costs .95€ ($1.10). At least 16 trains per day make the 3-hour run north from Lisbon. It costs 12€ ($14) one-way. From Figueira da Foz, there's one train per hour. The trip takes 1 hour and costs 2.10€ ($2.40) one-way.

BY BUS The **bus station** is on Avenida Fernão de Magalhães (✆ **23/985-52-70**). Fourteen buses a day arrive from Lisbon, after a 3-hour trip that costs 9.40€ ($11) one-way. Thirteen buses per day make the 6-hour trip from Porto (see chapter 11). The one-way fare is 8.90€ ($10).

BY CAR From Lisbon, take the express highway A1 north. The journey takes less than 2 hours, if there isn't too much traffic.

VISITOR INFORMATION

The **Coimbra Tourist Office** is on Largo da Portagem (✆ **23/948-81-20**). During the summer, the office is open Monday through Friday from 9am to 7pm, and Saturday and Sunday from 10am to 1pm and 2:30 to 5:30pm. Winter hours are Monday through Friday from 9:30am to 12:30pm and 2 to 5:30pm, and Saturday and Sunday from 10am to 1pm and 2:30 to 3pm.

WHAT TO SEE & DO IN COIMBRA

EXPLORING THE TOWN

Coimbra's charms and mysteries unfold as you walk up Rua Ferreira Borges, under the Gothic **Arco de Almedina** with its coat of arms. From that point, you can continue up the steep street, past antiques shops, to the old quarter.

Across from the National Museum is the **Sé Nova** (New Cathedral), Largo da Sé Nova, which has a cold 17th-century neoclassic interior. Admission is free. It's open Tuesday through Friday from 9am to 12:30pm and 2 to 5:30pm. More interesting is the **Sé Velha** (Old Cathedral) ★★, Largo da Sé Velha (✆ **23/982-31-38**), founded in 1170. The crenellated cathedral enjoys associations with St. Anthony of Padua. You enter by passing under a Romanesque portal. Usually a student is here, willing to show you (for a tip) the precincts, including the restored cloister. The pride of this monument is the gilded **Flemish retable** ★ over the main altar, with a crucifix on top. To the left of the altar is a

Coimbra

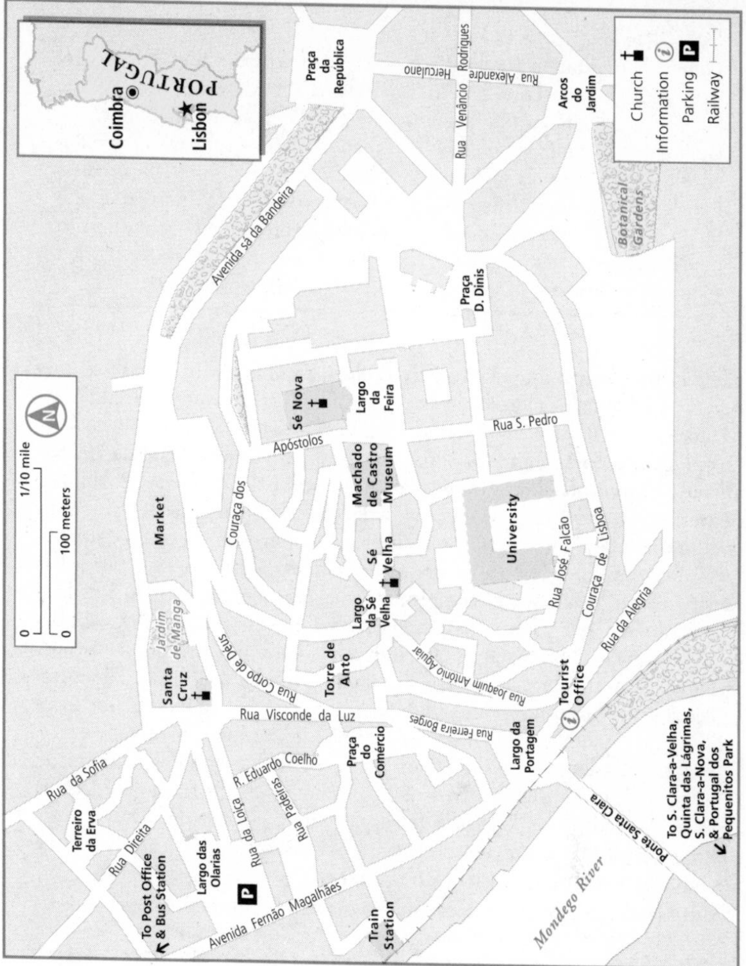

16th-century chapel, designed by a French artist, that contains the tomb of one of the bishops of Coimbra. Admission to the old cathedral is free; admission to the cloisters is 1€ ($1.15). The Sé Velha is open Monday through Saturday from 10am to 6pm.

Velha Universidade ★★ The focal point for most visitors is the University of Coimbra, established here in 1537 on orders of João III. Among its alumni are Luís Vas de Camões (the country's greatest poet, author of the national epic, *Os Lusíadas*), St. Anthony of Padua (also the patron saint of Lisbon), and the late Portuguese dictator, Dr. Salazar, once a professor of economics.

Ignore the cold statuary and architecture on Largo de Dom Dinis and pass under the 17th-century **Porta Pérrea** into the inner core. The steps on the right take you along a cloistered arcade, **Via Latina,** to the **Sala dos Capelos,** the site of graduation ceremonies. Inside you'll find a twisted rope ceiling, a portrait gallery of Portuguese kings, red-damask walls, and the inevitable *azulejos* (tiles).

Portugal's Romeo & Juliet

Coimbra's reputation for romance derives in part from the 14th-century story of Pedro the Cruel and Inês de Castro. The crown prince and the Spanish beauty, his wife's lady-in-waiting, fell in love at what's now the Quinta das Lágrimas, where Inês was then living. Unhappy with the influence Inês had over his son, Pedro's father, Afonso IV, eventually ordered her death. Three noblemen slit her throat in the quinta's garden. In the Igreja e Mosteiro da Santa Cruz (see below), Pedro forced his courtiers to pay homage to her corpse and kiss her hand. The lovers are buried together in Alcobaça's Mosteiro de Santa Maria (see chapter 7).

Afterward you can visit the **University Chapel,** decorated with an 18th-century organ, 16th-century candelabra, a painted ceiling, 17th-century tiles, and a fine Manueline portal.

The architectural gem of the entire town is the **Biblioteca Geral da Universidade** (University Library) ★★, also at Largo de Dom Dinis. Established between 1716 and 1723 and donated by João V, the library shelters more than a million volumes. The interior consists of a trio of high-ceilinged salons walled by two-story tiers of lacquer-decorated bookshelves. The pale jade and sedate lemon marble inlaid floors complement the baroque decorations of gilded wood. Chinese-style patterns have been painted on emerald, red, and gold lacquer work. The library tables are built of ebony and lustrous rosewood, imported from the former Portuguese colonies in India and Brazil. The three-dimensional ceilings and zooming telescopic effect of the room's structure focus on the large portrait of João V, set against imitation curtains in wood.

You might want to save the library for last; after viewing this masterpiece, other sights in town pale by comparison. To wind down after leaving the library, walk to the end of the belvedere for a panoramic view of the river and the rooftops of the old quarter. On the square you'll see a statue of João III and the famous curfew-signaling clock of Coimbra, known as *cabra* (goat).

Largo de Dom Dinis. ✆ **23/985-98-00.** Combined admission to Sala dos Capelos and Biblioteca 4€ ($4.60) adults, 2€ ($2.30) seniors, 2.80€ ($3.20) students and children 6–20; single admission to either Sala dos Apelos or Biblioteca 2.50€ ($2.90) adults, 1.25€ ($1.45) seniors, 1.75€ ($2) students and children 6–10. May–Sept daily 9am–7pm, Oct–Apr daily 9:30am–5:30pm.

Igreja e Mosteiro da Santa Cruz ★ This former monastery was founded in the late 12th century during the reign of Afonso Henríques, Portugal's first king. Its original Romanesque style gave way to Manueline restorers in 1507. This is where the story of Pedro the Cruel and Inês de Castro reached its climax. Tiles decorate the lower part of the walls inside. Groined in the profuse Manueline manner, the interior houses the Gothic sarcophagi of Afonso Henríques, his feet resting on a lion, and of his son, Sancho I. The **pulpit** ★ is one of the achievements of the Renaissance in Portugal, carved by João de Ruão in the 16th century. The **choir stalls** ★ preserve, in carved configurations, the symbolism, mythology, and historic import of Portuguese exploration. With its twisted columns and 13th-century tombs, the two-tiered Gothic-Manueline **cloister** ★ is impressive. The facade is decorated like an architectural birthday cake, topped with finials and crosses.

Praça do 8 de Maio. ✆ **23/982-29-41.** Admission 1€ ($1.15). Mon–Sat 9am–noon and 2–5pm; Sun 4–6pm.

NEARBY ATTRACTIONS

Convento de Santa Clara-a-Nova Commanding a view of Coimbra's right bank, the New Convent of St. Clara contains the tomb of St. Isabella. Built during the reign of João IV, it's an incongruous blend of church and military garrison. The church is noted for a rich baroque interior and Renaissance cloister. In the rear, behind a grille, is the original tomb of the saint (closed except on special occasions). In 1677, her body was moved here from the Convent of St. Clara-a-Velha. Instead of regal robes, she preferred to be buried in the simplest habit of the order of the Poor Clares. At the main altar is the silver tomb (a sacristan will light it for you), which the ecclesiastical hierarchy considered more appropriate after her canonization.

Rua Santa Isabel. ✆ **23/944-16-74.** Admission 1€ ($1.15). Daily 9am–noon and 2–5pm.

Portugal dos Pequenitos *Kids* For children, this mixture of miniature houses—"Portugal for the Little Ones"—from every province of the country is Coimbra's main attraction. You get there by crossing Ponte de Santa Clara and heading out Rua António Agusto Gonçalves. You'll feel like Gulliver strolling through a Lilliputian world. The re-creations include palaces, an Indian temple, a Brazilian pavilion (with photos of gauchos), a windmill, a castle, and the 16th-century House of Diamonds from Lisbon.

Jardim do Portugal dos Pequenitos. ✆ **23/980-11-70.** Admission 5€ ($5.75) adults, 2.50€ ($2.90) children. Daily Apr–Sept 9am–8pm; Oct–Mar 10am–5pm.

Quinta das Lágrimas The legendary poet Camões told the story of the "Garden of Tears." Inês de Castro, mistress of Pedro the Cruel, and their three illegitimate children lived in "sweet Mondego's solitary groves." Although the gardens have been the property of the Osorio Cabral family since the 18th century, romantics from many countries visit them. The house has been turned into a deluxe hotel (see "Where to Stay," below), and you can wander through the greenery to the spring fountain, known as the Fonte dos Amores.

Rua António Agusto Gonçalves. ✆ **23/980-23-80.** Admission .75€ (85¢). Daily 9am–7pm.

OUTDOOR ACTIVITIES

There are tennis courts at the university stadium and at the **Club Tênis de Coimbra,** Avenida Urbano Durate, Quinta da Estrela (✆ **23/940-34-69**). All are open to the public and cost 6€ ($6.90) per hour; call ahead to reserve a court. For horseback riding or excursions in the Beiras, contact **Centre Hippique de Coimbra,** Mata do Choupal (✆ **23/983-76-95**), open daily from 10am to 1pm and 3 to 7pm. A 1½- to 2-hour excursion along country trails costs 13€ ($14) per person.

For swimming, head for the trio of pools at the **Piscina Municipal,** Rua Dom Manuel I (✆ **23/970-16-05**). Take bus no. 5 from the center. Open daily from 10am to 1pm and 2 to 7pm, it charges 1.30€ ($1.50) admission.

SHOPPING

Many of Coimbra's most interesting shops lie near the Sé Velha, on the narrow streets radiating from **Rua de Quebra Costas.** Because of its steep inclines, its name (The Street That Will Break Your Back) seems appropriate. Look for lots of outlets selling products manufactured in the surrounding region. The best bookstore, with a number of English editions, is **Livraria Bertrand,** Largo da Portagem 9 (✆ **23/982-30-14**), a block from the tourist office.

Even the city's tourist authorities usually recommend short excursions into the suburbs and outlying villages for anyone seriously interested in shopping. Possibilities include the villages of **Lousa,** 21km (13 miles) southeast, and **Penacova,** 21km (13 miles) east, where unpretentious kiosks and stands beside the roads sell hand-woven baskets and ceramics. Contact the tourist office (see above) for directions.

A better destination is **Condeixa,** 17km (10½ miles) south; its shops are better stocked, and the staff members are prepared for foreigners who don't speak Portuguese. To reach the village, take EN1 and follow signs toward Lisboa. Condeixa is home to nine independent ceramics factories, source of most residents' income. The most appealing are **Ceramica Berardos,** Barreira, EN1, Condeixia (✆ **23/994-13-31**); and **Filceramica,** Avenal, Condeixa (✆ **23/994-18-38**). The merchants will usually agree (for a fee) to insure and ship your purchases. Because of the expense, it's usually a lot easier just to buy an extra suitcase, wrap your porcelain carefully, and haul it back with you on the plane.

WHERE TO STAY

Note that the **Pousada de Santa Cristina** (see "An Excursion to the Roman Town of Conimbriga," below) is nearby.

EXPENSIVE

Quinta das Lágrimas ★★★ The most luxurious place to stay in all the Beiras, the Estate of Tears gets its name from the story of Dom Pedro and Inês de Castro. Inês was murdered on the quinta's grounds, and her tears, it's said, were transformed into a pure, fresh stream of water. The red color of the rocks is said to be from her blood.

The duke of Wellington, the emperor of Brazil, and various kings of Portugal once occupied these rooms. They're now a hotel of great modern comfort that maintains the romanticism of its past. The midsize to spacious guest rooms are often sumptuous but not overly decorated, and everything is in traditional Portuguese style. All units maintain tidily kept bathrooms equipped with shower-tub combinations. You can find ample retreats in the drawing rooms and among the centenarian exotic trees, lovely fountains, and well-maintained gardens.

Rua António Agusto Gonçalves, Santa Clara, 3041-901 Coimbra. ✆ **23/980-23-80.** Fax 23/944-16-95. www.supernet.pt/hotelagrimas. 35 units. 133€–184€ ($153–$212) double; 300€–375€ ($345–$431) suite. Rates include breakfast. AE, DC, MC, V. Free parking. **Amenities:** Restaurant; bar; pool; golf; limited room service; babysitting; laundry service; nonsmoking rooms; 1 room for those w/limited mobility. *In room:* A/C, TV, minibar, hair dryer, safe.

Tivoli Coimbra ★ On a hillside above Coimbra's northern outskirts, a 15-minute walk from the town center, this is a favorite stop for bus tours. Built in 1991, it's a member of one of Portugal's most respected chains, the Tivoli Group, whose hotels in Sintra and Lisbon are among the finest in their four- and five-star categories. The midsize rooms are conservatively modern (too much so for some tastes) and filled with electronic gadgets such as bedside controls. All units are equipped with neatly arranged bathrooms with shower-tub combinations. Some rooms have city views. There's a small garden behind the hotel.

Rua João Machado 4–5, 3000-226 Coimbra. ✆ **23/982-69-34.** Fax 23/985-83-45. www.tivolihotels.com. 95 units. 134€–145€ ($154–$167) double; 200€ ($230) suite. Rates include breakfast. AE, DC, MC, V. Free parking. **Amenities:** Restaurant; bar; pool; health club; Jacuzzi; sauna; room service (9am–11pm); babysitting; laundry service; nonsmoking rooms. *In room:* A/C, TV, minibar, hair dryer, safe.

MODERATE

Hotel Astória ★ It has surrendered its role as market leader to the more glamorous Quinta das Lágrimas (see above), but the Astória is as inviting as ever. When it was built in 1927, the domed, triangular Astoria was the most glamorous hotel in Coimbra. It played host to Portugal's famous and infamous before falling into neglect and decay. It reopened in a streamlined and somewhat simplified format in 1990. The comfortable hotel retains a faded grandeur. Its cupolas and wrought-iron balcony balustrades rise from a pie-shape wedge of land in the city's congested heart. The guest rooms vary greatly in size, but all are comfortably furnished with well-maintained bathrooms equipped with shower-tub combinations. Five units are air-conditioned, but they're usually reserved in advance.

Av. Emídio Navarro 21, 3000-150 Coimbra. ✆ **23/985-30-20.** Fax 23/982-20-57. www.almeidahotels.com. 62 units. 80€–115€ ($92–$132) double; 125€–135€ ($144–$155) suite. Rates include breakfast. AE, DC, MC, V. **Amenities:** Restaurant; bar; limited room service; babysitting; laundry service. *In room:* A/C, TV, hair dryer.

INEXPENSIVE

Hotel Bragança This bandbox hotel next to the train station is a possible choice if you arrive late at night by rail and other, better hotels are full. Primarily catering to businesspeople, it does a thriving trade in summer. The rooms vary in size—a few have balconies that overlook the main road; others are airless and often hot. The furnishings are utterly basic and recall the 1950s. All are equipped with tidy bathrooms containing shower-tub combinations.

Largo das Ameias 10, 3000-024 Coimbra. ✆ **23/982-21-71.** Fax 23/983-61-35. www.maisturismo.pt/braganca.html. 83 units. 55€–65€ ($63–$75) double; 78€–90€ ($90–$104) suite. Rates include breakfast. AE, MC, V. Free parking. **Amenities:** Restaurant; bar; limited room service; laundry service. *In room:* A/C, TV, safe.

Hotel Dom Luís ★ Built in 1989, this is one of the most stylish hotels in the Coimbra area. Less than 1km (¾ mile) south of the city, it lies on the road to Lisbon. The comfortable, well-maintained guest rooms, though a bit small, offer good beds and well-maintained bathrooms with shower-tub combinations. The hotel has a pleasing modern design, brown-marble floors, and a restaurant that serves Portuguese and international food.

Quinta da Verzea, Santa Clara. 3040-091 Coimbra. ✆ **800/582-1234** in the U.S., or 23/980-21-20. Fax 23/944-51-96. www.bestwestern.com/prop_72044. 98 units. 68€ ($78) double; 100€ ($115) suite. Rates include breakfast. AE, DC, MC, V. Free parking. **Amenities:** Restaurant; bar; limited room service; laundry service; nonsmoking rooms; rooms for those w/limited mobility. *In room:* A/C, TV, dataport, minibar, safe.

Hotel Domus The Domus lies above an appliance store on a narrow commercial street. Machine-made golden-brown tiles cover its 1970s facade, and its rectangular windows are trimmed with slabs of marble. The reception desk is at the top of a flight of stairs, a floor above ground level. Rooms are usually large and well maintained, and all contain neatly kept bathrooms with mostly shower-tub combinations. Many have contrasting patterns of carpeting and wallpaper, creating a haphazardly functional but cozy family atmosphere. A stereo system plays in the TV lounge, which doubles as the breakfast room.

Rua Adelina Veiga 62, 3000-002 Coimbra. ✆ **23/982-85-84.** Fax 23/983-88-18. 20 units. 35€–50€ ($40–$58) double; 25€–35€ ($29–$40) apt w/no toilet. AE, MC, V. Free parking on street. **Amenities:** Breakfast room; TV lounge. *In room:* TV.

Hotel International This hotel is very simple and unabashedly Portuguese in its mentality and decor. It occupies a once-grand 1840s building whose interior has been updated over the years. The building became a hotel in 1949, and the aura of that time lingers. Members of the family that owns the property staff the insignificant lobby. After registering, you climb a series of steep staircases—the hotel is not wheelchair-accessible—to rooms that are often tiny, with furniture that's merely old instead of antique. Yet at busy times, finding any room in Coimbra is a welcome relief. All come with neatly kept bathrooms equipped with showers. Ten rooms have phones. Breakfast is not served.

Av. Emídio Navarro 4, 3000-150 Coimbra. ✆ **23/982-55-03.** 27 units. 30€–35€ ($35–$41) double. No credit cards. Limited free parking on street. **Amenities:** Laundry service. *In room:* A/C, TV.

Hotel Oslo This hotel lies on one of the busiest streets in town and was built during the 1960s craze for Scandinavian design and decor. In the '90s it underwent a complete overhaul and upgrade. The small rooms are conservatively modern, unpretentious, and simple. All are equipped with neatly kept bathrooms containing shower-tub combinations. Because of traffic noise, ask for a room at the rear, especially if you're a light sleeper.

Av. Fernão de Magalhães 25, 3000-175 Coimbra. ✆ **23/982-90-71.** Fax 23/982-06-14. www.hotel-oslo.web.pt. 36 units. 60€–70€ ($69–$81) double; 90€–100€ ($104–$115) suite. Rates include breakfast. AE, DC, MC, V. Free parking. **Amenities:** Breakfast room; bar; 24-hr. room service; babysitting; laundry service; nonsmoking rooms. *In room:* A/C, TV, dataport, hair dryer, safe.

WHERE TO DINE

MODERATE

A Taberna ★ PORTUGUESE Out of a lackluster lot, this tavern ranks at the top of the independent eateries of this university city. Popular with students, local residents, as well as visitors, its kitchen turns out a notable though typical cuisine set against a backdrop of regional decorations in 2 different dining rooms, one seating 20 patrons and another seating 50. Dedicated to his job, the chef goes to the market himself to look for the best and freshest of ingredients. Back in the kitchen, he turns out such specialties as goat meat roasted tender in wine or oven-cooked veal with roast potatoes soaking up the juice. The typical fishermen's favorite, codfish with potatoes, is another good dish. Freshly made pastries and cheeses round out the repast.

Rua Dos Combatentes da Grande Guerra 86. ✆ **23/971-62-65.** Reservations recommended. Main courses 8€–16€ ($9.20–$18). AE, MC, V. Sun–Fri noon–3pm and 7:30–10:30pm.

Dom Pedro PORTUGUESE/CONTINENTAL Dom Pedro is across from the bank of the river, near a congested part of town. After negotiating a vaulted hall, you'll find yourself in an attractive room with tables grouped around a splashing fountain. In winter, a corner fireplace throws welcome heat; in summer, the thick walls and terra-cotta floor provide a kind of air-conditioning. Full Portuguese and Continental meals might include codfish Dom Pedro, grilled squid, pepper steak, or pork cutlet Milanese. The food is basic; as our Portuguese host informed us at the end of the meal, "I didn't promise you a rose garden—only dinner."

Av. Emídio Navarro 58. ✆ **23/982-91-08.** Reservations recommended. Main courses 6.70€–16€ ($7.70–$18). AE, DC, MC, V. Daily 8am–10:30pm.

O Alfredo PORTUGUESE This restaurant lies on the less populated side of the river, on the street that funnels into the Santa Clara Bridge. The unobtrusive pink-fronted building looks more like a snack bar than a formal restaurant. The ambience is pleasant, albeit simple. Full Portuguese meals might feature pork Alentejo style, shellfish paella, Portuguese-style stew, several types of clam dishes, roast goat, and regional varieties of fish and meat. Although the wine is often better than the food, this is nonetheless a satisfying choice.

Av. João das Regras 32. ✆ **23/944-15-22.** Main courses 7€–25€ ($8.05–$29). MC, V. Daily noon–3pm and Tues–Sun 7–10:30pm.

INEXPENSIVE

Café Nicola PORTUGUESE Café Nicola is a plain but modern little restaurant over an old-fashioned delicatessen and pastry shop. It's spartan inside—even the flowers are usually wilted. Students gather here for strong coffee. The food is good but simple; the fish and meat platters are usually large enough for two. A nourishing bowl of the soup of the day begins most meals. After that, you can order filet of fish, roast chicken, chicken cutlets, or veal croquettes.

Rua Ferreira Borges 35. ✆ **23/982-20-61.** Main courses 6€–10€ ($6.90–$12). AE, MC, V. Mon–Sat 7am–10pm.

Café Santa Cruz ★ SANDWICHES This is the most famous coffeehouse in Coimbra, perhaps in the whole of northern Portugal. In a former auxiliary chapel of the cathedral, it has a high ceiling supported by flamboyant stone ribbing and vaulting of fitted stone. The paneled waiters' station boasts a marble top handsome enough to serve as an altar. A favorite gathering place by day or night, it has a casual mood; cigarette butts are tossed on the floor. Scores of students and professors come here to read the newspaper. There's no bar to stand at, so everyone takes a seat on an intricately tooled leather chair at one of the marble-topped hexagonal tables. If you order cognac, the shot will overflow the glass, but most patrons ask for a glass of coffee with milk.

Praça do 8 de Maio. ✆ **23/983-36-17.** Sandwiches 1.40€–3€ ($1.60–$3.45); coffee .60€ (70¢). No credit cards. Summer Mon–Sat 8am–2am; winter Mon–Sat 8am–midnight. Closed Sept 25–Oct 8.

COIMBRA AFTER DARK

The city's large student population guarantees an active, sometimes raucous nightlife. You'll find the bars around the Sé Velha and its square, Largo da Sé Velha, packed with students, professors, and locals, who drink, gossip, and discuss academic priorities. Our favorite experience is hopping randomly from bar to bar. If you want a definite address, consider the **Diligência Bar,** Rua Nova (✆ **23/982-76-67**), where folks drink and flirt early in the evening and then listen to the local fado diva's performances beginning at 10 or 10:30pm. A more Americanized option is the **Dixie Bar,** Rua Joaquim António d'Agiar 6 (✆ **23/982-74-26**), where live jazz by local performers sometimes evokes New Orleans.

The town's dance clubs rock at least 5 nights a week (sometimes 7, depending on how many students are in town). The glamour and desirability of the dance clubs we recommend below increase or decrease every season based on the whims of the danceaholic public. Depending on your mood and who's there at the time of your visit, the most worthwhile are **Via Latina,** Rua Almeida Garrett 1 (✆ **23/982-02-93**); and **Passarelle,** Machado Asses 22 (✆ **23/982-70-67**). Each becomes animated after 10:30pm and often stays open until around 3am or, on Friday and Saturday, until dawn. **Caffé,** Largo de Sé Velha 4-8 (✆ **23/983-81-64**), is not just an Internet cafe, but a hot new dance club, with African, Brazilian, or pop music blasting away. A cover of 2.50€ ($2.90) is imposed only after 11pm. It's open June to mid-September Monday through Saturday 11am to 4am, and September 16 to May Monday through Saturday 9am to 4pm

An Excursion to the Roman Town of Conimbriga

One of Europe's great Roman archaeological finds, **Conimbriga** ★ is 16km (10 miles) southwest of Coimbra. If you don't have a car, you can take a bus from Coimbra to Condeixa, 1.75km (1 mile) from Conimbriga. The bus, AVIC MONDEGO, leaves Coimbra at 9am and returns at 1 and 6pm. From Condeixa, you reach Conimbriga by walking or hiring a taxi in the village.

The site of a Celtic settlement established in the Iron Age, the village was occupied by the Romans in the late 1st century A.D. From then until the 5th century, the town knew a peaceful life. The site lay near a Roman camp but never served as a military outpost, though it was on a Roman road connecting Lisbon (Roman Olisipo) and Braga (Roman Braçara Augusta).

You can walk from the small **Museu Monográfico** along the Roman road to enter the ruins. The museum contains artifacts from the ruins, including a bust of Augustus Caesar that originally stood in the town's Augustan temple. The **House of Cantaber** ★ is a large residence, and in its remains you can trace the life of the Romans in Conimbriga. The house was occupied until intruders seized the family of Cantaber. The invaders also effectively put an end to the town in the mid–5th century.

Another point of interest is the **House of the Fountains** ★★, constructed before the 4th century, when it was partially destroyed by the building of the town wall. Much of the house has been excavated, and you can see remains of early Roman architecture as it was carried out in the provinces.

Roman mosaics in almost perfect condition have been unearthed in area diggings. The designs are executed in blood red, mustard, gray, sienna, and yellow; the motifs include beasts from North Africa and delicately wrought hunting scenes. In one of the houses you can see mosaics with mythological themes. The diggings attest to the ingenuity of Roman design. Columns form peristyles around reflecting pools, and the remains of fountains stand in courtyards. There are ruins of temples, a forum, patrician houses, water conduits, and drains. Feeding the town's public and private bathrooms were special heating and steam installations with elaborate piping systems. The town even had its own aqueduct.

The ruins are open daily from 9am to 8pm (until 6pm in winter). The museum is open Tuesday through Sunday from 10am to 8pm. Admission is 3€ ($3.45) for adults and free for children under 14. For more information, call ✆ **23/994-11-77.**

Student celebrations in Coimbra include the **Queima das Fitas** (Burning of the Ribbons), a graduation ritual during the first or second week of May. Then loosely organized *serenatas* (troupes of students who re-create the music and aura of medieval troubadours) sing and wander through Coimbra's streets at unannounced intervals. It's impossible to predict when and where you're likely to find these spontaneous reminders of yesteryear.

A PLACE TO STAY NEAR COIMBRA

Pousada de Santa Cristina ★★ One of Portugal's finest pousadas, this inn, which opened in 1993, is a modern four-story hotel whose design was vaguely inspired by a 19th-century palace. It replaced a gone-to-seed mansion, and many of that building's embellishments, including moldings, were used in the reconstruction. Other furnishings were imported from the site of a tragic fire at the Palácio de Sotomaior, near Lisbon. The guest rooms are generally spacious, light, and sunny. The furnishings are tasteful, with well-chosen fabrics and carpeting, plus a tiled bathroom with shower-tub combination.

Many guests visiting Coimbra, 15km (9⅓ miles) away, prefer to stay here.

Condeixa-a-Nova, 3150-142 Coimbra. ✆ **23/994-40-25.** Fax 23/994-30-97. www.pousadas.pt. 45 units. 97€–140€ ($112–$161) double. Rates include breakfast. AE, DC, MC, V. Free parking. **Amenities:** Restaurant; bar; pool; tennis court; room service; laundry service; nonsmoking rooms. *In room:* A/C, TV, dataport, minibar, hair dryer, safe.

Serra de Estrêla National Park

Portugal's largest national park, Serra de Estrêla ★★★, is one of the country's most popular rest and recreation areas. From January to May, the great granite mountain is a winter-sports center. In summer, campers, trout fishers, and mountain climbers replace the skiers.

Until the late 1800s, the land was almost completely isolated from the rest of Portugal. It was known mainly to local hunters and shepherds. It's the home of the *cão de sena* (dog of the mountain), a tough species of canine bred for its shepherding skill. The area is still a major sheep-raising district and is filled with wild animals, including boars, badgers, and packs of roving, often hungry, wolves. Traditional iron collars with long, sharp spikes protect the sheep dogs' throats from the wolves' teeth. Strangely, many of the dogs survive by sucking ewes' milk.

Roads link the region's major points of interest in the mountain range. One major auto route (N339) runs between Covilhã and Seia via the scenic mountain hamlet of **Torre,** the highest point in Portugal (1950m/6,396 ft.). Torre has been developed into a resort and boasts two ski lifts, but the facilities don't compare with those found in Austria, Switzerland, and parts of France. If you're driving, expect sheer drop-offs and hair-raising curves and turns as panoramic views of the **Zêzere Valley** unfold.

The best trout fishing in the park is in the Zêzere Valley, where the river drains one of the deepest glacial gorges in Europe. Fishermen also try their luck in the lakes of **Loriga** and **Comprida.**

The ideal time for hiking is spring, when wildflowers bloom. Well-marked trails cut through the park, meandering along the sloping terrain. Several official campsites are also in the park. The **Covilhã Tourist Office,** Praça do Município (✆ **27/531-95-60**), can supply you with maps and information. It is open Monday through Saturday from 9am to 12:30pm and 2 to 5:30pm.

The easiest way to reach the park is from Coimbra. Take N17 east and follow signs.

4 Buçaco ★★

28km (17⅓ miles) N of Coimbra, 232km (144 miles) N of Lisbon, 3.25km (2 miles) SE of Luso

The rich, tranquil beauty of Buçaco's forests was initially discovered by a humble order of barefoot Carmelite monks, following the dictates of seclusion prescribed by their founder. In 1628, they founded a monastery at Buçaco and built it with materials from the surrounding hills. Around the forest they erected a wall to isolate themselves further and to keep women out.

The friars had a special love for plants and trees, and each year they cultivated the natural foliage and planted specimens sent to them from distant orders. Buçaco had always been a riot of growth: ferns, pines, cork, eucalyptus, and pink and blue clusters of hydrangea. The friars introduced such exotic flora as the monkey puzzle, a tall Chilean pine with convoluted branches. The pride of the forest, however, remains its stately cypresses and cedars.

ESSENTIALS

ARRIVING

BY BUS Buçaco is best explored by car. However, if you're depending on public transportation, you can visit the forest on a day trip from Coimbra. Buses from Coimbra to Viseu detour from Luso through the forest and stop at the Palace Hotel do Buçaco. Five buses per day (three on Sun) make the 1-hour trip; a one-way ticket is 3€ ($3.45). For information and schedules, call ✆ **23/982-70-81.**

BY CAR From Coimbra, head northeast along Route 110 to the town of Penacova at the foot of the Serra do Buçaco. From there, continue north, following signposts along a small secondary road.

VISITOR INFORMATION

The nearest tourist office is at Luso (see section 5, below).

EXPLORING THE AREA

The forest created by the order of Carmelite monks who settled here in 1628 has been maintained through the ages. Such was the beauty of the preserve that a papal bull, issued in 1643, threatened excommunication to anyone who destroyed one of its trees. Though the monastery was abolished in 1834, the forest survived. Filled with natural spring waters, the earth bubbles with many cool fountains, the best known of which is **Fonte Fria** (cold fountain).

The Buçaco forest was the battleground where Wellington defeated the Napoleonic legions under Marshal André Massena. The Iron Duke slept in a simple cloister cell after the battle. A small **Museu da Guerra Peninsular** (Museum of the Peninsular War), less than 1km (¾ mile) from the Palace Hotel do Buçaco (✆ **23/193-93-10**), reconstructs much of the drama of this turning point in the Napoleonic invasion of Iberia. The small museum collection consists of engravings, plus a few guns. It's open June 15 to September 15 Tuesday through Sunday from 10am to 5:30pm, and from 10am to 4pm in the off season. Admission is 1€ ($1.15).

In the early 20th century, a great deal of the Carmelite monastery was torn down to make way for the royal hunting lodge and palace of Carlos I and his wife, Amélia. He hardly had time to enjoy it before he was assassinated in 1908. The Italian architect Luigi Manini masterminded the neo-Manueline structure of parapets, buttresses, armillary spheres, galleries with flamboyant arches, towers, and turrets. After the fall of the Braganças and the transformation of the palace into a hotel, wealthy tourists took their afternoon tea by the pools underneath the trellis hung with blossoming wisteria.

One of the best ways to savor Buçaco is to drive the 550m (1,804 ft.) up to **Cruz Alta** (high cross), through the forests and past hermitages. The view from the summit is among the best in Portugal. Take Carretera Nacionale No. 1 to get to the top.

WHERE TO STAY & DINE

Palace Hotel do Buçaco ★★★ Once a vacation retreat for Portuguese monarchs, this is one of the most mythical buildings in the country. In one of Iberia's most famous farewells, the deposed Amélia passed from the Earth after her final visit to Buçaco in 1945. The government had permitted the ailing queen a sentimental journey to all the places where she had reigned before her husband and son were assassinated in 1908. In 1910, the Swiss-born head of the kitchen, the former king's cook, persuaded the government to let him run the palace as a hotel.

The palace is an architectural fantasy, ringed with gardens and exotic trees imported from the far corners of the Portuguese empire. The designer borrowed heavily from everywhere: the Jerónimos Monastery in Belém, the Doge's Palace in Venice, and the Graustark Castles of Bavaria. One of Europe's most grandiose smaller palaces, it's in the center of a 100-hectare (247-acre) forest.

Despite the wear and tear caused by thousands of guests, the structure is intact and impressive. Especially notable is the grand staircase with ornate marble balustrades, 4.5m-wide (15-ft.-wide) bronze torchières, and walls of blue-and-white tiles depicting important scenes from Portuguese history. Each richly furnished drawing room and salon is a potpourri of whimsical architecture.

The most spectacular accommodation is the queen's suite, which has a private parlor, dressing room, sumptuous marble bathroom, and dining room. In the '90s many of the guest rooms were upgraded and restored, but they retain their dignified, conservative decor. All rooms have well-maintained bathrooms with shower-tub combinations.

Mata do Buçaco, Buçaco, 3050-261 Luso. ✆ **23/193-79-70.** Fax 23/193-05-09. www.almeidahotels.com. 60 units. 110€–210€ ($127–$242) double; 350€–1,100€ ($403–$1,265) suite. Rates include continental breakfast. Free parking. AE, DC, MC, V. **Amenities:** Restaurant; bar; tennis court; concierge; 24-hr. room service; laundry service. *In room:* A/C in some rooms, TV, minibar (in suites only), hair dryer.

5 Luso

31km (19 miles) N of Coimbra, 230km (143 miles) N of Lisbon, 8km (5 miles) SE of Cúria

Luso, a little spa town on the northwestern side of the Buçaco mountains, boasts a mild climate and thermal waters for both drinking and bathing. The radioactive and hypotonic water is low in mineral content. It is said to have great efficacy in the treatment of kidney ailments, alimentary complaints, circulatory problems, and respiratory tract or skin allergies.

Besides the health-oriented aspects of the spa, it's a resort area that shares many of its facilities with Buçaco, 3.25km (2 miles) away. During the spa season, festivities and sports events are held at the casino, nightclub, and tennis courts, as well as on the lake and at the two pools, one of which is heated. Thermal spa enthusiasts flock here from June to October.

ESSENTIALS

ARRIVING

BY TRAIN From Coimbra, line 110 extends west. There are three trains a day to Luso. The one-way fare is 1.80€ ($2.05).

BY BUS Five buses a day run to Luso from Coimbra, a 1-hour trip. Beginning at 7:45am, departures are about every 1½ hours. The one-way cost is 3€ ($3.45). For information and schedules, call ✆ **23/982-70-81.**

BY CAR From Coimbra, head north along the Lisbon-Porto motorway—the most important highway in the country—until you come to the signposted turnoff for Luso. Head east for another 6km (3½ miles).

VISITOR INFORMATION

The **Luso Tourist Office** is on Rua Emídio Navarro (✆ **23/193-91-33**). October through June it's open Monday through Friday 9:30am to 12:30pm and 2 to 6pm, Saturday and Sunday 10am to 1pm and 3 to 5pm. July through September it's open Monday through Friday 9am to 7pm and Saturday and Sunday 10am to 1pm and 3 to 5pm.

WHERE TO STAY

Grande Hotel de Luso ★★ With a backdrop of rolling forests, the vanilla-colored Grande Hotel, built in 1945, nestles in a valley amid abundant foliage. It's a sprawling place adjacent to the spa, offering comfortable, well-proportioned rooms with matching furnishings; some open onto private terraces with views of the tree-covered valley. All units have neatly kept bathrooms equipped with shower-tub combinations.

Guests praise the thermal spa facilities here. You can lounge and sunbathe on the grassy terrace, or relax under the weeping willows and bougainvillea arbor.

Rua Dr. Kid Oliveira 86, 3050-210 Luso. ✆ **23/193-79-37.** Fax 23/193-79-30. 143 units. 75€–100€ ($86–$115) double; 190€–250€ ($219–$288) suite. Rates include continental breakfast. AE, DC, MC, V. Free parking. **Amenities:** Restaurant; bar; 2 pools; 2 tennis courts; thermal spa; sauna; room service (8am–midnight); babysitting; laundry service; 1 room for those w/limited mobility. *In room:* A/C, TV, dataport, minibar, hair dryer, safe.

Vila Duparchy ★ *Finds* Half a kilometer (⅓ mile) from the center of Luso, this 8-hectare (20-acre) working horse farm is across from the town's only gas station. Conceived in the 19th century as a farmhouse, it was named after the French-born engineer who designed and built the town's rail station. He lived here during the late 19th century before selling it to the present owner's forebears. Today, under Oscar and Maria Santos, the place has some of the most appealing accommodations in the region. Rooms vary in shape and size; all are exceedingly comfortable, with fine bed linens. The Santos family's main business is rearing and training horses; if you're qualified, you can usually arrange to go horseback riding during your stay.

Luso, 3050-235 Mealhada. ✆ **23/193-07-90.** Fax 23/193-03-07. principe.santos@clix.pt. 6 units. 65€–75€ ($75–$86) double. Rates include breakfast. AE, MC, V. Free parking. **Amenities:** Dining room; bar; pool; TV room. *In room:* No phone.

WHERE TO DINE

Restaurant O Cesteiro PORTUGUESE This unpretentious restaurant is near the train station, about a 5-minute walk from the center. It's on the road leading out of town toward Mealhada. The popular bar does a brisk business with local artisans and farmers. The fare is likely to include duck stew, roast goat, roast suckling pig with saffron sauce, and an array of fish dishes, including cod. The food is decently prepared and fresh. On weekends, motoring Portuguese families fill the tables.

Rua Monseñor Raul Nira, 74. 3050-267 Luso ✆ **23/193-93-60.** Main courses 6.50€–11€ ($7.50–$13). AE, MC, V. Daily noon–3pm and 7–10pm.

6 Cúria

11km (6¾ miles) NW of Luso, 26km (16 miles) NW of Buçaco, 229km (142 miles) N of Lisbon, 19km (12 miles) N of Coimbra

Cúria, in the foothills of the Serra de Estrêla, forms a well-known tourist triangle with Luso and Buçaco. Its spa has long been a draw for people seeking the curative properties of the medicinal waters, which are slightly saline and contain calcium sulfates and sodium and magnesium bicarbonates. In addition, the town has tennis courts, swimming pools, roller-skating rinks, a lake for boating, cinemas, and teahouses. The season for taking the waters is April to October; June sees the beginning of the largest influx.

In the Bairrada wine-growing district, Cúria offers the fine wines of the region. The famous local cuisine includes roast suckling pig, roast kid, and sweets.

ESSENTIALS

ARRIVING

BY TRAIN Fifteen trains per day make the 25-minute trip between Coimbra and Cúria. If you're visiting Cúria by train from Lisbon, go first to Coimbra and change trains there.

BY BUS There is no bus service to Cúria.

BY CAR From Coimbra, head north along N1.

VISITOR INFORMATION

The **Cúria Tourist Office** is on Largo da Rotunda (✆ **23/151-22-48**). It's open daily 9am to 12:30pm and 2 to 6pm.

WHERE TO STAY & DINE

Grande Hotel de Cúria ★★ This is a grand old spa hotel in the old-fashioned tradition. The Grande Hotel was an elegant hideaway for many of Europe's crowned heads after it opened in the 1880s, but then it saw years of neglect. Following massive renovations by Portugal's Belver Hotel Group, it reopened in 1990. The most prominent structure in town, with a lavish Art Nouveau facade, the hotel reigns as the finest in the region. Decorative touches in the public rooms include marble floors and lavish upholstery and carpets. There's a carefully trained staff. The midsize to spacious guest rooms come in two styles: Art Deco nostalgic and conservative modern. All come equipped with neatly kept bathrooms containing shower-tub combinations. The hotel is a few steps west of the center of the village, less than a kilometer (¾ mile) from the railway station.

Tamingos-Anadia, 3780-541 Anadia. ✆ **23/151-57-20.** Fax 23/151-53-17. 84 units. 95€–105€ ($109–$121) double; 152€–190€ ($175–$219) suite. Rates include breakfast. AE, DC, MC, V. Free parking. **Amenities:** Restaurant; bar; 2 pools; gym; health spa; sauna; concierge; room service (7am–midnight); massage; babysitting; laundry service. *In room:* A/C, TV.

Hotel das Termas ★ You approach Hotel das Termas on a curving road through a parklike setting with lacy shade trees. The guest rooms have a homey feeling, with lots of floral chintz, wooden beds, and walls of wardrobe space. All units have well-kept bathrooms equipped with shower-tub combinations. The hotel has a British colonial atmosphere, with lots of brass and wicker. It offers facilities for health and relaxation, including a park with a rustic wooden bridge leading over a lake to walks.

Cúria, 3780-541 Tamingos. © **23/151-21-85.** Fax 23/151-58-38. 57 units. 60€–90€ ($69–$104) double. Rates include breakfast. AE, DC, MC, V. Free parking. **Amenities:** Restaurant; bar; pool; tennis courts; bike rentals; limited room service; laundry service. *In room:* A/C, TV, hair dryer, safe.

Pensão Lourenço *Value* Throughout the spa, a series of signs points motorists to this simple inn, which you'll find in a tree-lined hollow away from the town center. It occupies a pair of buildings on either side of a narrow road. One of the buildings contains a ground-floor cafe whose tables sometimes spill into the road. Guest rooms are small, with time-worn but comfortable furnishings. All units have well-kept bathrooms with showers or shower-tub combinations. Most of the guests are elderly; many are pensioners who come to Cúria season after season. They form a closely knit community of shared interests and needs.

Cúria, 3780-541 Anadia. © **23/151-22-14.** 38 units. 25€–30€ ($29–$35) double. Rates include breakfast. No credit cards. Closed Oct–May. Free parking on street. **Amenities:** Breakfast room. *In room:* TV.

Quinta de São Lourenço ★ *Finds* In the village of São Laurenço do Barrio, 3km (1¾ miles) from the center of Cúria, stands this unexpected discovery. A manor house, built in the 1700s and enveloped by vineyards and a pine forest, has been converted to receive paying guests. The bathrooms are modern, with tubs, but much of the house, including the antiques and wooden floors, evokes another time. Bedrooms are well maintained and comfortably furnished, much like a typical Portuguese family house. The main house has a modern extension containing the bedrooms, and there is also an apartment to rent.

3780-179 São Lourenço do Barrio. © **23/152-81-68.** Fax 23/152-85-94. 7 units. 75€ ($86) double or apt. Rates include breakfast. No credit cards. **Amenities:** Pool. *In room:* TV, kitchenette in apt, no phone.

7 Aveiro ★

56km (35 miles) N of Coimbra, 68km (42 miles) S of Porto

Myriad canals spanned by low-arched bridges crisscross Aveiro. At the mouth of the Vouga River, it's cut off from the sea by a long sandbar that protects clusters of islets. The architecture is almost Flemish, a good foil for a setting of low willow-reed flatlands, salt marshes, spray-misted dunes, and rice paddies.

On the lagoon, brightly painted swan-necked boats traverse the waters. Called *barcos moliceiros,* the flat-bottomed vessels carry fishers who harvest seaweed used for fertilizer. They're ever on the lookout for eels, a regional specialty, which they catch in the shoals studded with lotus and water lilies. Outside the town are extensive salt pits, lined with fog-white pyramids of drying salt.

ESSENTIALS

ARRIVING

BY TRAIN The **rail station** is at Largo da Estação (© **808/208-208**). At least 30 trains per day make the 40-minute run from Porto (see chapter 11). The fare is 9€ ($10) one-way. Some 29 trains arrive daily from Coimbra; the trip takes an hour and costs 9€ ($10) one-way. Twenty-six trains per day arrive from Lisbon; it's a 5-hour trip, and the one-way fare is 19€ ($22).

BY BUS The nearest Rodoviária (national express bus company) station is at Agueda, 19km (12 miles) from Aveiro. Buses connect Agueda with the train station at Aveiro. For information and schedules, call © **23/442-37-47.**

BY CAR Continue north along A1 from Coimbra to the junction with N235, which leads west to Aveiro.

VISITOR INFORMATION

The **Aveiro Tourist Office** is at Rua João Mendonça 8 (✆ **23/442-36-80**) and is open Monday through Sunday from 9am to 8pm.

EXPLORING THE AREA The town is quite congested, and many readers have expressed disappointment with the incessant whine of Vespas and the foul-smelling canal water. Others, however, find it worth the journey.

The lagoons and many secret pools that dot the landscape around Aveiro make for a fine **boat excursion.** Inquire at the tourist office (see above).

Convento de Jesús ★, Avenida Santa Joana Princesa (✆ **23/442-32-97**), is hailed as the finest example of the baroque style in Portugal. The Infanta Santa Joana, sister of João II and daughter of Afonso V, took the veil here in 1472. Her tomb, an inlaid rectangle of marble quarried in Italy, attracts many pilgrims. Its delicate pale pinks and roses lend it the air of a cherub-topped confection.

The convent, owned by the state and now called the **Museu de Aveiro** ★, displays a lock of the saint's hair, her belt and rosary, and a complete pictorial study of her life. A **portrait** ★ of her is exceptional. Painted in the late 15th century, it is attributed to Nuno Gonçalves. What's most noteworthy about the convent is its carved gilt work, lustrous in the chapel despite the dust.

In this setting is an assortment of 15th-century paintings, royal portraits of Carlos I and Manuel II (the last two Bragança kings), 16th-, 17th-, and 18th-century sculpture, and antique ceramics. There are also some well-preserved 18th- and 19th-century coaches and carriages. After viewing all this, you can walk through the cloisters, which have Doric columns. The museum is open Tuesday through Sunday from 10am to 5:30pm. Admission is 1.50€ ($1.75) for adults and free for children under 15.

On Rua Santa Joana Princesa is the 15th-century **Igreja de São Domingo,** with blue-and-gold altarpieces and egg-shape windows flanking the upper nave. The facade, in Gothic-Manueline style, is decorated with four flame finials. To the right (facing) is a bell tower.

After a meal of stewed eels and a bottle of hearty Bairrada wine, you might want to explore some of the settlements along the lagoon. In **Ilhavo,** about 5km (3 miles) south of Aveiro on the IC1, you can stop at the **Museu Maritimo,** Avenida Dr. Roca Madahil (✆ **23/432-96-08**). The unpretentious gallery offers an insight into the lives of people who live with the sea. It displays seascape paintings, fishing equipment, ship models, and other exhibits. The museum is open Tuesday through Friday from 10am to 12:30pm and 2 to 5pm, and Saturday and Sunday 2 to 5pm. Admission is 2€ ($2.30) for adults and 1€ ($1.15) for seniors and children 6 to 17.

From Ilhavo, you can drive less than 2km (1¼ mile) south to **Vista Alegre,** the famed village of the porcelain works. Britain's Elizabeth II and Spain's Juan Carlos have commissioned pieces of Vista Alegre porcelain. On a branch of the Aveiro estuary, the village is the site of an open market held on the 13th of every month, a tradition dating from the late 1600s.

Vista Alegre Museum, Fábrica Vista Alegre (✆ **23/432-07-55**), records the history of porcelain, starting in 1824 when the factory was founded here. It's open Tuesday through Sunday from 9am to 12:30pm and 2 to 5:30pm. Admission is 1.50€ ($1.75) and free for children under 12.

OUTDOOR ACTIVITIES In the Rota da Luz area near Aveiro, you can go **windsurfing** in many places, including Ria de Aveiro and Pateira de Fermentelos. The long stretches of sand and the formation of waves also provide ideal conditions for **surfing;** particularly good Rota da Luz **beaches** are Esmoriz, Cortegaça, Furadouro, Torreira, São Jacinto, Barra, Costa-Nova, and Vagueira. The whole stretch of the Ria estuary is ideal for **water-skiing,** and many rivers, notably the Pateira and the Ria, are suited for **canoeing** and **rowing.**

There's good **fishing** along the Rota da Luz. The tourist office (see above) provides helpful information. The local waterways contain carp, lampreys, and barbels, along with gray mullet, bass, and eels. The best places for trout are the rivers Paiva, Arda, Antuà, Caima, Alfusqueiro, and Agueda.

Horseback riders head for the **Escola Equestre de Aveiro,** Quinta Chão Agra, Vilarinho (✆ **23/491-21-08**), 6.5km (4 miles) north of Aveiro on N109. It offers trekking rides across the wetlands around Aveiro. The cost is 20€ ($23) per rider for 2 hours. Call for reservations and more information.

Many visitors to the area like to go **biking,** particularly along the traffic-free route between Aveiro and Ovar. You can get free bikes near the tourist office on Rua João Mendonça (✆ **23/442-00-80**).

SHOPPING You'll find handcrafts and the sophisticated porcelain manufactured in the village of Vista Alegre, 6.5km (4 miles) south. To visit the **Vista Alegre factory outlet** (✆ **23/432-06-00**), follow the signs from Aveiro's town center. Free visits to the manufacturing facilities are conducted Monday through Friday from 9am to 12:30pm and 2 to 4:30pm. The factory outlet is open Tuesday through Sunday from 9am to 12:30pm and 2 to 7pm.

Another outfit with worthwhile inventories of porcelain and pottery imported directly from a nearby factory is **O Buraco** (no phone), at Mercado Manuel Firmino, Losa 5.

The town's most visible and best-stocked shopping venues are on the main boulevard bisecting the town, **Avenida Dr. Lourenço Peixenho.** The shops on this street sell virtually everything a local resident might need to pursue the good life in the Portuguese and international style.

WHERE TO STAY

Arcada Hotel The family-owned Arcada enjoys an enviable central position, with a view of the traffic in the canal out front. In summer, white pyramids of drying salt on the flats are visible from the guest rooms. The modernized hotel retains its classic beige-and-white facade and its rooftop decorated with ornate finials. The hotel occupies the second, third, and fourth floors of the old building. Many of the midsize guest rooms open onto balconies, and each has a neatly kept bathroom equipped with a shower-tub combination. Some are in the traditional Portuguese style; others evoke 1950s international style, with blond furnishings. Some units can be noisy. Breakfast is the only meal served.

Rua Viana do Castelo 4, 3800 Aveiro. ✆ **23/442-30-01.** Fax 23/442-18-86. 49 units. 50€–60€ ($58–$69) double. Rates include breakfast. AE, DC, MC, V. Free parking. **Amenities:** Breakfast room; bar; limited room service; laundry service. *In room:* TV, hair dryer (on request).

Hotel Afonso V ★ We think this is the best place in town, though many people prefer the Imperial (below). If you're driving, signs will direct you to the hotel, in a residential, tree-lined neighborhood. Small sea-green tiles line the facade. A recent enlargement and renovation turned the original core into a contemporary structure. The midsize guest rooms are comfortably furnished. All rooms contain neatly kept bathrooms with shower-tub combinations.

Rua Dr. Manuel das Neves 65, 3810-101 Aveiro. ✆ **23/442-51-91.** Fax 23/438-11-11. 80 units. 60€–69€ ($69–$79) double; 74€–84€ ($85–$97) suite. Rates include breakfast. AE, MC, V. Parking 1.50€ ($1.75). **Amenities:** Restaurant; bar; laundry service. *In room:* A/C, TV, dataport, minibar, hair dryer, safe.

Hotel Imperial ★ Unexceptional but efficient and modern, the Imperial is often cited as the best hotel in town by those who prefer it over the Afonso V (see above). It attracts local young people, who gravitate to the lounge for drinks or to the airy dining room (a favorite with tour groups). Many of the small, neutrally decorated guest rooms and all of the lounges overlook the Ria de Aveiro and the garden of the Aveiro museum, the old convent. From the summer terrace, a view sweeps over the arid expanse of the district's salt pans. All rooms are furnished in contemporary style, with many built-in features, firm beds, and neatly kept bathrooms equipped with shower-tub combinations.

Rua Dr. Nascimento Leitão, 3810-108 Aveiro. ✆ **800/582-1234** in the U.S., or 23/438-01-50. Fax 23/438-01-51. 103 units. 63€–70€ ($72–$81) double; 105€ ($121) suite. Rates include breakfast. AE, DC, MC, V. Free parking. **Amenities:** Restaurant; bar; pool; gym; sauna; limited room service; babysitting; laundry service; nonsmoking rooms; rooms for those w/limited mobility. *In room:* A/C, TV, dataport, minibar, hair dryer, safe.

Hotel João Padeiro ★ *Finds* Beside the N109, 7km (4⅓ miles) north of Aveiro, João Padeiro is a sienna-colored building concealing an elegant hotel. It was a village cafe until the Simões family transformed it more than a decade ago. You enter a reception area filled with family antiques. Each unit is unique, and most contain an antique four-poster bed; all boast exuberantly flowered wallpaper, coved ceilings, and hand-crocheted bedspreads. Each unit has a well-maintained bathroom equipped with a shower-tub combination.

Rua da República 13, Cacia, 3800-533 Aveiro. ✆ **23/491-13-26.** Fax 23/491-27-51. 26 units. 55€ ($63) double; 60€ ($69) suite for 2. Rates include breakfast. AE, DC, MC, V. Free parking. **Amenities:** Restaurant; bar; limited room service; laundry service. *In room:* TV, dataport.

Mercure Aveiro ★ *Finds* This hotel occupies a Moorish-style building that was once an aristocratic private villa. An iron fence encloses the front courtyard, where trees, vines, and hand-painted tiles surround a fountain. The best rooms look out over the third-floor loggia onto a goldfish-filled basin in the garden. You'll find this well-preserved house (known in Portuguese as an *antiga moradia senhoria,* meaning "antique manor house") on a busy downtown street leading into the city from Porto. Most of the large guest rooms are old-fashioned; all are equipped with well-maintained bathrooms containing shower-tub combinations. Breakfast is the only meal served.

Rua Luís Gomes de Carvalho 23, 3800-211 Aveiro. ✆ **23/440-44-00.** Fax 23/440-44-01. www.mercure.com. 45 units. 62€ ($71) double. AE, DC, MC, V. Parking 4€ ($4.60). **Amenities:** Breakfast room; bar; limited room service; laundry service on weekdays; nonsmoking rooms; 1 room for those w/limited mobility. *In room:* A/C, TV, minibar, hair dryer, safe.

WHERE TO DINE

A Cozinha do Rei ★ PORTUGUESE/INTERNATIONAL A Cozinha do Rei is in the best hotel in town (see "Where to Stay," above). The formal restaurant serves regional and international meals in a modernized sun-washed room. You can order fresh fish with confidence. Service is among the best in town.

In the Hotel Afonso V, Rua Dr. Manuel das Neves 66. ✆ **23/448-37-10.** Regular main courses 9.50€–14€ ($11–$16); tourist menu 13€ ($15); seafood main courses 15€–53€ ($17–$60). AE, MC, V. Daily noon–midnight.

Restaurante Centenário PORTUGUESE Centenário stands at the side of Aveiro's version of Les Halles. From the front door you can see the teeming covered market; laborers often stream up to the elongated bar after unloading produce early in the morning. The high-ceilinged, modern room contains lots of polished wood and has a large window opening onto the street. The restaurant is also called *A Casa da Sopa do Mar,* and that shellfish-laden soup is the house specialty. In addition to a steaming bowl, you can order grilled pork or veal, fried or grilled sole, codfish *brasa* (cooked over charcoal), and an array of other good-tasting specials. This isn't gourmet fare, but it's good and satisfying.

Largo do Mercado 9–10. ✆ **23/442-27-98.** Main courses 9€–20€ ($10–$23). MC, V. Daily 9am–midnight.

WHERE TO STAY & DINE NEARBY

Pousada da Ria ★★ The government operates this pousada, about 30km (19 miles) northwest from Aveiro on a promontory surrounded by water on three sides. Between the sea and the lagoon, it's a contemporary building that makes good use of glass and has rows of balconies on its second floor. You can reach it by boat from Aveiro or by taking a long drive via Murtosa and Torreira. A waterside terrace opens onto views of fishing craft. The inn is popular with vacationing Portuguese families. The compact guest rooms are furnished with built-in pieces, including firm beds. All units come equipped with well-maintained bathrooms containing shower-tub combinations.

Bico do Muranzel, 3870-301 Torreira-Murtosa. ✆ **23/486-01-80.** Fax 23/483-83-33. 19 units. 102€–152€ ($117–$175) double. Rates include breakfast. AE, DC, MC, V. Free parking. **Amenities:** Restaurant; bar; pool; limited room service; laundry service. *In room:* A/C, TV, minibar, hair dryer, safe.

AVEIRO AFTER DARK

The core of the city's nightlife is the **Canal de São Roque,** near the Mercado de Peixe in the town center. Here you'll find a trio of 18th-century stone salt warehouses. They've been transformed into attractive, richly folkloric bars that draw loyal local patrons. One is **Cal Ponente** (✆ **23/438-26-74**), which functions from 7 to 10pm as a well-managed restaurant and then from 10:30pm to around 4am as a venue for live concerts. Expect to hear lots of Brazilian samba and rock—everything except fado. Cal Ponente is one of the few eateries in town with views that encompass both the lagoon and the town's age-old salt pans. Another choice is the **Eugência Bar** (✆ **23/442-80-82**).

If you want to go dancing, head for the town's most appealing dance club, **Disco Oito Graus Oeste** (Eight Degrees West Disco), Canal do Paraiso (✆ **23/442-32-97**).

8 Caramulo

81km (50 miles) NE of Coimbra, 280km (174 miles) N of Lisbon

Set against a background of mimosa and heather-laden mountains, this tiny resort between Aveiro and Viseu is a good place from which to view the surrounding country. About 3km (1¾ miles) north of town, at the end of a dirt road, is a watchtower that affords a panoramic view of the Serra do Caramulo.

ESSENTIALS

ARRIVING

BY TRAIN There is no train service to Caramulo.

BY BUS From Lisbon, you must go to Tondela and then make connections into Caramulo. You can also go from Lisbon to Viseu (see section 9, below) and then ride the bus to Caramulo, though you'll have to allow at least 5 hours. You can also take the train from Lisbon to Coimbra (see section 3 in this chapter), a bus to Tondela, and another bus to Caramulo.

BY CAR The village is usually approached from Viseu (see section 9, below). Follow N2 south for some 24km (15 miles) to Tondela, and then take a right onto N230 and follow signs for Caramulo for about 19km (12 miles).

VISITOR INFORMATION

The **Caramulo Tourist Office** is on Estrada Principal do Caramulo (✆ **23/286-14-37**). It's open daily 9am to 1pm and 3 to 6pm.

EXPLORING THE AREA

From the tip of the mountain, about 7km (4⅓ miles) from town at **Caramulinho,** you can see for miles. The panoramic sweep includes the Lapa, Estrela, Lousa, and Buçaco ranges; the Serras da Gralheira and do Montemura; and the coastal plain. To reach the best viewing place on the 1,000m-high (3,280-ft.-high) peak, take Avenida Abel de Lacerda from Caramulo west to N230-3 and then go less than 1km (¾ mile) on foot. Another panoramic vista spreads out from the summit of **Cabeça da Neve,** off the same road you'd take to go to Caramulinho.

Museu do Caramulo ★ (✆ **23/286-12-70;** www.museu-caramulo.net) houses at least 60 vintage cars, including a 1905 4-cylinder De Dion–Bouton, a 1909 Fiat, an 1899 Peugeot, a 1902 Oldsmobile, a 1911 Rolls-Royce, and a 1902 Darracq. The cars have been restored to perfect condition. A few early bicycles, one dating to 1865, and motorcycles are on exhibit. The museum also contains Portuguese and foreign paintings and art by such diverse artists as Dalí, Picasso, and Grão Vasco. Admission is 6€ ($6.90) for adults, 3€ ($3.45) for children 6 to 12, and free for children under 6. The museum is open daily from 10am to 1pm and 2 to 6pm.

WHERE TO STAY & DINE

Pousada de São Jerónimo ★★ *Finds* High as an eagle's nest, São Jerónimo is near the crest of a mountain ridge. The well-designed inn resembles a spread-out chalet. You ascend to the reception, living, and dining rooms; one salon flows into another. In winter, guests sit by the copper-hooded fireplace. Beyond the wooden grille is a pleasant dining room, with a window wall that overlooks the hills.

The guest rooms are small but attractive, with Portuguese antiques and reproductions. Wide windows open onto private balconies. All units come equipped with neatly kept bathrooms containing shower-tub combinations. If you enjoy fishing, the Agueda and Criz Rivers teem with trout and achigas, a local barbel. From here, you can follow the Besteiros valley, and from its terraces you can see the impressive Estrela mountains, 77km (48 miles) away.

3475-031 Caramulo. ✆ **23/286-12-91**. Fax 23/286-16-40. www.pousadas.pt. 12 units. 80€–118€ ($92–$136) double. Rates include continental breakfast. Free parking. AE, DC, MC, V. **Amenities:** Restaurant; bar; pool; playground; private park; room service; laundry service; 1 nonsmoking room; 1 room for those w/limited mobility. *In room:* A/C, TV, minibar, hair dryer, safe.

9 Viseu ★

97km (60 miles) E of Aveiro, 92km (57 miles) NE of Coimbra, 291km (180 miles) NE of Lisbon

The capital of Beira Alta, Viseu is a thriving provincial city. It's also a city of art treasures, palaces, and churches. Its local hero is an ancient Lusitanian rebel leader, Viriatus. At the entrance of Viseu is the Cova de Viriato, where the rebel, a combination Spartacus and Robin Hood, made his camp and plotted the moves that turned back the Roman tide.

Some of the country's most gifted artisans ply their trades in and around Viseu. Busy weaver women create the unique quilts and carpets of Vil de Moinhos, local artisans of Molelos produce the region's provincial pottery, and women with nimble fingers embroider feather-fine bone lace.

ESSENTIALS

ARRIVING

BY TRAIN The nearest rail station is at Nelas, about 24km (15 miles) south. For train information, call ✆ **808/208-208.** Buses run from Nelas to Viseu; the fare is 2.10€ ($2.40). The fare from Lisbon to Nelas is 12€ ($13).

BY BUS Nine Rodoviária buses per day make the 2-hour trip from Coimbra. Ten buses per day come from Lisbon, a 5-hour run. For information, call ✆ **23/985-52-70.**

BY CAR Viseu lies near the center of the modern expressway, IP-5, which cuts across Portugal. IP-5 hooks up with the Lisbon-Porto motorway. Coming from Spain, motorists enter Portugal at the Vilar Formoso Customs station and then head west to Viseu.

VISITOR INFORMATION

The **Viseu Tourist Board** is on Avenida Gulbenkian (✆ **23/242-09-50**). Hours vary throughout the year, so call ahead.

WHAT TO SEE & DO IN VISEU

EXPLORING THE TOWN

Viseu offers much to see and explore at random. Wander the cubistic network of overlapping tiled rooftops, entwining narrow alleys, and encroaching macadam streets. If your time is limited, head at once to **Largo da Sé,** the showplace of Viseu. Here, on one of the most harmonious squares in Portugal, you'll find the town's two most important buildings.

Largo da Sé (Cathedral) ★ The severe Renaissance facade of this cathedral evokes a fortress. Two lofty bell towers, unadorned stone up to the summit of the balustrades, with crowning cupolas, are visible from almost any point in or around town. The second-story windows—two rectangular and one oval—are latticed and symmetrically surrounded by niches containing religious statuary.

On your right, you'll first find the two-story Renaissance cloister, adorned with classic pillars and arcades faced with tiles. The cathedral interior is essentially Gothic but infused with Manueline and baroque decorations. Plain, slender Romanesque columns line the nave, supporting the vaulted Manueline ceiling with nautically roped **groining** ★. The basic color scheme inside plays brilliant gilding against muted gold stone. The emphasis is on the Roman arched chancel, climaxed by an elegantly carved **retable** ★ above the main altar. The chancel makes ingenious use of color counterpoint, with copper, green gold, and brownish yellow complementing the gilt work. The ceiling continues in the sacristy.

Largo da Sé. ✆ **23/243-60-65.** Free admission. Daily 8am–7pm.

Museu de Grão Vasco ★★ This museum, next door to the cathedral, was named after the 16th-century painter, also known as Vasco Fernandes. The Portuguese master's major works are on display; especially notable is *La Pontecôte,* in which lancelike tongues of fire hurtle toward the saints, some devout, others apathetic. There's also an intriguing collection of sculpture from the 13th to the 18th centuries, with a stunning **Throne of Grace** ★ from the 1300s.

Largo da Sé. ✆ **23/242-20-49.** Admission 1.50€ ($1.75), free for children under 15. Tues 2–6pm; Wed–Sun 10am–6pm.

SHOPPING

Viseu has many handcrafts shops. On **Rua Direita,** the main street, you'll find merchants selling pottery, wrought iron, and woodcarvings. The most comprehensive stock is at the **Casa de Ribiera,** Camera Municipal de Viseu, Praça da República (✆ **23/242-35-01**), which carries selections from many of the region's best artisans.

WHERE TO STAY

Grão Vasco ★ In the heart of town, near Praça da República, Grão Vasco sits amid gardens and parks. It's built like a motel; the guest room balconies overlook an oval pool. After days of driving in the lodging-poor environs, you'll find it a pleasure to check in here. The decor is colorful and contemporary, and the guest rooms are decorated with reproductions of traditional Portuguese furnishings. Most are large, and all have well-maintained bathrooms equipped with shower-tub combinations.

Rua Gaspar Barreiros, 3510-032 Viseu. ✆ **23/242-35-11.** Fax 23/242-64-44. hotelgraovasco@mail.telepack.pt. 110 units. 77€–86€ ($89–$99) double; 105€ ($121) suite. Rates include breakfast. AE, DC, MC, V. Free parking. **Amenities:** Restaurant; bar; pool; 24-hr. room service; laundry service; nonsmoking rooms; rooms for those w/limited mobility. *In room:* A/C, TV, dataport, minibar, hair dryer, safe.

Hotel Avenida *Value* Avenida is a personalized small hotel right off Rossio, the town's main plaza. It's the domain of the personable Mario Abrantes da Motto Veiga, who has combined his collection of African and Chinese antiques with pieces of fine old Portuguese furniture. The small guest rooms vary in size and character. For example, room 210B boasts a high-coved bed and an old refectory table and chair; an adjoining chamber has a wooden spindle bed and a marble-topped chest. All are equipped with neatly kept bathrooms containing shower-tub combinations.

Av. Alberto Sampaio 1, 3510-030 Viseu. ✆ **23/242-34-32.** Fax 23/243-56-43. www.turism.net/avenida. 29 units. 45€–55€ ($52–$63) double. Rates include breakfast. AE, DC, MC, V. Free parking. **Amenities:** Dining room; bar; 24-hr. room service; laundry service. *In room:* TV.

Hotel Montebelo ★★ This independent hotel is the best in town, with an enviable reputation based on the attentiveness of its multilingual staff. Less than .5km (⅓ mile) from the town center, on a rise providing a panorama over the countryside, it stands in a pleasant garden. The four floors incorporate hundreds of large windows. The midsize rooms are traditionally and comfortably furnished, and all come equipped with neatly kept bathrooms containing shower-tub combinations. Maintenance is all state-of-the-art.

Urbanização Quinta do Bosque, 3510-020 Viseu. ✆ **23/242-00-00.** Fax 23/241-54-00. 100 units. 95€ ($109) double; 120€ ($138) junior suite. Rates include breakfast. AE, DC, MC, V. Free parking. **Amenities:** Restaurant; 2 bars; pool; tennis court; health club; Jacuzzi; sauna; limited room service; laundry service. *In room:* A/C, TV, dataport, minibar, hair dryer, safe.

Quinta de São Caetano ★ *Finds* Less than 1km (¾ mile) north of the center of Viseu, this is one of the most renowned properties in the region. Built in the 17th century, with a chapel dating from 1638, it was the home for many years of the viscountess of St. Caetano. It was also the setting of the novel *Eugénia e Silvina,* by the prominent contemporary Portuguese novelist Agustina Bessa Luís.

Members of the Vieira de Matos family run the severely dignified hotel. On the premises are a garden with mature trees (including a century-old Atlantic cedar) and a greenhouse where flowers grow. Dark-grained, sometimes antique furnishings fill the thick-walled rooms. Guest rooms in various sizes and shapes are traditionally furnished, with excellent beds. All units have well-kept bathrooms containing showers. Breakfast usually is the only meal served. With prior notice, lunch and dinner can be prepared for groups. There's a billiard table on the premises, and horseback riding can be arranged with the owner of a nearby stable.

Rua Possa dos Feiticeiras 38, 3500-020 Viseu. ✆ **23/242-39-84.** Fax 23/243-78-27. bfe00894@mail.telepac.pt. 6 units. 75€ ($86) double. Rates include breakfast. AE, MC, V. Free parking. **Amenities:** Breakfast room; swimming pool. *In room:* A/C, no phone.

WHERE TO DINE

Cortiço PORTUGUESE In the oldest part of Viseu's historic core, close to the cathedral and upstairs from the Museo de Grão Vasco, this is one of the most appealing restaurants in town. A team of articulate, English-speaking locals prepares winning versions of time-tested dishes. You can select from several tasty versions of codfish, roasted breast of duck, stewed or roasted partridge (when available), and rack of rabbit simmered in red wine. One of the most prized dishes is octopus, grilled or fried, with herbs and lemon. Many diners consider it the best in the region. The wines, from throughout Portugal, are reasonably priced.

Rua de Augusto Helário. ✆ **23/242-38-53.** Main courses 7.50€–20€ ($8.65–$23). AE, DC, MC, V. Daily noon–3pm and 7–11pm.

Muralha da Sé ★ PORTUGUESE Next to the cathedral, this is the town's most rewarding dining stopover and has been since it opened. In the historic district, it is decorated in a regional style and secures some of the best of the bounty from the countryside, which its cooks fashion into delectable platters. We are especially found of their grilled lamb dishes, although their grilled baby beef tastes equally as good. Although hardly by the sea, the establishment manages to secure fresh fish from the Atlantic, which is cooked to perfection. The fresh vegetables make meals here a treat. The service is rather casual, and there is a respectable and most affordable wine list.

Adro da Sé 24. ✆ **23/243-77-77.** Reservations recommended. Main courses 10€–20€ ($12–$23). AE, DC, MC, V. Tues–Sun 12:30–3pm and 9:30–11pm.

11

Porto & Environs

Porto (Oporto in English) is Portugal's second-largest city and its capital of port wine. The 15th-century residence of the royal family, and a bastion of trade and mercantilism, the city is rich in the legacy of the past—art treasures, medieval cathedrals, famous museums, a fine library, and other attractions. Many old homes trace their beginnings to fortunes made in Portugal's overseas colonies and, in some cases, to events leading up to the Age of Discoveries.

Every year, port wine is brought from vineyards along either side of the Douro River to lodges at Vila Nova de Gaia, across the river from Porto, where it's aged, blended, and processed. In the past it was transported on flat-bottomed boats called *barcos rabelos.* With their long rudders and flapping sails, these boats with tails skirted down the Douro like swallows. Nowadays, they've nearly given way to the train and even the unglamorous truck.

The city, which is undergoing a major renovation and sprucing up, has never looked better. Some of its alleyways—especially those around the old port—look as if they haven't changed since the Middle Ages. Porto's labyrinth of steep streets, with their decorative *azulejos* (tiles) and wrought-iron balconies, often filled with potted flowers, is reason enough to visit the city.

Especially rewarding is the **Barredo** section, a UNESCO World Heritage Site. Architect Fernando Namora, a Porto citizen, is supervising the restoration of this old-fashioned district. The sectors of Miragaia and Ribeira are also being restored.

The city also boasts a lively arts and cultural scene. The **Serralves Foundation,** one of the country's most dramatic cultural centers, often sponsors events. Many art galleries are sprouting up in the hilly **Miragaia** district, near the river. Poetry readings, art exhibits, and live jazz and rock concerts characterize Porto today.

An underrated stretch of coastal resorts and fishing villages lies between Porto and the southern reaches of the **Minho** district. The Atlantic waters, however, are likely to be on the chilly side, even in July and August. In recent years the resorts have grown tremendously; they're known more to European vacationers than to Americans, who still prefer the Algarve. Overall, however, Porto and the coast to its north and south are among the most rewarding places to visit in Portugal.

Flying from Lisbon is the speediest way to Porto, though the express train or motorway takes only 3½ hours. Once in Porto, the transportation hub of the area, you can explore the coastal towns by bus or car.

1 Porto ★★★

314km (195 miles) N of Lisbon, 304km (189 miles) S of La Coruña, Spain, 589km (365 miles) W of Madrid, Spain

Porto (known also as the Port) gave its name not only to port wine but also to Portugal and its language. The name derives from the Roman settlement of

Portus Cale. The Douro, which comes from Rio do Ouro (River of Gold), has always been Porto's lifeblood. The city perches on a rocky gorge that the Douro cut out of a great stone mass. According to the writer Ann Bridge, "The whole thing looks like a singularly dangerous spider's web flung across space."

Porto's most interesting neighborhood is **Ribeira.** The steep, narrow streets and balconied houses evoke Lisbon's Alfama, though the quarter has its own distinctive character. Ribeira preserves the timeless quality of many of the old buildings and cobbled streets lining the riverbank.

Many visitors write off Porto as an industrial city with some spectacular bridges, but there's much to enjoy here. As the provincial capital and university seat, Porto has its own artistic treasures. The city beats with a sense of industriousness—it's not surprising that Henry the Navigator was born here in the late 14th century.

ESSENTIALS

ARRIVING

BY PLANE Porto stretches along the last 5km (3 miles) of the river Douro and is the hub of northern Portugal's communication network. The quickest and easiest way to get there is by plane. **TAP,** the Portuguese airline, provides connections between Lisbon and Porto, and there are daily flights year-round. Flights arrive at the **Aeroporto Francisco de Sá Carneiro** (© **22/943-24-00**). The main office of TAP is at Praça Mouzinho de Albuquerque 105 (© **22/608-02-00**) in Porto.

A taxi, the most convenient way to get from the airport into the city center, costs around 25€ ($29) for up to four passengers with luggage. Less expensive is the **Aerobus.** Painted white with a blue stripe, it picks up passengers on the sidewalk adjacent to the luggage-retrieval carrousels at the airport. Buses run at 30-minute intervals every day between 7am and 7pm, making stops at many of the city's major hotels and at strategic points within Porto. The fare costs 2.60€ ($3) per person each way. For more information, call © **22/507-10-54,** or click on www.stcp.pt.

BY TRAIN There are two main rail stations in Porto. The **Estação de São Bento,** Praça Almeida Garrett (© **808/208-208**), is in the city center, only a block from Praça de Liberdade. Trains from here serve the Douro Valley and destinations in the north, including Viana do Castelo and Braga. East of the center, but connected to São Bento by rail, is the **Estação de Campanhã,** Rua da Estacao (© **808/208-208**). It serves the south, including Lisbon, as well as international routes. For any other rail information, go to www.cp.pt.

Twenty-six trains arrive per day from Lisbon; the trip takes 3 to 5 hours and costs 21€ ($24) one-way. Ten trains a day make the 90-minute trip from Viana do Castelo; a one-way ticket costs 13€ ($15). Twelve trains per day arrive from Coimbra; it's a 75-minute trip and costs 11€ ($13) one-way. One train per day arrives from Paris; the trip takes 27 hours and costs 120€ ($138) one-way.

BY BUS There are at least five daily departures from Lisbon. The trip takes 3 to 4 hours and costs 14€ ($16) one-way. It ends at the **bus station,** Rua Alexandre Herculano 366 (© **22/200-69-54**). Service is provided by the national bus company, **Rodoviária Nacional** (© **22/605-24-20**). There are also 10 buses per day from Coimbra; the trip takes 1½ hours and costs 10€ ($12) one-way.

BY CAR The Lisbon-Porto superhighway cuts driving time between Portugal's two leading cities to just over 3 hours. For motorists, Porto is the center of

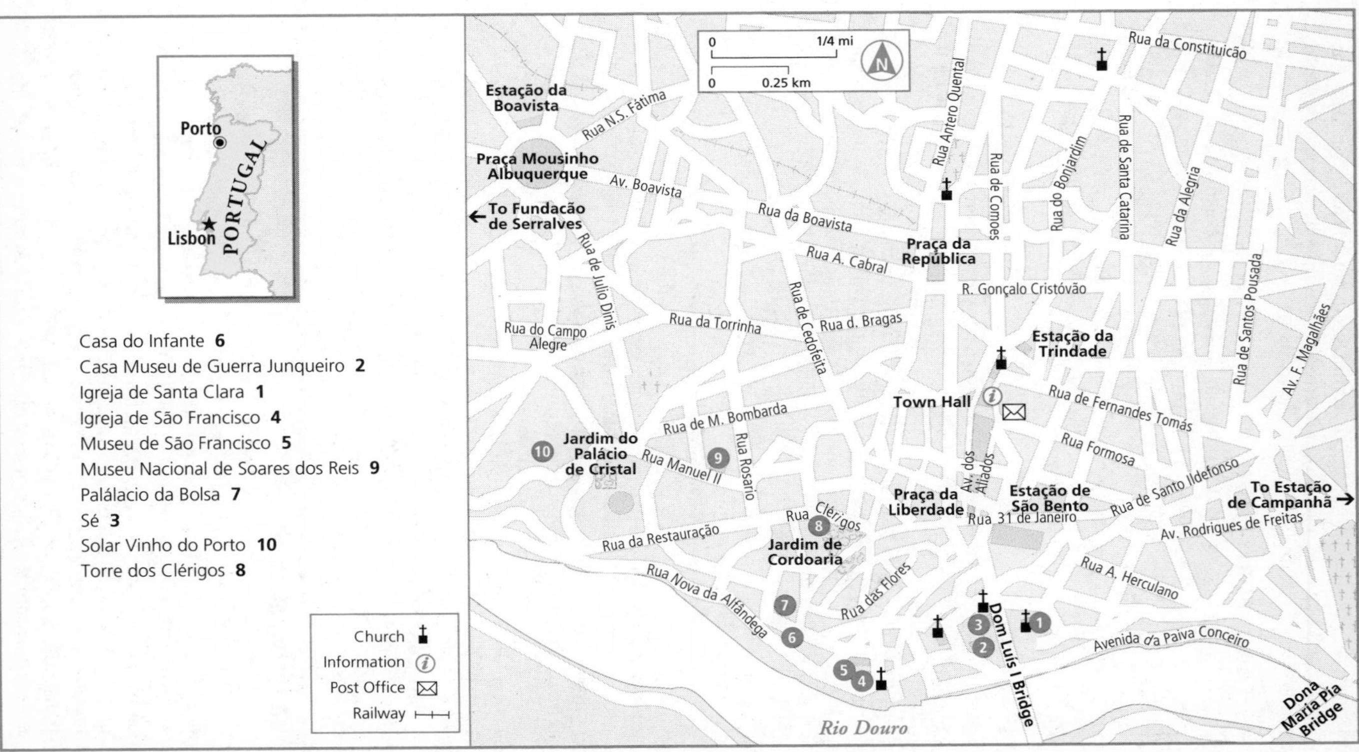
PORTUGAL
Porto
Lisbon
Casa do Infante 6
Casa Museu de Guerra Junqueiro 2
Igreja de Santa Clara 1
Igreja de São Francisco 4
Museu de São Francisco 5
Museu Nacional de Soares dos Reis 9
Palálacio da Bolsa 7
Sé 3
Solar Vinho do Porto 10
Torre dos Clérigos 8
Church
Information
Post Office
Railway
0
1/4 mi
0
0.25 km
N
Estação da Boavista
Rua N.S. Fátima
Praça Mousinho Albuquerque
Av. Boavista
To Fundacão de Serralves
Rua de Julio Dinis
Rua do Campo Alegre
Rua da Boavista
Rua A. Cabral
Rua da Torrinha
Rua de Cedofeita
Rua d. Bragas
Rua Antero Quental
Praça da República
Rua de Comoes
Rua do Bonjardim
Rua de Santa Catarina
Rua da Alegria
Rua da Constituicão
R. Gonçalo Cristóvão
Rua de Santos Pousada
Av. F. Magalhães
Estação da Trindade
Town Hall
Rua de Fernandes Tomás
Rua Formosa
Rua de M. Bombarda
Jardim do Palácio de Cristal
Rua Manuel II
Rua Rosario
Av. dos Aliados
Praça da Liberdade
Estação de São Bento
Rua 31 de Janeiro
Rua de Santo Ildefonso
To Estação de Campanhã
Av. Rodrigues de Freitas
Rua Clérigos
Rua da Restauração
Jardim de Cordoaria
Rua A. Herculano
Rua Nova da Alfândega
Rua das Flores
Dom Luís I Bridge
Avenida da Paiva Conceiro
Rio Douro
Dona Maria Pia Bridge

the universe—all major roads in the north fan out from here. From Spain, the nearest border crossing is at Tuy–Valença do Minho. After that, you can head south for some 125km (78 miles) to Porto on N13.

VISITOR INFORMATION

One of the most helpful tourist offices in Portugal is the **Porto Tourist Board,** Rua do Clube Fenianos 25 (✆ **22/205-27-40;** www.portoturismo.pt). The office is open July to September Monday through Friday from 9am to 7pm, and Saturday and Sunday from 9:30am to 4:30pm; in the off season, it's open Monday through Friday from 9am to 5:30pm, and Saturday from 9:30am to 4:30pm. Another tourist office at Rua de Infante Dom Henrique 63 (✆ **22/200-97-70**) keeps the same hours.

CITY LAYOUT

Regardless of your method of transport, you'll need to acquaint yourself with the geography of this complicated city. Its bridges are famous. Connecting the right bank to the port-wine center of Vila Nova de Gaia and the lands south is the **Ponte de Dona Maria Pía,** an architectural feat of Alexandre-Gustave Eiffel (of Eiffel Tower fame). Another bridge spanning the Douro is the **Ponte de Dom Luís I.** An iron bridge of two roadways, it was completed in 1886 by Teófilo Seyrig, a Belgian engineer inspired by Eiffel. Another bridge, Edgar Cardoso's **Ponte de Arrábida,** which opened in 1963, is bright and contemporary. Totally Portuguese in concept and execution, it's one of the largest single-span reinforced-concrete arches in Europe.

The heart of Porto is **Avenida dos Aliados,** with its parklike center where families sometimes go for a stroll. It's bounded on the south by **Praça General Humberto Delgado.** Two major shopping streets lie on either side of Praça de Liberdade: **Rua dos Clérigos** and **Rua 31 de Janeiro.** Rua Clérigos leads to the landmark **Torre dos Clérigos,** which some consider the symbol of Porto.

Foz do Douro, set about 5km (3 miles) to the northwest of Porto, stands adjacent to where the River Douro empties into the sea. Foz is scenic, calm, and mostly residential, a verdant, middle- and upper-class suburb whose income level is in distinct contrast to the grinding poverty of some neighborhoods in downtown Porto. Foz (and that's the way its name is shortened by most residents of North Portugal) is known as a "green lung" for Porto, with a rather high percentage of nightclubs and restaurants. It is connected to Porto by buses (especially bus no. 1), but an above-ground "metro" line should be completed around

Vila Nova de Gaia

For more than a century, the "other" bank of the Douro has sheltered representatives of the port wine industry, many of which maintain a sales outlet and, in most cases, warehouses. It lies just across the river from Porto, within a very short walk from the Praça de Ribeira, but spiritually, it's a long way away. Poverty is a bit more obvious on this side of the river, and the buildings are a bit less well maintained. Hotels are extremely limited here, and only a few of the restaurants are oriented to the tourist trade. The port wine lodges are by far the most visible entities here. Despite occasional flashes of bravura from the local tourist board, the mostly residential district has far fewer monuments and attractions than Porto. To reach it from Porto, take bus nos. 57 or 91.

2004. City planners predict that the route between Porto and Foz will become one of the new network's busiest lines.

Matosinhos is set about 11km (7 miles) to the northwest of Porto, beyond Foz. It is metallic, industrial, intensely commercial, and dominated by the heavy machinery that's in place to unload some of the biggest transport ships in the world. Much of it is devoted to vast warehouses, unloading docks, and cranes. But all is not purely industrial here: Matosinhos has at least one very well-known restaurant, Trinca Espinho (see "Where to Dine"), and about a half-dozen well-known dance clubs. When the much-awaited metro line is completed, Line 1 will connect it to both Foz and Porto.

GETTING AROUND

Porto is well serviced by a network of buses, trolleys, and trams; tickets begin at 1€ ($1.15). If you plan extensive touring in the area, a **Passe Turístico** is a good deal. It includes 3 days of transportation for 5€ ($5.75). Tobacco shops and kiosks around town sell the pass.

Taxis are available 24 hours a day. Call © **22/502-11-32** for radio taxis, or hail one on the street or at a taxi stand.

FAST FACTS: Porto

American Express The representative in Porto is **Top Atlantic Tours,** Rua Alferes Malheiro 96 (© **22/207-40-20**). It's open Monday through Friday from 9:30am to 1pm and 2:30 to 6:30pm.

Banks Most banks and currency-exchange offices are open Monday through Friday from 8:30 to 11:45am and 1 to 2:45pm. Two central ones are the **Banco Espírito Santo & Comercial de Lisboa,** Avenida dos Aliados 145 (© **22/209-00-00**), and the **Banco Pinto & Sotto Mayor,** Praça de Liberdade 26 (© **22/209-09-00**).

Consulates The United States and Canada don't maintain consulates in the north. There's a British Consulate at Avenida de Boavista 3072 (© **22/618-47-89**).

Drugstores Porto has many pharmacies. A centrally located one is the **Farmácia Central do Porto,** Rua do 31 Janeiro 203 (© **22/200-16-84**). If you don't speak Portuguese, ask someone at your hotel to call for you, or dial © 118 for a recording of pharmacies that remain open throughout the night.

Emergencies Emergency numbers include police (© **112** or **22/208-18-33**), fire (© **112** or **22/507-37-00**), Red Cross (© **22/600-63-53**), and Hospital de Santo António, Rua Prof. Vicente José de Carvalho (© **22/207-75-00**). Otherwise, phone © **112** for an ambulance.

Post Office The main post office is at Praça General Humberto Delgado (© **22/340-02-00**), near the tourist office. It sells stamps Monday through Friday from 9am to 10pm. You can send telegrams and faxes during those hours.

Telephone It's possible to place long-distance calls at the post office (see above). Otherwise, go to the **phone office,** Praça de Liberdade 62. It's open daily from 8am to 11:30pm. By placing your calls at these public institutions, you avoid hotel surcharges, which can be as much as 40%.

EXPLORING THE CITY

Seeing the sights of Porto requires some legwork, but your discoveries will compensate you for the effort. The tourist office suggests that you take at least 3 days to explore Porto, but most visitors spend only a day.

For those on a short schedule, the most famous things to do are visiting a wine lodge at Vila Nova de Gaia; taking in the panorama from the Torre dos Clérigos, with its view of the Douro; visiting the Sé (cathedral); strolling through the most important museum, the Museu Nacional de Soares dos Reis; walking through Ribeira, the old quarter; and, if time remains, seeing the Church of São Francisco, with its stunning and richly gilded baroque interior.

CHURCHES

Sé (Cathedral) ★ The cathedral grew and changed with the city—that is, until about the 18th century. Founded by a medieval queen and designed in a foreboding, basically Romanesque style, it's now a monument to changing architectural tastes. Part of the twin towers, the rose window, the naves, and the vestry are elements of the original 13th-century structure. The austere Gothic cloister was added at the end of the 14th century and later decorated with ***azulejos*** (tiles) ★ depicting events from the Song of Solomon. Opening off the cloister is the Chapel of St. Vincent, built in the late 16th century.

The main chapel was erected in the 17th century, and in 1736 the baroque architect Nicolau Nasoni of Italy added the north facade and its attractive loggia. Twisted columns flank the monumental **altar** ★, and the nave is adorned with fading frescoes. In the small baroque Chapel of the Holy Sacrament (to the left of the main altar) is an altarpiece fashioned entirely of silver. The work is so elaborate that the whole piece gives the illusion of constant movement.

Terreiro de Sé. ✆ **22/205-90-28**. Admission to Sé free; cloister 1.25€ ($1.45). Daily 9am–12:30pm and 2:30–6pm. Bus: 15.

Igreja de Santa Clara ★ Completed in 1416, the interior of the Church of St. Clara was transformed by impassioned 17th-century artists, masters of woodwork and gilding. Nearly every square inch is covered with carved and gilded **woodwork** ★ depicting angels, saints, cherubs, and patterned designs in an architectural mélange of rococo and baroque, one of the most exceptional examples in Portugal. The clerestory windows permit the sun to flood in, making a golden crown of the upper regions. In deliberate contrast, the building's facade is squat and plain. If the keeper of the keys takes a liking to you, he'll lead you on a behind-the-scenes tour of the precincts. In the Tribute Room, for example, you'll see a devil carved on the choir stalls.

Largo de 1 Dezembro. ✆ **22/205-48-37**. Free admission. Mon–Fri 10–11:30am and 3–7pm.

Igreja de São Francisco ★★ The Gothic Church of St. Francis, reached by steps leading up from the waterfront, was built between 1383 and 1410. In the 17th and 18th centuries, it underwent extensive **baroque decoration** ★★. The vault pillars and columns are lined with gilded woodwork: cherubs, rose garlands, fruit cornucopia, and frenzied animals, entwined and dripping with gold. Many of the wide-ribbed Gothic arches are made of marble. Soaring overhead, the marble seems to fade and blend mysteriously with the gray granite columns and floors.

The Romanesque rosette dominates the facade, whose square portal is flanked by double twisted columns. Above the columns, a profusely ornamented niche contains a simple white statue of the patron saint. In the rose window, 12 mullions emanate from the central circle in apostolic symbolism, ending in a swaglike stone fringe. The steps spill fanlike into the square, along the base of the curved walls. Nearby, through a separate entrance, is the Museu de São Francisco (see below).

Praça do Infante Dom Henríque. ✆ **22/206-21-00.** Admission (including church and museum) 2.50€ ($2.90). Daily 9am–6pm. Bus: 1, 57, or 88.

MUSEUMS

Casa Museu de Guerra Junqueiro The famous Portuguese poet Guerra Junqueiro lived here between 1850 and 1923. The Italian architect Niccolò Nasoni (1691–1773) built the house. The room arrangements preserve Junqueiro's private art collection and memorabilia. The collection includes Georgian and Portuguese silver; Flemish chests; Italian, Oriental, Spanish, and Portuguese ceramics; and ecclesiastical wood and stone carvings.

Rua de Dom Hugo 32. ✆ **22/200-36-89.** Admission .75€ (85¢), free for children under 10. Tues–Sun 10am–noon and 2–5pm. Bus: 15.

Museu de São Francisco The sacristan at the Museum of St. Francis estimates that 30,000 human skulls have been interred in the cellars. He could be exaggerating, but this dank building was once the burial ground for rich and poor. Nowadays it's a catacomb unique in Portugal. A section of it looks like an antique shop. There are also paintings, including one of St. Francis of Assisi worshiping Christ on the Cross. Curios include some of the first paper money printed in Portugal and an 18th-century ambulance that was really a sedan chair. The Sala de Sessões, built in rich baroque style, is now a meeting hall with a Louis XIV table and João V chairs. Wherever you go in the room, the painted eyes of framed bishops follow you.

Rua de Bolsa 44. ✆ **22/206-21-00.** Admission (including church and museum) 3€ ($3.45), free for children 9 and under. Mar–Oct daily 9am–6pm; Nov–Feb daily 9am–5:30pm. Tram: 1. Bus: 1, 57, or 91.

Museu Nacional de Soares dos Reis Created in 1833 by order of Dom Pedro IV, the museum was called the Museu Português when it opened in 1840. A hundred years later, it was declared a national museum and dedicated to Soares dos Reis (1847–89), the noted sculptor from Porto whose remarkable works include ***Desterrado*** ★ and *Flor Agreste.* Portraits and allegorical figures can be seen in the same gallery.

In the foreign painters collection, you'll find Dutch, Flemish, Italian, and French works, including two portraits by François Clouet (1522–72), and landscapes by Jean Pillement (1727–1808). The most representative and unified display is that of the Portuguese 19th-century painters, particularly from the Porto School. Henríque Pousão (1859–87) and Silva Porto (1850–93) are represented by fine naturalistic work. Also on display are decorative arts—ceramics, glassware, gold and silver work, furniture, and other objects.

Rua de Dom Manuel II 56. ✆ **22/339-37-70.** Admission 3€ ($3.45), free for children under 10. Tues–Sun 10am–noon and 2–6pm. Bus: 3, 6, 20, 35, 37, or 41.

Fundação de Serralves (Museu Nacional de Arte Moderna) ★ Run by the Gulbenkian Foundation in Lisbon, the National Museum of Modern Art, the most visited museum in Portugal, is an outpost of culture in western Porto. It occupies a new building in an 18-hectare (44-acre) **park** ★ next to the sherbet-pink Art Deco mansion where the collection was formerly displayed. Pritzker Prize–winning architect Álvaro Siza, a native son, designed the stark granite-and-stucco new structure. The building is Porto's finest example of

1930s Art Nouveau. The museum exhibits the work of an exemplary coterie of contemporary Portuguese painters, designers, and sculptors. Exhibits change constantly, but there's always something interesting. The descriptions of the works are in Portuguese, but you can ask to see an English-language video on the artists. It's also worth the time to wander through the sculptured gardens and see their fountains. There's even old farmland tumbling down toward the Douro.

Rua Don Joàn de Castro. ✆ **22/615-65-00.** Admission 4€ ($4.60). Tues–Wed and Fri–Sun 10am–7pm; Thurs 10am–10pm. Bus: 78.

MORE ATTRACTIONS

Casa do Infante Tradition has it that Porto's fabled hometown boy, Prince Henry the Navigator, was born in this house—now appropriately called the House of the Prince—which dates from the 1300s. In the 1800s the building was used as a Customs house. Today it contains a **Museu Histórico** with documents, manuscripts, and various archives relating to the history of Porto.

Rua de Alfândega 10. ✆ **22/608-10-00.** Free admission. Tues–Sat 10am–12:30pm and 2–5:30pm; Sun 2–5:30pm. Tram: 1. Bus: 1, 15, 57, or 91.

Palácio de Bolsa Late in the 19th century, Porto's municipal council decided to build a stock exchange so ornate that it would earn the instant credibility of investors throughout Europe. The result is this echoing testimonial to the economic power and savvy of north Portugal during the late Industrial Revolution. The podiums, desks, benches, and lecterns were removed long ago; the place functions today purely as a municipal showplace, without stock-trading activities of any kind. Instead you'll be ushered through something that might remind you of an abandoned royal palace, complete with massive staircases, a library, a "president's room," a domed "hall of nations" (site of stock trading activities of yesteryear), an intricately paneled General Assembly room, and a "portraits room" in the Louis XVI style, wherein six full-length portraits of the last six Portuguese monarchs are on permanent display. The architectural highlight is the **Arabian Hall** ★, a pastiche of the Alhambra in Granada. Ovoid in shape, it is adorned with arabesques, carved woodwork, and stained-glass windows, all evocative of the Moors of long ago. The garden in back is especially lovely.

Rua Ferreira Borges, 4050-253 Porto. ✆ **22/339-90-00.** Admission (w/guided 30-min tour in English, French, and Spanish included) 5€ ($5.75) adults, 2.50€ ($2.90) children under 12. Nov–Mar daily 9am–1pm and 2–6pm; Apr–Oct daily 9am–7pm. Bus: 1.

Torre dos Clérigos West of Praça de Liberdade, follow Rua dos Clérigos to the Clérigos Tower, which the Italian architect Niccolò Nasoni designed in 1754. The tower's six floors rise to a height of some 76m (249 ft.), which makes it one of the tallest structures in the north of Portugal. You can climb 225 steps to the top of the belfry, where you'll be rewarded with one of the city's finest views, of Porto and the river Douro. The Italianate baroque **Igreja dos Clérigos,** at the same site, was also built by Nasoni and predates the tower.

Rua Sạn Felipe De Nery. ✆ **22/200-17-29.** Admission to tower 1€ ($1.15); church free. Tower daily Nov–Mar 10am–noon and 2–5pm; Apr–Oct 9:30am–1pm and 2–7pm. Church Mon–Sat 10am–noon and 2–5pm; Sun 10am–1pm. Bus: 15.

SAMPLING PORT & TOURING THE LODGES ★★

No other city in Portugal is as devoted to port wine as Porto. The history of the city itself is largely dependent on this product, and hundreds of locals labor to promote the product in markets throughout the world.

The actual **port-wine lodges** (Taylor's, Porto Sandeman, Ferreira, Caves Porto Cálem, and Caves Ramos Pinto) lie across the river from Porto at Vila Nova de Gaia. Like the sherry makers at Jerez de la Frontera, Spain, these places are hospitable and run free tours for visitors.

Solar Vinho do Porto Head here if you're looking for a relatively fair and unbiased presentation of all of the ports in the region. Within the Quinta de Macieirinha, an elegant 18th-century villa ringed with roses, you can sample glasses of every port produced in Portugal, in a setting that evokes an upscale and very comfortable private home. Glasses of port cost 1€ to 2.50€ ($1.15–$2.90) each; bottles go for 7€ to 160€ ($8.05–$184) each. Don't expect anything approaching a nightclub (it's more like an upscale cocktail bar where the only drinks happen to be port) or even a bona-fide restaurant: There's a short list of simple foods (cheese, olives, breads, almonds, pistachios) that go well with port, and a staff that's prepared to offer educational insights into some aspects of the port-making process.

While you're here, make it a point to drop into the **Museu Romântico** (✆ **22/605-70-33**), which occupies the same 18th-century villa as the Solar Vinho do Porto. It's open Tuesday through Saturday from 10am to noon and 2 to 5pm, and Sunday 2 to 5pm. It charges .75€ (85¢) for adults and is free for students and for persons under 18 throughout the week. Admission is also free for everyone, regardless of their age, every Saturday and Sunday. Inside you'll find a collection of 18th- and 19th-century furniture, paintings, porcelain, and portraits that evoke the monarchical history of Portugal.

220 Rua de Entre-Quintas. ✆ **22/609-47-49.** Mon–Sat 2pm–midnight. Bus: 3, 56, or 78.

Taylor's The cellars of Taylor's are among the most interesting in Porto. The firm is the last of the original English port companies to remain family owned. Tours here are less rigidly orchestrated than those at the other wine lodges, and the atmosphere is less modernized. Known for its carefully selected grapes, Taylor's produces vintage ports, single Quinta wines, and even a rare 40-year-old tawny port. You'll be served a glass of wine on the terrace, which has a view of the city and the river.

Rua do Choupelo. ✆ **22/374-2800.** Mon–Fri 10am–6pm (in Aug open Sat). Bus: 57 or 91.

Porto Sandeman ★ The most famous port-wine center is Porto Sandeman, owned by Seagram's of Canada. In a former 16th-century convent, George Sandeman of Scotland established Sandeman in 1790. Originally founded in 1780, the company became notorious in the 1920s for its ad campaigns, which featured sex appeal in ways never before seen in the port wine industry. (Satyrs carrying gleeful, scantily clad flappers off into the forest for a glass of port or whatever . . . .) The Sandeman "Don," created in 1928, and inspired by the cape-clad troubadours of Coimbra, has been viewed as one of the most compelling and successful images in the world of advertising. Sandeman "Splash," wherein white port is used as a mixer with virtually anything, is the campaign-of-the-minute. The House of Sandeman also operates a museum that traces the history of port wine and of the company. You can purchase Sandeman products on the premises.

Largo Miguel Bombarda 3. ✆ **22/374-05-33.** Apr–Oct daily 10am–12:30pm and 2–6pm; Nov–Mar Mon–Fri 9:30am–12:30pm and 2–5pm. Bus: 57 or 91.

Finds "Porting" & Dining

Much of the character, architecture, and history of Porto is derived from its wine trade. As such, you'd be well advised to take a morning tour of two or three of the wine lodges of **Vila Nova de Gaia,** learning about the nuances of port and the vast amounts of time and labor that go into it. And if you happen to be on that side of the river already, consider a lunch at a restaurant that's richly permeated with the old-fashioned mystique of the port industry, **Barão Fladgate,** Rua do Choupelo 250, Vila Nova de Gaia (© **22/374-28-00**). Owned and operated by the Taylor Wine Company, and set within the walled compound the company maintains on a hillside high above the Douro, it's slow, graceful, and much more formal and old-world than any other restaurant in Vila Nova de Gaia. In some ways, it's a gastronomic showcase for the port wine industry and the Taylor Wine Company, in particular.

If you arrive on foot, expect to be seriously winded by the time you reach the restaurant, thanks to the steep uphill climb past forbidding-looking stone walls that line the narrow streets on either side. Once at a table, you'll be offered a glass of Taylor (white port) and then be presented with a list of the company's other products by a formally dressed battalion of waiters. Menu items are strictly Portuguese, including dried cod with fresh cream sauce, pork medallions with caramelized pineapple, and old-fashioned specials including a *cozhinado* (stew) of the day. As you dine, views of Porto, just across the river, spread out across the panorama. Main courses cost 8€ to 15€ ($9.20–$17) each. Meals are served Monday through Friday from 12:30 to 3pm. During the month of August, the restaurant is also open for dinner every Monday through Saturday from 7 to 10pm. Reservations are required.

Ferreira The legendary Ferreira is one of the biggest wine lodges. Dating from the early 1800s, it was launched by Dona António Adelaide Ferreira. From a modest beginning, with only a handful of vineyards, her company rose in power and influence, gobbling up wine estate after wine estate. At its apex, its holdings stretched all the way to the border with Spain, making its owner the richest woman in the nation. The fabled entrepreneur (known as Ferreirinha, or "Little Ferreira") nearly drowned in the Douro in 1861, but her voluminous petticoats kept her buoyant. (Her companion, an Englishman named Baron de Forrester, who did not wear petticoats, wasn't as lucky.)

Av. Diogo Leite 70. © **22/375-20-66.** Daily Mon–Fri 10am–12:30pm and 2–6pm. Bus: 57 or 91.

Caves Porto Cálem Founded in 1959 by the Cálem family, this wine-production company was taken over by a bank based in Vigo, Spain, in 2001. Its tour is much less formal than one at Sandeman, next door. A tour hostess will guide you through the barrel-making process, leading you past 75-year-old oaken casks, each laid out in an antique stone-sided warehouse whose walls are marked with the high-water marks of each of the floods of the past 200 years.

The tour eventually heads upstairs to an antique room whose displays of port evoke the great days of the wine trade at its best. The cellars are a bit newer than those at the more established firms, but the port, depending on the vintage, is just as good.

Av. Diogo Leite 26. ✆ **22/374-66-60.** May–Sept daily 10am–5:30pm (last visit); Oct–Apr Mon–Sat 10am–5:30pm (last visit). Bus: 57 or 91.

Caves Ramos Pinto ★★ This wine producer is usually acknowledged as the most interesting and best-preserved of any in Porto and Vila de Gaia. Owned since 1991 by the French champagne company Roederer, it showcases the creation in 1880 by Adriano Ramos Pinto of an outfit that placed enormous interest in the advertising campaigns of its era. You'll be given a guided tour of the cellars, with information about port and its manufacture, plus tastings at the end of the tour. But what you'll get in addition to the tour of the cellars is a visit to the corporate offices, each re-created in turn-of-the-20th-century style, complete with the artworks and furniture selected by the company founder or his cohorts. On the premises is one of the largest collection of posters ever assembled during the Belle Epoque, many of them works of art in their own right, each proclaiming the virtues of port as a defining factor of an elegant lifestyle. Tours are conducted in Portuguese, French, Spanish, and English, and because of the outfit's strong corporate links with France, you're likely to find goodly numbers of French tourists on board. Incidentally, one of the most celebrated and most frequently showcased products of this company is a 10-year-old tawny port named Quinta de Ervamoira. Named after a particularly beautiful villa in the region, around which some of the company's grapes are produced, it might be a good idea to haul a bottle of it home with you.

Av. Ramos Pinto 380. ✆ **22/370-70-00.** July–Aug daily 10am–5pm (last visit); Sept–June Mon–Sat 10am–5pm (last visit) and Sun 2–5pm (last visit). Bus: 57 or 91.

WALKING TOUR THE HEART OF PORTO

Start:	**Terreiro de Sé.**
Finish:	**Estação de São Bento.**
Time:	**2½ hours.**
Best Times:	**Any day between 10am and 4pm.**
Worst Times:	**Monday through Friday from 8 to 10am and 4 to 6pm, because of heavy traffic.**

The only suitable way to explore the heart of the inner city is on foot. Nearly all the major monuments are in the old part of town, and the major sights are close together. The streets are often narrow and sometimes confusing to the first-time visitor; even armed with a good map, you're likely to get lost from time to time. Long accustomed to entertaining foreigners, the people of Porto are generally friendly and hospitable, and will point you in the right direction.

Begin your tour in the heart of the old town, at:

❶ Terreiro de Sé

This square is dominated by the cathedral, founded as a fortress church in the 12th century and greatly altered in the 1600s and 1700s. Square domed towers flank the main facade. "Cathedral Square" is also bordered by an 18th-century former Episcopal palace, now municipal offices. Noted for its granite-cased doors and windows, it contains an exceptional stairway. Also on the square is a Manueline-style pillory and a statue of Vimara Peres, the warrior of Afonso III of León, who captured ancient Portucale in A.D. 868.

To the rear of the cathedral is one of Porto's most charming streets:

❷ Rua de Dom Hugo

If you continue along this street, you'll pass the Chapel of Our Lady of Truths. It's invariably closed, but you can peek through the grille at the gilded rococo altar, with a statue of the Virgin at the center.

Along this same street at no. 32 stands the:

❸ Casa Museu de Guerra Junqueiro

This white mansion—now a museum—was the home of the poet Guerra Junqueiro (1850–1923). The Italian architect Niccolò Nasoni designed this mansion.

Continue along Rua de Dom Hugo, a narrow street that curves around the eastern side of the Sé, until you come to some steep steps. These were carved through remaining sections of the town walls that existed in the Middle Ages. This brings you into one of the most colorful and poverty-stricken sections of Porto, the:

❹ Ribeira district ★★

The back streets of this historic neighborhood have much charm. The area abounds with arcaded markets, churches, museums, monuments, and once-elegant buildings.

Regardless of which alley you take, everything eventually merges onto the:

❺ Cais de Ribeira

The quayside section of the Ribeira district opens onto the Douro. Locals come here for the low-cost *tascas* (taverns) and seafood restaurants, which were constructed into the street-level arcade of the old buildings.

TAKE A BREAK
If you're walking around at midday, stop for lunch at the **Taverna do Bêbodos,** Cais de Ribeira 24 (✆ **22/205-35-65**), which has been serving locals since 1876. A dining room upstairs opens onto views of the Douro. You might happily settle for a glass of the local wine from a cask balanced on the bar.

The center of the district is:

❻ Praça de Ribeira

Locals sit in the sun here telling tall tales. From here, visitors can take in the port-wine lodges across the Douro at Vila Nova de Gaia.

Now head north to the:

❼ Ponte de Dom Luís I

This is the middle of the trio of bridges over the river Douro. The iron bridge was designed by Seyrig, a collaborator of Eiffel, in 1886. It has an upper and a lower span, both of which funnel traffic to Vila Nova de Gaia.

After viewing the bridge and the river, retrace your steps to Praça de Ribeira. At the west side of the square, walk up Rua de São João to the:

❽ Feitoria Inglesa (Factory House of the British Association)

This is the headquarters of the Port Wine Shippers' Association. One of the most fabled buildings in the Ribeira district, it stands where Rua do Infante Dom Henríque crosses Rua de São João. British consul John Whitehead designed the "factory" in 1786.

Follow Rua do Infante Dom Henríque to the:

❾ Casa do Infante

The Casa do Infante lies at the corner of Rua de Alfândega. Porto-born Henry the Navigator, who launched Portugal on the Age of Discovery, reputedly was born in this house.

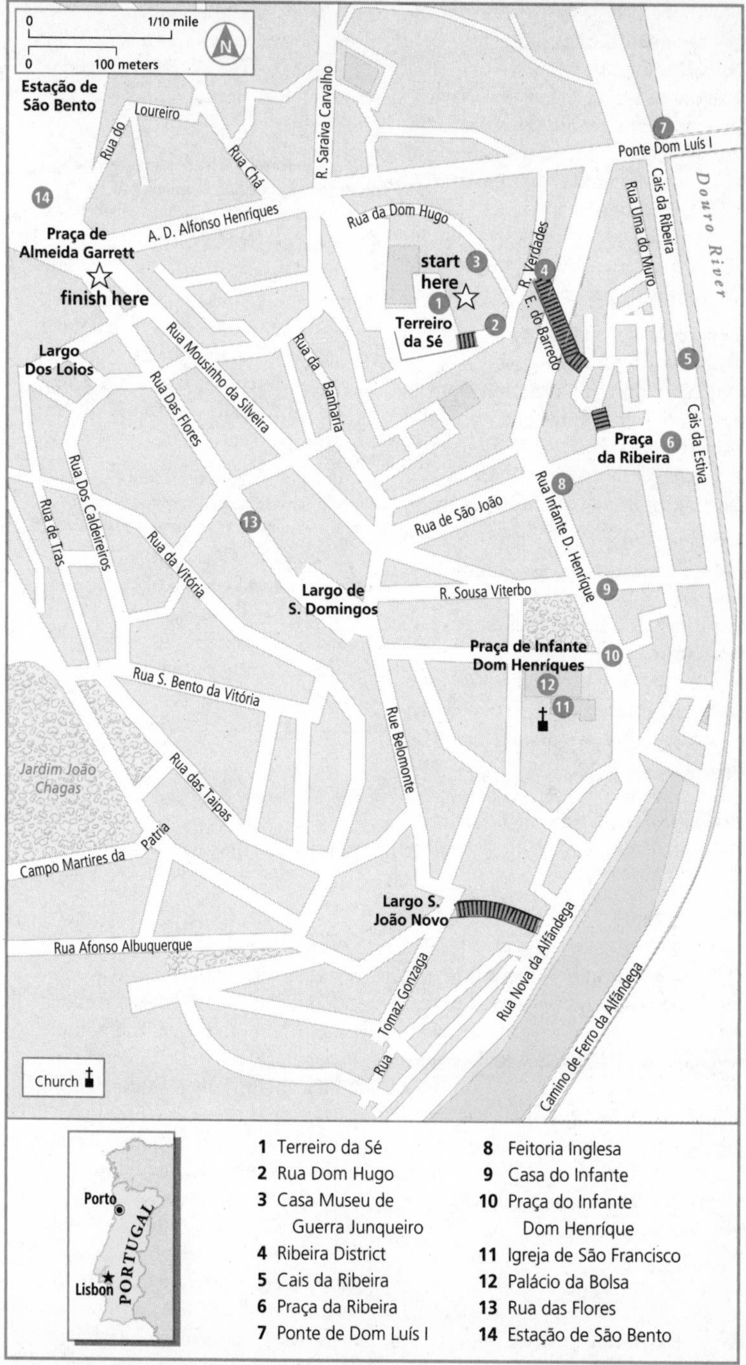
0 1/10 mile
0 100 meters
N
Estação de São Bento
Loureiro
Rua do
Rua Chá
R. Saraiva Carvalho
Ponte Dom Luís I
Douro River
Cais da Ribeira
Rua Uma do Muro
Praça de Almeida Garrett
A. D. Alfonso Henríques
Rua da Dom Hugo
start here
R. Verdades
E. do Barredo
finish here
Terreiro da Sé
Largo Dos Loios
Rua Mousinho da Silveira
Rua da Banharia
Rua Das Flores
Cais da Estiva
Praça da Ribeira
Rua Dos Caldeireiros
Rua de Tras
Rua da Vitória
Rua de São João
Rua Infante D. Henrique
Largo de S. Domingos
R. Sousa Viterbo
Praça de Infante Dom Henríques
Rua S. Bento da Vitória
Rue Belomonte
Jardim João Chagas
Rua das Taipas
Campo Martires da Patria
Largo S. João Novo
Rua Nova da Alfândega
Rua Afonso Albuquerque
Rua Tomaz Gonzaga
Camino de Ferro da Alfândega
Church
Porto
Lisbon
PORTUGAL
1 Terreiro da Sé
2 Rua Dom Hugo
3 Casa Museu de Guerra Junqueiro
4 Ribeira District
5 Cais da Ribeira
6 Praça da Ribeira
7 Ponte de Dom Luís I
8 Feitoria Inglesa
9 Casa do Infante
10 Praça do Infante Dom Henríque
11 Igreja de São Francisco
12 Palácio da Bolsa
13 Rua das Flores
14 Estação de São Bento

Follow Rua do Infante Dom Henríque to:

⑩ Praça do Infante Dom Henríque

A statue of Prince Henry the Navigator graces this square. Here you can visit a big covered food market, where tripe is sold in great quantities. Although shunned by much of the Western world (except by Florentines), tripe is said to be the favorite food of the denizens of Porto.

The highlight of this square is the:

⑪ Igreja de São Francisco

Originally this was a Gothic church. Its adjacent museum once was the property of a Franciscan monastery. This church boasts the most lavish, spectacular church interior in Porto—and the competition is keen.

Behind the church, facing the square, is Porto's:

⑫ Palácio de Bolsa (Stock Exchange)

It takes up a great deal of the site of what used to be a Franciscan monastery. It's known for an oval Arab Room whose stained glass and arabesques are said to imitate the style of the Alhambra in Granada, built by the Moors. The Stock Exchange stands at Rua de Bolsa and Rua Ferreira Borges.

Follow Rua Ferreira Borges west, veering north to Largo de São Domingos. At the top of this square, continue northwest along:

⑬ Rua das Flores (Street of Flowers)

Some visitors consider this the most romantic street in Porto. It has long been known for the quality of its silversmiths, but what makes the street so architecturally striking is its wrought-iron balconies.

This street eventually opens onto Praça de Almeida Garrett, named for the famed Portuguese writer. On this square is the:

⑭ Estação de São Bento

This is the most central of Porto's railway stations. Its grand main hall is decorated with large tiles tracing the history of transportation in Portugal. From this terminal you can catch a train to your next destination.

WHERE TO STAY

Porto provides the most interesting selection of superior accommodations north of Lisbon.

EXPENSIVE

Infante de Sagres ★★★ Plush, legendary, and elegant, this hotel is one of the most prestigious in Porto, with a roster of guests (members of the royal families of England and Belgium, European presidents from everywhere, and a long list of billionaires) that reads like a Who's Who of European society and politics. Although its rich, handcrafted ornamentation convinces most first-timers that it dates from the 19th century, it was actually built in 1951 by a wealthy textile manufacturer as a guesthouse for the clients of his firm. Later it evolved into a prestigious semiprivate address for executives of the wine and textile industries. Baronial and imposing, it boasts the most impressive public rooms of any hotel in the north of Portugal, thanks to stained glass, elaborate tile work, wrought iron, polished stone, acres of mahogany paneling, and brass. In the late 1990s, each of the suites was brilliantly redecorated by Fiorella Ferreira, the wife of the founder's grandson, in a style that evokes the baroque interior of an Italian palace, albeit with riveting contemporary paintings. It's extremely comfortable—a high-caliber staple among Porto Hotels, with a desirable location close to the commercial core of town. Other than the suites, which are spectacular, bedrooms are comfortable but somewhat conventional-looking, with dignified decors, high ceilings, quietly substantial furnishings, and marble-sheathed bathrooms with a combination shower-tub.

Praça Filippa de Lancastre 62, 4050-259 Porto. ✆ **22/339-85-00.** Fax 22/339-85-99. www.hotelinfantesagres.pt. 72 units. 210€ ($242) double; 350€–1,000€ ($403–$1,150) suite. AE, DC, MC, V. Rates include breakfast. Limited free parking on street, 15€ ($17) in nearby garage. Bus: 35 or 37. **Amenities:** Restaurant; bar; 24-hr. room service; babysitting; laundry; dry cleaning. *In room:* A/C, TV, minibar, hair dryer.

Ipanema Park Hotel ★★★ Built in 1991, this elegant hotel is the blockbuster choice for Porto, rising 15 floors and filled with grand comfort, a 15-minute taxi ride from the heart of Porto. Its good-size bedrooms open onto the ocean of the Douro estuary. With its array of facilities, it even outranks the traditional Infante de Sagres. Not to be confused with the cheaper Ipanema Porto (see below), the deluxe hotel is not typical of the region but could be any luxury palace anywhere. It is a study in good taste, with luxuriously furnished bedrooms and suites, each done in tasteful pastels with supercomfortable furnishings and marble-clad bathrooms. There are extra amenities everywhere you look, including extra phones in the bathrooms. Facing a winter garden, its on-site restaurant, Jardim d'Inverno, is one of the best in Porto, blending a Portuguese cuisine with international dishes. The facilities, such as an outdoor pool on the 15th floor, are the best in town.

Rua Serralves 124. 4150-702 Porto. ✆ **22/532-21-00.** Fax 22/610-28-09. www.ipanemaparkhotel.pt. 264 units. 90€–130€ ($104–$150) double; 275€ ($316) suite. Rates include breakfast. AE, DC, MC, V. Bus: 37 or 78. **Amenities:** Restaurant; bar; 2 pools; health club; 24-hr. room service; babysitting; laundry service; dry cleaning; nonsmoking rooms; rooms for those w/limited mobility. *In room:* A/C, TV, dataport, minibar, hair dryer, safe.

Le Méridien Park Atlantic Porto ★★ One of the most dramatically modern hotels in town, the Méridien offers three vertical rows of bay windows along its 13-floor concrete shell. The hotel, about 3km (1¾ miles) from the heart of the city, is owned by Air France and is a favorite of conventioneers. Though in the same price bracket, it's too big to offer the personalized service of Infante de Sagres. The well-furnished midsize guest rooms have well-kept bathrooms equipped with shower-tub combinations.

Av. de Boavista 1466, 4100-114 Porto. ✆ **22/607-25-00.** Fax 22/600-20-31. www.lemeridien-hotels.com. 232 units. 180€ ($207) double; 210€–520€ ($242–$598) suite. Rates include breakfast. AE, DC, MC, V. Parking .90€ ($1.05) per hr. Bus: 3 or 78. **Amenities:** Restaurant; bar; dance club; 24-hr. room service; babysitting; laundry; dry cleaning. *In room:* A/C, TV, dataport, minibar, hair dryer, safe.

Porto Carlton Hotel ★★ *Finds* This is one of the gemstones of the Pestana Hotel chain. It opened in 2000 in a portside location that every hotelier in town envied from the very beginning. Composed of 11 separate but interconnected buildings, each between 200 and 400 years old, it rises to dizzying heights in a tribute to the stonemason's art. Inside you'll find an intriguing blend of antique granite blocks and hypermodern minimalism, all bound together in a design that's the most appealing of any hotel in North Portugal. Expect an attentive and youthful staff, a sense of architectural zest and excitement, and rooms that are among the most comfortable and imaginative in Porto. Bathrooms are large and airy, combining glossy slabs of beige stone with hand-chiseled granite blocks, and modern plumbing fixtures as well as shower-tub combinations. Decorative schemes incorporate lots of full-grained hardwoods, sophisticated lighting, and all the modern electronics you'd expect. Overall, this is a spectacular hotel in a location that's virtually unbeatable, directly in the heart of medieval Porto.

Praça de Ribeira 1, 4050-513 Porto. ✆ **22/340-23-00.** Fax 22/340-24-00. www.pestana.com. 48 units. 128€–149€ ($147–$171) double; 231€ ($266) suite. Rates include breakfast. Parking 6€ ($6.90). AE, DC, MC, V. Bus: 1. **Amenities:** Restaurant; bar; salon; room service (7:30am–10:30pm); laundry service; dry cleaning. *In room:* A/C, TV, dataport, minibar, safe.

Porto Palacio Hotel ★ Opened with a flourish in 1986, this 23-floor tower is one of Porto's most stylish and desirable modern hotels. In the Boavista section, a short distance from the city's commercial center, it rises across from its major competitor, the Méridien. Set back from a busy street, its exterior has bands of stone and reflecting bronze glass. Each good-size guest room has a well-kept bathroom equipped with a shower-tub combination.

The premier restaurant, Madruga, serves mainly regional fare, with some international choices.

Av. de Boavista 1269, 4100-130 Porto. ✆ **22/608-66-00.** Fax 22/609-14-67. www.hotelportopalacio.com. 252 units. 88€–167€ ($101–$192) double; from 234€ ($269) suite. AE, DC, MC, V. Parking .85€ ($1) per hour. Tram: 2. Bus: Boavista 3, 78. **Amenities:** Restaurant; bar; indoor pool; squash court; health club; 24-hr. room service; babysitting; laundry; dry cleaning. *In room:* A/C, TV, dataport, minibar, hair dryer, safe.

Tivoli Porto Atlantico ★ This is a small hotel in the northwest of town off Avenida da Boavista in the vicinity of Fundação de Serralves. Rising three floors, this 1975 hotel enjoys a location in an exclusive residential neighborhood and a rather tranquil setting in bustling Porto. The government-rated five-star hotel was acquired by the famous Tivoli chain in 1989, which is known for having one of the best hotels in Lisbon. The Porto hotel is classical yet very modernized, its midsize to spacious bedrooms fully equipped with tasteful furnishings and thoughtful little extra touches, such as a magnifying mirror in the marble-clad bathrooms. An impressive buffet breakfast is served, but there is no restaurant. However, a good French restaurant, Foco, stands adjacent to the Tivoli.

Rua Afonso Lopes Vieira 66, 4100-020 Porto. ✆ **22/609-49-41.** Fax 22/607-79-00. www.tivolihotels.com. 58 units. 320€ ($368) double; 450€ ($518) suite. Rates include buffet breakfast. AE, DC, MC, V. Bus: 78. **Amenities:** Breakfast room; bar; outdoor pool; gym; sauna; limited room service; babysitting; laundry service; dry cleaning. *In room:* A/C, TV, dataport, minibar, hair dryer, safe.

MODERATE

Grande Hotel do Porto ★ Charming and evocative of a long-gone way of life, this is a carefully renovated relic of a hotel that's set on an all-pedestrian street with the densest collection of shops in central Porto. Radically renovated in 2001, it has an appealing combination of the 1950s with Belle Epoque accessories. It was originally built in 1891 in a five-story "Grand Hotel" format that's still visible in its late Victorian facade and elaborate exterior detailing. Today it's a three-star hotel with better-than-average service. Some noise might filter up through the open windows into the bedrooms above. But that's overcome by the charm of very wide stairwells and hallways, high-ceilinged accommodations with more space than you might have expected, and a contemporary decor that was spanking new in 2001 or early 2002, depending on the floor you're on. Each unit contains a midsize tiled bathroom with tub and shower combination.

Rua Santa Catharina 197. 4000-450 Porto. ✆ **22/207-66-90.** Fax 22/207-66-99. www.grandehotelporto.com. 99 units. 110€ ($127) double; 146€ ($168) suite. AE, DC, MC, V. Bus: 3, 52, or 78. **Amenities:** Restaurant; bar; room service (7am–midnight). *In room:* A/C, TV, dataport, minibar, hair dryer, safe.

Hotel Dom Henríque ★ Though designed for business travelers, Dom Henríque is equally accommodating to tourists. In the city center, the recently restored hotel is in a 22-story tower. Executive suites are available. While it's generally a moderately priced hotel, this place has some extra-large, amenity-filled rooms that fall into the "expensive" category. Rooms are equipped with well-maintained bathrooms with shower-tub combinations. The 17th-floor bar affords panoramic views. The cuisine in the ground-floor restaurant is often refreshingly imaginative.

Rua Guedes de Azevedo 179, 4049-009 Porto. ✆ **22/340-16-16.** Fax 22/340-16-00. www.hotel-domhenrique.pt. 112 units. 90€–108€ ($81–$97) double; from 125€ ($113) suite. Rates include buffet breakfast. AE, DC, MC, V. Parking nearby 6€ ($5.40). Bus: 29 or 59. **Amenities:** Restaurant; bar; room service; babysitting; laundry; dry cleaning. *In room:* A/C, TV, minibar, hair dryer.

Hotel Ipanema Porto ★ The four-star Ipanema (don't confuse it with the government-rated five-star Ipanema Park Hotel, above) is one of the best hotels in Porto. A sleek 10-story modern structure, it's a prominent feature of the city's skyline, with elongated rows of smoked glass that are visible from the highway to Lisbon. In fact, one of this hotel's assets is that it's easy to find. Exit the highway at the signs indicating the direction of Porto, and you'll find it on a cobblestone road leading to the town center, less than 2km (1¼ miles) away. The handsomely furnished midsize guest rooms have cedar accents and views of Porto. All units were renovated in 2001 and are equipped with well-maintained bathrooms containing shower-tub combinations.

Rua do Campo Alegre 156, 4100-168 Porto. ✆ **22/607-50-59.** Fax 22/619-41-40. www.ipanema-porto-hotel.pt. 150 units. 99€ ($114) double; 144€ ($166) suite. Rates include breakfast. AE, DC, MC, V. Parking 5€ ($5.75). Bus: 35, 37, or 78. **Amenities:** Restaurant; bar; room service (7am–10:30pm); babysitting; laundry service; dry cleaning. *In room:* A/C, TV, dataport, minibar, hair dryer, safe.

Hotel Mercure Porto Batalha ★ Opposite the National Theater, the Batalha reopened in 1992 following a complete renovation. Popular with international port wine buyers, it's about a 10-minute walk from the river. In one of the more colorful sections of the old town, it combines the traditions of yesterday with the modern comforts of today.

The lobby sets the tone, with old paintings, antique furniture, pillars, and cushioned seating. The guest rooms are also traditional; while not grand, they're tastefully decorated, with coordinated fabrics, French windows, and tiled bathrooms equipped with shower-tub combinations. In spite of soundproofing, traffic noise is audible from some front rooms. The hotel goes back to those halcyon years of the 1950s but is up-to-date, opening onto one of the busiest commercial squares of Porto. It's streamlined and efficient, with prices designed to sell rooms.

Porto Praça de Batalha 116, 4049-028 Porto. ✆ **22/204-33-00.** Fax 22/204-34-98. www.mercure.com. 149 units. 84€ ($97) double; 109€ ($125) suite. AE, MC, V. Parking 6€ ($6.90). Bus: 35, 37, or 38. **Amenities:** Restaurant; bar; room service; babysitting; laundry; dry cleaning. *In room:* A/C, TV, minibar, hair dryer, safe.

Quality Inn In the heart of the city, this six-story hotel lies in the Barredo section, which UNESCO has declared a historic heritage site. The hotel is severely modern and is not exciting in any way, but it's a practical, no-frills choice with very affordable prices. The streamlined, functional guest rooms have good comfort, well-kept bathrooms with shower-tub combinations, and deluxe toiletries. Some units are suitable for travelers with disabilities, and other accommodations are reserved for nonsmokers.

Praça de Batalha 127–130, 4000-102 Porto. ✆ **800/465-43-29** in the U.S., or ✆ **22/339-23-00.** Fax 22/200-60-09. www.ichotelsgroup.com/h/d/hi/1/en/hd/prtpo. 113 units. 125€ ($144) double. Rates include breakfast. Parking 6€ ($6.90). Bus: 35, 82, or 84. **Amenities:** Breakfast room; bar; laundry service; dry cleaning; some rooms for those w/disabilities. *In room:* A/C, TV, dataport, hair dryer.

INEXPENSIVE

Albergaria Miradouro ★ *Finds* Resembling an eagle's nest, Albergaria Miradouro is a slim 13-floor structure built atop a hill within a commercial and residential neighborhood not far from the heart of town. The Miradouro offers rooms with great vistas—you can watch ships laden with port making their way to the open sea. The corner guest rooms are preferable; two walls have wardrobes and chests (with a built-in pair of beds), and the other walls are glass. Every unit has a vestibule, luggage storage, a valet stand, desks, a sitting room, and a well-maintained bathroom equipped with a shower-tub combination. A 1950s aura pervades. The small-scale public rooms are tasteful. The lower bar is decorated with wall tiles from Japan and Portugal. The walls of the upper bar open onto a view. The Restaurante Portucale, which serves international cuisine, is the best in town.

Rua de Alegria 598, 4000-037 Porto. ✆ **22/537-07-17.** Fax 22/537-02-06. alb.miradouro@teleweb.pt. 30 units. 60€–68€ ($69–$78) double. Rates include breakfast. AE, DC, MC, V. Free parking. Bus: 20. **Amenities:** Restaurant; bar; room service (7am–10pm); laundry; dry cleaning. *In room:* A/C, TV, minibar, hair dryer, safe.

Castelo de Santa Catarina ★ *Finds* A former residential showplace, this hotel lies behind a high wall in a commercial neighborhood less than 2km (1¼ miles) from the center. In the 1920s, a Brazilian military officer returned to his native Porto determined to build the most flamboyant villa in town. He created a sprawling compound with greenhouses, terraced gardens, a chapel, and a sumptuous main house. A crescent of servants' quarters circles the other buildings. Today the tile-covered exterior walls almost give an encapsulated history of Portugal.

After ringing the bell, you'll be ushered down a labyrinthine series of halls and narrow stairways. To get to your room, you'll pass through opulent but disorganized sitting rooms and ballrooms, illuminated with chandeliers. Each of the small guest rooms contains carved antique furniture, often of rosewood. The plumbing fixtures are designed with a florid Art Nouveau flair. All units come equipped with neatly kept bathrooms containing shower-tub combinations. Breakfast is the only meal served.

Rua de Santa Catarina 1347, 4000-457 Porto. ✆ **22/509-55-99.** Fax 22/550-66-13. 26 units. 63€ ($72) double; 75€–90€ ($86–$104) suite. Rates include breakfast. AE, DC, MC, V. Free parking. Bus: 9, 29 or 59. **Amenities:** Breakfast room; lounge; babysitting; laundry; dry cleaning. *In room:* TV in some rooms.

Hotel de Bolsa ★ *Finds* Porto's newest centrally located hotel occupies what was originally built in 1908 as a private social club. About 30 years later, after a disastrous fire, it was rebuilt in the beaux arts style into the headquarters of an insurance company. In 1994, after several years of closure, it reopened as a well-managed and unpretentious government-rated three-star hotel. Bedrooms are compact but high-ceilinged, many with floor plans that were influenced by the building's former role as a private office. Each is comfortable and blandly decorated with Victorian prints, tiled bathrooms with shower-tub combinations, and uncontroversial contemporary furniture.

Rua Ferreira Borges 101. 4050-253 Porto. ✆ **22/202-67-68.** Fax 22/205-88-88. 36 units. 76€–90€ ($87–$104) double. Extra bed 17€ ($20). Rates include breakfast. AE, DC, MC, V. Bus: 1. **Amenities:** Bar; laundry; dry cleaning. *In room:* A/C, TV.

Residencial Rex *Value* The facade of this place fits in gracefully with its location on one of Porto's most beautiful squares. Its design, inspired by Art Nouveau, features sea-green tiles, cast-iron embellishments, and Roman-style window treatments. It was built by a Portuguese aristocrat around 1845 and transformed into a *pensão* (boarding house) in 1925. The present family-owners have been here since 1980. A majestic marble staircase leads from the street into the reception area. The lobby and small guest rooms are crowned with ornately molded plaster ceilings, and much of the furniture is antique. The bathrooms have been modernized and come equipped with shower-tub combinations. You can park on the adjacent driveway.

Praça de República 117, 4050-497 Porto. ✆ **22/207-45-90.** Fax 22/207-45-93. 21 units. 55€ ($63) double. Rates include breakfast. AE, MC, V. Bus: 7, 71, or 72. **Amenities:** Bar; car rental; laundry; dry cleaning. *In room:* A/C, TV, hair dryer.

IN FOZ DO DOURO

Hotel Boa-Vista *Finds* Set within an antique villa, a few steps from the São João do Foz fortress, this hotel evokes old Porto at its most nostalgic. It was originally built as a hotel around 1900, on the site of a ruined Franciscan monastery. In 2000, a team of architects added a modern wing and a rooftop swimming pool, enlarging the site from 39 rooms to today's total of 71. Views from most of them encompass the mouth of the Douro and are very clean, attractive, and simple, usually with wood-grained furniture. The more modern rooms have granite floors and a more streamlined look; the original ones have a slightly dated 1980s feel, with beige carpeting instead of granite floors, and somewhat nondescript but very comfortable decor. Each unit comes with a shower-tub combination.

Esplanada do Castelo 58. Foz do Douro, 4150-196 Porto. ✆ **22/532-00-20.** Fax 22/617-38-18. 71 units. 78€–88€ ($90–$101) double. Extra bed 8€ ($9.20). Rates include breakfast. AE, DC, MC, V. Bus: 1 or 24. **Amenities:** Restaurant; bar; pool; laundry; dry cleaning. *In room:* TV, minibar, hair dryer, safe.

WHERE TO DINE

When Prince Henry the Navigator was rounding up the cattle in the Douro Valley to feed his men aboard the legendary caravels, he shipped out the juicy steaks and left the tripe behind. The people of Porto responded bravely and began inventing recipes using tripe. To this day they carry the appellation "tripe eaters," and it has become their favorite dish. To sample this specialty, the adventurous can order *tripas à moda do Porto* (tripe stewed with spicy sausage and string beans).

EXPENSIVE

Churrascão do Mar ★★★ BRAZILIAN/PORTUGUESE Porto's most elegant restaurant is housed in what locals call an *antiga moradia senhorial* (antique manor house), built in 1897 and beautifully restored to its Belle Epoque glory. The setting and elegance alone might justify a dinner here—and the cuisine matches the setting. Under the direction of owner Manuel Rocha, some of the town's finest chefs turn out excellent cuisine from South America. The staff seems determined not to let anyone leave unsatisfied. The best items are grilled fish and grilled seafood. Grilled meats are also superb. Everything is served with Brazilian spices or mild sauces to enhance the flavor, not destroy it. Service is in one of four rooms, all of which are quite charming. If you are staying outside of Porto, the restaurant will provide transportation by bus to the grounds.

Rua João Grave 134. ✆ **22/609-63-82.** Reservations required. Main courses 20€–35€ ($23–$40). AE, DC, MC, V. Mon–Sat noon–3pm and 7–11pm. Closed last 2 weeks of Aug. Bus: 3 or 78.

Restaurante Escondidinho *Finds* PORTUGUESE Near the transportation hub of the Estação de São Bento, the Escondidinho (meaning "hidden" or "masked") restaurant is an 80-year-old regional tavern popular with port wine merchants and English visitors. The intimate 31-table dining area contains time-blackened beams and timbers, a baronial stone fireplace, and a collection of antique Portuguese ceramics. The chairs, with intricate carving and brass studs, are just right for a cardinal—or at least a friar. The waiters serve with old-world charm and will candidly tell you the day's best dishes. The restaurant serves excellent steaks, but most people come here for fresh seafood. Working with turbot, sole, hake, sea bass, shellfish, and anything else that's fresh, the chef creates well-seasoned grills, skewers, and other excellent dishes. Shellfish soup and charcoal-broiled sardines are always good choices. Specialties include hake in Madeira sauce and chateaubriand for two. For dessert, try a kirsch omelet or orange pudding.

Rua Passos Manuel 144. ✆ **22/200-10-79.** Reservations recommended. Main courses 20€–29€ ($23–$33). MC, V. Daily noon–3pm and 7–10pm.

MODERATE

Aquário Marisqueiro ★★ PORTUGUESE In business for more than half a century, Aquário Marisqueiro is one of the finest seafood restaurants in Porto. One of two restaurants connected by a central kitchen, it's within sight of the city hall and close to the Infante de Sagres hotel. Seafood reigns supreme at this "aquarium." Soup made by boiling the shells of mariscos (seafood) is a good starter. Main course options include cod, sole, and trout with ham. An excellent dish is clams Spanish style, but the grilled sea bass is delicious.

Rua Rodrigues Sampaio 179. ✆ **22/200-22-31.** Reservations recommended. Main courses 11€–20€ ($13–$23); fixed-price menu 15€ ($17). MC, V. Mon–Sat noon–10pm. Bus: 7, 77, or 79.

Don Tonho ★★★ CONTINENTAL/PORTUGUESE This consistently ranks as one of the most spectacular and relentlessly hip restaurants in Porto, with superb food and a physical layout that is a triumph of historical renovation. Opened in 1992 by a group of investors who included Portugal's most famous pop singer, Rui Velosa, it sits on the eastern edge of the town's medieval port, welcoming clients who have included French president Jacques Chirac, Italian superstar Marcello Mastroianni, Fidel Castro, and John Malkovich. You'll wait for your table in a street-level bar, amid an intriguing collection of 18th century stonework and latter-day poured concrete. The sprawling upstairs dining room contains a medley of different architectural styles, as well as once-concealed stairways and granite facades of elaborate 17th-century houses that were buried during excavations for a nearby traffic tunnel during the 18th century. They were recently unearthed during the renovations that led up to the opening of this restaurant.

Menu items are savory and superb. Stellar examples include a soup of very fresh green beans with herbs and tomatoes, at least four (and sometimes more) preparations of codfish, fresh sea bass roasted in a salt crust, roasted kid in red wine sauce, a wide selection of shellfish, and modernized versions of the kind of earthy rural food that many Portuguese remember fondly from their childhoods. The wine list is so comprehensive that some American gastronomy magazines have added it to their reference collection for research on the Portuguese wine industry.

13–15 Cais de Ribeira. ✆ **22/200-43-07.** Reservations required. Main courses 13€–29€ ($15–$33). AE, DC, MC, V. Daily 12:30–2:45pm and 7:30–11:15pm. Bus: 1.

Espaço Massaerelos ★ *Finds* INTERNATIONAL Two local merchants beautifully restored this 1830s town mansion with its panoramic terrace opening onto views of the Douro River. This is part of the exploding dining scene enveloping Porto's once-decaying historic core, as more old buildings are recycled and given a new lease on life. The food is well prepared using market-fresh ingredients. Start with one of the delicious cream soups or perhaps a carpaccio of lamb. The *gambas* (shrimp dishes), including one tempura styled, are especially noteworthy, as are the fresh fish of the day cooked as you like them. The chef also does *bacalhau* (dried codfish) in a number of tasty ways. The desserts, including vodka-laced sorbets, are soothing, especially several concocted from chocolate.

Rua do Boa Viagem 3. ✆ **22/600-87-32.** Reservations recommended. Main courses 14€–26€ ($16–$30). Tues–Sun noon–3pm and 8–11pm. Bus: 15.

Garrafão PORTUGUESE/SEAFOOD A traditional restaurant in the suburbs, Garrafão overlooks Praia Boa Nova. Although it's standard fare made according to time-tested recipes, the cuisine is quite good. The kitchen staff deftly handles the fresh ingredients. The wine cellar, which contains a large selection of the best Portuguese wines, is another draw. A la carte Portuguese specialties include shrimp omelet, shellfish soup, grilled sole, veal dishes, and caramel custard. Prices of the seafood specialties vary according to the season.

Rua António Nobre 53, Leça de Palmeira. ✆ **22/995-16-60.** Reservations recommended. Main courses 12€–30€ ($14–$35). AE, DC, MC, V. Mon–Sat noon–4pm and 7–11pm. Bus: 31 or 78.

Itmae JAPANESE The cuisine of Japan has finally arrived in Porto. Flanked by a denser concentration of art galleries than virtually any other restaurant in the city, this restaurant offers minimalist decor and superb dishes. The setting is within a basement, with a small courtyard that's available for summer dining. Sushi lovers will find comfort sitting in the zenlike environment. The fish is very fresh, and it's handled with skill by the highly trained chefs. The ruby-red tuna is a special delight, as are the crab rolls. Everything is impressively presented on Japanese ware, and there is also an excellent choice of sake.

Rua Miguel Bombarda 216. ✆ **22/205-12-40.** Reservations recommended. Main courses 5€–20€ ($5.75–$23). Lunch buffet Tues–Sat 18€ ($21). Dinner buffet Mon–Fri 23€ ($26). AE, MC, V. Tues–Sat 12:30–3pm and Mon–Sat 8–11:30pm.

Restaurante Portucale ★★★ INTERNATIONAL/PORTUGUESE This restaurant, one of the most courtly in Porto, is acknowledged by virtually everyone as one of the three or four finest eateries in a town that's loaded with worthy competitors. It opened in 1969 on the 13th (uppermost) floor of the same building that contains the also-recommended hotel, the Albergaria Miradouro, in a contemporary-looking residential and commercial neighborhood near the heart of town. Expect a combination of grandly aristocratic Portugal with a slightly dated 1970s-era decor (including some tangerine-hued tile work) and an unflagging sense of Portuguese courtesy and good manners. It offers wide panoramic views of the cityscape around it; tables that are elaborately set with fine silver, porcelain, and flowers; and absolutely superb food. Consider an aperitif in the cozy corner bar before the debut of your meal. Specialties usually include foie gras with truffles in puff pastry, wild boar in red wine sauce, roast capon with walnut sauce, braised escalopes of fresh foie gras, stewed kid in red wine; and two different preparations of partridge (our favorite is stuffed with foie gras and stewed in port). Grilled sea bass with tartar sauce is excellent, as is an old-fashioned and succulent dish, sole Walewski, wherein filets of sole are prepared with champagne, lobster, shellfish, and grated cheese.

In the Albergaria Miradouro, Rua de Alegria 598. ✆ **22/537-07-17.** Reservations required. Main courses 13€–28€ ($15–$32). AE, DC, MC, V. Daily 12:30–2:30pm and 7:30–11pm. Bus: 20.

INEXPENSIVE

Abadia PORTUGUESE This large and bustling restaurant stands on a short street with a patio entrance and an open-air mezzanine. It's straightforward, with a hardworking staff, and serves generous portions in a style that hasn't changed in as long as anyone can remember. The cook specializes in such fresh fish dishes as *Codfish Abadia* (oven-baked and served with potatoes) and *Codfish Gomes de Sá* (sautéed with garlic and lots of onions). He also offers tripe stew, savory fried pork, and succulent roast goat. Soups are hearty and full of flavor. English is definitely not spoken.

Rua do Ateneu Comercial do Porto 22. ✆ **22/200-87-57.** Main courses 9€–15€ ($10–$17). AE, MC, V. Daily noon–11pm. Bus: 3, 35, 52, or 58.

Farol de Boa Nova *Value* PORTUGUESE Set on the upper level of the two stone tiers overlooking the waterfront, this is a richly authentic staple on the Portuguese restaurant scene. There's a brightly lit service bar near the entrance, additional seating in the cellar, and an outdoor terrace. Menu items are straightforward and simple but good, with many recipes served virtually unchanged from the days when some of the patrons used to eat equivalent food prepared by their grandparents. The finest examples include fried filets of sole, veal cutlets, and Portuguese sausages.

Muro do Bacalhoeiros 115. ✆ **22/200-60-86.** Main courses 8€–15€ ($9.20–$17). No credit cards. Daily noon–3pm and 7–11pm. Closed 3 weeks at Christmas. Bus: 1.

La Merceria PORTUGUESE This is an appealingly affordable middle-bracket restaurant set directly on the port. It's authentic enough to attract locals and has a long history of coping with the annual midwinter floods from the nearby Douro. Look for signs of water damage, including warped turn-of-the-century wine racks and paint peeling from the ground-floor doors. There's a cozy upstairs dining room that's accessible via a very steep wooden staircase, and a decor that includes hanging hams and turn-of-the century accessories. Menu items include grilled octopus, several different preparations of codfish, steaks, and lots of very fresh fish. The food is fresh and well prepared, although hardly imaginative. Its patrons come here for the tried-and-true recipes familiar to them from their mothers' kitchen.

Cais do Ribiera 32. ✆ **22/200-43-89.** Reservations recommended Fri–Sat nights. Main courses 9€–23€ ($10–$26). AE, DC, MC, V. Daily noon–3pm and 7–11pm. Closed Tues Nov–Mar. Bus: 1.

O Muro *Finds* PORTUGUESE This is the kind of earthy, rough-and-ready fish restaurant that appears in Portuguese-language guidebooks and that a businessman visiting from, say, Lisbon, might search out for an evening meal. Don't expect grandeur: The decor is utilitarian and the staff is gruff. But there's a convivial amiability about the place, with an outdoor terrace that was built a very long time ago as part of the foundation buttresses for this medieval waterfront neighborhood a short walk from the Praça de Ribeira. Owned by a once-professional soccer player and his Mozambique-born wife, it specializes in the type of hearty and straightforward cuisine that used to make the Portuguese Empire run. The best dishes include codfish- or octopus-studded rice, red snapper or turbot, fried codfish, and steak with mushrooms, milk, cream, herbs, and lemon-flavored butter. Most dishes are at the lower end of the price scale listed below.

Muro do Bacalhoeiros 87–88. ✆ **22/208-34-26.** Main courses 8€–18€ ($9.20–$21). MC, V. Daily noon–2am. Bus: 1.

Restaurante Tripeiro *Value* PORTUGUESE If you want to sample tripe, the most famous dish of Porto, this is the place to go. Since 1942, this restaurant's textured stucco walls and elaborately crafted wooden ceiling have offered a cool, dark retreat from the glaring sunlight. It's a no-frills eatery with efficient waiters. The traditional cooking aims to please—and succeeds. You can enjoy *vinho verde* (green wine), which is ideal with the specialty, *tripas à moda do Porto* (tripe with sausage and beans). If you're not up to tripe, you might order codfish, beef, or shellfish. Though most prices are reasonable, shellfish is priced daily by the kilo.

Rua Passos Manuel 195. ✆ **22/200-58-86.** Main courses 8€–18€ ($9.20–$21). AE, DC, MC, V. Mon–Sat noon–3pm and 7–10:30pm. Bus: 35.

Taverna dos Bêbobos ★ *Finds* PORTUGUESE Taverna dos Bêbobos ("Tavern of Drunks"), on the riverside dock, is the oldest (founded in 1876) and smallest restaurant in Porto. The ground floor has a service bar with every sort of knickknack on its little tables. A narrow, open staircase leads to an intimate dining room with a corner stone fireplace and a coved ceiling. The portions are large enough to be shared. To begin your typically Portuguese meal, you might order a hearty bowl of *caldo verde* (soup of ham hocks, greens, and potatoes) or a plate of grilled sardines. For a main course, we suggest trout with ham, codfish with béchamel sauce, or pork prepared Alentejana style (with savory clam sauce). All these dishes show flair and technique. Seafood rice and any of a number of grilled fish are also popular.

Cais de Ribeira 21–25. ✆ **22/205-35-65.** Reservations required. Main courses 10€–24€ ($9–$21). MC, V. Tues–Sun 12:30–3pm and 7:30–11pm. Bus: 15.

IN VILA NOVA DE GAIA

Adega & Presuntaria Transmontana II PORTUGUESE Set within easy walking distance of most of the port wine sales outlets, across the river from the medieval core of Porto, this rustic-looking restaurant showcases the rich and hearty cuisine of Portugal's most remote province, Trás-os-Montes. The venue resembles a stone *tasca* (tavern) where at least two dozen cured hams hang from the ceiling. The best-tasting menu items include platters of cured ham, green cabbage soup, shrimp in garlic sauce, octopus with green sauce, and either stewed or grilled meat in the Minho style.

Av. Diogo Leite 80. Vila Nova de Gaia. ✆ **22/375-83-80.** Reservations recommended. Main courses 9€–17€ ($10–$20). AE, DC, MC, V. Daily 11am–2am. Bus: 57 or 91.

IN FOZ DO DOURO

Bar/Restaurant de Praia do Ourigo PORTUGUESE One of the most popular and appealing beachside restaurants in Porto lies in the residential suburb of Foz do Douro, at the bottom of a cement staircase that descends from the waterfront boulevard above. Its design might remind you of a giant glass-and-steel box. Windows take in views of a lighthouse and the jagged mouth of the Douro River as its waters merge with the sea. Your seating options will largely depend on the weather: Whenever it's clement, dozens of wicker-topped tables sprawl along a wide terrace nearby, protected from the wind by a Plexiglass breakfront. Most of the time, however, diners huddle inside, seeking protection from the wind, rain, and fog. We savored the grilled monkfish with garlic butter, although a wide array of shellfish was featured as well, including a garlic-flavored lobster Thermidor. The chef proves his considerable talent with the loin of venison with broccoli and foie gras. An unusual dish for Portugal is the tasty turkey stroganoff with wild rice.

Esplanada do Castelo, Foz do Douro. ✆ **22/618-95-93.** Reservations recommended. Main courses 11€–35€ ($13–$40). AE, DC, MC, V. Daily 12:30–3pm and 8–11pm. Bus: 1 or 24.

Cafeína ★ FRENCH/ITALIAN/INTERNATIONAL Set within a 19th-century villa, in an environment that combines high ceilings, dark colors, warm lights, and cool jazz, this is one of the most appealing restaurants-of-the-minute in Foz. You'll recognize it by the yellow-and-black tiles that cover the building's exterior. Just before it opened in 1995, its owners ripped out the walls among seven small and claustrophobic rooms to create the airy, big-windowed environment you'll see today. Menu items are thoughtfully presented and well prepared. The best examples include grilled turbot with herb butter, flame-grilled tiger prawns, magret of duckling, tenderloin of lamb with cassis sauce and a tapenade of black olives, and at least nine kinds of steak. A particularly popular dessert is a marquise of white and dark chocolate with an orange-flavored coulis.

Rua do Padrão 100. ✆ **22/610-80-59.** Reservations recommended. Main courses 12€–16€ ($14–$18). AE, DC, MC, V. Daily noon–2am. Bus: 37.

Rhino INTERNATIONAL Trend-conscious, post-modern, and good-looking, this well-designed restaurant has been a staple of Porto's haute bourgeoisie since it was established in 1999. A cooperative staff member, a semicircular bar area, a color scheme of aquamarine and café au lait, and touches of russet-colored marble will greet you at the entrance. Menu items are well prepared and savory, and the finest dishes include shellfish stew and prawn-studded rice, both prepared for two diners at a time; braised beef with peppers; and perfectly grilled versions of swordfish, sole, and turbot.

35 Rua M. Manuel Marinho, Foz. ✆ **22/618-19-45.** Reservations recommended. Main courses 9.50€–22€ ($11–$25). AE, DC, MC, V. Daily 12:30–2:30pm and Mon–Sat 7:45–10:30pm. Closed 1 week in Aug. Bus: 37 or 78.

IN MATOSINHOS

Trinca Espinhas ★★★ CONTINENTAL/PORTUGUESE Elegant, alert, and hip, this avant-garde restaurant attracts an urban crowd from throughout Portugal and the rest of Europe. It lies along a busy boulevard in the definitely unglamorous neighborhood of Matosinhos, an industrial-looking suburb, near modern dockyards. It was established in the late 1990s in a boxy-looking warehouse that a team of decorators softened with sinuously curved walls crafted from vertical planks of exotic hardwoods. You might want a predinner drink at the poured-concrete bar area. The chef's repertoire is seductive, with fresh spices and herbs used judiciously to highlight the flavor of the splendid, handpicked ingredients. Menu items include at least 4 kinds of carpaccio (including versions made from tuna, monkfish, swordfish, and cod), stuffed spider-crab, three kinds of risotto, pastas, and at least 20 kinds of fresh fish, any of which can be fried, poached with seaweed, roasted on a salt bed, or baked. There's also a sophisticated array of meats, including a salt-roasted magret of duckling with Cumberland sauce, prepared for two diners at a time. Consider the fixed-price *rodízio* menu: a staggering number of skewers are brought with fanfare, one by one, out of the kitchen, each containing different kinds of fish and vegetables. They're preceded with fish soup and followed by a fruit and chocolate fondue.

Av. Serpa Pinto 283, in Matosinhos. ✆ **22/935-02-46.** Reservations recommended. Main courses 13€–30€ ($15–$35); fixed-price menu 25€ ($29). Daily noon–4pm and 7:30pm–1am. Closed 1 week at Christmas. Bus: 1.

SHOPPING

Much of Porto's commercial space consists of shops that appeal mainly to residents and, except for their curiosity value, only rarely to international visitors. In recent years, many of these have clustered in shopping malls. The newest and most elegant are the **Centro Comercial Peninsular,** Praça do Bom Sucesso, and the particularly charming **Centro Comercial Via Caterina.** It's in the pedestrian zone of the city's most vital shopping street, **Rua de Santa Catarina,** at the corner of Rua Fernandes Tomar. The storefronts inside duplicate the facades you'd probably see in a folkloric village of northern Portugal.

If you're looking for the designer wares of noteworthy clothiers from France, Italy, and Spain, these malls will have them. Other shopping malls have a sometimes uneven distribution of upscale and workaday shops. They include the **Centro Comercial de Foz,** Rua Eugênio de Castro, which is adjacent to the sea and especially pleasant in midsummer, and the **Centro Comercial Aviz,** Avenida de Boavista, rather inconveniently located in the middle of the city's largest concentration of automobile dealerships. The big but seriously decayed Centro Comercial Brasilia, which is, to an increasing degree, being stocked with inexpensive manufactured goods from Asia, is on Praça Mouzinho de Albuquerque. More chic and upscale, with a greater emphasis on clothing, furniture, and housewares, is the **Centro Comercial Cidade de Porto,** Rua do Bom Sucesso, whose shops are interspersed with restaurants, bars, movie theaters, and cafes.

Open-air markets supplement the malls. You can buy caged birds at the **Mercado dos Passaros,** Rua de Madeira (near the San Bento railway station), every Sunday from 7:30am to 1pm; and potted plants at Mercado das Flores, Praça de Liberdade, every day of the week between April and October from 9am to 5pm.

For a glimpse of the agrarian bounty of northern Portugal, head for the Mercado de Bolão, where hundreds of merchants sell food, flowers, spices, and kitchen equipment from the city's most famous open-air market. Open Monday through Friday from 9am to 5pm, and Saturday from 9am to 12:30pm, it sprawls for several blocks beside one of the great shopping arteries of Porto, Rua de Santa Caterina.

Porto has always sheltered a community of artisans crafting gold jewelry from stones brought in from all parts of the once-mighty Portuguese empire. Two of the city's leading jewelers are **David Rosas,** Lda, Avenida de Boavista 1471 (✆ **22/606-10-60**), and its leading competitor, **Elysée Joias,** Praça Mouzinho de Albuquerque 113 (✆ **22/600-06-63**). Each is stocked with wristwatches, gemstones, and miles of gold chains.

The local showcase for the fabled Arraiolos carpets is **Casa dos Tapetes de Arraiolos,** Rua Santa Catarina 570 (✆ **22/205-48-16**). The nubby, pure wool carpets of Portugal that teams of women spend hours crafting are sold here in all their glory. Look for symmetrical patterns that make full use of the subtle palettes of grays, blues, greens, and soft reds that have attracted non-Portuguese homeowners to these carpets for many generations.

Cutting-edge home furnishings, most of them in a minimalist Iberian style that evokes the best of the *movida* movement that swept over Spain after the death of Dictator Francisco Franco, are sold at **Móvel,** Rua 1° de Maio 243 (✆ **22/961-70-20**). For high-quality leather ware, including suitcases, wallets, belts, briefcases, duffel bags, and handbags, go to Haity, Rua de Santa Catarina 247 (✆ **22/205-96-30**). At **Casa dos Linhos,** Rua da Fernandes Tomás 660 (✆ **22/200-00-44**), you'll find linen and embroideries—many of them excellent examples of the exquisite handiwork that has traditionally been produced in the north of Portugal. A bookstore that has been cited as the most beautiful in Iberia, stocking a small percentage of its titles in English, is the **Livrario Lello,** Rua das Carmelitas 144 (✆ **22/201-81-70**). Partly because of its inventories, but especially because of its lavish Art Nouveau design, this is the best-known and most prestigious bookstore in Porto. A fixture among readers in northern Portugal since around 1900, it has two floors of lavishly ornate iron and plasterwork, a small cafe on the second floor, and a staff that's congenial but impossibly slow. And if you're looking for any of the standard international perfumes, as well as more esoteric brands available for the most part only in Iberia, head for **Perfumaria Castilho,** Rua de Sá de Bandeira 80 (✆ **22/208-56-58**).

Among voguish women's fashion designers, **Ana Salazar,** Rua Nova de Alfândega 65 (✆ **22/203-97-01**), is the market leader. In Porto, she maintains a high-tech showroom with a minimum of architectural distractions. Here you'll find women's clothing that's sexy, clingy, and chic, at prices that are expensive compared to most other clothing outlets in Portugal but relatively reasonable when compared to the clothing of other designers in, let's say, Paris. In addition to office wear, eveningwear, and sportswear, you'll find bags, shoes, and other accessories.

To stock up on traditional Portuguese handcrafts, begin at the **Regional Center of Traditional Arts** (CRAT), Rua de Reboleira 33–37 (✆ **22/332-02-01**). In an aristocratic 18th-century town house, it sells the best handcrafts from artisans throughout the country's northern tier. Lively competitors in the handcrafts trade include the following: **Casa do Coração de Jesús,** Rua Mouzinho de Silveira 302 (✆ **22/200-32-17**); and **Casa Lima,** Rua de Sá de Bandeira 83 (✆ **22/200-52-32**), where the inventories include large numbers of gloves, umbrellas, crystal, and embroideries, many of them laboriously crafted within the region.

An especially noteworthy gift shop is **Casa Margaridense,** Travessa de Cedofeita 20A (✆ **22/200-11-78**). You'll find a scattering of Portuguese handcrafts inside, but it's best known for a smooth and subtle cake, *Pão de Ió,* which has been made here on site for at least a century. Eaten year-round, and especially at Easter, it's rich with eggs and sugar. (Each cake contains as many as 5 eggs and 20 egg yolks.) Ironically, because of Portuguese trade with Japan and Portuguese advertising campaigns in Japan, the confection is especially popular in Japan, where it's almost a household word. Consequently, expect to see several visitors from Japan lined up at the counter here, buying the authentic version of what they've already tasted back home. Also expect a display or two of chocolates and jams, especially marmalades.

One of the finest names in Portuguese porcelain is **Vista Alegre,** Rua Cândido dos Reis 18 (✆ **22/200-45-54**). It carries a variety of items and can arrange shipping. Prices vary greatly, depending on the handwork involved, how many colors are used, and whether a piece is decorated in gold.

PORTO AFTER DARK

Porto isn't as vital a center for fado music as Lisbon, so only a few clubs promote the art form. The most appealing is **Mal Cozinhado,** Rua do Outeirinho 13 (✆ **22/208-13-19;** bus: no. 1). The name translates as "badly cooked." Five singers and musicians (three women, two men) perform folkloric guitar music and the evocative, nostalgic lyrics that go with it. They perform in 6-hour stints to an enthusiastic crowd Monday through Saturday beginning at 9:30pm. A la carte dinners, priced at around 25€ to 30€ ($29–$35) per person, are served beginning at 8:30pm. After the music begins, most people opt just to drink, paying an initial 12€ ($14), which includes the first two drinks. After that, beer costs 5€ ($5.75) a bottle.

Many night owls simply walk through the commercial district, along streets radiating from Rua de Santa Catarina, and stop at any appealing tavern or cafe. If you're looking to dance, try the **Bar Indústria,** in the Centro Comercial de Foz, Avenida do Brasil 843 (✆ **22/617-68-06;** bus: no. 1). It has a stripped-down interior that caters to a crowd of artists, writers (and their readers), architects, and other well-behaved, cosmopolitan patrons. It's open Friday and Saturday from 10:30pm to 4am.

For years, **Disco Swing,** in the Centro Commercial Italia, Rua Julio Dinis 766, near Rotonda de Boavista (✆ **22/609-00-19;** bus: no. 3), has been one of Porto's most popular dance clubs, with a mixed, mainstream clientele that appreciates the broad spectrum of musical forms (rock 'n' roll, '80s-era disco, house, garage, and, in rare instances, rave music) that's presented here. The setting is a battered-looking and dusty shopping center in a residential neighborhood near the Rotonda de Boavista. It's open daily from 8pm to 4am. Minimum drink consumption is 4€ to 7€ ($4.60–$8.05).

If you're looking for a cocktail bar where people in their 50s won't feel hopelessly out of place, head for the **Bar Hiva-oa,** Rua de Boavista 2514 (✆ **22/617-96-63;** bus: no. 19).

Set within a graceful three-story 19th-century villa, **Triplex,** 911 Avenida de Boavista (✆ **22/606-31-64;** bus: no. 19), contains two bars and a dining room that glitters with crystal chandeliers, lots of room for socializing with strangers, and occasional bouts of live music. Its restaurant is open daily from 12:30 to 3pm and from 6 to 11pm, but frankly, we prefer the bars to the food-service areas. These don't become popular until after around 10pm; then they continue to rock and roll till at least 3am. Entrance is free; drinks begin at 4€ ($4.60) each.

O Libirinto, Rua Nossa Senhora de Fátima 334 (no phone; bus: no. 3), is an oddity in Porto. This town house art gallery and bar is as hard to classify as its clientele (mixed, straight, gay, whatever). It's set behind a yellow-tiled facade of a distinguished but battered-looking town house in the Boavista neighborhood, a 2-minute walk from the Rotunda de Boavista. After you admire the paintings from whatever exhibition is being conducted there at the time, head for the garden, a verdant refuge, or any of the several bars scattered amid its confusingly laid-out spaces. You'll be happiest here if you accept it as a kind of indoor/outdoor salon where paintings are displayed, drinks are served, and dialogues flow. It's open nightly from 9pm till 2am or later, depending on the crowd.

One of our favorite bars and nightclubs in Porto, **Aniki Bobo,** Rua de Fonte Taurina 38 (✆ **22/606-36-65;** bus: no. 1), is set within a 17th century building a few steps from the port. A team of designers transformed it into a triplex nightclub with three distinctly different ambiences and settings. Hip and counterculture, with an ambience you might have expected within a late-night watering hole in Lisbon, it's named after one of the three or four most famous Portuguese films ever made, a 1930s classic that's immediately recognizable to virtually everyone in Portugal. The clientele here is about 25% to 40% gay, as defined by one of the alert staff members, a percentage that helps transform this place into one of the most frequently recommended counterculture bars in Porto. There's a minimum drink charge of 5€ ($5.75).

A gay hot spot is **Moinho de Vento,** Rua Sá Noronha 78 (✆ **22/205-68-83;** bus: nos. 3, 35, or 37), set within a medieval building on a narrow street near the Infante do Sagres Hotel. Only a brass plaque and a bright light that's illuminated every night beginning around 11pm identify this place. Expect a bar area that's really busy only on weekends, a dance floor, some dungeon-inspired artifacts, and a scattering of Portuguese-speaking residents of Porto and the surrounding regions. Entrance is free, and beer begins at around 3€ ($3.45).

Boys 'R US, Rua Dr. Barbosa de Castro 63 (✆ **91/754-99-88;** Metro: Trinidade or San Bento), is one of Porto's newest dance clubs, a late-night celebration of loud house and garage-style music, flashing lights, and gay sexuality. Set within the warren of narrow medieval streets near the San Bento railway station, it's open Wednesday and Friday through Sunday from 11pm, remaining open till between 2 and 4am, depending on business. There's no entrance fee, but everyone is expected to order a minimum of 5€ ($5.75) of drinks during their time inside.

The most beautiful and historic cafe of Porto is **Café Majestic,** Rua de Santa Catarina 112 (✆ **22/200-38-87;** bus: nos. 29 or 53), set on an all-pedestrian stretch of the city's busiest shopping street. This cafe evokes the grand era of Porto's gilded age prosperity more artfully than any other establishment in town. It was built in 1921, but because of its neo-baroque detailing, an art historian might be fooled into thinking that it's at least 40 years older than that. Angels and cherubs cavort on the ceiling, leaded glass shimmers, and the Belle Epoque comes alive again within a setting that's surprisingly down-to-earth and workaday. If you don't stop by for a drink or coffee in the evening, you can come here for breakfast, priced from 9€ ($10), or a full-fledged afternoon tea for 8€ ($9.20), complete with jam, bread, and toast. And if you're looking for a meal, platters—which include codfish "Oporto style," omelets with port-soaked shrimp, and filet mignon with mushroom sauce—are priced from 8.25€ to 16€ ($9.50–$18) each.

Vila Nova de Gaia, on the opposite side of the Douro River, is a lot less interesting after dark than Porto. But if you happen to be here, or if you're interested in an evening stroll across one of Porto's bridges for a panoramic view of Porto's old harbor, **Contra Corrente Bar,** Avenida Diogo Leite 282, Vila Nova de Gaia (✆ **22/375-75-77;** bus: nos. 32 or 33), is a cozy bar with a waterfront terrace offering a superb vista of Porto at night. It manages to be both hip and traditional at the same time, welcoming a clientele of locals or workers in the port trade, along with an occasional foreign visitor. Drinks and platters of food are available.

Battered but hip, with hints of the psychedelic era of the 1960s, the **31 (Treintaeum) Bar,** 564 Rua do Passeio Alegre in Foz do Douro (✆ **22/618-57-21;** bus: no. 1), occupies a compact town house on the cobble-covered, seafront main avenue in the residential suburb of Foz. Immediately adjacent and under the same ownership is the **Cerveja Viva,** where the bar list contains mostly beers, as opposed to the cocktails that are available in the more cutting-edge 31. Many first-timers make it a point to duck into both establishments, just as a comparison, for a quick nip and taste of local nightlife.

For the best view of the raging Atlantic to go with your drink, head for **Praia da Luz,** Avenida do Brasil (✆ **22/617-32-34;** bus: nos. 1, 7, 8, or 24), which occupies prime real estate on a rocky shoreline near the point where the Douro empties into the Atlantic. Watching waves from the ocean breaking and frothing from behind large windows is reason enough to visit—that and catching the live music. It's open daily 9am to 2am.

Somewhat surprisingly, the industrial suburb of Matosinhos, easily reached by bus no. 1, is a new nightlife center for Porto. The site is about 11km (6¾ miles) northwest of the historic core of Porto.

The nightclub **La Movida,** Rua Brito e Cunha 584 (✆ **22/937-91-65**), is set behind what looks like the entrance to a car repair shop. There's no sign in front. Inside you'll find a sprawling warehouse outfitted with artificial palm trees, accessories you might find on a beach in Cuba, and vibrant tones of lime green, lemon yellow, and russet. Latino music prevails here as party-makers dance their nights away, usually with heavy doses of rum- and tequila-based cocktails. The restaurant opens at 8pm on Thursday and Saturday through Tuesday, with a dance action beginning at 11:30pm. The cover charge ranges from 7.50€ to 10€ ($8.65–$12), depending on the night of the week.

Estado Novo, Rua Sousa Arosa 722 (✆ **22/938-59-89**), in Matosinhos, is one of the most popular and crowded dance clubs in the Porto area, with a hard-dancing, hard-drinking clientele. It's set within a white-sided industrial building, originally built as a warehouse and canning factory. Its name was derived from a tongue-in-cheek reference to a slogan of Salazar, Portugal's once-all-powerful dictator whose call to arms for an *estado novo* (new state) catalyzed many changes, both good and bad, throughout Portugal. Expect lots of space to mingle and dance, and a catchall, late-night environment that could include just about anything. Hours are Thursday through Saturday from 11pm to 4am, with a cover of 9€ to 14€ ($10–$16). This entrance cost is credited against your drink tab. On Thursday, women enter and drink for free.

2 Espinho

18km (11 miles) S of Porto, 307km (190 miles) N of Lisbon

Espinho is a popular resort on the Costa Verde. It offers many activities for growing crowds of vacationers. The town has a range of shops, restaurants, hotels, and campsites in the pinewoods near the sandy beach. Sports enthusiasts will find tennis courts, a bullfighting ring, and an 18-hole golf course.

ESSENTIALS

ARRIVING

BY TRAIN From Porto, trains depart from the **Estação de São Bento** (✆ **22/536-41-41**) about every hour during the day. Trip time is 35 minutes. A one-way ticket to Porto-Espinho costs 1€ ($1.15).

BY BUS Buses depart about once an hour from Porto's **Autovia Espinho,** Rua Alexandre Herculano, near Praça de Batalha (✆ **22/734-03-23**). Trip time is 30 minutes. A one-way ticket to Porto-Espinho costs 1.50€ ($1.75).

BY CAR From Porto, head south along IC-1.

VISITOR INFORMATION

The **Espinho Tourist Office** is at Angulo das Ruas 6 (✆ **22/733-58-72**). It's open September to June Monday through Friday from 9:30am to 12:30pm and 2 to 5:30pm; and July to August Monday through Friday from 9:30am to 7pm, and Saturday and Sunday from 9:30am to 12:30pm and 2 to 5:30pm.

RELAXING IN ESPINHO

DAYTIME ACTIVITIES Sports-related activities in Espinho tend to revolve around the beach. At least four beaches are within an easy walk from the town center. Closest and most crowded is **Praia Baia;** most distant (though only

.5km, or ⅓ mile, east of the center) and least crowded is **Praia do Costa Verde.** Between the two stretch the beige sands of **Praia Azula** and **Praia Pop,** both of which boast clean sunbathing areas and access to not particularly dangerous surf. If you prefer calmer waters, head for the town's largest swimming-pool complex, **Solar Atlântico,** adjacent to Praia Baia (✆ **22/734-01-53**). Fed with seawater, it has separate pools for diving and swimming, hundreds of devoted aficionados (only some of whom actually swim), and lots of options for voyeuristic intrigue. It's open from mid-May to September.

Grass and hard tennis courts, soccer fields, and volleyball courts are in the **Nave Sportiva,** Rua 33 (✆ **22/731-00-59**). The cluster of outdoor playing fields on the eastern outskirts of town opened in 1996.

The **Oporto Golf Club** is on Rua do Golf (✆ **22/734-20-08**), about 2.5km (1½ miles) south of Espinho. The 18-hole course is the second oldest in continental Europe. Greens fees are 60€ ($69) per person.

SHOPPING The three most interesting products produced in the surrounding region are carved-wood models of Portuguese fishing boats painted in bright colors, woven baskets, and dolls in regional dress whose bodies are carved from wood or fashioned from clay. Some shops operate only seasonally. Many sell items like suntan oil, sunglasses, and cheap souvenirs. The town's main shopping street is Rua 19. If you're looking for authentic handcrafts, head for **Casa Ramos,** Rua 23, no. 49 (✆ **22/734-00-24**).

If you happen to be in town on a Monday, Espinho is home to one of the largest outdoor markets in the region. Known as the **Feira de Espinho,** it takes place every Monday from 7am to 8pm along the entire length of Rua 24, Rua 23, and Rua 22. Look for carloads of produce, meats, and foodstuffs, plus some clothing and other objects you'd expect at a flea market.

WHERE TO STAY & DINE

Hotel Praiagolfe ★ Espinho's accommodations are a generally unimpressive lot. The best place to stay is the Praiagolfe, a totally renovated hotel originally opened in 1972, offering many modern comforts. Many units were redecorated in 2000, and all are comfortable, with neatly kept bathrooms with shower-tub combinations. The streamlined hotel overlooks the sea, about 50m (164 ft.) from the railway station. Tennis courts and golf courses are nearby. In summer, the hotel is almost always booked, so reservations are imperative.

Rua 6, 4500-357 Espinho. ✆ **22/733-10-00.** Fax 22/733-10-01. www.praiagolfe.com. 133 units. 120€–139€ ($138–$160) double; from 185€–210€ ($213–$242) suite. Rates include continental or buffet breakfast. AE, DC, MC, V. Free parking. **Amenities:** 2 restaurants; 2 bars; indoor pool; health club; Jacuzzi; sauna; room service (7:30am–9:30pm); massage; babysitting; laundry service; dry cleaning. *In room:* A/C, TV, hair dryer.

WHERE TO STAY & DINE NEARBY

Hotel Solverde/Granja ★★★ *Value* Solverde/Granja is one of the most luxurious hotels in the north. Opened in 1989, it stands on the beach of Granja, about 16km (10 miles) south of Porto, less than 2km (1¼ mile) north of Espinho, and about 32km (20 miles) from the Porto airport. The rates are among the lowest in Portugal for a government-rated five-star hotel. The generally spacious guest rooms, each renovated in 2001, are well furnished, with excellent roomy bathrooms that contain shower-tub combinations. The hotel has a heliport.

Av. de Liberdade 4405-362, San Felix de Marinha. ✆ **22/731-31-62.** Fax 22/731-32-00. www.solverde.pt/. 166 units. 145€–180€ ($167–$207) double; 375€ ($431) suite. Rates include continental breakfast. AE, DC,

The Porto Region

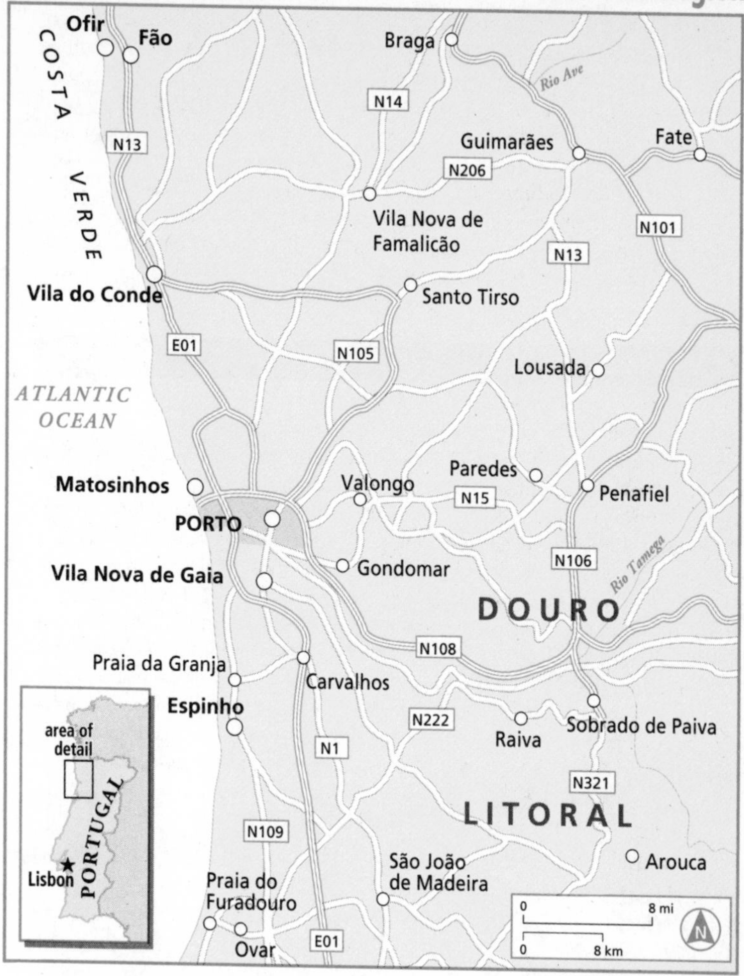

MC, V. Free parking. **Amenities:** 2 restaurants; cafe; 3 bars; 3 pools; minigolf course; 3 tennis courts; health club; Jacuzzi; sauna; 24-hr. room service; babysitting; laundry; dry cleaning. *In room:* A/C, TV, minibar, hair dryer, safe.

ESPINHO AFTER DARK

If you want to gamble, you're in luck. The big gray **Casino Solverde,** Rua 19 no. 85, 4500-858 Espinho (© **22/733-55-00**), offers roulette, French banque, baccarat, and slot machines. Open all year, it has a restaurant and nightclub in addition to the gaming tables. Admission is free for bingo and slot machines; to gain access to the gaming tables, you must show proper ID (such as a passport). The nightclub stages international cabaret. Dinner and the show cost between 25€ and 38€ ($29–$44) without drinks; the show alone is 14€ ($16), which includes one drink. The casino is open year-round (except Christmas Day) Sunday through Thursday from 3pm to 3am; Friday and Saturday, it's open from 4pm to 4am.

Espinho doesn't have any conventional dance clubs. The town does have eight or nine bars where somebody might actually get up and dance to recorded music, which includes healthy doses of Brazilian samba and whatever happens to be prevalent in London and Lisbon. If you're into nighttime prowling, head to the beachfront near the southern perimeter of the historic center and take your pick. Our favorites, each on Rua no. 2 and each immediately adjacent to the beach, include **Bombar, Bar Pasha, Surfing Bar,** and **Double "O" Bar.** Their busiest and most animated seasons are during the summer, with a breezy indoor-outdoor ambience that's conducive to chitchat. None of these has a listed phone number, and each has an outdoor terrace and a character that varies according to who's in town at the time of your visit.

3 Vila do Conde

27km (17 miles) N of Porto, 341km (211 miles) N of Lisbon, 42km (26 miles) S of Viana do Castelo, 3km (2 miles) S of Póvoa do Varzim

At the mouth of the river Ave, the charming little town of Vila do Conde has been discovered by summer vacationers who seek out its fortress-guarded sandy beaches and rocky reefs. Along the wharves, you might still see piles of rough hand-hewn timbers used in the building of the sardine fleet. Shipbuilding is a traditional industry here, and a few wooden-hulled vessels are still made, some for the local fishing fleet and others for use on the cod banks of Newfoundland.

The women of the town have long engaged in the making of lace using a shuttle, a craft handed down from generation to generation. So revered is this activity that the **Feast of St. John,** celebrated from June 14 to 24, features processions by the *rendilheiras* (lace makers) and the *mordomas* (women who manage the cottage-industry homes). The latter wear magnificent chains and other ornaments of gold. The famous hand-knit and hand-embroidered fishers' sweaters are also made here. The making of sweets (there's a famous confectionery that uses convent recipes) is another local occupation; sweets provide part of the rich local cuisine.

ESSENTIALS

ARRIVING

BY TRAIN From Porto, trains head north for Vila do Conde from the **Estação de Trindade,** Rua Alferes Malheiro (© **22/200-48-33**), several times a day. At press time, rail service into Vila do Conde had been temporarily discontinued because of repairs to the tracks, but local officials expected railway service from Porto's Estação de Trindade, Rua Alferes Malheiro (© **22/200-48-33**) to be reinaugurated sometime during the lifetime of this edition. Once it's reinstated, the trip to Vila do Conde will take about 35 minutes each way and cost around 2.80€ ($3.20) per person.

BY BUS Buses leave Porto from the **Autoviação do Minho,** Praça Filippa de Lancastre (© **22/200-61-21**). Three or four buses a day make the 40-minute trip. Tickets cost 2.50€ ($2.90).

BY CAR From Porto, head north along IC-1.

VISITOR INFORMATION

The **Vila do Conde Tourist Office** is at Rua do 25 de Abril 103 (© **25/224-84-73**). It's open Monday through Friday 9am to 6pm, Saturday and Sunday 10am to 1pm and 2:30 to 5:30pm September through June, and daily 9am to 7pm July and August.

EXPLORING THE RESORT

BEACHES OF VILA DO CONDE Both of the resort's beaches, **Praia do Forno** and **Praia de Senhora de Guia,** combine fine-textured white sand with smaller crowds—often much smaller—than at equivalent beaches on the Algarve or near Lisbon. A handful of kiosks and shops sell suntan lotion, sunglasses, and beachwear. Both beaches are within about a 3-minute walk from the resort's commercial center.

CHURCHES Sitting fortresslike on a hill, the large, squat **Igreja de Santa Clara (Convent of St. Clare)** ★, on the north bank of Rio Ave (✆ **25/263-10-16**), was founded in the 14th century. The present monastery was built in the 1700s, accompanied by construction of a 999-arch aqueduct to bring water from nearby Póvoa do Varzim. Part of the water conduit is still visible.

In the upper rooms, you can see relics and paintings collected through the centuries by the nuns. The building is now a charity home. Simplicity and opulence play against each other in a combination of Gothic and Romanesque styles. The plain altar of its church offers contrast to the gilded stalls behind the communion grilles and the ornately decorated ceilings. A side chapel contains 14th-century sarcophagi. One is the elaborately carved tomb of Dom Afonso Sanche, founder of the convent; the feet of his effigy rest on a lion. Also here are the tomb of his wife, Dona Teresa Martins, topped by a figure dressed in the habit of a Franciscan Tertiary nun, and those of two of their children. The convent is open daily from 9am to 12:30pm and 2 to 6pm. Admission is free.

The 16th-century parish church, **Igreja Matriz** (✆ **25/263-13-27**), is also worth seeing. It stands in the center of town near the market. Another national monument is the **pillory,** opening onto Praça Vasco de Gama. Built from 1538 to 1540, it consists of a graceful column, slightly twisted, which recalls many creations from the Manueline art style.

LACE MAKING Visitors are welcomed free at the **Museu Escola de Rendas,** the lace-making school on Rua de São Bento (✆ **25/224-84-70**). Here you can purchase the finest examples of lace for which the town is known. Vila do Conde guards its lace-making and pastry-making traditions with fierce pride. The Rendas school is devoted to perpetuating the traditions of Portuguese lace making, and it's one of the largest technical schools in the country. Some students enroll as early as age 4 and tend to have completed their technical training before they turn 15. A handful of the matriarchs, now in their 70s, associated with the school remember its importance in their town when they were young girls. You can buy most of the lace made in the school at its on-site boutique. The Museu Escola de Rendas is open Monday through Friday from 10am to noon and 2 to 7pm. For more information, contact the **tourist office** at ✆ **25/224-84-73.**

A nearby annex, **Centro de Artesanato,** Avenida Dr. João Canavarro, also stocks lace curtains and tablecloths, doilies, and trim. Most of the lace you'll see here is white, designed according to traditional patterns established long ago. In recent years, however, some limited experiments have been conducted using colored thread.

PASTRIES & SWEETS During the 18th and 19th centuries, the nuns of Vila do Conde developed recipes for pastries and sweets that their detractors claimed were thinly masked substitutes for their yearnings for love and affection. Examples of the sweets they invented are still sold in almost every cafe and about a dozen pastry shops in the village. The best known of these pastries are *papo de anjo* (angel's belly) and *doce de feijão* (bean sweets). The ones seemingly best appreciated by modern-day palates are the *Jesuitas* (Jesuits), concocted from lavish amounts of eggs, flour, and sugar. You'll see dozens of outlets for these confections. One of the most appealing is the **Pastelaria Santa Clara,** Rua 25 de Abril (no phone).

WHERE TO STAY

Estalagem do Brasão ★ This inn, in the center of the village, is styled like a gracious pousada. Its compact guest rooms are of contemporary design, with built-in headboards, comfortable armchairs, and firm beds. All units contain well-maintained bathrooms equipped with shower-tub combinations.

Av. Dr. João Canavarro, 4480-668 Vila do Conde. © **25/264-20-16.** Fax 25/264-20-28. 30 units. 52€–78€ ($60–$90) double; 78€–94€ ($90–$108) suite. Rates include buffet breakfast. AE, DC, MC, V. Free parking. **Amenities:** Bar; room service; babysitting; laundry; dry cleaning. *In room:* A/C, TV, minibar, hair dryer.

WHERE TO DINE

Ramon PORTUGUESE At the entrance into Vila do Conde stands this well-run restaurant decorated in a regional Portuguese style. It's small, with only 20 tables, but in summer it opens the terrace for overflow guests. Although many beachfront restaurants come and go seasonally, this is a reliable year-round choice. The fresh shellfish depends on daily market prices and can be quite expensive, but most dishes, including fish, are reasonable. The chefs make the best paella at the resort, and they also prepare a delicious array of grilled fish based on the catch of the day. A specialty is *tamboril à Ramon,* which is a white fish, known as "rape," served with potatoes and fresh garlic. Special attention is also paid to the soups.

Rua 5 do Octubro 176. © **25/263-13-34.** Reservations recommended in summer. Main courses 12€–20€ ($14–$23). AE, DC, MC, V. Wed–Mon noon–3pm and 7–11pm. Closed for 3 weeks in mid-Sept and mid-Oct.

4 Ofir & Fão

47km (29 miles) N of Porto, 364km (226 miles) N of Lisbon, 36km (22 miles) W of Braga

Once you pass through the pine forests of Ofir, you gaze down on a long white-sand spit dotted with windswept dunes and hear the sharp cries of seagulls. Ofir offers the best beach resort between Porto and Viana do Castelo. The beach is dramatic at any time of the year but is exceptional during summer. The **White Horse Rocks,** according to legend, were formed when fiery steeds from the royal stock of King Solomon were wrecked on the beach.

While Ofir's hotels offer every convenience in a secluded setting, the nearest shops and more local color are at Fão, 2 to 3km (1¼–1¾ miles) inland on an estuary of the Cávado River. Framed by mountain ridges in the background and a river valley, the village, which dates from Roman times, is the sleepy gateway to Ofir. The *sargaceiros* (gatherers of sargasso), with their stout tunics, rake the offshore breakers for the seaweed used in making fertilizer. On the quays, you can lunch on sardines off smoking braziers. At the end of the day, counteract your overdose of sunshine with a mellow glass of port wine.

ESSENTIALS

ARRIVING

BY TRAIN There's no direct rail service to Fão or Ofir. Passengers go to Póvoa do Varzim, 15km (9⅓ miles) south, and continue by bus.

BY BUS From Porto, buses depart from **Autoviação do Minho,** Praceto Regulo Maguana (© **25/880-03-41**). Three or four buses per day service the area. Trip time is 65 minutes; tickets cost 3€ ($3.45).

BY CAR From Póvoa do Varzim, continue north along Route 30.

VISITOR INFORMATION

The nearest tourist office is the **Esposende Tourist Bureau,** Avenida Arantes de Oliveira, Esposende (✆ **25/396-13-54**). Esposende lies on the opposite bank of the Rio Cávado Estuary from Ofir and Fão. It's open Monday through Saturday 9:30am to 12:30pm and 2 to 5:30pm September through June, and Monday through Saturday 9:30am to 7pm July and August.

WHERE TO STAY & DINE

Estalagem Parque do Rio This first-class modern inn on the Cávado River is in a pine-covered garden 5 minutes from the main beach. It has two excellent garden pools with surrounding lawns. The small guest rooms are well designed, with private balconies. All units come equipped with well-maintained bathrooms containing shower-tub combinations. The resort, planned for those who stay for more than a day, offers a full range of activities. In the beamed dining room, a snug wood-paneled bar sits against a stone wall.

Apdo. 1, Ofir, 4740-405 Esposende. ✆ **25/398-15-21.** Fax 25/398-15-24. www.parquedorio.pt. 36 units. 55€–80€ ($63–$92) double; 70€–106€ ($81–$122) suite. Rates include continental breakfast. AE, MC, V. Free parking. **Amenities:** Restaurant; bar; 4 lounges; outdoor pool; tennis court; room service (7am–11pm); laundry service; dry cleaning. *In room:* TV.

Hotel Ofir ★★ The older central core contains guest rooms furnished in traditional Portuguese fashion with reproductions of regional furniture; the adjoining wings are modern. A newer section is quite luxurious, built motel style right along the dunes, with a row of white tents and a pure-sand beach in full view of the second-floor balconies. All units come equipped with neatly kept bathrooms containing shower-tub combinations. There are well-styled public rooms, but the principal focus is on the wide oceanfront terrace, where guests sunbathe.

The hotel is a resort unto itself, with a vast playground terrace and a flagstone terrace bordering soft green lawns. The hotel is located near a golf course.

Av. Raul de Sousa Martins, Ofir, 4740-405 Esposende. ✆ **25/398-98-00.** Fax 25/398-18-71. 200 units. 57€–102€ ($66–$117) double; 70€–137€ ($81–$158) suite. Rates include buffet breakfast. AE, DC, MC, V. Free parking. **Amenities:** Restaurant; bar; outdoor pool; health club; room service (8am–1am); babysitting; laundry; dry cleaning. *In room:* A/C, TV, dataport, minibar, safe.

12

The Minho Region & Trás-os-Montes

The Minho, in the verdant northwest corner of Portugal, is almost a land unto itself. The region begins some 40km (25 miles) north of Porto and stretches to the frontier of Galicia, in northwest Spain. In fact, Minho and Galicia and their people are strikingly similar. The regions share a Celtic background.

Granite plateaus undulate across the countryside, broken by the green valleys of the Minho, Ave, Cávado, and Lima rivers. For centuries, the region's bountiful granite quarries have been emptied to build everything from the great church facades in Braga and Guimarães to the humblest village cottages. Green pastures contrast sharply with forests filled with cedars and chestnuts.

The small size of the district and the proximity of the towns make it easy to hop from hamlet to hamlet. Even the biggest towns—Viana do Castelo, Guimarães, and Braga—are provincial in nature. You'll sometimes see wooden carts in the streets, drawn by pairs of dappled and chocolate-brown oxen. These noble beasts are depicted on the pottery and ceramics for which the Minho (especially Viana do Castelo) is known.

Religious *festas* are occasions that bring people out into the streets for days of merrymaking and celebrations, including folk songs, dances, and displays of traditional costumes. The women often wear woolen skirts and festively decorated aprons with floral or geometric designs. Their bodices are pinned with golden filigree and draped with layers of heart- or cross-shape pendants.

The Minho was the cradle of Portuguese independence. From here, Afonso Henrîques, the first king, made his plans to capture the south from the Moors. Battlemented castles along the frontier are reminders of the region's former hostilities with Spain, and fortresses still loom above the coastal villages.

Porto (see chapter 11) is the air gateway to the Minho. A car is the best way to see the north if you have only a short time; if you depend on public transportation, you can visit some of the major centers by bus and rail.

The far northeast province of Portugal is a wild, rugged land—Trás-os-Montes, or "beyond the mountains." Extending from south of the Upper Douro at Lamego, the province stretches north to Spain. Vila Real is its capital. Rocky crests and deep valleys break up the high plateau, between the mountain ranges of Marão and Gerês. Most of the population lives in the valleys, usually in houses constructed from shale or granite. Much of the plateau is arid land, but swift rivers and their tributaries supply ample water, and some of the valleys have fertile farmland. The Tãmega River Valley is known for the thermal springs found there as far back as Roman days.

Vigo
SPAIN
N202
Melgaço
Valença
Monção
Riba de Mouro
Sierra do Suajo
Rio Coura
Vila Nova de Cerveira
Caminha
Moledo do Minho
N101
Vila Praia de Âncora
Lindosa
N203
Soajo
Rio Lima
Ponte da Barca
Ponte de Lima
N203
Rio Homem
Sierra do Barroso
Arcos de Valdevez
Viana do Castelo
Gerês
N103
Rio Cávado
Vieira do Minho
Cerdeirinhas
Mar
Póvoa de Lanhoso
Barcelos
Braga
Arosa
Esposende
Vila Nova de Famalicão
Cabeceiras de Basto
E01
N13
N14
Guimarães
Fafe
COSTA VERDE
Póvoa de Varzim
Vila do Conde
Caldas de Vizela
N101
Celorico de Basto
E82
ATLANTIC OCEAN
0
10 mi
0
10 km
N
Porto
N15
FRANCE
area of detail
SPAIN
PORTUGAL
Lisbon

This land is rich in history and tradition, offering the visitor a new world to discover, from pre-Roman castles to pillories and interesting old churches. The inhabitants are of Celtic descent, and most speak a dialect of Galician.

You can reach Trás-os-Montes by train from Porto. Service is to Régua, not far from Lamego, which serves as a gateway into the province in the Pais do Vinho, where grapes from vineyards on the terraced hills provide the wines that are credited to Porto. Lamego is actually in the province of Beira Alta. You can drive through this land of splendid savagery, but don't expect superhighways.

1 Guimarães ★★

48km (30 miles) NE of Porto, 69km (43 miles) SW of Viana do Castelo, 364km (226 miles) N of Lisbon

The cradle of Portugal, Guimarães suffers from a near embarrassment of riches. At the foot of a range of *serras* (mountains), this first capital of Portugal has preserved a medieval atmosphere in its core. The city was the birthplace of Afonso Henrîques, the first king of Portugal and son of a French nobleman, Henri de Bourgogne, and his wife, Teresa, daughter of the king of León and Castile. For her dowry, Teresa brought the county of Portucale, whose name eventually became Portugal. Portucale consisted of the land between the Minho and the Douro, taking in what is now the city of Porto. Teresa and Henri chose Guimarães as their court, and Afonso Henrîques was born here.

After Henri died, Teresa became regent for the baby king. She soon fell into disfavor with her subjects for having an affair with a count from Galicia and developing strong ties with her native Spain. As a young man, Afonso revolted against the regent's forces outside Guimarães in 1128. A major victory for Afonso came in 1139, when he routed the Moors near Santarém. He broke from León and Castile and proclaimed himself king of Portucale. In 1143, Spain recognized the newly emerged kingdom.

Guimarães had another famous son, Gil Vicente (1470?–1536?). Founder of the Portuguese theater, he's often referred to as the Shakespeare of Portugal. Although trained as a goldsmith, Vicente entertained the courts of both João II and Manuel I with his farces and tragicomedies. He also penned religious dramas.

Today Guimarães is a busy little town with an eye toward commerce, especially in weaving, tanning, and kitchenware and cutlery manufacturing. It's also known for its craft industries, especially pottery, silver- and goldsmithing, and embroidery.

ESSENTIALS

ARRIVING

BY TRAIN Fifteen trains daily make the 2-hour run between Porto and Guimarães; the one-way cost is 3.10€ ($3.55). Call © **808/208-208** for schedules.

BY BUS Guimarães is easily accessible from Braga (see section 2 in this chapter); buses make the 1-hour trip frequently during the day. A one-way bus ticket from Braga to the Guimarães bus station, Quinta das Lameiras, is 3.15€ ($3.60). For information call © **25/342-35-00.**

BY CAR Drive northwest from Porto on N105-2 and N105.

VISITOR INFORMATION

The **Guimarães Tourist Office** is at Alameda S. Damaso 83 (© **25/341-24-50**). It's open Monday through Friday from 9:30am to 12:30pm and 2 to 6:30pm.

EXPLORING THE TOWN

If you'd like to step into the Middle Ages for an hour or two, stroll down **Rua de Santa Maria** ★. It has remained essentially unchanged for centuries, except that nowadays you're likely to hear blaring music—in English, no less. Proud town houses, once the residences of the nobility, stand beside humble dwellings. The hand-carved balconies, aged by the years, are most often garnished with iron lanterns (not to mention laundry).

At the end, you'll come upon a charming square in the heart of the old town, **Largo da Oliveira** (Olive Tree Square). Seek out the odd chapelette in front of a church. Composed of four ogival arches, it's said to mark the spot where, in the 6th century, Wamba was asked to give up the simple toil of working his fields to become the king of the Goths. Thrusting his olive stick into the tilled soil, he declared that he would accept only if his stick sprouted leaves. So it did, and so he did—or so goes the tale.

The best excursion in the environs is to **Penha** ★, 5.5km (3½ miles) southeast of the center of town. At 620m (2,034 ft.), this is the loftiest point in the Serra de Santa Caterina. Penha can be reached from the end of Rua de Dr. José Sampaio by cable car for 2.50€ ($2.90) round-trip. The car runs from June to September daily from 10am to 7pm (Sun until 8pm). In the off season, the schedule depends on the weather. Call the tourist office (see above) for information.

Dominating the skyline of Guimarães itself is the 10th-century **Castle of Guimarães** ★, Rua Dona Teresa de Noronha, where Afonso Henrîques, Portugal's first king, was born. High-pitched crenels top the strategically placed square towers and the looming keep. The view is panoramic. For more information, contact the staff at the Paço dos Duques (✆ **25/341-22-73**). Almost in the shadow of the castle is the squat, rectangular 12th-century Romanesque **Igreja de São Miguel de Castelo,** where Afonso Henrîques was baptized. Nearby is a heroic statue of the mustachioed, armor-clad Afonso, helmeted with sword and shield in hand. The church keeps irregular hours. The castle (no phone) is open Tuesday through Sunday from 9:30am to 5pm (Aug until 7pm). Admission is free unless you visit the panoramic tower, **Torre Demanage,** which costs 1.30€ ($1.50).

Paço dos Duques de Bragança ★ From the keep of the castle you can see the four-winged Palace of the Dukes of Bragança. Constructed in the 15th century, it has been heavily restored. Many critics have dismissed the rebuilt structure with contempt. If you're not a purist, however, you might find a guided tour interesting.

Perched on the slope of a hill, the palace possesses an assortment of treasures. The portraits include one of Catherine of Bragança, who married Charles II of England, "the merrie monarch" and lover of Nell Gwynne. There are copies of the large Pastrana tapestries depicting scenes from the Portuguese wars in North Africa, scabbards and helmets in the armor room, Persian hangings, Indian urns, ceramics, and Chinese porcelains. The chapel opens onto the throne chairs of the duke and duchess. Nearby are the double-tiered cloisters.

Rua Conde Dom Henrîque. ✆ **25/341-22-73.** Admission 3€ ($3.45), free for children under 15. Daily 9:30am–5pm, until 7pm in August.

Igreja de São Francisco The Church of St. Francis contains by far the most dramatic church **interior** ★ in town. Entered through a Gothic portal, the spacious interior is faced with Delft blue and white ***azulejos*** ★ (tiles). In the transept to the right of the main altar is a meticulously detailed miniature recreation of the living room of a church prelate, from the burgundy cardinal's chapeau resting on a wall sconce to the miniature dog and cat. On the second altar to the right is a polychrome tree of life that represents 12 crowned kings and the Virgin, with her hands clasped and her feet resting on the heads of three cherubs. Entered through the south transept, the **sacristy** ★ rests under a beautiful coffered ceiling decorated with grotesques and a stunning Arrábida marble table.

Largo de São Francisco. ✆ **25/351-25-07.** Free admission. Mon–Sat 10am–noon and 2:30–5pm, Sun 7am–1pm.

Museu de Alberto Sampaio ★ The Alberto Sampaio Museum is in the Romanesque cloister and the buildings of the old monastery of the Collegiate Church of Our Lady of the Olive Branch. Besides a large silver collection, it displays the tunic worn by João I at the battle of Aljubarrota, which decided Portugal's fate. There are priestly garments as well as paintings, ceramics, and medieval sculpture. A fresco illustrates a gloating Salome, rapturous over the severed head of John the Baptist. In one of the rooms are pieces from a baroque chapel, with enormous wood-carved angels bearing torches.

Rua Alfredo Guimarães. ✆ **25/342-39-10.** Admission 2€ ($2.30), free for children under 14. Tues–Sun 10am–midnight. Closed holidays.

SHOPPING

In the town's historic core, two streets are particularly noteworthy. The narrow medieval **Rua de Santa Maria** is the street long acknowledged by art historians as the most beautiful. Here you'll find some outlets for handcrafts and souvenirs like ceramics, woodcarvings, handmade lace, and embroidered linen. More geared to the needs of residents is the main commercial thoroughfare, **Rua Gil Vicente.** For handcrafts, the best-stocked shop in town is **Artesanato de Guimarães,** Rua Paio Galvão (✆ **25/351-52-50**). Loosely affiliated with the municipal government, it functions as a showplace for the works of dozens of artisans from throughout the region, with an emphasis on textiles, woodcarvings, ceramics, and metalwork.

WHERE TO STAY

EXPENSIVE

Pousada de Santa Marinha da Costa ★★★ With foundations dating from the 12th century, this restored pousada is one of the most impressive in Portugal. Teresa, mother of Afonso Henríques, built it in 1154 as an Augustinian convent. It gained a baroque facade in the 18th century, when the soaring interior halls and spouting fountains were installed. The ornate Manueline church that occupies part of the building still offers mass on Sunday. The property lies at the end of a winding road about 2km (1¼ miles) north of the town center on N101-2. Signs indicate the direction.

Take the time to explore both the upper halls and the gardens. One of the best rooms is a beautifully furnished large salon. At the end of one of the soaring halls, a fountain bubbles beneath an intricate wooden ceiling, surrounded by an open arcade that encompasses a view of the faraway mountains.

The guest rooms are a pleasing blend of old stonework, modern plasterwork, regional fabrics, and Portuguese lithographs. About half are in a relatively modern wing attached to the medieval core. The modern units, decorated in traditional Portuguese style, are equipped with well-maintained bathrooms containing shower-tub combinations.

Costa, 4801-011 Guimarães. ✆ **25/351-12-49.** Fax 25/351-44-59. www.pousadas.pt. 51 units. 112€–181€ ($129–$208) double; 227€–301€ ($261–$346) suite. Rates include breakfast. AE, DC, MC, V. Free parking.

Amenities: Restaurant; bar; limited room service; babysitting; laundry service; dry cleaning; nonsmoking rooms. *In room:* A/C, TV, dataport, minibar, hair dryer, safe.

MODERATE

Hotel de Guimarães ★★ We still prefer to stay at either of the pousadas recommended below, but this sleepy town is now blessed with a big, government-rated four-star hotel. Flavored by business clients and tour groups, it lies at the center of the historic core. The decoration is in contemporary good taste, and the bedrooms are midsize to spacious, each with a good-size bathroom with a shower-tub combination. The hotel also offers the best facilities at the resort, including a gym and an indoor swimming pool. If you don't demand character and charm from your hotel but like to be buffeted in comfort with many distractions, including bars and on-site dining, this is obviously the best choice.

Rua Eduardo de Almeida, 4801-911 Guimarães. ✆ **25/342-48-00.** Fax 25/342-48-99. www.hotel-guimaraes.com. 116 units. 85€–110€ ($98–$127) double; 110€–160€ ($127–$184) suite. AE, DC, MC, V. Free parking. **Amenities:** Restaurant; bar; indoor pool; squash court; gym; Jacuzzi; sauna; solarium; limited room service; babysitting; laundry service; dry cleaning; nonsmoking rooms; 1 room for those w/limited mobility. *In room:* A/C, TV, dataport, minibar, hair dryer, safe.

Hotel Turismo de Braga ★ The best hotel in the town center, Turismo de Braga is in a sprawling 11-story 1950s building fronted with flowering gardens and a parking lot. The entrance lies beneath an arcade that shelters some cafes. The hotel offers uninspired comfort. The two-story lobby lies below a spacious wood-paneled lounge, bar, and restaurant. Each midsize guest room contains a spacious balcony opening onto traffic; the walls are covered with blue-and-white tiles. Furnishings are standardized but still comfortable, and the beds are firm. All units come equipped with well-maintained bathrooms containing shower-tub combinations. The hotel has a rooftop pool and an eighth-floor snack bar.

Praçeta João XXI, 4710-245 Braga. ✆ **25/320-60-00.** Fax 25/320-60-10. www.hotelturismobraga.com. 128 units. 69€–75€ ($79–$86) double; 99€–120€ ($114–$138) suite. Rates include breakfast. AE, DC, MC, V. Parking 5€ ($5.75). **Amenities:** Restaurant; snack bar; bar; pool; 24-hr. room service; laundry; dry cleaning; nonsmoking rooms. *In room:* A/C, TV, dataport, hair dryer.

Pousada de Nossa Senhora de Oliveira ★★ The ambience at the second pousada in town differs from the atmosphere at the Santa Marinha da Costa, which is bigger and livelier. This establishment was created when a handful of 16th-century stone town houses were combined into a single rambling hotel. Many of their original features have been preserved. The pousada has a loyal clientele, a location on one of Portugal's most beautiful medieval squares, and a distinctive country-inn flavor. The street is so narrow that you'll have to park (free) in a well-marked lot about 31m (102 ft.) away.

The front rooms are of good size, but those on the side tend to be smaller. The accommodations contain twin beds, regional fabrics, and rug-covered tile floors. All rooms also have well-kept bathrooms equipped with shower-tub combinations. This place exudes intimate warmth, heightened by the wooden ceilings, tavern bar, and fireplace in the restaurant, whose windows look out over the square.

Rua de Santa Maria, 4801-910 Guimarães. ✆ **25/351-41-57.** Fax 25/351-42-04. 16 units. 92€–140€ ($106–$161) double; 114€–169€ ($131–$194) suite. Rates include breakfast. AE, DC, MC, V. Free parking. **Amenities:** Restaurant; bar; limited room service; laundry service; dry cleaning; 1 nonsmoking room. *In room:* A/C, TV, minibar, hair dryer, safe.

INEXPENSIVE

Fundador Hotel This central hotel offers comfortable but small guest rooms in a medium high-rise. Though the pousadas are preferable, the Fundador is a decent place to spend the night. Rooms have piped-in music and well-kept bathrooms equipped with shower-tub combinations. The hotel isn't stylish, but it's functional and well kept, and boasts fine service. The penthouse bar serves snacks.

Av. Dom Afonso Henríques 740, 4810-431 Guimarães. ✆ **25/342-26-40.** Fax 25/342-26-49. www.hotelfundador.com. 63 units. 85€ ($98) double. Rates include breakfast. AE, DC, MC, V. Free parking. **Amenities:** Bar; limited room service; laundry service; dry cleaning; 1 nonsmoking room. *In room:* A/C, TV, dataport, minibar, hair dryer, safe.

WHERE TO DINE

MODERATE

Solar do Arco ★ PORTUGUESE/INTERNATIONAL The best independent restaurant outside of hotel dining is this winning eatery, which is installed in an antique house in the historic center with a rustic decor featuring lots of wood. The chef fashions superb dishes based whenever possible on local market-fresh produce. "We are rustic but also noble," our waiter assured us. The shrimp with white beans was a delight, as was the roast veal with potatoes and greens so fresh they tasted like they were just picked. And what respectable Portuguese dining room would not offer a codfish specialty of the day? On our most recent visit, the chef had prepared a savory codfish stew with onions, potatoes, and fresh greens. We launched our repast with a cream of shellfish soup and saved room for dessert, which was a tart of "summer fruits."

Rua da Santa Maria 48–50. ✆ **25/351-30-72.** Reservations recommended. Main courses 7€–24€ ($8.05–$28). AE, DC, MC, V. Daily noon–3pm and 6pm–midnight.

INEXPENSIVE

El Rei Dom Afonso REGIONAL PORTUGUESE In an enviable position in the heart of the medieval sector, this little restaurant opens onto the rear of the former town hall and the Pousada de Nossa Santa Maria da Oliveira. The patrons are mostly locals, joined by occasional foreigners. It offers good fish and tender meat dishes, including pork and codfish, plus country-fresh vegetables. Try hake filets or house-style steak. Service is efficient, albeit sometimes rushed.

Praça de São Tiago 20. ✆ **25/341-90-96.** Main courses 8€–12€ ($9.20–$14); tourist menu 14€ ($13). AE, DC, MC, V. Mon–Sat noon–3pm and 7–11pm.

GUIMARÃES AFTER DARK

There are a lot of folkloric-looking taverns in the city center, many on such thoroughfares as **Rua Gil Vicente** and **Rua de Santa Maria.** For dancing and insights into what the new hipsters of northern Portugal are doing, head about 5km (3 miles) east. On the opposite side of the mountain that looms above the town center, you'll find the **Penha Club,** Estrada A Penha (✆ **25/343-20-68**). It doesn't have a formal address, but it's signposted from the town center. Its leading competitors include our favorite, **Seculo XIX,** Localidade da Universidade (✆ **25/341-88-99**), a replica of a century-old tavern, with lots of paneling and the kind of music that attracts fun-lovers regardless of age.

2 Braga ★

50km (31 miles) N of Porto, 367km (228 miles) N of Lisbon

Nearly everywhere you look in Braga there's a church, a palace, a garden, or a fountain. Known to the Romans as Bracara Augusta, the town has resounded to the footsteps of other conquerors, including the Suevi, the Visigoths, and the Moors. For centuries it has been an archiepiscopal seat and pilgrimage site; the

Visigoths are said to have renounced their heresies here. Although aware of its rich history, the capital of Minho is very much a city of today. Its historic core and cathedral lie at the center, but the periphery bustles with commerce and industry, including a lot of manufacturing—brick making, soap making, textiles, smelting, engineering, and leather goods.

Politically, Braga is Portugal's most conservative city. In 1926, a coup here paved the way for Salazar to begin his long dictatorship. Paradoxically, Braga is a hot place at night, primarily because of its young people. In fact, its lively streets have earned it a reputation for being "Lisbon in miniature."

Braga is also a religious capital. It stages the country's most impressive observances of *Semana Santa* (Holy Week). Torchlit processions of hooded participants, eerily evocative of the KKK, parade by.

Sleepy Braga is gone forever. Today 65,000 residents live with noisy streets, increasing numbers of ugly and uninspired apartment blocks, and traffic congestion on streets that not long ago contained a few cars and maybe a donkey or two.

ESSENTIALS

ARRIVING

BY TRAIN The train station is on Largo da Estação (✆ **25/327-85-52**). Some 20 trains per day arrive from Porto after a 1½-hour trip. It costs 6€ ($6.90) one-way. From Coimbra, 15 trains a day make the 4-hour trip. A one-way ticket costs 9€ ($10). Eleven trains a day arrive from Viana do Castelo. The trip takes 2 hours and costs 4€ ($4.60) one-way.

BY BUS The bus station is at Central de Camionagem (✆ **25/320-94-00**), a few blocks north of the heart of town. Buses arrive every hour from Porto; the trip takes 1½ hours and costs 3.80€ ($4.35) one-way. From Guimarães, there are 12 buses per day; the trip takes an hour and costs 2.15€ ($2.45). From Lisbon, five daily buses make the 5½-hour trip. The fare is 15€ ($17) one-way.

BY CAR From Guimarães (see the preceding section), head northwest along N101.

VISITOR INFORMATION

The **Braga Tourist Office** is at Avenida da Liberdade 1 (✆ **25/326-25-50**). It's open Monday through Friday 9am to 12:30pm and 2 to 6:30pm, Saturday and Sunday until 5:30pm October through June, and daily 9am to 7pm July through September.

EXPLORING THE TOWN

Sé ★ Inside the town, interest focuses on the Sé (cathedral), which was built in the 12th century by Henri de Bourgogne and Dona Teresa. After he died, she was chased out of town because of an illicit love affair, but in death Henri and Teresa were reunited in their tombs in the Chapel of Kings.

The Sé has undergone decorative and architectural changes. The north triple-arched facade is austere and dominating, with a large stone-laced Roman arch flanked by two smaller Gothic ones. What appear to be the skeletons of cupolas top the facade's dual bell towers, which flank a lofty rooftop niche containing a larger-than-life statue of the *Virgin and Child.* Under a carved baldachin in the apse is a statue of Our Lady of the Milk—that is, the Virgin breast-feeding the infant Jesus. The statue is in the Manueline style but is somehow pious and restrained.

Inside you might think you've entered one of the darkest citadels of Christendom. If you can see them, the decorations, including a pair of huge 18th-century gilded organs, are profuse. In the 1330 **Capela da Glória** ★ is the sarcophagus of Archbishop Dom Gonçalo Pereira, with an unctuous expression on his face. It was carved by order of the prelate.

You can visit the **Treasury of the Cathedral** ★ and the **Museum of Sacred Art,** an upstairs repository of Braga's most precious works of art. On display are elaborately carved choir stalls from the 18th century, embroidered vestments from the 16th to the 18th centuries, a 14th-century statue of the Virgin, and a Gothic chalice from the same period. An 18th-century silver-and-gilt monstrance adorned with diamonds is by Dom Gaspar de Bragança. In the cloister is a pietà.

Sé Primaz, Rua Dom Paio Mendez. ✆ **25/326-33-17.** Free admission to Sé; to museum and treasury 2€ ($2.30), free for children under 12. Daily 8:30am–6pm.

Museu dos Biscainhos This museum is in Biscainhos Palace, a building from the 17th and 18th centuries that for about 300 years has served as the house of a noble family. The original gardens are still here. The museum has painted and ornamented ceilings and walls with panels of figurative and neoclassic tiles. Its exhibition rooms contain collections of Portuguese furniture and pottery, glassware, silverware, textiles, and Portuguese, Oriental, and Dutch Delft porcelain.

Rua dos Biscainhos. ✆ **25/320-46-50.** Admission 2€ ($2.30), free for children under 15. Tues–Sun 10am–5:30pm. Closed holidays.

Bom Jesús do Monte ★★ Bom Jesús do Monte is a hilltop pilgrimage site; it's reached on foot, on a funicular (the ride costs .60€/55¢), or by car along a tree-lined roadway. The baroque granite double staircase dating from the 18th century might look daunting, but if it's any consolation, pilgrims often climb it on their knees. The stairway is less elaborate than the one at Remédios at Lamego but is equally impressive. On the numerous landings are gardens, grottoes, small chapels, sculptures, and allegorical stone figures set in fountains.

N103-3, 5km (3 miles) SE of Braga. ✆ **25/367-66-36.** Free admission. Daily 7:30am–8pm.

SHOPPING

The town's best outlet for gifts and handmade souvenirs is in the **tourist office** (see "Essentials," above). You'll find an impressive array of appealingly textured linens, pottery and ceramics, and woodcarvings that evoke the values and traditions of northern Portugal.

Nearby is a textile factory that transforms flax into linens; the factory outlet boasts a rich stock of houseware linens, some of them of heirloom quality. Head 4km (2½ miles) north of the city, following signs to Prado. In the hamlet of Sanpaio Merelim, you'll find the factories of **Edgar Duarte Abreu,** Sanpaio Merelim (✆ **25/362-11-92**).

Camping & Pony Trekking

Parque Nacional da Peneda-Gerês ★★, named after the two mountains it encompasses, sprawls across Minho and Trás-os-Montes. Established in 1971, it's one of the best places for hiking in Portugal. The Lima River, running north-south, bisects the reserve. In the south, the Cávado marks the border. Although the park has a limited infrastructure, and walking maps and signposted paths almost don't exist, organized tours offer both pony trekking and camping. For **park information,** call ✆ **25/320-34-80.**

WHERE TO STAY

Albergaria Senhora a Branca ★ *Finds* Offering good value, this discovery in a four-story building lies on a historic square about a 7-minute walk from the exact center of town. Modern comforts have been installed in a restored antique building. Bedrooms are small to midsize, but they are attractively and comfortably furnished, each with a small bathroom and shower. The owner used to be in the antique business, and part of his former merchandise is used to decorate the hotel, giving it added charm. The hotel is well run and welcoming.

Largo da Senhora a Branca 58, 4710 Braga. ✆ **25/326-99-38.** Fax 25/326-99-37. www.albergariasrabranca.pt. 18 units. 50€ ($58) double; 60€ ($69) suite. Rates include breakfast. AE, DC, MC, V. Free parking. **Amenities:** Breakfast room; limited room service; laundry. *In room:* A/C, TV, dataport.

Dona Sofia *Value* The town's best bargain lies close to the cathedral, a business thriving for more than a decade in an antique but restored building. Bedrooms are midsize and traditionally furnished, often with handcrafted pieces. Each room comes with a small bathroom with a shower-tub combination. The place is basic and merely functional, but it's such good value and so tidily maintained that it's highly recommended. Although breakfast is the only meal served, there are several choices for dining nearby.

Largo São João de Souto 131, 4700 Braga. ✆ **25/326-31-60.** Fax 25/361-12-45. 34 units. 55€–60€ ($63–$69) double; 70€–75€ ($81–$86) suite. AE, MC, V. **Amenities:** Bar; laundry. *In room:* A/C, TV, minibar.

Hotel João XXI This is a good second-class hotel. On a tree-shaded avenue leading to Bom Jesús do Monte, it stands opposite Braga's leading first-class hotel. The midsize guest rooms have warm modern decor, with the accent on neatness and efficiency; the singles have double beds. Each unit comes with a neatly kept bathroom equipped with a shower-tub combination. The entry to this modern little place is a salute to the 19th century. The tiny street-floor reception room is decorated a la Louis XVI. The social center is the living room lounge, which has well-selected furnishings and an open fireplace.

Av. João XXI 849, 4715-035 Braga. ✆ **25/361-66-30.** Fax 25/361-66-31. 40 units. 35€–40€ ($40–$46) double. Rates include breakfast. AE, DC, MC, V. Limited free parking on street. **Amenities:** Breakfast room; lounge. *In room:* A/C, TV.

AT BOM JESUS DO MONTE

Castelo do Bom Jesús ★★ This 18th-century manor-turned-luxury-hotel is the area's best choice; at Bom Jesus, life is more tranquil than in the center of the city. The windows open onto views of Braga. A well-landscaped private park and a large lake with islets, ancestral trees, and tropical flora surround the building. The rooms have great charm; the rooftop unit is the most desirable. They're individually decorated in 18th-century traditional style, with swagged draperies, color-coordinated bedspreads and furnishings, and tasteful accessories. All come with well-maintained bathrooms containing shower-tub combinations. The nuptial chamber was a favorite of Dom Carlos, former king of Portugal, who installed his mistress, an actress, here.

Live music is presented on weekends. A few yards from the main building is a regional cellar that schedules vintage wine-tasting events on some evenings. Breakfast is served in the Oval Dining Room, frescoed by various artists. With advance notice, lunch or dinner can be served.

Bom Jesús do Monte, 4710-245 Braga. ✆ **25/367-65-66.** Fax 25/367-76-91. 11 units. 54€–68€ ($62–$78) double; 90€–113€ ($104–$130) junior suite; 180€ ($207) suite. Rates include breakfast. AE, DC, MC, V. Free parking. **Amenities:** Breakfast room; bar; pool; limited room service; babysitting; laundry service; dry cleaning. *In room:* A/C (only in suites), TV, hair dryer, safe.

Hotel do Elevador ★ Near the Bom Jésus do Monte, this traditionally styled hotel was completely rebuilt in 1998 and named for a nearby and still-working water-powered elevator from the 1800s. The hotel is mainly known for its 120-seat panoramic restaurant, opening onto the best views in Braga. But there is also much comfort here in the midsize bedrooms if you want to stay over. Decoration is in the classic style, and furnishings are tasteful; each unit comes with a small bathroom with a shower-tub combination. The location lies 3km (2 miles) outside of Braga on a wooded hillside.

Parque do Bom Jesus do Monte, 4700 Braga. ✆ **25/360-34-00.** Fax 25/360-34-09. www.hoteisbomjesus.web.pt. 22 units. 74€–90€ ($85–$104) double; 108€–130€ ($124–$150) suite. Rates include buffet breakfast. AE, DC, MC, V. **Amenities:** Restaurant; bar; limited room service; laundry service. *In room:* A/C, TV, minibar, hair dryer.

Hotel do Parque Originally a turn-of-the-20th-century villa, the Parque offers comfortably furnished but small rooms. They have modern amenities such as well-maintained bathrooms equipped with shower-tub combinations. The decor is traditional, and the grounds are well maintained. At dinner, the hotel serves cuisine of the Minho and of France. There's a spacious sitting room with an open fireplace.

Bom Jesús, Tenões, 4710-455 Braga. ✆ **25/360-34-70.** Fax 25/360-34-79. www.hoteisbomjesus.web.pt. 49 units. 85€–90€ ($98–$104) double; 108€–130€ ($124–$150) suite. Rates include breakfast. AE, DC, MC, V. Free parking. **Amenities:** Dining room; bar; lounge; limited room service; babysitting; laundry; dry cleaning. *In room:* A/C, TV, dataport, minibar, hair dryer.

EAST OF BRAGA

Casa de Requeixo ★★ *Finds* The area's most romantic place to stay is at Frades, near Póvoa de Lanhoso, 20km (12½ miles) east of Braga. Casa de Requeixo is a massive, elegant stone mansion from the 16th and 17th centuries. Dr. Manuel Artur Norton has beautifully furnished the guest rooms, each with a large living room and a well-maintained bathroom equipped with a shower-tub combination. The *quinta* (manor house) combines old-fashioned charm with modern-day comfort in a bucolic setting. While based here, you can explore the area, including the Minho and Peneda-Gerês national parks.

Frades, 4830-216 Póvoa de Lanhoso. ✆ **25/363-11-12.** Fax 25/363-64-99. 6 units. 55€ ($63) double; 65€ ($75) apt. Rates include continental breakfast. No credit cards. Free parking. From the national highway N103 from Braga to Chaves, exit after 16km/10 miles at the signposted stop in the village of Frades. From Braga, take a bus marked VENDAS NOVAS or CHAVES. **Amenities:** Breakfast room; lounge; kitchenette (in apt. only). *In room:* No phone.

WHERE TO DINE

O Alexandre PORTUGUESE Since the 1970s, this small eatery has attracted patrons from all walks of city life, including the mayor and church officials. It seems busiest at lunch, when businesspeople book most of the tables. Regional wines accompany most meals. There's an a la carte menu, but always ask about the daily specials. Portions are generous, and the cooking is rich. Roast *cabrito* (kid) is in season in June; the year-round favorite is *bacalhau* (dried salt cod), prepared in an infinite number of ways.

Campo das Hortas 10. ✆ **25/361-40-03.** Reservations recommended. Main courses 13€–17€ ($15–$19). DC, MC, V. Daily noon–3:30pm and 7–11pm.

O Inácio ★ REGIONAL PORTUGUESE Located in an old stone structure outside the Arco da Porta Nova (the town gate), O Inácio is the most popular restaurant in town. With rugged walls and hand-hewn beams from the 1700s, it has thrived as a restaurant since the 1930s. The owner has a well-stocked wine cellar and, in our opinion, serves the best cuisine in Braga.

In the colder months a fire burns in an open hearth. The rustic decor features regional pottery and oxen yokes. The Portuguese specialties usually include *bacalhau à Inácio* (codfish), *papas de sarrabulho* (a regional stew served in winter only), and *bife na cacarola* (pot roast). Roast kid is featured occasionally. Most fish dishes, which are fresh, are good alternatives. The dessert surprise is a rum omelet soufflé.

Campo das Hortas 4. ✆ **25/361-32-35.** Reservations recommended. Main courses 11€–16€ ($13–$18). AE, DC, MC, V. Wed–Mon 12:30–3:30pm and 7–10pm. Closed for 2 weeks in Sept.

BRAGA AFTER DARK

There aren't any dance clubs, and there isn't a lot to do after dark. You'll probably remain in the bar of your hotel or head for one of three tried-and-true bars, favorites of many generations of locals. They lie almost adjacent to one another, near the corner of Avenida Central and Praça da República: the **Bar Barbieri** (✆ **25/361-43-81;** open Wed and Fri–Sat 10pm–7am), the **Café Vianna** (✆ **25/326-23-36;** open daily 7am–2am), and the **Café Astoria** (✆ **25/327-39-44;** open daily from 8am to midnight). They serve coffee, wine, and whiskey in settings redolent of local gossip and intrigue.

3 Barcelos

23km (14 miles) W of Braga, 365km (226 miles) N of Lisbon

Barcelos is a sprawling river town that rests on a plateau ringed by green hills. Wrought-iron street lanterns glimmer late in the evening, long after the market in the open square of Campo da República has closed down.

The town doesn't feature any single major attraction, but it does have a famous symbol: the rooster. Although it was cooked and about to be served as the main course in a magistrate's dinner, the legend goes, the rooster crowed ecstatically to prove the innocence of a pilgrim wrongfully accused of theft.

ESSENTIALS

ARRIVING

BY TRAIN The station is on Avenida Alcaides de Faria (✆ **25/381-12-43**). Thirteen trains a day arrive from Braga; the trip takes 1¼ hours and costs 1.60€ ($1.85). Twelve trains a day make the 45-minute trip from Viana do Castelo that costs 1.80€ ($2.05).

BY BUS The station is on Avenida Dr. Sidónio Pais (✆ **25/381-43-10**). Fourteen buses a day arrive from Braga. It's a 50-minute trip that costs 1.80€ ($2.05).

BY CAR From Braga, follow N103 due west.

VISITOR INFORMATION

The **Barcelos Tourist Office** is at Torre da Porta Nova (✆ **25/381-18-82**). It's open daily from 10am to 6pm.

EXPLORING THE TOWN Try to visit Barcelos on Thursday, when the **market** (7am–6pm) takes over the **Campo da República,** almost 400 sq. m (4,306 sq. ft.), with a fountain at the center. You'll see local handcrafts—rugs, dyed pillows stuffed with chicken feathers, chandeliers, crochet work, pottery, and hand-painted earthenware cockerels, Portugal's most characteristic souvenirs and often a symbol of the country.

Opening onto the tree-studded main square are some of the finest buildings in Barcelos. The 18th-century **Igreja de Nossa Senhora do Terco** resembles a palace more than a church, with a central-niche facade topped by finials and a cross. The tile work around the baroque altar depicts scenes of monks at labor and a moving rendition of the Last Supper. Also fronting the *campo* is the **Hospital da Misericórdia,** a long, formal 17th-century building behind a spiked fence.

Of more interest is the small, octagonal **Igreja do Bom Jesús da Cruz,** with a tile-faced cupola. An upper balustrade, punctuated by large stone finials and a latticed round window about the square portal, contrasts with the austerity of the walls. The interior is more sumptuous, with crystal, marble, and gilt. There are no set hours for visits, though generally one can enter daily from 9am to noon and 3 to 6pm. Don't count on always finding someone to admit you, however.

Overlooking the swirling Cávado River are the ruins of the 1786 **Palace of the Braganças.** The original palace site, as well as the town of Barcelos itself, was bestowed on Nuno Álvares by João I as a gift in gratitude for his bravery in the 1385 battle at Aljubarrota.

On the facade is a representation of the palace, re-created in splendor. You can wander through the ruins, which have been turned into an archaeological museum filled with sarcophagi, heralded shields, and an 18th-century tile fountain. The **Museu Arqueológico** (© **25/382-47-41**) is open daily 9am to noon and 2 to 6pm. Admission is free. The **Museu Regional de Cerâmica** (© **25/382-47-41**) underneath the palace encapsulates the evolution of that handcraft (look for the blood-red ceramic oxen with lyre-shape horns). Enter on Rua Conego Joaquim Gaiolas. It is open Tuesday through Friday from 10am to 5:30pm, and Saturday and Sunday from 10am to 12:30pm and 2 to 5:30pm. Admission is 1.40€ ($1.60) for adults, and .70€ (80¢) for students and children.

The shadow from the high palace chimney stretches across the old pillory in the courtyard below. The structure even exceeds in height the bell tower of the adjoining **Igreja Matriz** (parish church). Fronting the river, the Gothic church contains a baroque altar and an interior whose sides are faced with multicolored tiles. The altar is an array of cherubs, grapes, gold leaf, and birds.

SHOPPING The unique **Centro do Artesanato de Barcelos,** Torre de Porta Nova (© **25/381-18-82**), is a gem. It displays some of the best regional handcrafts at the best prices we've encountered in the north. The center has an age-old stone tower that rises opposite the Church of São da Cruz. A wide display of goods is for sale on its street level and upper floor.

One outstanding collection is worth the trip to Barcelos. It consists of witty, sophisticated ceramics from the heirs of Rosa Ramalho, who was known as the Grandma Moses of Portuguese ceramics. Some of these figures show the influence of Picasso. Ms. Ramalho created figures depicting eerie people. For example, she put the heads of wolves on nuns and gave goats six legs—all in muted forest green or butterscotch brown. In addition, there's a good selection of the ceramic red-combed Barcelos cockerels, with many variations on the traditional motif in red and black. Local wares include black ceramic candlesticks, earthenware bowls used for *caldo verde* (a fortifying soup of greens and vegetables), hand-knitted pillows, handmade rugs in bold stripes, and hand-loomed bedspreads.

If this place doesn't have what you're looking for, head for **Largo do Dom António Barroso,** where a handful of other souvenir and handcrafts shops sell the products of local artisans.

WHERE TO STAY

Quinta de Santa Combra *Finds* In a little town without many places to stay, this 18th-century manor house comes as a welcome relief. Five kilometers (3 miles) from Barcelos on the road to Famalicão, it offers the best bed-and-breakfast in the area. The *quinta* (manor house) is decorated in rustic but grand style, with spindle beds placed against stone walls on tile floors. Accommodations vary in shape and size. All come equipped with tidily kept bathrooms containing showers. In the heart of Minho, this is grand country living—a true taste of Portugal, unlike the few dreary pensions in the area. The manor was converted into a small country inn in 1993.

Lugar de Crujães, 4755-531 Varzea (Barcelos). ✆ **25/383-14-40.** Fax 25/383-45-40. 6 units. 60€ ($69) double. Rates include breakfast. No credit cards. Free parking. **Amenities:** Breakfast room; lounge. *In room:* TV, no phone.

WHERE TO DINE

Bagoeira ★ PORTUGUESE This is the most charming little restaurant in town. You'll find oceans of local color along with good-tasting regional food based on recipes handed down by grandmothers. The setting boasts fresh flowers, wrought-iron chandeliers, and patina-coated wood surfaces. Try *feijoada,* the national dish of northern Portugal, redolent with beans and beef, or else fresh vegetable soup made with a bountiful harvest from the countryside. The chef also specializes in freshly caught fish, which is then grilled to perfection. Chicken with rice is a local favorite, and on market day (Thurs) people from the countryside fill up the tables, often ordering their favorite: stewed pork cooked with pig's blood.

Av. Sidónio Pais 495. ✆ **25/381-12-36.** Reservations required only for Thurs lunch. Main courses 7€–25€ ($8.05–$29). AE, DC, MC, V. Daily noon–10:30pm.

Dom António PORTUGUESE This local favorite, opening in the mid-1980s, lies on the street level of an old town house in the town's historic heart. It has a rustic interior and a polite staff. The restaurant features hearty soups, *bacalhau Dom António* (a popular house specialty concocted from codfish, onions, and potatoes), superb shellfish rice, grilled salmon, grilled steaks, and grilled pork chops.

Rua Dom António Barroso 87. ✆ **25/381-22-85.** Main courses 3€–15€ ($3.45–$17); tourist menu 13€ ($14). AE, MC, V. Daily 9am–midnight.

BARCELOS AFTER DARK

Save your raucous nightclubbing for bigger cities like Lisbon or Porto, and reconcile yourself to quieter nocturnal diversions. Our favorite watering hole is the **Café Conciliu,** Rua dos Duques de Bragança (✆ **25/381-19-75**), open Friday and Saturday from 11pm to 2am.

4 Esposende

20km (12 miles) S of Viana do Castelo, 48km (30 miles) N of Porto, 367km (228 miles) N of Lisbon

Esposende is a beach resort town where Atlantic breezes sweep the pines and sand dunes, and cows graze in nearby pastures. The surrounding countryside is no longer unspoiled—though you'll still see an occasional ox cart in the street, the area has been extensively developed, and a wide new road runs along the seafront. Men and women in broad-brimmed hats work the vineyards in the foothills. The beach, lining both sides of the Cávado estuary, is large and fine.

Small fishing vessels plod along the river carrying anglers to the bass upstream. Recent archaeological digs have revealed the remains of a Roman city and necropolis, but that doesn't seem to have disturbed Esposende in the least.

ESSENTIALS

ARRIVING

BY TRAIN There is no train service to Esposende.

BY BUS A bus trip from Porto to Esposende takes about an hour and costs 3.10€ ($3.55) one-way. Call © **25/396-23-69** for schedules.

BY CAR From Porto, take IC-1 north.

VISITOR INFORMATION

The **Esposende Tourist Office** is on Avenida Arantes de Oliveira (© **25/396-13-54**). It's open Saturday through Thursday from 9:30am to 12:30pm and 2 to 5:30pm, and Sunday 9:30am to 12:30pm.

WHERE TO STAY

Estalagem Zende ★★ Rated a luxury inn by the government, Estalagem Zende lies on the main road to Viana do Castelo, right outside Esposende. One third of the well-maintained, midsize guest rooms have minibars. Furnishings are worn but comfortable, with good beds and well-kept bathrooms equipped with shower-tub combinations. The restaurant, Martins, serves some of the best food in Esposende (see "Where to Dine," below). In winter, a fire blazes on the hearth.

Estrada Nacional 13, 4740-203 Esposende. © **25/396-90-90.** Fax 25/396-90-91. www.estalagemzende.com. 25 units. 39€–84€ ($45–$97) double; 108€–168€ ($124–$193) suite. Rates include breakfast. AE, DC, MC, V. Free parking. **Amenities:** Restaurant; bar; 24-hr. room service; laundry service; dry cleaning; 1 room for those w/limited mobility. *In room:* A/C, TV.

Hotel Suave Mar *Value* A semimodern hotel on the river, Suave Mar attracts frugal travelers who don't want to pay for the first-class accommodations at neighboring Ofir and Fão (see chapter 11). The midsize rooms are pleasant and comfortable, with well-kept bathrooms equipped with shower-tub combinations.

The food is among the best in the resort. The restaurant, which is open to nonguests, serves Portuguese and International cuisine, a nod to the 20 years the owners spent in Brazil.

Av. Eng. Arantes e Oliveira, 4740-205 Esposende. © **25/396-94-00.** Fax 25/396-94-01. www.suavemar.com. 84 units. 50€–146€ ($58–$168) double; 75€–130€ ($86–$150) junior suite; 120€–182€ ($138–$209) suite. Rates include breakfast. AE, DC, MC, V. Free parking. **Amenities:** Restaurant; 2 bars; 2 pools; tennis court; fitness room; limited room service; laundry service; dry cleaning; rooms for those w/limited mobility. *In room:* A/C, TV, minibar (in some), hair dryer, safe.

WHERE TO DINE

Restaurant Martins PORTUGUESE In the heart of Esposende, this large, bustling restaurant specializes in Portuguese seafood, often grilled lightly and seasoned with local garlic and herbs. Other choices include roast goat, smoked salmon, grilled filets of sole, shellfish rice, and several preparations of codfish. Prices are reasonable. The regional produce and fresh seafood keep this traditional restaurant packed with devotees. "It's reliable and it's classic," one satisfied diner told us. "That's why I keep coming back."

In the Estalagem Zende, Estrada Nacional 13. © **25/396-90-90.** Main courses 9€–25€ ($10–$29). AE, DC, MC, V. Daily noon–3pm and 7–10:30pm.

5 Viana do Castelo ★

71km (44 miles) N of Porto, 388km (241 miles) N of Lisbon, 25km (15½ miles) N of Esposende

Viana do Castelo, between an estuary of the Lima River and a base of rolling hills, is the most folkloric city in northern Portugal. An occasional ox cart with wooden wheels clacking along the stone streets enhances the atmosphere. Boatmen can be seen near the waterfront, offering to sell visitors a slow cruise along the riverbanks. After years of decline, Viana today is bustling and prosperous, once again a major center of deep-sea fishing. It's also the site of industries like pyrotechnics, wood manufacturing, ceramics, and boat building.

Viana do Castelo is noted for its pottery and regional handcrafts; you can buy many of them at the Friday market. It's even better known for its regional dress, best seen at the annual *Festa de Nossa Senhora de Agonia* (Festival of Our Lady of Agony), which takes place in late August. The women wear strident orange, scarlet, and Prussian blue, and layers of golden necklaces with heart- and cross-shape pendants.

ESSENTIALS

ARRIVING

BY TRAIN The station is on Avenida dos Combatentes da Grande Guerra (✆ **25/882-13-15** for information). Eleven trains per day arrive from Porto; the trip takes 2 hours and costs 4.60€ ($5.30) one-way.

BY BUS The station, **Central de Camionagem** (✆ **25/882-50-47**), is at the eastern edge of the city. Buses arrive every hour from Porto; the 2½-hour trip costs 4.10€ ($4.70) one-way. There are seven buses daily from Lisbon. It's a 6-hour trip, and a one-way ticket costs 14€ ($16). From Braga, eight buses a day make the 1½-hour trip; the fare is 3.20€ ($3.70) one-way.

BY CAR From Porto or Esposende, continue north along IC-1.

VISITOR INFORMATION

The **Viana do Castelo Tourist Office** is on Rua do Hospital Velho (✆ **25/882-26-20**). It's open Monday through Saturday from 9am to 12:30pm and 2:30 to 6pm, and Sunday from 9:30am to 1pm.

EXPLORING THE TOWN The town center is **Praça da República** ★, one of Portugal's most handsome squares. At its heart is the much-photographed 16th-century **Chafariz Fountain,** with water spewing from the mouths of its figures. The most impressive building on the square is the dour, squat three-story **Igreja da Misericórdia.** The lower level is an arcade of five austere Roman arches, and the two upper levels are ponderous Renaissance balconies. A rooftop crucifix crowns the structure. Each level's four supporting pillars are primitive caryatidlike figures. The church fronts Rua da Bandeira and adjoins the former charity hospice, Hospital da Misericórdia. It contains pictorial tiles made in 1714, ornate baroque altars, a painted ceiling, and woodcarvings.

The other building dominating the square is the 1502 **Paço do Concelho** (the former town hall), constructed over an arcade made up of three wide, low Gothic arches. The crenel-topped facade displays a royal coat of arms and wrought-iron balcony windows above each arch.

The best views of both turf and surf are from the ramparts of the **Castelo de São Tiago da Berra,** reached by following Rua General Luîs do Rego. In 1589, Philip I of Spain ordered that the walls of the *castelo* be built—this is the reason "do Castelo" was added to Viana's name. It's open Monday through Friday from 9am to 12:30pm and 2 to 5:30pm. Call ✆ **25/882-02-70** for more information.

To enjoy one of the great panoramas in the north of Portugal, you can visit the **Miradouro de Santa Luzia** ★★, a belvedere on the hill of Santa Luzia, where the view of Viana is especially stunning at night when all the lights go on. Located to the north of town, the belvedere is topped by the modern **Basilica de Santa Luzia,** (✆ **25/882-31-73**), constructed in a neo-Byzantine style. A trio of rose windows illuminates its interior, and the chancel and apse are adorned with frescoes. For another **panoramic view** ★★, you can climb 142 steps that begin in the sacristy. The basilica, reached along Estrada de Santa Luzia, is open daily from 8am to 7pm, and access to the dome is .50€ (60¢).

It's possible to drive the 7km (4½ miles) to the top following the signposts from the center pointing the way to Santa Luzia. The funicular no longer operates, but if you're in good shape, you can take a long, long series of steps up the 200m (656-ft.) climb. The steps begin behind the rail station.

SHOPPING The artifacts you'll find here tend to be earthier, more rustic, and less influenced by fads than what's usually available closer to Lisbon. In addition to the ceramics and woodcarvings that are widely available in other regions, look for linens and embroideries, sometimes in bewitchingly subtle patterns. The main shopping streets, **Rua Manuel Espergueira** and **Rua da Bandeira,** contain shops selling virtually everything you'd need to dress yourself or accessorize a house.

If you're looking for handcrafts, try **Casa Sandra,** Largo João Tomás da Costa (✆ **25/882-21-55**). It carries fine linens and embroideries in all possible degrees of intricacy. The oldest and biggest store in town is **Casa Fontinha,** Largo João Tomás da Costa (✆ **25/882-22-31**). Smaller, dustier, and confusingly arranged is **A Tenda,** Rua do Hospital Velho (✆ **25/882-28-13**). Three more worthwhile choices are **Arte Regional,** Avenida dos Combatentes da Grande Guerra (✆ **25/882-90-45**); **O Traje,** Rua do Poso (✆ **25/882-54-66**); and **Arte Minho,** Rua de São Pedro 21–23 (✆ **25/882-10-52**).

WHERE TO STAY

Estalagem Casa Melo Alvim ★★★ This is the oldest urban mansion in Viana do Castelo and an inn of such antique charm and character that it has quickly become one of the most coveted stopovers in the north of Portugal. Except for views, it clearly outdistances the Pousada do Monte de Santa Luzia, which was the reigning queen for many years. Built in the Manueline style in 1509, this inn had a long history before it was finally restored and turned into a luxurious place for overnight guests. In a massive restoration, much of the old architectural charm was maintained. In keeping with its original decor, the new inn still has an air of sobriety about it, a winning combination of natural light and natural materials. Access to the upper floors is along a baroque stairwell with banisters. The small to midsize bedrooms and suites are decorated in a sober but comfortable style, with excellent modern furnishings including a good-size bathroom with a tub and shower. Furnishings in the rooms reflect various ages and styles of Portuguese design.

Av. Conde da Carreira 28, 4900-343 Viana do Castelo. ✆ **25/880-82-00.** Fax 25/880-82-20. www.meloalvimhouse.com. 20 units. 115€–140€ ($132–$160) double; 139€–186€ ($159–$213) suite. AE, DC, MC, V. Free parking. **Amenities:** Restaurant; bar; 24-hr. room service; laundry service; dry cleaning. *In room:* A/C, TV, dataport, minibar, hair dryer, safe.

Hotel do Parque This government-rated four-star hotel, at the base of the bridge crossing the Lima River on the edge of town, is the second-best choice within the town center. It feels like a small resort, with lounges overlooking two pools (one reserved for children). The main floor has a lounge and an interior winter garden. The midsize guest rooms are quite contemporary, with built-in furnishings, balconies, and neatly kept bathrooms with shower-tub combinations.

Praça da Galiza, 4900-476 Viana do Castelo. ✆ **25/882-86-05.** Fax 25/882-86-12. www.hoteldoparque.com. 124 units. 110€–145€ ($127–$167) double. Rates include breakfast. AE, DC, MC, V. Free parking. **Amenities:** Breakfast room; bar; 2 pools; 24-hr. room service; laundry service. *In room:* A/C, TV, hair dryer, safe.

Hotel Viana Sol Behind a dignified granite-and-stucco facade, near a commemorative column and fountain in the town center, this well-designed hotel is 3 blocks south of Praça da República. In contrast to its elegantly severe exterior, its spacious public rooms are sheathed with white marble, capped with mirrored ceilings, and illuminated with a three-tiered atrium. The lobby bar is near a pagoda-shape fountain. The small to midsize guest rooms are sparsely furnished, and most don't have views. Nonetheless, they offer comfortable beds and well-equipped bathrooms with shower-tub combinations.

Largo Vasco da Gama, 4900-322 Viana do Castelo. ✆ **25/882-89-95.** Fax 25/882-34-01. 65 units. 48€–73€ ($55–$84) double. Rates include breakfast. AE, DC, MC, V. Limited free parking on street. **Amenities:** Breakfast room; bar; pool; tennis courts; squash courts; health club; sauna; limited room service; laundry service; dry cleaning. *In room:* TV, dataport, safe.

Pousada do Monte de Santa Luzia ★★ Some 6km (3¾ miles) from the center, the government-owned Santa Luzia sits on a wooded hillside high above the most congested part of the city. It's just behind the illuminated dome of the neo-Byzantine Basilica of Santa Luzia. Built in 1895, the hotel has neoclassical details and granite balconies, giving it the appearance of a royal palace, especially when it's floodlit at night. Winding cobblestone roads run through a forest to the entrance. At the summit, you'll find the area's best view of the city and river.

Guest rooms are spacious, and some bathrooms have Jacuzzis; all come equipped with shower-tub combinations. The high-ceilinged public rooms gained Art Deco sheen when the hotel was completely renovated in the '90s. It boasts long expanses of glistening marble, stylish Jazz Age accessories, a comfortable bar and restaurant, and enormous, echoing halls.

Monte de Santa Luzia, 4901-909 Viana do Castelo. ✆ **25/880-03-70.** Fax 25/882-88-92. www.pousadas.pt. 48 units. 97€–187€ ($112–$215) double; 217€–244€ ($250–$281) suite. Rates include breakfast. AE, DC, MC, V. Free parking. **Amenities:** Restaurant; bar; pool; tennis court; health club; 24-hr. room service; babysitting; laundry service; dry cleaning; nonsmoking rooms; 1 room for those w/limited mobility. *In room:* A/C, TV, minibar, safe.

Residencial Viana Mar Viana Mar is on the main commercial thoroughfare, behind a granite facade whose severity is relieved by colorful awnings. Near the nondescript reception area lies a sunken bar. Each small guest room has basic furnishings but comfortable beds. For the most part, bathrooms are equipped with shower-tub combinations. A few rooms are in two nearby but dull annexes.

Av. dos Combatentes da Grande Guerra 215, 4900-563 Viana do Castelo. ✆ and fax **25/882-89-62.** 36 units, 10 w/bathroom. 20€–33€ ($23–$37) double w/no bathroom; 25€–45€ ($29–$52) double w/bathroom. Rates include breakfast. AE, DC, MC, V. Parking 2€ ($2.30). **Amenities:** Breakfast room; bar; laundry service; dry cleaning. *In room:* TV.

WHERE TO STAY NEARBY

The most romantic places to stay in and around Viana do Castelo are the antique *quintas.* In these restored manor houses, you can literally stay with the Portuguese aristocracy. You can make reservations through **Turismo de Habitação,** Praça da República, 4990-062 Ponte de Lima (✆ **25/874-16-72;** fax 25/874-14-44). Payment is made by check sent directly to the owners, with

Finds A Village off the Beaten Path

Upriver 213km (132 miles) from Viana do Castelo is **Ponte de Lima,** which is exactly what one hopes a Portuguese village will be like. Spread lazily along the tree-lined banks of the Lima River, it's named for the Roman bridge with 27 arches spanning the water. Jagged ramparts surround Ponte de Lima, and massive towers, narrow winding streets, and fortified doors decorate the houses.

The drive along the north side of the river takes you through grape arbors, pastoral villages, and forests of cedar, pine, and chestnut. Red-cheeked locals stand silhouetted against moss-green stone walls as they interrupt their toil in the cabbage fields to watch you pass by. We've never recommended cabbages as a sightseeing attraction, but they are here. Jade green and monstrous, they grow to wild heights of 2m (6½ ft.). They're most often used to make *caldo verde,* the fabled regional soup.

The town, founded on the site of a Celtic settlement, was developed by the Romans, who named it Forum Limicorum. It was important for both river trade and river defense. Thick stone walls enclose the town, guarding the bridge across the Lima. Part of the Roman bridge is still in use. It has a buttressed extension, made under King Dom Pedro in 1355 because of changes in the river's course. Sometimes you'll see women wringing out their clothes along the riverbanks. At certain times of the year, the Lima is likely to be dry, but when it's full, anglers often catch trout.

The Roman wall has been partially destroyed to make room for roads, but you can walk along the top of what's left. An 18th-century fountain graces the town's main square, and houses of that era are still occupied. Ruins of ramparts from the Middle Ages and a solitary keep can be seen, opposite the old bridge. Go up the stone steps of the keep to visit the **Biblioteca Pública Municipal,** founded in the early 18th century. Its archives are rich in historic documents.

50% prepayment required when your reservation is made. A minimum stay of 2 nights is required, and reservations must be made at least 3 days before arrival.

The Viana do Castelo area has some of the most elaborate and stylized *quintas* in Portugal. A random sampling follows.

Casa de Rodas ★ *Finds* Constructed in typical *quinta* style with a red-tile roof and stucco walls, this large guesthouse is between a wooded area and a farm that grows grapes for consumption in Santiago de Compostela. It's less than a kilometer (about ¾ mile) from Monção, which is known for its *termas* (spa) treatments for rheumatism and respiratory ailments. Monção is 69km (43 miles) northeast of Viana do Castelo.

The house was built in the 16th century, destroyed by fire in 1658 during Portugal's battle for independence, and reconstructed soon afterward. Guest rooms come in a variety of shapes and sizes, but all are well maintained and traditionally furnished, with neatly kept bathrooms with shower stalls. The location along the border of Spain allows for day trips to the Spanish cities of

The Ponte de Lima **market,** held on alternate Mondays, is known throughout Portugal. The sellers show up in regional costumes. On the north side of the bridge is the cattle market where oxen and steers are sold. A little bag nestling between the horns of the animals contains a "magic potion" said to ward off the evil eye. Below the bridge is a place reserved for eating alfresco delights like roast sardines accompanied by glasses of *vinho verde* (green wine). Taking the riverside walk, you can survey the stalls of various craftspeople, including cobblers, carpenters, and goldsmiths.

In recent years, Ponte de Lima has opened a collection of beautiful antique properties as accommodations, ranging from farms to manor houses. Staying in one of these treasures is reason enough to go. There are about 60 such properties in the region. Information about them is available through **Turismo de Habitação,** 4990-062 Ponte de Lima (✆ **25/874-16-72;** fax 25/874-14-44).

Another stellar property is the **Paço de Calheiros,** Calheiros, 4990-062 Ponte de Lima (✆ **25/894-71-64;** fax 25/894-72-94). Perched on a hill overlooking the town, it's the best-known *solar* (country villa) in Ponte. The nine doubles and three apartments in converted stables go for 100€ ($115). Breakfast and parking are included. A splendid dinner can be arranged on request. The *solar* has lush gardens and a pool.

Back in Ponte de Lima, you can dine at **Encanada,** Rua do Castelo (✆ **25/894-11-89**), which serves the best regional cookery around. Try the special fried pork or homemade fish cakes. Eels with rice is a local specialty, but it's available only in winter. Meals are served Friday through Wednesday from noon to 3pm and 7 to 10:30pm; prices start at 12€ ($14).

Vigo and Santiago de Compostela, as well as the beach, about a 30-minute drive away.

4950-498 Monção. ✆ **25/165-21-05.** 10 units. 75€ ($86) double. Rates include breakfast. No credit cards. Free parking. **Amenities:** Breakfast room; lounge. *In room:* No phone.

Quinta do Convento de Val de Pereiras This hotel occupies a 15-hectare (37-acre) site and has been famous since the Middle Ages for its freshwater springs. According to legend, St. Francis of Assisi, who performed many miracles here on his way to Santiago de Compostela, blessed them. In 1316, a stone building on the site functioned as a monastery. Some 200 years later, the monks were evicted, and a community of Franciscan nuns controlled the premises for another 300 years. Around 1890, everything except one of the towers of the original monastery was demolished, and a new Minho-style monastery, similar in design to a large manor house, was erected. It lies 1.75km (1 mile) from Ponte de Lima, across the Douro from the town center. Bedrooms are well furnished and maintained, each with a private bathroom with a shower-tub combination. Don't expect any in-room amenities other than a phone. ***Warning:*** Always call and confirm a room before heading here because the inn is closed from time to time.

Lugar Val de Pereiras, 4990 Arcozelo, Ponte de Lima. © **25/890-00-69**. Fax 25/890-00-69. www.valdepereiras.pt. 11 units. 75€ ($86) double; 100€ ($115) suite. Rates include breakfast. No credit cards. Free parking. **Amenities:** Pool; 2 tennis courts; horseback riding arranged. *In room:* A/C, TV.

WHERE TO DINE

A Ceia *Value* PORTUGUESE This artfully rustic restaurant occupies a prime position in the heart of town. You enter through a prominent bar area, where you'll be tempted to linger with the many regulars who appreciate their wine and only rarely seem to want to rush in to dinner. Portions are generous, and the food is flavored in traditional and time-tested (but not particularly innovative) ways. It seems universally popular among the extended families who sometimes conduct their once-a-week powwows at long connected tables. Menu items include steaming bowls of bean-and-meat stew, tripe, roast pork with clams, succulent roast goat, veal and beef dishes, and steaming bowls of such soups as *caldo verde* (made from greens and vegetables).

Rua do Raio 331. © **25/326-39-32.** Reservations recommended Sat–Sun. Main courses 5€–14€ ($5.75–$16). AE, MC, V. Tues–Sun noon–3pm and 7–10pm.

Alambique REGIONAL PORTUGUESE You enter this typical Portuguese restaurant through a large wine vat. Inside you'll find many of the specialties for which the cooks of northern Portugal are known, including codfish Antiga Viana, *churrasco de porco* (pork), *cabrito* (goat), tripe Porto style, and lampreys bordelaise (an eel dish). One of the chef's most memorable dishes is baked *bacalau* (poached cod). To begin, you can order one of the soups, such as *sopa do mar* (seafood soup). Such food might be too authentic for those who grew up on the Big Mac, though.

Rua Manuel Espergueira 86. © **25/882-13-64.** Main courses 6.50€–13€ ($7.50–$14); tourist menu 15€ ($17). AE, DC, MC, V. Daily noon–3pm and 7–10pm.

Os 3 Potes ★★ PORTUGUESE/INTERNATIONAL Off Praça da República, this restaurant was an old bakery before its conversion into one of the best regional dining rooms in Viana do Castelo. The atmosphere is rustic. On Saturday, folk dancing is featured and the place takes on a touristy feel. Fado music is featured every other Friday. Have someone at your hotel call for a reservation. We recommend *caldo verde* (a soup made from greens and vegetables) to begin, followed by such main dishes as codfish, lampreys (eels), or fondue bourguignonne. The restaurant is somewhat hard to find but worth the search.

Beco dos Fornos 7-9. © **25/882-52-50.** Reservations recommended in summer. Main courses 10€–15€ ($12–$17). AE, DC, MC, V. Daily noon–3:30pm and 7–10:30pm. Closed Mon Oct–May. From Praça da República, take Rua de Sacadura Cabral.

Túnel REGIONAL PORTUGUESE Túnel is a good bet for regional cuisine. When they're available, you can order especially delectable quail or roast kid. The fresh fish dishes are usually the best, however. You might begin with rich vegetable soup made with fresh produce. The dining room is on the second floor, and you pass through a simple snack bar at ground level.

Rua dos Manjovos 9 (off Av. dos Combatentes da Grande Guerra). © **25/882-21-88.** Main courses 6.95€–14€ ($8–$16); tourist menu 12€ ($14). AE. Tues–Sun noon–3pm and 7–10pm. Closed Dec 20–Jan 15.

Viana's PORTUGUESE This well-managed restaurant has thrived here since 1991. The keys to its success are its generous portions, kindly staff, and flavorful dishes created from sometimes unappetizing-looking species of fish. In a historic-looking room that's close to the sea, you'll dine on fresh meat and locally caught fish. Codfish is everybody's justifiable favorite, but you can also order succulent cuts of meat braised or grilled according to your taste.

Rua Frei Bartolomeu Martas 4900. ✆ **25/882-47-97.** Reservations recommended. Main courses 9€–24€ ($10–$28). MC, V. Tues–Sat 12:30–3pm and 7:30–10pm; Sun 7:30–10pm.

VIANA DO CASTELO AFTER DARK

You won't lack for bars and cafes that serve alcohol and refreshments. If you're interested in music and energy, consider a visit to the town's most popular dance club: **Foz Café,** Praia do Cabedelo (✆ **25/833-24-85**), open Tuesday through Sunday from noon to 3pm and 7pm to 1am.

6 Vila Real

399km (247 miles) NE of Lisbon, 113km (70 miles) E of Porto

The capital of Trás-os-Montes is a lively little town built on a hilly plateau in the foothills of the Serra do Marão. Bridges across the ravines link some parts of town. Gorges cut by the Corgo and Cabril rivers, which flow together here, are visible from a terrace high above, where a castle once stood. The lookout is reached in a direct line from the cemetery. From this vicinity, you can also see houses overhanging the ravine of the Corgo.

You can spend a worthy 2 hours or so wandering through Vila Real's historic core and enjoy a glass of port in one of the cafes, which brim with youth. The main sights and buildings of interest are along the Avenida Carvalho Araújo.

The agricultural town makes a good base for many beautiful trips into the area, including the **Parque Nacional do Alvão** to the northwest, with its waterfalls, flower-filled valleys, and ravines. The tourist office provides maps and suggests places to visit. To drive to the park, follow the IP-4 west for 10km (6¼ miles), turning onto N304 heading for Mondim de Bastro and Campeã. This stretch takes you through some of the most scenic areas of Trás-os-Montes—once you've passed through the dreary modern suburbs of Vila Real, which are in marked contrast to the mellow historic core.

ESSENTIALS

ARRIVING

BY TRAIN Vila Real has awkward rail connections. The trip from Porto takes longer than the bus ride and requires a transfer at the town of Régua. There are seven trains a day from Porto via Régua. It's a 4½ hour journey and costs 7€ ($8.05) one-way. For information, call ✆ **808/208-208.**

BY BUS Buses from Porto take only 2 hours. There are 15 runs a day, and the one-way fare is 6€ ($5.40). Five buses a day make the 5-hour and 50-minute trip from Lisbon. The cost is 14€ ($16) one-way. For information and schedules, call ✆ **25/932-32-34.**

BY CAR From Porto, continue east along the express route, A4, following signs to Amarante, where you continue east along N15 into Vila Real.

VISITOR INFORMATION

The **tourist office** is at Avenida Carvalho Araújo 94 (✆ **25/932-28-19**). It's open Monday through Friday from 9:30am to 7pm, and Saturday from 9:30am to 12:30pm and 2 to 6pm.

EXPLORING THE TOWN You won't be dazzled by "must-see" monuments, although the historic core as a whole makes for an interesting walk. Vila Real is called a Royal Town because it contains many formerly aristocratic houses dating from the 16th to the 18th centuries. It's fun to poke your nose down the tiny offshoot streets, hoping to make discoveries. The main monuments are concentrated in and around Avenida Carvalho Araújo. However, the famous **Sé (Cathedral) of São Domingos** is currently closed for renovation.

Chief among these is the **Capela Nova** (New Chapel), sometimes called the Capel dos Clérigos (Chapel of the Clergy) by the locals. It is the finest baroque monument in Vila Real. The Italian architecture might have been the work of Niccolò Nasoni, the 18th-century master. It has a floral facade. The chapel lies 2 blocks east of the cathedral, between Rua Direita and Rua 31 de Janeiro. It is open daily from 10am to noon and 2 to 6pm. Admission is free.

Farther north is **Igreja São Pedro** (St. Peter's Church), at Largo de São Pedro, just off the main street. From 1528, though much altered over the ages, this church has an intriguing interior, with much baroque gilt carving and a chancel adorned with colorful tiles. Its main attraction, and reason enough for a visit, is the coffered ceiling of carved and gilded wood. It is open daily from 8am to 8pm. Admission is free.

The **Camera Municipal** (Town Hall), Avenida Carvalho Araújo (© **25/930-81-00**), also merits a look. It has an Italian Renaissance-style stone staircase constructed in the early 1800s. In front is a lantern pillory. It is open Monday through Friday from 9am to 5:30pm. Admission is free.

Although it's not open to the public, you can stop to admire the **Casa de Diogo Cão,** Avenida Carvalho Araújo 19. This is the reputed birthplace of the navigator who discovered the Congo River in 1482. The exterior of the house was altered, and it is now 16th-century Renaissance style. Although the explorer visited the legendary King Manicongo, and the powerful monarch reportedly was baptized as a Christian, little is know about Cão. Dom João II concealed all records in the Torre de Tombo in Lisbon to keep the discoveries from the Castilians. The earthquake of 1755 destroyed the archives.

The most interesting attraction lies not in Vila Real, but 4km (2½ miles) east of the city, on the N322 highway signposted to Sabrosa. The grapes of the original Mateus rosé wine were grown in vineyards here.

Solar de Mateus ★★ is a perfect example of baroque architecture, with a stunning **facade** ★★ preceded by a "mirror" of water. This is the building pictured on the Mateus wine label. Dating from the first half of the 18th century, the main section of the manor house has a stunning balustraded staircase and a high-emblazoned pediment surrounded by allegorical statues. Sacheverell Sitwell called it "the most typical and the most fantastic country home in Portugal." The twin wings of the manor advance "lobsterlike," in Sitwell's words.

An ornamental stone balustrade guards the main courtyard, and lovely pinnacles crown the roof cornices. The architect is unknown, although some authorities claim it was the work of Niccolò Nasoni, who might have designed the Capela Nova (see above).

The manor house and the gardens are open for tours (© **25/932-31-21**). The house contains heavy silk hangings, high wooden ceilings, paintings of bucolic scenes, and a tiny museum. You'll see vestments, Sèvres vases, and an 1817 edition of the Portuguese classic, *The Lusiads,* printed in Paris. The gardens are among the most beautiful in Europe, with a tunnel of cypress trees shading the path.

From March to September, the site is open daily from 9am to 7pm; off-season, it's open daily from 10am to 1pm and 2 to 5pm. A full guided tour costs 6€ ($6.90) per person. It's 3.50€ ($4.05) just to tour the gardens.

SHOPPING If you happen to be in Vila Real on June 28 and 29, you can purchase some of the region's fine black pottery, which is sold at St. Peter's Fair. At other times, you can find the pottery, made in the surrounding countryside, at little shops throughout the historic district. Many visitors also come here to buy sparkling rosé wine directly from Solar de Mateus (see above).

WHERE TO STAY

Hotel Miracorgo ★ This is the city's best choice for lodgings. It's in the commercial section, popular with businesspeople, but has an impersonal aura. The hotel spreads across 2 buildings—one has 5 floors, and the other has 12 floors. It is 2 decades old and was renovated in the mid–1990s. The sterile quality recedes somewhat when you enter the midsize accommodations, most of which open onto views of a scenic valley. All are comfortably furnished, with well-maintained bathrooms containing shower-tub combinations with excellent plumbing.

Av. 1 de Maio 78, 5000-651 Vila Real. ✆ **25/932-50-01.** Fax 25/932-50-06. 166 units. 62€–65€ ($71–$75) double; 90€ ($104) suite. Rates include breakfast. AE, DC, MC, V. Free parking. **Amenities:** Restaurant; bar; pool; limited room service; laundry service; dry cleaning; rooms for those w/limited mobility. *In room:* A/C, TV, minibar, hair dryer.

Hotel Mirameve This hotel, built in 1984, sits in the center of the city, facing the marketplace. It is the second-best choice in town, but don't get your hopes up. Although well maintained, it is simplicity itself. Rooms are a bit small but comfortable, with tidily kept bathrooms with shower-tub combinations.

Rua Dom Pedro de Castro, 5000-669 Vila Real. ✆ **25/932-31-53.** Fax 25/932-30-28. www.miraneve.pt. 26 units. 45€–65€ ($52–$75) double. Rates include breakfast. AE, DC, MC, V. Free parking. **Amenities:** Restaurant; bar; lounge; room service; laundry; dry cleaning. *In room:* A/C, TV, minibar, safe.

AT ALIJÓ

Barão de Forrester Pousada ★★ *Finds* Our favorite retreat in Trás-os-Montes lies in the village of Alijó, some 29km (18 miles) southeast of the center of Vila Real; it's a lovely stop for motorists who don't mind the short drive. The inn takes its name from the Scotsman, Baron Forrester, who in the 19th century plotted a map of the Douro River, opening it up to navigation. In time, the Forrester family became wealthy port vintners. The location of this retreat is in the heart of the Douro Wine Region, an area famous for its *quintas* (manor houses) filled with port wine vineyards that grow on terraces. The hotel staff can arrange cruises on the Douro for guests. The inn is decorated in a warm traditional style, with beautifully maintained and comfortable bedrooms along with tidily organized bathrooms with a tub-shower combination. The excellent on-site restaurant opens onto two terraces with views of the countryside, and on a chilly night you can retreat with a glass of port to a cozy nook in front of the fireplace.

Rua José Rufino, 5070-031 Alijó. ✆ **25/995-94-67.** Fax 25/995-93-04. www.pousadas.pt. 21 units. 126€–132€ ($145–$152) double. Rates include breakfast. **Amenities:** Restaurant; bar; pool; tennis court; fishing arranged; limited room service; laundry service; 1 nonsmoking room. *In room:* A/C, TV, minibar, hair dryer.

WHERE TO DINE

O Espadeiro ★ TRAS-OS-MONTES This is the finest independent restaurant in Vila Real. You climb a flight of stairs to the modern, rustically decorated restaurant, which has a large, sunny terrace and a bar with a panoramic view. The chefs are rightly proud of their region and its foodstuffs. A delectable specialty is trout stuffed with Parma-style ham. Seafood rice is a savory offering, and if you are leery of the meat by-products used in the *feijoada* (bean stew), you can always opt for baked ham instead. Some dishes—including stewed tripe and roast kid—are very regional and not for the unadventurous palate. The dining room with the fireplace is where everybody wants to dine in winter. The name, which means "the swordsman," honors a brave tramontane warrior, Lourenço Viegas.

Av. Almeida Lucena. ✆ **25/932-23-02.** Reservations recommended. Main courses 10€–22€ ($12–$25). AE, MC, V. Tues–Sun 9am–2pm and 6–11pm. Closed first 2 weeks of Oct.

7 Bragança ★

139km (86 miles) NE of Vila Real, 522km (324 miles) NE of Lisbon

The medieval town of Bragança (Braganza in English) was under the aegis of the House of Bragança, which ruled Portugal from 1640 until its overthrow early in the 20th century. On a hilltop, a long, fortified wall surrounds Bragança, the best-preserved medieval town in Portugal. It overlooks the modern town in the northeastern reaches of the country on a rise of ground in the Serra da Nogueira, some 600m (1,968 ft.) above sea level.

ESSENTIALS

ARRIVING

BY TRAIN There is no direct train service. The nearest station is in the town of Mirandela, which is connected by bus to Bragança. For information and schedules, call ✆ **808/208-208.**

BY BUS Rodonorte (✆ **27/330-01-83**) runs 10 buses a day from Porto via Mirandela. The trip takes 4 hours and costs 8.60€ ($9.90) one-way. The same company runs five buses a day to Lisbon. The journey takes 8 hours and costs 14€ ($16) one-way.

BY CAR From Vila Real, continue northeast on E82.

VISITOR INFORMATION

The **tourist office** is at Avenida Cidade de Zamora (✆ **27/338-12-73**). It's open Monday through Friday from 9am to 12:30pm and 2 to 8pm, Saturday from 9am to 12:30pm and 2 to 5:30pm, and Sunday 9am to 1pm.

EXPLORING THE TOWN Bragança lies at the edge of the **Parque Natural de Montesinho** (Montesinho Natural Park), one of the wildest regions on the continent. A walled citadel, or castle, on a hilltop crowns the town of Bragança. The **Upper Town** ★ grew up around this brooding old castle. In a small public garden within the citadel stands a Gothic pillory. A medieval shaft has been driven through the stone effigy of a boar, which has a depression carved in its snout. The boar is believed to date from the Iron Age, and it's possible that it was used in ancient pagan rituals.

A Cidadela (sometimes called O Castelo) dates from the 12th century. Dom João I reconstructed it in the 14th century. The heyday of this castle came under the fiefdom of the Dukes of Bragança, the ruling family of Portugal from 1640 until the monarchy collapsed in 1910. The Upper Town was also a major silk center in the 1400s—in part because of a prosperous Jewish merchant community. The Inquisition dispersed most of the merchants. The citadel's tall, square keep, Torre de Menagem, today contains the **Museu Militar** (✆ **27/332-23-78**). The military museum's displays range from medieval suits of armor to a World War I machine gun used in trench warfare. Unusual exhibits are collections of

African art, some from Angola, gathered by Portuguese soldiers. The museum is open Friday through Wednesday from 9am to noon and 2 to 5pm. Admission is 1.50€ ($1.75) for adults and free for children under 10.

Beside the castle, you can look at the **Torre da Princesa** (Princess Tower). Here the fourth duke of Bragança imprisoned his wife, Dona Leonor. She was said to be so beautiful that he didn't want other men to look at her. However, when he moved his court to Lisbon, he murdered her.

Also part of the castle complex in the Upper Town, the **Domus Municipalis** (Town Hall)—built over a cistern—dates from the 12th century. It is one of the few remaining Romanesque civic buildings in the country. The interior is a cavernous room lit by little round arches. It's open Friday through Wednesday from 9am to noon and 2 to 5pm. Admission is free.

A final building of note is the 16th-century **Igreja da Santa Maria** (St. Mary's Church; no phone). The interior is distinguished by a barrel-vaulted painted ceiling from the 18th century. The painting depicts the Assumption of the Virgin in many colors. Salomonic (twisted) columns frame the front door. Hours are Friday through Wednesday from 9am to 12:30pm and 2 to 5pm.

The citadel and Upper Town are the reasons to go to Bragança. If time remains, you can also explore the Lower Town, with its major boulevard and (in the summer) sidewalk cafes.

Museu do Abade de Baçal, Rua Abilio Beca 27 (© **27/333-15-95**), occupies a former bishop's palace. A local priest, Francisco Manuel Alves (1865–1947), created this bizarre assemblage. He collected everything from Iron Age depictions of pigs to ancient tombstones. He also collected antiques, ceramics, folkloric costumes, old coins, regional paintings, silver, archaeological artifacts—virtually anything that caught his eye, including church plates and vestments. The museum is open Tuesday through Friday from 10am to 5pm. Admission is 2€ ($2.30).

After exploring Bragança, visit the **Parque Natural de Montesinho** ★★. Pick up a map at the tourist office (see above). This forbidding but beautiful land of towering mountains and high plateaus stretches northwest and northeast of Bragança. Here you'll discover some of the most rugged—certainly the wildest—land in the country. It is still home to wolves, wild boars, and foxes, among other animals. In the little villages you'll see as you drive through the vast land, life is lived nearly the way it was a century ago, although modern intrusions have occurred.

At least until the outbreak of World War II, many pre-Christian rituals were still practiced here. The area stretches over 467 sq. km (182 sq. miles). In all, less than 9,000 people live in fewer than 100 villages. This is one of the best places in Portugal for trekking along well-worn mountain paths, most of which date from the fall of the Visigothic empire. Sometimes you can spot an endangered bird such as the black stork. Because trails are unmarked, the tourist office provides brochures, useful maps, and advice.

SHOPPING Head for the shops around **Largo da Sé** (sometimes called Praça da Sé), the cathedral precinct, for local handcrafts. You'll find locally produced copper and leather goods, plus woven fabrics. The shops also carry ceramics from the surrounding area. Many similar shops also lie within the walls of the citadel.

WHERE TO STAY

Classis This is the town's second-best choice, although its accommodations fall far short of the more luxurious ones in the pousada (below). But since the pousada might be fully booked in the summer, it's worth considering—you'll still sleep well here. The midsize guest rooms are comfortably furnished, with well-maintained bathrooms that, for the most part, contain shower-tub combinations. The hotel is convenient to the train and bus stations.

Av. João da Cruz 102, 5300-178 Bragança. ✆ **27/333-16-31.** Fax 27/332-34-58. 20 units. 40€–48€ ($46–$55) double. Rates include breakfast. AE, DC, MC, V. Limited free parking on street. **Amenities:** Breakfast room; bar; 24-hr. room service; laundry service; 1 room for those w/limited mobility. *In room:* A/C, TV, minibar.

Pousada de São Bartolomeu ★★ Built in 1959 and modernized since, this is the best accommodation in the area. It's on the heights of the Serra da Nogueira, with a panoramic view of the 12th-century castle of Bragança. The fairly spacious guest rooms were upgraded in the '90s. They're well furnished and maintained, with private balconies, firm beds, and neatly kept bathrooms equipped with shower-tub combinations.

The pousada makes an ideal stop for travelers entering the country from Spain at Alcanices-Quintanilha, about a 30-minute drive away. The view at night is the most spectacular in Bragança, taking in the crenellated fortifications of the old city. Guests enjoy the rustically decorated public rooms, especially the one with an open fireplace. The international and regional cuisine is the best in the area.

Estrada de Turismo, 5300-271 Bragança. ✆ **27/333-14-93.** Fax 27/332-34-53. www.pousadas.pt. 28 units. 92€–140€ ($106–$161) double. Rates include breakfast. AE, DC, MC, V. Free parking. **Amenities:** Restaurant; bar; pool; limited room service; laundry service; dry cleaning; nonsmoking rooms; 1 room for those w/limited mobility. *In room:* A/C, TV, dataport, minibar, hair dryer.

Residencia Santa Isabel The best budget-conscious choice in town is this small-scale hotel, set among a handful of stores and businesses in the center of town. View it as a stop for the night, and don't expect too much of the Portuguese-speaking staff. The guest rooms are well scrubbed but simply furnished, with worn but comfortable mattresses and well-kept bathrooms equipped with shower-tub combinations. Rooms tend to be small.

Rua Alexandre Herculano 67, 5300-075 Bragança. ✆ **27/333-14-27.** Fax 27/332-69-37. 14 units. 38€–45€ ($44–$52) double; extra bed 20€ ($23). Rates include breakfast. No credit cards. **Amenities:** Breakfast room; bar; lounge; limited room service. *In room:* A/C, TV.

WHERE TO DINE

La Em Casa *Value* TRAS-OS-MONTES/PORTUGUESE With pine-paneled walls and a rustic atmosphere, this modern, airy restaurant is one of the town's most consistently reliable. In the center of the city, it attracts the rare foreign visitor but has a devoted local following. Diners are drawn by the kitchen's deft handling of local produce. The rack or leg of lamb is aromatic and tender, and veal is served in the typical style of the province, grilled with potatoes and flavored with a sauce made with fresh garlic and vinegar. Octopus also appears on the menu, coated in egg batter and sautéed golden brown. Fresh seafood shipments arrive daily. Sometimes fado performances are staged here.

Rua Marquês de Pombal 7. ✆ **27/332-21-11.** Reservations required. Main courses 6€–14€ ($6.90–$16). AE, DC, MC, V. Daily 12:30–3pm and 7:30–11:30pm.

Pousada de São Bartolomeu ★ INTERNATIONAL/REGIONAL Though it might lack the local flavor of the various town taverns, this is the most refined place to dine in the area, with many chefs who have worked in Continental kitchens. Dishes are perfectly prepared and filled with robust country flavor. Among the favorites are stewed rabbit with peppers, grilled trout with smoked ham, and—a special delight—roasted veal on a spit with small baked potatoes. To launch your repast, try the French bean salad with fresh tuna fish or a codfish salad; the fish is served with fresh chopped onions and vine-ripened tomatoes. Every day a selection of fresh pastries appears on the "sweets buffet."

Estrada de Turismo ✆ **27/333-14-93.** Reservations not required. Main courses 12€–15€ ($14–$17). AE, DC, MC, V. Daily 1–3pm and 7–10pm.

Solar Bragançano ★★ TRAS-OS-MONTES In a 3-century-old house on the main square of town, this old-fashioned restaurant is our all-time favorite in the area. It serves the best, most flavor-filled regional dishes. You'll get a true taste of Trás-os-Montes here and will likely have a good time, too. The tiled stairway leads to a formal dining room decorated in a typical style, with handwoven regional rugs, chandeliers, and wood ceilings. You can also dine in an inside garden. The chef's local specialties include game dishes in autumn—perhaps pheasant with chestnuts or hare with rice. Spicy game sausages are another exciting choice, as is white Montesinho kid, perfectly roasted. Veal steak with wine sauce is available year-round. You might conclude your meal with regional goat cheese; discerning locals do, and we always follow their example.

Praça da Sé (Largo da Sé). ✆ **27/332-38-75.** Reservations recommended. Main courses 7.50€–20€ ($8.65–$23). Fixed-price menu 13€ ($14). AE, DC, MC, V. Daily 11am–3pm and 6–11pm.

13

Madeira & Porto Santo

The island of **Madeira** ★★★, 850km (527 miles) southwest of Portugal, is just the mountain peak of an enormous volcanic mass. The island's craggy spires and precipices of umber-dark basalt end with a sheer drop into the blue water of the Atlantic Ocean, which is so deep near Madeira that large sperm whales often come close to the shore. If you stand on the sea-swept balcony of Cabo Girão, one of the world's highest ocean cliffs (590m/1,935 ft. above sea level), you'll easily realize the island's Eden-like quality, which inspired Luís Vaz de Camões, the Portuguese national poet, to say Madeira lies "at the end of the world."

The summit of the mostly undersea mountain is at Madeira's center, where **Pico Ruivo,** often snowcapped, rises to an altitude of 1,860m (6,100 ft.) above sea level. It is from this mountain peak that a series of deep, rock-strewn ravines cuts through the countryside and projects all the way to the edge of the sea. The island of Madeira is only 56km (35 miles) long and about 21km (13 miles) across at its widest point. It has nearly 160km (99 miles) of coastline, but no beaches. In Madeira's volcanic soil, plants and flowers blaze like creations from Gaugin's Tahitian palette. With jacaranda, masses of bougainvillea, orchids, geraniums, whortleberry, prickly pear, poinsettias, cannas, frangipani, birds of paradise, and wisteria, the land is a botanical garden. Custard apples, avocados, mangoes, and bananas grow profusely throughout the island. Fragrances such as vanilla and wild fennel mingle with sea breezes and permeate the ravines that sweep down the rocky headlands.

In 1419, João Gonçalves Zarco and Tristão Vaz Teixeira of Portugal discovered Madeira after being diverted by a storm while exploring the west coast of Africa, some 564km (350 miles) east. Because the island was densely covered with impenetrable virgin forests, they named it Madeira (wood). Soon it was set afire to clear it for habitation. The blaze is said to have lasted 7 years, until all but a small northern section was reduced to ashes. Today the hillsides are so richly cultivated that you'd never know there had been such extensive fires. Many of the island's groves and vineyards, protected by buffers of sugarcane, grow on stone-wall ledges next to the cliff's edge. Carrying water from mountain springs, a complex network of man-made *levadas* (water channels) irrigates these terraced mountain slopes.

The uncovered levadas, originally constructed of stone by slaves and convicts (beginning at the time of the earliest colonization and slowly growing into a huge network), are most often .3 to .6m (1–2 ft.) wide and deep. By the turn of the 20th century, the network stretched for 1,000km (620 miles). In the past century, however, the network has grown to some 2,140km (1,327 miles), of which about 40km (25 miles) are covered tunnels dug into the mountains.

Madeira can be a destination unto itself, and, in fact, many Britons fly here directly, avoiding Portugal altogether. Most North Americans, however, tie in a visit to Madeira with trips to Lisbon. It isn't really suited for a day trip from Lisbon—the island deserves a minimum of 3 days, if you can afford that much. Madeira is an extremely popular destination in both summer and winter, and the limited number of planes flying here might not have seats at the last minute, so book well in advance.

Cruise ships sometimes anchor here, but there's no regular passenger boat service to Madeira from the mainland. That means you'll have to fly. Many charter flights link Funchal (Madeira's capital) with the capitals of Europe, though the regular route is from Lisbon to Funchal on TAP Air Portugal (see "Arriving" under "Essentials," below, for more details).

Madeira is both an island and the name of the autonomous archipelago to which it belongs. The island of Madeira has the largest land mass of the archipelago, some 460 sq. km (179 sq. miles). The only other inhabited island in the Madeira archipelago is **Porto Santo** ★ (about 26 sq. km/10 sq. miles), 40km (25 miles) to the northeast of the main island of Madeira. *Réalités* magazine called Porto Santo "another world, arid, desolate and waterless." Unlike Madeira, Porto Santo has beaches and has built several hotels.

There are also a series of other islands in the archipelago, including the appropriately named *Ihlas Desertas,* or The Empty Islands, 19km (12 miles) southeast of Funchal (the capital of the island of Madeira), and even more remote islands, called *Selvagens,* or Wild Isles, near the Canary Islands. The latter archipelago is a possession of Spain. However, none of these is inhabited.

1 Madeira Essentials

853km (529 miles) SW of Portugal, 564km (350 miles) W of the African coastline

ARRIVING

The quickest and most convenient way to reach Madeira from Lisbon is on a 90-minute **TAP** flight. The daily flights (9–13, depending on the season) stop at the Madeira airport then go on to Porto Santo.

Getting to Madeira's capital, Funchal, is easier and cheaper than you might think, especially if you fly aboard any TAP plane into Lisbon from anywhere outside of Portugal and then connect with a TAP commuter flight from Lisbon to Funchal. If you fly business class into Lisbon from virtually anywhere within TAP's overseas network (including flights to Portugal that originate in both the New York area and London), no additional funds are charged for passengers continuing on to Madeira. If you're flying coach class, however, with even the cheapest of APEX deals, the supplement you'll pay for the final round-trip leg into Funchal will rarely exceed $100 and, in many cases, might not even exceed $50. If you're going to Madeira, it is wise to book all legs of your trip to Portugal as part of the same ticketing process.

In addition, TAP has five direct flights daily, and British Airways flies nonstop (Mon, Wed, Fri, and Sat) from London to Funchal. Trip time is 4 hours.

In Madeira, planes arrive at **Aeroporto de Madeira** (✆ **291/52-07-00**), east of Funchal, at Santa Cruz. **Taxis** into Funchal's center can take from 15 to 20 minutes and cost 22€ ($25) for a typical fare. However, the taxis that wait at the airport will take airline passengers anywhere they want to go on the island.

Frommer's Favorite Madeira Experiences

Riding a Toboggan. Madeira's most fabled activity is taking a ***carro de cesto*** ride in a wicker-sided sled from the high-altitude suburb of Monte to Funchal. Two drivers run alongside the sled to control it as it careens across slippery cobblestones. It's a great joyride that lasts 20 minutes.

Escaping to the Golden Beaches of Porto Santo. Pirates of the Atlantic once romped on the 6.5km (4 miles) of beaches in this relatively forgotten part of the world.

Spending a Morning at the Mercado dos Lavradores (Market of the Workers). Go early—between 7 and 8am, at the latest—to see this market come alive. Flower vendors, fishers, and local terrace farmers sell an array of local wares (produce, fish, clothing, flowers, baskets, ceramics, prepared food, crafts) not seen anywhere else in Madeira. Check out the fish, everything from tuna to eel, that you'll be served later in local restaurants. It's open Monday through Saturday from 7am to 8pm.

Tasting the Local Wines. Go to any *taverna* (tavern) on the island and acquaint yourself with the array of local wines, all fortified with grape brandy. Before you leave the island, be sure to sample all the different selections: the world-renowned, light-colored **Sercial,** the driest of the Madeira wines; the golden-hued, slightly sweeter **Verdelho;** the decidedly sweet **Bual,** a dessert wine that's good with cheese; and the sweetest: rich, fragrant **Malmsey,** which is served with dessert.

Attending the End of the Year Festival. The most exciting (and most crowded) time to visit Funchal is during this festival, December 30 to January 1, when live music, food stalls, dancing, costumes, and parades fill the streets. At night, fireworks light up the bay, for which the mountains in the background form an amphitheater.

If you're going to Funchal or from Funchal back to the airport, you can also take a **bus,** run by the Sociedad de Automibiles de Madeira (✆ **291/20-11-50**), which can take from 40 minutes to 1 hour (depending on the number of stops) but costs only 4€ ($4.60) one-way. These busses run as needed and are timed to meet incoming and outgoing flights. They stop at three or four places in the town center as the need arises because there is no central bus station.

VISITOR INFORMATION

An English-speaking staff runs the desk at the **Madeira Tourist Office,** Avenida Arriaga 18 (✆ **291/21-19-02**), in Funchal. It's open Monday through Friday from 9am to 5pm, and Saturday and Sunday 9am to 6pm. The office distributes maps of the island, and the staff will make suggestions about the best ways to explore the beautiful landscape. They also have information about ferry connections to the neighboring island of Porto Santo.

TAP has an office in Funchal at Avenida das Comunidades Madeirenses 8-10 (✆ **707/205-700**). It's open Monday through Saturday from 9am to 6pm. However, British Airways' local office is located only at the **Aeroporto de Madeira** (✆ **291/52-08-70**).

Madeira

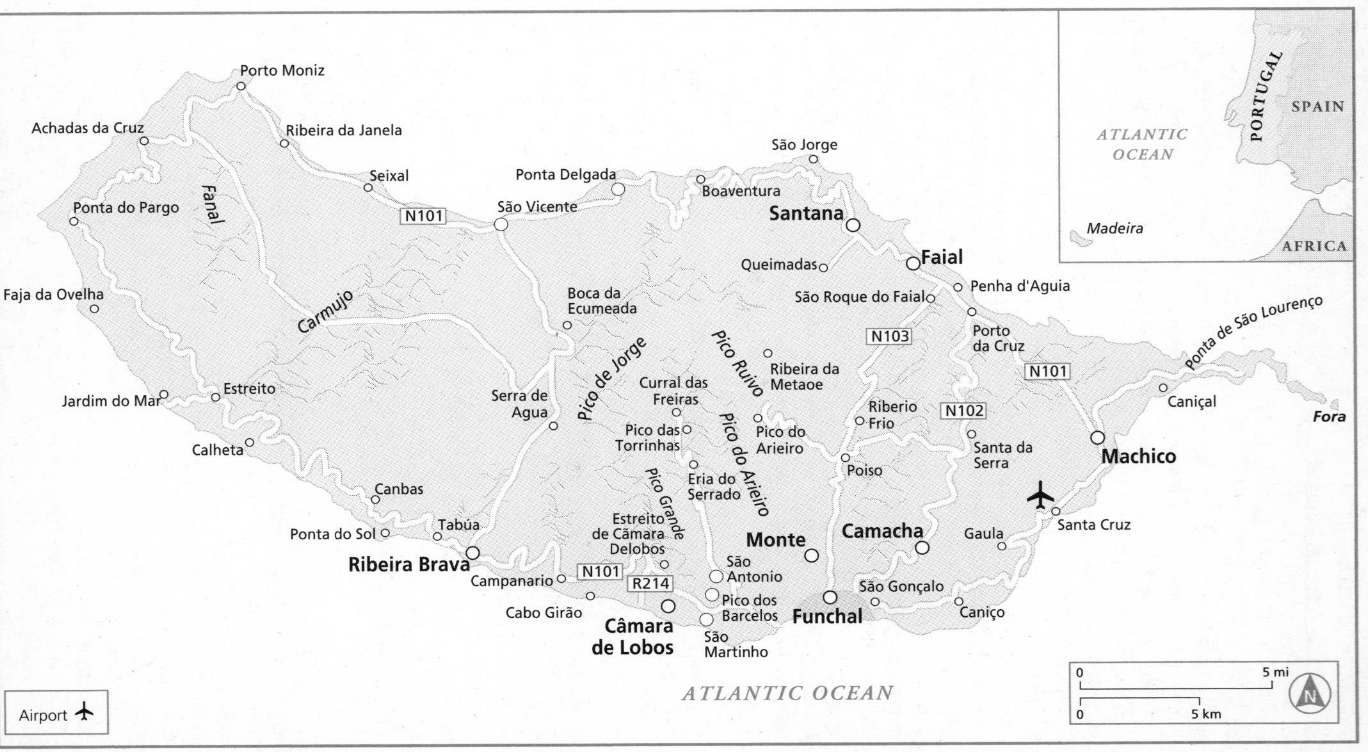

Porto Moniz
Achadas da Cruz
Ribeira da Janela
Seixal
Ponta do Pargo
Fanal
N101
São Vicente
Ponta Delgada
Boaventura
São Jorge
Santana
Faial
Queimadas
São Roque do Faial
Penha d'Aguia
Faja da Ovelha
Carmujo
Boca da Ecumeada
Porto da Cruz
Ponta de São Lourenço
N103
Pico Ruivo
Ribeira da Metaoe
N101
Caniçal
Fora
Jardim do Mar
Estreito
Serra de Agua
Pico de Jorge
Curral das Freiras
Riberio Frio
N102
Pico das Torrinhas
Pico do Arieiro
Pico do Arieiro
Calheta
Poiso
Santa da Serra
Machico
Eria do Serrado
Pico Grande
Canbas
Santa Cruz
Estreito de Câmara Delobos
Ponta do Sol
Tabúa
Monte
Camacha
Gaula
Ribeira Brava
São Antonio
Campanario
N101
R214
São Gonçalo
Pico dos Barcelos
Funchal
Caniço
Cabo Girão
Câmara de Lobos
São Martinho
ATLANTIC OCEAN
Airport
0
5 mi
0
5 km
ATLANTIC OCEAN
PORTUGAL
SPAIN
Madeira
AFRICA

ISLAND LAYOUT

The capital of Madeira, **Funchal** (pop. 100,000), is the focal point of the island and the gateway to its outlying villages. When Zarco landed in 1419, the sweet odor of wild fennel led him to name the town after the aromatic herb (*funcho* in Portuguese). Today this southern coastal city of hillside villas and narrow winding streets is the island's most luxuriant area, filled with fertile fields, hundreds of flowering gardens, and numerous exotic estates.

A long, often traffic-clogged street, **Avenida do Mar,** runs east-west along the waterfront. North of this is **Avenida Arriaga,** the "main street" of Funchal. At the eastern end of this thoroughfare is the *Sé* (cathedral), and at the western end is a large traffic circle that surrounds a fountain. As Avenida Arriaga, site of several hotels, heads west, it changes its name to **Avenida do Infante.** As it runs east, it becomes **Rua do Aljube.** Running north-south, the other important street, **Avenida Zarco,** links the waterfront area with the heart of the old city.

To explore and savor Madeira, adventurous visitors (definitely not the queasy), with time to spend go on foot across some of the trails strewn around the island. Hand-hewn stones and gravel-sided embankments lead you along precipitous ledges, down into lush ravines, and across flowering meadows. These dizzying paths are everywhere, from the hillsides of the wine-rich region of Estreito de Câmara de Lobos to the wicker-work center of Camacha. A much easier way to go, of course, is on an organized tour or on local buses, or you can rent a car and risk the hazardous driving on hairpin curves.

If you'd like to take a circular tour of the entire island, you can take N101 either east or west of Funchal, which traverses the coast of the entire island. Heading west from Funchal, you'll pass women doing their laundry on rocks, homes so tiny that they're almost like dollhouses, and banana groves growing right to the edge of the cliffs that overlook the sea. Less than 10km (6¼ miles) away is the coastal village of **Câmara de Lobos** (Room of the Wolves), the subject of several paintings by Sir Winston Churchill. A sheltered, tranquil cove, it's set amid rocks and towering cliffs, with hillside cottages, terraces, and date palms. The road north from Câmara de Lobos, through vineyards, leads to **Estreito de Câmara de Lobos** (popularly known as Estreito), the heart of the wine-growing region that produces Madeira's wine. Along the way you'll spot women sitting on mossy stone steps doing embroidery, and men who cultivate the ribbonlike terraces wearing brown stocking caps with tasseled tops. (Incidentally, the islanders' blond locks were inherited from early Flemish settlers.)

Lying 16km (10 miles) west of Câmara de Lobos, **Cabo Girâo** is one of the highest ocean-side cliffs in the world. You can stand here watching the sea crash 580m (1,902 ft.) below while also taking in a panoramic sweep of the Bay of Funchal.

From **Cabo Girão,** return to Funchal by veering off the coastal road past São Martinho to the belvedere at **Pico Dos Barcelos.** In one of the most idyllic spots on the island, you can see the ocean, mountains, orange and banana groves, bougainvillea, and poinsettias, as well as the capital.

By heading north from Funchal, you can visit some outstanding spots in the heart of the island. Past São António is **Curral das Freiras,** a village huddled around an old monastery at the bottom of an extinct volcanic crater. The site, whose name means Corral of the Nuns, was originally a secluded convent that protected the nuns from sea-weary, woman-hungry mariners and pirates.

If you go north in a different direction, one destination is **Santana,** which many visitors have described as something out of Disney's *Fantasia.* Picture an alpine setting with waterfalls, cobblestone streets, green meadows sprinkled with multicolored blossoms, thatched cottages, swarms of roses, and plunging ravines. The novelist Paul Bowles wrote, "It is as if a 19th-century painter with a taste for the baroque had invented a countryside to suit his own personal fantasy."

Southwest of Santana, is **Queimadas,** the site of a 900m-high (2,952-ft.-high) rest house. From here, many people make the 3-hour trek to the apex of **Pico Ruivo** (Purple Peak), the highest point on the island, 1,860m (6,101 ft.) above sea level. This is a difficult, long, hot climb and is recommended only for the hearty and those with no fear of heights. The best access to Pico Ruivo is from Pico de Arieiro (see below) because the trail from there is the most scenic. However, some visitors who are really into hiking prefer this more daunting challenge.

Southeast of Santana, heading for **Faial,** a colorful hamlet with tiny A-frame huts, the road descends in a series of sharp turns into a deep ravine. The lush terraces here are built for cows to graze on, not for produce.

In the east, about 30km (19 miles) from Funchal, is historic **Machico,** where Portuguese explorers first landed on Madeira. The town is now visited mainly because of the legend of "the lovers of Machico," an English couple who were running away to get married but whose ship is said to have sank here in 1346. In the main square of the town stands a Manueline church constructed at the end of the 15th century, supposedly over the tomb of the ill-fated pair. The facade contains a beautiful rose window. In the interior are white marble columns and a frescoed ceiling over the nave. Try to view the village from the belvedere of **Camoé Pequeno.**

On the way back from Machico, you can detour inland to the village of **Camacha,** perched in a setting of flowers and orchards. It's the island center of the wickerwork industry. You can shop here or just watch local craftspeople making chairs and other items. You'll find that though the stores in Funchal are amply supplied; some items are as much as 20% cheaper in Camacha.

2 Getting Around Madeira

Remember that distances are short on Madeira, but you should allow plenty of time to cover them because of the winding roads.

BY BUS The cheapest, albeit slowest, way of getting around Madeira is by bus. If you want to tour on your own, you can make excursions on local buses that go all over the island at a fraction of the cost the tour companies charge, but you will miss the commentary of an organized tour, of course. A typical fare in Funchal is 1.50€ to 1.90€ ($1.70–$2.20.); rides in the countryside can cost 4€ ($4.60). Sometimes only one bus a day runs to the most distant points. Some of the rides into the mountains can be quite bouncy and uncomfortable. There is no bus station in Funchal, but you can buy tickets for anywhere on the island at any of the newsstands in the center of Funchal. For information about schedules, go to the tourist office in Funchal.

Most buses depart from the large park at the eastern part of the Funchal waterfront bordering Avenida do Mar. Buses to Camacha or Camiço leave from a little square at the eastern sector of Rua da Alfândega, which runs parallel to Avenida do Mar near the marketplace.

BY TAXI The going taxi rate is about 90€ ($104) per day, but three or four passengers can divide the cost. Always negotiate (many taxi drivers speak English) and agree on the rate in advance. Most taxis are Peugeots or Mercedes, so you'll ride in relative safety and comfort and won't have to worry about navigating the nightmarish roads. If you're in Funchal, you'll usually find a line of taxis across from the tourist office along Avenida Arriaga.

BY CAR Unless you're a skilled driver used to narrow roads, reckless drivers, and hairpin turns, you should not rent a car on the island. If you need to, however, most hotels can make arrangements for car rentals.

Avis (✆ **800/331-2112** in the U.S.) has offices at the Aeroporto da Madeira in Santa Cruz (✆ **291/52-43-92**) and in Funchal at Largo António Nobre 164 (✆ 291/76-45-46). **Hertz** (✆ **800/654-3001** in the U.S.) has a branch in Funchal at Estrada Monumental 284 (✆ 291/76-44-10). **Budget Rent-a-Car** (✆ **800/472-3325** in the U.S.) has outlets at the airport (✆ 291/52-46-61) and in Funchal at Estrada Monumental 239 (✆ **291/76-65-18**). You can also rent vehicles at **Europcar,** Aeroporto da Madeira (✆ **291/52-46-33**), and **Atlas Car Rental,** Rua da Alegria 23 (✆ **291/22-31-00**), in Funchal.

ORGANIZED TOURS If you don't care to venture out on your own, you can take one of the many organized bus tours that cruises through the valleys and along the coast of Madeira. Participants can be picked up at their hotels in Funchal or at the tourist office. Those staying at hotels outside Funchal usually pay a small surcharge to be picked up. For more information, contact the tourist office (see "Essentials," above) or **Inter Tours,** Avenida Arriaga 30, 3rd floor (✆ **291/22-83-44**), in Funchal.

The most popular excursion is Inter Tour's **full-day island tour** that incorporates virtually every accessible point on Madeira, including the island's remote northwestern tip, **Porto Moniz,** and the lovely harbor of **Câmara de Lobos,** a few miles west of Funchal. The full-day tour, offered daily, is 40€ ($46) per person, including lunch.

Inter Tours also offers a less-strenuous **half-day volcano-and-toboggan tour,** which is 20€ ($23) per person; it departs (picking up passengers at their hotels around Funchal) twice a week, usually on Tuesday and Sunday. Another possibility, usually offered Monday and Wednesday, for 40€ ($46) is visiting the **wickerworks at Camacha,** where thousands of pieces of locally crafted work, from small baskets to entire groupings of furniture, are on sale. Tuesday through Friday night, there's a **dinner featuring fado and folkloric dancing** (appropriate for all ages) at the Restaurant Relogio at Camancha and Seta, costing 30€ ($35). It has some very talented local performers, but, of course, like all shows of this nature, it's very touristy and not something that a local would go to. The food is a combination of Portuguese and international cooking.

FAST FACTS: Madeira

American Express The representative in Madeira is **Top Tours Travel Agency,** Avenida do Mar 15 (✆ **291/20-62-60**), in Funchal. It's open Monday through Friday from 9:30am to 1pm and 2:30 to 6:30pm, and is a full-service American Express office.

Area Code The country code for Portugal is 351; the area code for Madeira is **291.**

Automated Teller Machines (ATMs) Most ATMs (available 24 hr. a day) are found in Funchal. But there are also some ATMs in towns throughout the island.

Business Hours **Shops** are usually open Monday through Friday from 9am to 1pm and 3 to 7pm, and Saturday from 9am to 1pm. They're closed Sunday. **Municipal buildings** are open Monday through Friday from 9am to 12:30pm and 2 to 5:30pm. All **banks** are open Monday through Friday from 8:30am to 3pm.

Consulates The Consulate of the **United States** is on Rua Alfãndega 10 (✆ **291/23-56-36**), off Avenida do Infante. The Consulate of the **United Kingdom** is at Avenida Zarco 2, second floor (✆ **291/22-12-21**). All other consulates are located only in Lisbon.

Dentist A good English-speaking dentist, **John de Sousa,** has an office in the Marina Forum Building, Avenida Arriaga (✆ **291/23-12-77**), in Funchal.

Doctor A good English-speaking doctor is **Francis Zino,** in the Edifício Jasmineiro, Rua do Jasmineiro (✆ **291/74-22-27**), in Funchal.

Drugstores Drugstores (chemists) are open Monday through Friday from 9am to 1pm and 3 to 9pm. The rotation emergency, night service, and Sunday schedules are posted on the door of all drugstores. A reliable, centrally located chemist is **Farmácia Honorato,** Rua da Carreira 62 (✆ **291/20-38-80**). Dial ✆ **118** to locate a pharmacy that's open.

Emergencies Call ✆ **112** for a general **emergency,** ✆ **291/22-20-22** for the **police,** ✆ **291/74-11-15** for the **Red Cross,** and ✆ **291/75-06-00** for a **hospital** emergency.

Hospital The island's largest hospital is the **Hospital Distrital do Funchal,** Cruz de Carvalho (✆ **291/70-56-00**).

Laundry/Dry Cleaning Try **Lavandaria Donini,** Rua das Pretas (✆ **291/22-44-06**), Funchal. Clothing can be laundered or dry-cleaned in 1 or 2 days. It's open Monday through Saturday from 9am to 7pm.

Lost Property Check at the island's main **police station** on Rua João de Deus in Funchal (✆ **291/22-20-22**).

Newspapers/Magazines The island stocks a good selection of such English-language publications as *Newsweek, Time,* and the *International Herald Tribune,* as well as periodicals in French, German, and Spanish. Especially useful is a locally produced English-language publication, the *Madeira Island Bulletin,* distributed free at the tourist office and in many of the island's more visible hotels, which features descriptions of island activities and lists special events.

Police Dial ✆ **291/22-20-22.**

Post Office If you've had your mail sent poste restante (general delivery), you can pick it up at Funchal's **Zarco Post Office,** Avenida Zarco 9, 9000-999 (✆ **291/20-28-31**), near the tourist office, as long as you bring your passport to identify yourself. From here, you can also place long-distance phone calls (without steep hotel surcharges) and send telegrams, faxes, and telexes. The office is open Monday through Friday from 8:30am to 8pm, and Saturday from 9am to 1pm.

Other post offices offering the same services are **Calouste Gulbenkian,** Avenida Calouste Gulbenkian (open Mon–Fri 9am–6:30pm), near the Monument of the Infante Dom Henríque; **Monumental,** on Estrada Monumental, near the Lido swimming pool (Mon–Fri 8:30am–7pm); and **Mercado,** Rua do Arcipreste, near the Municipal Market (Mon–Fri 8:30am–6:30pm). Signs in the center of Funchal that read CORREIOS point the way to the nearest post office, or look for mailboxes on the street.

Restrooms The airport, hotels, and some museums have public restrooms. However, there are not enough public toilets. Locals often use cafes or taverns, though, in theory, these facilities are reserved for customers.

Safety In terms of crime statistics, Madeira is safer than mainland Portugal, especially Lisbon. However, as in any area that attracts tourists, there is a criminal element that preys on visitors. Pickpockets and purse-snatchers are the major villains. Protect your valuables, as you would at any resort.

Taxes Madeira imposes no special taxes other than the value-added tax (VAT) on all goods and services purchased in Portugal. Refer to "Fast Facts: Portugal," in chapter 2 for more information.

Weather Call ✆ **291/22-15-86** for a report in English.

3 Where to Stay in Funchal

Madeira enjoys year-round popularity, though April through May and September through October are the most comfortable and, in many ways, the most beautiful times to visit. It has become hard to get a plane seat in the peak summer season without reservations made way in advance. August is still not the most desirable month to visit because of the *capacete,* a shroud of mist that often envelops the island because it is so hot—remember that Madeira is close to Africa. If you're visiting in the summer, air-conditioning might be vital to you—unless you're at a retreat in the mountains.

Madeira's hotels range from some of the finest deluxe accommodations in Europe to attractively priced old-fashioned *quintas* (manor houses) for budget travelers. Chances are, you won't be staying in the center of Funchal, but on the outskirts, where many of the best hotels with pools and resort amenities are. However, these make travelers dependent upon transportation into town, and only the first-class and deluxe hotels lying outside of Funchal offer vans taking guests at frequent intervals into town. There are also downfalls to staying in the center of town; because heavy traffic fills the center of Funchal most of the day, hotels there tend to be noisy. Nevertheless, for shopping and the widest selection of restaurants, Funchal is a magnet.

VERY EXPENSIVE

Choupana Hills Resort & Spa ★★★ An oasis of charm, elegance, and tranquility, there is nothing like this newly opened resort and spa on Madeira. An elite retreat, it lies in the hills 4km (2½ miles) north of Funchal. Its public and private rooms lie on top of a mountain just above the Botanical Gardens and stand in a well-landscaped 8-hectare (20-acre) plot of land opening onto views of the bay and the Atlantic Ocean. The choice way to stay here is in one of four unique suites set apart from the resort's other pavilions and designed as a total

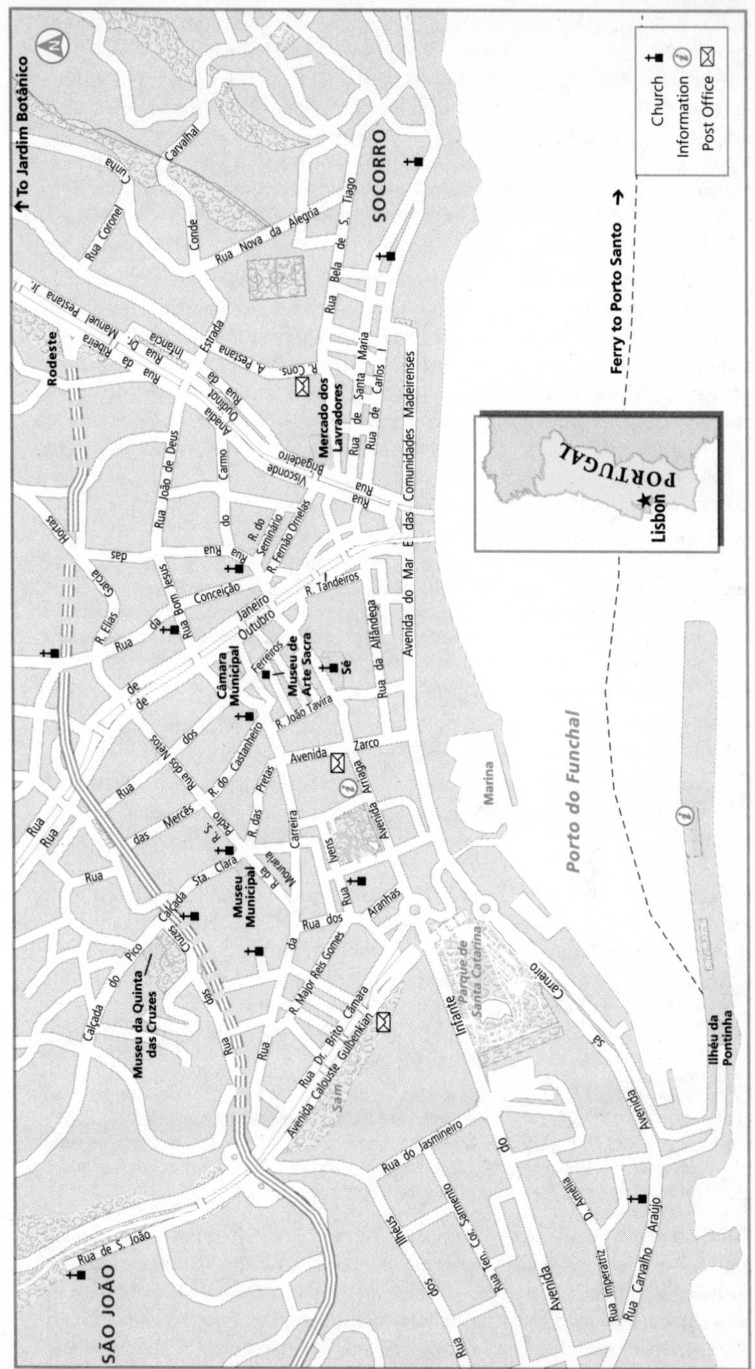

To Jardim Botânico
Rodeste
SOCORRO
SÃO JOÃO
Mercado dos Lavradores
Câmara Municipal
Museu de Arte Sacra
Sé
Museu Municipal
Museu da Quinta das Cruzes
Parque de Santa Catarina
Marina
Porto do Funchal
Ilhéu da Pontinha
Ferry to Porto Santo
PORTUGAL
Lisbon
Church
Information
Post Office
Rua Coronel
Cunha
Carvalhal
Conde
Rua Nova da Alegria
Rua Bela de S. Tiago
Rua Dr. Manuel Pestana Jr.
Rua da Ribeira
Rua Infancia
Estrada
R. Cons. A. Pestana
Rua de Santa Maria
Rua de Carlos I
Avenida do Mar E das Comunidades Madeirenses
Rua João de Deus
Rua da Anadia
Rua Oudinot
Visconde
Brigadeiro
Carmo
R. do Seminário
R. Fernão Ornelas
Rua do Carmo
Rua das Hortas
Rua Bom Jesus
Conceição
Janeiro
Outubro
R. Tandeiros
Rua da Alfândega
R. Elias Garcia
Ferreiros
R. João Tavira
Avenida Zarco
Arriaga
Avenida
Rua dos Netos
R. do Castanheiro
R. das Pretas
Carreira
Rua das Mercês
R. S. Pedro
Ivens
Calçada Sta. Clara
R. da Mouraria
Rua dos Aranhas
R. Major Reis Gomes
Calçada do Pico
Rua das Cruzes
Rua Dr. Brito Câmara
Avenida Calouste Gulbenkian
Infante
Carneiro
Sá
Rua do Jasmineiro
Rua de S. João
Rua dos Ilhéus
Rua Ten. Cor. Sarmento
D. Amélia
Rua Imperatriz
Rua Carvalho Araújo

hideway. But all the bedrooms have understated luxury and taste, and are most comfortable, spread across wooden bungalow-style buildings, each with a large terrace. The resort also boasts a first-class restaurant specializing in fusion cuisine and two bars. And there's the added attraction of one of the resort's best spas.

Travessa do Largo da Choupana, 9050-286 Funchal. ✆ **291/20-60-20.** Fax 291/20-60-21. www.choupanahills.com. 64 units. 230€–320€ ($265–$368) double; 430€–560€ ($495–$644) suite. Rates include breakfast. AE, DC, MC, V. **Amenities:** Restaurant; bars; indoor and outdoor pool; gym; spa; Jacuzzi; sauna; 24-hr. room service; babysitting; laundry service; dry cleaning; nonsmoking rooms. *In room:* A/C, TV, minibar, coffeemaker, hair dryer, safe.

The Cliff Bay ★★★ *Kids* One of the island's top lodgings, rivaled and surpassed only by Reid's (see below), this nine-story hotel is dramatically located on a craggy bluff towering over wave-lashed rocks, 1.5km (1 mile) west of Funchal's center. A group favorite, the deluxe hotel stands on the site of a former banana plantation. All but a dozen or so rooms have great exposure to ocean or harbor panoramas. Units are generally spacious, with such luxuries as sitting areas and roomy marble bathrooms with deluxe toiletries and shower-tub combos. The restaurants, from the Rose Garden to Il Gallo d'Oro to the Blue Lagoon (featuring Portuguese and international cuisine), are among the finest on the island, again surpassed only by the options at Reid's.

Estrada Monumental 147, 9004-532 Funchal, Madeira. ✆ **291/70-77-00.** Fax 291/76-25-25. www.cliffbay.com. 201 units. 205€–378€ ($236–$435) double; 340€–482€ ($391–$554) junior suite; from 409€ ($470) suite. AE, DC, MC, V. Free parking. Bus: 1, 2, or 35. **Amenities:** 3 restaurants; 3 bars; 2 pools; health club; spa; sauna; watersports; game room; 24-hr. room service; massage; babysitting; kindergarten; laundry service; dry cleaning; nonsmoking rooms; 1 room for those w/limited mobility. *In room:* A/C, TV, dataport, minibar, hair dryer, safe.

Hotel Classic Savoy ★★ *Kids* The Savoy is one of the leading government-rated five-star hotels not only in Madeira, but in all of Portugal. Long known for its overstated lushness and often-garish theatricality, it stands at the edge of Funchal. The hotel is superbly situated, opening onto both the ocean and the Bay of Funchal. With its vast public facilities, it captures a peculiar kind of Madeira *dolce vita.*

Each guest room has a balcony. The most expensive doubles are twins with sea views. The rooms have standard built-in furniture and elegant small bathrooms with dual basins and tub-shower combinations. Each generation of management (since its founding by a Swiss-trained hotelier at the turn of the 20th century) has introduced enlargements and improvements.

For deluxe dining, try the elegant Fleur-de-Lys, a grill room with a panoramic view. See "Where to Dine," later in this chapter.

Av. do Infante, 9004-542 Funchal, Madeira. ✆ **291/21-30-00.** Fax 291/22-31-03. www.savoyresort.com. 337 units. 220€–390€ ($253–$449) double; from 700€ ($805) suite. Rates include breakfast. AE, DC, MC, V. Free parking. Bus: 1, 2, 3, 4, 13, or 35. **Amenities:** 3 restaurants; 2 bars; 2 pools; 2 tennis courts; health club; sauna; children's playground; boutiques; salon; 24-hr. room service; babysitting; laundry service; dry cleaning; nonsmoking rooms. *In room:* A/C, TV, dataport, minibar, hair dryer, safe.

Reid's Palace ★★★ The legendary place to stay in Funchal is Reid's, founded in 1891 by William Reid but now owned by the Orient Express. Its position is "smashing," as the British say, along the coastal road at the edge of Funchal, on 4 hectares (10 acres) of terraced gardens that descend the hillside to the rocky ocean shores. The English who frequent the hotel in large numbers (Sir Winston Churchill stayed here) spend their days strolling the walks lined with hydrangeas, geraniums, gardenias, banana trees, ferns, and white yuccas.

The spacious guest rooms are conservative in the finest sense, with well-chosen furnishings (antiques or reproductions), plenty of storage space, sitting areas, and desks. The bathrooms have marble or tile walls and floors, plus shower-tub combinations, robes, and luxurious toiletries.

The gourmet restaurant, Les Faunes (see "Where to Dine," later in this chapter), is on the sixth floor, in the garden wing.

Estrada Monumental 139, 9000-098 Funchal, Madeira. ✆ **800/223-6800** in the U.S., or 291/71-71-71. Fax 291/71-71-77. www.reidspalace.orient-express.com. 164 units. 275€–400€ ($316–$460) standard double; 395€–520€ ($454–$598) superior double; 465€–590€ ($535–$679) premier double; 685€–885€ ($788–$1,018) junior suite; 885€–1,085€ ($1,018–$1,248) superior suite; 1,115€–1,295€ ($1,282–$1,489) executive suite; 2,535€–2,935€ ($2,915–$3,375) presidential suite. Rates include breakfast. AE, DC, MC, V. Free parking. Bus: 4, 8, 10, or 16. **Amenities:** 3 restaurants; 2 bars; 3 pools; 2 tennis courts; health club; spa/salon; sauna; watersports; children's programs; salon; 24-hr. room service; babysitting; laundry; dry cleaning; nonsmoking rooms; rooms for those w/limited mobility. *In room:* A/C, TV, dataport, minibar, hair dryer, safe,.

EXPENSIVE

Eden Mar ★ Last renovated in 1998, this decade-old hotel rises six floors from the swimming complex (the Lido). Though often booked by tour groups from England, it is still suitable for the individual traveler, especially families that like its rooms with kitchenettes. The midsize to spacious guest rooms open onto views of the sea. Decorated in lively flowery prints, the hotel has first-rate furnishings and excellent tiled bathrooms equipped with shower-tub combinations. The restaurant serves international and Portuguese cuisine.

Rua do Gorgulho 2, 9004-537 Funchal, Madeira. ✆ **291/70-97-00.** Fax 291/76-19-66. www.edenmar.com. 146 units. 127€–152€ ($146–$175) double. Extra bed 44€–72€ ($51–$83). AE, DC, MC, V. Free parking. Bus: 1, 2, 4, or 6. **Amenities:** Restaurant; 2 bars; 2 pools; health club; Jacuzzi; sauna; library; limited room service; massage; babysitting; laundry service; dry cleaning. *In room:* A/C, TV, dataport, kitchenette, safe.

Madeira Palácio ★★ This is a luxurious, contemporary hotel on the seaside route to Câmara de Lobos, about 3km (1¾ miles) from the center of Funchal. It's perched on a cliff over the sea, with a view of Madeira's famous high cliff, Cabo Girão, looming in the distance. Guest rooms are well appointed and generally spacious, with balconies. Bathrooms have combined tubs and showers, plus vanity areas and dual basins. Rooms opening onto the mountains are less desirable than those facing the sea and are priced accordingly. The main restaurant is Cristóvão Colombo, with a menu of local and international dishes, and the gourmet restaurant, Vicerei, offers international cuisine.

Estrada Monumental 265, 9001-250 Funchal, Madeira. ✆ **291/70-27-02.** Fax 291/70-27-03. www.hotelmadeirapalacio.com. 250 units. 138€–341€ ($159–$392) double; 385€ ($443) suite. Rates include breakfast. AE, DC, MC, V. Free parking. Bus: 1, 2, 4, or 35. **Amenities:** 3 restaurants; 2 bars; 2 pools; 2 tennis courts; health club; sauna; boutiques; salon; 24-hr. room service; babysitting; laundry service; dry cleaning; nonsmoking rooms. *In room:* A/C, TV, minibar, hair dryer, safe.

Pestana Carlton Madeira ★★ This is a luxurious 18-story structure near Madeira's only casino, with direct access to the sea via stairs that lead down from the hotel to a platform from which you can get into the sea for swimming. The hotel lies on a promontory overlooking Funchal Bay in the fashionable Vale-Verde Garden district, next to Reid's Palace (see above). All of the spacious accommodations, many furnished in provincial style, have private balconies and comfortable, tasteful furniture. The more expensive rates are for the deluxe sea-view rooms. The oceanfront exposure (to the south) of these rooms means the pool terraces and seaside guest-room balconies and patios receive dawn-to-dusk sunlight. Bathrooms are well organized and contain dual basins and shower-tub combos. The three restaurants serve fine cuisine, if only to tour groups at times: The Atlantico features a show with dinner, Os Arcos has an international and regional menu, and the Taverna Grill serves succulent meats.

Largo António Nobre, 9004-531 Funchal, Madeira. ✆ **291/23-95-00.** Fax 291/22-33-77. www.pestana.com. 361 units. 170€–240€ ($196–$276) double; 370€–450€ ($426–$518) suite. Rates include breakfast. AE, DC, MC, V. Bus: 1, 2 3, 4, 9, or 10. **Amenities:** 3 restaurants; 4 bars; night club; 3 pools; tennis courts; health club; sauna; solarium; game room; 24-hr. room service; babysitting; laundry service; dry cleaning; rooms for those w/limited mobility. *In room:* A/C, TV, dataport, minibar, hair dryer, safe.

Pestana Casino Park ★ Part of Madeira's Casino and Conference Centre, this deluxe citadel is a 7-minute walk from the town center, nestled in a subtropical garden overlooking the harbor. Designed by Oscar Niemeyer—one of the architects of Brasília, Brazil—the gray-concrete main building is low (only five stories) and undulating. The complex consists of the hotel as well as a conference center and a casino.

The small to midsize guest rooms (tastefully decorated in bright, sunny colors) have balconies with panoramic views over the harbor and town. Most rooms have only twin beds, but all boast first-class furnishings. Bathrooms have shower-tub combinations, dual basins, and bidets. Two comfortable lounge areas grace each floor. The luxurious dining room overlooks the port and town of Funchal, and the international Grill Room has an extensive wine cellar.

Rua Imperatriz Dona Amélia, 9004-513 Funchal, Madeira. ✆ **291/20-91-00.** Fax 291/23-20-76. www.pestana.com. 334 units. 160€–200€ ($184–$230) double; 245€–280€ ($282–$322) suite. Rates include buffet breakfast. AE, DC, MC, V. Free limited parking. Bus: 1, 2, 10, 12, or 16. **Amenities:** 3 restaurants; 2 bars; pool; 2 tennis courts; health club; sauna; 24-hr. room service; babysitting; laundry service; dry cleaning; nonsmoking rooms. *In room:* A/C, TV, dataport, minibar, hair dryer, safe.

Quinta da Bela Vista ★★ *Finds* The core of this hotel, in the hills above Funchal, dates from 1844, when it was built as a private villa. Its owner has added two outlying annexes in the Portuguese colonial style. The complex is now a government-rated five-star hotel. A verdant garden surrounds the annexes, which hold comfortable guest rooms. Rooms are slightly larger in the newer annex, constructed in 1991. Furnishings include high-quality mahogany reproductions and a scattering of English and Portuguese antiques. The bathrooms have combined showers and tubs, and deluxe toiletries. A well-staffed formal restaurant, Casa Mãe, is in the original villa. The more relaxed Avistas Navios offers sweeping views and regional and international cuisine.

Caminho do Avista Navios 4, 9000-129 Funchal, Madeira. ✆ **291/70-64-01.** Fax 291/70-64-11. www.qbvista.pt. 90 units. 160€–270€ ($184–$311) double; from 345€ ($397) junior suite. Rates include breakfast. AE, DC, MC, V. Free parking. Bus: 45. **Amenities:** 2 restaurants; 3 bars; pool; tennis courts; health club; sauna; 24-hr. room service; babysitting; laundry service; dry cleaning. *In room:* A/C, TV, hair dryer, safe.

Quinta da Casa Branca ★★★ *Finds* This grand country manor, surrounded by its own manicured grounds, is the personification of estate living on the island, and it was extensively renovated in 2002. Close to the city center, you are also vastly removed in a world apart from the hectic activity of Funchal. An old manor house dominates the grounds, but the living accommodations are entirely modernized and up-to-date, complete with spacious bathrooms with shower-tub combinations. You can expect the services and comfort of a first-rate hotel here. The dining room and bar area are in a restored outbuilding, and a swimming pool makes this a bit like resort living.

Rua da Casa Branca 7, 9000-088 Funchal, Madeira. ✆ **291/70-07-70.** Fax 291/76-50-70. www.quintacasabranca.pt. 43 units. 150€–230€ ($173–$265) double. Rates include breakfast. AE, DC, MC, V. Free parking.

Bus: 5 or 6. **Amenities:** Restaurant; bar; limited room service; babysitting; laundry service; nonsmoking rooms; rooms for those w/limited mobility. *In room:* A/C, TV, dataport (in some), minibar, hair dryer, safe.

MODERATE

Girassol *Kids* Girassol offers immaculate accommodations at reasonable rates. It's on the outskirts of Funchal, overlooking the Tourist Club (a small complex with a restaurant, pool, and platform for swimming in the sea), where guests are allowed access to the sea for a small charge. Most double rooms are actually suites, consisting of a bedroom, a bathroom equipped with a shower-tub combination, a small sitting room, and a veranda, which make them a perfect size for families. Each unit has a terrace or balcony overlooking the garden, the mountains, or the sea. One pool is set aside for children. The dining room, which serves regional and international cuisine, has sea views and, at dinner, live music.

Estrada Monumental 256, 9004-539 Funchal, Madeira. ✆ **291/70-15-70.** Fax 291/76-54-41. hotelgirassol@mail.telepack.pt. 136 units. 130€ ($150) double; 180€ ($207) suite. Rates include breakfast. AE, DC, MC, V. Free parking. Bus: 1, 3, 5, or 6. **Amenities:** Restaurant; 3 bars; 2 pools; health club; sauna; limited room service; babysitting; laundry service; dry cleaning. *In room:* TV, minibar, hair dryer, safe.

Hotel do Carmo Carmo provides modern accommodations in the center of Funchal. It's laid out in a cellular honeycomb fashion; most guest rooms open onto balconies overlooking the busy street scene below. Rates for rooms with and without balconies are the same. Guests gather at the rooftop pool, which affords a good view of the harbor. Created by the Fernandes family, the hotel was designed for thrifty guests who want to be near the heart of the city. The rooms are simple, with contemporary but well-used furnishings. All units are equipped with well-kept bathrooms containing shower-tub combinations. Meals are served in a spacious dining room or can be taken onto an open-air terrace on the second floor. The chefs specialize in a Portuguese and international cuisine, making use of the rich produce of Madeira when available.

Travessa do Rego 10, 9054-502 Funchal, Madeira. ✆ **291/20-12-40.** Fax 291/22-39-19. hoteldocarmo@mail.telepack.pt. 80 units. 90€ ($104) double; 122€ ($140) triple. Rates include breakfast. AE, DC, MC, V. Parking 5€ ($5.75). Bus: 1, 2, 4, 5, 6, 8, 9, or 10. **Amenities:** Restaurant; bar; pool; sauna; babysitting; laundry service; dry cleaning. *In room:* TV, safe.

Hotel Santa Isabel ★ *Kids* *Value* Adjacent to the Savoy and under the same management, this is a small hotel with a homelike feeling and a well-deserved reputation for service and comfort. It has a rooftop terrace with a lounge that overlooks the gardens. There are two grades of accommodations: The more expensive face the sea, and the cheaper units open onto a garden and a mountain view. Some suites cost the same as doubles, and early birds book them quickly, since they know these rooms will allow their children to have their own space (extra beds can be brought in). All rooms come equipped with well-maintained bathrooms containing shower-tub combinations. Color schemes are monochromatic, and the furniture is the kind of Nordic modern that was installed with fanfare in 1961 and hasn't been upgraded since. Overall, it's appealingly old-fashioned and especially popular with travelers from the British Midlands. The value derives from the access guests have to the resort facilities at the nearby Savoy, including the restaurants.

Av. do Infante, 9004-543 Funchal, Madeira. ✆ **291/21-30-50.** Fax 291/22-79-59. www.savoyresort.com. 69 units. 90€–190€ ($104–$219) double; 120€–230€ ($138–$265) suite. Children 2–11 free; 12–18 years 25€–42€ ($29–$48). Rates include breakfast. AE, DC, MC, V. Free parking. Bus: 2, 4, 6, 12, or 16. **Amenities:** Limited room service; laundry service; dry cleaning. *In room:* TV, hair dryer, safe.

Quinta da Penha de França ★★ Kids This gracious old manor house is now a guesthouse, with an annex containing 33 sea-view rooms, a balcony, and a terrace. Rooms in the older section have high ceilings, thick walls, casement windows, and a scattering of old-fashioned furniture, including some family antiques. Rooms in the modern annex, completed late in 1999, are more contemporary, with traditional country-house designs. All units have neatly kept bathrooms equipped with shower-tub combinations. Like a family home, the *quinta* is chock-full of antiques, paintings, and silver. Near the Savoy, it stands in a garden on a ledge almost hanging over the harbor. It's a short walk from Funchal's bazaars and is opposite an ancient chapel. Unlike most hotels on Madeira, many of this hotel's rooms have connecting doors, which can be opened and rented as two rooms for families with one to three children.

Rua da Penha de França 2, 9050-014 Funchal, Madeira. ✆ **291/20-46-50.** Fax 291/22-92-61. www.hotelquintapenhafranca.com. 77 units. 51€–115€ ($59–$13) double; 110€–130€ ($127–$150) suite. Rates include breakfast. AE, DC, MC, V. Free parking. Bus: 2, 12, or 16. **Amenities:** 2 restaurants; 2 bars; pool; babysitting; laundry service; dry cleaning. *In room:* A/C, TV, dataport, minibar, hair dryer, safe.

Quinta do Sol ★ The government-rated four-star Quinta do Sol is among the best in its category on Madeira. In an attractive setting, it offers well-furnished guest rooms; some have their own balconies, and all contain neatly kept bathrooms containing shower-tub combinations. Rooms are sun-flooded with big windows and contemporary furniture; some have balconies with views of the sea. Units without balconies are both larger and less expensive. The hotel has a bar-restaurant, Magnolia, which offers Portuguese and international food and wine.

Rua Dr. Pita 6, 9000-089 Funchal, Madeira. ✆ **291/70-70-10.** Fax 291/76-62-87. www.enotel.com. 158 units. 87€–103€ ($100–$118) double; 160€–232€ ($184–$267) suite. Rates include buffet breakfast. AE, DC, MC, V. Free parking. Bus: 2, 8, or 12. **Amenities:** Restaurant; 2 bars; 1 pool for adults and 1 pool for children; fitness room; sauna; solarium; limited room service; babysitting; laundry service; dry cleaning. *In room:* A/C, TV, dataport, minibar, hair dryer, safe.

INEXPENSIVE

Albergaria Catedral This is a good, budget-conscious choice if you want to be amid the commercial bustle of the center of town. Don't judge the hotel by its narrow, dark entrance, across the street from the cathedral. Climb a flight of stairs to a slick reception area and proceed to one of the cozy, comfortable guest rooms. Rooms in the rear are quieter; however, they don't have much of a view. In front, eight of the units have balconies—unfortunately, they open onto the street noise. The sunniest and most pleasant rooms occupy the two uppermost floors. Don't expect luxury—rooms are simple and somewhat spartan, with serviceable but battered furniture. All units come equipped with tidy bathrooms containing shower-tub combinations.

Rua do Aljube 13, 9000-067 Funchal, Madeira. ✆ **291/23-00-91.** Fax 291/23-00-92. 25 units. 40€–55€ ($46–$63) double. Rates include breakfast. AE, DC, MC, V. No parking. Bus: 1, 2, 4, 5, 6, 8, 9, or 10. **Amenities:** Breakfast room; bar. *In room:* TV.

Estrelícia This is a 20-year-old hotel that was renovated in the summer of 1999 and is now better than ever. Estrelícia is in the upper floors of a high-rise building, constructed up a hill from the main hotel drag. The location is a bit inconvenient, so rates seem low considering the quality of the rooms. Most units are midsize. All are well appointed, with durable modern furniture, neatly kept bathrooms equipped with shower-tub combinations, and a view of the sea. The hotel minibus runs to the center of Funchal several times a day.

Caminho Velho da Ajuda, 9000-113 Funchal, Madeira. © **291/70-66-00.** Fax 291/76-48-59. www.dorisol.pt. 148 units. 74€–85€ ($85–$98) double. Rates include breakfast. AE, DC, MC, V. Free parking. Bus: 1, 2, 4, 5, 6, or 35. **Amenities:** Restaurant; 2 bars; nightclub; pool; babysitting; laundry service; dry cleaning; nonsmoking rooms. *In room:* TV, dataport, minibar, hair dryer, safe.

Hotel Madeira ★ This five-story hotel sits in the center of Funchal, behind the tranquil Park of San Francisco. The rooftop pool has an extraordinary panoramic view of the town, mountains, and sea, and there's a solarium area with a bar and snack services. The small to midsize guest rooms surround a plant-filled atrium. One of the nicest features is the sheltered sun windows attached to each unit. Some rooms have balconies—the ones in the front overlook buildings and have no view, but those in the rear have views of the mountains above Funchal.

All are comfortably furnished, with worn but durable furniture and tidily kept bathrooms equipped with shower-tub combinations.

Rua Ivens 21, 9001-801 Funchal, Madeira. © **291/23-00-71.** Fax 291/22-90-71. www.hotelmadeira.com. 53 units. 66€–75€ ($76–$86) double; 80€ ($72) suite. Rates include breakfast. AE, DC, MC, V. Limited free parking on street. Bus: 2, 12, or 16. **Amenities:** Breakfast room; bar; pool; limited room service; laundry service. *In room:* A/C in some rooms, TV, hair dryer, safe.

Hotel Windsor ★ *Value* Opened with fanfare in 1987, this is one of the most stylish hotels in Funchal. The government-rated four-star hotel consists of two buildings connected by an aerial passage above a sun-flooded enclosed courtyard. The marble-sheathed lobby is laden with plants, wicker chairs, and Art Deco accessories. Rooms are not particularly large, and few have views, but they are comfortable and nicely decorated, with wall-to-wall carpeting and wooden furniture. They all come equipped with well-maintained bathrooms containing shower-tub combinations. The hotel has a cafe-bar designed to resemble a Jazz Age nightclub. The free parking garage is almost a necessity in this crowded commercial neighborhood. The formal Windsor Restaurant is a suitable choice if you are dining at the hotel. It serves a reasonably good and moderately priced Portuguese and international cuisine, with local swordfish as a specialty.

Rua das Hortas 4C, 9050-024 Funchal, Madeira. © **291/23-30-81.** Fax 291/23-30-80. www.hotelwindsor.pt. 67 units. 68€ ($78) double. Rates include breakfast. No credit cards. Free parking. Bus: 1, 12, or 16. **Amenities:** Restaurant; 2 bars; pool; laundry; dry cleaning. *In room:* TV, dataport, hair dryer, safe.

ON THE OUTSKIRTS OF FUNCHAL

EXPENSIVE

Casa Velha do Palheiro ★★★ This unique inn was constructed in 1804 as a hunting lodge for the first Count of Carvalhal and then was restored in 1996 to become Madeira's first government-rated five-star country house hotel, a type of accommodation more common in England. The hotel, a member of the Relais & Châteaux chain, adjoins the par-71 championship Palheiro golf course, about a 15-minute drive from Funchal. It is the only hotel in Madeira on a golf course. Rooms vary in shape and size, but all are richly furnished in an old-fashioned but comfortable way, with first-class furnishings and neatly kept bathrooms equipped with shower-tub combinations. The restaurant and bar serve quality international and Portuguese cuisine.

Palheiro Golf, Sao Conçalo, 9050-296 Funchal, Madeira. © **291/79-49-01.** Fax 291/79-49-25. www.relaischateaux.com/site/us/FicheAdherent?RcCode=casavelha. 37 units. 144€–299€ ($166–$344) double; 294€–358€ ($338–$412) suite. Rates include breakfast. AE, DC, MC, V. Free parking. Bus: 33. **Amenities:** Restaurant; bar; pool; golf course; sauna; 24-hr. room service; babysitting; laundry service; dry cleaning. *In room:* TV, dataport, minibar, hair dryer, safe.

MODERATE

Quintinha São João ★ *Finds* Dating from 1900, this *quinta* (manor house) is one of the best preserved in the Funchal area, surrounded by age-old trees and graced with classic architecture. Once an elegant private residence, it has been tastefully converted into a family inn. Most of the good-size, standard guest rooms contain twin beds; some suites are available. All are handsomely decorated, often with traditional embroidery and Madeiran handiwork covering the beds. Old-style furnishings and antiques appear throughout, but modern luxuries include neatly kept bathrooms equipped with shower-tub combinations. The restaurant, A Morgadinha, offers a variety of regional and international dishes, and features unusual Goan specialties. The terrace bar, Vasco da Gama, overlooks the Bay of Funchal and is one of the most scenic places in town for a drink.

Rua da Levada de São João, 9000-191 Funchal, Madeira. ✆ **291/74-09-20.** Fax 291/74-09-28. www.madeira-web.com/qsj. 43 units. 124€–168€ ($143–$193) double; 154€–187€ ($177–$215) junior suite; 179€–212€ ($206–$244) suite. Rates include breakfast. Half-board 28€–30€ ($32–$35). AE, DC, MC, V. Free parking. Bus: 11. **Amenities:** Restaurant; bar; pool; tennis court; health club; sauna; limited room service; babysitting; laundry; dry cleaning. *In room:* A/C, TV, dataport, minibar, hair dryer, safe.

4 Where to Dine in Funchal

Many guests dine at their hotels, but there's no reason you can't sneak away for a regional meal at one of the Funchal restaurants listed below. The list begins with the pick of the hotel restaurants.

EXPENSIVE

Chez Oscar/Restaurante Panorámico ★ INTERNATIONAL The smaller and more elegant of the Bestana Carlton Park Hotel's restaurants is Chez Oscar, housed in a large, modern room that opens onto a flowering terrace. Pin lighting, candles, and a polite uniformed staff add to the glamorous ambience. The Panorámico is larger and somewhat less personal but offers a cabaret performance on Sunday night. Both restaurants emphasize fresh ingredients. Chez Oscar's food is more exotic and experimental than at the Panorámico—for example, you might find grilled swordfish with sautéed pumpkin and basil-flavored marinara sauce. Dishes in either restaurant might include pork piccata, mixed grill of locally caught fish, roast lamb with thyme flowers, shellfish in saffron-flavored sauce, or chateaubriand for two.

Rua Emperatriz Doña Amelia, Quinta Vigia, Funchal. ✆ **291/20-91-00.** Reservations required. Chez Oscar main courses 8€–27€ ($9.20–$31). Buffet 28€ ($32). AE, DC, MC, V. Hours for both: Daily 7:30–9:30pm. Bus: 2, 12, or 16.

Fleur-de-Lys ★★ FRENCH Its most devoted admirers claim that this restaurant serves the finest food on Madeira. We rank it near the top. It's certainly scenic, with a panoramic view of the twinkling lights of Funchal. You can observe the activity in an open-grill kitchen. Reservations are important, and even with them you sometimes have a long wait. Meals are likely to include such well-prepared dishes as fresh lobster with mushrooms, shrimp in Pernod sauce, flavorful steak in peppercorn sauce, and veal medallions flavored with Calvados.

In the Hotel Savoy, Av. do Infante 9004-542. ✆ **291/21-30-00.** Reservations required. Main courses 16€–25€ ($18–$29). AE, DC, MC, V. Daily 7–11pm. Bus: 2, 6, 8, or 12.

Les Faunes ★★ FRENCH Try to dine at least once at Les Faunes, the island's finest hotel dining room, which takes its name from the series of Picasso lithographs decorating the walls. Live piano music accompanies your meal, and winter guests often dress for dinner, the men in black tie.

The chef offers a variety of French specialties and some typical Portuguese dishes. To begin, you can try everything from Portuguese soup to the chef's own smoked fish. Favorite entrees are *caldeirada* (fish stew) and lobster (grilled or poached). The chef's special pride is swordfish with banana. You can select from the dessert cart or ask for a hot soufflé, preferably made of passion fruit or strawberries.

In Reid's Palace, Estrada Monumental 139. © **291/71-71-71.** Reservations required. Jacket and tie required for men. Main courses 15€–28€ ($17–$32). AE, DC, MC, V. Daily 7:30–10:30pm. Closed in summer. Bus: 5 or 6.

Quinta Palmeira ★★ PORTUGUESE/INTERNATIONAL The best and most elegant restaurant in Madeira is in a beautiful country home dating from 1735. In fair weather, a table on the spacious veranda is the most desirable on the island. Manuel Jose da Sousa, the owner, insists on only the finest ingredients and the most talented chefs. They concoct such dishes as tender, perfectly seasoned grilled filet of beef on toast with Roquefort, served with Madeira wine. Among the fish selections, curried shrimp is a delight, and sautéed swordfish or salmon goes perfectly with lemon and butter sauce. Some meat dishes have island flair, appearing with regional fruit such as bananas or passion fruit. For a refreshing change of pace, opt for the homemade avocado ice cream.

Av. do Infante 17–19. © **291/22-18-14.** Reservations required. Main courses 17€–24€ ($19–$27). AE, DC, MC, V. Daily 11:30am–midnight. Bus: 9, 10, 12, 16, 43, or 44.

MODERATE

Casa Madeirense ★ PORTUGUESE/INTERNATIONAL Owner Filipe Gouveia extends a hearty welcome and is delighted when guests enjoy his elegant regional decor of *azulejos* (tiles) and hand-painted murals. The lively bar evokes a thatched-roof house in the village of Santana. Fresh fish and shellfish dominate the menu and are never better than in *cataplana de marisco* (savory shellfish stew). Tuna steak is grilled to perfection, and you can also enjoy tender, perfectly seasoned peppercorn steak or chateaubriand.

Estrada Monumental 153. © **291/76-67-00.** Reservations recommended. Main courses 15€–30€ ($17–$35). AE, DC, MC, V. Mon–Sat 1–3pm and 6:30–10:30pm. Closed Aug. Bus: 1, 2, or 4.

INEXPENSIVE

Casa da Carochinha (Lady Bird) *Kids* MADEIRAN/ENGLISH Casa da Carochinha faces the Centenary Gardens, near the tourist office. This is the only place on Madeira where the chef doesn't use garlic. Specialties include *coq au vin* (chicken cooked in wine), beef Stroganoff, roast beef with Yorkshire pudding, and duck with orange sauce. The cuisine is refined but hardly imaginative. You've had better versions of all these dishes, but the food is still satisfying and filling.

This is a favorite with families, especially those from Britain and the United States, because the cooks prepare familiar food without a lot of regional spicing and seasoning. Since all the food is cooked to order, families can come in here and request fish, meat, or poultry dishes pretty much as they'd like them (nothing too complicated, of course). There is no children's menu, but the cooks will prepare smaller portions for kids at reduced prices.

Rua de São Francisco 2A. © **291/22-36-95.** Reservations recommended for dinner. Main courses 6€–12€ ($6.90–$14). AE, DC, MC, V. Tues–Sat noon–3pm and 6–10pm. Tea Tues–Sat 3–5pm. Bus: 2, 12, or 16.

Dos Combatentes *Value* MADEIRAN This is a good choice for regional food. At the top of the Municipal Gardens, this simple restaurant serves well-prepared dishes, including rabbit stew, roast chicken, stewed squid, and sword-fish with bananas. Most dinners begin with a bowl of the soup of the day. Portions are ample, and two vegetables and a green salad come with the main dish. Desserts are likely to be simple—caramel custard, chocolate mousse, and fresh fruit. The waiters are efficient but not adept in English.

Rua Ivens 1. ✆ **291/22-13-88.** Main courses 5€–11€ ($5.75–$12). AE, DC, MC, V. Mon–Sat 11:45am–3pm and 6:30–10:30pm. Bus: 2, 12, or 16.

O Celeiro ★ *Finds* MADEIRAN This rustic restaurant serves some of the most authentic and best regional dishes in the capital. O Celeiro attracts visitors and businesspeople with reasonable prices and big helpings of delectable fare. Freshly caught swordfish is cooked with bananas, a longtime island favorite. Tuna steak is marinated in wine and garlic sauce and served with fresh mush-rooms. Our longtime favorite is *cataplana de marisco,* a kettle of seafood stew that tastes different every time we sample it. You might also opt for a tender steak in peppercorn sauce. With *espetada* (skewered beef on a spit), you'll want crusty bread for soaking up the juices.

Rua dos Aranhas 22. ✆ **291/23-06-22.** Reservations recommended. Main courses 10€–27€ ($12–$31). AE, DC, MC, V. Mon–Sat noon–3pm and 6–11pm. Bus: 2, 12, or 16.

O Patio *Kids* PORTUGUESE In the center of town, O Patio Jardim Tropi-cale is in the inner courtyard of a complex of commercial buildings, and its entrance, near a newspaper kiosk, is easy to miss. The restaurant is a welcome refuge from the noise and traffic outside. One of the best lunch bargains in Fun-chal is a heaping platter of the dish of the day, usually roast chicken or stewed codfish with onions. Meals, served on well-scrubbed wooden tables, might include beef or squid, or tuna steak with potatoes, followed by pineapple flambé. This is not the lightest fare on Madeira, but it can be satisfying and definitely filling, especially on a windy, rainy day. Though there is no particular menu for children, this restaurant attracts more family business, both visitors and locals, than any other restaurant in the center of Funchal. And kids like the many dishes that are familiar fare to them, including the roast chicken, the fresh fish, the roast beef, or the tuna steaks. The yummy desserts are also kid-pleasers.

Av. Zarco 21. ✆ **291/22-73-76.** Main courses 5€–11€ ($5.75–$13). AE, DC, MC, V. Mon–Sat noon–3pm and 7–10pm. Bus: 2, 12, or 16.

Pizzaria Xaramba *Value* PIZZA/PASTA The dining bargain of Funchal, and a magnet for young islanders, this pizza joint lies in the old town. It serves the best pizza in Funchal, as well as an array of succulent pastas, and does so long after other Funchal restaurants have closed for the night. You can watch as the cooks prepare your pie or opt for such rib-sticking fare as lasagna and ravioli Bolognese.

Rua Portão São Tiago 11. ✆ **291/22-97-85.** Reservations not accepted. Main courses 5€–12€ ($5.75–$14). No credit cards. Daily 6pm–4am. Bus: 2, 12, or 16.

ON THE OUTSKIRTS OF FUNCHAL

A Seta ★ MADEIRAN A Seta (The Arrow) specializes in supreme regional cuisine. It's almost midway between Funchal and Monte, 4km (2½ miles) from either, along winding roads. The mountainside restaurant, a favorite with tour groups, is a tavern where you can order inexpensive yet tasty meals. The rustic decor incorporates burned-wood trim, walls covered with pinecones, and crude pine tables.

First, a plate of homemade coarse brown bread still warm from the oven arrives at your table. Above each table is a hook with a long skewer of charcoal-broiled meat attached. You slip off chunks while mopping up juices with the crusty bread. There are three specialties: beef, chicken, and grilled dry codfish. Seasoned with olive oil, herbs, garlic, and bay leaves, these concoctions are called *espetadas*. Fried potatoes are always done well here (ask for some hot sauce).

Estrada do Livramento 80, Monte. ✆ **291/74-36-43.** Reservations recommended. Main courses 10€–22€ ($12–$25). AE, DC, MC, V. Thurs–Tues noon–3pm and 6–11pm. Bus: 19 or 23.

5 Exploring Madeira

SEEING THE SIGHTS IN FUNCHAL

Funchal's stately, beautiful **Praça do Município (Municipal Square)** is a study in light and dark; its plaza is paved with hundreds of black and white half-moons made from lava. (Masonry is a well-rehearsed Madeiran art form, and in Funchal, many of the sidewalks are paved with cobblestones that are arranged into repetitive patterns defined by contrasting colors.) The whitewashed buildings surrounding it have black-stone trim and ocher-tile roofs. On the south side of the square is a former archbishopric now devoted to a museum of religious art (see below). Rising to the east is the **Câmara Municipal** (city hall), once the 18th-century palace of a rich Portuguese nobleman. It's noted for its distinctive palace tower rising over the surrounding rooftops.

Sé (Cathedral) ★ The most intriguing of Funchal's churches is the rustic 15th-century Sé, with its Moorish carved cedar ceiling, stone floors, Gothic arches, stained-glass windows, and baroque altars. The cathedral is at the junction of four busy streets in the historic heart of town. Note that open hours are subject to change depending on church activities.

Rua do Aljube. ✆ **291/22-81-55.** Free admission; donation suggested. Mon–Sat 7am–1pm and 4–7pm, Sun 8am–8:30pm. Bus: 1, 2, 4, 5, or 6.

Museu da Quinta das Cruzes ★★ This museum is the former residence of João Gonçalves Zarco, who discovered Madeira in 1419. The surrounding park is of botanical interest and contains a noteworthy collection of orchids. The museum houses many fine examples of English furniture and China-trade porcelains brought to Madeira by expatriate Englishmen in the 18th century. You'll see rare Indo-Portuguese cabinets and the unique chests native to Madeira, fashioned from *caixas de açucár* (sugar boxes, dating from the 17th century). Also worth noting is a superb collection of antique Portuguese silver.

Calçada do Pico 1. ✆ **291/74-06-70.** Admission 3€ ($3.45). Tues–Sat 10am–12:30pm and 2–5:30pm, Sun 10am–1pm. Bus: 1, 2, 4, or 6.

Museu Municipal do Funchal The Municipal Museum displays land and aquatic animal life of the archipelago. Specimens include moray eels, eagle rays, scorpion fish, sea cucumbers, sea zephyrs, sharp-nosed puffers, and loggerhead turtles. Also on display are many of the beautifully plumed birds seen around Madeira, although the most interesting exhibit to us is the collection of ferocious-looking stuffed killer sharks, evocative of the film *Jaws*. Access is by private car or taxi; no buses are allowed. This is a very minor attraction and need not take up much more than 30 minutes of your time.

Rua da Mouraria 31. ✆ 291/22-97-61. Admission 2.10€ ($2.40), free for children under 12. Tues–Fri 10am–6pm, Sat–Sun noon–6pm. Bus: 1, 2, 4, or 6.

Museu de Arte Sacra The Museum of Sacred Art occupies an old bishop's house in the center of town. Many of its exhibitions came from island churches, some of which are no longer standing. Its most interesting collections are a series of paintings from the Portuguese and Flemish schools of the 15th and 16th centuries. The paintings are on wood (often oak); an outstanding example is the 1518 Adoration of the Magi. A rich merchant commissioned it and paid for it with sugar. A triptych depicts St. Philip and St. James, and there's an exceptional painting called Descent from the Cross. Ivory sculpture, gold and silver plate, and gilded wood ornamentations round out the collection.

Rua do Bispo 21. ✆ **291/22-89-00.** Admission 3€ ($3.45). Tues–Sat 10am–12:30pm and 2:30–6pm, Sun 10am–1pm. Bus: 1, 2, 4, 5, or 6.

Jardim Botânico ★ On the road to Camacha, about 4km (2½ miles) from Funchal, this botanical garden is one of the best in Portugal, with **faraway views** ★ of the bay. Opened by the government in 1960 on the grounds of the old Quinta do Bom Sucesso plantation, the garden includes virtually every tree or plant growing on Madeira. Some of the subtropical plants were imported from around the world, including anthuriums and birds-of-paradise from Africa and South America. A heather tree, discovered near Curral das Freiras, is said to be 10 million years old. The gardens open onto panoramic views of Funchal and its port.

Caminho do Meio. ✆ **291/21-12-00.** Admission 3€ ($3.45), children under 14 1€ ($1.15). Daily 9am–5:30pm. Bus: 29, 30, or 31.

EXPLORING THE REST OF THIS ISLAND

Funchal is an excellent launching pad for exploring the island's mountainous interior and lush coastlines. During your exploration of Madeira, you're likely to see many banana, date, and fruit trees. Please remember that these trees are grown to help local farmers make a living, and the fruity bounty should not be "harvested" for a picnic while touring the island.

THE OUTSKIRTS OF FUNCHAL

Immediately east of Funchal, the **Quinta do Palheiro Ferreiro** ★★ is a beautiful spot for a stroll. The mansion is the private property of the Blandy wine family, former owners of Reid's Palace. The 12-hectare (30-acre) estate, with some 3,000 plant species, is like a pleasure garden. The camellia blooms that burst into full flower from Christmas until early spring are reason enough to visit. You'll also see many rare flowers (often from Africa) and exotic trees.

The estate is open Monday through Friday from 9:30am to 12:30pm. Admission is 7€ ($8.05). Permission must be granted for picnics: Ask at the gate upon your arrival. Bus no. 36 from Funchal runs here. By car, drive 5km (3 miles) northeast of Funchal, following N101 toward the airport. Fork left onto N102 and follow signposts toward Camacha until you see the turnoff to the quinta.

The grandest *miradouro* (or belvedere) in Madeira is **Eira do Serrado** ★★★, at 1,175m (3,854 ft.). This belvedere looks out over the Grande Curral, which is the deep crater (nicknamed "the belly button" of the island) of a long extinct volcano in the center of Madeira. You can look down into this awesome crater, viewing farms built on terraces inside the crater itself. The panorama takes in all the craggy mountain summits of Madeira if the day is clear. You can drive all the way to the lookout point, where you can park your car and get out to take in the view. The location is 16km (10 miles) northwest of Funchal. To reach the lookout point, head west out of Funchal on Rua Dr. João Brito Câmara, which leads to a little road signposted to Pico Dos Barcelos. Follow the sign to Eira do Serrado until you reach the parking lot for the belvedere.

After taking in the view at the belvedere, head north along N107, which is signposted, to the stunningly situated village of **Curral das Freiras** ★, 6.5km (4 miles) north of Eira do Serrado. Meaning "Corral of the Nuns," the village in olden days was the center of the **Convento de Santa Clara,** where the sisters retreated for safety whenever Moorish pirates attacked Funchal. On the way to the village, the road goes through two tunnels cut through the mountains. Curral das Freiras sits in almost the exact geographic center of Madeira, lying in a valley of former volcanoes (all now extinct). The volcanoes surrounding Curral das Freiras were said to have been responsible for pushing up the land mass that is now Madeira from the sea. The village of whitewashed houses is centered on a small main square with a church of only passing interest. Most visitors stroll around the village, take in views of the enveloping mountains, have a cup of coffee at one of the cafes, and then head back to Funchal. Allow about 2 hours to make the 36km (22-mile) circuit of Eira do Serrado and Curral das Freiras.

Western Madeira

If time is limited, head for the western part of Madeira, where you'll find panoramic coastlines, dramatic waterfalls, and cliffs towering over the ocean. Leave Funchal on the coastal road, N101, heading west for 19km (12 miles) to the village of Câmara de Lobos, beloved by Sir Winston Churchill.

Câmara de Lobos

You approach the Room of the Wolves after passing terraces planted with bananas. The little fishing village of whitewashed red-tile-roofed cottages surrounds a cliff-sheltered harbor and rocky beach. If you come here around 7 or 8am, you can see fishers unloading their boats after a night at sea. There is nothing finer to do here than walk along the harbor taking in the view and perhaps deciding to follow Churchill's example and become a Sunday painter.

If you need a target for your sightseeing, head for **Henriques & Henriques Vinhos,** a winery at Estrada de Santa Clara 10, Sitio de Belém (✆ **291/94-15-51**), in the heart of the village, where you can tour the winery and buy wine. It is open Monday through Friday from 9am to 1pm and 2 to 5:30pm. Admission is free. The village also makes a good spot for lunch. The best place to eat is **Santo Antonio** (✆ **291/91-03-60**), some 5km (3 miles) from Câmara de Lobos, in the tiny village of **Estreito de Câmara de Lobos** (popularly known as Estreito). Near the little village church, owner Manuel Silvestro offers mostly grills, including golden chicken, cooked over an open hearth. A specialty is *espetada,* Madeira's most famous dish—delicately flavored skewered beef on a spit. Don't expect elegance—you dine at simple paper-covered tables on linoleum and mop up juices with crusty bread. Santo Antonio is open daily from noon to midnight; main courses cost 6€ to 14€ ($6.90–$16). Major credit cards are accepted, and no reservations are needed.

If you don't want to make the trek up to Estreito, try the **Coral Bar,** Largo da Republica 3 (✆ **291/94-24-69**), near the cathedral in Câmara de Lobos. The owner, Augustinho Ramos, secures the best of the day's catch for his Portuguese and international cuisine. His chefs turn out such dishes as the west coast's best *caldeirada* (fish stew) and swordfish grilled to perfection and topped with ham, cheese, and shrimp. Opt for a table on the rooftop terrace opening onto dramatic views of the fishing harbor itself and a backdrop of the cliffs of Cabo Girão. Hours are daily from 11am to 11pm, and reservations are suggested. Main courses cost 7.50€ to 17€ ($8.65–$20). Major credit cards are accepted.

Cabo Girão ★

The cliffs you might have seen from Câmara de Lobos lie 16km (10 miles) west of the village. To get to Cabo Girão, take R214 up a hill studded with pine and eucalyptus. From the 570m (1,870-ft.) belvedere, the panorama down the almost-sheer drop to the pounding ocean is thrilling. The terraced farms you'll see clinging to the cliff edges are cultivated entirely by hand because the plots are too small for either animal or machine.

Ribeira Brava

Continuing on the coast road west, you'll come to Ribeira Brava, which lies 15km (9⅓ miles) west of Cabo Girão and 48km (30 miles) west of Funchal. Meaning "Wide River," Ribeira Brava is a lovely little Madeiran village (founded in 1440) and the sunniest spot on the island. It even has what locals refer to as a "beach," although you might view it as a strip of pebbles along the water.

We like to visit the village for its bustling seafront fruit market, which is active every morning except Sunday. Even if you don't buy anything, it's worth a stroll through the market to take in the amazing bounty grown in the mountains of Madeira. It also provides a great photo opportunity. As you stroll through the village, you'll encounter locals selling island handcrafts, and you can visit a little 16th-century church in the center of the village. It has absolutely no artistic treasures, but locals are fond of pointing it out to visitors anyway. There is one more sight, the ruins of the 17th-century **Forte de São Bento.** This towered fort once protected the fishing village against pirates from the African coast to the east. From Ribeira Brava, head north along N104 to the center of the island, toward Serra de Agua.

Serra de Agua

Serra de Agua, a little village 6.5km (4 miles) north of Ribeira Brava, is reached by trasversing a sheer canyon. One of the best centers for exploring Madeira's lush interior, it's also the site of one of the island's best *pousadas* (government-sponsored inns). Surrounded by abundant crops, jade-green fields, ferns, bamboo, weeping willows, and plenty of waterfalls, the village enjoys one of the loveliest settings in Madeira. Come here not for attractions, but for pure scenic beauty, though you should be warned that mist and clouds often shroud the town.

For dining and lodging, seek out the **Pousada dos Vinháticos,** Estrada de São Vicente Serra de Agua, 9350 Ribeira Brava (✆ **291/95-23-44;** fax 291/95-25-40), near the top of a pass on the winding road to São Vicente. You can visit for a meal or spend the night. The solid stone pousada, a tavern-style building with a brick terrace, opened in 1940. The tasty food is hearty and unpretentious, often depending on the catch of the day. Specialties include *espetada* (a swordfish version), ox tongue with Madeira sauce, and local beef flavored with regional wines. Main courses cost 10€ to 20€ ($12–$23); hours are daily from noon to 6pm and 7 to 9pm. Reservations are recommended.

Most of the immaculate guest rooms are done in Portuguese modern style; a few contain antiques. All have good views. The price of a double is 80€ ($92), including breakfast. Major credit cards are accepted, and parking is free.

From Serra de Agua, the route climbs to the 990m (3,247 ft.) **Boca de Encumeada** ★, or Encumeada Pass, 6.5km (4 miles) north of Serra de Agua. It's one of the island's best centers for hiking (information about hiking is available from the tourist office in Funchal), and a belvedere affords great panoramas over both sides of Madeira.

Following the route northwest of Boca de Encumeada, you reach the village of São Vicente, 14km (8⅔ miles) northwest of Boca de Encumeada and 56km (35 miles) northwest of Funchal.

São Vicente

One of the best-known towns on the north coast lies where the São Vicente River meets the ocean. Again, you come here for the sweeping views, some of the most dramatic on the island. Part of the fun of going to São Vicente is taking the one-lane north coast route. In a miraculous and costly feat of engineering, it was chiseled out of pure cliff face. It's a nightmare if you encounter one of the bloated tour buses taking this highway. You'll often have to back up because the drivers rarely give way. Constructed in 1950 and nicknamed the "gold road," the drive offers views of water cascading down the slopes. Many locals have planted vineyards in this seemingly inhospitable terrain.

In such a remote outpost, an inn comes as a welcome relief. You'll find good food and lodging at **Estalagem do Mar,** Juncos, Fajã da Areia, 9240 São Vicente (✆ **291/84-00-10;** fax 291/84-00-19). Most visitors pass through here only to dine on the excellent regional and international cuisine. Specialties include swordfish prepared in almost any style. Many versions of sea bass are served, and the meat dishes—especially perfectly grilled veal chop and beef filet in mushroom cream sauce—are also good. Main courses cost 10€ to 20€ ($12–$23), with a set menu for 15€ ($17); it's open daily from noon to 3pm and 7 to 9:30pm. Reservations are recommended.

If you decide to spend the night, the 90-room inn offers rather simply furnished accommodations opening onto views of the ocean. The inn has a provincial look, with flowery curtains and spreads, but rooms are modern with tiled bathrooms, TVs, and phones. On the premises are an indoor and outdoor pool, a tennis room, a Jacuzzi, a sauna, a gym, and a game room. Limited room service is available. The three-floor hotel was built in the early 1990s and was last renovated in 1998. A double costs 60€ ($69) and a suite costs 80€ ($92), including breakfast. Parking is free. Major credit cards are accepted, and reservations are recommended.

From São Vicente, you can continue west along N101 to the town of Porto Moniz, 16km (10 miles) away in one of the remotest parts of Madeira.

Porto Muniz ★

This portion of the "gold road" is one of the most difficult but dramatic drives in Portugal, requiring nerves of steel. The road is boldly cut into the side of a towering cliff that plunges vertically into the ocean below. Eventually you arrive at Porto Moniz, a fishing village of great charm built at the site of a sheltered anchorage shaped by a slender peninsula jutting out toward an islet, Ilhéu Mole. This is the only sheltered harbor on the north coast of Madeira. Porto Moniz boasts no major sights other than the old village itself, with its fishermen's cottages and cobbled lanes. The adventure is surviving the trip.

For the best food in the area, head for **Residencial Orca,** Vila do Porto Moniz, Porto Moniz 9270 (✆ **291/85-00-00;** fax 291/85-00-19). The former inn also serves excellent regional cuisine. Tasty options include swordfish in mushroom and cream sauce, filet of beef served with dates, and fresh tuna steak breaded in corn flour and then sautéed and served with country cabbage and potatoes. Main courses cost 8.50€ to 35€ ($9.80–$40). Food is served daily from noon to 4pm and 7 to 9:30pm. Major credit cards are accepted, and reservations are recommended.

Aquário ★ is a real discovery, serving some of the freshest and finest fish dishes on the island, all at very affordable prices. This waterfront restaurant (Seixal, Porto Moniz; ✆ **291/85-43-96**) is too often ignored by visitors who flock to the other dining spots in Porto Muniz. Your meal begins here when the waiter comes around and serves you a heaping basket of homemade bread and a carafe of the local wine. The soups—especially the wonderfully spicy fish soup—are hearty and the portions are generous. The best main courses are the grilled fish of the day. The filet of swordfish with rice studded with morsels of seafood is our favorite. The cooks also prepare a nightly selection of fresh vegetables. Main courses are 8€ to 9€ ($9.20–$10). Major credit cards are accepted. It's open daily from noon to 7pm.

After leaving Porto Moniz, you can continue southwest along N101, going back along a winding road via Ribeira Brava and Câmara de Lobos until you finally make the full circuit back into Funchal.

SANTANA & CENTRAL MADEIRA

For a final look at Madeira, you can cut through the center of the island, heading north from Funchal. This route takes you to such scenic highlights as Pico do Arieiro and Santana, and is one of the finest parts of Madeira for mountain hiking.

Pico do Arieiro ★★

This mountain and the settlement built on its side, 36km (22 miles) north of Funchal, really evoke the island's volcanic nature. When the 1,780m (5,838-ft.) peak is not covered by clouds (it's likely to be obscured Dec–Mar), the panoramas are stunning. Pico do Arieiro is the third-tallest mountain on the island. To reach it, follow Rua 31 de Janeiro out of Funchal, and take N103 as it climbs to Monte. When you reach the pass at Poiso, some 10km (6¼ miles) north of Monte, take a left and continue to follow the signposts into Pico do Arieiro. The best access (and most scenic route) to Pico Ruivo is from Pico do Arieiro. The hike is 8km (5 miles) on foot and takes approximately 4 hours.

Once at the **miradouro** ★ (belvedere) at Pico do Arieiro, you'll have a panoramic sweep of the central mountains of Madeira. To the southeast is the village of Curral das Freiras (see above). To the immediate northeast you can take in a panorama of Penha d'Aguia (Eagle's Rock), a rocky spike that is one of the most photographed sites in Madeira. You will also have a view of Pico Ruivo to the northwest (Madeira's highest point, at 1,860m/6,101 ft.), which can be accessed from Pico do Arieiro by a difficult 8km (5-mile) hill walk.

One of the island's most delightful pousadas is up in the mountains at Pico do Arieiro. The 25-unit **Pousada do Arieiro,** Santa Ana, 9230, Funchal (✆ **291/23-01-10;** fax 291/22-86-11), offers some of the finest lodgings and the best cuisine in the area. Built in 1989, the inn was last renovated in 1998. Its midsize rooms are comfortably furnished, with fine mattresses, TVs, phones, and neatly kept and efficiently organized private bathrooms, each medium in size and lined with tiles and containing a shower-tub combination. Doubles cost 90€ to 131€ ($104–$151) with half-board. There is no actual address or route number; however, the place is signposted along the road and is easy to spot. Driving time from Funchal is 1 hour and 15 minutes. Santana, the closest town, lies 45 minutes away.

The view from the pousada's rustic dining room is reason enough to eat here, but the food is good, too. The international and regional dishes include everything from codfish in creamy onion and garlic sauce to rack of lamb flavored with rosemary and honey and served with sweet potatoes. Pepper steak is flambéed at the table, and you can also order such classics as veal Marsala or marinated tuna steak sautéed with onions. Main courses cost 12€ to 15€ ($14–$17), and hours are daily from noon to 3pm and 7 to 9pm; major credit cards are accepted. Reservations are recommended.

Ribeiro Frio ★

Instead of taking the left fork at Poiso (see above) and heading for Pico do Arieiro, you can go straight to reach Ribeiro Frio, an enchanting spot 11km (6¾ miles) north of Poiso.

Ribeiro Frio (Cold River) is a little village in the Madeira Forest Park (a protected area of trees and mountains in the center of Madeira that is spared from development) that occupies a dramatic setting in view of waterfalls, jagged peaks, and sleepy valleys.

You can take one of the most dramatic walks in Madeira from Ribeiro Frio. Just follow the signposts from Ribeiro Frio directing you to the **Balcões** ★★. This walk passes along Levada do Furado and takes you on footpaths cut out of basalt rock until you reach the belvedere, whose dizzying perch overlooks the jagged peaks of the Pico do Arieiro, Pico das Torres, and Pico Ruivo. This 40-minute walk is of only moderate difficulty and is suitable for the average visitor with no special hiking skills.

If the mountain air gives you an appetite, head south from Balcões for a 5-minute drive to **Victor's Bar,** on N103 in Ribeiro Frio (✆ **291/57-58-98**), a chaletlike mountain restaurant known for afternoon tea and good regional food and wine. Trout from the area hatchery (prepared in a variety of ways) is a specialty; we prefer it grilled golden brown. You'll also find typical Madeiran cuisine, including lamb stew with potatoes, and swordfish with bananas. Main courses cost 10€ to 14€ ($12–$16). The restaurant is open daily from 9am to 7pm; reservations are recommended. Major credit cards are accepted.

Follow N103 out of Ribeiro Frio, heading north toward the coast. In the village of Faial, you'll find a connecting route, signposted west, to the village of Santana.

Santana ★

Eighteen kilometers (11 miles) northwest of Ribeiro Frio and 40km (25 miles) north of Funchal, Santana is the most famous village in Madeira and certainly the prettiest. It is noted for its A-framed, thatched-roof cottages called *palheiros.* Painted in bright, often flamboyant colors, they are the most-photographed private residences on the island. On a coastal plateau, Santana lies at an altitude of 742m (2,434 ft.).

You can find food and lodging at one of the most frequented establishments on the north coast, **Quinta da Furão,** Achado do Gramacho, 9230, Santana (✆ **291/57-01-00;** fax 291/57-35-60). The 43-unit inn lies in a vineyard on a cliff-top setting that opens onto a panorama of the ocean. Most visitors stay just for the day to sample the cuisine, which is the finest on the north coast. The rustic dining room serves Madeiran, Portuguese, and international cuisine. Dishes include swordfish cooked with banana, grilled T-bone steak in garlic butter, and filet of beef baked in a pastry case and served with Roquefort sauce. The goat cheese of the region is a delight. Main courses cost 10€ to 13€ ($12–$15).

Open hours are daily from noon to 3pm and 7 to 9:30pm. Reservations are recommended.

The inn is also a delightful place to stay. The ample guest rooms are well furnished in the regional style, with excellent mattresses, TVs, phones, and small to midsize bathrooms that are tiled and neatly kept, each with a shower-tub combination. Some accommodations open onto sea views, and others face the mountains. The inn has a swimming pool, gym, Jacuzzi, and pub. Doubles with half-board cost 115€ to 125€ ($132–$144), including breakfast. Parking is free. Major credit cards are accepted at the hotel and the restaurant.

6 Sports & Outdoor Activities on Madeira

The pleasant climate on Madeira invites visitors to enjoy outdoor activities, even if they consist mainly of strolling through Funchal and along park pathways and country lanes.

DEEP-SEA FISHING This is a popular sport on Madeira. The catch is mainly longtail tuna, blue marlin, swordfish, and several varieties of shark. Most boat rentals are moderately priced. The tourist office (see "Essentials," earlier in this chapter) can supply information about boat rentals and rates.

GOLF The island maintains two l8-hole courses, both open to the public and accustomed to foreigners. The easier and better established is the **Campo de Golfe de Madeira,** in the hamlet of Santo da Serra (✆ **291/55-01-00**), on the island's northeastern side, about 24km (15 miles) from Funchal. Greens fees are 70€ ($81) for 18 holes. On rocky, steep terrain that some golfers find annoying is the **Pelero Golf Course,** in the hamlet of **São Gonçalo,** 9050 Funchal (✆ **291/79-01-20**), about 5km (3 miles) north of Funchal. It charges 70€ ($81) for 18 holes. Clubs and carts are for rent at both establishments, and local caddies are available. At both courses there's a clubhouse with a bar and restaurant, and both are abundantly accented with mimosas, pines, and eucalyptus trees.

SWIMMING Madeira doesn't have beaches. If your hotel doesn't have swimming facilities, you can use those of the **Complexo Balnear do Lido** (Lido Swimming Pool Complex), Rua do Gorgulho (✆ **291/76-22-17**), which has an outdoor Olympic-size pool as well as a spacious outdoor pool for children. It's open daily in summer from 8:30am to 8pm, and off season from 9am to 7pm. Adults pay 2.60€ ($3). Children under 10 are free with parents; otherwise, they pay 1.30€ ($1.50) to use the pool. You can rent lounge chairs and umbrellas for 2€ ($2.30). The complex has a cafe, a restaurant, an ice-cream parlor, bars, and facilities for exercising in the water. To get there from Funchal, take N101 west for 5 minutes until you see the turnoff for Rua do Gorgulho, at which point you head south along this road to the Lido complex. The Lido is signposted from N101—you shouldn't have any trouble finding it. By public transit, take bus no. 6.

TOBOGGAN RIDES By far the most entertaining rides on the island are on the two- or three-passenger toboggans, which resemble big wicker baskets resting on wooden runners. You get into one of the cushioned passenger seats for a ride down the slippery-smooth cobblestones, which takes about 20 minutes to reach Funchal. Runners are greased with suet to make them go smoother. Trained sled drivers run alongside the sled. If the sled starts to go too fast, they can hop on the back of it and slow it down. Originally, these sleds were used to transport produce from Monte to Funchal. But over the years tourists began to request rides in them, and an island attraction was born. When you pass Terreiro da Luta, a point along the way of your ride (at a height of 875m/2,870 ft.), you'll enjoy a panoramic view of Funchal and see monuments to Zarco and Our Lady of Peace.

Before you begin your descent, visit the **Church of Nossa Senhora do Monte,** which contains the iron tomb of the last of the Hapsburgs, Emperor Charles, who died of pneumonia on Madeira in 1922. From a belvedere nearby, you can look down on the whole of Funchal.

Toboggan rides from Monte to Funchal cost 10€ ($11.50) per passenger and end up at Strada do Lebramento in Funchal. For more information, contact **Carreiros dos Montes** (✆ **291/78-39-19**).

WATERSPORTS The activities desks of several major hotels, including the **Hotel Savoy** and **Reid's Palace** (see "Where to Stay," earlier in this chapter), can arrange water-skiing, windsurfing, and rental of boats or sailing dinghies for guests and nonguests. If you want to go snorkeling or scuba diving, check with the **Madeira Carlton Hotel,** Largo António Nobre 9004-531 (✆ **291/23-95-00**).

7 Shopping in Madeira

Crafts are rather expensive on the island, but collectors might want to seek out exquisite Madeira embroidery or needlework. Check to see that merchandise has a lead seal attached to it, certifying that it was made on Madeira and not imported. The businesses listed in this section are all in Funchal.

At the factory **Patricio & Gouveia,** Rua do Visconde de Anadia 33 (✆ **291/22-29-28**), you can see employees making stencil patterns on embroidery and checking for quality of materials, though the actual embroidery is done in private homes and this process is not likely to be of great interest to anyone not seriously interested in embroidery. Of the several embroidery factories of Funchal, this is not only the most famous but also the best place to buy embroidery because many of the routine souvenir shops scattered throughout the island sell embroidery from Taiwan and other places. The embroidery at Patrico & Gouveia, however, is the real thing—every item is guaranteed to be handmade on the island. **Bordac-Bordados de Madeira,** Rua Doctor Ferñao Ornelas 77 (✆ **291/22-29-65**), also carries an outstanding selection of completed embroidery.

A German family introduced needlepoint and tapestry making to Madeira at the turn of the 20th century. It has been a tradition ever since. You can visit the needlepoint and tapestry factory of **Kiekeben Tapestries,** Rua da Carreira 194 (✆ **291/23-12-01**), or its nearby shop, **Bazar Maria Kiekeben,** Avenida do Infante 2 (✆ **291/22-78-57**). This is the most famous needlepoint factory on Madeira, established in 1938 by the Kiekeben family from Germany who began making tapestries almost like Impressionist paintings, often evoking the most famous tapestries in the world from the Gobelins factory outside Paris. Other subjects include reproductions of famous paintings, flowers of Madeira, and island landscapes. Original commissions are also accepted.

CRAFT SHOPS & FACTORIES

Camacha Wickerworks This is a showcase for the wickerwork for which Madeirans have long been noted. Most of the products—everything from giraffes to sofas—were made in the village of Camacha, about 10km (6¼ miles) from Funchal. The store arranges shipment of items too large to carry home. Avenida Arriaga. ✆ **291/92-21-14.**

Casa do Turista Near the waterfront in Funchal, this is the best place on the island for Madeira handcrafts. On the patio, with a fountain and semitropical greenery, is a miniature village, with small-scale typical rooms furnished in the local style. The merchandise includes handmade embroideries in linen or cotton (the fabric is often imported from Switzerland and Ireland), tapestries, wickerwork, Portuguese pottery and ceramics, Madeiran wines, fruit, and flowers. You'll find all types of embroidery and appliqués, as well as "shadow work" (a technique in which stitching takes place on the reverse of a transparent fabric, with the design showing through to the front in a very subtle manner). Prices are determined by the number of stitches. Rua do Conselheiro José Silvestre Ribeiro 2. ✆ **291/22-49-07.**

Casa Oliveira There's an embroidery factory on the premises of this shop. The store is primarily a retail outlet for one of the largest embroidery manufacturers in town, and everything sold in this shop is handmade on the island. It turns out everything from embroidered towels to delicate negligees to elegant "heirloom" tablecloths. The outlet is also known for its handmade ceramics, which are hand painted. For those seeking island souvenirs such as T-shirts, there is a large selection here, too. Rua da Alfândega 11. ✆ **291/22-93-40.**

Lino and Araujo, Ltd. The specialty here is hand-embroidered and hand-knitted goods, one of the island's best selections. Many non-Portuguese residents of Madeira frequent the shop, which sells towels, exquisite tablecloths, and traycloths. The place also offers an unusual collection of island ceramics, based on designs of original pieces created in the 17th century. For shoppers who don't want to make "serious" purchases, the outlet sells a collection of T-shirts and towels printed (not embroidered) with the word *Madeira.* Rua das Murcas 15. ✆ **291/77-31-17.**

Madeira Superbia This shop, known for its fine embroidery, also specializes in handmade tapestries. The embroideries and tapestries are virtually the same as in the other shops we recommend. What sets this store apart, however, is its large assortment, including embroidered towels, tablecloths, and bed coverings. Most of the tapestries sold here are modern but based on antique designs, often going back to the 17th century. This shop also stocks merchandise in a wide price range, from inexpensive to prohibitive. Rua do Carmo 27. ✆ **291/22-40-23.**

WINE

MADEIRA WINE Funchal is the center of Madeira's **wine industry.** Grapes have grown in the region since the early 15th century, when Henry the Navigator introduced vines and sugarcane to the island's slopes. Every Madeira wine is fortified, brought up to full strength with high-proof grape brandy. The distinctive flavor of Madeira comes from being kept for months in special rooms called *estufas.* These estufas have high temperatures instead of the cool chambers where most bottles of wine are stored. *Madeira* refers to a whole body of wines that ranges from very sweet to very dry. Even the cheapest Madeira is quite remarkable, and the French, among others, use the least expensive Madeira for cooking, which adds more flavor than sherry or Marsala.

The light-colored Sercial, with a very dry taste, is gently scented. This wine is often compared to a Fino Sherry, although Sercial has its own special bouquet and character. Bual (sometimes known as Boal) is more golden in color and is a medium sweet wine, sometimes served as a dessert wine. It is velvety in content, its color ranging from a dark gold to a brown. Mainly a dessert wine, Malmsey is sweet, chestnut brown Madeira. The grapes that today produce Malmsey were the first ever shipped to the island.

Madeira Wine Company, Avenida Arriaga 28 (© **291/74-01-00**), a well-stocked wine shop next to the tourist office, offers samples from the diverse stock, which covers virtually every vintage produced on the island for the past 35 years. The shop is housed in a former convent dating from 1790. The building contains murals depicting the wine pressing and harvesting processes, which proceed according to the traditions established hundreds of years ago. You can savor a wide range of Madeira wines in a setting of old wine kegs and time-mellowed chairs and tables made from kegs. Admission is free; it's open Monday through Friday from 9:30am to 6:30pm, and Saturday from 10am to 1pm. **Guided tours,** conducted at 10:30am, 2:30pm, and 3:30 pm, cost 4€ ($4.60). Tours last 1 hour and take visitors into a museum of antique wine-making equipment and past displays of some of the oldest bottles of Madeira wine. The highlight of the tour, however, is when visitors are taken into a cellar bodega for an actual wine-tasting.

MARKETS AND BAZAARS

The Workers' Market, **Mercado dos Lavradores,** at Rua Hospital Velho, is in full swing Monday through Saturday from 7am to 8pm but is liveliest in the morning. Flower vendors dressed in typical Madeiran garb of corselets, leather boots, and striped skirts will generally let you photograph them if you ask them—especially if you buy some flowers. The market is filled with stalls selling island baskets, crafts, fruits, and vegetables, and offers Madeira's largest array of that day's fish catch.

In Funchal's **bazaars,** you can purchase needlepoint tapestries, Madeiran wines, laces, embroidery on Swiss organdy or Irish linen, as well as local craft items like goat-skin boots, Camacha basketry, and other eclectic merchandise. The colorful **City Market,** at Praça do Comércio Monday through Saturday, offers everything from yams to papaws to a wide array of handcrafts including products in wicker and leather. Bazaars are found throughout the center of Funchal.

At these bazaars, there are good deals on handmade shoes and tooled leather. However, prices on other items (embroidery, needlework, table linens, and tropical flowers) can be high, so have an idea of what you want to pay for certain items and sharpen your bargaining skills before going. Madeira is an excellent place to buy tropical (though expensive) flowers such as orchids and birds of paradise, all of which can be shipped to the United States. U.S. Customs allows flowers of Madeira into the United States, as long as they are inspected at any American airport upon arrival.

8 Madeira After Dark

The glittering **Entertainment Complex at the Casino Park Hotel,** Avenida do Infante, Funchal (© **291/20-91-00**), is the most obvious entertainment venue for first-time visitors. The complex offers an array of options. Foremost is a **casino,** the only one on Madeira, which offers roulette, French banque, craps, blackjack, and slot machines. To be admitted, you must present a passport or other form of identification and pay a 3€ ($3.45) government tax. The casino is open daily from 4pm to 3am.

Nearby, on Avenida do Infante, is a dance club, **Copacabana,** that's liveliest after 11pm Thursday through Saturday; it charges a cover (including one drink) of 6€ ($6.90). On Sunday at 9pm, the hotel offers a Las Vegas–style cabaret show. For the show only, there's a minimum bar tab of 14€ ($16) per person; dinner, two drinks, and a view of the show costs 42€ ($48). In addition, the complex contains bars, kiosks, and boutiques. You must be 18 or older to enter.

Options outside the casino complex are limited, although some hotels present dinner shows. Funchal isn't the best place in Portugal to hear fado, but you can sample the music at **Arsênios,** Rua de Santa Maria 169 (✆ **291/22-40-07**), which serves dinners from 15€ ($17). It's open daily from 6 to 10pm.

Teatro Municipal Baltazar Diaz, Avenida Arriaga (✆ **291/23-35-69**), in the center of Funchal, presents plays (in Portuguese only) and occasional classical music concerts. The tourist office has information, and tickets can be purchased at the box office.

There's limited dance club action, notably at **Vespas,** Avenida Sá Carneiro 7 (✆ **291/23-48-00**), a warehouselike club near the docks. This postmodern place attracts a young crowd. It's open Thursday through Saturday from 10pm to either 2 or 3am (depending on business). If you're over 35, you might head for the spacious **O Farol,** Largo António Nobre 9007 (✆ **291/23-95-00**), in the Madeira Carlton Hotel. It features modern dance music and hits from the 1970s and '80s. Hours are Thursday through Saturday from 10:30pm to 3am. Neither club has a cover charge.

Prince Albert, Rua da Imperatriz Dona Amélia (✆ **291/23-57-93**), is a Victorian pub complete with plush cut-velvet walls, tufted banquettes, and English pub memorabilia. Next to the Savoy, it serves English spirits and oversize mugs of beer at the curved bar and at tables under Edwardian fringed lamps. It's open daily from noon to midnight.

You also might try the restaurant/taverna **A Seta,** where you can sample the local wine until 11pm. (See "Where to Dine Nearby," earlier in chapter.)

9 Porto Santo ★

39km (24 miles) NE of Madeira

The second major island of the Madeira archipelago is Porto Santo, an arid landmass that presents a marked contrast to the lushness of the main island. It is 14km (8⅔ miles) long and 5km (3 miles) wide, with a 6.5km (4-mile) strip of fine sandy beach along the southern shore. The island is not as hilly as Madeira: Its highest elevation is about 509m (1,670 ft.) above sea level, at **Pico do Facho.**

João Gonçalves Zarco and Tristão Vaz Teixiera, who discovered Madeira, landed on Porto Santo in 1418 when they took refuge from a storm. To express gratitude for their survival, they named the island Porto Santo (Holy Port). It was not until 1419 that the men were able to sail on and make landfall on the main island. Prince Henry the Navigator gave Teixiera and Zarco authority to run Madeira, but he placed Porto Santo in the hands of Bartolomeu Perestrello.

The island gets very dry in summer, which makes it popular with beachgoers but not good for crops. The foodstuffs grown on Porto Santo in the winter include grain, tomatoes, figs, and melons, as well as grapes, from which sweet wines are made. A few remaining unusual windmills crown the island's low hills.

The water of Porto Santo supposedly has therapeutic value. It's a popular drink not only on the island, but also in Madeira and Portugal. The water-bottling plants, fish canneries, and a lime kiln make up the island's industries.

ESSENTIALS

ARRIVING

BY PLANE The flight from Madeira to the little **Campo de Cima** airport, Strada Regionale 101, at Porto Santo takes only 15 minutes. (The views are spectacular.) Always reserve well in advance for July and August, when beach lovers descend en masse. Flights generally cost 42€ ($48) one-way and 84€ ($97) round-trip. In peak season, count on eight flights per day; frequency diminishes in the off season. For ticket reservations and information, call ✆ **707/205-700** or 291/98-21-46. (See "Essentials," earlier in this chapter, for information on arriving from Lisbon or international destinations.) The airport lies right outside of town, a 30-minute walk from the center. Taxis meet all arriving flights, and a fare into town typically costs 4€ ($4.60). There is no bus service from the airport to the center of town.

BY BOAT Regularly scheduled ferry service connects Madeira and Porto Santo. The Lobo Marinho departs Funchal Harbor daily. Tickets cost 53€ ($61) round-trip if you return the same day. If you stay more than 1 night, a round-trip ticket costs 44€ ($51).

Saturday through Thursday, the ferry usually departs Madeira at 8am and arrives in Porto Santo at 10:30am. The departure from Madeira on Friday isn't until 6pm. Always check the schedules for return trips from Porto Santo, which vary. Tickets can be purchased at the **Lobo Marinho** office, Rua da Praia, Funchal (✆ **291/98-29-38**), Monday through Friday from 9am to 12:30pm and 2:30 to 6pm. On weekends, you can buy a ticket at any travel agency in Funchal.

The boats arrive at a little port about a 30-minute walk from the center of town. Taxis await arriving boats and will take you into the center or to one of the nearby hotels for 5€ ($5.75). There is also bus service into the center, which costs 1€ ($1.15) per passenger.

VISITOR INFORMATION

The **tourist office** is on Avenida Vieira de Castro (✆ **291/98-23-61**) in Vila Baleira, the island's capital. It's open Monday through Friday from 9am to 5:30pm, and Saturday from 10am to 12:30pm.

GETTING AROUND

Most visitors get around on foot or rely on a **taxi** (✆ **291/98-23-34**) for excursions. In town, you can usually pick up a taxi along Rua Doctor Nuno Teixeira. Car rentals can be arranged at **Mainho,** at Porto Santo Airport (✆ **291/98-27-80**).

EXPLORING THE ISLAND

Most visitors come here strictly for the wide beach of golden sand along the southern coast. It's ideal for swimming in unpolluted waters or for long strolls. If you tear yourself from the beach for a day, you will find some minor attractions. **Vila Baleira,** a sleepy town of whitewashed stucco houses, merits an hour of your time. You'll be following in the footsteps of Christopher Columbus as you make your way along its cobblestone streets.

Locals call the town Vila, and it lies at the center of the 6.5km-long (4-mile-long) beach. Stop for a drink at Café Ballena on **Largo de Pelourinho** ★, the main square. Shaded by palm trees, it is the center of life on the island. To the right of the Church of Our Lady of Piedad, follow a sign along the alley to the Casa de **Cristovão Colombo,** Travessa de Sacristia 4 (✆ **291/98-34-05**). The explorer is said to have lived here with his wife, Isobel Moniz. Documentation about the Columbus visit to Porto Santo is skimpy, but it appears that he did live here for a short time. In an annex, you can view maps and engravings depicting major events in his life. The museum is open Tuesday through Friday from 10am to 6pm, and Saturday and Sunday from 10am to 1pm. Admission is free.

Later you can follow Rua Infante Dom Henrique, off Largo do Pelourinho, to a beach-surrounded, flower-filled **park** with a statue dedicated to Columbus. This is one of the most restful and scenic spots on the island.

After seeing the town and its meager attractions, you can visit some of the island's scenic highlights. They include **Pico do Castelo,** north of Vila Baleira, on a small and difficult road. It affords a perspective on the whole island and endless views of the sea. Pick up picnic provisions at one of the little shops in Vila Baleira. A fortified castle once stood here to guard Vila Baleira from attacks by pirates. Only four cannons remain—islanders removed most of the castle's stone for building materials. The island government has planted pine trees to keep the air moist, but they never grow beyond 3m (9¾ ft.), so as not to obscure the view. From Pico do Castelo, you can follow signs to **Pico do Facho,** the tallest point on the island.

At the southwestern tip of the island, **Ponta da Calheta** is another scenic destination. To get there, take the road west out of Vila Baleira. It has a view of the little offshore island of Baixo, across a dangerous channel riddled with reefs. The beach is made of black basalt rocks, so it's not suitable for swimming.

Directly north lies another of the island's great lookout points, **Pico dos Flores.** Access is over a pothole-riddled dirt road. The cliffs here also have a panoramic view of the islet of Baixo, to your left. The tiny islet to your right is Ferro.

While in the southwestern part of the island, you can also follow the signs to **A Pedreira** ★, on the slopes of Pico de Ana Ferreira. The amazing basalt rock formation brings to mind organ pipes stretching toward the sky.

WHERE TO STAY

MODERATE

Porto Santo ★ Right on the beach, a 15-minute walk from the center of town, this has been one of the leading hotels on the island since it opened in 1979, although it is now surpassed by the Torre Praia Suite Hotel. Outside your window, you'll see a wide stretch of beach. The government-rated four-star hotel, renovated in 1996, is 1.75km (1 mile) from the town of Vila Baleira. It's a two-story building decorated in contemporary style in a peaceful garden setting. The midsize rooms are standard but well furnished. All have well-maintained bathrooms containing shower-tub combinations. Make reservations far in advance if you plan to visit in August. There's a bar in the restaurant, which serves regional and international cuisine, plus another on the beach. In the summer, the lavish Wednesday night buffet is the hottest ticket on the island.

Campo Baixo, 9400-015 Porto Santo. ✆ **291/98-01-40.** Fax 291/98-01-49. 94 units. 100€–159€ ($115–$183) double. Rates include breakfast. AE, DC, MC, V. Free parking. Bus: 3 or 4. **Amenities:** Restaurant; 2 bars; 2 pools; minigolf; tennis courts; health club; sauna; babysitting; laundry service; dry cleaning. *In room:* A/C, TV, dataport, minibar, hair dryer, safe.

Torre Praia Suite Hotel ★★ The island's premier hotel is on the outskirts of Vila Baleira, adjacent to its own beach. Opened in the summer of 1993 and rated four stars by the government, it offers midsize to spacious guest rooms. Spread over three stories, they're well furnished, with excellent beds and state-of-the-art plumbing. All have neatly kept bathrooms equipped with shower-tub combinations. Most have water views. Despite the name, the hotel has only three suites. The restaurant, constructed around an old watchtower, is one of the island's best. There is a bar with a great view on top of the hotel.

Rua Goulart Medeiros, 9400-164 Porto Santo. ✆ **291/98-04-50.** Fax 291/98-24-87. www.torrepraia.pt. 66 units. 77€–160€ ($89–$184) double; 150€–185€ ($173–$213) triple; 120€–225€ ($108–$203) suite. Rates include breakfast. AE, DC, MC, V. Free parking. **Amenities:** 2 restaurants; 2 bars; pool; health club; Jacuzzi; sauna; game room; room service; babysitting; laundry service; dry cleaning. *In room:* A/C, TV, minibar, hair dryer, safe.

INEXPENSIVE

Praia Dourada This is the third-best hotel within the center of Vila Baleira. It opened in 1980 and was last renovated in 1998. Its three floors contain standard, motel-like rooms. Rooms are light, airy, and well furnished, though they lack any particular luster. Many units have private balconies. All units are equipped with well-maintained bathrooms with either shower-tub combos or showers only. The hotel, about a 5-minute walk from a beach, attracts many frugal Madeirans in the summer. Breakfast is the only meal served.

Rua D. Estevão d'Alencastre, 9400-161 Porto Santo. ✆ **291/98-04-50.** Fax 291/98-24-87. www.torrepraia.pt. 100 units. 48€–80€ ($55–$92) double. Rates include breakfast. AE, DC, MC, V. Free parking on street. **Amenities:** Breakfast room; bar; pool; solarium; laundry; dry cleaning. *In room:* TV.

Residential Central When it opened some 40 years ago, the Central was the only decent place to stay in Porto Santo. Although the other accommodations we list have surpassed it, it remains a well-maintained and decent place to stay. The hotel shows a bit of wear and tear, but reception is friendly and the comfort level is high—although there is no air-conditioning. Many rooms have views over the town to the sea, and there is a sun terrace and a garden. All units come with well-maintained bathrooms containing shower-tub combinations. In the summer, the hotel has a real family atmosphere; you'll find more businesspeople in the off season. Breakfast is the only meal served.

Rua Abel Magno Vasconcelos, 9400-150 Porto Santo. ✆ **291/98-22-26.** Fax 291/98-34-60. 42 units. 35€–56€ ($40–$64) double; 45€–70€ ($52–$81) suite. Rates include breakfast. No credit cards. Limited free parking on street. **Amenities:** Breakfast room; bar; private garden; laundry service; dry cleaning. *In room:* TV.

WHERE TO DINE

Most guests dine at their hotels, which are also open to nonguests (see above). Some little eateries around the island specialize in fresh fish.

MODERATE

A Gazela PORTUGUESE/MADEIRAN We're not turned on by this modern restaurant's location near the little Campo de Cima Airport, but it's a local favorite because of its tasty regional food and low prices. Islanders flock here for weddings, anniversaries, and family reunions. Always look for the catch of the day, or try the classic Madeiran specialty, *espetada* (skewered and grilled beef), or excellent fresh grilled tuna with sautéed onions. Another specialty is beef loin a la Gazela (cooked with ham and cheese). The restaurant is 1.75km (1 mile) from the center of town and about a 10-minute walk from the Hotel Porto Santo.

Campo de Cima. ✆ **291/98-44-25.** Reservations recommended. Main courses 5.50€–20€ ($6.35–$23). AE, DC, MC, V. Daily noon–3pm. Bus: 3.

INEXPENSIVE

Baiana PORTUGUESE Near the town hall in the center of Vila Baleira, this is a regular rendezvous, popular with visitors and locals alike. In fair weather, guests select a table on the sidewalk and order drinks, sandwiches, or full regional meals. The tasty dishes include filet of beef cooked at your table and served with a selection of sauces. Instead of beef, *espetada* comes with skewered squid and shrimp, delicately flavored and served with fresh lemon. Pork in wine and garlic marinade is another delectable offering.

Rua Dr. Nuno S. Texeira. ✆ **291/98-46-49.** Reservations recommended. Main courses 9€–14€ ($10–$16). AE, DC, MC, V. Daily noon–3:30pm and 6:30–11pm.

Teodorico ★ *Finds* MADEIRAN Our longtime island favorite, this restaurant occupies a former farmhouse. It has made its reputation on only one dish: *espetada* (skewered and grilled beef), which is tender and filled with flavor. The dish comes with fried potatoes, a salad, and two other vegetables. Locals wash this dish down with a dry red wine that's made on the island and sop up the juices with hearty regional bread, *páo de caco.* The restaurant is in the hills, 3.5km (2¼ miles) northeast from the center of Vila Baleira. In fair weather, you can dine outside (where the chairs are made from tree stumps). If it's cold, you can join the locals inside at a little table in a room warmed by an open fire.

Sera de Fora. ✆ **291/98-22-57.** Reservations recommended. Main courses 8€–15€ ($9.20–$17). No credit cards. Daily 7:30pm–midnight.

10 Porto Santo After Dark

Porto Santo's nightlife is relatively sleepy, with few bars and one dance club. One of the best bars on the island, popular with a young crowd, is **Tatos Bar,** Sitios do Las Pedras Pretas (✆ **291/98-44-20**), open Tuesday through Saturday from 11pm till early in the morning (depending on business). There's no cover, with beer costing 1.25€ ($1.45). Another bar, drawing a mostly European crowd of all ages, is **João de Cabezo,** Sitio de Cabezo (✆ **291/98-21-37**), open Tuesday through Saturday from 9:30am until closing (which varies).

Appendix: Portugal in Depth

Portugal, positioned at what was once thought to be the edge of the Earth, has long been a seafaring nation. At the dawn of the Age of Exploration, mariners believed that two-headed, fork-tongued monsters as big as houses lurked across the Sea of Darkness, waiting to chew up a caravel and gulp its debris down their fire-lined throats.

In spite of these paralyzing fears, Portugal launched legendary caravels on explorations that changed the fundamental perceptions of humankind: Vasco da Gama sailed to India, Magellan circumnavigated the globe, and Dias rounded the Cape of Good Hope. In time, Portuguese navigators explored two thirds of the Earth, opening the globe to trade and colonization and expanding the intellectual horizons of Western civilization for all time.

In spite of its former influence, Portugal still suffers from one of the most widespread misconceptions in European travel—that it's simply "another Spain," and a poorer version, at that. Before its European political and economic integration in 1986, some dared to call it "the last foreign country of Europe."

1 Portugal Today

Portugal is moving deeper into the 21st century in more ways than one as it struggles to take its place among the leading capitalist economies of Western Europe, experiencing steady economic growth, falling interest rates, and low unemployment.

Portugal today is a land in transition. It exhibits signs of the fever of national renewal, with a giant new bridge spanning the Tagus in Lisbon and its entry into the European market.

The country is long past the quasi-fascism of the Salazar era and the leftist excesses (including revolution) that followed when the government fell in 1974. Portugal has moved forward since then, although its growth rate still runs at only half the productivity rate of the EU average.

An increasing trend toward revitalization has targeted the horribly inefficient state-run companies, including the national bus company. Banks and other financial institutions, newspapers, petroleum refineries, and food processors, among others, continue to fall into private hands.

Workers, however, continue to earn only about a third of the pay of their counterparts in the United Kingdom and France. Life expectancy for men between the ages of 40 and 65 is among the worst in the European Union, roughly on the level of someone living in Mexico City. Nearly half of the people can barely read or do simple math, according to a literacy study. One quarter of Portuguese households remain below the poverty level.

Portugal joined the European Union in 1986, instigating a major overhaul of the country. Fellow members of the European Union, along with investors in the United States and elsewhere, continue to pump money into Portugal, fueling industry and improving infrastructure. The use of that money is apparent in vastly improved railways, new highways, better schools, more sophisticated hospitals, and vastly upgraded port and airport facilities. Telecommunications and transport are improving, and greater numbers of young Portuguese are receiving on-the-job training to help them compete in the modern world, especially in the computer industry. Resort hotels continue to sprout around the country, and many old palaces are being reconditioned and opened to paying guests for the first time in their long histories.

Regrettably, however, all this refurbishing has led to Portugal's becoming quite expensive. Before the late 1990s, it was the unequivocal bargain vacation paradise of Western Europe. Now, in the 21st century, its hotels and restaurants are as expensive as those elsewhere in Europe—although, even in Lisbon, the prices are nowhere near as staggering as those in London or Paris.

There's a general feeling of optimism in Portugal; people have more disposable income and high hopes for the new century. Lisbon's sidewalks are as crowded in the evening as Madrid's. Young Portuguese are much better tuned in to Europe than their parents were. The younger generation is as well versed in the electronic music coming out of London and Los Angeles as in fado repertoires, and more taken with French and Spanish films than with Portuguese lyric poetry. Still, as Portugal advances with determination into the 21st century, its people retain pride in their historic culture.

2 A Look at the Past

THE ROMANS ARRIVE Starting in 210 B.C., the Romans colonized most of Iberia. They met great resistance from the Celtiberian people of the interior. The Lusitanian (ancient Portugal was known as Lusitania) leader, Viriatus, looms large in Portuguese history as a freedom fighter that held up the Roman advance; he died about 139 B.C. The Romans were ultimately unstoppable, however, and by the time of Julius Caesar, Portugal had been integrated into the Roman Empire. The Roman colonies included Olisipo (now Lisbon).

Christianity arrived in Portugal near the end of the 1st century A.D. By the 3rd century, bishoprics had been established at Lisbon, Braga, and elsewhere. Following the decline of the Roman Empire, invaders crossed the Pyrenees into Spain in 409 and eventually made their way to Portugal. The Visigothic Empire dominated the peninsula for some 2 centuries.

Dateline

- 210 B.C. The Romans invade the peninsula, meeting fierce resistance from the Celtiberian people.
- 60 B.C. During the reign of Julius Caesar, Portugal is fully integrated into the Roman Empire.
- A.D. 409 Invaders from across the Pyrenees arrive, establishing a Visigothic empire that endures for some 2 centuries.
- 711 Moorish warriors arrive in Iberia and conquer Portugal within 7 years.
- 1065 Ferdinand, king of León and Castile, sets about reorganizing his western territories into what is now modern Portugal.
- 1143 Afonso Henríques is proclaimed the first king of Portugal and begins to drive the Moors out of the Algarve.
- 1249 Afonso III completes the Reconquista of the Algarve, as Christians drive out the Moors.
- 1279–1325 Reign of Dinis, the Poet King. Castile recognizes Portugal's borders.

THE MOORS INVADE & RETREAT In 711, a force of Moors arrived in Iberia and quickly advanced to Portugal. They erected settlements in the south. The Christian Reconquest—known as the Reconquista—to seize the land from Moorish control is believed to have begun in 718.

In the 11th century, Ferdinand the Great, king of León and Castile, took much of northern Portugal from the Moors. Before his death in 1065, Ferdinand set about reorganizing his western territories into Portucale.

Portuguese, a Romance language, evolved mainly from a dialect spoken when Portugal was a province of the Spanish kingdom of León and Castile. The language developed separately from other Romance dialects.

PORTUGAL IS BORN Ferdinand handed over Portugal to his illegitimate daughter, Teresa. (At that time, the Moors still held the land south of the Tagus.) Unknowingly, the king of Spain had launched a course of events that was to lead to Portugal's development into a distinct nation.

Teresa was firmly bound in marriage to Henry, a count of Burgundy. Henry accepted his father-in-law's gift of Portugal as his wife's dowry, but upon the king's death, he coveted Spanish territory as well. His death cut short his dreams of expansion.

Following Henry's death, Teresa ruled Portugal; she cast a disdainful eye on and an interfering nose into her legitimate sister's kingdom in Spain. Teresa lost no time mourning Henry and took a Galician count, Fernão Peres, as her lover. Teresa's refusal to conceal her affair with Peres and stay out of everyone else's affairs led to open strife with León.

Teresa's son, Afonso Henríques, was incensed by his mother's actions. Their armies met at São Mamede in

- 1385 Battle of Aljubarrota. João de Avis defeats the Castilians and founds the House of Avis to rule Portugal.
- 1415 Henry the Navigator sets up a school of navigation in Sagres. Madeira is discovered in 1419; the Azores are discovered in 1427.
- 1488 Bartholomeu Dias rounds the Cape of Good Hope.
- 1498 Vasco da Gama rounds India's west coast, opening up trade between the West and the East.
- 1500 Brazil is discovered. Peak of the reign of Manuel the Fortunate (1495–1521). Portugal's Golden Age begins.
- 1521 Portugal becomes the first of the great maritime world empires, dominating access to the Indian Ocean.
- 1521–57 Reign of João III, ushering in Jesuits and the Inquisition.
- 1578 João's son, Dom Sebastião, disappears in the battle of Morocco, leaving Portugal without an heir.
- 1581–1640 Philip II of Spain brings Hapsburg rule to Portugal.
- 1640 Following a nationalist revolution, João IV restores independence and launches the House of Bragança.
- 1755 A great earthquake destroys Lisbon and parts of Alentejo and the Algarve.
- 1822 Portugal declares Brazil independent.
- 1908 Carlos I, the Painter King, and his son, the crown prince, are assassinated in Lisbon.
- 1910 The monarchy is ousted and the Portuguese Republic is established.
- 1916 Portugal enters World War I on the side of the Allies.
- 1926 The Republic collapses and a military dictatorship under Gomes da Costa is established.
- 1932–68 António de Oliveira Salazar keeps a tight hold on the government during his long reign as dictator. Portugal is officially neutral in World War II, but Salazar grants the Allies bases in the Azores.

continued

1128. Teresa lost, and she and her lover were banished.

Afonso Henríques went on to become Portugal's founding father. In 1143, he was proclaimed its first king, and official recognition eventually came from the Vatican in 1178. Once his enemies in Spain were temporarily quieted, Afonso turned his eye toward the Moorish territory in the south of Portugal. Supported by crusaders from the north, the Portuguese conquered Santarém and Lisbon in 1147. Afonso died in 1185. His son and heir, Sancho I, continued his father's work of consolidating the new nation.

Successive generations waged war against the Moors until Afonso III, who ruled from 1248 to 1279, wrested the Algarve from Moorish control. The country's capital moved from Coimbra to Lisbon. After Portugal became independent in the 11th century, its borders expanded southward to the sea.

- **1955** Portugal joins the United Nations.
- **1974** The April "flower revolution" topples the dictatorship; Portugal collapses into near anarchy.
- **1976–83** Sixteen provisional governments reign over a Portugal in chaos.
- **1986** Portugal joins the European Union. Mário Soáres is elected president.
- **1989** Privatization of state-owned companies begins.
- **1991** Soáres is re-elected.
- **1992** Portugal holds the presidency of the European Union.
- **1995** Portugal is designated the cultural capital of Europe.
- **1998** Millions flock to Lisbon for EXPO '98, celebrating the heritage of the oceans.
- **1999** Portugal officially adopts the euro as its soon-to-be standard currency.
- **2002** Portugal abandons the escudo and switches to the euro.

The Moors left a permanent impression on Portugal. The language called Mozarabic, spoken by Christians living as Moorish subjects, was integrated into the Portuguese dialect. The basic language of today, both oral and written, was later solidified and perfected in Lisbon and Coimbra.

Castile did not recognize Portugal's borders until the reign of Pedro Dinis (1279–1325). Known as the Poet King or the Farmer King (because of his interest in agriculture), he founded a university in Lisbon in about 1290; it later moved to Coimbra. Dinis married Isabella, a princess of Aragon who was later canonized. Isabella was especially interested in the poor. Legend has it that she was once smuggling bread out of the palace to feed them when her husband spotted her and asked what she was concealing. When she showed him, the bread miraculously turned into roses.

Their son, Afonso IV, is remembered today for ordering the murder of his son Pedro's mistress. During Pedro's reign (1357–67), an influential representative body called the Cortes (an assembly of clergy, nobility, and commoners) began to gain ascendancy. The majority of the clergy, greedy for power, fought the sovereign's reform measures, which worked to ally the people more strongly with the crown. During the reign of Pedro's son, Ferdinand I (1367–73), Castilian forces invaded Portugal, Lisbon was besieged, and the dynasty faced demise.

In 1383, rather than submit to Spanish rule, the Portuguese people chose the illegitimate son of Pedro as regent. That established the house of Avis. João de Avis (reigned 1383–1433) secured Portuguese independence by defeating Castilian forces at Aljubarrota in 1385. His union with Philippa of Lancaster, the granddaughter of Edward III of England, produced a son who oversaw the emergence of Portugal as an empire—Prince Henry the Navigator.

HENRY BUILDS A MARITIME EMPIRE Henry's demand for geographical accuracy and his hunger for the East's legendary gold, ivory, slaves, and spices drove him to exploration. To promote Christianity, he joined the fabled Christian kingdom of Prester John to drive the Muslims out of North Africa.

To develop navigational and cartographic techniques, Henry established a community of scholars at Sagres, on the south coast of Portugal. He was responsible for the discovery of Madeira, the Azores, Cape Verde, Senegal, and Sierra Leone, and he provided the blueprint for continued exploration during the rest of the century. In 1482, Portuguese ships explored the mouth of the Congo, and in 1488, Bartholomeu Dias rounded the Cape of Good Hope. In 1497, Vasco da Gama reached Calicut (Kozhikode), on India's west coast, clearing the way for trade in spices, porcelain, silk, ivory, and slaves.

The Treaty of Tordesillas, negotiated by João II in 1494, ensured Portugal's possession of Brazil. Using the wealth of the whole empire, Manuel I (the Fortunate; reigned 1495–1521) inspired great monuments of art and architecture whose style now bears his name. His reign inspired Portugal's Golden Age. By 1521, the country had begun to tap into Brazil's natural resources and had broken Venice's spice-trade monopoly. As the first of the great maritime world empires, Portugal dominated access to the Indian Ocean.

João III (reigned 1521–57) ushered in the Jesuits and the Inquisition. His son, Sebastião, disappeared in battle in Morocco in 1578, leaving Portugal without an heir. Philip II of Spain claimed the Portuguese throne and began 60 years of Spanish domination. In the East, Dutch and English traders undermined Portugal's strength.

THE HOUSE OF BRAGANÇA A nationalist revolution in 1640 brought a descendant of João I to the throne as João IV. That began the House of Bragança, which lasted into the 20th century. João IV arranged an English alliance, arranging his daughter's marriage to Charles II. For her dowry, he "threw in" Bombay and Tangier. In 1668, Spain recognized Portugal's independence with the Treaty of Lisbon.

On All Saints' Day in 1755, a great earthquake destroyed virtually all of Lisbon. In 6 minutes, 15,000 people were killed. The marquês de Pombal, adviser to King José (reigned 1750–77), later reconstructed Lisbon as a safer and more beautiful city. Pombal was an exponent of absolutism, and his expulsion of the Jesuits in 1759 earned him powerful enemies throughout Europe. He curbed the power of the Inquisition and reorganized and expanded industry, agriculture, education, and the military. Upon the death of his patron, King José, he was exiled from court.

In 1793, Portugal joined a coalition with England and Spain against Napoléon. An insane queen, Maria I (reigned 1777–1816), and an exiled royal family facilitated an overthrow by a military junta. A constitution was drawn up, and Maria's son, João VI (reigned 1816–26), accepted the position of constitutional monarch in 1821. João's son, Pedro, declared independence for Brazil in 1822 and became a champion of liberalism in Portugal.

FROM REPUBLIC TO DICTATORSHIP Between 1853 and 1908, republican movements assaulted the very existence of the monarchists. In 1908, Carlos I (reigned 1889–1908), the Painter King, and the crown prince were assassinated at Praça do Comércio in Lisbon. Carlos's successor was overthrown in an outright revolution on October 5, 1910, ending the Portuguese monarchy and making the country a republic.

Instability was the watchword of the newly proclaimed republic, and revolutions and uprisings were a regular occurrence. Portugal's attempt to remain neutral in World War I failed when—influenced by its old ally, England—Portugal commandeered German ships in the Lisbon harbor. This action promptly brought a declaration of war from Germany, and Portugal entered World War I on the side of the Allies.

The republic's precarious foundations collapsed in 1926, when a military revolt established a dictatorship headed by Gomes da Costa. His successor, António de Carmona, remained president until 1951, but only as a figurehead. António de Oliveira Salazar became finance minister in 1928 and rescued the country from a morass of economic difficulties. He went on to become the first minister, acting as (but never officially becoming) head of state. He was declared premier of Portugal in 1932, and he rewrote the Portuguese constitution along Fascist lines in 1933.

In World War II, Salazar asserted his country's neutrality, although he allowed British and American troops to establish bases in the Azores in 1943. After Carmona's death in 1951, Salazar became dictator, living more or less ascetically and suppressing all opposition. He worked in cooperation with his contemporary, the Spanish dictator Francisco Franco.

In 1955, Portugal joined the United Nations. Salazar suffered a stroke in 1968 and died in 1970. He is buried in the Panteão Nacional in Lisbon.

MODERN PORTUGAL WRESTLES WITH DEMOCRACY Dr. Marcelo Caetano replaced Salazar. Six years later, following discontent in the African colonies of Mozambique and Angola, revolution broke out. The dictatorship was overthrown on April 25, 1974, in a military coup dubbed the "flower revolution" because the soldiers wore red carnations instead of carrying guns. After the revolution, Portugal drifted into near anarchy. Finally, after several years of turmoil and the failures of 16 provisional governments from 1976 to 1983, a revised constitution came into force in the 1980s.

In 1976, Portugal loosened its grasp on its once-extensive territorial possessions. The Azores and Madeira gained partial autonomy, and Macau (which reverted to Chinese control in 1999) received broad autonomy. All the Portuguese territories in Africa—Angola, Cape Verde, Portuguese Guinea, Mozambique, and São Tome and Prîncipe (islands in the Gulf of Guinea)—became independent countries. Portugal also released the colony of East Timor, which Indonesia immediately seized.

From the time of the revolution until 1987, Portuguese governments rose and fell much too quickly for the country to maintain political stability. Moderates elected Gen. Ramalho Eanes as president in the wake of the revolution, and he was re-elected in 1980. He brought the military under control, allaying fears of a right-wing coup to prevent a socialist takeover. However, Eanes appointed a socialist, Mário Soáres, prime minister three times.

In the 1985 elections, the left-wing vote was divided three ways, and the Socialists lost their vanguard position to the Social Democratic Party. Their leader, Dr. Anîbal Cavaco Silva, was elected prime minister. In January 1986, Eanes was forced to resign the presidency. He was replaced by Soáres, the former Socialist prime minister, who became the first civilian president in 60 years.

Although his administration had its share of political scandal, President Soáres won a landslide victory in the January 1991 elections.

With the elections of 1995, constitutional limitations forced Soáres to step down. He was replaced by Jorge Sampaio, the former Socialist mayor of Lisbon. The Socialists currently remain a minority government, holding only 112 of 230 parliamentary seats.

In 1997, ugly headlines questioned Portugal's role in World War II. It was revealed that Portugal sold tungsten and other goods to Nazi Germany and profited greatly from its neutral status in the conflict. The German government paid with gold bullion looted from conquered countries and, it's suspected, from victims of the Holocaust. After Switzerland, Portugal was the largest importer of Nazi gold.

Portugal took a major leap in 1999 when it became part of the euro community, adopting a single currency along with other European nations such as Spain, Italy, Germany, and France.

On February 28, 2002, the nation of Portugal made a bold step forward into its union with the other countries of Western Europe. It officially assigned its longtime currency, the escudo, to permanent mothballs and started trading in euros. This officially launched Portugal, along with 11 other European nations, into the European Monetary Union.

3 Manuelino: Portugal's Unique Architectural Style

The style known as Manueline or Manuelino is unique to Portugal. It predominated between 1490 and 1520, and remains one of the most memorable art forms to have emerged from the country. It's named for Manuel I, who reigned from 1495 to 1521. When Dom Manuel I inaugurated the style, Manueline architecture was shockingly modern, a farsighted departure from the rigidity of medieval models. It originally decorated portals, porches, and interiors, mostly adorning old rather than new structures. The style marked a transition from the gothic to the Renaissance in Portugal.

Old-timers claim that Manuelino, also called Atlantic Gothic, derived from the sea, although some modern-day observers detect a surrealism that foreshadowed Salvador Dalí's style. Everything about Manueline art is a celebration of seafaring ways. In Manuelino works, Christian iconography combines with shells, ropes, branches of coral, heraldic coats of arms, religious symbols, and imaginative waterborne shapes, as well as with Moorish themes.

Many monuments throughout the country—notably the Monastery of Jerónimos in Belém, outside Lisbon—offer examples of this style. Others are in the Azores and Madeira. Sometimes Manuelino is combined with the famous tile panels, as in Sintra's National Palace. The first Manueline building in Portugal was the classic Church of Jesus at Setúbal, south of Lisbon. Large pillars in the interior twist in spirals to support a flamboyant ribbed ceiling.

Although it's mainly an architectural style, Manuelino affected other artistic fields as well. In sculpture, Manuelino was usually decorative. Employed over doorways, rose windows, balustrades, and lintels, it featured everything from a corncob to a stalk of cardoon. Manuelino also affected painting; brilliant gemlike colors characterize works influenced by the style. The best-known Manueline painter was Grão Vasco (also called Vasco Fernandes). His best-known works include several panels, now on exhibition in the Grão Vasco museum, that were originally intended for the Cathedral of Viseu. The most renowned of these panels are *Calvary* and *St. Peter,* both dating from 1530.

The Lady in the Tutti-Frutti Hat

She was called the Brazilian Bombshell. In the 1940s, one critic labeled her Brazil's most famous export. But the great Carmen Miranda, the star of big Hollywood musicals in the 1940s and '50s, was actually Portuguese. She was born Maria de Carmo Miranda da Cunha in 1909 in the little village of Marco de Cavavezes, in the north of Portugal.

Costumed garishly, with bowls of fruit perched on her head, she wriggled outrageously through kitschy numbers like "Tico Tico" in such 20th Century-Fox films as *Down Argentine Way* and *The Gang's All Here.* Although she appeared with a number of other stars, fans best remember her appearances with Cesar Romero and Alice Faye.

In 1911, she moved with her family to Rio de Janeiro, where she learned to make outrageous hats for wealthy customers. One of them asked her to sing at a party. With her sambas and tangos, she was an immediate hit. At age 19, she made her first record on the RCA Victor label. Called *Tai,* it sold a record-breaking (for the era) 35,000 copies. Her career was launched, eventually leading to 140 records and 6 films produced in Brazil.

The United States soon discovered her, and she was lured to Hollywood, where her career soared. By 1943, she was one of the highest-paid performers in the United States. Her act captured (and still does!) the fantasy of drag queens around the world. With her colored dresses, stylized bananas, turbans, outrageous platform shoes, dangling earrings, and shimmering dance steps, Carmen Miranda emerged as an ambassador of the Lusophone world like no star before or since.

Although she was a hit with American audiences, she did not always meet with approval in her native Latin world. Many Latin Americans objected to the stereotype she projected—that of an oversexed, vivacious, clownish cartoon of a Brazilian woman.

Regrettably, her career also degenerated into caricature. After a failed marriage and a severe bout of depression, she ended up making farcical appearances in the 1950s. She appeared on TV with Milton Berle, also dressed in Carmen Miranda drag. On August 5, 1955, she collapsed on the set of *The Jimmy Durante Show* and died of a heart attack shortly after.

Today, decades after her death, legions of impassioned fans keep alive the memory of the Portuguese-Brazilian legend. A biography, *Carmen Miranda,* by Cássio Emmanuel Barsante, was the result of 20 years of exhaustive research. The film *Bananas Is My Business* was made of her life. Even the Film Forum in New York has honored her with retrospectives.

Coveted, adored, ridiculed, and eulogized, Carmen Miranda has been adopted as a Lusophone legend.

4 Portuguese Cuisine: Teeming with Seafood

In her *Invitation to Portugal,* Mary Jean Kempner gets to the heart of the Portuguese diet: "The best Portuguese food is provincial, indigenous, eccentric, and proud—a reflection of the chauvinism of this complex people. It takes no sides, assumes no airs, makes no concessions or bows to Brillat-Savarin—and usually tastes wonderful."

DINING CUSTOMS & TAXES Much Portuguese cooking is based on olive oil and the generous use of garlic. If you select anything prepared to order, you can request that it be *sem alho* (without garlic).

It's customary in most establishments to order soup (invariably a big bowl filled to the brim), followed by a fish and a meat course. Potatoes and rice are likely to accompany both the meat and fish platters. In many restaurants, the chef features at least one *prato do dia* (plate of the day). These dishes are prepared fresh that day and often are cheaper than the regular offerings.

Service is usually included in your restaurant bill, but it's customary to leave about 5% to 10% extra as a tip; 10% is usually de rigueur in first-class or deluxe restaurants. In addition, a 17½% IVA, or value-added tax, is added to restaurant bills, which means you'll be paying supplements on all your food and drink orders.

CUISINE *Couverts* are little appetizers, often brought to your table the moment you sit down. These can include bread, cheese, and olives. In many restaurants they are free; in others you are charged extra. It's a good idea to ask your waiter about extra costs. In many places, the charge for these extras is per person. ***Remember:*** Not everything served at the beginning of the meal is free.

Another way to begin your repast is to select from *acepipes variados* (hors d'oeuvres), which might include everything from swordfish to olives and tuna. From the soup kitchen, the most popular selection is *caldo verde* (green broth). Made from cabbage, sausage, potatoes, and olive oil, it's common in the north. Another ubiquitous soup is *sopa alentejana,* simmered with garlic and bread, among other ingredients. Portuguese cooks wring every last morsel of nutrition from their fish, meat, and vegetables. The fishers make *sopa de mariscos* by boiling the shells of various shellfish and then richly flavoring the stock and lacing it with white wine.

The first main dish you're likely to encounter on any menu is *bacalhau* (salted codfish), faithful friend of the Portuguese. As you drive through fishing villages in the north, you'll see racks and racks of the fish drying in the sun. Foreigners might not wax rhapsodic about bacalhau, although it's prepared in imaginative ways. Common ways of serving it include *bacalhau cozido* (boiled with such vegetables as carrots, cabbage, and spinach, and then baked), *bacalhau à Bras* (fried in olive oil with onions and potatoes, and flavored with garlic), *bacalhau à Gomes de Sá* (stewed with black olives, potatoes, and onions, and then baked and topped with a sliced boiled egg), and *bacalhau no churrasco* (barbecued).

Aside from codfish, the classic national dish is *caldeirada,* the Portuguese version of bouillabaisse. Prepared at home, it's a pungent stew containing bits and pieces of the latest catch.

Next on the platter is the Portuguese sardine. Found off the Atlantic coasts of Iberia as well as France, these 6- to 8-inch-long sardines also come from Setúbal. As you stroll through the alleys of the Alfama or pass the main streets of small villages throughout Portugal, you'll sometimes see women kneeling in front of braziers on their front doorsteps grilling the large sardines. Grilled, they're called *sardinhas assadas.*

Shellfish is one of the great delicacies of the Portuguese table. Its scarcity and the demand of foreign markets, however, have led to astronomical price tags. The price of lobsters and crabs changes every day, depending on the market. On menus, you'll see the abbreviation *Preço V.,* meaning "variable price." When the waiter brings a shellfish dish to your table, always ask the price.

Many of these creatures from the deep, such as king-size crabs, are cooked and then displayed in restaurant windows. If you do decide to splurge, demand that you be served only fresh shellfish. You can be deceived, as can even the experts, but at least you'll have demanded that your fish be fresh and not left over from the previous day's window display.

When fresh, *santola* (crab) is a delicacy. *Santola recheada* (stuffed crab) (*santola recheada*) might be too pungent for unaccustomed Western palates. *Amêijoas* (baby clams) are a reliable item. *Lagosta* is translated as "lobster" but is, in fact, crayfish; it's best when served without adornment.

The variety of good-tasting, inexpensive fish includes *salmonette* (red mullet) from Setúbal, *robalo* (bass), *lenguado* (sole), and sweet-tasting *pescada* (hake). Less appealing to the average diner, but preferred by many discriminating palates, are *eiros* (eels), *polvo* (octopus), and *lampreas* (lampreys, a seasonal food in the northern Minho district).

Piri-piri is a sauce made of hot pepper from Angola. Jennings Parrott once wrote: "After tasting it you will understand why Angola wanted to get it out of the country." Unless you're extremely brave, consider ordering something else. Foreigners accustomed to hot, peppery food, however, might like it.

Porto residents are known as tripe eaters. The local specialty is *dobrada* (tripe with beans), a favorite of workers. The *cozido á portuguesa* is another popular dish. This stew often features both beef and pork, along with fresh vegetables and sausages. The chief offering of the beer tavern is *bife na frigideira* (beef in mustard sauce), usually served piping hot in a brown ceramic dish with a fried egg on top. Thinly sliced *iscas* (calves' livers) are usually well prepared and sautéed with onion.

Portuguese meat, especially beef and veal, is less satisfying. The best meat in Portugal is *porco* (pork), usually tender and juicy. Especially good is *porco alentejano* (fried pork in a succulent sauce with baby clams), often cooked with herb-flavored onions and tomatoes. *Cabrito* (roast kid) is another treat, flavored with herbs and garlic. Chicken tends to be hit or miss and is perhaps best when spit-roasted golden brown (*frango no espeto*). In season, game is good, especially *perdiz* (partridge) and *codorniz estufada* (pan-roasted quail).

Queijo (cheese) is usually eaten separately and not with fruit. The most common varieties of Portuguese cheese are made from sheep or goat's milk. A popular variety is *queijo da serra* (literally, cheese from the hills). Other well-liked cheeses are *queijo do Alentejo* and *queijo de Azeitao.* Many prefer *queijo Flamengo* (similar to Dutch Gouda).

Locked away in isolated convents and monasteries, Portuguese nuns and monks have created original sweet concoctions. Many of these desserts are sold in little pastry shops throughout Portugal. In Lisbon, Porto, and a few other cities, you can visit a *salão de chá* (tea salon) at 4pm to sample these delicacies. Regrettably, too few restaurants feature regional desserts.

The most typical dessert is *arroz doce,* cinnamon-flavored rice pudding. Flan, or caramel custard, appears on all menus. If you're in Portugal in summer, ask for a peach from Alcobaça. One of these juicy, succulent yellow fruits will spoil you forever for all other peaches. Sintra is known for its strawberries, Setúbal for its orange groves, the Algarve for its almonds and figs, Elvas for its plums, the Azores for its pineapples, and Madeira for its passion fruit. Some people believe that if you eat too much of the latter, you'll go insane.

Portugal doesn't offer many egg dishes, except for omelets. However, eggs are used extensively in many sweets. Although egg yolks cooked in sugar might not sound appealing, you might want to try some of the more original offerings. The best known are *ovos moles* (soft eggs sold in colorful barrels) that originate in Aveiro. From the same district capital comes *ovos de fio* (shirred eggs).

WINE One of the joys of dining in Portugal is discovering the regional wines (see "The Best Wines," in chapter 1). With the exception of port and Madeira, they remain little known in much of the world.

Among the table wines, our personal favorites are from the mountainous wine district known as Dão. Its red wines are ruby colored, and their taste is often described as velvety; its white wines are light and delicate enough to accompany shellfish. From the sandy dunes of the Colares wine district, near Sintra, emerges a full-bodied wine made from Ramisco grapes. A Portuguese writer once noted that Colares wine has "a feminine complexion, but a virile energy."

The *vinhos verdes* (green wines) have many adherents. These light wines, low in alcohol content, come from the northwestern corner of Portugal, the Minho district. The wine is gaseous because it's made from grapes that are not fully matured. Near Estoril, the Carcavelos district produces an esoteric wine commonly served as an aperitif or with dessert. As this wine mellows, its bouquet becomes more powerful. The Bucelas district, near Lisbon, makes a wine from the Arinto grape, among others. Its best-known wine is white, with a bit of an acid taste.

Port wine is produced on the arid slopes of the Douro. Only vineyards within this area are recognized as yielding genuine port. The wine is shipped from Portugal's second-largest city, Porto. Drunk in tulip-shape glasses, port comes in many different colors and flavors. Pale dry port makes an ideal aperitif, and you can request it when you might normally order dry sherry. Ruby or tawny port is sweet or medium dry and usually drunk as an after-dessert liqueur. The most valuable ports are vintage and crusted. Crusted port does not mean vintage—rather, it takes its name from the decanting of its crust. Vintage port is the very best. In a decade, only 3 years can be declared vintage.

Port is blended to ensure consistent taste. Matured in wooden casks, the wood ports are white, tawny, or ruby red. At first the wine is a deep ruby; it turns the color of straw as it ages.

Port wine "perpetuated and glorified the fame of Porto," as one citizen put it. The first foreigners won over by it were the English in the 17th century. More recently, however, the French have imported more of the wine than the British.

Its greatest fame has passed, but Madeira wine remains popular. It was highly favored by the early American colonists. Made with grapes grown in volcanic soil, it's fortified with brandy. The major types of Madeira are Sercial (dry, drunk as an aperitif), Malmsey (a dessert wine), and Boal (a heady wine used on many occasions, from a banquet following a hunt to a private tête-à-tête).

BEER *Cerveja* (beer) is gaining new followers yearly. One of the best of the home brews is sold under the name Sagres, honoring the town in the Algarve that enjoyed associations with Henry the Navigator.

Index

See also Accommodations and Restaurant indexes, below.

General Index

Accommodations

Restaurants

FROMMER'S® COMPLETE TRAVEL GUIDES

Alaska
Alaska Cruises & Ports of Call
Amsterdam
Argentina & Chile
Arizona
Atlanta
Australia
Austria
Bahamas
Barcelona, Madrid & Seville
Beijing
Belgium, Holland & Luxembourg
Bermuda
Boston
Brazil
British Columbia & the Canadian Rockies
Brussels & Bruges
Budapest & the Best of Hungary
California
Canada
Cancún, Cozumel & the Yucatán
Cape Cod, Nantucket & Martha's Vineyard
Caribbean
Caribbean Cruises & Ports of Call
Caribbean Ports of Call
Carolinas & Georgia
Chicago
China
Colorado
Costa Rica
Cuba
Denmark
Denver, Boulder & Colorado Springs
England
Europe
European Cruises & Ports of Call
Florida
France
Germany
Great Britain
Greece
Greek Islands
Hawaii
Hong Kong
Honolulu, Waikiki & Oahu
Ireland
Israel
Italy
Jamaica
Japan
Las Vegas
London
Los Angeles
Maryland & Delaware
Maui
Mexico
Montana & Wyoming
Montréal & Québec City
Munich & the Bavarian Alps
Nashville & Memphis
New England
New Mexico
New Orleans
New York City
New Zealand
Northern Italy
Norway
Nova Scotia, New Brunswick & Prince Edward Island
Oregon
Paris
Peru
Philadelphia & the Amish Country
Portugal
Prague & the Best of the Czech Republic
Provence & the Riviera
Puerto Rico
Rome
San Antonio & Austin
San Diego
San Francisco
Santa Fe, Taos & Albuquerque
Scandinavia
Scotland
Seattle & Portland
Shanghai
Sicily
Singapore & Malaysia
South Africa
South America
South Florida
South Pacific
Southeast Asia
Spain
Sweden
Switzerland
Texas
Thailand
Tokyo
Toronto
Tuscany & Umbria
USA
Utah
Vancouver & Victoria
Vermont, New Hampshire & Maine
Vienna & the Danube Valley
Virgin Islands
Virginia
Walt Disney World® & Orlando
Washington, D.C.
Washington State

FROMMER'S® DOLLAR-A-DAY GUIDES

Australia from $50 a Day
California from $70 a Day
England from $75 a Day
Europe from $70 a Day
Florida from $70 a Day
Hawaii from $80 a Day
Ireland from $60 a Day
Italy from $70 a Day
London from $85 a Day
New York from $90 a Day
Paris from $80 a Day
San Francisco from $70 a Day
Washington, D.C. from $80 a Day
Portable London from $85 a Day
Portable New York City from $90 a Day

FROMMER'S® PORTABLE GUIDES

Acapulco, Ixtapa & Zihuatanejo
Amsterdam
Aruba
Australia's Great Barrier Reef
Bahamas
Berlin
Big Island of Hawaii
Boston
California Wine Country
Cancún
Cayman Islands
Charleston
Chicago
Disneyland®
Dublin
Florence
Frankfurt
Hong Kong
Houston
Las Vegas
Las Vegas for Non-Gamblers
London
Los Angeles
Los Cabos & Baja
Maine Coast
Maui
Miami
Nantucket & Martha's Vineyard
New Orleans
New York City
Paris
Phoenix & Scottsdale
Portland
Puerto Rico
Puerto Vallarta, Manzanillo & Guadalajara
Rio de Janeiro
San Diego
San Francisco
Savannah
Seattle
Sydney
Tampa & St. Petersburg
Vancouver
Venice
Virgin Islands
Washington, D.C.

FROMMER'S® NATIONAL PARK GUIDES

Banff & Jasper
Family Vacations in the National Parks
Grand Canyon
National Parks of the American West
Rocky Mountain
Yellowstone & Grand Teton
Yosemite & Sequoia/Kings Canyon
Zion & Bryce Canyon

Frommer's® Memorable Walks

Chicago
London
New York
Paris
San Francisco

Frommer's® With Kids Guides

Chicago
Las Vegas
New York City
Ottawa
San Francisco
Toronto
Vancouver
Washington, D.C.

Suzy Gershman's Born to Shop Guides

Born to Shop: France
Born to Shop: Hong Kong, Shanghai & Beijing
Born to Shop: Italy
Born to Shop: London
Born to Shop: New York
Born to Shop: Paris

Frommer's® Irreverent Guides

Amsterdam
Boston
Chicago
Las Vegas
London
Los Angeles
Manhattan
New Orleans
Paris
Rome
San Francisco
Seattle & Portland
Vancouver
Walt Disney World®
Washington, D.C.

Frommer's® Best-Loved Driving Tours

Britain
California
Florida
France
Germany
Ireland
Italy
New England
Northern Italy
Scotland
Spain
Tuscany & Umbria

Hanging Out™ Guides

Hanging Out in England
Hanging Out in Europe
Hanging Out in France
Hanging Out in Ireland
Hanging Out in Italy
Hanging Out in Spain

The Unofficial Guides®

Bed & Breakfasts and Country Inns in:
- California
- Great Lakes States
- Mid-Atlantic
- New England
- Northwest
- Rockies
- Southeast
- Southwest

Best RV & Tent Campgrounds in:
- California & the West
- Florida & the Southeast
- Great Lakes States
- Mid-Atlantic
- Northeast
- Northwest & Central Plains
- Southwest & South Central Plains
- U.S.A.

Beyond Disney
Branson, Missouri
California with Kids
Central Italy
Chicago
Cruises
Disneyland®
Florida with Kids
Golf Vacations in the Eastern U.S.
Great Smoky & Blue Ridge Region
Inside Disney
Hawaii
Las Vegas
London
Maui
Mexio's Best Beach Resorts
Mid-Atlantic with Kids
Mini Las Vegas
Mini-Mickey
New England & New York with Kids
New Orleans
New York City
Paris
San Francisco
Skiing & Snowboarding in the West
Southeast with Kids
Walt Disney World®
Walt Disney World® for Grown-ups
Walt Disney World® with Kids
Washington, D.C.
World's Best Diving Vacations

Special-Interest Titles

Frommer's Adventure Guide to Australia & New Zealand
Frommer's Adventure Guide to Central America
Frommer's Adventure Guide to India & Pakistan
Frommer's Adventure Guide to South America
Frommer's Adventure Guide to Southeast Asia
Frommer's Adventure Guide to Southern Africa
Frommer's Britain's Best Bed & Breakfasts and Country Inns
Frommer's Caribbean Hideaways
Frommer's Exploring America by RV
Frommer's Fly Safe, Fly Smart
Frommer's France's Best Bed & Breakfasts and Country Inns
Frommer's Gay & Lesbian Europe
Frommer's Italy's Best Bed & Breakfasts and Country Inns
Frommer's Road Atlas Britain
Frommer's Road Atlas Europe
Frommer's Road Atlas France
The New York Times' Guide to Unforgettable Weekends
Places Rated Almanac
Retirement Places Rated
Rome Past & Present